W0232742

THE
$10 TRILLION
DREAM
DENTED

THE
$10 TRILLION
DREAM
DENTED

The State of the Indian Economy and Policy Reforms during Modi 2.0 (2019-24)

SUBHASH
CHANDRA GARG

PENGUIN
BUSINESS

An imprint of Penguin Random House

PENGUIN BUSINESS

Penguin Business is an imprint of the Penguin Random House group of companies whose addresses can be found at global.penguinrandomhouse.com

Published by Penguin Random House India Pvt. Ltd
4th Floor, Capital Tower 1, MG Road,
Gurugram 122 002, Haryana, India

First published in Penguin Business by Penguin Random House India 2024

Copyright © Subhash Chandra Garg 2024

All rights reserved

10 9 8 7 6 5 4 3 2 1

The views and opinions expressed in this book are the author's own and the facts are as reported by him which have been verified to the extent possible, and the publishers are not in any way liable for the same.

Please note that no part of this book may be used or reproduced in any manner for the purpose of training artificial intelligence technologies or systems.

ISBN 9780143467434

Typeset in Adobe Garamond Pro by MAP Systems, Bengaluru, India
Printed at Manipal Technologies Limited, Manipal

This book is sold subject to the condition that it shall not, by way of trade or otherwise, be lent, resold, hired out, or otherwise circulated without the publisher's prior consent in any form of binding or cover other than that in which it is published and without a similar condition including this condition being imposed on the subsequent purchaser.

www.penguin.co.in

To Anjali, my wife, soulmate and protector

*To we, the people of India that is Bharat (and also Hindustan),
who want to build a developed, high-income country with
a per capita income of $25,000 by 26 January 2050,
when we celebrate the 100th anniversary of our republic*

Contents

Part V: Money, Finance and Wealth

Part VI: Budgets and Debt

Prologue

The May 2019 Lok Sabha elections returned the Narendra Modi-led Bharatiya Janata Party (BJP) with a thumping majority of 303 members of Parliament (MPs), enabling it to form a single party majority government quite comfortably. The depth of Narendra Modi's electoral victory was attested to by the fact that about 75 per cent of elected BJP MPs got more than 50 per cent votes in their constituencies and, in some states, such as Rajasthan and Gujarat, no non-BJP MP was elected. Without a doubt, the Indian electorate expressed its complete confidence in the leadership of Narendra Modi.

I attended the swearing-in ceremony of the government on 30 May 2019 in the forecourt of Rashtrapati Bhavan as a serving Finance Secretary to the Government of India. The inability of Arun Jaitley to join the government on health grounds (he died three months later) and the absolute hold that Narendra Modi had on the party and the government made him choose a Rajya Sabha member—Nirmala Sitharaman—as the Finance Minister of India.

I worked with Nirmala Sitharaman to present the regular 2019–20 Budget on 5 July 2019. Certain developments made me choose to take voluntary retirement. I filed my application on 24 July 2019 and bade adieu to the IAS and the government on 31 October 2019. A detailed account of what led to it and my encounter with policy and institutional issues in the government during my two years in the Ministry of Finance is available in my book *We Also Make Policy*.

After that, I have been engaged seriously in observing Indian budgets, economy, state, businesses and people quite closely. I published my first book—*The $10 Trillion Dream: The State of the Indian Economy and the Policy Reforms Agenda*—in February 2022. My next book—*Subhash Chandra Garg's Explanation and Commentary on Budget 2023–24*—was published in March 2023.* I have been writing blogs and opinion pieces regularly since I left the government, commenting on all aspects of economic policy affecting people, businesses and the economy.

---

* Budget book 2024–25, published in August 2024.

The goal of growing Indian Gross Domestic Product (GDP) to $10 trillion by the middle of the 2030s was announced by the Modi government in the Interim Budget 2019–20, while I was the economic affairs secretary to the government, in charge of the budgets. The book in your hands critically assesses the policies and performance of the Modi government during 2019–24, their second tenure, which we can call Modi 2.0, towards their professed goal of making India a $10 trillion GDP economy.

Growth

The economy did well during the first term (2014–19)

Presenting the Interim Budget in 2019–20, Finance Minister Piyush Goyal rightly noted that India was 'the fastest growing major economy in the world with an annual average GDP growth during last five years higher than the growth achieved by any Government since economic reforms began in 1991'.

The notion of 'minimum government, maximum governance' captured the essence of the Modi government's economic agenda to deliver faster private sector-led economic growth. The government banished the ghosts of policy paralysis after Narendra Modi assumed India's prime ministership in May 2014. Many far-reaching policy decisions were taken and implemented. Privatization of public sector enterprises and monetization of infrastructure assets were initiated. Air India was completely privatized. As many as six major airports were successfully monetized and concessioned for fifty years.

The government successfully reformed India's fragmented indirect taxation system with the enactment and implementation of the Goods and Services Tax (GST) Act from 1 July 2017, institutionalizing the 'one nation, one value added tax system' all over the country. Enactment of the Bankruptcy and Insolvency Code (IBC) pulled the rug from under the feet of the capitalist cronies and enabled banks to recover billions of rupees stuck in non-performing loans.

'Sabka saath, sabka vikas' defined and operationalized an ambitious, universal and effective redistribution and people's empowerment agenda. PM Awas Yojana for housing, Saubhagya for electricity, Ujjwala for LPG connections, Swachh Bharat Abhiyan for toilets and Ayushman Bharat for medical insurance reached out to all people without basic living facilities and delivered benefits without discrimination. The universal Aadhaar identity and widespread use of fintech applications for direct benefit transfers made delivery of government benefits efficient and eliminated corruption.

Adoption of ambitious renewable energy goals—first 175 gigawatts (GW) by 2022 and then 450 GW by 2030—offered great hopes of saving India from pollution and controlling carbon emissions to make life in the soon-to-be-most-populous-country in the world qualitatively better.

Aided by falling crude oil prices and a surge of global interest, India did quite well in terms of GDP growth as a result of these policy initiatives, despite the demonetization misadventure, in the first term of the Modi government during 2014–19 (Modi 1.0).

India's real GDP (2011–12 prices) grew from Rs 98.01 trillion in 2013–14 to Rs 139.93 trillion in 2018–19. India recorded a compounded annual growth rate (CAGR) of 7.38 per cent during this period, with annual growth rates of 7.4 per cent, 8 per cent, 8.3 per cent, 6.8 per cent and 6.5 per cent respectively, for 2014–15 to 2018–19.

GDP growth peaked in 2016–17 at 8.3 per cent. There was a notable, though not alarming, decline in the growth rate during the last two years 2017–18 and 2018–19 at 6.8 per cent and 6.5 per cent. There were, however, worrying signs in the quarterly data as GDP growth in the fourth quarter of 2018–19 declined to 5.8 per cent, as per the National Statistical Office (NSO) press release dated 31 May 2019.

Pathetic growth in 2019–20

The second term of the Modi government started on an ominous note. India's GDP, at constant 2011–12 prices, could rise to only Rs 145.35 trillion in 2019–20 (from Rs 139.93 trillion in 2018–19), recording a pathetic growth of only 3.87 per cent—the slowest annual growth rate in the post-1991 economic reforms era.

The growth debacle was hideously mirrored in the quarterly gross value added (GVA) data. The GVA growth rate fell continuously in every succeeding quarter in 2019–20—from 5.4 per cent in Q1 to 4.6 per cent in Q2 to 3.3 per cent in Q3 and to only 3 per cent in Q4. The total lockdown announced by Prime Minister Narendra Modi on 24 March 2020 to 'eliminate' Covid-19 capped the economic growth misfortune of the year.

The GDP, at current prices, was Rs 188.87 trillion in 2018–19. It was expected to touch Rs 225 trillion in 2019–20, which, at Rs 75 to a dollar, was tantalizingly close to making India a $3 trillion economy. Instead, the GDP, at current prices, turned out to be only Rs 201 trillion, making the Indian economy a shade lower than $2.7 trillion in dollar terms.

Investment also slumped in that miserable year. The gross fixed capital formation (GFCF) recorded a pedestrian growth. At Rs 46.11 trillion at constant prices, GFCF grew by a paltry Rs 1.25 trillion over the GFCF of Rs 44.86 trillion in 2018–19, a growth rate of barely 2.8 per cent. This was one of the lowest investment growth rates in years.

The most stringent lockdown anywhere in the world imposed by the government on 24 March 2020 gave migrants no time to reach their homes. The day the lockdown was imposed, there were only about 500 people infected with Covid-19 in India.

If the lockdown had been better planned and imposed from 1 April, the economy would have been saved a considerable avoidable economic hit in the last week of the year. The devastating effect of the lockdown was starkly visible in the downward revision of GDP growth estimates for 2019–20. The NSO had projected 5 per cent growth for 2019–20 in its first advance estimates (FAE) released in January 2020. This growth estimate was revised down to 4.2 per cent in the PE released on 29 May 2020. The 2019–20 growth finally turned out to be only 3.87 per cent.

The first year of Modi 2.0 was a wasted year.

Worst contraction in 2020–21

The lockdown gutted the Indian economy in 2020–21.

The GDP at Rs 27.2 trillion in 2020–21 Q1 contracted by a humungous 23.2 per cent compared to the 2019–20 Q1 GDP of Rs 35.5 trillion. The nominal GDP also declined from Rs 49.42 trillion in 2019–20 Q1 to Rs 38.81 trillion in 2020–21 Q1, which amounted to an income loss of over Rs 10.6 trillion to Indians in one quarter. India's labour lost about 12–13 crore jobs in the immediate aftermath of the lockdown, a reduction of about 30 per cent from the normal employment level of about 40 crore.

The government was reluctant to ease the lockdown quickly. Consequently, the lockdown conditions spilled over into the second quarter of 2020–21 as well, though less stringently than the first quarter. The second quarter (2020–21 Q2) also recorded a GDP contraction. The nominal GDP was lower at Rs 47.3 trillion in 2020–21 Q2, compared to the nominal GDP of Rs 48.6 trillion in 2019–20 Q2. India lost about Rs 1.4 trillion income in the second quarter as well.

With the lockdowns practically removed, the second half of 2020–21 did not see any contraction, with the fourth quarter recording decent growth in the circumstances. The GDP recorded growth of 0.7 per cent and 6.5 per cent in 2020–21 Q3 and 2020–21 Q4, respectively. The nominal GDP recorded growth of 6.4 per cent in 2020–21 Q3 (Rs 54.6 trillion) and 12.01 per cent in 2020–21 Q4 (Rs 57.6 trillion).

The NSO revised 2020–21 GDP numbers many times. Advance GDP estimates, released on 7 January 2021, estimated GDP at Rs 134.40 trillion, with GDP contracting by (-)7.7 per cent. The second advance estimates (SAE) released on 26 February 2021 increased the estimated GDP contraction to (-)8 per cent. In the PE released on 31 May 2021, GDP was revised to Rs 135.13 trillion and its contraction reduced to (-)7.3 per cent. In the first revised estimates

(I RE) released in February 2022, the 2020–21 GDP was further increased to Rs 135.58 trillion, bringing the contraction down to (-)6.6 per cent. In the second revised estimates (II RE) of GDP 2020–21, released in February 2023, the GDP was revised upward to Rs 136.87 trillion, bringing down the rate of contraction further down to (-)5.7 per cent. Finally, the GDP was revised marginally up to $136.95 trillion in the third and final revised estimates (III RE) in February 2024, with GDP growth contraction placed finally at (-)5.8 per cent. The 2020–21 GDP contraction was a full 2.2 per cent less than the contraction first estimated in January 2021.

India has never seen such a humungous contraction since its independence. In nominal terms, Indians' loss of GDP/income in 2020–21 was estimated at Rs 2.45 trillion over 2019–20 (Rs 198.30 trillion in 2020–21 against Rs 200.75 trillion in 2019–20). However, in the context of nominal GDP of Rs 223 trillion estimated in Budget 2020–21, Indians lost an income of about Rs 25 trillion in the lockdown-ravaged year of 2020–21.

GDP bounced back in 2021–22 but not enough

Provisional GDP numbers for 2021–22 were released by the NSO on 31 May 2022. India's GDP, at constant prices, was estimated at Rs 147.36 trillion. In the I RE released in February 2023, the estimated GDP was increased to Rs 149.26 trillion and, in the II RE released in February 2024, to Rs 150.22 trillion. The GDP growth for 2021–22 turned out to be a pretty decent 9.7 per cent.

At current prices, the GDP was estimated at Rs 236.65 trillion in PE, recording annual growth of a massive 19.5 per cent. The GDP, at current prices, was reduced to Rs 235.97 trillion in the II RE released in February 2024, which brought down the growth marginally to 18.9 per cent.

The GDP growth of 9.7 per cent in 2021–22, following a contraction of (-)5.8 per cent in 2020–21 did make India record a 7.35 per cent absolute growth over the 2018–19 GDP of Rs 139.93 trillion. Yet, the CAGR over three years of Modi 2.0 (2018–19 to 2021–22) was still a lowly 2.39 per cent. The 2021–22 growth bounce back was clearly not enough to reclaim India's normal GDP growth trajectory.

There were greater worries in the GVA numbers.

The NSO had reported India's GVA growth in PE at 8.1 per cent for 2021–22. Worryingly, GVA growth for Q3 (October–December 2021) and Q4 (January–March 2022) was only 4.7 per cent and 3.9 per cent, respectively. Effectively, this meant that the second half of 2021–22 generated a tepid GVA growth of only 4.3 per cent.

This unimpressive GVA growth in the second half of the year appeared more problematic if one also took note of GVA growth in the second half of

2020–21. In the Q3 and Q4 of 2020–21 (more or less free of lockdowns), the GVA growth was uncomfortably low at 2.1 per cent and 5.7 per cent (3.9 per cent for the second half as a whole). Strangely, in 2019–20, the first year of Modi 2.0, also free of the Covid-19 pandemic, the GVA growth was only 3.4 per cent in Q3 and 3.7 per cent in Q4, averaging barely 3.6 per cent in the second half of 2019–20.

Abysmally low growth in the second half for three years continuously indicated a deep-seated structural pattern. Sub-4 per cent growth in the second half for three years running! India seemed trapped in a serious low-growth quagmire.

Added to GVA, net taxes on products (taxes on products received minus subsidies on products paid) make up the GDP. Declining net taxes on products in 2021–22 signalled a fiscal logjam.

The GVA numbers for 2021–22 improved in the first and second revisions. The GVA of Rs 136.05 trillion in PE improved to Rs 137.98 trillion in the I RE and further to Rs 138.77 trillion in the II RE, which has been treated as the final estimates as well. Despite these improvements, the three-year GVA growth (in 2021–22 over 2018–19) was still a middling 2.91 per cent.

The sectoral GVA story for 2021–22 was quite discouraging as well. The GVA of mining and quarrying at Rs 3.09 trillion in the final estimates was still less than the GVA of Rs 3.27 trillion in 2018–19, yielding a negative CAGR of (-)1.8 per cent. Likewise, the trade, hotels, transport, communication and services related to the broadcasting group, otherwise a very large and good growth group, also remained in the negative at Rs 24.80 trillion, with a negative three-year CAGR of (-)0.77 per cent.

In the final revised numbers for 2021–22, the net taxes of Rs 11.45 trillion added to the GVA of Rs 138.77 trillion yielded India's GDP of Rs 150.22 trillion. Net taxes on products were Rs 12.59 trillion in 2018–19 and Rs 12.96 trillion in 2019–20. The net taxes got drastically reduced to Rs 10.08 trillion in 2020–21 as the government cleared food and other subsidy arrears. Taxes' growth, particularly that of GST, was quite robust in 2021–22. However, subsidies also grew. Consequently, the net taxes on products for 2021–22 (final revised) of Rs 11.45 trillion were still Rs 1.53 trillion lower than the net taxes in 2019–20. Juxtaposed against the net product taxes of 2018–19, the last year of Modi 1.0, the net product taxes had a negative growth of (-)3.12 per cent per annum.

Worsening net product taxes also hurt the government's ability to contribute to GDP on the expenditure side. The government's final consumption expenditure (GFCE) had, as a consequence, also stagnated despite the government running large fiscal deficits. GFCE was Rs 14.35 trillion in 2018–19 and Rs 14.92 trillion in 2019–20. It was still only Rs 14.80 trillion in 2021–22, which turned out to be lower by Rs 12,000 crore in nominal numbers over 2019–20.

Two numbers captured the injured state of consumer happiness; one, the private final consumption expenditure (PFCE), which measures people's total consumption, and second, per capita GDP, which is a good measure of Indians' average income.

PFCE at Rs 87.33 trillion in 2021–22 had grown by merely 3.61 per cent over consumption of Rs 78.50 trillion in 2018–19. This insignificant growth gets further reduced if one takes into account the increase in population during this period. The per capita real income, Rs 1,05,448 in 2018–19, which had actually fallen to Rs 1,01,038 in 2020–21, recovered only to Rs 1,09,762 in 2021–22. This amounted to an abysmally low growth of 3.29 per cent per annum. Without a doubt, Indian consumers suffered for three years running.

Nothing to feel smug about growth in 2022–23

The NSO estimated provisional GDP growth for 2022–23 at 7.2 per cent in May 2023, which was better than 7 per cent growth estimated in January 2023 (FAE). The 2022–23 GDP growth was lowered to 7 per cent in the I RE for the year released in February 2024.

In the first quarter of 2022–23, the GDP grew by a decent 12.8 per cent year on year. There was considerable chest-thumping by the circles close to the government about this 'high' growth rate, bordering on smugness. Was this warranted?

The 2022–23 quarterly GDP growth came down to 5.5 per cent in the second quarter and only to 4.3 per cent in the third quarter. In the fourth quarter, there was an uptick to 6.2 per cent, though the yearly growth rate remained at 7 per cent per annum. The quarterly growth readings of the second and third quarters were enough to make every one realize that there was nothing to feel smug about. The annual growth of 7 per cent was not a great growth performance in our development context. Excluding 2022–23 Q1 growth, GDP growth was not even 5.5 per cent.

The sectoral GVA growth performance told the real story of severe underperformance in many sectors.

Three sectors—agriculture, livestock, forestry and fishing (referred to usually as the agriculture sector); electricity, gas, water supply and other utility services (which can be conveniently referred to as utilities); and financial, real estate and professional services (which includes IT services; let us call these financial and professional services), which were, by their very nature, structure and pandemic-neutral, i.e., not adversely impacted by the Covid-19 pandemic and lockdown—recorded GVA growth of 4.7 per cent, 9.4 per cent and 9.1 per cent in 2022–23, as per the last available I RE. Their steady-state performance was more or less in line (in case of agriculture) and much higher (for the other two) compared to their four-year GVA growth of 4.87 per cent, 4.29 per cent and 5.8 per cent, respectively, since 2018–19.

Three sectors—manufacturing, construction and public administration; defence; and other services (public services), which had suffered convulsions on account of Covid-19—had recovered by 2021–22 to surpass (after three years) their 2018–19 GVA levels, registering growth of 3.22 per cent, 5.14 per cent and 1.94 per cent, respectively.

In 2022–23, manufacturing recorded a negative growth of (-)2.2 per cent, which brought the four-year Modi 2.0 GVA growth down to 1.83 per cent only. Construction recorded a massive growth jump of 9.44 per cent in 2022–23, raising the four-year growth to 6.20 per cent. Public services recorded 8.92 per cent growth in 2022–23, raising the four-year GVA growth to 3.64 per cent. Clearly, there was a continuing logjam in manufacturing while construction remained volatile.

Two other sectors—mining and quarrying (for short, mining) and trade, hotels, transport, communication and services related to broadcasting (commerce and communications)—had suffered badly on account of Covid-19 and did not recover to their 2018–19 levels.

The mining sector recorded an annual growth of 1.93 per cent in 2022–23, which reduced the compounded negative growth since 2018–19 to only (-)0.90 per cent from (-)1.82 per cent up to the year before. The commerce and communications sector did very well in 2022–23, with all Covid-19 restrictions and inhibitions gone, recording a fabulous growth of 11.99 per cent. This stupendous growth brought the four-year CAGR of the sector into positive territory in 2022–23 with cumulative growth of 2.77 per cent over 2018–19.

The message in sectoral GVA analysis for 2022–23 was quite sanguine. Agriculture and utilities were stuck in their low-growth groove of 3–4 per cent. Commerce and communications, financial and professional services, and public services had recovered fully but were still in a mediocre growth range of 5–8 per cent. Manufacturing and construction were quite volatile despite the government-induced high CapEx contributing to growth. The mining sector was in its long-term sclerosis and seemed incapable of contributing meaningfully to India's GDP growth.

Expenditure-side data, taking into consideration the latest available I RE, confirmed persisting misery. People's consumption (represented by PFCE) grew by 6.77 per cent to reach Rs 93.24 trillion in 2022–23. The annual consumption growth, over four years of Modi 2.0, improved but was still only 4.39 per cent. Even assuming consumption was evenly spread, which certainly was not the case, 4.39 per cent growth indicated very low improvement in the quality of life of ordinary Indian people. Inflation continued to buffet people as the PFCE, at current prices, grew by a whopping 15 per cent.

The government expenditure on current consumption, represented by GFCE, captured the story of the government's stinginess tellingly. The GFCE grew quite slowly in 2022–23 (Rs 16.13 trillion versus Rs 14.80 trillion in 2021–22) bringing down the four-year growth to only 2.98 per cent. The government remained quite tight-fisted, except for the capital expenditure which, as the data suggested, did not help in improving people's consumption standard.

The story of 2022–23 capital formation growth is quite bizarre.

The PE released in May 2023 indicated a faster recovery and good growth in capital formation in 2022–23. GFCF, at Rs 54.35 trillion in 2022–23, grew by a decent 11.4 per cent over GFCF of Rs 48.79 trillion in 2021–22, seemingly on account of the government pushing capital expenditure.

However, the picture changed drastically in the I RE released in February 2024. The 2022–23 GFCF was revised down to Rs 53.46 trillion (from Rs 54.35 trillion) whereas the 2021–22 GFCF was increased to Rs 50.14 trillion (from Rs 48.79 trillion). This brought down the 2022–23 GFCF growth to barely 6.62 per cent.

The GFCF three-year CAGR in 2021–22 was a pathetic low of 3.54 per cent. The four-year CAGR improved to only 4.17 per cent in 2022–23. This certainly was not a great number in the context of India's growth needs. The government's CapEx seemed to be shallower than hyped.

The 7 per cent GDP growth in 2022–23 was the fastest growth in the G20. India, though, was not the fastest growing country in the comity of countries with $100 million GDP and 10 million population in 2022–23.

2023–24 GDP growth high but somewhat suspect

The NSO announced an impressive 7.6 per cent GDP growth for the second quarter of 2023–24 (2023–24 Q2), which raised the first half-year growth (2023–24 H1) to 7.7 per cent. Advance GDP growth estimates released on 5 January 2024 placed India's 2023–24 GDP, at constant prices, at Rs 171.78 trillion, indicating annual growth at 7.3 per cent. In the estimates for the third quarter (2023–24 Q3) released on 29 February, the quarterly growth was pegged as the best quarterly growth for the year at 8.4 per cent. The annual GDP growth estimate for 2023–24 was also raised to 7.6 per cent.

In the latest available PE released on 31 May 2024, India's GDP for 2023–24 has been estimated at Rs 173.82 trillion and growth at 8.2 per cent. This certainly is an impressive growth rate. The quarterly growth story for 2023–24 has also been quite strong in all quarters—8.2 per cent in Q1, 8.1 per cent in Q2, 8.4 per cent in Q3 and 7.8 per cent in Q4. The second half growth is also quite impressive at 8.1 per cent .

The GVA growth, however, was a full 1 per cent less than the GDP growth—7.2 per cent. There was much greater worry about GVA numbers, which actually measure growth in the production of goods and services in the economy. The quarterly growth was curiously moving down every quarter. As per the provisional GDP press release of 31 May 2024, India's quarterly GVA growth was 8.3 per cent, 7.7 per cent, 6.8 per cent and 6.3 per cent in Q1, Q2, Q3 and Q4, respectively. The GVA growth going down every quarter and that too at such high rates, declining a full 2 per cent between the first and the fourth quarter, is quite ominous.

What can explain the big gap in GDP and GVA growth, and what does it say about India's growth performance in the last year of Modi 2.0?

The GDP growth in the first half of 2023–24 was 8.15 per cent and the GVA growth was 8.0 per cent—not much difference. However, in the second half of 2023–24, GDP growth has been estimated at 8.2 per cent whereas GVA growth is down to 6.55 per cent; GDP growth is more than 1.6 per cent higher than GVA growth.

This is abnormal. There is no extraordinary growth in the government's indirect taxes in 2023–24 and no extraordinary fall in product subsidies either. The NSO had estimated net taxes growth of 19.1 per cent for 2023–24 (from Rs 12.67 trillion in 2022–23 to Rs 15.08 trillion in 2023–24). It seems fairly certain that the NSO's estimates of net taxes growth are inaccurate and will be revised down in subsequent estimates. This has implications for the estimated GDP growth of 8.2 per cent as well. The actual GDP growth for 2023–24 might be closer to 7.5–7.6 per cent.

The agriculture sector suffered from the El Niño effect in 2023–24 and produced a trend-defying low GVA growth of only 1.4 per cent (PE). This brought the five-year agriculture sector GVA growth to 4.02 per cent; still quite healthy in the context of trend growth in agriculture and allied sectors.

The four industrial sectors—mining, manufacturing, utilities and construction, which together make up the real industry—did quite well in 2023–24 and produced decent GVA growth of 7.1 per cent, 9.9 per cent, 7.5 per cent and 9.9 per cent, respectively. Despite this excellent performance in 2023–24, the five-year annual growth of these four sectors in Modi 2.0 remained quite low at 0.65 per cent, 3.39 per cent, 4.93 per cent and 6.94 per cent, respectively; certainly much less than the growth in the first term (except for construction) and for which the country cannot really feel satisfied about.

The services in three broad sectors—commerce and communications, financial and professional services, and public services—which make up 55 per cent of the total GVA, also recorded a decent growth of 7.6 per cent during 2023–24, with financial and professional services turning out excellent growth of 8.4 per cent. The trade and communications sector GVA growth was quite muted at only 6.4 per cent. Public services recorded GVA growth of 7.8 per cent during the year. Again, all across services, the five-yearly growth during Modi 2.0 was quite underwhelming with commerce and communications recording GVA growth of only 3.09 per cent, financial and professional services of 6.34 per cent and public services of 4.46 per cent respectively.

The real growth dynamics reflected in GVA numbers was that India's growth was still not high enough. If we view the five-year growth dynamics together, India remained in a low-growth trap in Modi 2.0.

There was another mysterious story lurking in the nominal GDP growth numbers, which might hide downside surprises when the PE are revised in subsequent estimates.

India's nominal GDP for 2023–24 (advance estimates) at Rs 296.58 trillion recorded growth of 8.9 per cent. The nominal GDP was revised downwards (when the real growth was revised upwards) in the SAE to Rs 293.90 trillion. Despite the reduction of Rs 2.68 trillion in nominal GDP, the nominal GDP growth for the year was revised upwards to 9.1 per cent. The real GDP growth of 7.6 per cent and nominal GDP growth of 9.1 per cent indicated that there is very little inflation in India!

The nominal GDP for 2023–24 was revised upwards to Rs 295.36 trillion in PE released on 31 May 2024, albeit still lower than the advance estimates of Rs 296.58 trillion. On the back of this upward revision, the nominal GDP growth for 2023–24 was revised upward to 9.6 per cent. The net taxes conundrum was evident in the case of nominal GDP growth as well with net taxes rising by as much as 21.1 per cent in PE. 9.6 per cent nominal growth and 8.2 per cent real growth in PE reinforced the suspicion about the inflation/deflator element in GDP.

One more dimension was quite notable. There were some sectors where real GVA growth was higher than nominal GVA growth, indicating serious price depression in the sector. Mining recorded real GVA growth of 7.1 per cent whereas nominal GVA growth was only 6.63 per cent. For manufacturing, real GVA growth was 9.9 per cent, whereas nominal GVA growth was much lower at 8 per cent. In commerce and communications, while real GVA growth was 6.4 per cent, nominal growth was lower at 6.2 per cent. In construction also, real GVA growth was 9.9 per cent whereas nominal growth was reported at 9.4 per cent. On the other hand, for public services, real GVA growth was 7.8 per cent whereas nominal growth was the highest at 13.5 per cent.

The expenditure-side story continued to indicate weak consumption. The NSO revised the PFCE for 2023–24 from Rs 97.74 trillion in FAE to Rs 96.05 trillion in SAE and back again to Rs 96.99 trillion in PE. The PFCE, which represents people's consumption, recorded growth of only 4.03 per cent in 2023–24 over FAE of 2022–23. For the five years of Modi 2.0, private consumption growth remained abysmally low at 4.32 per cent.

The gross fixed capital formation (GFCF) story was more encouraging for the year with the GFCF recording a decent 8.99 per cent growth in 2023–24 (Rs 58.27 trillion in 2023–24 PE over Rs 53.46 trillion in 2022–23 I RE), although the five-year growth of GFCF remained quite weak at 5.12 per cent.

The larger message in the provisional 2023–24 GDP numbers was that the Indian economy was back to its normal groove—growing at about 7 per cent annually—but possibly on the back of debt-funded government capital expenditure and household sector investment in housing. People's consumption growth was highly constrained both on account of loss of income/very slow growth of income and also the inflationary effect on consumption goods.

Worst growth track record

The 2023–24 GDP (PE) was Rs 173.82 trillion. India's GDP in 2018–19, the last year of Modi 1.0, was Rs 139.93 trillion. In the five years of Modi 2.0, India's GDP recorded CAGR of 4.43 per cent. This GDP growth was nothing but quite dismal.

The GVA growth story was also quite similar. India's GVA, at basic prices, in 2018–19 was Rs 127.34 trillion. The GVA in 2023–24 (PE) was Rs 158.74 trillion, yielding five-year GVA growth of only 4.51 per cent—nothing to write home about either.

Modi 2.0 (2019–24) witnessed the lowest GDP growth in the full term of any government post-1991. This growth performance was quite disappointing compared to Modi 1.0's GDP growth of 7.38 per cent as well.

While Piyush Goyal could rightly claim in the Interim Budget 2019–20 that GDP growth in Modi 1.0 was the highest GDP growth of any government after the 1991 reforms, Nirmala Sitharaman did not have the courage, in the Interim Budget 2024–25, to accept that Modi 2.0 delivered the lowest GDP growth of any government after the 1991 reforms. Instead, she presented a 'white paper' which attempted to obfuscate the issue to show the Modi government's ten-year economic track record was better than Manmohan Singh's ten-year track record.

$5 trillion GDP goal drifted further

India's nominal GDP growth in 2023–24, at current prices, was revised to Rs 295.36 trillion by the NSO in the PE released on 31 May 2024. With the dollar averaging about Rs 83 for 2023–24, India's GDP in US dollars was about 3.56 trillion for the year. This turned out to be much less than $3.75 trillion, which the International Monetary Fund (IMF) had projected as India's 2023 GDP a year before.

The Prime Minister had announced with big fanfare, in 2019, India's $5 trillion GDP goal, to be attained by 2024–25. India's nominal GDP was $2.70 trillion in 2018–19. India could progress to increase its GDP (in dollar terms) by only $0.86 trillion in five years to $3.56 trillion, at an average growth of $0.172 trillion per annum.

There is still a big gap of $1.44 trillion left to attain the GDP of $5 trillion, a little less than double the distance covered in five of the six years envisaged to attain the $5 trillion goal. There is no way India can reach the $5 trillion GDP goal by 2024–25. India will most likely miss this goal by about three years.

There is another dimension, which the government and commentators tend to forget, which will further delay the attainment of the actual $5 trillion GDP goal.

The $5 trillion goal, announced in June 2019, was implicitly expressed it in terms of the 2019 US dollar. The US dollar has depreciated since then by about 20 per cent (urban consumer price in October 2023 at 307.67 against 257.35 in October 2019—base 1982). The $5 trillion goal thus becomes a $6 trillion goal in 2023–24 in 2019 US dollars. India's $3.56 trillion economy in 2023–24 (in current US dollars) is behind by about $2.54 trillion in the context of the inflation-adjusted $5 trillion goal making the goal still harder to achieve.

Notable Successes

There were no major economic policy and legislative reforms like the GST Act and IBC in the second term. There were not many new big developmental programmes like Swachh Bharat Mission other than the Jal Jeevan Mission either. There still were significant achievements in certain operational, developmental and legislative fields.

I pick four major transformative programmes and policies initiated and implemented exceedingly well during Modi 2.0.

Clean-up of off-budget borrowings

The borrowings raised by the government outside the budget for meeting fiscal expenditures and not accounted for in the Consolidated Fund of India (CFI) are off-budget borrowings. The Government of India (GoI) started raising such off-budget borrowings in 2016–17, in the first term of the Modi government (earlier, the UPA government had raised such borrowings up to 2007–08).

The government had deployed two instruments primarily for this purpose. First, fully serviced bonds (FSBs) were the off-budget borrowings guaranteed by the GoI for the payment of both interest and principal. The government issued letters of guarantee to the organizations/special purpose vehicles (SPVs) that raised such off-budget borrowings. The second device was to provide loans to public sector organizations like the Food Corporation of India (FCI) from the National Small Savings Fund (NSSF) in lieu of the food subsidy due from the budget.

These off-budget borrowings, also termed extra-budgetary resources (EBRs), continued until the financial year (FY) 2020–21. The highest EBRs were raised in 2019–20, at Rs 1,48,316 crore (FSBs Rs 22,006 crore and loans from the NSSF Rs 1,26,310 crore). The government acknowledged the existence of EBRs in the 2019–20 Budget and started rolling it back from 2020–21. The government did away with off-budget borrowings completely from 2021–22. Annexure 2 to the Budget Speech 2022–23 provided complete details.

Through FSBs, the government raised off-budget borrowings of Rs 9,167 crore in 2016–17, Rs 15,095 crore in 2017–18, Rs 65,602 crore in 2018–19, Rs 22,006 crore in 2019–20 and Rs 26,665 crore in 2020–21. For 2021–22, no FSBs, except Rs 752 crore in 2021–22 RE for PM Awas Yojana, was budgeted. Off-budget borrowings through FSBs ceased to be an instrument of financing budget expenditures from that year.

Meeting fiscal expenditures through the NSSF was a much larger operation.

In 2016–17, Rs 70,000 crore was given to FCI from the NSSF as loan in lieu of the food subsidy payment by the government. During 2017–18, the NSSF loan to FCI was for Rs 65,000 crore and another Rs 8,000 crore was lent to the Building Materials and Technology Promotion Council (BMTPC) for affordable housing subsidy. In all, NSSF loans supported fiscal expenditures of Rs 73,000 crore in 2017–18. For 2018–19, Rs 87,000 crore went to the FCI from the NSSF as loan for food subsidy.

In 2019–20, the first year of Modi 2.0, the NSSF loan for the food subsidy amounted to Rs 1,10,000 crore. The NSSF also lent Rs 15,000 crore to the BMTPC and another Rs 1,310 crore to the Metals and Minerals Trading Corporation (MMTC). Off-budget borrowing from the NSSF thus amounted to Rs 1,26,310 crore in 2019–20. Total outstanding NSSF loans to FCI at the end of 2019–20 increased to Rs 2,54,600 crore, as per the statement annexed to the Budget Speech 2021–22.

The government decided to unwind food subsidy payments through NSSF loans effectively from FY 2020–21 sometime around the presentation of the Budget 2021–22 on 1 February 2021. Net food subsidy expenditure payments through NSSF loans amounted to only Rs 84,636 crore in 2020–21. No food subsidy was paid through the NSSF in 2021–22.

Off-budget borrowings to fund fiscal expenditures distort budget expenditures and government liabilities. These are resorted to when the government wants to show a lower fiscal deficit, which is a kind of misinformation to markets and the public. The government used the opportunity offered by Covid-19 and the demand for fiscal stimulus to bring all the off-budget borrowings on the budget and discontinue the system. This contributed somewhat to the government raising fiscal deficit to GDP ratio to more than 9 per cent in 2020–21.

The good thing, however, was that the pernicious practice of off-budget borrowing was given a decent burial.

Mainstreaming digital payments

Debit cards used to be the principal mode of digital payments before the Modi government took over in 2014 (6,701 million out of total digital payments of 8,640 million in 2013–14). After undertaking the misadventure of demonetization in November 2016, the government decided to push digital payments. The Unified Payments Interface (UPI) was not a significant mode of digital payments until that time. The Reserve Bank of India's (RBI) monthly bulletins did not recognize UPI as an independent mode of digital payments until 2018–19 if you look at the Payment System Indicators data, which brings out statistics relating to all modes of payments.

The new format of Payment System Indicators statement in 2019–20 began providing UPI data. UPI had a humble beginning in 2016–17, clocking a total of 18 million transactions. Thereafter, it took off and became the torchbearer of the government's success in digital payments. The government claimed in November 2023 that the initiatives taken by it and the RBI resulted in the volume of UPI transactions growing from 92 crore in 2017–18 to 8,375 crore in 2022–23, at a CAGR of 147 per cent.

UPI transactions continued to record scorching growth in 2023–24. In October 2023, UPI recorded 1,141 crore transactions (against 731 crore in October 2022), generating over 50 per cent year-on-year growth. In December 2023 again, it clocked a 50 per cent plus year-on-year growth. For 2023–24, UPI transactions amounted to 13,113 crore, which was an outstanding growth of 57 per cent over 8,371 crore transactions undertaken in 2022–23. The UPI transactions in 2023–24 constituted 80 per cent of total digital payments. In terms of amount, UPI transactions amounted to Rs 200 trillion, which was 25 per cent of total digital retail payments.

Indeed, UPI has transformed India's retail payments landscape. In 2018–19, UPI transactions were 22.24 per cent of all non-cash retail payment transactions. In 2023–24, UPI commanded 80 per cent share of such retail payments.

Payments are the lynchpin of the economy. Payments made exactly at the point of transaction work the best. Cash serves this purpose very well but requires the parties to meet in person to exchange cash. Cash has many other deficiencies as well, including non-availability of the exact amount, weight to carry and risk of loss. UPI solves all these problems.

At the root of UPI's success lies the instant payment it enables from one bank account to another. The National Payments Council of India (NPCI) has digitally pooled all bank accounts into one single system. This enables UPI to make instant digital transfers through mobile phones and other devices. This instantaneous, secure and convenient payment system underlines the stupendous success of UPI.

UPI has been widely adopted by crores of retailers and small enterprises; and also by more than 25 crore individual account holders. You can see the tiniest of vendors and service providers in villages, small towns and metros nonchalantly accepting UPI payments through mobile phones or QR codes.

The RBI does not collect and provide data of the quantum of retail transactions taking place in cash. Until 2018–19, it was anecdotally believed that about 90 per cent of all retail transactions were undertaken in cash. Cash transactions are likely to have fallen to less than 50 per cent of all retail transactions by now.

The RBI, however, provides data on paper-based transactions (mainly cheques). Such transactions have come down from 125.73 crore in 2013–14 to 71.09 crore in 2022–23, falling by a whopping 44 per cent. In 2023–24, paper-based transactions further declined to 66.32 crore.

Digital payments enabled through UPI have been an unqualified success during Modi 2.0.

Jal Jeevan Mission

The Modi government successfully implemented a number of beneficiary-oriented schemes which improved the living conditions of the masses in its first term (2014–19). These included Housing for All, for providing a *pucca* house to everyone in rural and urban areas; Ujjwala, for providing cooking-friendly LPG gas connections to over 8 crore families; Ayushman Bharat, to provide medical coverage of Rs 5 lakh to over 10 crore poor households; Swachh Bharat Abhiyan, to provide toilet facilities in all households and make the country free of open defecation; and Saubhagya, for reaching out to every household to provide an electricity connection. These schemes were also implemented quite well.

In the second term (2019–24), there was only one large new beneficiary-oriented scheme—the Jal Jeevan Mission (JJM), formally announced by the Prime Minister on 15 August 2019. JJM's goal is to provide every rural household with a functional household tap connection (FHTC) with a minimum service level of 55 litres per capita water per day (lpcd).

On the day JJM was formally launched, there were 3.24 crore households in rural areas with tap water connections, out of a total estimated 19.24 crore rural households. The FHTC coverage was thus only 16.8 per cent. As many as 16 crore rural households needed to be provided tap water connections in five years if the goal of providing every rural household with a tap water connection was to be realized—a truly gigantic task. JJM was expected to cover the 11.98 crore rural households with the rest of the households covered under other GoI and states' schemes.

The government approved (as per the JJM website updated at end May 2024) the schemes for creating infrastructure to provide FHTC connections to as many as 12.83 crore households under the JJM. By the end of the government's term, work on 10.46 crore connections could start, which meant that the work to provide tap connections was still to commence for as many as 2.37 crore households.

The JJM website further informs that the number of total rural households had increased to 19.31 crore households and 16.07 crore households were without connections on 15 August 2019. Further, a total 11.60 crore connections were provided during the term of Modi 2.0, which meant that 4.47 crore rural households were without tap water connections when the government completed its second term.

The provision of tap water connections is a basic minimum necessity of every household. The quality of life and economic progress depends upon the availability of assured water in every home. While Modi 2.0 could not achieve its goal of providing a tap water connection to every rural household (27.8 per cent households were still to receive a connection), the provision of as many as 11.60 crore water tap connections against the required 16.07 crore families was no mean achievement.

Data protection law

In July 2017, the Modi government constituted a Committee of Experts under the chairmanship of Justice B.N. Srikrishna to deliberate upon a data protection framework for India. The committee did present its report, along with a draft personal data protection (PDP) bill on 28 July 2018. The government, however, could not complete its deliberations to take the next step of introducing the PDP Bill to the Parliament before its first term concluded in May 2019.

In its second term, the Modi government invested its digital policy capital in getting a draft law prepared, based on the recommendations of the Justice Srikrishna Committee. The government introduced the Personal Data Protection Bill, 2019, in the Lok Sabha on 11 December 2019, which unfortunately was far more restrictive in the use of personal data than the 2018 Bill.

The PDP Bill was referred to a joint committee of the Parliament, which deliberated for about two years on the bill and presented its report, with considerable dissent, on 16 December 2021. The committee turned the personal data protection into an all data protection law, by including non-personal data in the scope of the bill. It suggested wholesale changes exceeding more than eighty. Everyone, including the government, found the PDP Bill 2021 recommended by the committee going beyond the scope of a modern digital privacy law. On 3 August 2022, the government withdrew the PDP Bill 2019 from the Parliament.

The government took some time to draft an all-new Digital Personal Data Protection Bill 2023. The Cabinet approved it on 5 July 2023 and it was introduced in the Lok Sabha on 3 August 2023. The bill was passed by the Lok Sabha on 7 August 2023 and by the Rajya Sabha on 9 August 2023. The President provided her assent on August 2023. The act was notified in the official Gazette on 12 August 2023. India finally had a digital personal data protection and usage law.

The act has been drafted in simple, business-like language and applies only to the processing of digital personal data within India where such data is collected online or offline and is digitized. It also applies to the processing of data collected abroad if it was for offering goods or services in India. The act provides for the processing of digital personal data in a manner that recognizes both the rights of the individuals to protect their personal data and the need of businesses to process such personal data for lawful purposes. The bill protects digital personal data (that is, the data by which a person may be identified) by providing for the obligations of data fiduciaries (that is, persons, companies and government entities who process data) for data processing (that is, collection, storage or any other operation on personal data) and the rights and duties of data principals (that is, the person to whom the data relates).

There are several provisions that the Central government is required to prescribe by making rules or issuing notifications. The Digital Personal Data Protection (DPDP) Act 2023 uses the word 'prescribed' thirty-one times, signifying that the Central government would have a lot of authority to exercise and frame subordinate legislation before the DPDP Act comes into effect fully. Section 1 (2) of the act provides that it shall come into force on such date as the Central government may, by notification in the official Gazette, appoint and that different dates may be appointed for different provisions of the act, and any reference in any such provision to the commencement of this act shall be construed as a reference to the coming into force of that provision.

The Ministry of Electronics and Information Technology (MeitY), the administrative ministry for the DPDP Act, 2023, initiated the work for framing rules immediately after the DPDP Act was passed. On 19 September 2023, it held consultations with industry stakeholders. Besides important policy issues, they flagged the issues involved in getting the technical preparations for bringing the digital systems of the industry in alignment with the requirements of the

DPDP Act, 2023. The government stated its intention in the meeting to frame necessary rules within the next thirty days and also to form the Digital Data Protection Board soon.

This unfortunately was the last time the government communicated to the public its intent of operationalizing the law. No rules were finalized and notified in its remaining tenure. Neither was the Digital Data Protection Board established.

No provision of the DPDP Act, 2023, was brought into effect until Modi 2.0 completed it tenure. Yet, the enactment of the DPDP Act, 2023, was a major milestone and achievement of Modi 2.0.

Big Initiatives with Mixed Results

Capital expenditure-led infrastructure growth

Capital expenditure (CapEx) was the biggest fiscal policy pitch and the unique selling proposition (USP) of the Modi government from 2021–22 when the Finance Minister provided Rs 5.54 trillion for CapEx—an increase of 34.5 per cent over CapEx provided in the 2020–21 Budget Estimates (BE). She doubled down on stepping up the CapEx in both the 2022–23 and 2023–24 budgets as well. Terming CapEx as the 'driver of growth and jobs', Nirmala Sitharaman blew the CapEx bugle in her 2023–24 speech: 'Capital investment outlay is being increased steeply for the third year in a row by 33 per cent to Rs 10 trillion' which would be 'almost three times the outlay in 2019–20'. Increased CapEx from the 2021–22 Budget was a new-found policy preference as, curiously, there was almost no mention of CapEx in the 2019–20 and 2020–21 Budgets.

In the five years of Modi 2.0, the nominal budgetary CapEx grew impressively from Rs 3.08 trillion in 2018–19 to Rs 10.01 trillion in 2023–24 BE, reduced to Rs 9.50 trillion in 2023–24 revised estimates (RE), with a CAGR of 26.6 per cent (25.3 per cent for RE CapEx). The total CapEx for the five years (including 2023–24 RE) was Rs 30.45 trillion—an average of Rs 6,09,038 crore per annum.

The nominal budgetary CapEx, however, was quite deceptive. I will deal with the subject in greater detail in Chapter 17—Expenditures. Three types of expenditures included in the CapEx were actually not the real capital expenditure of the GoI. In addition, the government also substituted public sector CapEx with budgetary CapEx in a big way during Modi 2.0.

First, the 'loans and advances' provided to state governments and others, which might be the CapEx of the recipients but not the CapEx of the GoI, amounted to Rs 4.52 trillion. Second, the capital outlays on buying arms and armaments for the defence services, while absolutely necessary from a national security perspective, are not economic growth-generating CapEx. The government budgets the non-economic growth promoting CapEx under the General Services and Social Services heads. The defence outlays of Rs 6.84 trillion during Modi 2.0 were part of the total General Services CapEx of Rs 7.64 trillion. Including Social Services capital expenditure of Rs 0.48 trillion, total non-growth promoting CapEx amounted to Rs 8.11 trillion during the second term. Finally, certain CapEx was phony. The government provided Rs 0.62 trillion as 'equity' to Air India Assets Holding Ltd for clearing the liabilities of Air India Ltd and also infused equity of Rs 1.36 trillion in zombies BSNL and MTNL to cover their losses, provide funds to pay the licence fee for 4G and take care of other dues. In all, a CapEx of Rs 1.99 trillion was quite an artificial and phony CapEx.

These three types of CapEx—loans and advances of Rs 4.52 trillion, non-economic growth promoting General and Social Services CapEx of Rs 8.11 trillion and Rs 1.99 trillion of phony CapEx—which were actually not real CapEx, totalled Rs 14.62 trillion, out of the total budgetary CapEx of Rs 30.45 trillion. The non-growing generating CapEx was as much as 48 per cent of the total, bringing down the real capital expenditure to Rs 15.83 trillion only.

The substitution of public sector CapEx was massive as well. I provide more detailed calculations of the substituted CapEx in Chapter 17—Expenditures. By my estimate, the government substituted at least an estimated Rs 2.29 trillion of railways CapEx and Rs 2.49 trillion of the National Highways Authority of India (NHAI) CapEx, totalling to Rs 4.78 trillion.

The real budgetary CapEx of Rs 15.83 trillion, adjusted for the substituted CapEx of Rs 4.78 trillion, shrinks to Rs 11.05 trillion—about 36 per cent of the claimed CapEx of Rs 30.45 trillion. The government did make capital expenditure the high point of its expenditure policy. The capital expenditure usually is much more productive than revenue expenditure. The big CapEx story was, however, much hollower than Modi 2.0 would have liked everyone to believe.

Financial turnaround of public sector banks

The public sector banks (PSBs) were in a terrible position in the first term of the Modi government. Of Rs 61.42 trillion of the PSBs' loans and advances portfolio in 2017–18, as much as Rs 8.96 trillion, a whopping 14.6 per cent of total advances, was non-performing. As most of these non-performing loans were concentrated in the industries and infrastructure segment, industrial credit had a gross non-performing ratio in excess of 20 per cent. The net non-performing loan ratio (gross non-performing loans minus provisions made) of 8 per cent in 2017–18 of the PSBs made them among the worst performers globally.

The Modi government started paying serious attention to repairing the PSBs' balance sheets by addressing the gross and net non-performing loans issue from 2017–18. The IBC was enacted and enforced. The first large chunk of twelve large non-performing loans, with gross non-performing loans in excess of Rs 2 trillion, were taken to IBC in 2018. The government began providing large capital infusion in PSBs as well, to enable them to make provisions to bring down the net non-performing loans ratio.

Demand for products of many non-performing companies—particularly steel, sugar and power—picked up from 2018–19, more particularly after the Covid-19 pandemic in 2020. This development led to such IBC companies being acquired by others with relatively smaller haircuts. In 2018–19, the financial creditors, mostly PSBs, realized Rs 1.07 trillion out of the admitted claims of Rs 1.95 trillion (over 55 per cent of admitted claims). In 2019–20, the realization was still healthy, though lower, at 35.33 per cent of the admitted claims. Until 2020–21, financial creditors could realize about 40 per cent of their admitted claims.

The government infused capital in excess of Rs 2.75 trillion in PSBs. This enabled PSBs to write-off a good part of their gross non-performing loans. When the written-off loans yielded recovery, it added to the profitability of the PSBs. The RBI also linked interest rates on personal loans—housing, vehicles, etc.—to the external benchmark, mostly the repo rate. The emergency credit line guarantee scheme (ECLGS) allowed banks to lend about Rs 3 trillion to small and medium enterprises (SMEs) and others with zero loss.

PSBs also shifted their lending from industry to personal loans, directly and through non-banks. When the RBI raised interest rates by 2.5 per cent after February 2022, PSBs could widen their net interest spreads on expanded personal loans, raising interest rates on loans while not passing on higher interest rates to depositors. The deposit rate started moving up only from the latter part of 2023–24.

All these measures made the PSBs balance sheets turn around and their profitability perk up. PSBs had a consolidated net loss of Rs 85,370 crore in 2017–18 and Rs 66,636 crore in 2018–19, the last two years of Modi 1.0. PSBs made a consolidated profit of Rs 66,543 crore in 2021–22 and Rs 1,03,000 crore in 2022–23. The PSBs balance sheet and profitability turnaround was nothing less than spectacular in Modi 2.0.

The profitability growth seem to have peaked in 2023–24. Banks' net interest margin started coming down. There is developing stress in the personal loan portfolio, which has grown massively. I will discuss this in greater detail in Chapter 16—Finance and Credit.

PSBs, though, continue to lose market share to private banks. PSBs don't have the right risk assessment systems and attitude in the matter of credit. It is no surprise that every ten to fifteen years, PSBs end up accumulating humungous amounts of non-performing and loss-making loans. This cycle is not going to end. Private banks have admirably taken up the bank-lending business in the last three decades. It is high time the government, in addition to consolidating the existing twelve PSBs into smaller numbers, lets go of most of the PSBs by privatizing them.

It was perhaps with this objective in mind that Nirmala Sitharaman announced, in Budget 2021–22, the privatization of two PSBs. The sense of urgency was reflected in her announcement in the same Budget speech that the government would bring the necessary bills to amend the two nationalization laws in that very Budget session to ensure their privatization without any loss of time.

Unfortunately, the government soon developed cold feet, as it has done in the case of farm laws and labour codes. No amendment bills were brought. Nor was any work done to identify the two banks to be privatized. The government had three years to accomplish this task in its second tenure. That much time has passed without any action towards privatization of two PSBs.

The government quietly abandoned the idea. Excellent profitability turnaround of PSBs but without any significant structural change and privatization, another round of weak performance and a bulge in non-performing loans might not be very far.

Production-linked incentive schemes

The Modi government brought in the Make in India policy in its first tenure to give a boost to manufacturing in the country. The Make in India policy was a curious mixture of greater opening up to foreign investment and technology by permitting automatic and higher foreign direct investment (FDI) limits, protection to manufacturing in India by higher import tariffs on final products, improving ease of doing business and investing in infrastructure.

The policy did not succeed much. The share of manufacturing and industry (mining, manufacturing, utilities and construction) barely moved up during 2013–14 (last year of the UPA government) and 2018–19 (last year of Modi 1.0). The share of manufacturing (GVA Rs 15.6 trillion) in 2013–14 was 17.2 per cent (total GVA Rs 90.64 trillion). By 2018–19, it moved by about 1 per cent with manufacturing GVA (Rs 23.29 trillion) amounting to 18.29 per cent of total GVA of Rs 127.34 trillion. For the larger industry, which was what Make in India really targeted, the share of mining, manufacturing, utilities and construction together, which was 31.16 per cent in 2013–14 (GVA Rs 28.24 trillion), remained flat at 31.22 per cent in 2018–19 (GVA Rs 39.77 trillion).

In the last year of the first term, the Modi government started changing tack. The global production structure of mobile manufacturing suggested that if India could make up for the profitability disadvantage in manufacturing mobile phones in India, besides the assemblers, even the top five mobile brand owners could be expected to shift a part of their global manufacturing to India. This realization gave birth to the PLI schemes in Modi 2.0.

The Finance Minister brought in visibility to the thirteen PLI schemes, which had been announced by different ministries/departments, in Budget 2021–22. The Finance Minister underlined the government's commitment to PLIs by assuring that nearly Rs 1.97 trillion would be spent over five years, starting 2021–22, for the PLI schemes. These PLIs offered a cash incentive of 4–6 per cent of the additional production achieved by the firms, approved under the schemes. The investors were expected to bring investments in additional/new capacity creation, create new direct and indirect employment and export a good chunk of the additional production.

The PLI schemes, however, did not succeed as envisaged.

In June 2023 (after two of five years, 2021–22 and 2022–23 had gone by), the government informed that, as on that date, a total of 733 applications had been approved in fourteen sectors with an expected investment of Rs 3.65 trillion. There were as many as 176 micro, small and medium enterprises (MSMEs) among these PLI beneficiaries in sectors such as bulk drugs, medical devices, pharma, telecom, white goods, food processing, textiles and drones. It was further stated that actual investment of Rs 62,500 crore had been realized till March 2023, which had resulted in incremental production/sales of over Rs 6.75 trillion and employment generation of around 3,25,000.

These claims, however, were not supported by PLI disbursements, which remained quite slow during the entire Modi 2.0. There was no expenditure on any of the PLIs in 2020–21. In 2021–22, the government budgeted a nominal amount of Rs 1 crore for PLI (on white goods). At the RE stage, budget provision expanded to Rs 197.5 crore for ten PLIs. Actual expenditure on PLIs in 2021–22 was, however, only Rs 10.45 crore. 2022–23 saw some, but very little traction. A total of Rs 2,917 crore of PLI were disbursed during the year. In the first two years of PLI schemes' implementation, the government could disburse only 1.48 per cent of the PLI budget of Rs 1.97 trillion.

Actual PLI numbers of 2023–24 are still not officially available. The government pegged the revised estimates for PLI for 2023–24 at Rs 8,007 crore. A newspaper report, citing an official, claimed that Rs 6,800 crore was released as PLI during 2023–24. If this report is taken into account, the government could disburse only Rs 9,727 crore in the first three years of PLI schemes (only about

4.92 per cent). If the 2023–24 RE numbers are taken into account, Rs 10,935 crore would have been disbursed (only about 5.5 per cent).

Make in India in the first term and PLI schemes in the second term made a lot of promises. Some good movement (as in the case of Apple shifting about 10 per cent of its global mobile production to India) also took place. The PLIs with their actual performance, however, largely made no difference to manufacturing and industry in India.

Big Failures

Covid-19 lockdowns

India was not in the pink of economic health in 2019–20 with a GDP, at 2011–12 fixed prices, of Rs 145.35 trillion, generating a faltering low growth rate of barely 3.87 per cent over 2018–19 GDP of Rs 139.92 trillion. Yet, by a decision, which can only be called a highly impulsive sledgehammer, India was placed under a twenty-one-day lockdown, without any notice or warning, on 24 March 2020. The decision locked up 135 crore Indians in their homes, or wherever they were stranded on that evening and closed all production and transportation activities in the economy, barring some essential health services and a few exceptions.

Originating in China in December 2019, the Covid-19 virus had spread swiftly to all parts of the world in the next three months. The world struggled to deal with this mighty virus with different countries trying different solutions. Quite a few leading pharmaceutical firms had started investing in developing vaccines but that was a few months away. In March 2020, when India imposed total lockdown, we had the benefit of knowing how the Covid-19 virus was effectively handled in China and South Korea and how badly it was handled in Italy and Iran. The big lesson apparent at that time was that the best way to contain the spread of the virus was a localized total lockdown in the areas where the virus had spread, to cut off all unprotected contacts between the infected (both symptomatic or asymptomatic) and the uninfected outside the affected local zone.

The Modi government, however, decided to lock up the entire country, all its businesses and all its people. There were only 519 known cases of Covid-19-affected persons in India on 24 March 2020, with 470 active cases, when the lockdown was clamped. The country had recorded only ten deaths by then. The virus had reached some of the urban areas, largely from the people who returned from abroad or who had come in contact with visitors. More than 99 per cent of the country, including all its rural areas, were completely unaffected on the day the total countrywide lock-down was imposed. The lockdown was imposed with a naive belief that India would be able to eliminate the virus in three weeks' time.

India had more than 8 crore individual, tiny, small, medium and large businesses with more than 95 per cent businesses employing no one else. All the businesses producing goods and services got completely knocked down upon being locked down. India also had a workforce of over 40 crore people. More than 12 crore workers, all in industry and businesses, were rendered jobless overnight. Many of these workers serving in metro and other cities of the country started walking hundreds of kilometres, as all means of transportation were also stopped, to the illusive safety of their rural homes.

India's lockdown strategy was clearly faulty. A total economic, social and human lockdown is like the Brahmastra, the most lethal and devastating weapon. It has to be exercised with enormous care and applied with the complete precision of a nuclear option. However, India decided to use this weapon on the entire country when only tiny parts of the country (areas where visitors from infected parts of the world had landed) and very few people (about 500 in all) were actually infected.

There were several versions of lockdowns to follow. Lockdowns 1 and 2 (the last week of March and the entire month of April) turned out to be extremely severe. Realizing that the rabi crop was waiting to be harvested and there was no spread of the Covid-19 virus in rural areas, agriculture operations were exempted on 28 March 2020. Only agriculture and government operations, which constituted about 25 per cent of GVA, remained exempt and largely unaffected during this lockdown period. The rest of the economy (mining, construction, manufacturing and services included), which made up about 75 per cent of GVA, was massively impacted. Some services shifted to digital mode. About 70 per cent of the economy remained largely shuttered for the entire month of April. Lockdown 3 (the first half of May) opened up India a little and Lockdown 4 (the second half of May) allowed some more productive activities, including construction work, to resume. Yet the country lost about 25 per cent of monthly output in May as well.

Unlocking India became more effective from the first week of June 2020. As time went by, most sectors were unlocked in phases. However, education, entertainment, metros and a few other services remained completely shuttered until August–September 2020. As other services gradually opened, some of them, which required close human contact, such as transportation, travel and personal salon services, remained substantially subdued for many more months. A semblance of normality returned only in the third and fourth quarter of 2020–21.

The Purchase Managers' Index (PMI) collapsed for months. It was no surprise that the PMI for services was below 35 in July 2020, though PMI for manufacturing had crawled to about 46 (though still in a contraction zone) in

July 2020. The PMI manufacturing and services indices returned to positive territory only in August and October 2020, respectively. The Index of Industrial Production (IIP) remained in negative growth territory until August 2020, and had a low, volatile performance thereafter (from negative 3.2 per cent in February 2021 to plus 4.5 per cent in October 2020) before it recorded the big bump of 24.2 per cent in March 2021, reflecting a rebound from the fall of 18.7 per cent in March 2020. The Index of Core Industries remained in the negative zone all through 2020–21.

For 2020–21, the country recorded a final contraction of 5.8 per cent (first estimated at 7.3 per cent) in the GDP as recounted in the earlier section. The story of destruction of GDP caused by the lockdowns was more visibly played out in the quarterly numbers—(-)23.8 per cent, (-)6.6 per cent, 0.7 per cent and 2.5 per cent.

Per capita GDP fell from Rs 1,08,247 in 2019–20, at 2011–12 prices, to Rs 1,00,981 in 2020–21, forcing people to reduce consumption. The per capita private final consumption came down from Rs 61,594 in 2019–20 to Rs 57,728 in 2020–21. The distress was writ large over the entire country, caused by both Covid-19 and the government's decision to impose mindless lockdowns—probably the worst policy decision of Modi 2.0.

Runaway fiscal deficits

Restoring the fiscal deficits (from 4.5 per cent in 2013–14 to 3 per cent of GDP) was one of the highest policy priorities of Modi 1.0. Though some off-budget borrowings made the fiscal deficit higher, the budgetary fiscal deficit came pretty close to the stated goal when the government could limit it to 3.4 per cent of GDP in the terminal year 2018–19.

In complete contrast to the rigorous fiscal discipline approach of the first term, Modi 2.0 abandoned fiscal deficit control completely in the second term (2019–24). Taking 2023–24 provisional fiscal deficit (Rs 16,53,670 crore against 2023–24 RE of Rs 17,34,773 crore) into account, Modi 2.0 ended up running massive aggregate fiscal deficits of Rs 76,96,415 crore in these five years. This aggregate fiscal deficit was Rs 48,76,801 crore higher than the total fiscal deficit of Rs 28,19,614 crore incurred during the first term—an increase of 173 per cent.

The annual fiscal deficit averaged 6.43 per cent of GDP (taking provisional numbers for 2023–24 into consideration) during Modi 2.0. No government since 1991, the year when the economic and fiscal reforms began and fiscal deficits came to be recognized, ran fiscal deficits of such high magnitude.

Amended in 2018, the Fiscal Responsibility and Budget Management (FRBM) Act enshrined the mandatory fiscal deficit limit of 3 per cent of GDP from 2020–21.

In the very first year of Modi 2.0 in 2019–20, the government abandoned the fiscal deficit rigour when it raised the fiscal deficit to 4.7 per cent of GDP in the 2019–20 RE. It did make some noises to signal a return to the fiscal discipline path in Budget 2020–21, promising to keep the fiscal deficit under 3.5 per cent of GDP. However, Covid-19 provided a good excuse to the government to abandon the fiscal deficit discipline for good.

In Budget 2021–22, the government revised the 2020–21 fiscal deficit to an unprecedented level of over 9.2 per cent of GDP, though it did bring a lot of off-budget liabilities inside the Budget. The fiscal deficits of 2021–22 and 2022–23 exceeded 6.7 per cent and 6.4 per cent of the respective GDP. The fiscal deficit (RE) for 2023–24 turned out to be 5.8 per cent of GDP. The actuals of the first four years of Modi 2.0 (2019–23) and the revised estimates of 2023–24 amounted to a whopping average fiscal deficit of over 6.5 per cent! The government borrowed Rs 42.48 trillion over and above the 3 per cent of GDP fiscal deficit ceiling in its five-year period (Rs 40.87 trillion if we take the provisional numbers of 2023–24 into account).

The Narasimha Rao (1991–96) government began controlling the fiscal deficits. From the high of 7.6 per cent in 1990–91, the fiscal deficits averaged 5.5 per cent in its five-year term. Three more governments with five-year terms, before Modi assumed power in 2014, also attempted to rein in the fiscal deficits. The Atal Bihari Vajpayee-led National Democratic Alliance (NDA, 1999–2004) averaged a fiscal deficit of 5.3 per cent of GDP. The Manmohan Singh-led UPA-I (2004–09), despite the global financial crisis, recorded the fiscal deficit average of 4 per cent of GDP. Despite running a lax stimulus policy, the Manmohan Singh-led UPA-II averaged a fiscal deficit of 5.2 per cent of GDP. The short-lived Deve Gowda (1996–98) and the first Atal Bihari governments (1998–99) recorded fiscal deficits of 5.2 per cent and 6.3 per cent in their respective tenures.

Modi 1.0 delivered the best performance since 1991, clocking fiscal deficit average of 3.6 per cent of GDP. Modi 2.0 delivered the worst fiscal deficit performance, generating a fiscal deficit of 6.4 per cent of GDP. The award for the best and the worst performance goes to the government led by the same Prime Minister! There cannot be a bigger irony and better proof of a complete about-turn in fiscal deficit policy and approach.

Maximum government

Narendra Modi had led the BJP to a single-party majority government in 2014 on the big promise of 'minimum government, maximum governance'. In sum, this promise implied that the government's interference in economic and social life would be drastically reduced, whereas governance would be significantly improved to make citizens' lives better by provision of efficient and sufficient delivery of public goods and services.

The Planning Commission was replaced by the NITI Aayog and the system of plan expenditure and budget was done away with in 2017 to wean away the government from production and distribution of private goods and services in the economy. The policy of privatizing public sector undertakings (PSUs) was adopted in 2015 to signal the end of expansion of the public sector and its gradual dismantling. Privatization of Air India was initiated. Aadhaar, direct benefit transfer in digital bank accounts and basic ease-of-life schemes like electricity, LPG, health insurance and toilets were initiated to improve delivery and quality of public goods and services.

There was a palpable sense of the government shrinking and governance improving in the first term. In the second term, however, there was an inescapable reversal of this policy and approach.

The government established more ministries and departments. As soon as the Modi government returned to power for the second term, a separate Department of Fisheries was established under the elevated Ministry of Fisheries, Animal Husbandry and Dairying on 31 May 2019. The Ministry of Jal Shakti was formed in the same month by combining the Department of Drinking Water, earlier under the Ministry of Rural Development, with the Department of Water Resources, River Development and Ganga Rejuvenation. The Ministry of Cooperation was established in June 2021, carved out of the Ministry of Agriculture. There was a lot of chopping, adding and renaming of departments/ministries in the second term. The government was clearly expanding instead of downsizing.

The privatization programme was completely abandoned. Monetization of six airports, initiated in the first term and completed in 2019, was not followed up. No more privatization took place after Air India. All the privatization proposals initiated—BPCL, Container Corporation of India Limited (CONCOR), Shipping Corporation of India, IDBI Bank and four others—were abandoned one by one. Even disinvestment of minority shares in PSUs was diverted to a slow lane. Instead, investment in PSUs mushroomed. The government invested trillions in structurally non-commercial entities like railways and national highways. The government provided financial packages of over Rs 3 trillion to perennially loss-making and irremediable entities like BSNL and MTNL. It seemed the government had a complete change of heart. More government became the default policy.

The government embarked on a massive centralization exercise. States' fiscal independence was curtailed massively by providing them interest-free capital expenditure loans, unleashing cesses and surcharges to take away shareable tax shares and even bringing many purely local funds, such as the mineral fund, under effective central control. Enforcement and investigative agencies such as CBI, ED, etc. went after political opponents and businesses.

The second term was marked more by maximum government and minimum governance.

Atmanirbhar Bharat

In the first term, it was the call for making a New India by 2022, the year when India completed seventy-five years of Independence. The New India was never defined clearly and no specific policy or programme was undertaken to put India on the path of becoming a New India by 2022. Of course, the term was rhetorically used at many places and also as a preamble to many programmes and policies during the first term. You cannot judge whether India became a New India by 2022 as there were no defined parameters and indicators for measuring the same.

When Covid-19 hit, suddenly, the Prime Minister brought out the notion of Atmanirbhar Bharat in May 2020. During his Independence Day address from the Red Fort on 15 August 2020, he elaborated on the theme. He provided the context by citing the example of India not manufacturing PPE kits for protection from the Covid-19 virus before the pandemic hit, but in a short time thereafter, India could not only manufacture PPE kits to take care of domestic needs but also began to export.

While the ministers and other spokesmen tried to explain the call of Atmanirbhar Bharat in a larger context, the intent became clearer by the day when tariffs started going up on imports, schemes like PLI were brought in to shift manufacturing to India, export incentives were expanded, imports from some countries were sought to be banned and so on.

It is not for the first time that India was turning inwards. The policy of producing everything in India and import substitution was practised for more than three decades after Independence with disastrous results. India's manufacturing growth remained stunted whereas the East Asian tigers, including China, got industrialized, became rich and abolished poverty by importing technology and capital and exporting goods. Liberalization and reforms after 1991 clawed back some manufacturing and exports space for India.

Exports remained subdued for a long time after the Narendra Modi-led government took over in 2014.

In 2013–14, India exported $314.46 billion worth of goods. The goods exports went down to an embarrassingly low level of $262.29 billion in 2015–16 before rising to $330.07 billion in 2018–19. In the five years of Modi 1.0, exports recorded an annual growth rate of less than 1 per cent (0.93 per cent). Imports rose at a somewhat higher rate, from $450.21 billion in 2013–14 to $514.08 in 2018–19.

No lessons were learnt from earlier failures. Despite Atmanirbhar rhetoric, exports of goods went down in 2019–20 to $313.36 billion and further to

$291.81 billion in 2020–21. Covid-19-induced global disruptions and increased demand globally led to India recording significant growth in goods exports in 2021–22 when exports rose to $422.01 billion. India's goods exports peaked at $450.96 billion in 2022–23, but declined to $437 billion in 2023–24. In the second term, the Modi government could achieve annual export growth of about 5.78 per cent.

Chinese merchandise exports grew from $2,487 billion in 2018 to $3,594 billion in 2022, recording a growth of 7.64 per cent. Chinese exports declined to $3,380 billion in 2023 bringing down the five-year growth rate to 6.33 per cent. The policy of Atmanirbhar was not able to compete with Chinese growth despite the Chinese economy slowing down and the world moving away from China under the friendshoring and China Plus One policies.

Amrit Kaal

The Prime Minister shifted the narrative of New India and Azadi Ka Amrit Mahotsav related to the seventy-five years of India's independence on 15 August 2022 into Amrit Kaal in his Independence Day speech, though the expression had been in currency for a year or so.

On 1 February 2022, while presenting her 2022–23 Budget, the Finance Minister said, 'We are marking Azadi Ka Amrit Mahotsav, and have entered into Amrit Kaal, the twenty-five-year-long lead up to India @100.' She further stated that the 2022–23 Budget sought to lay the foundation and give a blueprint to steer the economy over the Amrit Kaal of the next twenty-five years 'from India @75 to India @100'.

In his Independence Day speech on 15 August 2022, the Prime Minister outlined his notion of Amrit Kaal in terms of five resolutions or 'Panch Pran of Amrit Kaal'. He mentioned the goal of a Developed India among these five resolutions in addition to four others—to remove any trace of the colonial mindset, take pride in our roots, unity and sense of duty among citizens. He further stated that the twenty-five-year Amrit Kaal had started from that day and would culminate on 15 August 2047 with India having become a developed nation.

What defines a Developed India?

This was not outlined on 15 August 2022 or explained any time thereafter. Many ministers and governmental institutions have made claims about the size of India's economy in 2047. Industries and Commerce Minister Piyush Goyal claimed on 20 August 2023 that India's growth would take the country to a GDP of $35 trillion by 2047. The NITI Aayog chief executive officer, referring to the Centre's Vision Document under preparation, surmised that India is estimated to be a $30 trillion developed economy by 2047.

India has attained a GDP of $3.56 trillion in 2023–24 and is the fifth largest economy in the world. With her 140 crore people, India, which has overtaken China, is the most populous country in the world. The per capita income, which measures economic poverty/prosperity of the people, of India is about $2,500, making it languish as one amongst the 140–150 poorest countries of the world.

The global GDP crossed $100 trillion in 2023. With the global population exceeding a little over 8 billion, global average per capita GDP exceeds $12,500. The US, Japan and Germany, three of four countries ahead of us in terms of national GDP, clock average per capita income exceeding $50,000. China, the other country ahead of us, averages $12,500 per capita. India's per capita GDP is way behind the four countries ahead of us in GDP and is not even 20 per cent of the global average. India will certainly overtake Germany and Japan in the next few years to become the nation with the third-largest GDP in the world when our per capita income GDP would still be below $3,000.

India started out in 1947 as one of the least developed countries (LDC) according to the UN system of development classification. With 80 per cent of her people extremely poor, India got categorized as a low-income country (LIC) in the World Bank's classification of countries, based on average per capita income. It took India more than fifty years to move out of the class of LICs.

To adopt the path to redeem the pledge of becoming a developed nation by 2047, we need to first define our benchmark of a developed nation as there is no globally accepted definition of a developed country.

Breaking into the club of high-income countries (HICs) can be one such indicator. The World Bank threshold for an HIC for 2022–23 is per capita income in excess of $13,845. China is on the verge of getting into the HIC club. It clocked over 8 per cent GDP growth for forty years to attain this milestone when its population growth was also constantly declining.

Per capita income of $13,845 is about five to six times India's current per capita income. Attaining this in 2023 dollars by 2047 looks quite improbable. With India's population expected to stabilize around 155–160 crore in 2050, an average per capita income of $10,000 in 2023 dollars will mean a GDP of about $15 trillion. This might be an ambitious and decent goal to consider India a developed nation.

The government's fuzzy notion of Amrit Kaal, without defining what a Developed India would mean in terms of per capita dollar income in 2022/2023 dollars, is not going to take India anywhere. The bigger trouble with these long-term, undefined goals, without intermediate indicators, is that no one can hold the government accountable for making or not making any progress towards the goal.

Such notions are big distractions from the real task of building India and bringing economic prosperity to Indian people. The sooner such vague notions are junked the better.

The $10 Trillion Dream Dented

US and China added an India in three years of Covid-19

The IMF GDP database informs that the world GDP crossed $100 trillion, at current US dollars, in 2022 for the first time ever. The global GDP, at current US dollars, was about $34 trillion at the turn of the century. The global GDP trebled in twenty years.

In 2019, the year before the Covid-19 pandemic, global GDP was a little over $87 trillion, with the GDP of the US, China and India amounting to $21.38 trillion, $14.34 trillion and $2.84 trillion, respectively. In 2022, three years after the Covid-19 breakout, the US GDP grew to $25.46 trillion, the Chinese GDP to $18.1 trillion and the Indian GDP to $3.39 trillion. The US and China added GDP of $4.08 trillion and $3.76 trillion respectively, in these three years. India could add only $0.55 trillion. Both the US and China added more than India's 2022–23 GDP ($3.39 trillion) in this three-year period alone.

The cheerleaders forget that GDP in current US dollars factor in double depreciation of the rupee vis-à-vis the US dollar. We all see rupee-US dollars in terms of nominal exchange rates. Roughly Rs 69 equalled one US dollar on 31 December 2019. On 31 December 2022, it required nearly Rs 83 to get one US dollar. The rupee depreciated by about Rs 14 or 20 per cent in these three years. The nominal GDP, though boosted by Indian inflation, is reduced by the rupee depreciation.

There is another factor—the US inflation—the effect of which, however, usually gets missed out. The US real GDP growth is worked out after adjusting the US dollars for the US inflation. The US GDP was $21.38 trillion in 2019. If we were to take into account the inflation-adjusted real US growth, a contraction by (-)2.8 per cent would bring down US real GDP to $20.78 trillion in 2020, 5.9 per cent growth in 2021 will take it to $22.01 trillion and 2.1 per cent growth in 2022 will make real US GDP amount to $22.47 trillion. This, however, is not done. The US GDP is stated by the IMF in current US dollars.

Therefore, to compare apples with apples to assess India's relative performance, its GDP of $2.67 trillion, $3.15 trillion and $3.39 trillion in 2020–21, 2021–22 and 2022–23 needs to be juxtaposed against the US nominal GDP of $21.06 trillion, $23.06 trillion and $25.46 trillion and not the inflation-adjusted real GDP.

Measuring US GDP in current dollars dramatically transforms its low GDP growth during 2019–22 from 1.67 per cent in real terms to considerably high growth of 5.99 per cent. Our GDP growth at 6.08 per cent during this period looks impressive against US real GDP growth of 1.67 per cent but is not so great compared to 5.99 per cent growth in current US dollars. The Chinese yuan did not depreciate much against US dollars in this period, delivering a robust GDP growth of 8.07 per cent per annum, much higher than India's growth.

The US and China added GDP of $4.08 trillion and $3.76 trillion respectively during these three years, which was way higher than India's total GDP of $3.39 trillion. We were not catching up with the US and China: the GDP gap was only widening.

India, the fastest growing G-20 country, underperformed

In July 2023, Finance Minister Nirmala Sitharaman, in a boast-like post, termed India a bright star again, having become a $3.75 trillion economy—the fifth-largest. The Finance Minister, other ministers, senior government officials, party spokesmen and many analysts and commentators always highlighted, citing IMF and other multilateral agencies, that India was the fastest-growing major economy from 2021–22 onwards.

The IMF did speak about India being the fastest-growing major economy in 2022. In 2023, the IMF's tone changed to India being one of the fastest-growing economies. The IMF did project India's GDP to grow to $3.75 trillion in 2023–24.

India's GDP, in current US dollars, was $1.86 trillion in 2013–14. It grew to $3.58 trillion in 2023–24 (latest IMF data). Our annual compounded GDP growth for the period 2013–14 and 2023–24 was 6.76 per cent. The US dollar growth turned out to be lower at 5.73 per cent during the second term of the Modi government from 2018–19 to 2023–24 (first term growth 7.80 per cent).

India's annual compounded GDP growth from 1990–91, the year after the economic reforms began, to 2013–14, the year before Ms Sitharaman's party came to power, was 7.81 per cent over a twenty-three-year period. India's compounded dollar GDP growth between 2003–04 ($0.52 trillion) and 2013–14 ($1.86 trillion) was much higher at 11.82 per cent (14.56 per cent in UPA I and 9.14 per cent in UPA II)! Against this backdrop, India's five-year GDP growth of 5.73 per cent in dollar terms in the second term of the Modi government did not look exceptionally bright at all.

India grew at a slower pace than its real growth competitors

The IMF classifies 196 countries in two broad groups: advanced economies (AEs) and emerging market and developing economics (EMDEs), further divided into two groups: low-income developing countries (LIDCs) and emerging market and middle-income economies (EMMIEs), based on the income classification of the World Bank. The IMF does not classify the countries in AEs and EMDEs on the basis of any 'strict criteria, economic or otherwise' and says that it has evolved over time. The World Bank considered, in 2022 current US dollars, the countries with per capita gross national income (GNI) between $1,135 and $13,845 as middle-income countries (MICs) and the countries with per capita GNI up to $4,465 as lower middle-income countries (LMICs). India with per capita GNI of $2,380 is an LMIC and an EMMIE.

In reality, the transition of predominantly agricultural economies into industrialized and later services-oriented economies has constituted economic advancement. Industrialization required advancement in educational standards and skills leading to higher incomes and then the peaking/decline of their populations. All the forty-one AEs have a low share of agriculture incomes, high per capita incomes and stagnating/declining populations. Consequently, AEs need to and can generate only low GDP growth. India, with a high share of agriculture, particularly in employment, low per capita incomes and growing population is not in competition with AEs for GDP growth rates.

Of the 217 countries in the World Bank database, eighty-three are HICs, which include all the forty-one AEs, 108 MICs, divided in upper middle-income countries (UMICs) and LMICs—fifty-four each—and twenty-six LICs. India is primarily in competition with the 108 MICs. Many MICs, though, are quite small in terms of population or GDP or both. There are twenty-five major MICs with at least $100 million annual GDP and minimum 10 million population in 2022. Excluding Cuba, for which all data is not available, the remaining twenty-four MICs constitute India's real competitors in the matter of GDP growth and improving the quality of life of their people.

India recorded dollar GDP growth of 6.8 per cent in 2022. Five countries of the twenty-four competitor group recorded higher GDP growth than India—Bangladesh (7.1 per cent), Colombia (7.5 per cent), Malaysia (8.7 per cent), Philippines (7.1 per cent) and Vietnam (8 per cent). Compounded annual GDP growth rate between 2019 (the pre-Covid-19 year) and 2022 of nine countries in the peer group was higher than India's 6.1 per cent growth in this period—Angola (12.8 per cent), Argentina (11.9 per cent), Bangladesh (9.4 per cent), China (8.1 per cent), Dominican Republic (8.1 per cent), Egypt (14.3 per cent), Iran (13.4 per cent), Kazakhstan (7.5 per cent) and Vietnam (7 per cent).

If we take growth performance over a longer period—between 2013 and 2022—three countries—Bangladesh (11 per cent), China (7.3 per cent) and Vietnam (7.5 per cent)—recorded higher GDP growth than India's growth of 6.9 per cent.

Looked at from any of the standpoints, India's growth performance was not the best and the brightest. Bangladesh, China and Vietnam, India's big competitors in the development and growth sweepstakes in our close neighbourhood, did much better. India did better than many of its MIC peers. That, however, cannot provide any great satisfaction to us as India has the most formidable challenge of generating much higher growth for uplifting its millions out of poverty and affording them at least a decent middle income quality of life.

The $10 trillion dream got dented

The $10 trillion GDP goal for India was envisioned in the Interim Budget 2019–20 presented on 1 February 2019. The Budget Speech spoke about achieving this goal 'by the middle of 2030s', which can be inferred as 2034–35, i.e. in about sixteen years' time.

As per IMF data, the Indian GDP was $2.70 trillion in 2018, which takes on board India's performance data for FY 2018–19. To get to $10 trillion in current dollars (i.e. without adjusting for US dollar depreciation), India needed annual GDP growth in US dollars of 8.52 per cent per annum for sixteen years.

India's growth rate, during the Modi 2.0 period, of only 5.37 per cent in current US dollars against the required growth rate of 8.52 per cent per annum was a highly disappointing underperformance indeed. A 5.73 per cent annual dollar GDP growth takes India's GDP of $3.58 trillion in 2023–24 to only about $6.59 trillion in 2034–35, in the eleven years remaining—a far cry from the $10 trillion goal. Please remember, this is without making any adjustment for the depreciation in dollars.

The dream of $10 trillion GDP by the middle of the 2030s indeed got a big dent during Modi 2.0.

Part I

Production of Value
(Supply-Side Economics)

1

Agriculture

The production of food by humans gave birth to what we call agriculture. Production of excess food and trading/exchanging it with others gave birth to what we now call a market. Production and exchange of other goods and services followed. Trading of goods and services, first by barter and then intermediated by money, aided by the invisible hand of markets, gave birth to what we describe as the economy.

Agriculture is the mother of markets and the economy. In this chapter, agriculture is referred to in its widest sweep, which includes animal husbandry, fishery and products from forests. It is also coterminous with the first industry group in the national accounts—agriculture, livestock, forestry and fishing.

Since the Industrial Revolution, the production and exchange of industrial goods and services has overtaken value creation in agriculture. More recently, with the digital revolution unleashing the production and exchange of digital goods and services, the value created in agriculture has gone down substantially as a proportion of the GDP.

In advanced countries, the dependence of people on earning income from agriculture has also reduced enormously. People in developing countries, like India, still depend significantly on agriculture for their employment, income and sustenance. More than 40 per cent of labour is still engaged in agriculture in India, though the agriculture sector produces only about 16 per cent of GDP in the country. Agriculture policy and programmes are, therefore, of utmost importance in the Indian context.

Agriculture is primarily carried out on land. In India, the land for agriculture is very thinly spread in over 120 million operational holdings, more than 95 per cent of which are small and marginal holdings, of less than 2 hectares and 1 hectare respectively. Land policies are also, therefore, of tremendous economic significance.

Excessive governmental interference has been built into agriculture and farmers' lives in India, particularly after the mid-1960s with the introduction of the system of government procuring wheat and rice, the predominant cereals consumed in the country, at 'minimum' support prices (MSP).

Indian agriculture began producing overall surplus over the domestic demand and need of food for Indians by the mid-1980s. India today exports about $50 billion of agriculture goods and our agriculture trade account is in net surplus with annual agriculture imports not exceeding $25 trillion.

Agriculture is a List II (State) subject in the Constitution. There are some subjects—e.g. agriculture census and plant quarantine—in the List I (Union), which the GoI is directly concerned with.

There are some subjects in the List III (Concurrent)—economic planning for agriculture, price control of most of the agricultural commodities, general policy relating to the marketing of agriculture produce including pricing, exports, etc., agriculture produce grading and the like—which also provide material jurisdiction to the GoI and the Department of Agriculture and Farmers' Welfare. Finally, numerous centrally sponsored schemes (CSSs) provide a dominant role to the GoI in the field of agriculture.

This chapter reviews the Modi government's policies, programmes and performance on the agriculture front, especially in the second term (2019–24).

Agriculture sector contributed small output and GVA in 2018–19

The national accounts provide two kind of estimates—first, the output value and second, the GVA. The output is the aggregate value/final price realization of all agricultural goods produced and sold in the economy. GVA is the aggregate of actual value added in the agriculture sector out of the agriculture output sold. GVA equals the value of output minus the value of the inputs used in producing the output.

The agriculture, forestry and fishing sector is the first out of eight major sectors of the economy. The output value (at constant 2011–12 prices) of agriculture and allied sector products was Rs 20.74 trillion in 2013–14 and Rs 24.20 trillion in 2018–19. The total output value of all the goods and services produced in India in 2018–19 was Rs 272.08 trillion at 2011–12 prices. Agriculture sector output thus made up only 7.62 per cent of total output value in Indian economy.

The readers are more familiar with the output values/prices of products and services, including agriculture produce, at their current prices. In 2018–19, the output value of all agriculture and allied sector produce at current prices was Rs 38.03 trillion, which was approximately 183 per cent of the agriculture output value at constant prices. The element of 83 per cent represents inflation between 2011–12 and 2018–19.

The output value of Rs 38.03 trillion comprised Rs 20.99 trillion of crops, Rs 11.50 trillion of livestock products, Rs 3.05 trillion of forestry and logging produce and Rs 3.05 trillion of fishery and aquaculture products. As the total aggregate output value at current prices in 2018–19 was Rs 347.67 trillion, agriculture produce output value made up 10.93 per cent of total output value in the Indian economy.

GVA in the agriculture sector, at constant prices, was Rs 16.09 trillion in 2013–14 and Rs 18.79 trillion in 2018–19. This GVA was made up of Rs 10.49 trillion of crops, Rs 5.40 trillion of livestock products, Rs 1.64 trillion of forestry and logging products and Rs 1.24 trillion of fishery and aquaculture products.

With total GVA at constant prices amounting to Rs 127.34 trillion, agriculture GVA made up 12.63 per cent of total GVA in 2018–19. At current prices, agriculture sector GVA was Rs 30.30 trillion, which was 17.64 per cent of the aggregate GVA of Rs 171.75 trillion in 2018–19.

It is very interesting to note that total agriculture and allied sector output in 2018–19 was only 7.62 per cent at constant prices and 10.93 per cent at current prices of the total respective output value in India.

In terms of GVA, which is usually highlighted as the share of the sector in overall production, the agriculture and allied sector's contribution was only 12.63 per cent of total GVA at constant prices. Only at current prices, GVA of agriculture and allied sector was 17.64 per cent of total GVA. This vast difference confirms a high inflation element in agriculture products.

Rice and wheat has outsized importance in policy

In 2018–19, at current prices, cereals contributed Rs 5.87 trillion worth of output, which was only 28 per cent of crops output of Rs 20.99 trillion and 15.4 per cent of agriculture and allied sector output value of Rs 38.03 trillion.

The output value of rice was only Rs 3.10 trillion (14.8 per cent of crops and 8.2 per cent of agriculture sector output). Wheat contributed still less at Rs 2.01 trillion of output value (less than 10 per cent of crops and about 5.3 per cent of agriculture sector output).

The share of cereals in the monthly per capita consumption expenditure (MPCE) is also constantly declining, at rates much faster than the decline in the overall share of food in MPCE. As per the Household Consumption Survey (HCS) conducted by the Modi government with 2022–23 as the reference year, the share of cereals in MPCE declined from 22.23 per cent in 1999–2000 to 4.91 per cent in 2022–23 in rural areas and from 12.39 per cent in 1999–2000 to 3.64 per cent in 2022–23 in urban areas. A part of this decline can be attributed to the expansion of the free food scheme, but the fall by more than 75 per cent in rural areas and about 70 per cent in urban areas is best explained by the declining consumption share of cereals in India.

From a policy perspective, rice and wheat corner all discussion and programmes. The MSP programme, which ends up costing the country in excess of Rs 2 trillion in food subsidies every year, is essentially a rice and wheat procurement, storage, transportation and distribution programme. With a total output value of Rs 5.11 trillion in 2018–19, wheat and rice food subsidies cost more than one-third of total output value.

There are bigger issues connected with water scarcity, heavy pollution on account of rice stubble burning and the poverty of farmers in states where wheat and rice procurement is not strong. The outsized importance of wheat and rice in our scheme of things needs to be seriously looked at.

Among other foodgrain crops, pulses contributed an output value of Rs 1.08 trillion with gram contributing more than half of the pulses output of Rs 57,306 crore. Oilseeds' contribution was Rs 1.52 trillion with soybeans, rapeseed/mustard, groundnut and coconut being the largest four contributors with Rs 43,800 crore, Rs 36,205 crore, Rs 30,970 crore and Rs 24,678 crore of output contribution, respectively.

Horticulture produce exceeds cereals in output value

Fruits, vegetables and other horticulture products have emerged as a major contributor to the agriculture sector output, bigger than the cereals output value. In 2018–19, the output value of horticulture produce was Rs 6.08 trillion.

Mango (output value Rs 76,167 crore) was the largest horticultural crop. Banana (output value Rs 69,571 crore) followed close behind. Oranges with an output of Rs 23,248 crore was the third fruit crop with an output value exceeding Rs 20,000 crore.

Among the vegetable crops, potato with an output value of Rs 49,214 crore was the leader. Tomato (Rs 35,111 crore), onion (Rs 25,929 crore), brinjal (Rs 26,797 crore) and cauliflower (Rs 21,269 crore) were the other vegetable crops that contributed an output value of more than Rs 20,000 crore or more individually.

The floriculture produce amounted to Rs 34,776 crore.

Other crops

The sugar output value was Rs 1.17 trillion with sugarcane contributing the bulk of it with an output value of Rs 1.02 trillion.

The fibres output production was Rs 83,882 crore with cotton contributing Rs 75,478 crore of output.

Spices contributed an output value of Rs 1.21 trillion with arecanut, garlic and chillis having an output of Rs 28,657 crore, Rs 22,420 crore and Rs 19,730 crore, respectively.

Beverages contributed Rs 53,933 crore of output with tea pitching in an output of Rs 14,562 crore.

Other crops, such as fodder, grass and rubber, made the remaining output contribution.

Milk is the largest single contributor

Of the livestock production output value of Rs 11.50 trillion in current prices in 2018–19, the milk group contributed an output value of as much as Rs 7.76 trillion (67.5 per cent). The milk group's output value exceeded the cereals' output value of Rs 5.87 trillion by a cool 32 per cent.

The milk output value of Rs 7.76 trillion generated, for farmers, 2.5 times of the output value of rice (Rs 3.10 trillion) and 3.9 times the output value of wheat (Rs 2.10 trillion). Milk has virtually no MSP and the milk output of farmers procured by governmental and cooperative agencies did not exceed 10 per cent of total output.

Among other livestock products, the meat group contributed an output value of Rs 2.51 trillion, comprising Rs 2.34 trillion of meat. Eggs also had a decent contribution of Rs 36,592 crore. Wool and hair, dung (Rs 58,537 crore), silk worm cocoons and honey (Rs 10,973 crore) and others contributed the rest of the livestock product value.

Forestry and fisheries produce

Industrial wood (forest and trees outside forests) contributed a product value of Rs 1.99 trillion of the total forestry and logging output of Rs 3.04 trillion in 2018–19. Fuelwood (Rs 65,400 crore) and non-timber forest produce (Rs 39,437 crore) made up the other produce.

Inland fish (Rs 1.37 trillion) and marine fish (Rs 1.12 trillion) contributed almost equally to the total output of Rs 2.49 trillion of fishery and aquaculture output value in 2018–19.

Growth

Agriculture turned out decent growth

India is atmanirbhar in agriculture products with an annual production of calorie-providing cereals much higher than the consumption requirement of its total population. India is a net exporter of agriculture produce with its exports far exceeding its imports.

Agriculture and allied sectors of livestock, forestry and fishery grow at a relatively slower pace than industries and services. With the population growth falling below 1 per cent per annum, India can well afford lower growth in agriculture. India recorded a decent growth of agriculture during the second tenure of the Modi government.

Agricultural production was not affected by the Covid-19 disruption either. The first lockdown in March 2020 was thrust upon everyone, including the vast rural areas of India where agricultural production takes place, at a time when the rabi crop was being harvested and was to be brought to the markets. The government very soon realized that keeping the agriculture operations suspended on account of Covid-19, which had hardly reached rural areas, would be disastrous not only for rural people but would make the agriculture crops waste away. In any case, many farmers and workers were defying the lockdown. The government soon, within four days, exempted agricultural operations from the lockdown.

Agriculture production growth depends more on the monsoon, availability of water and spread of technology than on economic cycles or pandemics like Covid-19. In the first three years of Modi 2.0 (2019–22), agriculture GVA increased from Rs 18.79 trillion in 2018–19, at constant 2011–12 prices, to Rs 21.70 trillion in 2021–22, recording a decent growth rate of 4.93 per cent per annum. This growth rate was exceedingly better than the 3.14 per cent per annum growth recorded during the five years of Modi 1.0. In 2022–23, agriculture GVA growth was slightly lower at 4.71 per cent (Rs 22.72 trillion I RE), bringing the four-year CAGR to 4.87 per cent.

Agriculture value added growth suffered for the first time in Modi 2.0 in 2023–24. As per the PE, the agriculture and allied sector GVA for the year was Rs 23.05 trillion at constant 2011–12 prices, recording an annual growth of only 1.44 per cent. This brought down the five-yearly GVA growth to 4.18 per cent per annum. Still, the five-yearly growth was much better than the 3.14 per cent growth rate of Modi 1.0.

Capital formation received a leg-up

Agriculture has suffered from lack of faster capital formation in India—greenhouses are being set up, agriculture machinery is being deployed but all at a very slow pace. The gross capital formation (GCF) in agriculture grew by a pathetic 0.84 per cent per annum during Modi 1.0—from Rs 2.84 trillion, at constant prices, in 2013–14 to Rs 2.97 trillion in 2018–19.

Capital formation national account data are currently available only up to 2022–23 (I RE), i.e. for the first four years of Modi 2.0. In this period, the agriculture sector did witness excellent capital formation, especially during 2020–21, the period of the acute Covid-19 pandemic.

The GCF increased to Rs 3.03 trillion in 2019–20, the first year of Modi 2.0, and then shot up to Rs 3.54 trillion in 2020–21 (annual increase of 16.9 per cent) before nudging up to Rs 3.84 trillion in 2021–22 and to Rs 4.52 trillion in 2022–23. In these four years, the GCF in agriculture increased by 11.08 per cent per annum, a fabulous rate considering the long-term trend and the performance in Modi 1.0.

This performance was distinctly creditable considering the fact that total GCF during the three-year period for the economy as a whole was a paltry

3.58 per cent (from Rs 48.03 trillion in 2018–19 to Rs 55.30 trillion in 2022–23). As a complete contrast to the capital formation performance in this term, the total capital formation had grown by 7.64 per cent per annum during Modi 1.0.

Government increased subsidy on inputs

Farmers receive output prices but their real profit is reflected in the GVA. The GVA is the output value minus the input costs. Agriculture inputs—seeds, fertilizer, water, electricity, etc.—are heavily subsidized. If the government increases input subsidies more, farmers would receive higher GVA except in the situation when the output value gets depressed to the extent of or higher than additional input subsidies.

In 2018–19, agriculture sector output was Rs 24.20 trillion, inputs Rs 5.42 trillion and the GVA Rs 18.79 trillion. Farmers received 77.6 per cent of the output value as GVA. The GVA minus labour cost is the actual profit of the farmer. The input cost was Rs 4.65 trillion in 2013–14, the year before the Modi government took over, and had grown by 3.09 per cent per annum in the first term.

In the second term, in the first four years for which data is available in the national accounts, the agriculture sector output, input consumption and GVA grew to Rs 28.87 trillion, Rs 6.15 trillion and Rs 22.72 trillion respectively in 2022–23 (I RE). The input cost grew by 3.21 per cent per annum whereas the output and GVA grew by 4.51 per cent and 4.87 per cent respectively.

The agriculture inputs are subsidized both by the Central government and the states. Together, the governments ensured that the inputs grew at more or less the same rate in the first four years of Modi 2.0 at 3.21 per cent per annum as in the first term (3.09 per cent). Farmers' real value receipt or GVA grew at a much higher rate of 4.87 per cent in this period compared to 3.14 per cent in the first term.

As the output value growth was not as high as GVA growth, the GVA to output value ratio increased to 78.7 per cent.

Dependence on agriculture for employment increased

The government's own Periodic Labour Force Survey (PLFS) data confirms that the dependence of India's labour class on agriculture unfortunately went up during Modi 2.0.

In 2017–18, the first year for which PLFS data is available, 44.1 per cent of workers (employed as per usual status) were employed in agriculture. In the matter of rural urban employment, 59.4 per cent of total workers in rural areas and 6.1 per cent in urban areas were employed in agriculture. On gender matrix, 40.2 per cent of total male workers and 57 per cent of total female workers were principally employed in the agriculture sector.

There was distinct improvement in the next year (employment data is July–June), the last year of the Modi 1.0 government and the full year before Covid-19. The share of agriculture in total employment went down to 42.5 per cent with both male (38.3 per cent) and female (55.3 per cent) workers experiencing a shift away from agriculture.

The year 2019–20, with agriculture operations largely unaffected after the lockdown and other sectors witnessing migration to rural areas, saw the share of workers in agriculture shooting up to 45.6 per cent. This was a massive 3.1 per cent higher than the year before and even 1.5 per cent higher than 2017–18.

The share of agriculture in employment went up a per cent more to 46.5 per cent in 2020–21, indicating very clearly that migration of workers from urban areas to rural areas caused by Covid-19 and lockdown-related disruptions was highly impactful. A 4 per cent point increase in the share of labour dependent on agriculture between 2018–19 and 2020–21, in two years, is clear evidence of about 2.5 crore workers losing their jobs in the industrial and services sector and being forced to rely on agriculture, mostly as disguised labour.

There was a small decline in the share of agriculture workers in total employment in the next two years, 2021–22 and 2022–23, for which the PLFS data is available at the time of writing this book. Agriculture employment share declined to 45.5 per cent in 2021–22 but went back up slightly again to 45.8 per cent in 2022–23.

Agriculture was loaded with 3.3 per cent more of total labour in the fourth year of Modi 2.0 than it was in the last year of its first term.

Doubling farmers' income target fell woefully short

In 2016, Prime Minister Narendra Modi promised to double the farmers' income by 2022 when India celebrated its seventy-fifth Independence Day. This was quite a catchy promise. The Prime Minister and the government never defined precisely what it meant by doubling the farmers' income. The period in which farmers' income was to double was also somewhat unclear.

Farmers' income can best be understood in terms of the GVA in the agriculture and allied sector as this alone actually represents the profits/income of the farmers. There are practically no product taxes on agriculture produce and GVA is by and large profits as the share of paid wages is relatively smaller. For the period, as the promise was made in 2016, FY 2016–17 can be considered as the base year and FY 2022–23, in which the seventy-fifth anniversary of Independence fell, the terminal year. As the Modi government took office in 2014–15, it might also be given the benefit of a larger period by comparing the farmers income/GVA over eight years—from 2013–14 to 2021–22.

In 2013–14, the GVA from agriculture and allied sectors was Rs 16.09 trillion at constant 2011–12 prices. In 2021–22, the GVA from agriculture and allied sector was estimated at Rs 21.70 trillion (II and final RE). The GVA grew by only 34.86 or 35 per cent during the eight-year period. There was a whopping shortfall by 65 per cent from the goal of doubling the farmers' income. While the government was required to generate annual growth of 9.05 per cent, farmers' income grew by only 3.81 per cent per annum.

There was indeed a gross failure in terms of achieving the goal of doubling the farmers' income.

Another worrying aspect has also to be taken into consideration if we want to ascertain the true income growth of farmers during the Modi period. As noted above, the number of farmers and agriculture workers increased during the period 2017–18 to 2022–23. To the extent of increase in the number of workers dependent on agriculture, per capita income growth was that much lower. Obviously, per capita income of farmers grew at rates lower than the measly growth of 35 per cent in farmers' income measured by growth in the GVA.

Development Programmes

The agriculture and allied sector predominantly fall within the domain of states. Agriculture, including agricultural education and research, protection against pests and prevention of plant diseases (Entry 14), preservation, protection and improvement of stock and prevention of animal diseases; veterinary training and practice (Entry 15), land, that is to say, rights in or over land, land tenures including the relation of landlord and tenant, and the collection of rents; transfer and alienation of agricultural land; land improvement and agricultural loans; colonization (Entry 18) and fisheries (Entry 21) are all in the second schedule, the State List of the Seventh Schedule of the Constitution.

Yet, there are numerous ministries and departments in the Central government overseeing and meddling in agriculture and allied sectors of the economy. Two departments—the Department of Agriculture and Farmers' Welfare and the Department of Agriculture Research and Education—make up the Ministry of Agriculture and Farmers' Welfare. Two other departments—the Department of Fisheries and the Department of Animal Husbandry and Dairying—make up the Ministry of Fisheries, Animal Husbandry and Dairying. The Department of Land Resources in the Ministry of Rural Development concerns itself with land matters. There is a separate Ministry of Cooperation now. There is a Department of Food and Public Distribution, which manages the procurement of foodgrains and distribution/sale thereof.

These ministries and departments, as they deal with state subjects, have designed and operate a plethora of development schemes under the broad rubric of CSSs. These schemes serve a variety of objectives. Some are meant to increase production and productivity of agriculture and allied sector produce. These schemes are growth-oriented in that sense. There are others which are meant to alleviate the poverty of farmers like the PM Kisan scheme, as part of which the government provides Rs 6,000 per annum to about 10 crore farm families. The government operates the MSP scheme to provide remunerative prices to farmers as well.

In this section and chapter, I will review the performance of growth-oriented schemes in the agriculture and allied sector.

Outlay of growth-oriented schemes quite small

In the 2023–24 Budget of the Department of Agriculture and Farmers' Welfare (DoA and FW), the total schematic outlay of Rs 1.14 trillion is spread over central sector schemes (Rs 98,980 crore) and CSSs (Rs 14,676 crore).

Of the central sector schemes outlay, most of the budget is dedicated for income transfer schemes instead of being allocated for the growth of crops. Rs 60,000 crore is allocated for the PM Kisan scheme and Rs 23,000 crore for modified interest subvention scheme (which provides 3 per cent subvention on interest rate payable on crop loans). Other schemes play an indirect role in protecting farmers' crops and prices like the Crop Insurance Scheme (Rs 13,625 crore) and Market Intervention Scheme (Rs 800 crore). Other schemes with smaller outlays are also welfare schemes only—e.g. PM Kisan Mandhan with an outlay of Rs 100 crore.

The CSS schemes, on the other hand, are all growth-oriented. If we take the outlays of crop protection schemes as growth-oriented, the total budget outlay of Rs 14,425 crore of central sector schemes and Rs 14,676 crore of CSS, can be classified as growth-oriented schemes, in all, with an outlay of Rs 29,100 crore.

Of the total schematic outlay of Rs 1.14 trillion, only Rs 29,100 crore or about 25.2 per cent of outlay was growth-oriented. The total outlay of the DoA and FW, including non-schematic expenditures for 2023–24 BE was Rs 1.16 trillion.

Krishionnati—another name change

There used to be two major production and productivity enhancement schemes for crop agriculture for all the field and horticultural crops, operated by the Department of Agriculture and Farmers' Welfare, until 2021–22.

The first one, the Green Revolution, was one big umbrella scheme made up of Rashtriya Krishi Vikas Yojana (RKVY) and seventeen other sub-programmes. The other was Pradhan Mantri Krishi Sinchai Yojana (PMKSY)—More Crop Per Drop. Actual expenditure of Rs 11,758 crore was incurred for the Green Revolution scheme in 2018–19 and Rs 2,918 crore for the PMKSY.

In 2021–22, the last year when the schemes operated with this arrangement, the Green Revolution scheme witnessed actual expenditure of Rs 6,747 crore and the PMKSY scheme of Rs 1,796 crore. The expenditure on these two principal growth-oriented schemes in the agriculture sector had come down collectively from Rs 14,676 crore to Rs 8,543 crore, a drop of 41.8 per cent.

The new scheme—Krishionnati Yojana—subsumed ten programmes, which were the National Food Security Mission, Edible Oil—Oil Palm, Edible Oil—Oilseeds, Organic Value Chain Development for Northeast Region, Integrated Development of Horticulture, Seed and Planting Material Scheme, Agriculture Extension, Digital Agriculture, Agriculture Census and Statistics and Agriculture Marketing. Krishionnati Yojana did not include the RKVY. There was a separate budget allocation for each of these ten sub-schemes in the Budget 2022–23. However, in the 2023–24 BE, only a single allocation for the Krishionnati Yojana at Rs 7,066 crore was made.

The Expenditure Budget still describes Krishionnati Yojana as 'an Umbrella Scheme' comprising many CSSs, which aims to develop the agriculture and allied sector in a holistic and scientific manner to increase the income of farmers by enhancing production, productivity and better returns on produce.

The lasting legacy of Modi 2.0 is that the umbrella schemes kept getting new nomenclatures with nothing really changing with respect to their constituent sub-schemes.

Rashtriya Krishi Vikas Yojana

The RKVY is the other major production and productivity enhancing scheme in the budget of DoA and FW with an outlay of Rs 7,150 crore in 2023–24 BE.

The RKVY aims at promoting high growth in agriculture, generating higher returns for farmers and for integrated development by focusing on food security, sustainable agriculture, production of oilseeds, oil palm and agricultural extension. Six development schemes (PMKSY—sub-component More Crop Per Drop, National Project on Soil Health and Fertility, Paramparagat Krishi Vikas Yojana, Rashtriya Krishi Vikas Yojana, Rainfed Area Development and Climate Change and Sub-Mission on Agriculture Mechanization) were bundled into the RKVY from 2022–23 with no separate budget allocation for constituent schemes.

The combined allocation of RKVY was Rs 10,433 crore in 2022–23 BE, which was revised substantially lower to Rs 7,000 crore in 2022–23 RE. The actual expenditure for RKVY for 2022–23 came to Rs 5,248 crore.

With income distribution schemes like PM Kisan and interest subvention schemes coming to the centre stage and assuming the mantle of 'developmental' programmes in the agriculture sector, the growth-oriented programmes, the mainstay of the Green Revolution in India, have now got dislodged to a back-seat.

Biofuels programme takes off

India started its engagement with biofuels in 2003. In 2006, the government issued directions to the oil marketing companies to supply 5 per cent ethanol-blended petrol. A National Policy on Biofuels (NPB–2006) was adopted by the government with an indicative goal of 20 per cent blending of biofuels, both for biodiesel and bio-ethanol, by 2017. Nothing much came out of this policy. In June 2018, when the National Policy on Biofuels 2018 (NPB–2018) was adopted, it was noted that the ethanol blending percentage in petrol was around 2.0 per cent and biodiesel blending percentage in diesel was less than 0.1 per cent. The government notified the NPB–2018 with the indicative target of 20 per cent blending of ethanol in petrol and 5 per cent blending of biodiesel in diesel by 2030.

Modi 2.0 implemented the policy with all seriousness. In September 2019, the government included new sources—sugar and sugar syrup—for producing ethanol. In August 2020, registration of ethanol suppliers for the long-term was started to give them visibility of five years' supply contracts. In September 2020, the oil marketing companies (OMC) started providing offtake guarantees. OMCs also started investing in building their ethanol storage capacities. The NPB–18 was amended in May 2022 to advance the ethanol blending target of 20 per cent to the ethanol supply year (ESY) 2025–26 from 2030. In addition, some other minor amendments were also made, including allowing more feedstocks for production of biofuels and promoting production of biofuels by units located in Special Economic Zones (SEZ)/Export Oriented Units (EoUs) under the Make in India programme. The government lowered the GST rate to 5 per cent from 18 per cent on ethanol meant for blending under the Ethanol Blended Petrol Programme (EBP Programme) as well.

The government brought two major policy interventions for promoting ethanol (biodiesel and other small biofuels did not take off) under the rubric of EBP Programme, which expanded the supply sources for production of ethanol for blending in petrol. Prior to the NPB–18, the ethanol for the EBP Programme was produced primarily from molasses, a by-product of the sugar industry. This constrained the supply of molasses (C-heavy Molasses) to about 13 million metric tonnes (MMT) a year on average, which was sufficient to produce only about 300 crore litres of alcohol/ethanol. The NPB–18 allowed the use of B-heavy Molasses (produced from sugar) for ethanol production as well. One MMT of sugar could produce about 60 crore litres of ethanol. In some years, it was possible to divert 5–6 MMT of sugar, and this new source could yield 300–350 crore litres of additional ethanol supply. By permitting this option, the government hoped to improve participation of distilleries in ethanol production. This policy allowed ethanol to be produced directly from sugarcane juice to increase the blending percentage. The second change the government made was to permit the use of 'other alternate raw materials' for production of ethanol such as sugar containing materials like sugar beet, sweet sorghum, etc., and starch containing materials such as corn, cassava, rotten potatoes, etc., using first-generation fully developed technologies 2nd generation or 2G ethanol. During the years when there was surplus availability of foodgrains, ethanol was also allowed to be produced from foodgrains like rice, wheat, corn, etc.

The government also made many operational changes. For assured procurement of ethanol produced from other non-food feedstock, the public sector OMCs began signing Ethanol Purchase Agreements (EPAs) with 2G ethanol suppliers for a period of fifteen years.

The principal incentive to promote production of ethanol has been to provide a remunerative procurement price for the ethanol procured by the OMCs. The procurement price of ethanol produced from sugarcane-based feed stocks like C and B-heavy molasses, sugarcane juice, sugar and sugar syrup is fixed by the government and from foodgrain-based feed stocks by public sector OMCs on an annual basis. While the government had been notifying the administered price of ethanol since 2014, it introduced a differential price of ethanol based on raw material utilized after NPB-18 came into force.

The Ethanol Supply Year (ESY) runs from December to November. ESY 2018–19 was the first year of Modi 2.0 as it extended to 30 November 2019. For this supply year, the government increased the ex-mill price of ethanol derived from C-heavy molasses to Rs 43.46 per litre from Rs 40.85 per litre paid in ESY 2017–18. The government also fixed, for the first time, the ex-mill price of ethanol derived from B-heavy molasses/partial sugarcane juice at Rs 52.43 per litre and from 100 per cent sugarcane juice at Rs 59.19 per litre for ESY 2018–19. These prices were regularly increased during the 2019–2024 tenure of Modi 2.0.

For ESY 2020–21, the ex-mill price of C-heavy molasses was fixed at Rs 45.69 per litre, for B-heavy molasses at Rs 57.61 per litre, for sugarcane juice/sugar/sugar syrup at Rs 62.65 per litre, for damaged foodgrain/maize at Rs 51.55 per litre and from surplus rice from FCI at Rs 56.87 per litre. The prices were marginally increased for ESY 2021–22. For ESY 2022–23, the ethanol prices from C-heavy molasses, B-heavy molasses and sugarcane juice/sugar/sugar syrup were fixed at Rs 49.41, Rs 60.73 and Rs 65.61 per litre, respectively.

The result of all these initiatives was visible in the increase of ethanol supplied to the OMCs. For ESY 2018–19, 188.57 crore litres of ethanol was supplied.

The supply reduced slightly to 173.03 crore litres in ESY 2019–20. For ESY 2020–21, the ethanol procured for the blending programme increased to 302.30 crore litres. For ESY 2021–22, the ethanol procured by OMCs increased further to 433.6 crore litres.

The annual ethanol production capacity in the country increased to approximately 1,037 crore litres in ESY 2022–23, which had a tentative target of 542 crore litres of ethanol production. However, the government faced challenges in the path of EBP for the first time during its second term. Reduced production of rice and maize led to disruption in the supply of damaged rice from the FCI to ethanol producers. The Press Information Bureau (PIB) release on 20 December 2023 informed that 'about 502 crore litres' was supplied to OMCs in ESY 2022–23.

For ESY 2023–24, a half of which was part of Modi 2.0, OMCs called for tenders for the supply of 825 crore litres of ethanol. By the end of February 2024, they received commitments/offers for the supply of 560 crore litres comprising 270 crore litres of sugarcane-based ethanol and approximately 290 crore litres of grain-based ethanol. The sugar industry did not commit to diverting sugar production for ethanol in view of a likely reduction in the production of sugar from 36.6 million tonnes in the 2022–23 season to 33.7 million tonnes in the 2023–24 season. The OMCs and the government did not make any press releases about ethanol production after February, which indicated a constrained supply of ethanol in the year.

Policy and Reforms

Crazy case of three farm laws

The government moved at a very swift speed to bring reforms in agriculture marketing, contract farming and essential commodities. The third tranche of the stimulus package announced by Finance Minister Nirmala Sitharaman specified reforms in three farm laws, as part of the governance and administrative reforms package.

The first announcement stated that the government would, to enable better price realization for farmers, bring amendments to the Essential Commodities Act (ECA) to 'deregulate agriculture food stuffs including cereals, edible oils, oilseeds, pulses, onions and potato' and 'stock limit to be imposed under very exceptional circumstances like national calamities, famine with surge in prices'. She also announced that 'no stock limit shall apply to processors or value chain participants, subject to their installed capacity or to any exporter subject to the export demand'. The second announcement related to agriculture marketing reforms to provide marketing choices to farmers. For this purpose, the Finance Minister announced that 'a Central law will be formulated to provide adequate choices to farmers to sell produce at attractive price; barrier free inter-state trade and a framework for e-trading of agricultural produce'. The third announcement related to 'agriculture produce price and quality assurance'. For this purpose, the Finance Minister said that 'a facilitative legal framework will be created to enable farmers for engaging with processors, aggregators, large retailers, exporters, etc. in a fair and transparent manner' and that 'risk mitigation for farmers, assured returns and quality standardization shall form integral part of the framework'.

The government moved pretty fast thereafter.

The President of India promulgated two ordinances 'with the aim of giving a boost to rural India for farmers engaged in agriculture and allied activities': The Farmers' Produce Trade and Commerce (Promotion and Facilitation) Ordinance 2020 and The Farmers (Empowerment and Protection) Agreement on Price Assurance and Farm Services Ordinance 2020. It was claimed that the first Ordinance 'will provide for the creation of an ecosystem where the farmers and traders enjoy the freedom of choice relating to sale and purchase of farmers' produce which facilitates remunerative prices through competitive alternative trading channels'. Further, 'it will promote efficient, transparent and barrier-free inter–State and intra-State trade and commerce of farmers' produce outside the physical premises of markets or deemed markets notified under various State agricultural produce market legislations'. Besides, it was claimed that 'the Ordinance will provide a facilitative framework for electronic trading and matters connected therewith or incidental thereto'. The second Ordinance, it was emphasized in the Press Release 'will provide for a national framework on farming agreements that protects and empowers farmers to engage with agri-business firms, processors, wholesalers, exporters or large retailers for farm services and sale of future farming produce at a mutually agreed remunerative price framework in a fair and transparent manner and for matters connected therewith or incidental thereto'.

Together, the two measures, it was reiterated, 'will enable barrier-free trade in agriculture produce, and also empower the farmers to engage with sponsors of his choice'. The government seemed satisfied to have realized its objective and claimed that 'the freedom of the farmer, which is of paramount importance, has thus been provided'. The government also promulgated the Essential Commodities (Amendment) Ordinance 2020 on the same day, i.e. 5 June 2020.

Three bills: 1. The Farmers' Produce Trade and Commerce (Promotion and Facilitation) Bill, 2020, 2. The Farmers (Empowerment and Protection) Agreement of Price Assurance and Farm Services Bill, 2020 and 3. The Essential Commodities (Amendment) Bill, 2020 were introduced in the Lok Sabha on 14 September 2020 to replace the ordinances promulgated on 5 June 2020. The Bills were pretty much on the same lines as that of the Ordinances.

The Farmers' Produce Trade and Commerce (Promotion and Facilitation) Bill, 2020 sought to provide for the creation of an ecosystem where farmers and traders enjoy the freedom of choice relating to the sale and purchase of farmers' produce, which facilitates remunerative prices through competitive alternative trading channels to promote efficient, transparent and barrier-free inter-state and intra-state trade and commerce of farmers' produce outside the physical premises of markets or deemed markets notified under various state agricultural produce market legislations; to provide a facilitative framework for electronic trading and for matters connected therewith or incidental thereto. The Farmers (Empowerment and Protection) Agreement of Price Assurance and Farm Services Bill, 2020, sought to provide for a national framework on farming agreements that protects and empowers farmers to engage with agri-business firms, processors, wholesalers, exporters or large retailers for farm services and sale of future farming produce at a mutually agreed remunerative price framework in a fair and transparent manner and for matters connected therewith or incidental thereto. The Essential Commodities (Amendment) Bill, 2020 sought to remove commodities like cereals, pulses, oilseeds, edible oils, onions and potatoes from the list of essential commodities. This would remove the fears of private investors of excessive regulatory interference in their business operations. The freedom to produce, hold, move, distribute and supply would lead to harnessing of economies of scale and attract private sector/foreign direct investment into the agriculture sector.

There was an extraordinary hurry to pass the three farm laws. They were passed on 17 September 2020, within three days of their introduction, without much discussion, examination and division of vote. The President gave his assent to all the three laws on 27 September 2020 and, immediately thereafter, they became the law of the land.

The farmers in some parts of the country protested. Punjab farmers announced a rail roko agitation on 24 September. Farmer unions in Punjab and Haryana gave the call for 'Delhi Chalo' on November 2020. The farmers laid siege to Delhi borders from all sides soon and disrupted the movement of vehicles in and out of Delhi for many months.

The Farmers' Produce Trade and Commerce (Promotion and Facilitation) Act, 2020, introduced agriculture products marketing reforms by striking at the root of the agriculture produce marketing committees' (APMCs) monopoly over wholesale agricultural produce trading. In terms of marketing reforms, this law was truly revolutionary. The act granted complete freedom to farmers to sell their produce at the APMCs or anywhere outside. It also enfranchised any businessman to set up a physical trading station outside the APMC market yard or establish an electronic trading system anywhere in the country. The law also effectively abolished the system of *mandi* fees by exempting the businesses set up outside APMCs from the payment of mandi fees. Together, these two measures, brought about by the law, allowed farmers and traders to undertake inter-state and intra-state transactions without any restrictions. As there was a distinct comparative advantage to set up shop outside the APMCs, both in terms of trading freedom and non-payment of mandi fees, it was expected that trading of agriculture produce would soon shift outside the APMC market yards.

The Farmers (Empowerment and Protection) Agreement on Price Assurance and Farm Services Act, 2020 sought to institutionalize a Central government-controlled and regulated contract farming regime in the country. This did not bring any new reforms. Many states had institutionalized contract farming in their respective states though there was not much success in bringing the advantages of contract farming in the country. The central law, however, only envisaged a centralized policy and management of contract farming in the country. There was no real value addition. This was more of circumscribing states' authority and initiative without bringing any additional reform.

The amendment in the Essential Commodities Act was intended to circumscribe the government's authority to place restrictions on storage, pricing and export of agriculture produce. This again did not really bring any real reform. In fact, it was the government that was unnecessarily putting ad hoc restrictions on marketing, storage and transportation. There was a need to fully junk the Essential Commodities Act.

The states stood to suffer the loss of significant mandi tax revenues. The agriculture trade would have also shifted outside the APMCs controlled by them. However, barring some Opposition-ruled states, which also passed meaningless resolutions in their assemblies, the states did not wince much. Unfortunately for the GoI, the farmers of Punjab and two adjoining states decided to protest by blocking roads to Delhi, which created considerable visible opposition to the three farm laws. The Supreme Court suspended the implementation of the three laws. Later, the government also announced suspension of these three laws for a period of eighteen months. The government invited the farmers for talks. Nothing worked. Farmers continued to block the roads and agitate for more than one year.

Finally, the government gave in. In November 2021, the Prime Minister announced that the three farm laws would be repealed. The laws were duly repealed by the Parliament in December 2021. The repeal of these farm laws not only meant that the agriculture produce marketing would remain shackled in the country, the climb-down signalled that the will of the government to bring economic reforms was quite weak and further dissipating.

No follow-through for land leasing reform announcement

In her 2020–21 Budget Speech, Finance Minister Sitharaman announced that the government will encourage those state governments who undertake implementation of Model Agriculture Land Leasing Act, 2016, in addition to two other model laws—the Model Agricultural Produce and Livestock Marketing (Promotion and Facilitation) Act, 2017 and the Model Agricultural Produce and Livestock Contract Farming and Services (Promotion and Facilitation) Act, 2018.

The Model Agricultural Produce and Livestock Marketing (Promotion and Facilitation) Act, 2017 got subsumed in the Farmers' Produce Trade and Commerce (Promotion and Facilitation) Act, 2020. The Model Agricultural Produce and Livestock Contract Farming and Services (Promotion and Facilitation) Act, 2018 was overtaken by the Farmers (Empowerment and Protection) agreement on Price Assurance and Farm Services Act 2020. As discussed in the previous section, after being first enacted through respective ordinances and later replaced by hurriedly passed laws in the Parliament and lawfully notified, these two laws were cancelled by the enactment of another law in 2021.

The Model Agriculture Land Leasing Act, 2016, did not share this excitement. Nor was it followed through with the states. There was a complete contrast in the de-facto and de-jure situation in the country as far as land leasing was concerned.

Almost all land reform laws passed in all the states of the country after Independence either completely disallowed land leasing or made it subject to so many conditions that formal land leasing is just not practised in the country. The statutory bans and restrictions, however, could not overcome the real economic necessity of leasing land. There are many reasons why agricultural lands are given to other farmers for cultivation, though the system operates entirely informally. The lessor and the lessee enter into an informal agreement, commonly described as *batai*, or a sharecropping arrangement.

Land leasing restrictions have been relaxed in some states marginally over the years. The Andhra Pradesh Licenced Cultivators Act was passed in 2011. Some other states brought in contract farming through amendments in other laws. Yet, there are millions of landowners who still cannot formally lease land.

NITI Aayog constituted an Expert Committee on Land Leasing in 2015, which also stated that 'restrictive land leasing laws have forced tenancy to be informal, insecure and inefficient' and 'restrictions on land leasing have reduced the occupational mobility of many landowners'. The committee had rightly concluded that 'the restrictive tenancy laws have proved to be anti-growth and anti-poor even though India's policymakers thought it differently while making such laws.'

The committee recommended negating all the provisions in the land laws of the states banning and restricting land leasing. It also proposed a new Model Agricultural Land Leasing Act, 2016. The Model Act is quite business-like in nature and protects the legitimate interests of both the lessor and lessee. It also recommended a standard land leasing agreement. This is the leasing law which the Finance Minister had referred to in her Budget Speech 2020–21.

The government turned lukewarm soon after making this Budget announcement. After the fiasco over the three farm laws, the motivation to push the Modern Agricultural Land Lease Law simply vanished. Understandably, no progress was made on this reform during Modi 2.0.

Land records digitization yields limited results

By merging the two existing schemes for computerization of land records and strengthening of the land revenue administration system, the government had initiated the National Land Record Modernization Programme in 2008 to usher in a system of updated digital land records, automated and automatic mutation, integration between textual and spatial records, interconnectivity between revenue and registration to replace the present deeds' registration and presumptive title system with that of conclusive titling with a title guarantee.

The Modi government, during its first term, revamped and converted the programme into a Central Sector Scheme with effect from 1 April 2016 with 100 per cent funding by the Centre and named it the Digital India Land Records Modernization Programme (DILRMP). The objective of DILRMP is to develop a modern, comprehensive and transparent land record management system with the aim to develop an Integrated Land Information Management System which will inter alia: (i) improve real-time information on land; (ii) optimize use of land resources; (iii) benefit both landowners and prospectors; (iv) assist in policy and planning; (v) reduce land disputes; (vi) check fraudulent/benami transactions; (vii) obviate the need of physical visits to revenue/registration offices and (viii) enable sharing of information with various organizations/agencies. The government approved its extension as DILRMP 2.0 for a period of five years—2021–22 to 2025–26—during Modi 2.0.

As per the DILRMP-MIS 2.0 dashboard, as of end-May 2024, there are 6,54,388 villages in the country with 34.13 crore Records of Rights (RoRs). The RoRs have been completed in 6,26,327 villages (95.71 per cent) and the work was in progress in 1,624 villages (0.25 per cent). This implies that the RoRs' updating work was still to commence in the remaining 26,437 (4.04 per cent) villages.

The government brought in the concept of a unique land parcel identifier number (ULPIN), also called Bhu-Aadhaar number, in 2020–21, to assign an alpha-numeric fourteen-digit unique ID to each land parcel in the country based on geo-coordinates of vertices of the land parcel. The ULPIN uses the international standard—Electronic Commerce Code Management System (ECCMA). The programme aims at mapping the ownership (record of rights) status and other useful information to the ULPIN.

Thirteen states/UTs launched the ULPIN programme in March 2021 and the rest gradually followed. At the end of FY 2022–23, twenty-six states had adopted the programme and a total number of 9.026 crore land parcels had been assigned ULPIN/Bhu-Aadhaar numbers. In the seven states/UTs—Karnataka, Puducherry, Telangana, Manipur, Andamans and Nicobar, Delhi and Chandigarh—the pilot testing had been done and the decision was pending in two states/UTs—Arunachal Pradesh and Lakshadweep. By the end of 2023–24, the ULPIN programme was in operation in all thirty-six states and UTs.

Notable progress was made in digitizing cadastral maps and generating Bhu-Aadhaar numbers. Of the 3.03 cadastral maps in good condition in the country, as many as 2.53 crore maps could be digitized by the end of May 2024. Of the 6,54,388 villages, spatial data of as many as 4,99,887 villages had been verified and cadastral maps of 3,50,613 villages (53.58 per cent) geo-referenced. Of 23.61 crore land parcels, 8.59 crore could be geo-referenced and 7.22 crore ULPINs implemented. Indeed a creditable performance.

There are three major deficiencies in DILRMP 2.0/ULPIN. First, ULPIN seeks to computerize and assign ULPIN to all land parcels. However, there is no standard system of merging and dividing land parcels in the country. ULPIN assigned to a land parcel becomes ineffective the moment it is subdivided into more than one land parcel. Second, the DILRMP is computerizing the RoR as it exists in the states. There are many right-holders to one land parcel and one right-holder may own many land parcels. There is no national template for identifying right-holders to a land parcel. Third, the two most important land records—RoRs and land parcels (*khasra*)—are only available in local languages. As a result, there is no national land rights registry.

There are some other issues as well. The land records essentially state the status of tenancy/ownership of a person over the surveyed plot/parcel of land. If the land has been converted into non-agricultural use, at best a note is recorded in the last column of the record to that effect. It is also a limited and static record; assignment of different rights in the land, such as leasing, mortgage, etc., are either not recorded or remain un-updated. Thus, it is not a comprehensive record of ownership and other attributes of ownership over land. It is not a live record of 'ownership rights' in the land. Finally, the record is maintained basically for agricultural land. Urban areas or *abadi* areas usually get clubbed into one or a few survey numbers. The responsibility of maintaining a record of buildings is entrusted to urban bodies. In practice, there is no system of recognizing land in non-agricultural areas (residential, industrial and infrastructure). The record thus accounts for only a part of the land parcels in the country.

The DILRMP/ULPIN system need to address these issues and create/build an integrated system of land survey and record, covering both rural and urban areas—a National System of Land Records.

Land acquisition reforms left untouched

The Land Acquisition Act, 1894, was the principal instrument of land acquisition for public and private projects after Independence. As development required a good amount of land to be used for non-agricultural purposes, the act came to be used quite frequently. Both by design and operation, the Land Acquisition Act worked against the landholder farmer. Land could be acquired for almost any purpose as 'public purpose' was widely interpreted in practice. The compensation payable was the market value of similar land. This value, as recorded in the Registrar's record, was quite depressed on account of agriculture being a poor value creator and real transaction prices not being disclosed in registration documents. A solatium was offered, but it was a meagre 30 per cent. For the first thirty to forty years, farmers literally received a pittance as compensation and not only became poorer but in many cases rootless. As land was usually possessed much before compensation was provided, lakhs of farmers were rendered destitute.

The UPA government brought in the Right to Fair Compensation and Transparency in Land Acquisition, Rehabilitation and Resettlement Act, 2013. This law moved the pendulum to the other extreme. Compensation was made four times in rural areas and twice in urban areas. Such multiples hurt more as the base price recorded was also rigged/manipulated to be much higher than the normal market price. Further, compensation and assistance were mandated to be provided to not only landowners but various other affected persons. Provisions of social assessment and obtaining the free consent of a large number of people (70–80 per cent) in case of projects with private participation were made stringent. The process became impossible to navigate.

The private sector stopped acquiring land under the 2013 Act. The government began making payments that are way above anything justifiable. Even NHAI road projects, which are exempt from some procedural provisions, like taking prior consent of 80 per cent of farmers, have been paying massive amounts as land compensation. Paying Rs 10 crore per acre for an NHAI project had become quite normal in 2018/2019. Land costs began exceeding 50–60 per cent of the cost of a road project.

The NDA/Modi government tried to roll back in 2014–15 some provisions (prior consent and social impact assessment) in five specified types of acquisition: projects vital for national security or defence; rural infrastructure projects; affordable housing and housing for the poor; industrial corridors; and infrastructure, including social infrastructure projects. However, the 2015 Amendment Bill, brought for this purpose, could not get through the Rajya Sabha and the government abandoned the effort. The scene then shifted to the states—some states, including Tamil Nadu, Gujarat, Maharashtra, Telangana and Jharkhand, have enacted the provisions of the Amendment Law, by taking the consent of the Centre, However, irreparable damage had already been done. Urbanization, industrialization and infrastructure-building collapsed. Capital expenditure kept constantly coming down and infrastructure in the private sector became a casualty.

Everyone recognizes that two fundamental reforms are required in the 2013 Law. First, the applicability of the law needs to be severely limited. It should only be used for projects that require land for the government to produce public goods and services. Defence, policing, health, regulation, etc., should be the purposes for which land could be 'acquired'. The 2013 Law extends the liability to provide for a relief and rehabilitation package even for purely private purchase of land through private negotiations if the land involved is more than the limit prescribed by the government. These provisions need to be dropped. For private projects, the acquisition law should be used only where the private entrepreneur is able to buy more than 80 per cent of the land by private negotiations, but some minority landowners are unjustifiably holding up the remaining land. In such a situation, the Law should be used just to determine a reasonable price. Second, all the confusions and contradictions of the 2013 Law should be sorted out. The environmental and social impact consideration should be made applicable to the project, not the land acquisition. The price paid for land should be related to the market price plus compensation. If the underlying market price is not reflective of the true price, the same should be objectively determined by the acquisition officer. Other interests in the land property should be recognized and compensated in a fair manner. Requirements of giving jobs and annuities should be done away with.

Unfortunately, Modi 2.0 had no interest in getting anywhere close to the subject of reopening the 2013 Law. The government kept paying excessive amounts of compensation for the land acquired for public infrastructure. The private sector would either take the land from the government agencies or purchase the land directly from farmers or would co-opt the farmers/land owners to bring land as equity in housing and other projects. Hardly any road project was taken on a build, operate and transfer (BOT) basis as the land acquisition cost made such projects completely non-viable.

Legal guarantee for MSP demanded

The farmers of Punjab and Haryana re-launched their agitation for a legally-guaranteed MSP in February 2024, threatening to enter Delhi with their tractors. The farmers of Punjab, Haryana and Western UP have benefited the most from the system of assured procurement under the MSP. The maximum proportion of their principal crops—wheat and rice—grown for the last fifty years now, have been consistently purchased under the MSP system.

They also wanted prices higher than the current MSP formula. The current MSP provides the farmers with a 50 per cent income margin over all the paid costs (called A2) and imputed cost of their unpaid family labour (FL). The farmers demanded the 50 per cent margin to be fixed over the cost (called C2) which, in addition to A2 and FL, take into account return on the capital cost.

The logic of demanding a legal guarantee is quite flawed. If a legal guarantee to procure the produce at MSP is provided by bringing a law, the only additional element to the present system of procurement is that the farmers would be able to go to a court to enforce the procurement at MSP if the government does not do so. Hoping that courts would be able to enforce procurement under MSP is as dysfunctional and illusory as the state of enforcement of legal rights for education, employment and many other rights.

In reality, the MSP system has outlived its utility. The MSP grand bargain was offered when India used to face an acute food deficit. That situation no longer exists. The current agriculture system in India has excessive government involvement and interference. There are massive subsidies on every agriculture input—from seeds to fertilizers to power to water to crop loans.

Roughly about 140 million hectares of area is sown in India every year. The Government spends about Rs 6 trillion in food, fertilizers, interest, PM Kisan and other farmer-related subsidies every year. The state governments are estimated to spend another Rs 8 trillion in explicit and implicit subsidies. Even after excluding non-cash subsidies and subsidies attributable to consumers, the subsidies for farmers are not less than Rs 7 trillion. This gives an average subsidy of Rs 50,000 per hectare. Barring a few, the farmers do not get Rs 50,000 per hectare as profit.

Our current system makes the government spend a lot, yet the farmers remain steeped in poverty. Indian farmers who grow pulses, edible oils and coarse grains still remain quite poor. India is also supply-deficient in pulses and edible oils.

Our present situation calls for a fundamentally different policy solution. Let the governments consider giving the equivalent of what they spend today in cash subsidies to farmers as direct cash transfer in farmers' bank accounts on a per hectare basis. This will provide the farmers an income higher than the full price of their produce, which they get today. As part of the grand bargain, the farmers will stop receiving all input subsidies and their produce would not be bought by the government under the MSP system. Instead, they would be completely free to grow whatever they consider the best and sell their produce in the market. The government can continue the MSP system only for pulses and edible oil farmers if it likes. However, the farmers may get an option to receive the cash grant or sell their produce to the government at the MSP.

The Modi government did not try to resolve the MSP issue. Thankfully, it did not accept the demand to provide a legal guarantee for procurement under the MSP system. It also did nothing for moving India towards fundamental reform of the deeply flawed MSP system offering the grand bargain.

2

Industry and Construction

In the twentieth century, manufacturing was the biggest growth generator worldwide. Manufacturing primarily involves transforming agricultural and mineral raw materials into useful value-added products. Manufacturing also gave a big boost to assets construction—factories, residential building complexes, road networks, warehouses and so on. Four heads in national accounts, out of eight—mines and minerals, manufacturing, utilities and construction—together make up industry.

India, an agricultural giant for centuries, did not innovate industrial technologies, processes and products, contented as perhaps it was with its agricultural produce, income and prosperity. India realized much later how the Industrial Revolution, which transformed Europe and America, undermined its agricultural products-based economy, e.g. cotton textiles, massively.

In pre-Independence India, many Indian entrepreneurs began setting up manufacturing plants—cotton textiles, steel and the like. Post-Independence, India went the wrong way. It nationalized basic manufacturing by and large, by reserving it for the public sector. Whatever private industry was permitted in consumer products was also stifled massively by subjecting every production capacity creation and expansion to the draconian licence and permit system. Indian manufacturing did not really take off in the first forty years.

The 1991 reforms dismantled this largely failed system and Indian industry began to breathe. Private investment, including foreign investment, took off and India became something of a manufacturing nation. India's real GVA growth in manufacturing, construction and utilities (economic survey 2022–23, 2011–12 prices) was 5.38 per cent per annum for the forty-year period from 1950–51 to 1990–91. The same table informs that real GVA growth increased significantly to 6.70 per cent per annum in the twenty-three-year period between 1990–91 and 2013–14. Industrial growth was still higher at 7.87 per cent per annum in the ten-year period of the UPA government (2003–04 to 2013–14).

India, despite this reasonably creditable industrial growth record after the 1991 reforms, was not quite satisfied when the change of government took place in May 2014. The challenge before the Narendra Modi government was to boost industrial growth rate still higher. In the first term, the government came up with the Make in India programme. Industrial growth slowed down a little to 7.34 per cent per annum in Modi 1.0. That set the stage for the second term of the Modi government.

Growth

Converting agricultural and mineral produce into industrial products and making machines to manufacture industrial products is the core of manufacturing. Likewise, extracting mineral products from the mines and primary processing them to produce beneficiated minerals is an important industrial process. So is generating power and other utility services, and constructing buildings and other infrastructure.

In this chapter, I will assess the progress of the Modi government for manufacturing as such, which is separately accounted for in the national accounts, and also for industry as a whole, taking three other sectors of the economy in national accounts—mining and quarrying, utilities (electricity, gas, water supply and others) and construction.

Manufacturing growth slowed down

Manufacturing GVA, at constant 2011–12 prices, was of the order of Rs 23.29 trillion in 2018–19, the last year of Modi 1.0. The manufacturing growth rate was quite stupendous at 8.34 per cent per annum in the first term.

Covid-19 and the lockdowns imposed by the government hit manufacturing hard in the first two years of Modi 2.0. Manufacturing GVA was completely flat, at constant prices, at Rs 23.29 trillion in 2020–21. The year 2021–22 put manufacturing back on its feet with the GVA rising to Rs 25.61 trillion with annual growth of 9.96 per cent, raising the three-year growth rate during Modi 2.0 to 3.22 per cent.

Manufacturing growth remained volatile during Modi 2.0 with its GVA witnessing a bad year again in 2022–23. The GVA fell to Rs 25.05 trillion (I RE), which meant the manufacturing GVA contracted by (-)2.20 per cent in that year. In 2023–24, manufacturing switched again to the expansion mode. Manufacturing GVA was estimated at Rs 27.88 trillion (FAE) and at Rs 27.17 trillion in the SAE. The provisional numbers released on 31 May 2024 pegged manufacturing GVA at Rs 27.52 trillion. Over the five-year period of Modi 2.0, manufacturing recorded annual growth of only 3.39 per cent.

Compared to the 8.34 per cent annual growth in the first term (2014–19), the manufacturing growth of only 3.39 per cent per annum in the second term was quite disappointing and underwhelming. Manufacturing growth in Modi 2.0 was only about 40 per cent of the growth witnessed in Modi 1.0.

Metal and metal products group recorded respectable growth

The manufacturing data is classified into two groups of corporate and household sectors. The corporate sector is quite dominant. In 2018–19, the corporate sector's share in manufacturing value added was as much as 88 per cent (Rs 20.40 trillion out of a total GVA of Rs 23.29 trillion).

There are six industry groups in corporate manufacturing—a. manufacture of food products, beverages and tobacco, b. manufacture of textiles, apparel and leather products, c. manufacture of metal and metal products, d. manufacture of machinery and equipment, e. manufacture of coke, petroleum, rubber, chemical and related products and f. others. In the national accounts, GVA data is available for these industry groups only at GVA plus financial intermediary services indirectly measured (FISIM), which in 2018–19 for the corporate group was Rs 21.17 trillion.

In the first term of the Modi government, the manufacturing GVA (with FISIM) had grown at a decent rate of 8.36 per cent over GVA (with FISIM) of Rs 13.51 trillion in 2013–14. The first four years of Modi 2.0 (2019–23), for which the industry group GVA data is available at the time of finishing this book, witnessed a tepid growth of 1.80 per cent, lower than the overall GVA growth, in corporate manufacturing, with the GVA (with FISIM) growing to only Rs 22.74 trillion in 2022–23.

More granular analysis reveals that two out of six industry groups actually recorded negative growth during this period. The manufacture of food products, beverages and the tobacco group saw a contraction of (-)5.91 per cent per annum. The manufacture of textiles, apparel and leather products recorded negative growth of (-)2.62 per cent.

Three groups recorded lower growth. The manufacture of machinery and equipment group recorded annual growth of only 0.13 per cent; the manufacture of coke, petroleum, rubber, chemical and related products recorded growth of 3.52 per cent and the 'others' group was 1.14 per cent.

It was the metal and metal products group only that bucked the trend. The GVA of this group was Rs 3.04 trillion in 2018–19 and it rose to Rs 4.22 trillion in 2022–23, recording a decent growth rate of 8.52 per cent per annum. In the first term, this group had recorded growth of only 2.99 per cent. Clearly, the impact of government capital expenditure and outlays for housing schemes were doing their work.

Mining and quarrying had the worst outing

Mining and quarrying constitutes a smaller proportion of total GVA and also of industry GVA. In 2018–19, this group had a GVA, at constant prices, of Rs 3.27 trillion only, out of total GVA of Rs 127.34 trillion (2.56 per cent) and industry GVA of Rs 39.77 trillion (8.22 per cent).

During Modi 1.0, the mining and quarrying group had recorded growth of 4.43 per cent, not very impressive, though. In the second term, the growth in this group simply tanked. Mining and quarrying GVA collapsed to Rs 2.91 trillion in 2020–21, recording a two-year negative CAGR of 6.7 per cent. There was recovery in the next two years (Rs 3.09 trillion in 2021–22 and Rs 3.15 trillion in 2022–23). Still, at the end of four years, mining and quarrying GVA was lower than the GVA in 2018–19. Four years' CAGR was still negative at (-)0.90 per cent.

Fortunes turned only in 2023–24, with FAE placing mining and quarrying GVA at Rs 3.51 trillion, overtaking the 2018–19 GVA. The mining and quarrying GVA was revised down to Rs 3.41 trillion in the SAE and further to Rs 3.38 trillion in the PE. The 2023–24 growth was still good at 7.09 per cent, which also brought the five-year CAGR into positive territory, albeit at an abysmal annual rate of 0.65 per cent.

Fuel minerals—coal, petroleum and natural gas—make up more than half of the total output value of the mining and quarrying group. In 2018–19, at constant prices, the output value of coal was Rs 1.13 trillion and that of petroleum and natural gas Rs 1.67 trillion, in total Rs 2.81 trillion. The output value of the fuel group declined to Rs 2.70 trillion in 2022–23 with the petroleum and natural gas group output value declining massively to Rs 1.20 trillion. This affirms the continuous decline in the domestic production of petroleum and natural gas in the country for many years. The output value of coal on the other hand rose to Rs 1.50 trillion in 2022–23 reflecting much better growth in coal production, feeding rising thermal power generation demand.

Iron ore (Rs 84,161 crore in 2018–19) makes up the big chunk of the metallic mineral group output (Rs 1.24 trillion). There was a small decline in the output value of the metallic mineral group in the first three years (Rs 1.19 trillion in 2021–22) with iron ore remaining almost completely unscathed (Rs 83,170 billion). In 2022–23, the metallic minerals group output value at Rs 1.28 trillion just exceeded Modi 1.0's output value.

Utilities sector was lacklustre overall

The utilities group (electricity, gas, water supply and other utilities) has a strong government and public sector presence. The demand for electricity is rising massively on the back of growing charging infrastructure for both electric vehicles and electronic equipment. Yet, the group recorded lower annual growth during the second term in comparison to the first term, though its growth rate was higher than the overall industry group.

Thanks to the highly subsidized nature of the utility services pricing, the utilities group is a small group out of the eight GVA groups in national accounts. In 2018–19, the total value added by the utilities group was Rs 2.94 trillion at constant 2011–12 prices, smaller than even the mining and quarrying group. In 2023–24 (PE), the GVA of the utilities group reached Rs 3.74 trillion, recording growth of 4.93 per cent per annum during Modi 2.0.

This growth rate (4.93 per cent) was much smaller than the growth rate of 8.06 per cent recorded in the utilities group in the first term, though it was higher than the overall industry group GVA growth rate of 4.26 per cent per annum.

The electricity sector dominates the utilities output value and GVA. In 2018–19, the GVA of electricity, at constant 2011–12 prices, was Rs 2.21 trillion out of a total GVA of 2.94 trillion (a little over 75 per cent) with water supply (Rs 33,184 crore), natural gas (Rs 16,863 crore) and remediation and other utilities (Rs 22,655 crore) accounting for the rest. The electricity sector GVA rose to Rs 2.59 trillion in 2022–23 (CAGR 4.05 per cent) while the water supply GVA increased to Rs 45,439 crore and the gas sector GVA declined to Rs 14,753 crore (CAGR minus 2.69 per cent).

Heavy government ownership and highly suppressed prices, on account of subsidies, make the utilities sector appear much smaller in overall GVA than what its economic role actually is.

Construction recorded higher growth

Of the four groups that are part of the industry group, the construction group is the only one that recorded higher growth in Modi 2.0, again underlying the fact that the growth in the industry group was largely on the back of enhanced government CapEx and housing subsidies. The construction group is a fairly large group as well, and is of the size of about half the manufacturing group.

In 2018–19, the construction group GVA, at constant prices, was Rs 10.27 trillion. The group had recorded a growth of 5.10 per cent per annum during the first term of the Modi government, rising from a GVA of 8.01 trillion in 2013–14. In the five years of Modi 2.0, the construction group GVA grew to Rs 14.36 trillion (PE), recording five-year CAGR growth to 6.94 per cent, 1.84 per cent higher than in Modi 1.0.

The construction group comprises residential buildings (dwellings in national accounts), non-residential buildings, roads and bridges, other constructions and land improvements, plantation and mineral exploration. By its very nature, the construction of these physical assets use up large amounts of construction material and inputs—cement and cement products, iron and steel, bricks, tiles and the like.

In 2018–19, the output value of constructed assets, in constant terms, was Rs 28.43 trillion. To generate this output, inputs of Rs 17.74 trillion and FISIM of Rs 0.42 trillion were used, generating a GVA of Rs 10.27 trillion. The GVA produced by the construction group was only 36.12 per cent of its output value.

Construction majorly suffered the pangs of Covid-19 lockdowns with its GVA declining to Rs 9.95 trillion in 2020–21 (from Rs 10.27 trillion in 2018–19). The sector, however, bounced back handsomely in 2021–22 (GVA Rs 11.94 trillion), recording a whopping growth of 19.91 per cent, bringing the three-year growth CAGR to 5.14 per cent. In 2022–23, the construction group GVA rose to Rs 13.06 trillion (four-year CAGR 6.20 per cent).

The non-residential buildings group—office complexes, malls, warehouses, etc.—has the largest output value in the construction group with Rs 11.96 trillion of value in 2018–19 (about 42 per cent of all constructed assets). The non-residential buildings had witnessed a robust growth of 7.41 per cent per annum in Modi 1.0. In the second term also, in the first four years for which data is available, this group recorded higher output growth (6.89 per cent) than the overall construction group growth at 6.53 per cent, registering output of Rs 15.61 trillion in 2022–23.

The residential dwelling group is relatively smaller with an output value, at constant prices, of Rs 58,331 crore only (2 per cent) of the total output value in 2018–19. What has been visibly witnessed in under-construction and stalled constructions across the country is evident in the national accounts data as well. The residential building construction value recorded a negative growth rate of (-)2.63 per cent in Modi 1.0. In the first two years of the second term as well, growth in residential buildings continued to be negative at (-)5.69 per cent per annum. Only in the next two years (2021–22 and 2022–23), there was a positive turnaround in residential buildings with the output value rising to Rs 6.48 trillion in 2022–23, which resulted in a four-year CAGR of 2.65 per cent.

Iron and steel occupies primacy of place in terms of inputs used in construction. In 2018–19, iron and steel of Rs 7.51 trillion (42.3 per cent of all inputs) was used in construction. Iron and steel input consumption in construction grew by 2.84 per cent per annum in Modi 1.0. In the first four years of the second term, the consumption of iron and steel took off at a higher rate of 9.84 per cent per annum, reaching Rs 10.94 trillion in 2022–23.

Industry did not witness decent growth

The GVA of all the four constituents of the industry group (mining and quarrying, manufacturing, utilities and construction) put together was Rs 39.77 trillion in

2018–19 at constant 2011–12 prices. The industry growth in the first term was healthy at 7.08 per cent per annum (GVA Rs 28.24 trillion in 2013–14).

As noted above, mining and quarrying's annual CAGR growth was almost stagnant (0.65 per cent) in Modi 2.0. Manufacturing also recorded overall tepid growth (3.39 per cent). It was basically the construction group that recorded reasonably good growth (6.94 per cent). Utilities also had only an average performance (4.93 per cent). Consequently, the industry group GVA increased to Rs 49 trillion, at constant prices, in 2023–24 (PE) generating an overall industrial growth rate of 4.26 per cent per annum.

Industrial performance was certainly below par by all accounts during Modi 2.0.

Production-Linked Incentive Schemes

PLIs with big outlay of Rs 1.97 trillion announced

The government had taken up the first production-linked incentive (PLI) scheme for mobile manufacturing and specified electronic components (Rs 40,951 crore) in 2018–19. Two more PLIs—i. critical key starting materials/drug intermediaries and active pharmaceutical ingredients (Rs 6,940 crore) and ii. manufacturing of medical devices (Rs 3,420 crore)—were announced in 2020. These three PLI schemes were to cost the government a total of Rs 51,311 crore.

The government, thereafter, decided to make the PLIs its principal instrument of promoting industrialization in the country. On 11 November 2020, the government approved introduction of PLI schemes in ten additional key sectors to enhance India's manufacturing capabilities and increase exports.

These ten PLI schemes were: 1. Advance chemistry cell (ACC) battery—Rs 18,100 crore, 2. Electronic/technology products—Rs 5,000 crore, 3. Automobiles and auto components—Rs 57,042 crore, 4. Pharmaceuticals drugs—Rs 15,000 crore, 5. Telecom and networking products—Rs 12,195 crore, 6. Textile products: Man-made fibres (MMF) segment and technical textiles—Rs 10,683 crore, 7. Food products—Rs 10,900 crore, 8. High-efficiency solar PV modules—Rs 4,500 crore, 9. White goods (ACs and LEDs)—Rs 6,238 crore, and 10. Speciality steel—Rs 6,322 crore. In all, these ten newly announced PLIs were estimated to cost a total of Rs 1,45,980 crore.

Together with the three PLIs announced earlier, the total estimated outlay for the thirteen PLIs increased to Rs 1,97,291 crore.

One more PLI—Drone and drone components, with an outlay of Rs 120 crore, was announced in September 2021. With that, the total PLIs expanded to fourteen and the total outlay to Rs 1,97,411 crore. The government indicated its intent to bring two more (toys and leather goods) PLIs from time to time. However, no more PLIs materialized during Modi 2.0.

Budget commitments and investment approvals

Finance Minister Nirmala Sitharaman mentioned the government's policy push for the PLIs in her Budget Speech 2021–22 and its commitment to provide nearly Rs 1.97 trillion, to be spent over five years starting 2021–22. No provision was, however, made for the PLI schemes in Budget 2021–22.

In a press release issued on 1 December 2021, the government informed about the status of investment approved for the thirteen PLI schemes. Under the three older PLIs, an investment of Rs 4,347 crore was approved under the scheme of critical key starting materials/drug intermediaries and active pharmaceutical ingredients, Rs 3,000 crore under the scheme for large-scale electronics manufacturing and Rs 799 crore under the scheme for manufacturing of medical devices. In all, a total investment of Rs 8,146 crore was said to have been approved for the three older PLIs. Of the ten new PLI schemes, investments were approved under two schemes (PLI for IT hardware—Rs 17 crore and PLI for telecom and networking products—Rs 183 crore) only, totalling to Rs 200 crore.

In the 2022–23 Budget, the Finance Minister made an announcement about a new PLI scheme for design-led manufacturing to build a strong ecosystem for 5G. This was not a new PLI; but a modified PLI scheme in place of telecom and networking products. The modified scheme was approved by the government on 20 June 2022 without any alteration in its original approved outlay of Rs 12,195 crore. Later, to facilitate domestic manufacturing of high efficiency solar modules for realizing the goal of 280 GW of installed solar capacity by 2030, an additional allocation of Rs 19,500 crore was promised.

Very poor financial performance

The incentives disbursements under PLI schemes in 2021–22, 2022–23 and 2023–24, which marked three of the five years of the life of PLI schemes, have been nothing short of pathetic.

There was no expenditure on any of the PLIs in 2020–21.

In 2021–22, the government budgeted a nominal amount of Rs 1 crore for PLI on white goods. At the RE stage, the budget provisions expanded to Rs 24.5 crore, spread over eight PLI schemes. The largest provision was for the PLI on food processing (Rs 10 crore). For the other seven PLIs, the government made only nominal provisions, ranging from Rs 0.5 crore to Rs 3.5 crore.

The actual expenditure on PLIs in 2021–22 turned out to be still smaller at Rs 10.45 crore with the PLI on food processing accounting for the bulk of it (Rs 9.27 crore). The PLI on white goods reported an expenditure of Rs 1.18 crore. The six other PLI schemes for which a budget provision was made could not disburse incentives.

The government became a little more ambitious for the implementation of PLI schemes in 2022–23. A total budget provision of Rs 7,480.79 crore was made for nine PLI schemes in 2022–23 BE with the largest provision of Rs 5,300 crore made for PLI on large-scale electronics manufacturing. Rs 1,022 crore was budgeted for the food processing PLI, Rs 528 crore for the telecom and networking products PLI, Rs 390 crore for the key starting materials PLI and Rs 216 crore for the domestic manufacturing of medical devices PLI.

As the implementation progress did not appear to match, total production-linked incentives provisions were reduced to Rs 3,879.80 crore in 2022–23 RE. Incentive provision for PLI on pharmaceutical drugs was increased from Rs 3 crore in BE to Rs 694.20 crore. All other provisions were reduced significantly, with the provision for PLI on large-scale electronics manufacturing getting slashed to Rs 2,203 crore.

The actual disbursement of PLIs in 2022–23 amounted to only Rs 2,916.97 crore. The large-scale electronics manufacturing PLI disbursed to the extent of Rs 1,654.96 crore, the pharmaceutical drugs PLI for Rs 655.15 crore and food processing PLIs for Rs 489.83 crore. Seven other PLIs witnessed small disbursements ranging from Rs 1.65 crore (PLI on advanced batteries) to Rs 39.22 crore (PLI on telecom and networking products). The total disbursement of PLIs during the year was only 1.48 per cent of the PLI schemes' overall outlay of Rs 1.97 trillion.

The PLI schemes did not show any notable acceleration during 2023–24 either. The government made a total budget provision of a paltry Rs 8,082.84 crore for eleven PLI schemes. The provision of Rs 4,499.04 crore for the large-scale electronics PLI made up 56 per cent of total budget provision. No budget provision was made for three PLIs—speciality steel, high efficiency solar modules and telecom and networking products. The food processing PLI again had the second largest provision of Rs 1,529.08 crore (18.92 per cent). The pharmaceutical drugs PLI had a provision of Rs 1,000 crore. The government made an enhanced provision of Rs 604 crore for the automobiles and auto parts PLI. Other PLIs had small provisions ranging from Rs 1 crore (advanced batteries) to Rs 146 crore (electronics hardware PLI).

The government maintained more or less similar provisions in 2023–24 RE of Rs 8,007.3 crore. The government has not released the actual PLI disbursement numbers of 2023–24 at the time of writing this book.

A newspaper report, citing an official, claimed that Rs 6,800 crore was released as PLIs during 2023–24. If this report is taken into account, the government could disburse only Rs 9,727 crore in the first three years of PLI schemes (only about 4.92 per cent). If the 2023–24 RE numbers are taken into account, Rs 10,935 crore would have been disbursed (only about 5.5 per cent).

The overall financial performance of PLIs (despite 60 per cent of the implementation period having gone by in Modi 2.0) was nothing short of pathetic.

Only four PLIs made notable progress

Four PLIs disbursed more than 2 per cent of their approved outlays, taking actuals of 2021–22 and 2022–23 and RE of 2023–24 into consideration. The PLI on drones and drone components disbursed the largest outlay (52.5 per cent). Three other PLIs—large-scale electronics manufacturing, food processing and pharmaceutical drugs—disbursed a little over 15 per cent.

As many as six PLIs either saw no disbursement or disbursed incentives of amounts less than 0.5 per cent of their outlays. The PLI on high efficiency solar modules had an absolutely clean record—it did not disburse even a single rupee of incentives. The speciality steel PLI disbursed 0.04 per cent of its Rs 6,322 crore outlay. The PLI on advanced batteries with a large outlay of Rs 18,100 crore disbursed pathetically low incentives of 0.08 per cent. The textiles product PLI (outlay Rs 10,683 crore) could disburse 0.11 per cent of its outlay. The telecom and networking products PLI disbursed 0.32 per cent of its Rs 12,195 crore outlay. Finally, the key starting materials PLI, for which large budgetary provisions were made, also disbursed 0.50 per cent of its Rs 6,940 crore outlay.

The remaining four PLIs had no better than a very lukewarm start. The automobile and auto components PLI with the largest outlay of Rs 57,042 crore hardly moved and disbursed 0.86 per cent of its approved incentives. The electronics hardware PLI, brought with considerable noise, disbursed 1.41 per cent of its Rs 5,000 crore (raised to Rs 17,000 crore in May 2023) outlay only. Another high profile PLI on medical devices also could disburse only 1.74 per cent of its approved outlay of Rs 3,420 crore. The last slow-moving PLI in the group is white goods, which disbursed 1.12 per cent of its Rs 6,238 crore outlay.

The PLIs were the biggest and most high-decibel initiative of Modi 2.0 to kick-start manufacturing in India. The progress of most of the PLIs suggests that this proved to be a damp squib.

PLI for large-scale electronics manufacturing

The government adopted the National Policy on Electronics 2019 (NPE-19) to promote domestic electronics manufacturing and set the goal of $400 billion electronics manufacturing for 2025.

India could rustle up electronics production of only $59 crore in 2017–18, which was a paltry 3 per cent share of global production of $2 trillion. Raising electronics production to $400 billion in seven years (2018–25) required a CAGR growth of 31.4 per cent. The NPE-19 relied in a big way on the manufacture of mobile handsets (goal: production of 1 billion mobile handsets valued at $190 billion). The PLI for large-scale electronics manufacturing (PLI-LSEM) notified in April 2020 was meant to deliver this goal.

The NPE-19 and PLI-LSEM both, despite hundreds of mobile handset manufacturing units being set up, did not deliver. Domestic electronics production rose to $80 billion in 2021–22, with mobile phones contributing 43 per cent.

India's electronics production grew by a paltry $21 billion in four years. Realizing the impossibility of the goal, the government decided to tweak the target to $300 billion by 2026.

The PLI-LSEM offered a production-linked incentive of 4 per cent to 6 per cent on incremental sales to boost domestic manufacturing and attract large investments in mobile phone manufacturing and certain specified electronic components for a period of five years.

According to the publication 'PLI schemes of the Ministry of Electronics and IT for 2022–23', i.e. PLI schemes for mobile phones of the invoice value of Rs 15,000 or more—were approved for three contract manufacturers of Apple (Foxconn, Pegatron and Wistron) and Samsung. A PLI for mobile phones without any specified invoice value and for specified electronics components were approved for twelve domestic companies. In all, thirty-two beneficiary companies, with total investment promised of Rs 7,000 crore, were approved in two rounds of applications. The production plans approved were expected to lead to an incremental production of Rs 8,12,550 crore, of which around Rs 4,87,530 crore (60 per cent) was expected to be exported.

Scheme-specific regular progress updates are not publicly available. The publication referred to above stated that, by March 2023, the PLI-LSEM had resulted in an investment of Rs 6,559 crore. The production and exports of approximately Rs 2.84 trillion (about $35 billion) and Rs 1.29 trillion (about $15 billion) respectively were achieved. Apple seemed to be doing quite well under the scheme. However, as I noted above, operational performance was not reflected in financial disbursement. Still, this scheme remained the best advertisement of the government's PLI initiative.

PLI for IT hardware

The PLI for IT Hardware (PLI-ITH) offered incentives of 4 per cent to 2 per cent/1 per cent to eligible companies on net incremental sales over the base year of 2019–20 for a period of four years (2021–22 to 2024–25) on targeted production of laptops, tablets, all-in-one personal computers and servers.

Applications were received until 30 April 2021 and a total of fourteen companies were approved, which included four global companies—Dell, Wistron, Flex and Rising Star—and ten domestic companies, including Lava, Dixon and Saharsa. These fourteen approved companies were expected to lead to a total production of about Rs 1.6 trillion, of which about Rs 60,000 crore (37 per cent), was expected to be exported. Additional investment promised was Rs 2,500 crore. As per the March 2023 Quarterly Review Report (QRR), the PLI-ITH has resulted in an investment of Rs 195 crore. Additional production of Rs 5,715 crore was also reported.

The government came up with the PLI Scheme 2.0 for IT hardware (PLI-ITH 2.0) in May 2023 with an outlay of Rs 17,000 crore. The PLI-ITH 2.0 was expected to result in the broadening and deepening of the IT hardware manufacturing ecosystem by encouraging localization of components and sub-assemblies and to develop the supply chain within the country. Semiconductor design, integrated circuit (IC) manufacturing and packaging have also been included as incentivized components of the PLI-ITH 2.0.

The scheme extends an average incentive of around 5 per cent on net incremental sales to eligible companies for a period of six years. The operational guidelines for the scheme were notified on 14 July 2023. The application window was open until 31 August 2023. The government informed on 18 November 2023 that applications of twenty-seven IT hardware manufacturers were approved with a promised investment of Rs 3,000 crore.

The scheme did not take off during Modi 2.0.

PLI for automobiles and auto components

The biggest PLI scheme (outlay Rs 57,042 crore) was notified on 23 September 2021. The scheme envisaged incentivizing industry to overcome the cost disabilities in the manufacture of advanced automotive technology products in India. It was expected that, starting from 2022–23, the PLI scheme would lead to fresh investments of over Rs 42,500 crore, incremental production of over Rs 2.3 trillion, create additional employment opportunities of over 7.5 lakh jobs and increase India's share in the global automotive trade.

The champion incentive component of the PLI was a 'sales value linked' incentive on battery electric vehicles and hydrogen fuel cell vehicles. A minimum 50 per cent domestic value addition was required.

The incentive for champion OEM ranged from 13 to 16 per cent.

A total of 115 companies filed their applications under the scheme, out of which five auto OEM companies applied for both parts of the scheme within the time the scheme was open, i.e. up to 9 January 2022. The Ministry of Heavy Industries (MHI) processed the applications received under the Champion OEM

Incentive scheme and twenty applicants (along with their twelve subsidiaries) were approved under the scheme by February 2022 (their investment value and incentive to be claimed were not indicated).

The SOPs were released on 27 April 2023 for submission of applications for the testing and certification of nineteen vehicles and 103 components covered under the scheme. The scheme made very slow progress. On 4 March 2024, the government announced the award of the first PLI Automotive Certificate.

PLI for advanced batteries

The government, on 12 May 2021, approved the PLI scheme 'National Programme on Advanced Chemistry Cell (ACC) Battery Storage' for achieving manufacturing capacity of 50 giga watt hours (GWh) of ACC and 5 GWh of 'Niche' ACC with an outlay of Rs 18,100 crore.

Each selected ACC battery storage manufacturer was expected to commit to setting up an ACC manufacturing facility of minimum 5 GWh capacity and ensure a minimum 60 per cent domestic value addition at the project level within five years.

The government issued a Request for Proposal (RFP) on 22 October 2021. Ten companies submitted their bids within the time stipulated.

A total of four companies were selected, which included Reliance New Energy Solar Ltd (5 GWh); Ola Electric Mobility Pvt. Ltd (20 GWh); Hyundai Global Motors Company Ltd (20 GWh) and Rajesh Exports Ltd (5 GWh). Three selected bidders (other than Hyundai) signed the programme agreement under the PLI scheme for advanced chemistry cell (ACC) battery storage on 28 July 2022.

The government cancelled the allocation of PLI of Rs 7,240 crore (20 GWh) to Hyundai Global Motors, a company which was found to be impersonating South Korea's Hyundai Motor Co. No replacement was approved until Modi 2.0 completed its term.

PLI for drones and drone components

To promote the indigenous drone industry, the government notified the PLI scheme for drones and drone components on 30 September 2021. The PLI had a total incentive allocation of Rs 120 crore spread over three financial years.

This PLI provided incentives equal to 20 per cent of the value addition, which is one of the highest among PLI schemes. The value addition is calculated as the annual sales revenue from drones and drone components (net of GST) minus the purchase cost (net of GST) of drone and drone components. The minimum value addition norm was set at 40 per cent of net sales for drones and drone components instead of 50 per cent, which is another exceptional treatment for the industry. The eligibility norm for MSMEs and start-ups is at nominal levels. The coverage of the scheme included developers of drone-related software also.

The scheme, though with the smallest outlay of Rs 120 crore, had the best incentive disbursal record, which confirmed that the scheme had been implemented very well on the ground.

PLI for food processing

The PLI for food processing, approved on 11 November 2020, supported food manufacturing entities with stipulated minimum sales and willing to make a minimum stipulated investment for expansion of processing capacity and branding abroad to incentive the emergence of strong Indian brands. The scheme also aimed at the creation of global food manufacturing champions.

The scheme was expected to result in incremental sales of Rs 1.2 trillion, cumulative additional investment of Rs 6,057 crore, increase in exports of Rs 27,816 crore and increased employment of 2.28 lakh persons. Additionally, the PLI Scheme for Millet-based Products (PLI-MBP) was launched in FY 2022–23 with an outlay of Rs 800 crore, utilizing savings from PLI on food processing.

The products manufactured under the scheme did not require any high technology investment. The government approved 158 applications for availing incentives. Additionally, sixteen applications were approved under the category of innovative and organic products and twenty-two under the PLI-MBP. The government informed that an investment of Rs 7,427 crore was made by approved entities by 31 March 2023.

Pharma PLIs

The Department of Pharmaceuticals controlled three PLIs.

The PLI scheme for pharmaceuticals was launched in 2021 with a financial outlay of Rs 15,000 crore over a period of six years. In all, fifty-five applicants were selected under the scheme, including twenty MSMEs for three different categories of products—biopharmaceuticals, bulk drugs (except those forty-one eligible products notified under the PLI scheme for bulk drugs) and drugs not covered under Category 1 and Category 2 such as repurposed drugs, etc. The incentives on incremental sales to selected participants under these categories were promised at varying rates over the years, ranging from 10 per cent to 3 per cent. Against the expected investment of Rs 17,425 crore in the pharmaceutical sector over the scheme period, the scheme garnered an investment of Rs 16,199 crore.

Under the PLI scheme for bulk drugs, with a financial outlay of Rs 6,940 crore, the objective was to boost domestic production of forty-one select critical bulk drugs in the country. In all, fifty-one projects were selected for thirty-four notified bulk drugs. Out of this, twenty-two projects were commissioned till the end of FY 2022–23. Incentive rates for fermentation-based products are 20 per cent and chemical-based products are 10 per cent for the initial four years of the scheme, which will taper for the subsequent two years. Against a committed investment of Rs 4,138 crore over the scheme period of six years, an investment of Rs 2,019 crore was reported up to the end of FY 2022–23.

Under the PLI scheme for medical devices, with a financial outlay of Rs 3,420 crore, a total of twenty-one applicants were selected. The objective of this scheme was to establish domestic manufacturing capability of high-end medical devices under four target segments: cancer care/radiotherapy medical devices, radiology and imaging medical devices (both ionizing and non-ionizing radiation products) and nuclear imaging devices, anaesthetics and cardio-respiratory medical devices, including catheters of the cardio-respiratory category and renal care medical devices and all implants, including implantable electronic devices. Against a committed investment of Rs 1,059 crore over the scheme period of five years, an investment of Rs 714 crore was reported by the end of 2022–23 and fourteen projects were commissioned for thirty-four products.

Other PLIs

The PLI scheme for white goods for manufacture of components and sub-assemblies of ACs and LED lights was approved by the government on 7 April 2021 to be implemented over a seven-year period from 2021–22 to 2028–29, and has an outlay of Rs 6,238 crore. The scheme is operational now. Of the sixty-four selected beneficiaries, fifteen, who opted for the gestation period up to 31 March 2022, started commercial production before 2022–23. The rest, who opted for the gestation period up to 31 March 2023, were at different stages of implementation. The PLI scheme for white goods is designed to create a complete component ecosystem for the air conditioners and LED lights industry in India and make India an integral part of the global supply chains. Domestic value addition was expected to grow from the current 15–20 per cent to 75–80 per cent. Altogether, sixty-one applicants were approved in two rounds. They were expected to bring in investments to the tune of Rs 6,632 crore and to lead to a total production of components of ACs and LED lights of about Rs 1,22,671 crore over five years. In October 2023, the government made some important changes in the scheme. Adoption of the cost-plus method in place of the comparable uncontrolled price (CUP) method for calculation of sales prices in case of captive consumption or supplies to group companies was permitted.

Four PLI schemes—PLI for speciality steel (outlay Rs 6,332 crore), PLI for high efficiency solar modules (outlay Rs 4,500 crore), PLI for telecom and networking products (outlay Rs 12,195 crore) and PLI for textile products (Rs 10,683 crore)—did not make any appreciable progress.

The government signed MoUs with twenty-seven selected companies covering fifty-seven applications, which were expected to bring in an investment of Rs 29,530 crore for the PLI for speciality steel. The government allocated 39,400 MW of domestic solar PV module manufacturing capacity under PLI (Tranche II) in March 2023. A total integrated capacity of 8,737 MW was earlier allocated under Tranche I of the scheme in November 2022. These two PLI tranches on solar PV modules were expected to cost the government Rs 18,500 crore.

The PLI scheme for telecom and networking products announced in 2021 was modified into a design-led PLI scheme for telecom and networking products in October 2022 with an additional incentive of 1 per cent for products that are designed and manufactured in India. Forty-two companies were approved under the original scheme and seventeen applied under the design-led PLI. Sixty-one applicants were approved under the PLI for textile products as per the information note posted on 14 April 2022.

Semiconductor Mission

Government launches Semiconductor Mission

Integrated-circuit chips, fabricated on semiconductors, are the real building blocks and enablers of the Digital Age where the bulk of production, transmission and consumption of goods and services, and building of assets takes place on electronic equipment, machines and processes run on semiconductor chips. The semiconductor chip fab industry was $500 billion in 2023 and is heading strongly to reach $1 trillion by 2030.

India had virtually no presence in the semiconductor fab ecosystem in 2021. We did not manufacture silicon or any other semiconductor material or any semiconductor fab worth the name. Many Indians designed semiconductor chips for global companies in their development centres abroad and also those set up in India. Many Indian companies use semiconductor chips for manufacturing their relatively low-tech equipment and products. India has a great demand for semiconductor chips as well as a lot of talent to design chips.

In December 2021, the government announced its ambition of fabricating the most sophisticated sub-28 nanometre semiconductor chips in India and committed to subsidize 50 per cent of the cost of fab projects, besides providing a host of other benefits.

Indian governments did have semiconductor fab ambitions earlier as well. The Manmohan Singh government had formulated a semiconductor policy and offered major sops costing about Rs 39,000 crore in 2012.

Two proposals—one from the Jai Prakash group, along with IBM and the other from Hindustan Semiconductor Manufacturing (HSMC)—were received but died a slow death.

The Modi government's plan is more ambitious—to make India a semiconductor fabrication hub of the world. The government issued four notifications in December 2021, to incentivize semiconductor chips fabrication and design in the country, putting fiscal support of Rs 76,000 crore (at that time $10 billion) on the table.

The government invited companies/consortia/JVs to set up silicon CMOS-based semiconductor fab in India for manufacturing logic, memory, digital ICs, analogue ICs and other kinds of chips, promising graded fiscal support ranging from 30 per cent to 50 per cent of the project cost. The pride of place was reserved for sub-28 nm chips, which were promised 50 per cent of the cost as incentive.

Proposals were also invited for setting up manufacturing in India for display fabrication units/panels (50 per cent incentive), compound semiconductors, silicon photonics, sensors, etc. (30 per cent incentive) and encouraging chip designing by domestic companies, start-ups and MSMEs, etc. (50 per cent of the eligible expenditure subject to a ceiling of Rs 15 crore per application).

With additional support from state governments, fiscal subsidies were expected to range from 40 per cent–70 per cent of the capital cost. Other incentives were also offered, including support for development of infrastructure/common facility centre under the modified electronics manufacturing clusters (EMC 2.0) scheme. The government also promised purchase preference in procurement under the Public Procurement (Preference to Make in India) Order 2017. Some estimates suggested that the governments together were offering about 80 per cent of the cost of semiconductor fab project for sub-28 nm.

No initial take-off

MeitY reported, in its 2022–23 Annual Report, that five applications were received for semiconductor and display fabs, with a total investment to the tune of $20.5 billion (Rs 1,53,750 crore). In addition, two applications were received for semiconductor packaging units and sixteen applications for the Design Linked Incentive Scheme. None of these applications, except five small chip design applications, were approved.

Three consortiums—Vedanta-Foxconn, IGSS Ventures and ISMC—made applications to set up semiconductor fabs to manufacture Si CMOS chips and invest an estimated amount of $13.6 billion. They sought fiscal support of about $5.6 billion. The Vedanta-Foxconn JV promised to set up a 28 nm fab and asked for an estimated $3.7 billion fiscal support. None of the principal partners had any semiconductor chip fabrication experience, though Foxconn is the largest electronic products contract manufacturer/assembler in the world. The JV failed to locate a fab manufacturer partner or a technology supplier. Though the project received the approval of the Gujarat government and an MoU was signed in Dholera in the presence of IT Minister Ashwini Vaishnaw, the project proposal was stalled with Foxconn finally exiting the JV.

The other two proposals made equally nondescript progress. The ISMC Consortium, promoted by Abu-Dhabi based Next Orbit Ventures, wanted to fabricate analogue chips (65 nm and higher). IGSS Ventures, a Singapore-based investment holding company, also wanted to fabricate chips of 65 nm. Two proposals were received for fabricating the display chips—one from Vedanta and the other from Elest with Rajesh Exports as its partner. None of these proposals made any progress.

Government lowers ambition and relaxes

Looking at very little enthusiasm for sub-28 nm chips, the government decided to change tack. The scheme was reframed and three new notifications were issued in October 2022, providing uniform fiscal support at 50 per cent of the project cost for all types of chip fabs. The government, through these notifications, also advised the earlier applicants to apply afresh, effectively shelving all earlier applications, barring the five design-related applications which had been approved.

The government also issued comprehensive guidelines for all the three types of semi-conductor fabs—a. principal chips: logic, memory, digital, analogue, etc.; b. display fabs; and c. compound semiconductors in October 2022. The guidelines for the first two types of semiconductors were later modified again in May 2023 and for the compound semiconductors in June 2023. The government initiated a fresh round of applications on 31 May 2023 for setting up semiconductor and display fabs as per the Modified Semicon India Programme, where applications could be filed at any time until 31 December 2024, i.e. on a tap basis.

New formulation generates good interest

The first real progress came in the middle of 2023. American semiconductor major Micron Technology Inc. announced, on 22 June, its plans to build a new semiconductor assembly and test facility (not a chips fabrication facility, though). The Union Cabinet immediately approved fiscal support of Rs 11,000 crore for this proposed facility. Micron has started construction of its facility at Sanand in Gujarat.

Significant activity was generated just before the announcement of the Lok Sabha elections. The government, on 29 February 2024, approved establishment of three more semiconductor units.

The first proposal was for a semiconductor fab with 50,000 wafer starts per month (WFSM) capacity to be established by Tata Electronics Private Limited

(TEPL) in partnership with Powerchip Semiconductor Manufacturing Corp (PSMC), Taiwan. This fab was announced to be constructed in Dholera, Gujarat and would lead to an investment of Rs 91,000 crore. The fab will make high-performance computer chips with 28 nm technology and power management chips for electric vehicles (EV), telecom, defence, automotive, consumer electronics, display, power electronics, etc.

The second proposal was also from the Tatas and related to setting up a semiconductor Assembly, Testing, Marking, and Packaging (ATMP) unit. A Tata company—Tata Semiconductor Assembly and Test Pvt. Ltd (TSAT)—will set up this semiconductor unit in Morigaon, Assam, with an investment of Rs 27,000 crore. It was informed that TSAT was developing indigenous advanced semiconductor packaging technologies, including flip chip and integrated system in package (ISIP) technologies. The fab will have a capacity of 48 million chips per day and cover segments of automotive, EV, consumer electronics, telecom, mobile phones, etc.

The third proposal was from CG Power which, in partnership with Renesas Electronics Corporation, Japan, and Stars Microelectronics, Thailand, will set up a semiconductor unit in Sanand, Gujarat with an investment of Rs 7,600 crore. The CG Power semiconductor unit will manufacture chips for consumer, industrial, automotive and power applications and will have a capacity of 15 million chips per day.

The government claimed that with the approval of these three additional proposals, the India Semiconductor Mission had achieved four big successes. It was informally stated that, with the approval of these four proposals, the government had committed Rs 66,000 crore in subsidies, leaving only Rs 10,000 crore of the original Rs 76,000 crore outlay uncommitted.

The government had also received a big proposal from Israel-based Tower Semiconductors, which possibly envisages investment of Rs 91,000 crore. The government deferred the proposal for consideration after the Lok Sabha elections ostensibly for two reasons—one, the available subsidy allocation left was only Rs 10,000 crore, whereas the Tower Semiconductors proposal would have required a commitment of Rs 45,500 crore in subsidies, and second, the proposal was quite complex and required more time for examination.

The Semiconductor Mission could attract many proposals and the government did approve four major proposals by the time Modi 2.0 completed its tenure. Construction work also formally commenced with ground-breaking ceremonies being held. There is always some possibility of even the approved proposals getting abandoned. It is quite likely that the Micron and Tata projects will see the light of day. We will know for sure in the next few years.

Real opportunity in the chips space

India's educated and technical labour talent is our real strength. This makes seizing the opportunity in semiconductor chips-related services our best opportunity to bring us the best economic returns. This opportunity is most visible in chip-designing. Fab enterprises or fab-less ones—everyone uses Indian technological talent to design chips. It is estimated that about 20 per cent of all the global chips are designed by Indians. Indian fab designers earn decent salaries and bonuses, which contribute to our GDP and inward remittances. If India and Indians can become the chip designers of the world, and in times to come, the chip design enterprises of the world, a good part of the semiconductor chips gravy train can accrue to India.

The chips do not add value on their own. These unlock the real value in data which the chips help process and store. Data processing is the big service function and value creator in the digital world. Indian talent again is very proficient in data processing and crunching. If India can get global markets and companies to open doors for Indian data processors, by getting our data privacy and localization policies right, we can get global data processed in India, and we can become the data processor of the world.

Everything on semiconductors works with programmes written in computer codes. Again, Indian talent in programming and providing programming services—software as a service included—is globally acknowledged. If we can become the programmers of the world, we can take a good part of global digital value addition home.

The government does have an incentive programme for chip design as part of the Semiconductor Mission. However, that is too small and focuses on small enterprises.

Policy and Reforms

Start-up policy got messed up

While producing and delivering goods and services, largely digitally, is the foremost identity of a start-up, the Indian government adopted a highly diluted definition of a start-up. The Department of Promotion of Industry and Internal Trade (DPIIT), the nodal department for start-ups, recognizes any 'original entity', less than ten years in existence, incorporated as a private limited company or a registered or limited liability partnership, with turnover of less than Rs 100 crore in a year in any sector of the economy as a start-up. This loose definition has resulted in more than 6 lakh firms becoming part of the Start-up India Hub with over 1,27,400 firms getting officially recognized as start-ups by DPIIT by end March 2024. In the process, nurturing of digital economy start-ups has been wholly diluted.

The government made profits of start-ups registered by the CBDT before 31 March 2023 tax-free for any period of three years within a period of ten years under section 80-IAC of the Income Tax Act. The VC/PE industry recognizes over 50,000 digital/Internet start-ups; of which more than 5,000 have received funding from angel investors, PEs and VCs. However, for tax exemption purposes, there were only 1,162 start-ups in the country as on that date, that too not necessarily digital start-ups. These start-ups get no real benefits. The government does not provide the details of tax forgone under this section in the Budget papers.

Budget 2023–24 pushed the Indian start-up system into a still worse policy blind spot. Section 56(2)(viib) of the Income Tax Act, effectively provides, in the context of start-ups, that capital infusion in any new round at a price higher than the price of the previous round, will be taxed as capital gains. This tax is also colloquially termed angel tax. Despite the fact that most start-ups make losses in the growth phase and burn their capital, the tax officers have gleefully assessed such higher valuation of shares in subsequent rounds as capital gains and raised tax demands. This has been a major heartburn for the start-ups.

Until FY 2022–23, foreign investors in start-ups were exempt from this angel tax. The Finance Minister proposed in Budget 2023–24 that this exemption would no longer be available to foreign investors and there would be a tax on such higher valuations. Until that year, this provision did not affect start-up funding for the simple reason that most of their capital was coming from abroad. It should be quite clear to everyone who cares that this amendment will sound the death knell of foreign VCs/PEs funding in Indian start-ups in future.

Start-ups bring enormous efficiencies to industrial-age businesses by making extensive use of digital technology and data sets. The start-ups require a policy and regulatory environment in which they can innovate and experiment liberally using foreign funding, technology and Indian data sets. They don't need government tax incentives and small funding support.

To build such a vibrant start-up ecosystem, the current policy environment needs to be drastically changed. Some specific policy changes required are: First, angel tax for start-ups needs to be abolished by repealing section 56(2)(viib) of the Income Tax Act or exempting all start-ups from its application. Second, no one seems to be really availing the tax exemption available under section 80-IAC as it is highly restrictive. The government rubs it in further by increasing the eligibility period every year by one year. Budget 2023–24 raised it to 31 March 2024. The exemption needs to be extended to all the digital start-ups and the eligibility time limit should be increased in one go to 2030. Third, the government established a Fund of Funds (FoF) for providing equity capital to start-ups. In the last eight years of its existence, it has not even disbursed half a billion dollars. This little funding seems to have also gone to non-genuine, non-digital start-ups. This FoF can be simply disbanded. The government may, if it still wants to do something, establish a professionally run majority private VCs/PEs/Sovereign Fund-owned alternate investment fund (AIF) on the lines of National Infrastructure Investment Fund (NIIF), with a large capital base of, say, about $5 billion. Fourth, access to personal data, of course with willing consent, is the basic building block of digital age start-ups. Start-ups need to be provided liberal access to personal data barring critical personal data.

Modi 2.0 did not take any of these four key policy decisions to liberate the start-ups in India[*].

Industrial policy never arrived

On 29 August 2017, the Modi government issued a draft of an Industrial Policy and invited feedback and comments thereon (PIB release titled 'Formulation of a New Industrial Policy').

The press release informed that the Department of Industrial Policy and Promotion (DIPP, later renamed as DPIIT) had initiated the process of formulation of a new Industrial Policy in May 2017 to replace the last Industrial Policy announced in 1991. The new Industrial Policy was to subsume the National Manufacturing Policy (NMP).

The industrial policy would focus, it was also stated, on six thematic focus groups—manufacturing and MSME; technology and innovation; ease of doing business; infrastructure; investment, trade and fiscal policy; and skills and employability for the future.

In addition, a Task Force on Artificial Intelligence for India's Economic Transformation was also constituted to provide inputs for the Industrial Policy. The new Industrial Policy was to aim at making India a manufacturing hub by promoting Make in India and suitably incorporate the use of modern smart technologies, such as the Internet of Things (IoT), artificial intelligence and robotics for advanced manufacturing.

The government kept working on the draft policy in the remaining term. In 2018, Suresh Prabhu replaced Nirmala Sitharaman as Minister of Industry. In October 2018, while speaking in a meeting organized by the World Economic Forum (WEF) in New Delhi, he stated that the new Industrial Policy being framed by the government embodied the government's intention to align India with the emerging technologies of drones, artificial intelligence and blockchain.

The government kept promising the new Industrial Policy but did not take it up for approval in its first tenure.

---

[*] The Modi government, in its third term, finally abolished the angel tax in the July 2024 Budget with effect from FY 2024–25.

The government was keen on bringing out the new Industrial Policy when its second term began in May 2019. In the very first joint session of the Parliament in June 2019, President Ram Nath Kovind stated that India was on the way to becoming the world's fifth largest economy in terms of GDP.

To maintain the high growth rate and to make India a $5 trillion economy by 2024, the President committed to continue with the reform process. He said that the work was underway in full earnest to transform India into a global manufacturing hub and, keeping in view Industry 4.0, a new Industrial Policy would be announced shortly.

Literally thereafter, the government seemed to have lost interest in the Industrial Policy. No new draft came. No proposal was taken to the Cabinet.

Instead, the government focused on the PLIs, as its preferred mode of boosting manufacturing. Many PLIs were announced. Some other policy measures also saw the light of day.

The Logistics Policy was unveiled. PM Gati Shakti system came into being as a project building up and coordination tool.

The new Industrial Policy, however, got buried deep in red tape. It did not see the light of day during the entire Modi 2.0 and its draft was removed from the website.

No small industry reforms either

The second term of the Modi government would be known more for its benign neglect of small industries, formally described as the medium, small and micro enterprises (MSME) sector in India. The MSME Act governs the sector. In the second tenure, the government took only three measures concerning the MSMEs.

The definition of the three constituents of MSMEs were revised in June 2020. These definitions in India have always been based on the mix of investment in capital assets and turnover criterion. Investment and turnover limits for the micro manufacturing and services units was increased to Rs 1 crore of investment and Rs 5 crore of turnover. For the small units, the limit was increased to Rs 10 crore of investment and Rs 50 crore of turnover and for the medium units, to Rs 50 crore of investment and Rs 250 crore of turnover.

The government strengthened the Udyam registration portal on 1 July 2020 to make it a fully online, free of cost, hassle-free and a no-documentation-requirement portal. The government, on 11 January 2023, launched an Udyam Assist Platform (UAP) for enterprises not having GST. The MSMEs registered on the portal have access to the National Career Service Portal of the Ministry of Labour and Employment. Registration on the portal can be made through the Common Service Centre (CSC). Udyam registrations picked up speed in 2023. From 1.31 crore as on 31 December 2022, with the addition of 88.89 lakh registrations in 2023, total Udyam registrations reached 2.19 crore by the end of 2023. The UAP registrations on that date crossed 1.11 crore.

The third measure was to bring the government guarantee-backed Emergency Credit Line Guarantee Scheme (ECLGS) in May 2020, in the wake of Covid-19 and lockdown disruptions, to nudge the banks and non-banks to provide 20 per cent additional credit to the MSMEs over and above existing loans/credit sanctioned, with default, if any, for the additional credit, guaranteed by the government.

The MSMEs remained, by and large, on the sidelines of policy during Modi 2.0. Many MSMEs also folded up. The government, at one point in time, wanted a National Identity Register of MSMEs. Udyam is no unique identity register, nor is it universal. Of the estimated 8–10 crore MSMEs in the country, only about 30–40 per cent are registered on Udyam and UAP. Udyam/UAP also does not provide any functional service for MSMEs, like generation of GST vouchers, providing KYC services, filing of documents to any public registry and so on.

Successful coal block auctions

After wholesale nationalization of coal mining in 1972, the coal sector became a symbol of inefficiency, low growth, corruption and environmental pollution. Thermal power generation suffered. Indian power companies found it cheaper to import coal from Indonesia and Australia than to use the domestically produced coal by Coal India Ltd and its subsidiaries.

Provision of coal blocks to power plants and other users began, albeit through the back door, in the 1990s under the policy of captive use. Private and public sector power companies were allotted coal blocks to be developed by them but were subject to many restrictions, such as they could not produce more than what was required for their plants and sale of extra coal produced to outsiders was illegal. No wonder coal scams happened. Some senior officials went to jail as well and 204 coal blocks were cancelled by the Supreme Court in 2014.

The Modi government finally mustered up the courage in 2019–20 and removed all the cobwebs from the coal block auction policy. Mineral laws were amended to open up the coal sector, to provide a level playing field to the public and private sector players. Coal block auctions were permitted without any restriction on end use. The coal from these mines could be utilized towards own consumption, sale or for any other purpose.

Important reforms were also initiated in the auction process, participation and bid criteria. No technical or financial eligibility criteria were stipulated to enable wider participation. The winners were permitted to relinquish part of the coal mines in case of partially explored ones. The government migrated to a revenue-sharing mechanism in place of fixed rupees per tonne based auctions. 100 per cent FDI was allowed under the automatic route.

While the anticipated foreign participation did not materialize, the government could launch many rounds of coal block auctions and successfully allotted coal blocks. The first-ever tranche of commercial coal mine auctions was launched in June 2020. In less than three years (until FY 2022–23), six tranches of auctions were concluded successfully and eighty-seven coal mines were auctioned, which are estimated to generate revenue of around Rs 332 billion. On 29 March 2023, the government launched the process for the seventh round of auctions for a total of 106 coal blocks.

The government viewed commercial coal mine auctions 'a tremendous success'. On 20 October 2023, a PIB press release informed that a total of ninety-one coal mines had been successfully auctioned in seven tranches under the commercial coal mining policy. Of these, nine had received all the permissions and five could start production as well with production from commercial mines amounting to 7.2 million tonnes in 2022–23.

3

Services

Goods or merchandise like wheat, soap or laptops have value as these satisfy human wants and needs. So have services like trade, transport and entertainment, as these also satisfy human wants and needs. There is no difference between goods and services, in terms of 'value' created, except that goods are tangible whereas services are experienced without being tangible.

Services help create better value in goods—application-controlled, appropriately-delivered water, fertilizer, etc. help produce better agriculture products; products transported to the places and persons who don't have normal access command higher prices as the persons consuming them experience better value; films and shows produced with advanced technologies and delivered using digital technologies provide better entertainment and so on.

The national accounts system collects data relating to three broad groups of services: a. trade, hotels, transportation and communications; b. financial, real estate and professional services; and c. public administration, defence and other services. Services have been growing at a much faster clip than agriculture and industry for many years now.

The GVA of the services in India in 1950–51 was Rs 1.32 trillion (economic survey 2022–23, 2011–12 prices). This formed 27.5 per cent of India's total GVA of Rs 4.79 trillion. The services GVA had increased to 38.3 per cent of total GVA in 1990–91. Industrial reforms positively impacted services growth. All the services expanded, including the government services. In 2012–13, services GVA crossed 50 per cent of total GVA (Rs 43.01 trillion out of Rs 85.46 trillion). The services GVA share was 51.09 per cent in 2013–14, the year before Narendra Modi and the BJP assumed power at the Centre.

There is significant churning happening across all the three services groups. In the trade, hotels, transport and communication group, e-commerce is fast chewing the brick-and-mortar trading system, Airbnb types of hospitality services are giving traditional hotels a run for their money despite the massive expansion in travel boosting the hotel industry, electric vehicles are providing more environment-friendly transportation services in place of internal combustion (IC) engine-driven vehicles and cellular telephony and over-the-top (OTT) media services are making big inroads into traditional communication and entertainment industry film and television services. Similarly, financial services and public services are also undergoing massive digital transformation.

This chapter reviews the Modi government's policies, programmes and performance in services, primarily in the second term 2019–24. There aren't many government programmes and incentive schemes in the services sector barring the public goods, such as defence services and merit goods, such as health and education. The policy framework is also more attuned to the specific group of services instead of the omnibus services sector like an industrial policy or a manufacturing policy. The growth dynamics also need to be understood more for the specific set of services.

Accordingly, this chapter is organized in terms of specific services and groups of services in which I review the structure, role, growth, programmes and policies together for each type/sector of services.

Services Growth

Services growth slowed down

The services GVA in the national accounts is presented in three broad groups—a. Trade, hotels, transport, communication and services related to broadcasting, b. Financial, real estate and professional services, and c. Public administration, defence and other services.

In 2018–19, the GVA of the services together, at constant 2011–12 prices, was Rs 68.78 trillion. The services GVA grew, as per the latest available PE, in 2023–24 to Rs 86.69 trillion. The services thus recorded an annual growth of only 4.74 per cent in Modi 2.0. Quite a climb-down from the high services growth rates witnessed by India in the last three decades.

This growth performance was, however, better than the overall GVA growth of 4.51 per cent (PE). Services growth was also considerably lower than the GVA growth of 7.04 per cent per annum recorded during Modi 1.0.

The financial, real estate and professional services group witnessed the best growth of 6.34 per cent per annum among the services during Modi 2.0 (growing from Rs 27.14 trillion in 2018–19 to Rs 36.92 trillion in 2023–24, as per PE). In the first term, the GVA growth of this group was 7.77 per cent. While this was the lowest among the three services in the first term, despite being lower than the first term, it happens to be the best services sector group in the second term. The financial, real estate and professional services group, which includes information technology services, performed better, partly on account of the fact that the services in this group remained the least disrupted in the Covid-19 and lockdown period.

Public administration, defence and other services, which include health and education services, recorded a GVA growth of 4.46 per cent (PE) during the five years of Modi 2.0 (growing from Rs 16.25 trillion in 2018–19 to Rs 20.22 trillion in 2023–24). Despite the fact that the GVA of this group is excessively influenced by the government expenditure on salaries of public servants, the GVA growth of the group in Modi 2.0 was far lower than the growth of 7.91 per cent per annum in Modi 1.0.

The fortunes of the third services group—trade, hotels, transport, communication and services related to broadcasting—saw the biggest disruption and dip in the second term. This group had recorded an annual growth of 8.97 per cent per annum in the first term, the highest among all the eight GVA groups. In the second term, however, the growth dipped to a low of 3.09 per cent per annum (GVA Rs 25.39 trillion and Rs 29.56 trillion in 2018–19 and 2023–24 PE, respectively).

Services are the best growth engine in India's context, yet this growth engine also literally sputtered in Modi 2.0. There were signs of its revival only in the terminal year 2023–24, when services recorded a GVA growth rate of 7.58 per cent, taking into account PE for 2023–24 (Rs 86.69 trillion) and I RE for 2022–23 (PE) (Rs 80.59 trillion).

It is quite disconcerting to see the services growing by only 4.74 per cent annually during Modi 2.0 despite our enormous talent and prowess in financial and information technology services, the global growth engines of today.

Covid-19 badly affected trade and restaurant services

In the national accounts, published up to 2022–23 (covering four years of Modi 2.0), we have more granular information about the output, value added, capital formation, etc., and also for the three broad services groups divided into six.

The trade, hotels, transport, communication and services related to the broadcasting group is divided into services sub-groups of i. trade, repair, hotels and restaurants, and ii. transport, storage, communication and services related to broadcasting.

The trade, repair, hotels and restaurants group had recorded an outstanding annual growth rate of 10.55 per cent in the first term of the Modi government but became the worst-affected services sub-group during Covid-19. As most of the restrictions on restaurants and hospitality services were lifted only in the second half of 2021–22, the three-year GVA growth was negative at the end of 2021–22, (-)1.85 per cent over 2018–19, and could reach the positive territory (1.86 per cent per annum) at the end of four years in 2022–23.

The total value of output produced in the sector came down from Rs 26.86 trillion in 2019–20 to Rs 23.81 trillion in 2021–22 before recovering to Rs 27.81 trillion in 2022–23 (II RE). The GVA of the sub-group also reduced from Rs 18.29 trillion in 2019–20 (the last pre-Covid-19 year) to Rs 16.17 trillion in 2021–22 and recovered to Rs 18.39 trillion in 2022–23.

The other part of the trade, hotels, transport, communication and services related to the broadcasting group, i.e. sub-group transport, storage, communication and services related to broadcasting, was not that badly affected. This sub-group did record a positive GVA growth albeit of a lower order of 1.37 per cent per annum during the first three years of Modi 2.0, rising from Rs 8.31 trillion in 2018–19 to Rs 8.66 trillion in 2021–22, and further to Rs 9.39 trillion in 2022–23 (four-year growth of 3.10 per cent per annum).

In the following sections, I discuss growth, programmes and policy development for the three sub-groups of commerce and hospitality, transport and communications separately.

Commerce and Hospitality

I have recounted the growth performance of the two sub-groups of the larger trade, hotels, transport, communication and services related to the broadcasting group above. There were important policy and programme developments in the sector.

Constant tussle between traditional markets and e-commerce

The fast development of digital infrastructure, specially the ability to buy and sell on mobile phones, accompanied by quicker delivery to buyers' homes by the mushrooming force of delivery agents, has given wings to e-commerce in India. There are large e-commerce platforms like the foreign-owned Amazon and Flipkart and also lakhs of domestic start-ups offering all sorts of products now on the Internet.

This has naturally impacted the traditional mom-and-pop stores/*kirana* shops in physical markets, which had virtually sold all products until the arrival of e-commerce in the last few years. They have understandably been asking the government to put restrictions on the e-commerce players in the name of providing a level playing field. Traditional shopkeepers are organized under the banner of the Confederation of All India Traders or CAIT, which claims to represent 9 crore small businesses.

In their representation dated 4 January 2024, CAIT urgently requested the Prime Minister for an early roll-out of the e-commerce policy and the rules under the Consumer Protection Act. CAIT argued that a swift implementation of the policy and rules would foster a fair and competitive business environment, which is crucial for safeguarding the interests of consumers, promoting small businesses and ensuring a level playing field.

This representation followed many others and specifically mentioned that the e-commerce policy and rules were pending before the Prime Minister. No action was taken until the close of the Modi 2.0 term.

Controversial draft e-commerce rules not enacted

The new Consumer Protection Act 2019 provided for consumer protection in digital businesses and digital goods. For preventing unfair trade practices in e-commerce, the government notified the Consumer Protection (E-Commerce) Rules, 2020, in July 2020.

CAIT and many traditional traders were not satisfied and made several representations against unfair trade practices in the e-commerce ecosystem, dominated by two major foreign owned platforms—Amazon and Flipkart. The grievances included manipulating search results to promote certain sellers, preferential treatment to some sellers, selling their own goods, selling goods close to expiration and so on. There were complaints against the flash sales by third party sellers on e-commerce platforms as well.

Sympathetic to the traditional traders lobby, the government prepared and shared a draft of amendments to the Consumer Protection (E-Commerce) Rules, 2020, ostensibly to bring transparency in e-commerce platforms and strengthening the regulatory regime.

The proposed changes included appointment of a chief compliance officer, a nodal contact person for 24x7 coordination with law enforcement agencies, officers to ensure compliance to their orders and a resident grievance officer for redressing of the grievances of consumers on e-commerce platforms.

The draft changes also sought to provide a framework for registration of every e-commerce entity with the DPIIT. Selling private label goods or the goods and services entities of the e-commerce entity by misrepresentation of information was also sought to be curbed. A filter mechanism to identify imported goods based on country of origin and suggesting alternative domestic goods was also sought to be built in. There were other provisions as well, responding to almost every ask of the traditional traders.

There was an understandable outcry from not only foreign-owned e-commerce entities but also from domestic ones. The Prime Minister's Office took notice of the push-back. Several sessions were held between the commerce, industry and consumer affairs minister and officials with the e-commerce industry and traditional trading community.

The government found it difficult to push the draft amendments. At some point in time, even the draft amendments were removed from the website of the

Consumer Affairs Ministry. The draft amendments did not become the rule until the term of Modi 2.0 got over.

ONDC made its debut

To replicate the UPI ecosystem in the e-commerce space and break the dominance of foreign owned e-commerce giants Amazon and Flipkart, the government established and promoted a new entity, Open Network for Digital Commerce (ONDC), in 2021. ONDC aimed at enabling buyers and sellers to be digitally visible and transact through an open network, irrespective of whatever platform/application they used. ONDC was intended to empower merchants and consumers by breaking silos and forming a single network transforming all businesses from retail goods and food to mobility.

The government constituted an Advisory Council for ONDC in July 2021 to guide and mentor design, implementation and national roll-out of ONDC. It was to be based on certain key principles—ensure confidentiality and privacy of data in the network, no mandatory sharing of transaction-level data, publish only anonymized aggregate metrics on network performance without compromising on confidentiality and privacy and be fully compliant with the IT Act, 2000 and the Personal Data Protection Bill.

ONDC's beta version was actually launched on 29 September 2022 though it celebrated one year of its establishment on 22 May 2023.

In a press release on 22 May 2023, the ONDC management stated that the network had expanded to 236 cities. Further, ONDC had scaled to 36,000 sellers, 45+ network participants and 8+ categories, with a weekly average of 13,000+ retail orders and 36,000+ mobility rides per day with peak transactions reaching 25,000 retail orders on one day. While the management sounded quite confident, the widespread feeling in the market and analysts was that ONDC was nowhere close to the magic of UPI.

Several issues, mostly systemic and operational, cropped up as the roll-out happened—sellers not updating inventory listings, payment reconciliation, delivery frauds, logistical glitches, no clarity about returns and inherent contradictions of unintegrated design of buyers and sellers operating separate applications on the network.

The government, which was promoting ONDC very aggressively until the middle of 2023, seemed to have cooled off somewhat in the latter half of 2023. The dominance of the private e-commerce sector, by and large, remained largely unimpacted by ONDC when the term of Modi 2.0 ended.

E-commerce policy did not see the light of day either

Trade and commerce, like any other service sector, are an economic service and extremely amenable to digitalization. Transacted digitally, e-commerce has enormous advantages of cost, time and distance, owing to which it is disrupting traditional trade and commerce the world over.

There is no legitimate rationale for a separate law or policy for e-commerce, just as there is no logic for a separate law or policy for e-banking, e-accounting or BPO. However, Indian policymakers have been very sensitive to foreign companies selling products in India through both the brick-and-mortar model and in e-commerce mode. Likewise, they have been averse to permitting foreign companies to invest in the trade and commerce business segment in India, again both in traditional and e-commerce modes.

The Department for Industrial Policy and Promotion (DIPP), renamed the Department of Promotion for Industry and Internal Trade (DPIIT), has been in charge of FDI policy. India has evolved a restrictive FDI policy for trade and commerce over the years. There are distinctions in terms of wholesale trade and retail trade; multi-brand and single-brand stores; brick-and-mortar trade and commerce and e-commerce; and platform e-commerce companies and own product inventory/direct selling e-commerce companies. There are also numerous conditionalities on local content, minimum investment amount, export obligation, localities where the business can be established and extent of foreign ownership. The policy is quite complex.

For no good reason, DPIIT decided to take over the mantle of controlling digital aspects of e-commerce as well, notably data. In February 2019, it announced a Draft National E-Commerce Policy with the theme, 'India's Data for India's Development'. It was hardly an e-commerce policy. Rather, it was clearly a trade data control and regulation policy. It aimed to 'regulate cross-border data flow'; lay down 'conditions to be adhered to by business entities which have access to sensitive data of Indian users stored abroad'; ban 'sharing of such data with third-party entities, even with customer consent'; mandate 'e-commerce companies to ensure that all product shipments from other countries are channelized through the Customs route'; and propose creation of industrial standards for smart devices and IoT equipment.

The government continued to toy with the idea of bringing out an e-commerce policy focused on data. In a reply to the Lok Sabha question, Minister of Commerce and Industry Piyush Goyal informed on 26 June 2019, after the Modi 2.0 government had assumed office, that 'a draft National e-Commerce policy has been prepared and placed in public domain. The policy addresses six broad areas of the e-commerce ecosystem, viz. data, infrastructure development, e-commerce marketplaces, regulatory issues, stimulating domestic digital economy and export promotion through e-commerce'.

The inherent contradictions and excessive protectionism proposed in the policy did not allow it to progress much. The government, though, kept insisting that the e-commerce policy was coming. On 5 February 2021, a senior official of the DPIIT asserted that the government was 'definitely' working on a new e-commerce policy which would have various features, such as those related to data and consumer rights. In June 2023, the DPIIT publicly stated that the draft e-commerce policy was undergoing inter-ministerial consultations.

There is absolutely no need for the government to frame an e-commerce policy to regulate data and digitalization of trade and commerce services. The policy draft needed to be simply scrapped. After the Digital Personal Data Protection (DPDP) Act 2023, which deals with personal data comprehensively, there was no need for any e-commerce policy dealing with data issues in any case.

Though the government never officially informed that it would not bring the e-commerce policy, as nothing came out of it during the entire tenure of Modi 2.0, the same can be presumed as good as dead.

Transport Services

The national accounts provide more granular data of output and value added for the four constituents of the transport sub-sector—railways, road transport, water transport and air transport. There is also a fifth segment—services incidental to transport. This data is, however, available only up to 2022–23 at the time of writing this book.

The road sector dominates the transport sector in India. In 2018–19, the output and GVA in the road transport segment, at constant 2011–12 prices, were Rs 9.18 trillion and 4.18 trillion, respectively. The total output and value addition in the broader transport group were Rs 13.96 trillion and Rs 6.20 trillion respectively.

The road transport segment had a 65.8 per cent (Rs 9.18 trillion) and 67.35 per cent (Rs 4.18 trillion) share of the total output and value addition in the transportation sector in 2018–19. In 2021–22, the share of the road transport sector went up further to 72.04 per cent of output (Rs 9.13 trillion) and 70 per cent (Rs 4.27 trillion) of GVA. In 2022–23, the last year for which data is available, the share of road transport in output and GVA fell to 67.05 per cent and 67.72 per cent, still higher than in 2018–19.

Railways losing share despite heavy capital investment

Railways, on the contrary, has a relatively smaller share in transport sector output value and GVA. In 2018–19, Railways' share of transport sector GVA was 14.43 per cent (Rs 91,350 crore) only.

The value added share of Railways also consistently declined in Modi's two tenures. Railways' GVA share was 16.15 per cent in 2013–14 (Rs 73,685 crore out of a total GVA of Rs 4.56 trillion). After declining to 14.73 per cent in 2018–19 (Rs 91,350 crore out of a total GVA of Rs 6.20 trillion crore), Railways' share further declined to 13.10 per cent in 2021–22 (Rs 79,827 crore out of a total GVA of Rs 6.10 trillion). In 2022–23, by the time Railway services were fully normalized, its GVA share went up to 14.34 per cent (Rs 94,504 crore out of Rs 6.59 trillion), which was still less than in 2018–19.

The GCF in Railways, almost entirely government-funded, has been consistently high. The GCF, at constant 2011–12 prices was Rs 42,700 crore in 2013–14, Rs 73,028 crore in 2018–19, Rs 90,096 crore in 2021–22 and Rs 1.11 trillion in 2022–23.

It is amazing that the GVA to GCF ratio, which represents output to capital investment ratio, has been deteriorating during the Modi government tenure, in both the first and the second terms. This ratio was 184 per cent in 2013–14 (GVA Rs 78,724 crore and GCF Rs 42,700 crore). This deteriorated to 169 per cent in 2018–19 (GVA Rs 1.24 trillion and GCF Rs 73,028 crore). In 2021–22, the GVA to capital invested ratio fell to a low of 1.56 per cent as the capital expenditure raced up to Rs 93,249 crore whereas GVA grew to Rs 1.46 trillion. The deteriorating capital output ratio was evident in 2022–23 as well, the last year for which the data is available, with GVA to GCF ratio further declining to 148 per cent (GVA Rs 1.64 trillion and GCF Rs 1.11 trillion).

This is the most powerful evidence of poor capital productivity of Railways' CapEx.

Water and air transport has insignificant share

In 2018–19, the GVA of the water transport and air transport sectors was Rs 12,628 crore and Rs 9,402 crore respectively.

Of the transport sector GVA of Rs 6.20 trillion in 2018–19, the water transport and air transport sectors had a puny share of 2.04 per cent and 1.52 per cent respectively.

The saving grace, though, is that the share of both these sectors, though small, has been on a growing trajectory. In 2013–14, the respective share of these two sectors was only 1.61 per cent and 1 per cent.

The Covid-19 pandemic impacted the air transport sector the most. In 2020–21, the worst Covid-19 year, the GVA of the air transport sector came down to only 0.71 per cent (actual GVA Rs 3,433 crore). It recovered though it continued to remain below pre-Covid-19 levels even until 2022–23, the last year for which data is available. In 2021–22, the GVA was Rs 5,443 crore (0.89 per cent) and in 2022–23, Rs 8,750 crore (1.33 per cent). Hopefully, the sector would have returned to the pre-Covid-19 growth path by the time Modi 2.0 completes its term in 2023–24.

PPP in railways did not take off

The public private partnership (PPP) initiatives of the Ministry of Railways (MoR) were conceptualized on three tracks—constructing railway lines, redeveloping railway stations and running of trains. The construction of railways lines to connect ports, factories and mines had been going on for a long time. Railway station redevelopment in PPP mode was initiated in the first term of the Modi government. Running trains through PPP was largely initiated in the second term.

The government, it was informed in a press release in March 2020, had formulated a Participative Policy 2012 to encourage private investment in providing Railways connectivity. Under this policy, thirteen projects of Rs 6,176 crore had been completed through the PPP mode by that time and eleven projects of Rs 22,098 crore were under implementation, including coal connectivity and port connectivity projects.

The government had announced an ambitious programme to undertake redevelopment of 500 railway stations in the first term. However, the initiative made only very limited progress. The development of Habibganj Station only could be undertaken through the PPP mode in the first term and requests for qualification (RFQ) were invited for four more stations, i.e. Nagpur, Gwalior, Amritsar and Sabarmati.

In a press release issued by the MoR on 23 September 2020, it was stated, referring to the reply given by the Minister of Railways in the Rajya Sabha, that the Indian Railways would need capital investment of around Rs 50 trillion up to 2030 for network expansion and capacity augmentation, rolling stock induction and other modernization works to enable better delivery of passenger and freight services and to improve its modal share in transport. It was further informed that, to bridge this gap in capital funding and to induct modern technologies and improve efficiencies, Railways planned to use the PPP model extensively.

One of the PPP initiatives, it was mentioned, was to invite partners to invest and induct modern rakes over select routes to provide world-class services to passengers. For this purpose, the MoR issued twelve RFQs on 1 July 2020 for operation of passenger trains over approximately 109 origin-destination pairs (divided into twelve clusters) through PPP on a design, build, finance and operate (DBFO) basis.

The seeds of potential failure of the initiative were sown in the RFP design itself. The press release stated that the responsibility of train operations and safety certification rested with Indian Railways in all PPP cases and it was also decided that the crew (drivers and guards) required for operation of trains through the PPP mode would be provided by the Indian Railways. In effect, the private sector partners were to primarily provide the trains on the routes they selected and everything else was practically to be done by Railways.

The bids for PPP in passenger train operations projects were opened on 23 July 2021. The MoR received bids to operate only twenty-nine pairs of trains with around forty modern rakes, entailing an investment of around Rs 7,200 crore. Not an encouraging response.

The scheme ran into more problems. Labour unions also protested. The private sector saw no business case in the scheme. No trains were awarded on a PPP basis to the private sector. The government slowly forgot about it. By the time the term of Modi 2.0 ended, the government and MoR were not even talking about it.

Government frames logistics policy

Goods production and shipping for consumption markets depends on enormous logistics, as the World Bank Logistics Performance Index (LPI) measures in six core components—efficiency of customs and border management, quality of trade and transport infrastructure, ease of arranging competitively priced shipments, competence and quality of logistics services, ability to track and trace consignments, and frequency with which shipments reach consignees within scheduled and expected delivery times.

In more practical terms, the cost of logistics and rank in the LPI captures the state of logistics in a country. India's logistics cost has been estimated at about 12–13 per cent of GDP (though some academics dispute it, arguing that it is about 8–9 per cent) against the global benchmark of about 6–7 per cent. Less logistics cost—of freight, storage, delivery, etc.—would make the final product cost lower and competitive. Logistics, therefore, matter. India ranked 44 out of 139 countries in the World Bank LPI in 2018.

The government created a Division of Logistics in the Department of Commerce in 2018 and began talking about bringing in a logistics policy. In the second term, it did, besides creating a Gati Shakti projects preparation and approval tool to make Indian logistics more efficient. After missing many deadlines, the government finally announced the National Logistics Policy (NLP) in September 2022.

The press release issued on the day claimed that the policy laid down an overarching interdisciplinary, cross-sectoral, multi-jurisdictional and comprehensive policy framework for the logistics sector and it complemented the PM Gati Shakti National Master Plan.

The NLP was envisaged to bring efficiency in logistics services and human resources through streamlining processes, regulatory frameworks, skill development, mainstreaming logistics in higher education and adoption of suitable technologies. The vision was to develop a technologically enabled, integrated, cost-efficient, resilient, sustainable and trusted logistics ecosystem for accelerated and inclusive growth.

A lot of words, though the policy did not clearly lay out the policy reforms and the action plan. It, however, set clearer targets—to reduce the cost of logistics in India to be comparable to global benchmarks by 2030, to improve the LPI ranking, to be among the top twenty-five countries by 2030, and create a data-driven decision support mechanism for an efficient logistics ecosystem.

The press note further said that the focus would be on enabling adequate development of warehouses with optimal spatial planning, promotion of standards, digitization and automation across the logistics value chain and better track and trace mechanisms. Further measures to facilitate seamless coordination between different stakeholders and speedy issue resolution, streamlined EXIM processes and human resource development to create an employable pool of skilled manpower would also be taken.

Along with the policy, a Unified Logistics Interface Platform (ULIP), the Ease of Logistics Services platform, e-handbook on warehousing, and training courses on PM Gati Shakti and logistics on iGot platform were also launched.

On completion of one year of the NLP, the government issued another press note claiming rapid progress in improving logistics. It claimed to be undertaking numerous consultations and initiating new initiatives. However, in terms of progress made in reduction of logistics costs, there was no mention in the press release.

Earlier, in April 2023, when the World Bank came out with its LPI 2023, India improved its logistics ranking by six places to rank 38 out of 139 from 44 in 2018. The government attributed it to numerous initiatives taken since 2015. The press release also noted that India witnessed improvement on four out of six LPI indicators, which also meant that India slipped on the two remaining indicators.

Communication and Broadcasting

The national accounts statistics provide output and GVA details for storage and communications services. Further, within the communications sector, the data is available for three sub-sectors of: a. post and courier services, b. communications, and c. cable operators, recording, publishing and broadcasting services.

Communication services make up the bulk of the storage and communications group and telecommunications services make up the bulk of the communications sub-group output and GVA.

Telecommunications sector was gutted

In 2012, the Supreme Court cancelled 122 telecommunication licences after the Comptroller and Auditor General (CAG) saw a big scam of Rs 1.75 trillion in the allocation of 2G licences. Both the CAG and the Supreme Court were perhaps trying to safeguard government non-tax income without paying due regard to the telecommunication services to people and also growth of the furiously evolving telecom business in India.

The consequences of these ill-thought CAG notional loss calculations and the Supreme Court judgment are discernible in the national accounts data. Self-defeating competition by Jio and the imbroglio caused by another Supreme Court intervention in the matter of adjusted gross revenue (AGR) added its cost as the Modi government ran its government in the first term.

The telecommunications GVA, unadjusted for FISIM, was Rs 1.10 trillion, at constant 2011–12 prices, in 2013–14, the year before the Modi government took over. The telecommunications GVA was rising, albeit at a slower rate, until 2015–16 when it reached 1.41 trillion. Thereafter, the collapse started with GVA falling to Rs 1.33 trillion in 2016–17, to Rs 1.12 trillion in 2017–18 and finally to Rs 1.09 trillion in 2018–19, the last year of Modi 1.0. The GVA of Rs 1.09 trillion in the telecommunications services sector in 2018–19 was 99.4 per cent of GVA in 2013–14, registering a negative growth during the five-year period of Modi 1.0.

Telecom sector fortunes revived

In September 2021, the government approved a number of structural and process reforms in the telecom sector. The government claimed to have made nine structural reforms and five procedural reforms, and also provided relief measures for the telecom service providers (TSPs). I will discuss this in greater detail in Chapter 6 on Infrastructure.

The rationalization of the AGR regime and bank guarantees made a considerable difference. Lowering of interest rates and penalties also helped. Removal of spectrum usage charge (SUC) for spectrum acquired in future spectrum auctions brought a welcome change. Moratorium/deferment of up to four years in annual payments of dues arising out of the AGR judgement improved cashflows of telecom companies.

The telecom sector revenues and GVA began improving from 2019–20 itself. The GVA rose to Rs 1.30 trillion in 2019–20. Covid-19 actually helped raise demand for telecommunication services. In 2020–21, GVA rose to Rs 1.46 trillion. In 2021–22, the telecom GVA climbed to Rs 1.57 trillion. By this year, the telecom sector was literally out of the woods with the two largest players returning to profits. The sector recorded GVA growth of 13.66 per cent in the first three years of Modi 2.0.

The GVA data for the specific telecom sector has become available for 2022–23 in August 2024. Telecommunications GVA rose to Rs 1.79 trillion in

2022–23, signalling further strengthening of turnaround. The AGR data also records the same. The AGR receipts were Rs 2.06 trillion in 2021–22 and increased to Rs 2.49 trillion in 2022–23. The 2023–24 AGR climbed to Rs 2.7 trillion, growing 8.24 per cent year on year.

Government kept flogging dead horse BSNL

BSNL is in the business of providing telecom services. It has only a small share and its quality of services is nothing to write home about. It has also been bleeding for long, almost always being one of the top loss-making public sector enterprises. It has been, like Air India, a perfect candidate for the government to exit from—by privatizing or shutting down. Yet, the government steadfastly held on to this appalling business. Instead of closing it down, Modi 2.0 provided three 'revival' packages to BSNL costing over Rs 3 trillion!

Modi 2.0, during 2019–24, approved the third and final revival package on 7 June 2023 for BSNL with a total outlay of Rs 89,047 crore. The first package was approved in its first year on 23 October 2019 for Rs 69,000 crore and the second package for Rs 1,64,000 crore on 27 July 2022. The three revival packages aggregated to a whopping Rs 3,22,047 crore, almost equal to 1 per cent of India's GDP! These packages were termed as revival packages. In fact, these were desperate rescue packages and failed miserably in effecting any 'revival'.

Most of the package cost was in the form of equity and grants from the Budget of the Central government. As this equity was sham, the government ended up spending in excess of all the revenues it received in the form of spectrum auction prices, licence fees, AGR dues, etc., from all the private telecom operators put together. This was nothing short of robbing Peter to pay Paul.

Yet, BSNL continued to financially bleed. BSNL's revenue was Rs 19,321 crore in 2018–19, the year before the first revival package was granted. Its revenue fell to Rs 19,053 crore in 2021–22. In 2022–23, its revenue was only Rs 20,699 crore. Three years of revival packages; yet BSNL was earning the same ballpark revenues as before, even in absolute numbers.

Private telecom operators were making large losses when Modi assumed office in 2019 thanks to the flawed AGR burden. Two of them, who had more than two-thirds of the market share, returned to making decent profits. BSNL, on the other hand, despite so much injection of equity and grants, continued to make humungous losses. In 2020–21, its net loss was Rs 6,982 crore. In 2022–23, its losses widened to Rs 8,161 crore.

BSNL kept steadily losing market share as well in all the three segments—wireless, wireline and broadband.

In March 2019, BSNL had 9.96 per cent of wireless subscribers; in March 2023, it came down to 9.06 per cent. In three years, BSNL lost more than

1.2 crore subscribers and 10 per cent of its even otherwise small market share. For broadband, the biggest growing telecom segment during Modi 2.0, BSNL was only a bit player in the segment with a market share of only 3.92 per cent in March 2019, which went down further to below 3 per cent in March 2023. Even in the small fixed wireline business segment, BSNL's bread and butter for decades, its market share came down from 51.6 per cent in March 2019 to only 25 per cent in March 2023. BSNL lost the number one position in the fixed wireline segment in October 2022 and slid down to the number three position in March 2023.

There was no revival of BSNL by any definition. The rescue packages were more of the nature of pretending to provide sustenance to a near-dead person by keeping it on a ventilator.

Being a public enterprise, BSNL is subject to stifling governmental policy control even if these policies impede its business. BSNL was mandated to provide 4G services in the first revival package but was subjected not to obtain 4G technology from certain countries. For three and a half years, BSNL, constrained by the requirement of sourcing the network equipment only from indigenous sources, failed to launch its 4G services. It could finally place a limited order for deployment of 1,00,000 4G sites to TCS in early 2023–24 with pilot 4G connections to be provided in a couple of districts in Tamil Nadu. Ironically, BSNL is entering into the 4G space when it is time to move to 5G and India had been virtually saturated with 4G connections.

In the third revival package, the government again subjected BSNL to use India's own 4G/5G technology stack, developed under the Atmanirbhar programme. As could have been easily expected, there was no progress in delivering 5G connections during the entire Modi 2.0 period. Moreover, unable to compete with the private operators on technology and quality of services, and saddled largely with unremunerative legacy 2G/3G subscribers, there was and is no chance that BSNL would be able to get any subscribers from its private sector competitors even if it succeeds in installing 4G/5G systems.

The government had no hesitation in distorting the market and continuing to pump fiscal resources into BSNL. All the three packages provided for meeting the cost of spectrum through equity infusion by the government. Tragically, the government's fiscal managers justified these expenditures by terming them fiscal/cash neutral—equity infusion by the government came back to the government as licence fees. The first package provided for administrative allotment of spectrum for 4G services to BSNL and MTNL by a capital infusion of Rs 20,140 crore in addition, along with a GST amount of Rs 3,674 crore. The second package also provided for administrative allotment of spectrum in the 900/1800 MHz band at the cost of Rs 44,993 crore through equity infusion to improve existing services and provide 4G services. The third revival package of Rs 87,048 crore is exclusively for allotment of 4G/5G spectrum for BSNL through equity infusion, which was infused in 2023–24. More than 1.5 trillion of equity was provided for 4G and 5G spectrum to BSNL. Private operators have to buy this spectrum at a hefty cost. BSNL gets it virtually free and without any accountability. There cannot be a worse case of capital mismanagement.

Being a public sector undertaking and under the misconceived notion that employing more people is creating employment in the country, BSNL (including its earlier version of a departmental undertaking DoT), employed thousands of unnecessary and wrongly qualified clerks and workers. No wonder the first revival package provided for meeting the entire VRS cost as well. In addition, servicing the debt on the balance sheet, payment of AGR dues and miscellaneous other expenditures constituted the revival package.

Government policy constraints and unprofessional management did not allow sale or monetization of non-core assets either. In the first revival package, it was decided that BSNL would monetize its assets to raise resources for retiring debt, servicing of bonds, network upgradation, expansion and meeting the operational fund requirements. BSNL could not monetize any of its assets in Modi 2.0.

BSNL, like Air India, is a highly misgoverned and mal-operated organization. It is a zombie public enterprise—a perfect example of why the government should not be in business.

Financial Services

The financial services sector, more commonly known as banking, financial services and insurance (BFSI), is very well captured in the national accounts in the statement 8.12 titled value added from financial services.

There are three sub-groups: a. monetary financial institutions, which are essentially banks plus the RBI (banking sector), b. other financial corporations, which are more or less the entire set of non-banking finance companies (non-bank financial companies or NBFCs), and c. insurance corporations and pension funds, which cover the insurance and pension sectors (insurance and pension).

The banking sector is the largest. In 2018–19, the GVA in the banking sector was Rs 4.12 trillion out of total group GVA of Rs 7.58 trillion (53.6 per cent). The non-banking sector contributed GVA of Rs 2.61 trillion (34.4 per cent) and the insurance and pension fund sector Rs 0.85 trillion (11.2 per cent).

I review the growth performance of these three segments here. There was considerable policy development, more by the central bank and other sector regulators. I will review the policy developments in the fourth part of the book in the chapters relating to money, credit and wealth.

Non-banking sector most dynamic growth sector

In 2013–14, the NBFCs had a GVA of Rs 1.67 trillion out of a total GVA of 5.78 trillion. This gave the NBFCs a slice of 28.9 per cent in the total GVA.

By the time the Modi government completed its first term in 2018–19, the GVA of NBFCs had grown to Rs 2.61 trillion out of a total GVA of the financial sector of Rs 7.58 trillion, giving the sector a share of 34.4 per cent. The NBFCs recorded a decent annual growth rate of 9.33 per cent.

In the pandemic-impacted first three years of Modi 2.0, the NBFC sector recorded a positive growth, though a smaller one, at 3.98 per cent (GVA Rs 2.93 trillion in 2021–22), significantly lower than the first term. It is also notable that the growth of NBFCs' GVA was higher than the remaining two sub-sectors of banking and insurance and pension sector as well as the overall growth of the financial sector at 3.12 per cent.

The GVA (Rs 3.09 trillion) growth in 2022–23 was better (5.19 per cent), taking the four-year growth to 4.28 per cent (still higher than 4.22 per cent) for the sector as a whole.

Banking sector regained its place

The banking sector suffered massively in the first term of Modi 1.0 thanks to asset quality reviews, mounting non-performing loans and slowdown in credit offtake.

The banking sector GVA at Rs 3.30 trillion in 2013–14 made up 57 per cent of the financial sector GVA of Rs 5.78 trillion. On account of the factors mentioned above, the banking sector recorded a much slower growth rate of 4.28 per cent in the first term, rising to an aggregate GVA of Rs 4.12 trillion in 2018–19. This GVA at 53.6 per cent was a full 3.5 percentage points lower than the GVA share of 57.04 per cent in 2013–14.

The government infused over Rs 3 trillion of equity in the public sector banks to clean up their NPAs and provide them capital to work with to grow. Although the annual growth rate of 3.50 per cent in the first three years of Modi 2.0 was much slower than the growth recorded in the first term, it was higher than the overall growth of the financial sector during this period (3.12 per cent). The banking sector blossomed in the last two years of Modi 2.0. The GVA increased from Rs 4.57 trillion in 2021–22 to Rs 4.79 trillion in 2022–23, taking the four-year growth to 4.28 per cent.

Both life and non-life recorded very low growth

The insurance and pension funds sector has three services—life insurance, non-life insurance and pension funds. The GVA in the life and non-life sectors is almost quite equal (Rs 40,055 crore in life and Rs 42,915 crore in non-life) in 2018–19. Pension funds' GVA was quite small at Rs 2,171 crore.

The financial sector in general, and the insurance and pension sector in particular, are not highly labour-intensive. In addition, these companies do not earn hefty profits. Consequently, their value addition is quite small, which is reflected in the low GVA of Rs 2,171 crore in 2018–19.

To make matters worse for the insurance industry, the claims went up significantly during the Covid-19 period. As a result, the sector GVA, which was growing at a small rate of 2.08 per cent per annum during Modi 1.0 (from Rs 76,797 crore in 2013–14 to Rs 85,141 crore in 2018–19), recorded a negative growth rate of (-)1.62 per cent during the first three years of Modi 2.0, recording a GVA of Rs 81,070 crore in 2021–22. There was a decent recovery in 2022–23 with the sector GVA growing to Rs 1.03 trillion, raising four-year growth to a positive 4.99 per cent.

The non-life insurance sector recorded a larger negative growth—from positive 3.51 per cent per annum during 2014–2019 to (-)2.02 per cent during 2019–2022 (recovered to have positive CAGR of 3.19 per cent in 2022–23). The pension sector, although small, recorded a positive growth of 2.22 per cent (increased to 4.52 per cent in 2022–23) though it was much smaller than the growth rate of 17.53 per cent recorded during the first term.

Real Estate and Ownership of Buildings

The real estate sector services include brokerage, consulting, property maintenance and other related services. The ownership of buildings also earn rental incomes. The national accounts capture the GVA in this sector in two subheads of real estate and ownership of buildings.

The ownership of buildings contributes much higher GVA, unadjusted for FISIM, (Rs 7.39 trillion in 2018–19) than the real estate sector (Rs 92,289 crore in 2018–19). The real estate sector had witnessed a much better growth rate (8.03 per cent per annum) during Modi 1.0 than the ownership of buildings (3.08 per cent per annum).

Fortunes reversed in the second term—with the pandemic impacting both the sectors, the real estate segment got affected much more. Real estate GVA of Rs 91,483 crore in 2021–22 generated an annual growth rate of (-)0.29 per cent whereas the GVA of ownership of buildings of Rs 7.99 trillion was the result of 2.63 per cent growth per annum. Both the sub-sectors (real estate and ownership of buildings) had positive GVA CAGR of 2.38 per cent and 2.80 per cent respectively in 2022–23.

Information Technology

Information technology and computer-related services is the big segment of India's services sector value added. A great part of these services are also exported. In GVA, services consumed domestically and exported abroad are both included.

In nominal prices, the output value of information technology services in 2021–22 was Rs 16.56 trillion, which at Rs 75 a dollar in 2021–22 was equivalent to $220 billion-plus that year.

At constant 2011–12 prices, the output of IT services in 2018–19, the last year of Modi 1.0, was Rs 8.90 trillion and the GVA Rs 6.39 trillion. The IT services had recorded outstanding growth of 14.91 per cent per annum with the GVA growing from Rs 3.19 trillion in 2013–14. The IT services GVA doubled in the five years of Modi 1.0.

The growth trajectory of IT services continued very well in the first four years of Modi 2.0 as well, although the growth rate was somewhat lower than that recorded in the first term. The GVA grew to Rs 9.46 trillion in 2022–23, recording a growth of 10.29 per cent per annum.

Other Professional Services

Other professional and support services are grouped in two heads of: a. professional, scientific and technical services, including R&D, and b. administrative and support service activities and other professional services.

The size of professional, scientific and technical services, including R&D services, in India is still relatively small. These services contributed a GVA of Rs 50,631 crore in 2018–19. They had recorded an excellent growth of 10.70 per cent per annum during the first term, growing from the base of Rs 30,461 crore in 2013–14. In the second term, in the first four years as well, these services maintained the momentum, growing at a slightly higher rate of 11.01 per cent per annum and were of the size of Rs 76,876 crore in 2021–22. It is noteworthy that the global capability centres (GCCs) form part of this group. The handsome growth of this sub-group emanates from the excellent growth of GCCs in India.

The size of administrative, support and other professional services is much larger. In 2018–19, their GVA was Rs 4.43 trillion. It had also grown at a splendid rate of 11.98 per cent per annum during the first term, from Rs 2.52 trillion in 2013–14.

The pandemic and lockdowns did arrest the growth rate of the segment. In 2020–21, the GVA of administrative, support and other professional services actually declined to Rs 4.49 trillion from Rs 4.97 trillion in 2019–20. However, the segment more than made up by 2022–23, growing to Rs 5.72 trillion GVA, mustering an annual growth rate of 6.61 per cent in the first four years of Modi 2.0.

Public Administration and Defence

The eighth supply side group in the national accounts—public administration, defence and other services—is further broken down into two sub-groups of: a. public administration and defence, and b. other services.

The GVA growth in public administration and defence was good at 7.22 per cent in the first term (Rs 5.10 trillion in 2013–14 to Rs 7.23 trillion in 2018–19). This segment also slowed in the second term to 3.47 per cent in the first four years (GVA Rs 8.28 trillion in 2022–23).

A very interesting aspect of gross value creation in the public administration and defence is a high proportion of capital formation out of the GVA. The GCF in this sector was Rs 4.09 trillion in 2018–19 and Rs 5.28 trillion in 2022–23, resulting in GCF to GVA ratio for this segment of 56.6 per cent in 2018–19, which went up to 63.4 per cent in 2022–23. This is largely on account of a good part of defence outlays being accounted for as capital expenditure.

Other Services

The other services part of the public administration, defence and other services group has major services of education and health as its components. Private personal services are also part of this group. In addition, there are small groups of a. services of membership organizations, b. arts, entertainment and recreation, and c. private households with employed persons.

The GVA in the other services was Rs 9.03 trillion in 2018–19. In the first term, the other services recorded a decent growth rate of 8.49 per cent per annum, growing from Rs 6.01 trillion in 2013–14. Like most other segments of the economy, other services also suffered the slowdown in growth caused by Covid-19 and the indiscriminate lockdowns imposed. In the first four years of Modi 2.0, with the GVA rising to Rs 10.47 trillion, the growth rate of other services declined to 3.78 per cent per annum.

I will discuss the growth, programmatic and policy interventions for education, health and personal services, being the large segments of value addition, separately in subsequent sections.

Education

Education GVA slowed down during pandemic

The pandemic led to the closure of schools but that did not impact the salaries of teachers and fees students paid. Online coaching and other interventions also made up for the gap. India saw many education start-ups maturing and taking centre stage during Modi 2.0.

Education services have a decent size of GVA, despite education in government schools not contributing much output revenue and GVA. The salary of teachers in government schools is mostly counted in the public administration and defence sector.

In 2018–19, the value of output and GVA of education services recorded in the national accounts was Rs 6.01 trillion and Rs 4.73 trillion respectively. In the first term, the education services recorded a decent growth rate of 9.55 per cent, growing from a GVA of Rs 3 trillion in 2013–14.

The education services GVA grew to Rs 6 trillion in 2021–22, recording a decent growth rate of 6.11 per cent per annum.

EdTech prospered and slumped

Education, at its core, is teachers/masters imparting knowledge (of, for example, the human body, culture and geography) and skills (e.g. literacy, numeracy, use of machines, construction and computers) to the learners. Schools (or any other institution) are only mediums for enabling the delivery of knowledge and skills. Knowledge and skills constantly evolve and accumulate. The mediums of delivering education also evolve and change to suit the demands and technologies of the times. In agricultural societies, teachers/masters acquired knowledge by committing it to memory and delivered it to students using their voice and bodily actions (the Vedas came to us in this manner). They also acquired and delivered skills by physically performing them. In the industrial society, teachers/master-trainers acquired knowledge and skills, committed it to books and used the infrastructure of schools and other aids to transfer the same to students.

Industrial societies are fast morphing into digital societies. Data is the basic building block of digital society. New knowledge is fast accumulating about data, data sciences, databases, data-based products, services and assets, digital technologies and so much more. In the emerging digital societies, students need to learn this new knowledge and skills in addition to the relevant knowledge and skills of agricultural and industrial societies. The medium of delivering education and skills in the digital society is rapidly changing. Education technologies or EdTech is fast emerging as the medium of delivering knowledge and skills in the digital society.

EdTech is a much more powerful and productive medium. Education can be delivered directly by one teacher to many students or customized for an individual student. EdTech removes the constraint of teacher and student to be in close physical proximity. The versatility of Ed-Tech allows the organization of knowledge in words, pictures, videos, etc., to deliver education and skills in a much better and more understandable manner. EdTech is evolving fast to permit use of even machines to deliver education and skills using artificial intelligence. There are certain perceived advantages of physical schools. While EdTech is evolving to match the experiences of real schools, the school teachers, aided and empowered by EdTech solutions, can combine the advantages of both.

Education is over-regulated in India. Only schools set up or recognized by the government can impart education. Further, education is only 'not-for-profit'. Even skills education is completely not-for-profit. Only tuition/coaching is unregulated and can be 'for-profit'. No wonder EdTech enterprises have made the most forceful entry in the coaching/tuition/test preparation segment. Some EdTech enterprises do enter into speciality segments where regulatory loopholes exist. There is no concept of digital schools as yet where education and skills can be delivered fully or partially using EdTech. The world is going digital. Banks, commerce, games, entertainment and whatever services are fast becoming digital. It is time India conceptualizes and accepts digital schools and EdTech.

The government issued an advisory on 23 December 2021. Parents and students were advised to be careful while opting for online content and coaching offered by EdTech companies. EdTech enterprises were classified as e-commerce enterprises and consumer protection (e-commerce) rules 2020 were extended to them. The Advertising Standards Council of India's code regulating advertisements was also made applicable. The government also announced its intention to frame a policy for the EdTech sector. To ward off the government's potential interference, EdTech institutions, after forming an India EdTech Consortium, adopted a code of conduct and established a two-tier grievance redressal mechanism for addressing the areas/concerns underlined in the government's advisory.

The government, education community and EdTech industry should work together to form a policy and regulatory regime for digital schools and EdTech education. First, to seize the competitive advantage for India, recognize that the fast-developing digital society and economy requires mainstreaming of digital education and that education is best delivered using EdTech. Second, current laws and regulations need to be rewritten to evolve both fully digital and part physical-part digital schools with shared physical facilities and EdTech at the core of education. Third, free the skills education system from the constraint of not-for-profit. Permit private enterprise in skills education system. Many services in the traditional education system can also be opened for EdTech enterprises. Fourth, open the education system to foreign competition and obtain concessions from other nations on a reciprocal basis for the Indian EdTech industry to capture global education markets.

India did exceedingly well in capturing the global IT services market as there were no constraining regulations as there are in the present education system. We can repeat this success in the education field with the right policy mix of digital schools, EdTech and light-touch regulations. No EdTech policy emerged during Modi 2.0.

Health

Like education, a good proportion of health services are also in the governmental sector. With the government health services considered largely public good and accordingly not costed and priced, the GVA from the sector is relatively quite small in the country.

In 2018–19, the GVA from the health services was Rs 1.90 trillion. It had recorded a decent growth rate of 9.05 per cent per annum over the GVA of Rs 1.23 trillion in 2013–14.

Despite the expansion of vaccine and other hospital services during the second term consequent upon the Covid-19 pandemic, growth recorded in the first four years of Modi 2.0 was slower at 5.05 per cent (GVA Rs 2.31 trillion in 2022–23).

There is not much of health-tech in the country still. That perhaps explain the slower growth in health services in comparison to education services, which grew at 5.51 per cent per annum in the first three years of Modi 2.0.

With the growth in health services GVA being smaller than education services, the health services GVA as a proportion of education services GVA is steadily declining, albeit at a very small pace. In 2013–14, the health services GVA was 41.11 per cent of education services GVA. It declined to 40.18 per cent in 2018–19. In 2022–23, this proportion declined further to 38.60 per cent.

Personal Services

Personal services, the services which are delivered by a person to another person— e.g. hair-cutting, housemaid, personal attendant and so on—are becoming an important segment of the economy.

Personal services with a GVA of Rs 1.68 trillion in 2018–19 had recorded a growth rate of 5.69 per cent per annum over a GVA of Rs 1.28 trillion in 2013–14. In 2018–19, the personal services GVA was 88.5 per cent of the GVA of health and social work. In 2019–20, this proportion was 90.7 per cent.

Personal services, which required close personal contact, were very adversely impacted by the Covid-19 pandemic. From the level of Rs 1.84 trillion in 2019–20, the year before the pandemic struck, the GVA of personal services nosedived to Rs 1.20 trillion in 2020–21, declining by about 35 per cent in a year.

Some recovery was made in 2021–22 when the GVA of personal services was assessed at Rs 1.33 trillion. It was still only 72 per cent of the GVA of 2019–20. For the three years (2019–2022), the personal services GVA recorded a growth rate of (-)7.61 per cent per annum. In 2022–23, the personal services GVA rose to Rs 1.49 trillion. This was still less than the GVA in 2018–19. The four-year CAGR for personal services was still (-)2.92 per cent.

Part II

Consumption and Investment
(Demand-Side Economics)

4

Consumption

The value generated in goods and services produced in the economic sectors—agriculture, industry and services—gets consumed by households and the government (termed consumption in national accounts) or becomes part of the assets/capital created in households, corporate and public sectors (GCF in national accounts) or is exported to the rest of the world. We also import goods and services, which are either consumed or become part of the capital formation.

On the production/value creation side, as we noted in Part I of this book, the GVA plus net of product taxes and subsidies equals gross domestic product (GDP). On the expenditure side, the total of the consumption of goods and services, the GCF and net exports (exports minus imports) equals the GDP.

Any economy, more particularly a large economy like India, is quite complex with a multitude of goods and services produced in the corporate and public sectors, and millions of households, that are consumed by about 140 crore people or form part of the stock of capital. Collecting data and computing the GDP separately from both the production and expenditure sides understandably leads to some discrepancy.

In the national accounts, this discrepancy is taken on/accounted for on the expenditure side. Therefore, the GDP on the expenditure side actually equals consumption plus GCF plus net of exports plus the discrepancy. The consumption part is the largest component of the expenditure side GDP. Capital formation also makes a substantial contribution. The net exports and discrepancies make up a relatively smaller part.

In 2018–19, the last year of Modi 1.0, at constant 2011–12 prices, of the GDP of Rs 139.93 trillion, consumption aggregated to Rs 92.85 trillion (66.4 per cent) and capital formation Rs 52.26 trillion (37.3 per cent). Together, the consumption and capital formation at Rs 145.11 trillion were more than 100 per cent of GDP (103.7 per cent). As India imported more (Rs 33.50 trillion) than it exported (Rs 29.12 trillion), the net negative exports of Rs 4.38 trillion explained 3.1 per cent of the 3.7 per cent excess in GDP. The balance 0.6 per cent excess was accounted for by the discrepancy (Rs 1.50 trillion).

The expenditure side GDP represents the demand side of the economy, whereas the GVA/production side GDP, the supply side. While the government does consume, the bulk of the consumption takes place in private households. Household consumption is termed the private final consumption expenditure (PFCE) in the national accounts, whereas the government consumption is accounted for as the government's final consumption expenditure (GFCE).

Of Rs 92.85 trillion of consumption in 2018–19, the government consumption, formally termed GFCE was Rs 14.35 trillion (10.3 per cent of GDP), whereas the private consumption, formally termed PFCE was Rs 78.50 trillion (56.32 per cent of GDP).

The consumption demand arises primarily from the disposable income of the households. Households get their disposable income from four principal sources—the income earned out of goods and services produced in the household sector, the income earned as wages from the corporate and government sectors, the net income transfers from the rest of the world (e.g. remittances by Indian immigrants) and the grants/transfers from the government. A part of the demand is also fuelled by credit availed by the household sector. The disposable income plus credit availed minus the income saved/spent on capital formation represents the net demand for household consumption and equals the PFCE.

Businesses of all types form capital by investing in plants and machinery, buildings and other assets. New investment in factories for manufacturing goods, in office and other establishments to provide services and infrastructure, physical and digital, for facilitating production of goods and services adds up to the total capital formation.

In this chapter, I will review the state of and growth in consumption, including macro-economic policies of the Modi government which impacted consumption during 2019–24. The state of and growth in capital formation, along with the policies and programmes impacting capital investment in the economy during this period, will be analysed and commented upon in the next chapter.

Growth

Human health, happiness and well-being depends to a great extent on the consumption of goods and services. Food provides nutrition for human sustenance and growth. Clothes and homes protect and preserve the body and soul. Transport services take you around. Entertainment keeps your spirits high. Financial services help manage your income and assets. Numerous other goods and services take care of other needs and aspirations of the people.

The worst poverty is typically on account of someone's inability to consume adequate goods and services, principally food, on account of a lack of income. India is still a poor country with about 20 crore people estimated to be multidimensionally poor. In the absence of comprehensive consumption surveys (effectively discontinued by the Narendra Modi government; the last one was done in 2011–12), there is no real household survey data/information about consumption. We, therefore, have to look at the national accounts and other data for understanding the consumption pattern, poverty and growth in India.

Household consumption growth fell sharply

At constant prices, household consumption, represented by PFCE, was Rs 55.57 trillion in 2013–14, the year before Narendra Modi took the reins of the Central government. The household consumption expenditure had grown to Rs 78.50 trillion in 2018–19, when Mr Modi completed the first term. Annual consumption growth of 7.15 per cent in the first term, though not stupendous, was quite satisfactory. The consumption growth was in step with the GDP growth, as it was only slightly less than the GDP growth of 7.38 per cent.

Modi 2.0 began on a highly disappointing note. Though not impacted by Covid-19 in 2019–20, the annual household/private consumption growth rate collapsed to 5.2 per cent with the PFCE increasing to Rs 82.56 trillion.

The ill-fated decision to impose highly stringent lockdowns in the wake of Covid-19 all over the country led to severe destruction of household incomes. The decision of the government not to provide cash support to millions of persons who were uprooted from their jobs and had to trudge long distances to return to their villages, in many cases barefoot or after handing over their savings to transporters, led to a consumption collapse in the country. The 2020–21 PFCE came in at only Rs 78.24 trillion, a reduction by (-)5.2 per cent in that year. Indian households, even otherwise poor consumers in normal years, witnessed a significant reduction in their consumption. It is easy to imagine the state of distress and disease the contraction in consumption must have caused to crores of people.

There was a sharp recovery in 2021–22, ironically the year that witnessed the worst Covid-19 wave (as the government decision not to impose lockdowns allowed people to work and earn incomes), with PFCE growing to Rs 87.04 trillion and registering growth by more than 11.2 per cent over the previous year. In the process, private consumption overtook the 2018–19 and 2019–20 consumption levels. However, the three-year household consumption growth rate still remained quite subdued at 3.5 per cent per annum.

Reasonably satisfactory, at least in the year-on-year perspective, consumption growth continued in 2022–23 as well with the household consumption (PFCE) coming at Rs 93.59 trillion, registering an annual growth rate of 7.5 per cent.

Consumption growth, however, collapsed in 2023–24 again with PFCE for the year coming at Rs 97.74 trillion (FAE), recording an annual growth rate of only 4.4 per cent. There was something seriously wrong with the consumption story of India in 2023–24, as the PFCE was further reduced to Rs 96.06 trillion in the SAE, a reduction of about Rs 1.68 trillion over the space of less than two months. The PFCE was increased in the PE to Rs 96.99 trillion, higher than the SAE but still lower than the FAE.

The five-yearly household/private consumption growth, taking PE released on 31 May 2024 into account, was quite low at 4.43 per cent for Modi 2.0. This low growth in private consumption captured the income and consumption distress of the people faced in general during Modi 2.0.

Consumption growth collapsed except for food

The national accounts provide us much more granular information on household consumption in twelve sub-categories by purpose (food and non-alcoholic beverages, alcoholic beverages, tobacco and narcotics, clothing and footwear, housing, water, electricity, gas and other fuels, furnishings, household equipment and routine household maintenance, health, transport, communication, recreation and culture, education, restaurants and hotels, and miscellaneous goods and services) and four sub-categories by durability of goods purchased (durable goods, semi-durable goods, non-durable goods and services).

As we noted above, the household consumption/PFCE was Rs 78.50 trillion in 2018–19. This consumption data is about the private consumption of residents in India. The granular/category-wise details of consumption referred to above uses a slightly different definition of consumption by Indians by including the consumption of all residents in India but excluding the consumption of Indians living abroad, though this difference is minor. For 2018–19, the granular/category-wise PFCE was Rs 78.93 trillion.

Food and non-alcoholic beverages formed the largest proportion of household consumption in 2018–19 (Rs 21.38 trillion out of a total Rs 78.93 trillion; 27.1 per cent). Transport services made up the second largest (Rs 14.07 trillion; 17.8 per cent). Miscellaneous goods and services were the third-largest item of consumption (Rs 12.51 trillion; 15.9 per cent) and housing, water, electricity, gas and other fuels the fourth-largest consumption expenditure (Rs 10.77 trillion; 13.7 per cent).

The misery caused by income loss during Modi 2.0 is reflected in the data for 2020–21. The PFCE of Rs 83.07 trillion in 2019–20 declined to Rs 78.05 trillion in 2020–21, a reduction of 6.04 per cent. This made the people cut down on every item of consumption expenditure except the food and non-alcoholic beverages group, which grew by 3.34 per cent. During the four-year period of 2019–23, the annual growth of the PFCE turned out to be 4.24 per cent (Rs 93.21 trillion in 2022–23). The food and non-alcoholic beverages group growth increased at a slightly higher rate of 5.33 per cent per annum.

The restaurants and hotels group witnessed absolute reduction in the consumption of their services, reflecting the lockdown reality. The PFCE for this category was Rs 1.33 trillion in 2021–22 against Rs 1.86 trillion in 2018–19 with the expenditure on restaurants and hotels consumption declining by (-)10.51 per cent annum, which, in fact, meant an absolute reduction of over 28 per cent in three years. In 2022–23, however, the restaurant and hotels group recovered fully, with their consumption expenditure growing to Rs 2.07 trillion, recording a four-year growth of 2.68 per cent.

The transport services group witnessed a significant fall in growth. While in the first term, the transport services consumption of Rs 14.07 trillion in 2018–19 had grown at 11.9 per cent per annum, the annual growth collapsed to a tepid 2.45 per cent per annum in the first three years of Modi 2.0 (recovered to 5.06 per cent in 2022–23). The communications group also saw a sharp fall (expenditure Rs 2.27 trillion in 2021–22); annual growth only 1.58 per cent during 2019–22 against 11.56 per cent per annum during the first term. The sub-group growth improved to 3.95 per cent in 2022–23 with consumption expenditure rising to Rs 2.53 trillion.

The same trend was discernible in the durability-classified consumption expenditure data. Non-durable goods consumption, with a preponderance of food consumption, recorded the least fall in growth—from 5.51 per cent per annum in the first term to 4.86 per cent (Rs 30.44 trillion in 2018–19 and Rs 36.80 trillion in 2022–23). The other three sub-groups witnessed sharper cuts in growth with the durable goods consumption declining the steepest—from 10.76 per cent in the first term to 7.47 per cent in 2022–23.

Bread, cereals and pulses consumption got smaller

There is clear evidence in consumption data about the declining importance of cereals and pulses in Indian's consumption basket. In 2018–19, the consumption expenditure on breads, cereals and pulses was Rs 4.61 trillion, 21.6 per cent of the total food and non-alcoholic consumption expenditure of Rs 21.38 trillion and 5.8 per cent of the total household consumption expenditure of Rs 78.94 trillion.

The pandemic-impacted first four years saw a higher growth in the consumption expenditure (Rs 5.83 trillion in 2022–23) of breads, cereals and pulses at 6.01 per cent per annum as against an almost flat growth rate of 1.11 per cent during the first term. This growth was, however, less than the growth in meat, fish and seafood, eggs and oil and fats consumption expenditure.

The milk, cheese and eggs group consumption expenditure has, in most years, exceeded or is close to the expenditure on bread, cereals and pulses expenditure. In 2018–19, consumption expenditure on milk, cheese and eggs at Rs 4.64 trillion, at constant prices was a little over 100 per cent that of breads, cereals and pulses, which was of the order of Rs 4.61 trillion. The gap widened in 2021–22 with consumption of milk, cheese and eggs rising to Rs 5.51 trillion whereas that of breads, cereals and pulses came to Rs 5.22 trillion. In 2022–23, though, the expenditure on breads, cereals and pulses was somewhat higher than that of milk, cheese and eggs.

Oil and fats (Rs 1.44 trillion in 2022–23; annual growth 8.18 per cent during 2019–23) and fruits (Rs 3.49 trillion in 2022–23; annual growth 4.85 per cent) recorded higher growth than that in the first term of the Modi government. Vegetables (Rs 2.76 trillion in 2022–23; annual growth 4.09 per cent) consumption grew at almost the same rate in both the terms. The consumption of the sugar, jam, honey, chocolates and confectionery group witnessed sharp contraction in the first four years of Modi 2.0 (growth 5.01 per cent in the first term and 1.37 per cent during 2019–23).

There are unmistakable signs of India's food consumption basket changing materially.

Government consumption expenditure pushes household consumption

The GFCE (which is the government's consumption of goods and services) witnessed surprisingly lower growth during Modi 2.0 than in the first term.

In 2013–14, the GFCE was Rs 9.80 trillion in constant 2011–12 terms. It grew to Rs 14.35 trillion in 2018–19, when the Modi government completed its first term—a decent annual growth rate of 7.93 per cent per annum.

In the slowdown first year of 2019–2020, the GFCE grew by a lowly 3.95 per cent (Rs 14.92 trillion). In 2020–21, it actually fell marginally to Rs 14.80 trillion. In 2021–22 also, it remained flat at Rs 14.80 trillion. At the end of the slowdown and pandemic-impacted three years (2019–22), the GFCE at Rs 14.80 trillion generated annual growth of only 1.04 per cent.

The GFCE perked up in 2022–23, recording expenditure of Rs 16.14 trillion—a good growth of 9.01 per cent during the year. The last year of Modi 2.0 again witnessed poor growth (as per the latest available PE) recording annual growth of only 2.45 per cent with GFCE estimated to rise to Rs 16.53 trillion.

This unspectacular growth in government consumption expenditure during the entire five years capped GFCE growth to barely 2.87 per cent per annum for the five years of Modi 2.0. As GFCE records growth in government revenue expenditure on goods and services purchased and provided to people, this indeed was a sad commentary on what the government did for wiping away the tears of the pandemic and economic slowdown-affected Indian people.

As part of the government consumption expenditure, the government meets certain expenditure which substitutes households' consumption expenditure. In 2018–19, this kind of government household-oriented expenditure was Rs 4.02 trillion. The largest component of it was expenditure on education (Rs 2.70 trillion), followed by health (Rs 0.80 trillion).

The government effectively cut down on education and health expenditure in the first two years of its second term. The household services-oriented GFCE grew to only Rs 4.12 trillion in 2019–20 and remained almost flat at Rs 4.17 trillion in 2020–21. During this two-year period, education expenditure simply refused to budge, coming to Rs 2.71 trillion in 2019–20 and at Rs 2.73 trillion in 2020–21. In 2021–22, it grew to Rs 2.85 trillion and in 2022–23 to Rs 3.12 trillion, capping the four-year growth rate to only 3.67 per cent. Health expenditure performed no better with 2022–23 expenditure at 0.97 trillion, generating an annual growth rate of 5.15 per cent.

Consumption Survey

India finally had a consumption survey in February 2024, the last year of the Narendra Modi government. The National Sample Survey Office (NSSO) released a short document called the 'Household Consumption Expenditure Survey (HCES): 2022–23 Fact Sheet'.

HCES 2022–23 carries an introduction about the household consumption surveys in India. It notes that NSSO has been conducting household surveys on consumption/consumer expenditure at regular intervals as part of its rounds, normally of a one-year duration. The data on household consumer expenditure was collected in every round up to the 28th (1973–74) from the first round (1950–51) of the National Sample Survey (NSS).

The introduction further notes that, after the 26th round of the survey, the then Governing Council of NSSO decided to conduct the surveys on consumer expenditure and employment-unemployment together on a large scale, once in every five years. Accordingly, quinquennial surveys were conducted and results were published in the 27th (1972–73), 32nd (1977–78), 38th (1983), 43rd (1987–88), 50th (1993–94), 55th (1999–00), 61st (2004–05), 66th (2009–10) and 68th (2011–12) rounds of NSS, at roughly five-year intervals, barring the last one which was carried out and published after two years.

Without specifically noting that the employment-unemployment part of the survey has been done away with and the quinquennial survey conducted in 2017–18 was not released by the government, the introduction finally notes that the 2022–23 Survey titled 'Household Consumption Expenditure Survey' is the latest one on the subject.

Second term began with controversy about household consumption survey

In November 2019, a newspaper in India released leaked findings from the 2017–18 Consumption Expenditure Survey (CES), which showed that inflation-adjusted average monthly per capita consumption expenditure (MPCE) declined by 3.7 per cent in the country between 2011–12 and 2017–18, a very serious comment on consumption poverty in the country. There were other adverse findings as well.

The government had to issue an unusual press release titled 'Household Consumption Expenditure Survey' on 15 November 2019.

The press release acknowledged that the National Statistical Office (NSO) had carried out an all-India survey on household consumption expenditure in the 75th round during the period July 2017 to June 2018. It also noted that the CES was usually conducted at quinquennial intervals and the last survey on consumer expenditure was conducted in the 68th round (July 2011 to June 2012). It mentioned that the NSS' CES generates the estimates of household MPCE and the distribution of households and persons over the MPCE classes. The press release further stated that the Ministry had seen the media reports regarding the NSS' CES and that consumer spending was falling and the report had been withheld due to its 'adverse' findings.

The government then noted that the results of the 2017–18 Survey were examined and there was a significant increase in the divergence in not only the levels in the consumption pattern but also the direction of the change when compared to the other administrative data sources, such as the actual production of goods and services. It further said that concerns were also raised about the ability/sensitivity of the survey instrument to capture consumption of social services by households, especially on health and education.

The Ministry informed that the matter was referred to a committee of experts, which noted the discrepancies and came out with several recommendations, including a refinement in the survey methodology and improving the data quality aspects on a concurrent basis. The recommendations of the committee were being examined for implementation in future surveys. It also noted that the Advisory Committee on National Accounts Statistics had also separately recommended that for rebasing of the GDP series, 2017–18 was not an appropriate year to be used as the new base year.

Finally, the press release said, in view of the data quality issues, the Ministry had decided not to release the CES results of 2017–2018. The Ministry promised to separately examine the feasibility of conducting the next CES in 2020–21 and 2021–22, after incorporating all data quality refinements in the survey process.

The quinquennial consumer survey system died with that episode. The next CES did not come out in 2020–21 or 2021–22. It came finally, in a much shortened form, in 2023–24 with the reference year 2022–23.

Consumption Survey 2022–23 brings out interesting trends

The HCES: 2022–23 provides two sets of consumption data.

One, the consumption based on actual expenditure, including the imputed value of the consumption out of a. home-grown/home-produced stock, and b. gifts, loans, free collection and goods received in exchange of goods and services. This consumption value is based on the practice followed in earlier NSS household surveys. Second, the actual consumption as worked out by the frame cited above plus the imputed value of consumption of items received free of cost through social welfare programmes of a. food items—rice, wheat/atta, etc., and b. non-food items such as laptops, tablets, mobile handsets, bicycles, etc.

The HCES: 2022–23 estimated that average MPCE in rural India was Rs 3,773, comprising food expenditure of Rs 1,750 and non-food expenditure of Rs 2,023. For urban India, the total MPCE was estimated at Rs 6,459 comprising Rs 2,530 of food and Rs 3,929 of non-food expenditure. The MPCE, with imputed value of free-of-cost items included, went up to Rs 3,860 (food Rs 1,832 and non-food Rs 2,028) for rural India and Rs 6,521 (food Rs 2,589 and non-food Rs 3,932) for urban India. The difference between the two estimates is less than 2 per cent.

The HCES: 2022–23 provides relative consumption data for 1999–2000 (55th round), 2004–05 (61st round), 2009–10 (66th round), 2011–12 (68th round) and 2022–23 HCES. The rural MPCE went up from Rs 579 in 2004–05 to Rs 1,430 in 2011–12 and to Rs 3,773 in 2022–23. The urban MPCE went up from Rs 1,105 in 2004–05 to Rs 2,630 in 2011–12 and to Rs 6,459 in 2022–23.

As the HCES: 2022–23 does not provide consumption data coterminous with Modi 2.0, we have to take the next best approximate available for comparing the performance of the Modi government with its predecessor.

For the seven-year period (from 2004–05 to 2011–12), entirely attributable to the UPA government, the consumption of rural India grew at annual compound rate of 13.79 per cent and that of urban India at 13.19 per cent. The MPCE total consumption expenditure in rural India during the eleven-year period (2011–12 to 2022–23), largely attributable to the NDA government, increased at the compounded rate of 9.22 per cent per annum and in urban India at the rate of 8.51 per cent. The consumption growth during this largely NDA period was distinctly lower as per the HCES: 2022–23 data.

An interesting finding of HCES: 2022–23 is that the share of cereals in average MPCE had declined massively from 17.45 per cent in 2004–05 to 10.75 per cent in 2011–12 and further to merely 4.91 per cent in 2022–23 in rural areas and from 9.63 per cent in 2004–05, to 6.66 per cent in 2011–12 to only 3.64 per cent in 2022–23. The share of total food expenditure did not see this massive slide. It was still 46.38 per cent in 2022–23 (against 52.90 per cent in 2011–12) in rural areas and 39.17 per cent (against 42.62 per cent in 2011–12) in urban areas. Very obviously, cereals consumption declined very sharply for twenty years and has now become increasingly marginal in the consumption basket in both rural and urban areas.

As the government provides free food to over 81 crore persons, the share of cereals in average MPCE with imputed value is somewhat higher, though not still significantly higher. In rural India, for 2022–23, it has been estimated at 6.92 per cent of MPCE and for urban India at 4.51 per cent of MPCE.

One big takeaway from the HCES: 2022–23 is that the government must seriously reform production of cereals undertaken at the cost of enormous subsidies, procurement thereof with minimum (which tend to be maximum) support prices and massive public sector storage and distribution costs.

Support Programmes

Cereals supplied free of cost

The HCES: 2022–23 data set provides MPCE information divided in ten sub-groups of items as part of the food group and eleven sub-groups as part of the non-food group. A comparison of the MPCE without imputation for the items supplied free of cost by the government and MPCE with inclusion of the items supplied free of cost tells a very interesting story.

The absolute difference between these two MPCEs (with inclusion of free of cost supplied items and without inclusion of free of cost items) in rural areas is Rs 87 per month (Rs 3,861 and Rs 3,774 respectively. Of this difference, Rs 82 is accounted for by the cereal group with the rest accounted for by clothing, bedding and footwear (Rs 3 per month) and by durable goods (Rs 2 per month). Similarly for urban areas, the absolute difference is Rs 62 with cereals accounting for Rs 59, clothing, bedding and footwear Re 1 and durable goods (Rs 2 per month).

Durable goods include free laptops, mobile phones and many other items. The average MPCE per person in India for the cost of these freebies is only Rs 2 per month per capita. A lot is made of the freebies culture prevalent in the country. The fact of the matter is that the beneficiaries received free cereals of only Rs 82 per person per month in rural areas and Rs 59 per person per month in urban areas.

This leads to another very important conclusion that the Indian state primarily woos consumers through the provision of cereals, mainly wheat and rice. The average benefit is rather small, about 2.25 per cent of total MPCE in rural areas and 0.95 per cent in urban areas. Looked at from another perspective, even with respect to cereals expenditure (which otherwise is minuscule), as much 70 per cent in rural areas (Rs 185 out of Rs 267) and 80 per cent (Rs 235 out of Rs 294) in urban areas is incurred by households on their own.

Is the gargantuan cereal food subsidy based system on which the government ends up spending over Rs 2 trillion a year on average worth it? Does the programme provide any real benefit to the people? Should it not be discontinued or at least be replaced with a food discount coupon system, allowing people to buy whatever food they think they need?

Agriculture support programmes commented upon elsewhere

The government consumption support, other than cereals, is almost nil for all the other items.

The mammoth programmes which the government runs for poverty alleviation, other than free food programmes, such as MGNREGA, PM Kisan, etc., work from the income side of the households. Households receive these incomes and then use the same on consumption items. I have extensively reviewed these programmes as part of the chapter on Labour Incomes.

Likewise, there are numerous input subsidy programmes on agriculture and some other sectors. These subsidies contribute at best to the reduction of market prices of related produce. The households can then expect to spend lower amounts on these items to maintain their level of consumption. These agriculture subsidy programmes have been reviewed in the chapter on Agriculture.

5

Capital Formation

Investment, or the gross capital formation (GCF), is the growth-promoting expenditure. The GCF primarily consists of investments in fixed assets like buildings and machinery, termed gross fixed capital formation (GFCF) in the national accounts. Excess of stocks in goods produced and opening stock over the goods sold (termed change in stock or CIS) also counts as GCF. There is one more element of the GCF—valuables—which represents the expenditure incurred on acquisition of valuables like gold and diamonds. The GCF, thus, is made up of GFCF plus CIS and the valuables.

The GFCF stock is built in all industries, including agriculture and services, but the largest amount of capital has been, for many decades, formed in manufacturing. The national accounts classify the capital formed in four broad categories of buildings, machinery, intellectual property and biological resources.

The capital formation results in building new capacity to produce goods and services. Goods and services that go into making assets, e.g. steel and cement in constructing factory buildings and roads are part of the GVA of the year in which these goods and services are produced and used in forming the capital asset. The capital asset adds to the capital stock of the country and creates capacity to produce additional goods and services for times to come. The growth in the economy is, therefore, substantially attributable to the building of new capital stock and putting it to use to produce new goods and services.

The government participates in forming the capital stock as well, that too in numerous ways. Public buildings and other assets created to deliver public administration services, such as defence, law and order, etc., is one such important way. The governments in India also produce economic goods and services, e.g. the railways provide rail transport services. Rail infrastructure assets created for providing these services, therefore, become part of capital formation.

The governments, primarily the Central government, also provide equity and other fiscal support to public sector organizations for capital formation.

Public sector entities using these resources and also their own also create capital stock, e.g. National Thermal Power Corporation (NTPC) constructs thermal power plants to augment capacity to produce electric power. The governments also undertake specific programmes and provide budgetary allocations and expenditures for promoting private sector investments in manufacturing, such as through the scheme of production-linked incentives (PLIs). However, the private sector builds the capital stock mostly with its own and borrowed resources.

The national accounts provide details of capital formation in government, public sector, private sector and households, which also build a considerable amount of capital—primarily by building residential houses and investment in small enterprises.

Growth

Gross capital formation collapsed and then recovered

In 2013–14, the year before the Modi government took over, at constant 2011–12 prices, the Indian economy generated GCF of Rs 34.48 trillion. There was decent growth in capital formation during the first term of the Modi government. The GCF reached Rs 52.26 trillion in 2018–19, producing a respectable growth rate of 8.67 per cent per annum.

The second term began on a very ominous note on the capital formation front. In 2019–20, the last pre-pandemic normal year, the GCF nosedived to Rs 49.11 trillion, contracting by more than (-)6 per cent, instead of generating a positive growth. This was highly unusual and indicated bad times ahead for economic growth. The GCF further declined to Rs 43.92 trillion in 2020–21, the first year of Covid-19, recording a massive (-)10.6 per cent contraction.

Only in 2021–22, did the GCF prosper, in a remarkable V-shape type of recovery, and amounted to Rs 55.08 trillion (final/second revised estimates) for the year, recording an outstanding growth of 25.40 per cent. This recovery brought the GCF to a level higher than 2018–19 (Rs 56.40 trillion against Rs 52.26 trillion). Yet, the three-year growth of the GCF in the first three years of Modi 2.0 at 1.76 per cent per annum was nothing to write home about.

The GCF growth was quite muted in 2022–23, rising only to Rs 56.16 trillion (FAE), yielding a growth of only 1.96 per cent. The GCF performance was better in 2023–24 (PE) at Rs 62.99 trillion, raising the five-year GCF CAGR to 3.81 per cent—capping a not very comforting story of India's capital investment push in Modi 2.0.

Fixed capital formation story was relatively better

The GFCF, the investment in real capital assets such as buildings and plant and machinery, normally makes up about 90 per cent of the GCF, with the change in stocks and valuables accounting for the rest. In tight supply situations, the stock decline and the proportion of GFCF goes up.

The GFCF was Rs 31.95 trillion in 2013–14. Again, delivering a commendable performance, the annual GFCF grew to Rs 45.41 trillion in 2018–19, the terminal year of Modi 1.0, generating a CAGR of 7.28 per cent per annum.

Unlike GCF, the GFCF did not fall into negative growth territory in 2019–20 (the unused stock declined sharply); although at Rs 45.93 trillion, it barely generated a 1.15 per cent growth. Indiscriminate lockdowns in 2020–21, however, struck a blow to GFCF as well. It fell to Rs 42.67 trillion, contracting by (-)7.1 per cent.

Increasing capital expenditures became the buzzword of government policy from 2021–22 onwards when the government provided the first big jump in budgetary capital expenditure outlay. This switching of stance and normalization of the investment process in 2021–22 resulted in GFCF rising significantly to Rs 50.14 trillion (second and final revised estimates) that year, generating massive year-on-year growth of 17.52 per cent and also bringing the three-year GFCF growth rate of Modi 2.0 to 3.36 per cent per annum.

The decent GFCF growth story continued in the last two years of Modi 2.0 as well, although there were significant variations in GFCF numbers from provisional to revised estimates. In 2022–23 (I RE), the GFCF rose by 6.62 per cent to Rs 53.46 trillion (it was 10.66 per cent for Rs 54.46 trillion in PE). In 2023–24, the GFCF rose by another 8.99 per cent to Rs 58.27 trillion (PE).

Though not something to be quite proud about, Modi 2.0 ended its term with a not-so-bad GFCF annual growth rate of 5.12 per cent, though not an inspiring one, in its five years.

Government CapEx saved the blushes

The national accounts provide granular details of capital formation in six institutional sectors: a. public non-financial corporations or public sector non-financial enterprises such as NTPC and Powergrid, b. private non-financial corporations, i.e. private sector companies such as Tata Steel and Maruti Udyog, c. public financial corporations such as State Bank of India and Power Finance Corporation, d. private financial corporations such as HDFC Bank and Bajaj Finance, e. general government, which includes central and state governments, and f. households. The data, at the time of finishing this book, is available only until FY 2022–23 (covering four years of Modi 2.0).

The household sector contributes the largest share of the GFCF. In 2018–19, this sector generated GFCF of Rs 18.75 trillion out of a total GFCF of Rs 45.41 trillion, contributing as much as 41.3 per cent of total fixed capital formation.

Private non-financial corporations, the real Corporate India, had generated GFCF of Rs 15.64 trillion, which contributed 34.5 per cent of the total GFCF.

The general government, the central and state governments together, had invested Rs 5.30 trillion of goods and services in capital formation (11.7 per cent of total GFCF). The public sector, recognized as the public non-financial sector, invested Rs 5.26 trillion in fixed capital formation (11.6 per cent of total GFCF), almost at par with the government capital formation. Together, the general government and the public sector contributed Rs 10.56 trillion to fixed capital formation, commanding a share of 23.3 per cent.

The national accounts data now confirms that enhanced capital expenditure saved the blushes for not only generating the small GFCF growth but also made up for significantly declined public sector CapEx.

Of the total GFCF of Rs 53.46 trillion in 2022–23 (I RE), all five sectors (other than general government) saw investment of Rs 46.52 trillion, which was 87 per cent of the total fixed capital formation. In 2018–19, the total capital investment by all five non-general government sectors was Rs 40.11 trillion, which was 88.3 per cent of the total GFCF. In the first four years of Modi 2.0, the non-general government fixed capital formation proportionally declined by 1.3 per cent or about Rs 69,500 crore, which was made up by an equal increase in the share of general government fixed capital formation.

The general government fixed capital formation saved the embarrassment from significant reduction in the public sector fixed capital formation. The fixed capital formation funded by the internal and extra-budgetary resources (IEBRs) of the public sector enterprises declined in absolute numbers. The GFCF produced by the non-financial public corporations was Rs 5.26 trillion in 2018–19 (having grown at an annual rate of 8.49 per cent during Modi 1.0 from Rs 3.50 trillion in 2013–14). The GFCF contribution of these non-financial public corporations, in common parlance, the real public sector corporations, declined to Rs 4.70 trillion in 2019–20, Rs 4.13 trillion in 2020–21 (final estimates) and Rs 4.74 trillion in 2021–22 (second revised and final estimates). In the fourth year, 2022–23, the fixed capital formation by the public sector enterprises amounted to Rs 5.05 trillion, still Rs 21,478 crore less than their GFCF contribution in 2018–19. The real public sector four-year growth rate of GFCF was a disappointing (-)1.04 per cent per annum.

Interestingly, the GFCF by the general government and public sector corporations together declined as a proportion of total GFCF in the first four years of Modi 2.0 (from 23.3 per cent in 2018–19 to 22.4 per cent in 2022–23). While the general government increased its share in fixed capital formation (13 per cent in 2022–23 against 11.7 per cent in 2018–19), the capital expenditure by the public sector declined sharply (from 11.6 per cent in 2018–19 to 9.4 per cent in 2022–23). The increase in general government fixed capital investment could not make up for the sharp reduction in public sector CapEx and overall share declined by 0.9 per cent.

Visible lack of animal spirits in investment in machinery

The GFCF is accounted for in four broad categories of capital assets. Dwellings, other buildings and structures form the largest component. In 2018–19, the capital formation in this class of assets was Rs 22.18 trillion, which made up almost half (48.8 per cent) of the total fixed capital formation of Rs 45.41 trillion. Machinery and equipment accounted for another big chunk—at Rs 18.36 trillion, the investment in machinery and equipment was more than 40 per cent of the fixed capital formation.

Intellectual property products (IPPs), the third-largest class of fixed capital formation, though still relatively small, has been witnessing rising capital accumulation. In 2013–14, the IPPs' capital formation was Rs 3.48 trillion, which increased to Rs 4.81 trillion in 2018–19, recording annual growth of 6.71 per cent. The cultivated biological resources (CBRs) were and still are a nascent class of capital formation in India with only about Rs 5,378 crore of GFCF formed in this class in 2018–19.

Animal spirits is a widely used figure of speech in the economic world, denoting the entrepreneurial risk-taking urge of the industrialists in setting up manufacturing facilities and establishing business ventures to produce goods and services. The new manufacturing factories, transportation and other businesses are represented by new capital formation in machinery and plants in new factories, transportation engines and rolling stocks, cranes and other modern machinery in the construction industry and so on.

In Modi 1.0, the animal spirits were quite visible in the industry. The GFCF in machinery and equipment, Rs 10.69 trillion in 2013–14, grew to Rs 18.36 trillion in 2018–19, recording a very healthy growth of 11.42 per cent per annum.

In the second term though, the animal spirits deserted the Indian industrialists and entrepreneurs. Despite the government reducing corporation tax to only 15 per cent plus surcharge on the new manufacturing facilities in September 2019, the machinery and equipment capital formation declined to Rs 17.6 trillion in 2019–20. Covid-19 and lockdowns took a further toll in 2020–21 and the GFCF in machinery and equipment declined further to Rs 16.32 trillion. In two years, the machinery and equipment capital formation had declined by more than 11 per cent. There was good recovery in 2021–22 and machinery and equipment capital formation reached Rs 18.36 trillion (II RE) in that year, which was almost at par with the machinery and equipment GFCF in 2018–19.

It was flat growth in plant and machinery investment in the first three years of Modi 2.0!

Nirmala Sitharaman taunted industrialists as 'Sleeping Hanumans' in September 2022, perhaps with the knowledge of pathetic machinery and equipment CapEx performance until 2021–22. The industrialists did not listen to her. The capital formation in machinery and equipment declined to Rs 18.15 trillion in 2022–23 (I RE). Fixed capital investment in machinery and equipment in India, in the first four years of Modi 2.0, achieved a negative growth of (-)0.29 per cent. So much for public sector CapEx exerting a multiplier effect on private CapEx.

Transportation industry suffered most

The national accounts provide the details of capital formation (at GCF level excluding valuables) for each of the industries generating GVA. The GCF was Rs 33.25 trillion in 2013–14 and had grown in 2018–19 to Rs 48.03 trillion, recording an annual growth of 7.64 per cent per annum in Modi 1.0. This GCF, at Rs 55.30 trillion (I RE) for 2022–23, grew at an annual growth rate of 3.58 per cent during the first four years of Modi 2.0.

Transportation, storage, communications and services relating to the broadcasting group (transportation and communications group), along with the utilities group and construction group, recorded negative capital formation growth in the first four years of Modi 2.0. The transportation and communications group had a GCF, in 2013–14, of Rs 3.11 trillion, which was 9.3 per cent of the total GCF of Rs 33.25 trillion. Railways, road transport, water transport, air transport, services incidental to transport, storage and communications are among the constituents of the group. In 2018–19, the GCF in the group rose to Rs 6.41 trillion, growing at a spectacular rate of 15.57 per cent during Modi 1.0. The fortunes of the transportation and communications group received a beating during Covid-19 and the lockdowns. The group's annual growth declined to (-)2.73 per cent in the first four years of Modi 2.0. A pathetic performance by any account, despite massive investment from the budget.

Within the broader transport, communication, storage and broadcasting sector, the road transport segment GCF had grown at a superlative annual growth rate of 33.7 per cent per annum during Modi 1.0, growing from Rs 52,237 crore in 2013–14 to a whopping Rs 2.23 trillion in 2018–19.

Thanks to the slowdown first and then Covid-19 and lockdowns imposed, the new road transportation capital formation collapsed to Rs 1.51 trillion in 2019–20 and then to only Rs 63,647 crore in 2020–21. The GCF in the road transportation industry fell by more than 70 per cent in these two years. There was a good partial recovery in 2021–22 with the road sector GCF reaching

Rs 1.42 trillion in 2021–22 (II RE). There was some slide-down in 2022–23 with the GCF reducing to Rs 1.28 trillion (I RE). In four years of Modi 2.0, the road sector GCF growth rate was the worst (-)12.87 per cent per annum in the broader transportation and communication sector.

The air transport segment recorded a spectacular growth of 37.92 per cent per annum with the GCF growing from Rs 5,242 crore in 2018–19 to Rs 19,007 crore in 2022–23 (I RE). The railways also recorded a decent growth of 10.91 per cent per annum in the capital formation with the GCF growing from Rs 73,028 crore in 2018–19 to Rs 1.11 trillion.

The GCF in storage and communications segments also declined. Communications and services relating to broadcasting is a large group with a GCF of Rs 3.03 trillion in 2018–19. This GCF declined to Rs 2.71 trillion in 2022–23 (FAE).

The decline in road transport and communications largely was responsible for negative growth in the GCF of the transportation and communication group during Modi 2.0.

Public sector CapEx full of unproductive investment

The national accounts provide one more statement where all the capital expenditure of the public sector—general government, public non-financial corporations and public financial corporation—is aggregated and presented for the industry of use (statement 7.2A) and by assets (statement 7.3A). The GFCF details by assets and by industry for the public sector (statement 7.3A) is available only in current prices.

The statement 7.3A provides an industry-wise breakup of GFCF for the total public sector capital expenditure of Rs 18.76 trillion in 2022–23 (total of general government—Rs 10.91 trillion, public non-financial corporations—Rs 7.70 trillion and public financial corporations—Rs 0.15 trillion).

The largest chunk of this GFCF is generated in the public administration and defence industry, which hardly leads to production of economic goods and services. In 2022–23, the GFCF formed in this class was Rs 8.27 trillion (44.1 per cent of the total). It is notable that the share of public administration and defence in the government CapEx/GFCF has grown from 38.8 per cent in 2013–14 and 38 per cent in 2018–19.

Of the remaining GFCF, a good deal goes for the sectors that don't generate any real positive GVA as the prices charged for these services are typically very low—much lower than the cost of their production. The utilities sector had the second-largest GFCF of Rs 2.99 trillion (16 per cent) comprising electricity, water, gas and other utilities. The utilities in electricity and water sectors particularly lose so much money that their GVA is much smaller.

The railways sector generated GFCF of Rs 1.30 trillion in 2022–23 and the transport, storage and communication sector, as a whole, of Rs 1.59 trillion. This level of GFCF is much lower than the budgetary capital expenditure outlays of these sectors in the Central government budget. Obviously, a good part of the budgetary capital expenditure does not actually lead to formation of capital. It may be used in servicing interest payments and other non-capital creating expenditures or simply to fund the losses.

The construction GFCF of Rs 2.28 trillion in 2022–23 might be the only good quality capital formation from the larger public sector, primarily in the public sector non-financial corporations. Other remaining industries' GFCF was quite small.

Programmes and Policies

The government plays a highly significant role in promoting capital formation/investment in the economy. There are primarily two channels for doing so. First, the government and its public sector agencies make large capital investments themselves. Second, the government provides tax and investment incentives and also adopts policies that engender capital investment by the private sector and the households.

In this section, I take stock of the programmes and policies of Modi 2.0 in promoting capital investment.

Big corporate tax cut in 2019

In September 2019, the government, in a surprise move and in the middle of the year, reduced the base corporate tax rate from 30 per cent to 22 per cent for all companies that opt for this regime, which required forgoing of certain specified incentives. The government brought the base corporate tax rate to a still lower level of 15 per cent for all new manufacturing companies that complete the investment by a specified date and brings the unit to production within specified timelines.

This big policy move made India's corporate tax rates globally competitive and quite attractive. The income tax data presented by the government as part of the Budget papers confirm that the actual effective tax rates for the companies came down by about 6 percentage points by 2021–22. A massive increase in the profitability of Indian companies after Covid-19 and formalization of the economy, accompanied by the big cut in corporate tax rates, boosted the net profits of the companies, and also sent their share prices up.

I have described the government decision to slash the corporate tax rates so drastically and dramatically and its impact in Chapter 18—Revenues. The tax rate cuts do influence corporates' investment decisions but this is not the only factor. However, as we noted in the sections above, capital formation in the economy did not receive any big boost during Modi 2.0.

PLIs did not contribute much

PLI schemes, as described in detail in Chapter 2—Industries, were the biggest expenditure-side programme to boost capital investment in private sector manufacturing, brought in specifically and with big fanfare during Modi 2.0.

The schemes (fourteen in all) have an incentive outlay exceeding Rs 1.97 trillion and envisaged investment exceeding Rs 6 trillion in the economy over a five- to six-year period.

The PLI schemes witnessed a slow roll-out despite the lead provided by the large-scale electronics manufacturing (LSEM) PLI and also that of the bulk drugs and medical devices PLI, which actually had a good head start in the first term of the government, without being formally designated as PLI schemes. As per the press release of 13 June 2023, on that date, 733 applications had been approved in fourteen sectors with an expected investment of Rs 3.65 trillion, including 176 MSMEs. Actual investment of only Rs 62,500 crore was reported till March 2023.

Another official release by the PIB on 17 January 2024 informed that the number of approved applications increased to 746 (an increase of thirteen only since June 2023) with the expected investment of 'over Rs 3 trillion' by that date. This was hugely disappointing regarding investment taking place. While a more specific investment number of Rs 3.65 trillion was mentioned in the June 2023 release, its replacement by a lower round number of Rs 3 trillion seemed designed to hide that there might have actually been some reduction in the investment proposed on that day. There was no change in the number of 176 MSMEs as the PLI beneficiaries either.

In terms of investment realized, there was a notable increase to Rs 1.03 trillion as at end-November 2023. The amount disbursed as incentive was minuscule at around Rs 44.15 crore until the end of December 2023.

The PLIs unfortunately did not contribute meaningfully in raising private sector capital investment in the second term as the data of investment in machinery indicates.

Capital expenditure by government helped but was not enough

The government launched a major capital expenditure programme beginning FY 2021–22.

The nominal budgetary capital expenditure was only Rs 3.08 trillion in 2018–19. In 2021–22, this expenditure went up to Rs 5.93 crore. In 2022–23, the capital expenditure went further to touch Rs 7.40 trillion. The budgetary capital expenditure growth continued to be quite bullish in 2023–24 with the 2023–24 RE recording capital expenditures of Rs 9.50 trillion.

For the five years of Modi 2.0, the budgetary capital expenditure recorded an unprecedented CAGR of as high as 25.30 per cent per annum. The total budgetary capital expenditure for the same period amounted to Rs 30.45 trillion, giving an annual average nominal capital expenditure of Rs 6.09 trillion per year.

The government capital expenditure, besides forming capital in the government and public sector, is supposed to have significant impact on private capital investment. The private industry sets up production capacities to supply industrial and other goods needed for infrastructure and other public sector investment unleashed by the capital expenditure.

I have discussed the government's capital expenditure programme extensively in Chapter 17—Expenditures.

Capital formation remained unspectacular

There is significant discordance in the capital formation during Modi 2.0 as captured in the GCF and GFCF data, while both indicate an overall underwhelming capital formation performance during the period.

The GFCF fared the better of the two. The GCF went into a negative growth territory in both 2019–20 and 2020–21 before re-crossing the 2018–19 levels in 2021–22. The three-year GCF growth (with second revised and final numbers for 2021–22) turned out to be 1.76 per cent per annum. The GCF growth further improved to 3.81 per cent per annum by the end of 2023–24, taking the 2023–24 PE numbers into account.

The GFCF never fell in the negative territory though its growth was quite low. In 2021–22, at the end of three years of Modi 2.0, the GFCF recorded growth of 3.36 per cent per annum.

The GFCF for 2023–24 as per the PE was placed at Rs 58.27 trillion. This raised the fixed capital formation growth for Modi 2.0 to 5.12 per cent. It was certainly better than the GCF growth but not quite impressive and sufficient for putting India on a sustainable high growth path.

The overall GFCF growth subsumes the impact of all the programmes and policies of the Modi government—corporate rate cut, PLI initiative and big capital expenditure push. Tepid annual growth of only 5.12 per cent during the high-voltage capital investment tenure of the Modi government was quite a come-down as it was much less than the capital investment growth of 7.28 per cent in its first term.

Very clearly, there was more noise than real music in the capital formation story of Modi 2.0.

6

Infrastructure

Infrastructure means the assets providing services such as roads facilitating transportation of vehicles or telecom networks built on electromagnetic waves providing communication services or cold storages keeping food fresh and unspoilt, among others. Infrastructure constitutes the biggest part of the capital formation now and economic growth is critically dependent on it.

In the national system of accounts, on the GVA/supply side, there is no separate industry group to present the GVA in and by infrastructure. Infrastructural services GVA is part of all the eight broad industry groups. The utilities group—electricity, gas, water supply and other utility services—primarily comprises infrastructure services. Likewise, the industry group—trade, hotels, transport, communications and services relating to broadcasting—also have a fair bit of infrastructure services.

On the expenditure side, the GCF includes investment made in the creation of infrastructure assets. The GVA and the GFCF are formally classified into four broad heads of buildings, machinery, intellectual property and biological assets. The GCF/GFCF data is also presented for each industry group and many sub-groups thereof. While there is no specific group classified as infrastructure in the national accounts, it is possible to segregate the data relating to industries like roads and railways, which are typically infrastructure industries.

Infrastructure has become extremely important as an asset class and has an enormous impact on value creation across the entire economy—be it in agriculture, industry or services. A good part of infrastructure is still in the public domain. The Modi government, more particularly in the second term, places utmost emphasis on infrastructure investment.

In this chapter, I review the policies, programmes and performance of the Modi government, especially in the second term, in the infrastructure space.

Growth

Infra investment suffered in first three years

The national accounts statistics (NAS) provide details of capital formation by 'industry of use'. This helps in finding the estimates of capital investment made by the typical infrastructure industries—roads, railways or air transport. Investment made by all the infrastructure industries identified and aggregated from this table provides a good estimate of capital formation in the country's infrastructure.

This table (1.10) in the NAS has details of the GCF in the electricity, gas, water supply and other utilities services, which correspond with the infrastructure group of utilities. It also has sub-sector-wise data of transport, storage, communications and services relating to broadcasting, which provides details of capital formation in railways, road transport, water transport, air transport, services incidental to transport, storage and communications and services relating to broadcasting. While this data includes investment in infrastructure assets as well as in machinery like wagon cars, etc., this provides a good estimate of infrastructure capital investment. Likewise, there is data available for the construction and real estate industries.

In 2013–14, total capital formation in the four industry groups of utilities, transport and communication, construction and real estate was Rs 16.23 trillion, at constant 2011–12 prices, out of total capital formation of Rs 33.25 trillion, which was as much as 48.83 per cent of total capital formation. In 2018–19, the last year of Modi 1.0, the capital investment in these four infrastructure industry groups increased to Rs 23.88 trillion, which at 49.71 per cent was very close to being half of the total capital formation of Rs 48.03 trillion. Infrastructure industry sectors' capital formation recorded a reasonably decent growth of 8.02 per cent per annum, higher than the overall capital formation growth of 7.64 per cent.

The first three years of Modi 2.0 turned out to be quite horrific from the viewpoint of infrastructure industries capital formation. The capital investment in the four industries group of utilities, transport and communication, construction and real estate was only Rs 21.82 trillion (I RE) in 2021–22, as much as 8.6 per cent lower in absolute terms than the infrastructure capital formation of Rs 23.88 trillion in 2018–19. As a result, there was actually a negative annual growth rate of (-)2.96 per cent in the first three years of Modi 2.0. However, the picture became a lot better in the second and final revised estimates for 2021–22, which placed GCF in these infrastructure industries at Rs 22.94 trillion, still lower than the GCF of Rs 23.88 trillion in 2018–19, but by a much smaller annual negative growth of (-)1.32 per cent.

The economy-wide infrastructure capital formation did come out of negative territory in 2022–23 and at Rs 24.56 trillion (I RE) recorded positive compounded growth of 0.71 per cent. It also improved in 2023–24 but by how much, we will need to await the availability of national accounts data for the year to ascertain.

Index of core industries confirm poor infrastructure recovery

The Ministry of Commerce and Industries (MoCI) produces an Index of Eight Core Industries, which does not measure the progress in the infrastructure services industries of roads, railways, air transport, etc., as such but measures the production in basic goods industries such as steel, cement, etc., which go into the capital formation and operations of the infrastructure services besides servicing the industry sector.

The overall index of eight core industries was at 106.5 in 2013–14 and grew to 131.2 in 2018–19, recording an annual growth of 4.26 per cent. In 2022–23, after four years of Modi 2.0, the overall index recorded a reading of 146.7. This yielded a four-year annual growth of 2.83 per cent per annum, which of course was not only lower than the growth recorded during the first term, but also indicated the poor state of affairs in the basic/infrastructure industry in the country.

There are eight industry groups—electricity, coal, steel, cement, crude oil, petroleum products, natural gas and fertilizers—which make up the Index of Core Industries. All the industry groups, except fertilizers, recorded lower growth in the first four years of Modi 2.0 compared to Modi 1.0. Electricity recorded annual growth of 4.23 per cent (index moved to 182.2 in 2022–23 from 156.9 in 2018–19) against growth of 7.30 per cent in the first term (from 110.3 in 2013–14). Crude oil recorded a higher negative growth of (-)3.90 per cent per annum in the first four years of the second term against (-)1.97 per cent in the first term. Fertilizer production recorded higher growth of 3.98 per cent per annum in the second term against growth of 1.75 per cent in the first term.

The performance of the Index of Core Industries does vindicate the capital formation performance indicated by the national accounts. As we noted in the previous chapter, as per the first revised estimates for 2022–23, the overall GCF growth was 3.58 per cent only in the first four years of Modi 2.0.

The growth of GCF in the four infrastructure industry groups (a. utilities, b. construction, c. transportation and communications, and d. dwellings and buildings) was still worse. The GCF in these infrastructure industries increased to Rs 24.56 trillion in 2022–23 from Rs 23.88 trillion in 2018–19, recording a pathetic growth of only 0.71 per cent.

Stalled infrastructure credit

Credit is absolutely essential for the expansion of infrastructure investment. While some credit is available from external commercial borrowings and other domestic sources of finance, the bulk of credit still comes, or at least used to come, from the banks. The statement—Industry-wise Deployment of Gross Bank Credit—provided by the RBI does provide specific infrastructure sector-wise deployment of bank credit, in addition to all the major industries/groups. The statement has details of gross bank credit outstanding in overall infrastructure and specific sectors of power, telecommunications, roads, airports, ports, railways (other than Indian Railways, which does not avail any bank finance) and the remaining infrastructure industries clubbed as other infrastructure. In 2013–14, all sectoral infrastructure industries other than power, telecommunication and roads were clubbed as other infrastructure.

The total outstanding bank credit to infrastructure sectors at the end of FY 2013–14 was Rs 8.36 trillion, with the power sector accounting for the bulk of it at Rs 4.87 trillion (58 per cent), followed by the roads sector (Rs 1.58 trillion, 19 per cent). The outstanding credit to infrastructure sectors grew to Rs 10.56 trillion at the end of FY 2018–19, recording annual growth of 4.78 per cent. The power sector outstanding credit rose to Rs 5.70 trillion with annual growth of 3.20 per cent. The telecom sector recorded the highest (though quite small from the normal credit growth perspective) growth rate of 4.7 per cent taking the outstanding credit to Rs 1.16 trillion. This might as well be on account of the big stress telecom sector companies were facing at that time. As road sector investments had shifted primarily to the government-funded route, the outstanding credit to this sector increased to Rs 1.87 trillion, only recording annual growth of 3.43 per cent.

The outstanding credit data for the five years of Modi 2.0 indicate a volatile and not-so-rosy picture of infrastructure capital formation in the private sector. The outstanding credit to the infrastructure sector in the first two years virtually stalled, with the outstanding credit rising to only Rs 10.92 trillion at the end of FY 2020–21 (recording growth of 1.71 per cent only).

There was some traction in 2021–22 with the credit disbursal of Rs 1.03 trillion (growth rate 9.41 per cent) taking outstanding infrastructure credit to Rs 11.95 trillion and boosting three-year CAGR to 4.21 per cent. The fourth year again witnessed a complete standstill with outstanding infrastructure credit rising only to Rs 12.02 trillion (growth 0.58 per cent) at end 2022–23. It also brought down four-year CAGR to 3.29 per cent.

There was somewhat better performance in 2023–24 with the outstanding infrastructure credit increasing to Rs 12.80 trillion (with the net dispersal of Rs 78,275 crore during the year) with an annual growth rate of 6.51 per cent. In five years, the outstanding credit grew by only Rs 2.24 trillion, at an annual growth rate of 3.93 per cent, still smaller than the otherwise very timid growth of 4.54 per cent in the first term.

Two infrastructure sub-sectors—roads and airports—recorded excellent growth during the second term. The outstanding credit to the roads sector increased to Rs 3.03 trillion at end 2023–24, recording a hefty annual growth of 10.17 per cent per annum in the five years of Modi 2.0. The outstanding credit to airports, reflecting the privatization of six airports and the awarding of the construction of a couple of new greenfield airports, increased from Rs 4,424 crore in 2018–19 to Rs 7,206 crore in 2023–24, recording a spectacular growth rate of 10.25 per cent.

With the impasse in the telecommunication sector getting resolved and banks stopping to provide further credit to the weakest entity in the sector, the outstanding credit to the sector grew from Rs 1.16 trillion in 2018–19 to only Rs 1.39 trillion in 2023–24, reflecting a very weak credit growth of 3.71 per cent per annum. The outstanding credit to the power sector rose to Rs 6.45 trillion in 2023–24, again indicating a tepid growth rate of 2.55 per cent.

The status and dynamism of the bank credit growth to infrastructure during Modi 2.0 also confirmed the general low growth scenario in infrastructure industries during this period.

Government became principal infrastructure investor

The weak infrastructure investment growth reflected in the bank credit, index of infrastructure industries and also the capital formation data made the government adopt the infrastructure investment as its own key priority.

The government chose to make infrastructure investment in primarily three sectors—railways, roads and telecommunication. The government's capital expenditure shot up, though the public sector infrastructure investments through IEBR shrunk.

I have discussed the conscious and sudden policy shift to make public investment in the infrastructure sector through the budgets in Chapter 5—Investment and Chapter 17—Expenditure.

Infrastructure undertakings work like government departments

The government's public enterprises and infrastructure authorities, such as Railways and NHAI, are half-way houses between the government departments and private enterprises. Sound policy can push them towards being more like real commercial/private enterprises. Bad policy like reckless CapEx can slide them back towards being more like the government departments.

Railways and NHAI were set up to establish and run infrastructure services as commercial enterprises. NHAI was encouraged to adopt a commercial approach from 2001 onwards by nudging them to grant road construction concessions on a build, operate and transfer (BOT) basis with the government taking care of the unviability element through the viability gap funding. In the last few years, the process of commercialization has actually taken a sharp about-turn.

NHAI has not granted any concessions on a BOT basis for many years. All constructions have been undertaken with full expenditures being borne by the government or from loan resources raised by NHAI. As NHAI's debt piled up and a good deal of its borrowings were going to service its debt, the government stopped NHAI from raising borrowing from the market from 2021–22. Instead, the government started providing all the required resources from the budget, making NHAI literally a fully dependent organization of the government.

Railways have always been reluctant to commercialize or concession its assets. The government expected a big chunk of its national monetization pipeline (NMP) to come from Railways. Unfortunately, the execution of the government's monetization programme by Railways has turned out to be the weakest. No railway assets were monetized in the entire Modi 2.0.

Since 2021–22, Railways increased its dependence on budgetary resources massively. Its funding organizations, like Indian Railway Finance Corporation (IRFC), also stopped raising resources from the market. In the bargain, Railways has moved completely away from being a commercial operating entity. The government is now providing budgetary resources to meet Railways' deficit in its operating ratio as well.

The operating mantra—government has no business to be in business—got turned on its head during Modi 2.0. Instead, it is only government's business to be in the infrastructure business, became the principal guiding force.

Power

India had a 356.10 GW installed electricity generation capacity at the end of 2018–19 when the Narendra Modi government completed its first tenure.

There are four major classes of electricity generation—renewable sources (RES), hydroelectric, thermal and nuclear. RES and hydro generation are now referred to as renewable generation capacity. The thermal power generation capacity, based on the fuel sources, is also further sub-classified into coal (including lignite), gas and diesel.

Satisfactory growth and compositional change in first term

Total installed capacity had increased by a CAGR of 7.46 per cent in the first tenure of the Modi government. The growth of hydroelectric power generation has been literally stalled for quite some time, which was reflected in a tepid growth rate of 2.29 per cent during the first term (capacity increased from 40.53 GW at end 2013–14 to 45.4 GW at end 2018–19). Nuclear power generation had increased from 4.78 GW to 6.78 GW during the first term, recording growth of 7.24 per cent per annum.

Thermal power generation is India's mainstay. Steam power generation, the primary thermal power generation source, grew from 145.27 GW in 2013–14 to 200.70 GW in 2018–19, recording an impressive growth of 6.68 per cent. Gas power generation had faced the problem of economic unviability on account of costlier gas prices and its growth had stalled at 24.98 GW at the end of FY 2018–19, having grown at only 2.74 per cent per annum. Diesel thermal power generation, a small source, in any case was deinstalling capacity, reducing from 1.2 GW at end 2013–14 to 0.64 GW at end 2018–19. The total thermal power generation capacity grew from 168.3 GW in 2013–14 to 226.3 GW at an annual growth rate of 6.10 per cent.

The star performer in the first term was renewable power generation, most spectacularly, wind and solar. Wind power generation capacity had grown impressively from 21.04 GW in 2013–14 to 35.63 GW in 2018–19 at a high rate of 11.10 per cent per annum. Solar power generation did much better. The solar power generation capacity was only 2.63 GW in 2013–14. The installed capacity grew to 28.18 GW during Modi 1.0, recording a spectacular CAGR of 60.67 per cent.

Total renewable energy generation capacity, including small hydro and bio-energy generation, increased from 34.99 GW in 2013–14 to 77.64 GW in 2018–19, recording a highly impressive rate of 17.28 per cent per annum.

India seemed to be firmly getting on with renewable energy power generation.

Significant increase in renewable installed capacity in Modi 2.0

Significant changes took place in the new power generation capacity mix during Modi 2.0 as well.

Thermal power generation did not see any notable addition in the first three years of the second term (until March 2022). The gas power generation capacity actually declined to 24.90 GW. The coal-based steam power generation capacity also saw a modest increase of about 10 GW only during this period. In all, the thermal power generation capacity recorded a growth of only 1.43 per cent per annum in the first three years. Nuclear and hydro capacities also remained unchanged.

The renewable power generation space remained the playground of activity, although the pace of new capacity creation went down. New wind power generation capacity installed during the first three years of Modi 2.0 was only 4.73 GW at an annual growth rate of 4.24 per cent per annum.

The solar power capacity addition saw excellent action with the solar power generation capacity reaching 54 GW at the end of FY 2021–22, recording still a very high annual growth rate of 24.20 per cent. India's renewable power generation capacity touched 109.89 GW at end March 2022, recording annual growth of 12.27 per cent per annum, though less than the 17.28 per cent per annum recorded during the first term but still reasonably high.

The capacity addition seemed to have slowed down in 2022–23. A total of 12.24 GW capacity was added during the year—8.73 GW from renewables, 2.76 GW from thermal and 0.7 GW from nuclear. The annual growth of solar power generation capacity came down to 12.1 per cent during the year. In fact, addition in the wind power generation capacity was only 5.2 per cent. While the government had announced ambitious targets for renewable power generation, the actual performance seemed to be underwhelming.

2023–24 proved much better in terms of the capacity generation. India's total installed capacity went up by 25.91 GW, clocking growth of 6.23 per cent. The bulk of the new capacity came from renewables (18.48 GW—over 71 per cent). The solar generation capacity grew by 15.03 GW. Much better performance in 2023–24 improved the five-year power generation CAGR to 4.42 per cent per annum.

One discomforting message was the slowdown in renewable power generation. Total renewable capacity recorded growth in Modi 2.0 of 13.09 per cent per annum, which was less than 17.28 per cent in the first term. The wind power programme seemed to be losing steam much more with the wind power generation capacity growing by only 5.19 per cent per annum during the second term. It seemed that the government was not really on the top of the situation to maintain the steep pace in installing the renewable power generation capacity needed for achieving the 500 GW and Net Zero commitments.

Government resuscitates thermal power generation

The Modi government decided to change the policy of not building coal-based thermal power plants late in its first term. In the second term, the plan was formally incorporated in the National Electricity Plan for 2022–32, which envisaged building coal and lignite-based installed capacity of 283 GW by 2031–32 as against the installed capacity of 214 GW in 2022. Various projects, almost all in the public sector, taken up added up to 27 GW thermal power plants (TPP) capacity under construction until 2023.

On 18 January 2024, the government approved investment proposals for Coal India Limited (CIL) to set up two pithead coal-based TPP through its subsidiaries. One 1×660 MW supercritical TPP at Amarkantak in Madhya Pradesh is to be set up through a JV between CIL's subsidiary South Eastern Coalfields Ltd (SECL) and Madhya Pradesh Power Generating Co. Ltd (MPPGCL). The other 2×800 MW supercritical TPP would come up in Sundergarh District of Odisha, through Mahanadi Basin Power Ltd (MBPL), a wholly owned subsidiary of Mahanadi Coalfields Limited (MCL).

India is back to installing coal power plants.

Pump storage power generation on faster track

India, with a reported potential of about 103 GW of pumped storage power (PSP) generation, had not invested much in the sector. Consequently, India had around 4.7 GW of installed capacity of PSPs only in 2022–23 of which 3.3 GW was operational. Globally, China leads the PSP market with a total installed capacity of 36 GW, followed by the United States at 22 GW and Japan at 22 GW.

The Draft Electricity Plan 2022 prepared by the Central Electricity Authority (CEA) envisages the establishment of a PSP capacity of 18.8 GW by the end of 2031–32. The Ministry of Power issued draft guidelines in February 2023.

In January 2024, the Ministry of Environment, Forest and Climate Change (MoEFCC) granted environmental clearance to eight PSP projects with a projected capacity of 11.98 GW to be set up with an investment of Rs 81,981 crore. All these projects, except one by Andhra Pradesh Energy Development Corporation (of 1.2 GW capacity), are to come up in the private sector with Greenko Energy's 3.66 GW project being the largest of the lot.

Power generation faced intermittent crises

Power supply faltered in the hot summer of April 2022. On 28 April, India's power system supplied 4,567 million units (MU) and met the maximum demand of 204.65 GW. The day, however, witnessed a peak power shortage of 10.78 GW and energy shortage of 192 MU. Many states had to face blackouts. Rajasthan, Haryana, Punjab, UP, Bihar and MP were the worst affected. Only six months earlier, in October 2021, India had seen the highest power shortage in over five years. The power demand in April 2022 was barely a little over half of India's installed generation capacity of approximately 400 GW. However, the Indian power system struggled to meet it.

The Power Ministry panicked and went into overdrive to take many short-term, ad-hoc measures to stave-off/bottle the crisis. The Power Minister, on 2 May, set coal import targets for each state government and private-sector power companies. They were mandated to import 38 million tons (MT) of coal with 50 per cent coal imported by end-June. Central Public Sector Enterprises (CPSEs) were directed to import an additional 20 MT of coal. The Power Ministry also directed the thermal power plants, closed on account of having gone bankrupt, to start generating power. Natural gas was ordered to be purchased at whatever prices available to put closed/low-capacity operating gas power stations on generation. On 5 May, the Power Ministry issued statutory directions to the imported coal-based power plants (about half closed for years and the rest working at very low capacities thanks to unresolved pricing-related disputes) to immediately start generating power. It was with the knowledge that, with international coal prices hitting the roof, imported coal would certainly cost India a bomb.

Railways cancelled passenger trains first to provide fast-track passage to coal-carrying freight-trains. On 3 May, Railways decided to press into service its almost entire open wagon fleet (85 per cent) for movement of coal only, knowing fully well that this would create problems for the movement of other goods, including foodgrains. With demand outstripping supply, average spot prices touched Rs 18.7 per unit on India's energy exchanges on 25 March 2022. To 'control' exchange prices, the Power Ministry decided to put an artificial cap of Rs 12 per unit. In the absence of any market-clearing prices, it had only brought down trading volumes in power exchanges. Some generators preferred not to produce power in this non-market situation.

While this crisis caused by ad-hocism in policy passed over after a few weeks, increased demand after 2021–22 for various reasons kept the power generation industry on edge throughout the remaining period of Modi 2.0.

DISCOMs remained unreformed

Electricity is fundamental to India's growth and development. It continues to be almost entirely in the government's ownership and control. Power distribution and supply, the lynchpin in the power sector, housed in state distribution companies (DISCOMs) entirely under the thumb of state governments, are the real pain-point. DISCOMs are, to put it bluntly, bankrupt. They don't pay for the coal they buy, power purchased from generating companies (GENCOs) and also don't service their loans in time. DISCOMs have brought sickness to the entire power-sector ecosystem.

The Power Ministry continues to mollycoddle DISCOMs, including bringing out schemes for arrears financing time and again through financing companies like Power Finance Corporation (PFC), etc. There was a Rs 90,000-crore package as part of the stimulus package in 2020. The DISCOMs were perennially in an unpaid overdue position. In April-May 2022, their overdues exceeded Rs 1 trillion (PRAAPTI portal). In the last twenty years, there have been four 'reform packages' (including the much-publicized UDAY programme) to bring down aggregate transmission and collection (AT&C) losses and eliminate the uncovered gap between the per unit cost of power supply and price realization. All these packages have failed miserably. Still we refused to learn. The government started another UDAY type programme—Revamped Distribution Sector Scheme (RDSS)—in 2021. While it claims to be a reforms-based and results-linked programme, there was nothing to separate it from UDAY. The Executive Summary, put out by the Central Electricity Authority for the state of the power sector as on 31 March 2024, states that AT&C losses in 2013–14 were 22.62 per cent and 22.23 per cent in 2020–21. For 2021–22, it mysteriously notes 'under process'. No data is disclosed for 2022–23 and 2023–24. It is a no-brainer that, despite ten years of the Modi government and two big reform and investment programmes, there is no discernible reduction in AT&C losses.

Power generation had been opened up over time and the private sector owns about a half of generation capacity now. However, they are forced to sell through the DISCOM pipe. As DISCOMs don't pay, several private sector generation companies are with the National Company Law Tribunal (NCLT) for bankruptcy resolution/liquidation. Regulators levy usurious charges on surplus power sold by the captive power plants as cross-subsidy, forcing them to prefer not to produce rather than sell under such parasitical arrangements. Power exchanges were beginning to provide some direct sell market mechanisms. However, the practice of putting administrative price caps (Rs 12 per unit) and a later attempt to discover uniform prices across the exchanges (not implemented; the announcement itself caused considerable disruption) made the exchanges lose credibility as well.

The government follows arbitrary policies without regard to their long-term implications. On 28 April 2020, the Power Ministry had directed GENCOs to desist from importing coal to contribute towards making India 'atmanirbhar' in coal. The mad rush to import coal in April-May 2022 exposed the arbitrariness of such policies. The Power Ministry had frustrated all attempts to sell off power sector CPSEs. When pushed, one power sector CPSE bought another (NTPC bought NEEPCO and THDC and PFC bought REC) without any dilution of control of the Power Ministry.

Yet another distribution 'reform' programme

The government launched yet another programme in 2021–22—the Revamped Distribution Sector Scheme (RDSS)—officially named the Reforms Linked Distribution Scheme in Budget papers, with two objectives which have been the rationale/excuse for bringing a new programme every five to six years, with an outlay of Rs 3.04 trillion and estimated gross budgetary support (GBS) from the Central government of Rs 97,631 crore for the duration of five years, i.e. until 2025–26.

The RDSS aimed to reduce India's AT&C losses to 12–15 per cent and average cost of supply (ACS)—average revenue realized (ARR) gap to zero by 2024–25. Incidentally, UDAY, the programme launched by Modi 1.0 with considerable fanfare in 2015, had also aimed at reducing AT&C losses to 15 per cent by 2018–19 with zero ARR gap.

The RDSS focuses massively on prepaid smart metering and system metering and also upgradation of the distribution infrastructure. The government provides financial assistance to DISCOMs based on meeting pre-qualifying criteria and achieving a basic minimum benchmark in reforms.

The RDSS saw actual expenditures of Rs 814 crore in 2021–22. For 2022–23, the government had made a budget provision of Rs 7,566 crore, which was reduced to Rs 6,000 crore in RE. The actual expenditure for 2022–23 was only Rs 2,738 crore. While the scheme was hardly rolled out in 2021–22, the government claimed that the AT&C losses had been brought down from 22.32 per cent in 2020–21 to 16.44 per cent in 2021–22. As I noted in the previous section, the CEA, even after 2023–24 is over, is categorizing AT&C loss determination for 2021–22 'under process'. For 2023–24, the budget provision was kept at Rs 12,072 crore, which was reduced to Rs 10,400 crore in RE.

Promotion of smart metering is the principal intervention of the RDSS. The government wanted to install 25 crore smart meters in the country, covering more than 50 per cent of the consumer connections. As per the data placed by the National Smart Grid Mission (NSGM), as on 8 March 2024, the government had sanctioned a total of 22.2 crore meters. Of these, the agencies concerned had awarded 10.93 crore meters, i.e. a little less than 50 per cent of the meters sanctioned. However, the bigger disappointment was in the matter of actual installations. Until 8 March, only less than 1 crore smart meters had been installed.

This RDSS scheme is turning out to be another UDAY. Its investment component will take years to complete. There remains no link between its reform package, investment component and actual improvement in financial and technical performance of DISCOMs.

Roads

Like industrial growth, construction of road networks, so essential for the movement of people, goods and service providers, was slow until the economic liberalization reforms commenced in 1991. In 1951, 19,811 km of roads, mostly of no good standards, were designated as national highways. The national highways grew to a total length of 33,650 km in 1991, an increase of only 13,839 km in forty years. Almost all of the national highways were either single lane or at best double lane.

The 1990s witnessed a big upsurge when more than 24,000 km of roads were upgraded to national highways. The NDA government (1999–2004) laid massive emphasis on networking the whole of India with modern highways. The golden quadrilateral connecting the four metros—Delhi–Mumbai–Chennai–Kolkata—and the East–West and North–South corridors began to be built. Four-lane highways and expressways made their beginning in India. The length of the national highways increased at a steady pace to reach 70,934 km in 2011. At the end of calendar year 2013, India had 79,116 km of national highways.

Nitin Gadkari remained in charge of the Ministry of Road Transport and Highways (MoRTH) for the entire period of ten years of the Narendra Modi-led government. At the initiative of Nitin Gadkari, the government decided in 2014 to convert as many state highways as possible into national highways, creating a new class of 'in-principle national highways' made 'subject to the outcome of their Detailed Project Reports (DPRs)' by relaxing the criterion for declaring a highway a national highway.

As a result of this policy, as per the note issued by the PIB in July 2019, as many as 71,898 km of state highways were approved as 'in-principle national highways'. In due course, a good stretch of these 'in-principle national highways' got upgraded/declared as national highways. At the end of calendar year 2018, coinciding with the conclusion of Modi 1.0, the length of national highways reached 1,26,350 km, recording a humungous growth of 47,234 km in five years.

This scorching pace of construction was reflected in the roads constructed in a year. The year 2013–14 had seen construction of 4,260 km of national highways. In 2015–16, construction of national highways increased to 6,061 km. The pace gathered further momentum in the next three years: 8,231 km in 2016–17, 9,829 km in 2017–18 and 10,855 km in 2018–19.

The construction of national highways was the signature highlight of Modi 1.0.

Bharatmala project central pivot

The government had approved Bharatmala Pariyojana Phase-I in October 2017, with an aggregate length of about 34,800 km (including 10,000 residual kilometre stretches from numerous national highways development projects initiated since 2003) at an estimated outlay of Rs 5.35 trillion.

The new road construction programme of 24,800 km (out of total identified highways of 53,000 km for improvement of national corridor efficiency) included development of 9,000 km length of 'economic corridors', 6,000 km length of 'inter-corridor and feeder roads', 5,000 km length of national corridors efficiency improvement, 2,000 km length of border and international connectivity roads, 2,000 km length of coastal and port connectivity roads, and 800 km length of expressways. The project was to be completed over a period of five years (2017–18 to 2021–22, both years included).

The government had about one and a half years in the first term to execute the programme. During this period, the government reported that road construction of 6,400 km was awarded and DPRs of 25,000 km were under progress.

The government had a few other programmes also for road construction directed to specific geographies like the Special Accelerated Road Development Programme for North-Eastern region (SARDE-NE) for construction of 6,418 km in the Northeast and the Left Wing Extremism (LWE) programme for 6,085 km for road connectivity projects in left-wing extremist affected areas. The Bharatmala, however, was the flagship programme, many times more ambitious, and extremely important from the economic perspective as it targeted bringing very fast and convenient connectivity between economically important centres of production, import-export and consumption.

Bharatmala faced large cost escalation and slower execution

The original mandated period of the Bharatmala project got over on 31 March 2022.

As per the MoRTH's Annual Report 2022–23, construction of a total of 11,789 km of Bharatmala project highways was completed until the end of December 2022, i.e. after nine months of the original period fixed. The MoRTH could award Bharatmala road projects of 25,713 km with a total capital cost of Rs 7.81 trillion until 31 December 2022.

The project approval activity stopped thereafter as the project cost had already exceeded the original approved outlay. The Department of Expenditure asked, in November 2023, the MoRTH not to create any new liability under the Bharatmala programme before obtaining the approval of the revised cost.

The media reported that the MoRTH moved a Cabinet Note for approval of the revised cost of Rs 10.6 trillion in November 2023 for completing the Bharatmala project.

The flagship project's cost has surged to Rs 10.6 trillion from its initial approval estimate of Rs 5.35 trillion in October 2017. The primary factor contributing to the drastic cost escalation was reported to be the higher cost associated with land acquisition, which now accounted for nearly 35 per cent of the total construction cost of highways.

The cost of constructing highways has been going up sharply over the years. In 2019, according to the statements attributed to the officials from the MoRTH, the cost of constructing a kilometre of four-lane national highway had gone beyond Rs 25 crore per km; and for an expressway, it exceeded Rs 35 crore per km.

The government does not provide any reliable project-by-project information about the cost of constructing a kilometre of national highway. For the projects offered by NHAI in January 2024 on a build, operate, transfer (BOT) basis, the per kilometre cost worked out to Rs 37.45 crore for six projects in UP (project cost Rs 50,333 crore, length 1,344 km) to Rs 75.63 crore for four projects in Tamil Nadu (project cost Rs 39,477 crore, length 737 km).

The revised cost of the Bharatmala project was not approved until the end of Modi 2.0. It was indicated though, that the Bharatmala project would now be made part of the Vision 2047 plan, for all the roads that need to be built up, including the unawarded work of Bharatmala.

BOT projects disappeared

The BOT mode of constructing highways brings private capital and entrepreneurship in the road sector. Except for the pre-committed and bid-ascertained viability gap funding, the project awardee brings all the capital and debt required for building the roads as per the standards laid down in the bid, operates it and recovers its investment and cost of operation through tolling.

The BOT method was the most favoured method of road construction until 2008–09. However, artificial escalation in the land cost, economic slowdown and corruption led to BOT becoming the least-favoured method of constructing highways. In its place, the Engineering, Procurement and Construction or EPC mode, which requires the government to pay the entire cost of constructing roads through contractors upfront, and Hybrid Annuity Mode (HAM), which requires the government to pay 40 per cent cost upfront as EPC and the remaining 60 per cent, brought in by the awardee initially, in a fixed number of annuities, became the dominant mode of national highways construction. No wonder, the government's share of cost of constructing highways went up.

The Bharatmala project envisaged 60 per cent road project construction on HAM, 30 per cent on EPC mode and a smaller share of 10 per cent on BOT basis.

While implementing the project, NHAI/the government could not bid out and award even 10 per cent of the projects on BOT basis. The Annual Report 2022–23 informs that, of the aggregate length of 25,713 km of Bharatmala projects awarded, roads of an aggregate length of 14,317 km were approved on EPC mode, 10,989 km on HAM and only 408 km on BOT (Toll) mode. The projects awarded on EPC basis at 56 per cent were almost twice the proportion envisaged. HAM projects at 42 per cent almost made up the rest. However, the BOT projects at a lowly 2 per cent of the projects awarded were only 20 per cent of the unambitious target of 10 per cent.

Perhaps out of the inability to get the revised cost approved, the MoRTH asked NHAI to revive the BOT mode of national highways construction. NHAI, in January 2024, identified fifty-three highway projects of a total length of 5,214 km in eight states costing Rs 2.1 trillion to be developed on a BOT basis. While the projects envisaged the element of viability gap funding, no progress was made in awarding these projects by the time the second term of the government came to an end.

NHAI lost its creditworthiness

NHAI had the mandate of developing 22,016 km of the new 24,800 km of road programme under Bharatmala. The increasing cost of constructing national highways and small revenues from toll and other transfers by the government compelled NHAI to borrow a large amount of funds for constructing the Bharatmala and other national highway projects. This led to the piling up of debt on the books of NHAI. At the end of FY 2018–19, NHAI had a debt of Rs 1.8 trillion.

NHAI debt kept increasing when the Modi government began its second innings in May 2019. The year 2021–22 proved to be the watershed year.

NHAI debt, as per its Annual Report, crossed Rs 3.49 trillion (Rs 2.07 trillion of secured loans of various types and Rs 1.42 trillion of unsecured debt) at the end of 2021–22, almost doubling from the level of debt in 2018–19. That year, NHAI borrowed secured debt of Rs 0.06 trillion and unsecured debt of Rs 0.36 trillion, in all 0.42 trillion of loans. That year, NHAI spent Rs 0.47 trillion in repayment of loans and interest thereon.

The government found the business of NHAI unsustainable. The government had always funded a good proportion of NHAI's total expenditure on road construction by providing equity support, funded from receipts of road and infrastructure cess, ploughing back of toll revenues, against receipts from bilateral and multilateral loans and other means. In 2021–22, as per statement 26 in Budget 2023–24, of the capital outlay of Rs 1.22 trillion, NHAI had raised IEBR of Rs 0.57 trillion.

From 2022–23, the government stopped NHAI from raising any IEBR. The Budget 2022–23 provided the entire capital outlay of Rs 1.34 trillion to NHAI in the form of budgetary support. This was revised to Rs 1.416 trillion out of the total outlay of Rs 1.424 trillion in 2022–23 RE (actual Rs 1.417 trillion). For the Budget 2023–24, the government again provided the entire Rs 1.622 trillion of capital outlay from the budget, which was revised to Rs 1.674 trillion in 2023–24 RE.

NHAI has literally become the road contract awarding and execution managing agency of the GoI.

Railways

CapEx binge by Modi 2.0 did not accelerate capital formation

Railways have been investing heavily in capital formation for many years although the capital investment, being thinly spread across numerous capital-guzzling projects, did not make any real difference to its revenue-earning capacity and profitability.

As per the National Accounts Statistics 2023, Railways had seen capital formation of Rs 42,700 crore, at constant 2011–12 prices, in 2013–14. The steady state capital investment in Railways, largely funded from its own IEBRs, during the first term of the Modi government, saw the capital formation increase to Rs 73,028 crore in 2018–19, the last year of the first term. The capital formation in Railways increased by a robust 11.33 per cent per annum rate during the first term.

The second term began with an almost stagnant level of capital formation of Rs 75,185 crore in 2019–20. The capital formation suffered a massive fall to Rs 42,275 crore in the Covid-19 pandemic year of 2020–21. There was a smart recovery in 2021–22, after the government began shifting significant part of Railways' capital investment outlay to its general budget, to Rs 93,249 crore (II RE). This extent of capital formation in 2021–22 increased the investment CAGR to 8.49 per cent in the first three years of Modi 2.0.

The government-funded Railway CapEx continued to increase in 2022–23. As per the I RE, released by NSO, it turned out to be Rs 1.11 trillion, marking an excellent growth rate of 18.52 per cent. The four-year CAGR of 10.91 per cent per annum was not any smaller than the first term capital formation growth of 11.33 per cent. When the 2023–24 numbers become available, Railways' fixed capital formation is most likely to exceed its first-term investment growth.

The real challenge, however, was the utter lack of productivity of this CapEx, which I have recounted in Chapter 5—Investments.

Dedicated western and eastern freight corridors biggest infra project

Two dedicated freight corridor (DFC) projects for operating freight trains of much higher lengths and tonnage carrying capacity on tracks dedicated only for freight traffic (no passenger trains on these tracks)—one termed Eastern Dedicated Freight Corridor (EDFC) and another Western Dedicated Freight Corridor (WDFC)—were approved in 2008.

The EDFC (Ludhiana to Dankuni) was to construct a dedicated freight corridor of 1,875 km and the WDFC (Dadri to JNPT Mumbai) a dedicated corridor of 1,506 km. The total corridor length is 3,381 km. The entire DFC was entrusted to a special purpose vehicle—Dedicated Freight Corridors Corporation of India Ltd (DFCCIL). However, the 538-km Sonnagar-Dankuni corridor of the EDFC was envisaged to be constructed in PPP mode. The rest of the corridors—2,843 km—was to be constructed by DFCCIL as a project and operated under a thirty-year contract.

As per information furnished to the Parliament on 15 December 2023, the EDFC work entrusted to DFCCIL from Ludhiana to Sonnagar (1,337 km) had been fully completed and the WDFC (1,506 km) construction of 1,176 km out of 1,506 km had been completed. The cost incurred on the project, until October 2023, was informed to be Rs 1.09 trillion.

The Sonnagar-Dankuni PPP segment has been a non-starter even after sixteen years of project approval. While the government continued to acquire land for the project, the unviability of the project as a PPP came in the way of its making any progress. A few years ago, the government divided the PPP segment into two phases, Sonnagar-New Gomoh (approx. 263 km) and New Gomoh-New Dankuni (approx. 273 km). It was also decided to develop the Sonnagar-New Gomoh section through a hybrid-design, finance, build, operate and maintain and transfer (Hybrid-DBFOT) model. Inquiries were floated. However, the private sector showed no interest. Later, the DFCCIL approached the government to construct this segment through HAM in which the private contractor assumes no revenue/profitability risk. The government took no action until its term was over.

It is strange that the Sonnagar-Dankuni section, which will actually connect the corridor to the port, is not even monitored and reported by the government. The DFC project status reflected on the Gati-Shakti webpage talks about the DFC project as between Ludhiana and Sonnagar and the EDFC project states specific exclusion of the Sonnagar-Dankuni section.

The moth-eaten EDFC has been operational. DFCCIL claims to have operated 62,277 trains and 7,100 crore Gross Tonne Kilometres (GTKM) on operational sections of the two DFCs, yet its operational revenue was reported to be only Rs 3,141 crore in 2022–23, which also is not actual revenue but some kind of contract price recognized in the accounts (not received in cash) on a formula designed to pay enough to cover its costs. There is no authentic information available about how much freight actually moved on DFCs and how much revenue DFCCIL earned on a competitive basis is nowhere disclosed.

While there have been numerous inaugurations of various sections/subsections of the two DFCs, its real objective—of moving India's freight fast and efficiently to its ports—is still far.

India's first bullet train still awaiting flag-off

Prime Minister Narendra Modi and Japanese Prime Minister Shinzo Abe laid the foundation stone for India's first bullet train in Ahmedabad on 17 September 2017. This high-speed train from Ahmedabad to Mumbai, on the pattern of the Shinkansen bullet trains of Japan, was to run on a completely elevated track. Japanese companies were to supply the train stacks. The bullet train project was estimated to cost about Rs 1.1 trillion.

PM Modi wanted the project to become operational by 15 August 2022, when India completed her seventy-five years of independence. At the foundation stone-laying ceremony, he was very effusive of Japanese cooperation in terms of providing the technology of the train and yen loans of about Rs 88,000 crore at an abysmally low interest rate of 0.1 per cent per annum. The actual dollar cost of the financing package with Japanese yen depreciating heavily against the dollar was many times over, though.

The project got into land acquisition and other problems right after the foundation stone was laid. It has made excruciatingly slow progress. About seven years have gone since laying the foundation stone and the project has already gone two years beyond its originally expected completion.

The National High Speed Rail Corporation Ltd (NHSRCL), the special-purpose vehicle for the bullet train project(s), in its Annual Report 2022–23, informed that 99.6 per cent of overall land required had been acquired. In addition, the company had awarded all the civil contract packages covering the entire alignment of 508 km of the project.

In terms of specific implementation, the Annual Report noted physical progress in only 352 km of the Gujarat stretch, where also it reported that foundations on 257 km was completed until August 2023. In addition, 111 km of girder casting and 84 km of girder launching was also completed. In terms of financial progress, the Annual Report noted that capital work in progress of Rs 25,995 crore was achieved until 31 March 2023. The government had provided equity capital of Rs 14,751 crore by this date. The rest was in the form of loans (mostly Japanese-funded) routed by the government to NHSRCL.

The Modi government stopped talking about the bullet train project once it slid into the slow lane. In a reply to the Parliament on 9 February 2024, the government perfunctorily mentioned the status of its civil works only. In addition, it repeated that the sanctioned cost of the Mumbai-Ahmedabad High Speed Rail (MAHSR) project was Rs 1.08 trillion, which is certainly totally out of date.

While it stated that till that date, 290.64 km of pier foundation, 267.48 km of pier construction, 150.97 km of girder casting and 119 km of girder launching had been completed, it dismissively stated that 'the anticipated timeline and final cost can only be ascertained after award of all contract packages'.

The country has no idea when the first bullet train will run in India and at what cost the first high speed corridor of Ahmedabad-Mumbai will get completed.

Airports

As I noted above, the airports capital formation received the highest growth rate during the first four years of Modi 2.0 despite no progress in airport monetization in the second tenure.

During Modi 1.0, the government had finalized the award of six airports—Ahmedabad, Jaipur, Lucknow, Guwahati, Thiruvananthapuram and Mangalore—for an operations, management and development agreement (OMDA) contract model under PPP for a period of fifty years in February 2019 (the actual award was made in 2020–21).

These airport were concessioned on very uniquely crafted terms and conditions, which drew an excellent response. The competition between the parties ensured that the government got highly remunerative prices for the transaction. These unique terms included no requirement for bidders to have any prior airport experience (instead, any infrastructure construction experience was counted), no cap on number of airports for which a participating entity could bid for and simple per passenger fee as a bidding parameter instead of revenue-sharing.

The concessions also had a very long period of fifty years with complete liberty to the awardee for city-side development. The usual transactional roadblocks, such as fixing a total project cost (TPC) upfront, etc., were also done away with.

Unfortunately, the government could not replicate the model in its second term and did not monetize any more airports. The government claimed to have clubbed six small airports (Kangra, Kushinagar, Gaya, Hubballi, Aurangabad and Tirupati) with five major airports (Amritsar, Varanasi, Bhubaneswar, Raipur and Trichy) and publicly stated a number of times that these clubbed airports would be bid on a fifty-year OMDA model. Yet, no effective steps were taken to bid out these airports.

While the Airports Authority of India (AAI) does make capital investment as it still has 110 airports under its wing, the bulk of capital formation on airports now takes place in the private sector. Noida International Airport Jewar is being developed by Zurich Airport with a comprehensive four-phase master plan that aims to handle 60 million passengers per year in the future. Likewise, Navi Mumbai is the other big greenfield airport that is seeing substantial investment.

The airports at Delhi, Mumbai, Bangalore and Hyderabad, the biggest airports of India, and also the six airports concessioned by the government, are witnessing the largest amount of capital formation in the airport sector. This is expected to witness large investments, despite the failure of Modi 2.0 to undertake any monetization.

Telecommunications

Government sells 5G spectrum

5G electromagnetic spectrum is the most valuable natural resource in the modern world for the fast-emerging global digital economy and society. The government, the custodian of common resources, is the owner of the 5G spectrum, currently identified in the 700 MHz, 3 GHz and 26 GHz bands. The government has to allocate it to businesses to build the 5G services network and deliver services thereon. Unsold spectrum is spectrum lost for the time that has passed when it remained unsold.

The 2G notional loss kept troubling the government for five years (2017–22). The government tried to sell the 5G spectrum at prices exceeding Rs 5 trillion after 2018, but without any success. Finally, with some reduction in spectrum prices and by abolishing spectrum usage charges, the government could finally put up 5G spectrum for sale on 15 June 2022.

The government did succeed, though partly. It had offered a total of 72 GHz spectrum for sale in the auction. All bidders got the requisite spectrum in all twenty-two circles in the 26 GHz and 3 GHz bands. The spectrum was sold at the reserve price only. About one-third of this spectrum remained unsold. One bidder bought spectrum in the 700 MHz band as well at its steep reserve price. The government had not been able to sell 700 MHz spectrum in previous auctions. This time also, 60 per cent of 700 MHz spectrum remained unsold. The spectrum in some other bands was also on offer. Except in one or two circles for the 1800 MHz band, there was no demand/competition. The spectrum in some bands like 600 MHz and 800 MHz saw no interest at all. The other bands like 2100 MHz and 2300 MHz saw highly muted demand. The government would collect Rs 1.5 trillion in revenues from this spectrum sale. However, considerable spectrum still remained unsold and continues to get wasted.

Pricing spectrum has been a major policy failure. India's policy affair with telecom licensing and spectrum sale has been torrid right from its beginning in the 1990s. In the first phase lasting until 1998, the government wanted fixed prices. Chasing unknown dreams, the industry overbid. Within a few years, the system collapsed. The government had to rescue the sector by migrating telecom operators from the fixed price regime to the revenue-sharing regime.

This change and a rapidly growing economy made the pendulum swung to the other extreme. The telecom operators made a huge killing. The government allocated new spectrum virtually free on a first-come-first-served basis. This phase, lasting until 2010, corrupted the system, culminating in the horrible 2G scam. The CAG computed the notional loss to the exchequer at Rs 1.76 trillion. The Supreme Court cancelled the licences and the sector collapsed again.

This fallout, accentuated by the AGR imbroglio, has made India literally a two-horse telecom country. The collateral damage of this entire episode made the TRAI, the regulator and the government completely risk-averse. Spectrum reserve prices were fixed at levels at which none wanted to buy. The government wanted over Rs 5 trillion from 5G spectrum sale. For three years until 2021–22, there were repeated failures in attempts to sell 5G spectrum at such ridiculously high prices.

The fact that 3 GHz and 26 GHz had no history to align its reserve price with anything received in the past, made the government a little more reasonable in fixing the reserve price thereof. However, 700 MHz, despite 40 per cent reduction from earlier levels, was still considered too pricey. Perhaps comforted by the fact that they would have pricing power, the only two incumbent 5G operators in the sector bought the minimum necessary 5G spectrum at the reserve price. The reserve price is not the market price.

It will be advisable if the government rescues itself from this trap of over-fixing reserve prices. The government should have fixed the right reserve price and offered the remaining 5G spectrum for sale soon after June 2022. They did talk about it in 2023–24. A date was fixed in 2024–25. The fact was that no spectrum sale took place in the rest of Modi 2.0 after the only auction in June–July 2022.

Part III

Labour and Quality of Life
(Income-Side Economics)

7

Labour Income and Welfare

The GDP broadly represents the collective value of all the goods and services produced by the residents, collective incomes of all the households, received directly through wages earned and indirectly through return on their investment and the collective consumption of all the resident households and their savings.

To be considered inclusive, therefore, GDP and its growth need to be generated by the participation of all households/work-age individuals, either as entrepreneurs or labour. This results in the generation of income adequate for every household to live life comfortably, meeting at least the minimum needs for a happy, healthy and reasonably prosperous life.

GDP primarily gets divided into three parts: a. salary and wages to the workers employed as income, b. interest, dividends and profits to the entrepreneurs and investors of capital, and c. tax incomes of the government. A dominant majority of all households earn their incomes by working jobs and getting paid in the form of salaries and wages or from the profits of their small household enterprises. The larger the share of wages accruing to as big a proportion of the population as possible, the larger the inclusiveness of GDP growth.

The households/individuals in any country/society fall into three groups broadly: a. those who have the ability to earn for living a good life, b. those who have innate abilities to work and earn, but for various reasons—inappropriate/inadequate education and skills, lack of entrepreneurial and employment opportunities, poor policy framework and so on—are not able to do so, and c. those who have physical, mental or other disabilities that prevent them from earning an adequate income.

The first set of households/individuals do not need any financial support from the government. The government, however, has a major responsibility of framing policies and maintaining a fall-back mechanism for the second set of households/individuals, to create a conducive ecosystem for these households/individuals and private sector entrepreneurs to rectify/supplement their skills, take the right education and manage other inadequacies, to enable these individuals/households to set up their businesses or work as productive workers.

The way the economic system works, in the absence of or despite running inclusive development programmes, there will still be some or many households/individuals not in a position to take economic care of themselves. Those who cannot work and those who don't get employed adequately are the ones who fall into the poverty trap. Governments have a duty to take care of them.

Inclusive governance demands that the governments adopt redistribution policies and undertake redistribution programmes for taking care of the households/individuals not in a position to take care of themselves and provide skilling and hand-holding to the households/individuals who can take care of themselves, but with some temporary support from the government. The redistribution programmes would require fiscal means which an inclusive government would raise by taxing the income and wealth of the rich and providing support through appropriate welfare programmes, including provision of what these days have come to be called freebies.

In this chapter, I take stock of the policies, programmes and performance of the Modi government in the second tenure for inclusive growth and growth in labour incomes.

Labour Income and Growth

Inclusive growth is all about improving labour incomes

Most households buy goods and services from the income they earn from their labour—manual, skilled or intelligence. Their labour is essential for producing goods and services and contributes enormously to the total value generated in the goods and services produced in the economy.

The value generated is primarily divided between the labour and the capital. The government gets its share from the value added, as taxes from the businesses/consumers (product taxes) and from the value/income received by the labour and capital providers (income taxes).

Depending upon how much of the growth in value created goes as the share of labour, the growth will be inclusive or otherwise. If there is growth in the economy and the additional value so created goes completely or predominantly to the capital, it is jobless or non-inclusive growth. If the labour share is at least higher than the existing share of labour, the growth is inclusive. Growth in the share of labour is contributed by one or both of the factors—new labour employed and increase in the wages of the existing workforce.

PLFS projected significant growth

The government initiated the Periodic Labour Force Survey (PLFS) in April 2017 to provide estimates of the principal employment and unemployment indicators (labour force participation rate—LFPR, worker population ratio—WPR and unemployment rate—UR) in both 'usual status' (which combines principal status—PS, plus subsidiary status—SS) and current weekly states (CWS) in both rural and urban areas annually.

The PLFS, carried out by the NSSO using a July–June year framework, provides a host of useful data-points relating to the employment, wages and other dimensions of the state of labour incomes. The PLFS 2022–23, released on 9 October 2023, is the latest in the annual series of data available since 2017–18 and also the last released in Modi 2.0.

The PLFS provides data for LFPR, WPR and UR in three distinct series: a. for the working-age population, i.e. for persons aged fifteen and older, which is compatible with the definition used by the International Labour Organization (ILO) and other international organizations, b. for persons of all ages, i.e. for the entire population, and c. for persons between age fifteen and twenty-nine to capture the status of the younger population entering the job market. In this book, I use the ILO-compatible data series for persons of age fifteen years and older to draw my conclusions and make comments.

The Centre for Monitoring Indian Economy (CMIE) also conducts an employment survey—called the Consumers Pyramid Household Survey (CPHS)—and provides the same set of data. The CPHS uses the same definition as the PLFS but their results/findings are very different from each other. For example, the PLFS informs that the LFPR was 57.9 per cent for 2022–23, whereas the LFPR, as per the CMIE's CPHS, was only 39.5 per cent for the year. I use the official PLFS for all my conclusions/comments barring at some places to highlight some significant variations in the data-points of the two surveys for credibility.

The LFPR increased significantly as per the PLFS during the first four years of the Modi government. For 2022–23, all-India LFPR—taking the rural and urban areas together—in the usual status was 57.9 per cent for all persons aged fifteen years and higher. The all-India LFPR for all persons in 2017–18 was 49.8 per cent and for 2018–19, the last year of Modi 1.0, it was 50.2 per cent.

There was a notable increase of 8.1 per cent (from 49.8 per cent to 57.9 per cent) in the five years between 2017–18 and 2022–23 and 7.7 per cent in the first four years of Modi 2.0 (from 50.2 per cent in 2018–19). On the face of it, the absolute increase of 16.3 per cent (8.1 per cent/49.8 per cent) or annual growth rate of 3.06 per cent between 2017–18 and 2022–23 was an impressive achievement. The annual growth rate between 2018–19 and 2022–23 was still better at 3.63 per cent.

The UR and WPR are derived from the LFPR. The LFPR is made up of two parts: those who get employed (workers) and those looking for employment but not getting employed (unemployed). The ratio of workers to the total working age population, which is the base for LFPR as well, is the WPR. The ratio of those remaining unemployed despite looking for jobs to those employed is the UR. As per the PLFS, the unemployment rate declined consistently from 2017–18 (6 per cent) to 2022–23 (3.2 per cent).

As more people joined the workforce and the unemployment ratio declined, the WPR or the employment ratio increased. The employment ratio (WPR) rose from 46.8 per cent in 2017–18 to 56 per cent in 2022–23.

Job growth claim is quite suspect

More intensive analysis of the PLFS data, however, makes the claim of impressive growth in the employment metrics suspect.

The first factor which makes the claim suspect is the fact that the LFPR increase was heavily concentrated in female labour.

The LFPR, for all-India male persons, during the five-year period, rose from 75.8 per cent in 2017–18 to 78.5 per cent in 2022–23. The LFPR for all-India females during the same period in contrast rose from 23.3 per cent in 2017–18 to 37 per cent in 2022–23. While the increase in all-India male persons' LFPR was only 2.7 per cent in absolute percentage (3.6 per cent in relative percentage terms), the increase in all-India female persons' LFPR was massive—13.7 per cent in absolute percentage (58.8 per cent in relative percentage terms).

India's working age population is approximately 100 crore, roughly 52 crore male and 48 crore female. The increase in LFPR of all persons from 49.8 per cent to 57.9 per cent in the five years translates to an increase of 8.1 crore active workers, both male and female, during this period, assuming the population to be broadly constant. The male LFPR increase of 2.7 per cent in this period would mean an increase of 1.40 crore male workers, whereas the increase of 13.7 per cent in female LFPR implies a humungous increase of 6.58 crore active female workers. Taking into account the increase in the male and female workforce, as much as 81 per cent increase in overall LFPR in five years of the Modi government between 2017–18 to 2022–23, as per the government's PLFS, was contributed by female workers. On the face of it, it does not reflect ground reality and makes it suspect.

Another dimension in the LFPR increase, the rural and urban division, strengthens the suspicion further.

The urban all-person LFPR increased from 47.6 per cent in 2017–18 to 50.4 per cent in 2022–23, increasing by 2.8 percentage points. The rural all-persons LFPR, on the other hand, increased from 50.7 per cent to 60.8 per cent, recording an astounding increase of over 10.1 percentage points.

The LFPR represents the labour force getting employment or actively looking for employment, which invariably gravitates to where there are increasing employment opportunities. Urban areas are the engines of growth in our industrial and services-oriented economy and providers of jobs. Rural areas, on the contrary, are constantly shedding jobs on account of fast reduction in the employment intensity of agriculture and allied services. Contrary to this economic and obvious truth, the PLFS data suggests that there was a massive increase in labour workforce participation in rural areas!

In the rural areas, the male LFPR increased from 76.4 per cent in 2017–18 to 80.2 per cent in 2022–23, a marginal increase of less than 5 per cent over the base year. The female LFPR in the rural areas, on the other hand, increased massively from 24.6 per cent to 41.5 per cent, an increase of 68.7 per cent—an obviously unbelievable feat.

It requires a thorough investigation to decipher what kind of employment opportunities the female workers have got in the rural areas of India to make the female LFPR in rural areas shoot up so much.

The CMIE CPHS reports virtually no increase in the rural female workforce participation rate. The combination of high growth in rural areas and in female employment make the PLFS claim quite suspect.

Unpaid family helper provides the clinching clue

PLFS has a table which provides details of the 'employment type' of workers employed. There are three principal divisions of employment type of labour: self-employed, regular wage/salary and casual. The self-employed worker category is further subdivided into two sub-classes: a. own account worker and employer, and b. unpaid helper in household enterprises.

The Tables (Statement 6 in 2022–23 PLFS, Statement 12 in PLFS 2019–20 and Statement 14 in PLFS 2017–18) provide details of the type/category employment break-up of workers.

In 2017–18, 13.6 per cent of all workers were employed as 'helper in household enterprises'. This class of 'workers' came to occupy a larger share of employment in subsequent PLFS surveys. In 2017–18, their proportion increased to 15.9 per cent, which went up further to 17.5 per cent in 2021–22. In 2022–23, their proportion rose to the highest share of 18.3 per cent of workers, which meant an increase of 4.8 per cent of all employed workers. For the employed workforce of 58 crore (57.9 per cent of total workforce of the estimated 100 crore working age population), as many as 10.6 crore workers were helpers in the household enterprises. Their tribe increased by about 2.8 crore workers in five years between 2017–18 to 2022–23.

The helpers in household enterprises are unpaid workers. They work without being paid any wages. Is this employment? Such 'workers' do not increase overall wages available to the labour. Their employment only means wageless jobs and ends up reducing the average earnings of the self-employed workers.

The PLFS data provides evidence of unpaid workers depressing the average earnings of self-employed workers. In 2022–23, the rural regular wage/salary female workers earned, on average, income between Rs 10,367 (in the July–September quarter) and Rs 13,825 (April–June quarter) per month. Casual female workers earned between Rs 259 and Rs 287 per day in works other than public works or between Rs 7,770 and Rs 8,610 per month. Self-employed workers earned the least—between Rs 4,725 and Rs 5,071 in the last thirty days, equivalent to a month's earning/wages. Self-employed workers' wages are the least as they included the big cohort of the unpaid helper in households enterprises.

There is another set of data in PLFS that substantiates this. The quarterly ratio of female wages to male wages in rural areas for the regular wage/salary jobs for 2022–23 ranged between .64 to .80 and for casual workers between .60 to .69. On the other hand, this ratio for the self-employed was woefully low at only .35 to .39. This also suggests quite credibly that the unpaid helpers in household enterprises are predominantly female.

The solid chain of predominant increase in rural employment, that too in female employment and finally as unpaid helpers in household enterprises, is quite credible to believe that the increase claimed in employment is phony. Female members of the households assisting without wages in small enterprises like selling pakoras have been added to boost the employment data.

Labour stress reflected in lower consumption growth

There was distinct suppression in consumption expenditure during Modi 2.0.

In the first term, the private final consumption expenditure (PFCE), at constant 2011–12 prices, grew from Rs 55.57 trillion in 2013–14 to Rs 78.50 trillion in 2018–19. In the second term, however, this consumption expenditure increased to only Rs 97.74 trillion in 2023–24 (FAE), revised further down to Rs 96.99 trillion in the PE released on 31 May 2024.

It is distressing to note that the consumption growth in the second five-year term was lower in absolute numbers, at constant prices values—from Rs 22.93 trillion in the first term to Rs 18.49 trillion in the second term—a reduction of roughly one-fifth. The slowdown in the consumption growth was dramatically reflected in the PFCE annual growth petering out to only 4.32 per cent in the second term of the Modi government against 7.15 per cent in the first term.

Private consumption is supported substantially from wage incomes. Without a doubt, the lot of workers remained under stress in Modi 2.0.

Labour Welfare Programmes

EPS provided low welfare contribution

The Employee Pension Scheme (EPS), the long-running primary pensions scheme for workers in the organized sector, might be severely underfunded.

EPS was launched in 1995 to provide pensions to the workers of organized establishments (establishments subject to the Employee Provident Fund and Miscellaneous Provisions Act). An Employee Pension Fund (EPF) was established in the Employees Provident Fund Organization (EPFO) to manage the contributions, investments and payment of pensions. The scheme provides that 8.33 per cent out of the 12 per cent contribution made by employers is credited in the EPF fund account with EPFO, subject to a limit of Rs 1,250 per month. The government contributes 1.6 per cent of the employees' pay, subject to a pay ceiling of Rs 15,000. Employees get a monthly pension that broadly corresponds to their average salary of the past five years (subject to a ceiling of Rs 15,000) multiplied by the number of years served and divided by 70.

At the end of FY 2018–19, there were 64,51,746 pensioners of the EPS, including 43,25,413 member pensioners with the rest belonging to various other categories of pensioners like spouse pensioners, children pensioners, nominee pensioners and so on. By the end of FY 2021–22, the number of EPS pensioners increased to 72,73,898, recording a CAGR of 4.08 per cent. The EPF disbursed Rs 11,207 crore as pensions in 2018–19 and Rs 12,933 crore in 2021–22. The average pension was Rs 17,370 per annum (Rs 1,447 per month) in 2018–19 and Rs 17,780 (Rs 1,482 per month) in 2021–22.

The EPF received an annual contribution of Rs 40,260 crore from employers and Rs 6,402 crore from the government in 2018–19. It also earned an interest of Rs 32,982 crore that year. However, after disbursement of pensions, withdrawal benefits and other expenditures, the increase in the EPF corpus amounted to Rs 44,159 crore, taking the corpus to Rs 4,37,763 crore. The corresponding numbers in 2022–23 amounted to Rs 56,171 crore (employer contribution), Rs 8,715 crore (government contribution) and Rs 51,986 crore (interest). The net increase in the EPF was Rs 91,098 crore with the EPF corpus rising to Rs 7,80,309 crore, recording four-year growth at a compounded rate of 15.55 per cent per annum.

The EPS provides for a minimum pension of Rs 1,000 per month. As many as 20.56 lakh EPS pensioners (27.20 per cent of total 75.59 lakh pensioners) received the benefit at the minimum Rs 1,000 pension rate in 2022–23.

There have been doubts about the financial viability of EPS. On a current basis, it still receives much higher inflow than what it pays as pension and other benefits. The scheme provides for a mandatory annual actuarial valuation (para 32 of the Employees' Pension Scheme, 1995—the Central Government shall have an annual valuation of the Employees' Pension Fund made by a Valuer appointed by it). The EPFO/Central government got the actuarial valuation reports of the scheme for 2017–18 and 2018–19. The reports received were forwarded to the government for acceptance/action but are still 'under process' at the time of finishing this book. Apparently, the Central government is sitting tight on these reports without taking the requisite action.

The EPFO temporarily stopped appointing actuaries thereafter. In August 2022, it last issued a fresh request for proposal (RFP) for actuarial valuation of EPS-95 as on 31 March 2020, 2021 and 2022. Whether any actuary has been appointed and whether any reports have been received has not been publicly disclosed. In the absence of this information, there is no way to know what the lifecycle/actuarial assessment of the gap in financial assets and liabilities of EPS-95 is currently.

Contribution pension schemes simply failed

The Modi government initiated contributory pension schemes for: a. unorganized sector workers, b. farmers, and c. traders with considerable fanfare in 2018–19 and 2019–20. All these schemes have got virtually grounded.

On 5 March 2019, after the approval in the Interim Budget 2019–20, the government introduced the contributory new pension types of scheme for all unorganized sector workers. The scheme was eloquently named Pradhan Mantri Shram Yogi Maandhan (PM-SYM).

Two more such contributory pension schemes were launched after the Modi government returned to power in 2019–20 for small traders named Pradhan Mantri Karma Yogi Maandhan (PM-KYM) and Pradhan Mantri Kisan Maandhan Yojana (PM-KMY) for farmers. All these three contributory pension schemes put together literally cover the entire universe of unorganized/informal sector workers in India, with both farm and non-farm workers in their scope.

These three schemes remained in operation during the entire tenure of Modi 2.0. There was considerable energy/activity in rolling out the schemes and enrolling the 'beneficiaries' in the first full year of their implementation, i.e. 2019–20.

PM-SYM provides for a monthly pension of Rs 3,000 to unorganized sector workers in the age group of eighteen to forty, on a self-declaration basis, provided they make a monthly contribution determined by taking into account the age at which they join. For a worker who is twenty-nine years old, the monthly contribution is fixed at Rs 100 per month. The monthly contribution for the youngest worker (eighteen years) is Rs 55; for the oldest (forty years), it is Rs 200 per month. The benefits promised under PM-KYM and PM-KMY are broadly similar to PM-SYM.

The government did assume major financial responsibility under the schemes as well. The schemes are administered by LIC, which makes the investment of the corpus as per the investment pattern approved by the government. The government makes a contribution equal to that of the enrolled worker, trader and farmer. The government guarantee is to meet the underwritten shortfall, if any, in the corpus in discharging its pensionary obligations.

The government had announced, at the time of launching the PM-SYM scheme, that it envisaged providing post-retirement pensions to about 50 crore workers in the unorganized sector.

By the end of the first full year of the operation of the PM-SYM scheme, i.e. 2019–20, a total of 43.64 lakh informal sector workers were registered, a little less than 1 per cent of the targeted 50 crore. The enrolments under the scheme slowed down in FY 2020–21. A total of 1.31 lakh unorganized sector workers registered under PM-SYM in that year, taking the scheme total to 44.95 lakh. The performance during 2021–22 was no better, with total registration reaching 46.56 lakh only, indicating fresh registration of only 1.61 lakh.

In 2022–23, there was some pick-up with 2.76 lakh workers registering, taking total membership at the end of year to 49.33 lakh. The last year of Modi 2.0 saw the scheme getting almost completely stalled. As on 31 March 2024, the PM-SYM dashboard reported total registrations to be 49.98 lakh. This meant in 2023–24, less than 65,000 workers joined. Instead of registering 50 crore workers under the scheme, the Modi government managed to attract less than 1 per cent of the target in five years.

The PM-KYM almost collapsed before it began. The government does not even have a functional dashboard for a scheme like the PM-KYM. A total of 53,218 traders probably registered under the people-oriented scheme. The PM-KMY did relatively better enrolment at about 17.8 lakh.

These schemes have operated for the full five years of Modi 2.0. However, they could not muster even 70 lakh of enrolments. In the last four years, new enrolments were not even 10 lakh put together. The schemes are as good as flops. This is reflected in financial expenditures as well.

For the PM-SYM, the government incurred an expenditure of Rs 355.20 crore in the first year, 2019–20. The amounts spent in the subsequent two years were lower—Rs 319.71 crore in 2020–21 and Rs 324.23 crore in 2021–22—which reflected the reality that new beneficiary addition had become a trickle and the workers who joined in 2019–20 were also not contributing regularly. In 2022–23, the expenditure was reduced further to Rs 269.91 crore and for 2023–24 RE, the government provided for only Rs 205.21 crore. This is the surest evidence that a good proportion of the registered cohort have abandoned the scheme and are not making their due contributions.

PM-KYM for traders has completely disappeared. The government spent only Rs 0.02 crore in 2022–23 and kept 0.10 crore provision in 2023–24 RE.

PM-KMY for farmers did have some notable contribution in the first two years—Rs 125 crore and Rs 110 crore, respectively. However, this scheme also lost its mojo by 2022–23. In that year, the government spent only Rs 12.50 crore on the scheme. While it kept a provision of Rs 138 crore in 2023–24 RE, the actual expenditure is unlikely to exceed Rs 10 crore.

ABRY kept EPFO rolls mustered up

The Covid-19-era provident fund contribution payment scheme, Atmanirbhar Bharat Rozgar Yojana (ABRY), served the interests of employers and added numbers to the EPFO payroll data. The Modi government had launched a scheme—Pradhan Mantri Rozgar Protsahan Yojana (PMRPY)—in August 2016 to encourage industries to create new employment by paying employers' contribution to the employee pension scheme and provident fund.

In Modi 2.0, the PMRPY emerged with a different name and an enlarged package—as ABRY in December 2020 'to boost employment in formal sector and incentivize creation of new employment opportunities during the Covid-19 recovery phase under Atmanirbhar Bharat Package 3.0', to be implemented during 2020–23 with an outlay of Rs 22,810 crore.

Under ABRY, the government committed to provide subsidies for two years in respect of new employees engaged on or after 1 October 2020 and up to 30 June 2021. Going beyond the PMRPY package, the government promised to pay both the employees' and employers' contributions (12 per cent each; 24 per cent in total) in establishments employing up to 1,000 employees for a period of two years for such eligible persons employed. For establishments with more than 1,000 employees, only employees' contribution was to be paid.

Only new employees drawing monthly wages of less than Rs 15,000, not working in any establishment registered with EPFO and not having a Universal Account Number or EPFO number prior to 1 October 2020 were made eligible. To extend the benefit to workers adversely affected by the Covid-19 lockdowns, EPF members with a Universal Account Number (UAN), drawing pay less than Rs 15,000 per month and losing their job between 1 March 2020 and 30 September 2020, who did not join employment in any EPFO establishment until 30 September 2020, were also made eligible.

The government extended the registrations under the scheme from 30 June 2021 to 31 March 2022 when the fresh registrations finally closed. Total registrations under the scheme reached 60.44 lakh. The government spent Rs 405 crore on the scheme in 2020–21, Rs 3,931 crore in 2021–22, Rs 4,636 crore in 2022–22 and made provision of Rs 1,350 crore in 2023–24 RE.

The scheme did help in boosting new EPFO employee registrations.

MGNREGA relieved Covid-19 distress

The Mahatma Gandhi National Rural Employment Guarantee Act (MGNREGA) scheme is structured to provide survival jobs to labour not finding any formal or informal jobs in the economy as backstop/the last resort. Rural labour does not have full-time work all around the year in agriculture operations and also as unskilled construction workers in rural and urban areas. They fall back on MGNREGA work for as many days as possible within the overall household limit of 100 days' work in a year.

MGNREGA is a demand-based programme. Every household that wants to work as labour under the programme can register and get a job card. There are about 10 crore active job cards and about 15.2 crore active workers registered with the MGNREGA programme. Typically, a little over 5 crore households get employment on MGNREGA works every year.

In 2020–21, the year of Covid-19 distress, the number of households and individuals that sought work under MGNREGA shot up to 7.57 crore and 11.20 crore. The intensity of survival jobs continued in 2021–22 as well. In 2022–23, when the Covid-19 effect was over, the demand came down significantly.

Labour Reforms

Organized sector workers

India has numerous labour laws, and massive compliance and reporting requirements about different dimensions of labour employment in its factories and workplaces. The labour laws, however, concern only a small fraction of workers in the organized sector.

The basic law dealing with working conditions is the Factories Act. It applies to factories/workshops/undertakings that employ more than ten workers with the use of power or more than twenty workers without the use of power.

The annual survey of industries (ASI) collects statistics for all factories satisfying the above criterion and establishments registered under seven specified laws, employing over 100 employees.

These factories, workshops, undertakings and establishments make up broadly the organized sector in India. In 2019–20, there were 2.46 lakh factories; 1.98 lakh considered operating by the ASI and the rest 47,876 non-operating/zero units. These factories and establishments employed a total of 1.31 crore workers, which was less than 2.5 per cent of the country's estimated 55 crore labour force.

These survey reports are routinely delayed (the 2020–21 survey was available only at the time I completed this book). In a reply to the Rajya Sabha on 11 December 2023, the Minister of Statistics informed that 'no results of ASI have been published in 2023. The fieldwork of ASI 2021–22 has been completed in 2023. Further data validation and scrutiny is being done before release'.

Government consolidated twenty-nine labour laws

The government undertook consolidation of twenty-nine labour laws in four codes in 2019–20, the first year of Modi 2.0.

The Labour Code on Wages was passed by the Parliament on 30 July 2019. This code consolidated four dimensions of pay and allowances by bringing four existing laws—the Minimum Wages Act, 1948; the Payment of Wages Act, 1936; the Payment of Bonus Act, 1965; and the Equal Remuneration Act, 1976—under a single code.

The three other labour codes—the Occupational Safety, Health and Working Conditions Code, 2020, which deals with workplace conditions; the Industrial Relations Code, 2020, which deals with aspects relating to organization of labour and resolution of labour disputes; and the Code on Social Security, 2020, which deals with social security, including for workers of unorganized sectors—were passed by the Parliament on 22 September 2020.

These four codes were duly notified immediately thereafter. The codes only required the rules to be framed and notified before they came into effect and became enforceable.

The Draft Code on Wages (Central) Rules 2020 under the Code on Wages was notified on 24 August 2020. The Draft Occupational Safety, Health and Working Conditions Code (Central) Rules 2020 were notified on 19 November 2020 and the Draft Central Rules on Industrial Relations Code were notified on 29 October 2020. The Draft Rules on Social Security were also published on 13 November 2020.

Codes bring uniformity in definitions

The twenty-nine laws on labour had variously described and defined industrial labour in different ways: workman, worker, employee, organized worker, unorganized worker, etc.

The new Code on Wages defined 'worker' to mean any person (excluding an apprentice) employed in any industry to do any manual, unskilled, skilled, technical, operational, clerical or supervisory work for hire or reward, whether the terms of employment were express or implied, and included working journalists and sales promotion employees. This code also provided a definition of 'employee' similar to 'worker' except that it included administrative and supervisory workers.

The Industrial Relations Code and the Workplaces Conditions Code use exactly the same definition of employee and worker. The Social Security Code uses almost the same definition of employee and worker but also brings in additional types of workers—'platform worker', 'home-based worker' and 'gig worker'—within their scope.

Bringing greater uniformity in different forms/nomenclature of labour, irrespective of occupations, is the most significant contribution of the consolidation exercise. Otherwise, the consolidation made largely cosmetic changes.

The Occupational Safety and Health Code (OS&H Code), which consolidated thirteen laws relating to workplaces/working conditions/working relationships, defines all workplaces as 'establishments' using a single definition and does away with different conditions for registration of different type of workplaces.

The OSH&WC Code, however, continues with mandatory registration of all workplaces as was required under the consolidated laws earlier. The code fails to recognize that most office and service establishments today have very minor risks to safety, health and working conditions. Without making any distinction between hazardous and non-hazardous establishments, the OSH&WC Code subjects them all to the same registration conditions.

Wages code the least dynamic

The Code on Wages displays the least dynamism. While merging four existing laws, it continues with all their existing prescriptions and deformities without any change, e.g. payment of mandatory bonus continues for establishments making no profit.

The code prescribes only one 'form' of wages, treating the employees working on a salary as the universal form of wage. It ignores newer forms of labour and compensation, like the gig economy, contractor-employee relationship and so on. It does not recognize the 'cost-to-company' approach or the total package cost as well.

Government could not fix minimum wages

Among many benefits, the government claimed that the Code on Wages would guarantee minimum wages to all workers/employees.

Fixation of minimum wages was required under the standalone Minimum Wages Act, 1948 as well.

Before undertaking the consolidation exercise, the government appointed a committee under the chairmanship of Dr Anoop Satpathy in January 2018 on minimum wages, which submitted its report in January 2019.

Taking into account a minimum intake of 2,400 calories, 50 gms of protein and 30 gms of fat per adult per day, the committee recommended minimum wages of Rs 375 per day as of July 2018 (Rs 9,750 per month), irrespective of sectors, skills, occupations and rural-urban location. In addition, house rent allowance up to Rs 55 per day for urban workers was also recommended.

The government did not formally accept or implement these recommendations.

The Code on Wages stipulates that minimum wages be fixed for all establishments covered after factoring in unspecific elements like 'skills of workers required for working under the categories of unskilled, skilled, semi-skilled and highly-skilled', etc., for different 'geographical areas', taking into account 'variation in the cost of living index number applicable to such workers' and 'cash value of the concessions in respect of supplies of essential commodities at concession rate' and so on. It is estimated that the government would need to fix about 2,400 different minimum wages to comply with the code's stipulations.

In June 2021, the government appointed another expert committee 'to provide technical inputs and recommendations' for 'minimum wages' and 'national floor minimum wages', and gave it three years to provide its report.

The expert committee did not submit its report before the end of the Modi government's second term.

Social security code promise remained unrealized

The Social Security Code 2020 consolidates the existing nine laws dealing with social security and expands the coverage of workers for benefits. In terms of intent, the code is most progressive.

The Social Security Code materially expands coverage and benefits in five principal ways.

First, it allows non-covered establishments to voluntarily join EPF and EPS and also offers the choice between the new pension scheme (NPS) or EPFO, if they decide to provide such retirement savings-related benefits to employees.

Second, the code defines new forms of employment, such as aggregator, gig worker and platform worker, and includes them within the ambit of the law. It defines an establishment excluding the condition of a minimum of ten employees, which means all establishments in the country—micro and small— will come within its scope.

Third, the code seeks to establish an electronic system of registration of establishments which has the potential to create a complete database of establishments in the country.

Fourth, it makes employees on fixed-term contracts eligible for gratuity.

Fifth, the code provides for registration of every unorganized worker, including gig workers and platform workers, electronically and that too on the basis of their self-declaration.

The only downside is that the code left the responsibility to develop programmes and schemes to deliver these benefits only to the government. Unfortunately, the government did not do anything to implement the Social Security Code either. Its promise remained totally unfulfilled in Modi 2.0.

Industrial Code attempted to solve old problems

The Industrial Relations (IR) Code brought reforms for factories of the bygone era.

First, it included fixed-term employment as a regular mode of employment.

Second, it eliminated the misuse of casual leave as a weapon of industrial action by bringing the same within the scope of 'strike'.

Third, it eliminated multiplicity of negotiating trade unions in an establishment by mandating that only a trade union with the support of 51 per cent or more workers would be allowed to participate in negotiations. Further, it eliminates strong-arm tactics by any one union by providing a seat on the council for the support of every 20 per cent of workers.

Fourth, it made the life of enterprises employing less than 300 workers simpler, by making certain restrictive conditions—mandatory certification of complete standing orders and taking prior permission before layoff, retrenchment and closure—applicable only to industrial establishments that have over 300 workers on their rolls.

Fifth, it prohibits strikes and lockouts in all industrial establishments without fourteen days' notice.

These changes could tilt the balance in favour of entrepreneurs as there are only a few thousand industrial establishments in India with over 300 workers.

Consolidated laws remained unimplemented

The four codes needed detailed rules to implement their provisions. The rules are framed by the 'appropriate government'.

The Central government is the appropriate government for establishments of the Central government, Railways, mines, oilfields, major ports, air transport service, telecommunication, banking and insurance company, or a corporation or other authority established by a Central Act or CPSUs or their subsidiaries or autonomous bodies owned and controlled by the Central government, including contractors for any of these establishments.

The state governments are the appropriate government for the rest of the establishments. Almost 99 per cent of the establishments/enterprises/bodies to whom the labour codes would apply would have the respective state governments as the appropriate government.

The Central government called the consolidation exercise the 'biggest labour reforms in independent India'. The Central government framed all the required rules for the four codes—in all ten rules—two each for the three codes and four rules under the IR Code very quickly, in 2020–21 itself.

Most state governments also notified the requisite rules under the four codes before the end of 2021–22. Only four states—West Bengal, Sikkim, Nagaland and Meghalaya—did not notify any of the rules. Some states did not notify some rules. Andhra Pradesh and Arunachal Pradesh did not notify rules under two codes—Occupational Safety and Social Security. Maharashtra and Goa did not notify under the Occupational Safety Code. Some UTs—most prominently Delhi—did not notify rules under all or some of the codes.

Soon after passing the consolidated codes and notifying the draft rules, the GoI, particularly after the fiasco over the three farm laws, lost interest in the labour laws. While most of the states had framed the required rules and it did not need all the states to frame rules before bringing the consolidated codes into force, the GoI used the excuse of some states not framing the rules for not notifying the central rules and implementing the consolidated labour codes.

None of the four codes were notified for implementation by the end of Modi 2.0 in 2024.

8

Poverty and Redistribution

All income in an economy, in the final analysis, gets distributed to its households.

The GDP, in the first round, gets divided into three broad categories of income: labour income for the working households and individuals, profit income to capital owners—both real and financial capital—and tax income to the government.

Labour income accrues to the households and individuals directly. The profits on capital assets, whether rents, interest or dividends, get redistributed to households and individuals in the second round. Even the retained profits get reflected in higher valuation of assets owned by households and individuals. The tax income of the governments also goes back to the households and individuals as labour incomes of employees and benefits/redistribution made to the people.

Net incomes from the rest of the world also land finally with the households and individuals.

This final distribution of all income in the economy is grossly unequal. Typically, in the industrial-digital economy we live in today, a good chunk of incomes gets concentrated in the hands of only 1–10 per cent of the households and individuals. These are rich people with incomes far more than their consumption needs. There is a large middle section of people (20–88 per cent) who get enough income to be able to meet all their normal consumption needs.

The rest of the people are poor. They do not earn enough income to meet their minimum consumption requirements to afford a healthy life. They make the bulk of population in low income/poor countries. There is a lot of noise about lifting such poor people out of poverty. The Prime Minister and the government claimed credit for lifting 25 crore people out of poverty in the country during the ten years of Modi 1.0 and Modi 2.0.

Poverty is measured using different concepts and methodologies. The three most prominent are: multidimensional poverty, income poverty and consumption poverty.

Let me take stock of India's progress on the poverty front during Modi 2.0.

Multidimensional Poverty

Started by the United Nations Development Programme (UNDP) in 2010, the Multidimensional Poverty Index (MPI) has gained prominence over the last two decades. The MPI measures the progress of households/individuals out of a set of nutritional, social and economic deprivations to ascertain the reduction in multidimensional indicators of poverty over the years.

Government claims lifting 135 million out of MPI poverty

'India lifts 135 million Indians out of multidimensional poverty (MPI)' was the big headline in the media and prime-ministerial pronouncements in mid-July 2023, intended to create the impression that India had trumped poverty.

This claim was made based on the Indian edition of 'MPI-National Multidimensional Poverty: A Progress Review-2023', produced by the NITI Aayog, using and modifying the UNDP MPI Report. The UNDP report, also published in 2023, documents India's progress in MPI using data for three years 2005–06, 2015–16 and 2019–21.

The NITI Aayog Review and UNDP MPI have ten common deprivation indicators organized in three groups of health, education and standard of living, each group with an equal one-third weight. The group weight is divided further in its constituent sub-indicators. The health group has nutrition and child and adolescent mortality as two constituent indicators with one-sixth weight each. The education group again has two indicators in the global MPI—years of schooling and school attendance—again with equal one-sixth weight. The standard of living has six constituent indicators—cooking fuel, sanitation, drinking water, housing, electricity and assets—with each indicator having an individual weight of one-eighteenth.

NITI Aayog has added two indicators in its national MPI: maternal health in the health group, taking away half of the weight assigned to child and adolescent mortality, and bank account in the standard of living group with a weight equal to the other six indicators. Consequently, in India, the three indicators in the health group have weights of nutrition: one-sixth, child and adolescent mortality: one-twelfth, and maternal mortality: one-twelfth. There is no change in the two constituents of the education group. The seven indicators of the standard of living with the inclusion of bank accounts has 1/21 weight in India's MPI. These changes do make some difference between the UNDP and NITI Aayog assessment of MPI poverty reduction in India.

The UNDP MPI Report confirmed that the MPI poor reduced from 370.5 million in 2015–16 to 230.7 million in 2019–21 or by 139.8 million. The NITI Aayog MPI reduction claim was perfectly in line with the UNDP Report.

Nothing exceptional about MPI poverty reduction though

As per the UNDP MPI 2023 Report, the MPI poor people in India were 645.7 million in 2005–06, 370.5 million in 2015–16 and 230.7 million in 2019–21. The number of MPI poor reduced by 275.6 million between 2005–06 and 2015–16 (27.56 million per year on average) and by 139.8 million between 2015–16 and 2019–21 (27.96 million per year).

The poverty reduction in both the periods was remarkably similar as per the UNDP report. The NITI Aayog Review, while claiming reduction of MPI poverty by 135 million in the period 2015–16 and 2019–21, entirely covered by the Modi government, did not highlight the poverty reduction during the earlier period 2005–06 and 2015–16, which straddled largely the Manmohan Singh government and covered the first two years of the Modi government. There was nothing exceptional about the MPI poverty reduction during the BJP government period.

India still has large MPI poverty

The NITI Aayog report also did not bring out and highlight the number of remaining MPI poor in India. The UNDP Report did.

As per the UNDP Report 2023, there were as many as 270.7 million (about 16.4 per cent of India's population) multidimensionally poor in 2021. This is an uncomfortably large number of poor people. The war on poverty is not over yet.

There was no justification to blow the trumpet on vanquishing poverty when over 27 crore of Indians still remained trapped in MPI poverty.

Real MPI poverty is more deeply entrenched

There is a big deficiency in measuring poverty reduction by the MPI method.

As many as 31.52 per cent of people surveyed (approximately 44.5 crore of India's 140 crore population) were assessed to be nutritionally poor in India's National Family Health Survey (NFHS), on which MPI poor count is actually based. Likewise, 43.9 per cent of those surveyed were found suffering deprivation on the cooking fuel and 41.37 per cent on the housing indicator.

The MPI methodology does not consider an individual/household MPI poor unless a household scores minimum 33.33 per cent, taking all the MPI deprivation indicators together. The three indicators—nutritional deficiency, inappropriate access to clean cooking fuel and lack of adequate housing—individually do not have 33.33 per cent weight in the MPI formula. Therefore, all households found deprived on any one or two out of these three parameters are not considered MPI poor if their MPI score does not add up to minimum 33.33 per cent.

Any household/individual who is nutritionally poor or does not have access to cooking fuel or adequate housing, is actually poor even if the MPI score of that household/individual does not add up to 33.33. If we consider a household/individual deprived if he/she satisfies at least one of these three deprivation indicators, 44.5 crore (on nutritional deprivation) to 61.8 crore (on cooking fuel deprivation) Indians would be considered MPI poor in India.

Catchy 25 crore poverty reduction claim

NITI Aayog came up with a discussion paper in early January 2024 titled 'Multidimensional Poverty in India Since 2005–06'. UNDP had published an MPI report and data for 2005–06. NITI Aayog had earlier published an MPI report for 2015–16 and 2019–21 based on NFHS data of these two respective years. Therefore, data on reduction of MPI poverty between 2015–16 and 2019–21 was available, but not for the period 2014–2024 which is coterminous with the tenure of the Modi government.

To find the number of poor people lifted out of poverty between 2013–14 and 2022–23 in the nine years of the Modi government, NITI Aayog decided to resort to using arithmetical averages. It calculated that the MPI poverty reduction between 2005–06 and 2015–16 took place at an annual compound rate of 7.69 per cent. Likewise, it calculated the annual compound rate reduction of 10.66 per cent between 2015–16 and 2019–21.

NITI Aayog broke the period 2005–06 and 2015–16 into two periods: 2005–14 and 2014–16 to interpolate the reduction in MPI poverty in the first two years of the Modi government. It also extended the CAGR of the period between 2015–16 and 2019–21 to extrapolate the MPI poverty reduction for the period 2021–22 and 2022–23.

Based on these interpolations and extrapolations, NITI arithmetically calculated the estimated absolute change in the headcount MPI poverty over the nine-year period from 2013–14 to 2022–23 to be 17.89 percentage points, which, when converted into numbers based on assumed population, produced the number of poor reduced at 24.82 crore. With this arithmetical estimate, the government decided to go to town and claimed to have lifted 25 crore poor people out of poverty in the nine years of the Modi government.

Such an arithmetical exercise to arrive at a designer reduction of the poor does not have any credibility. Using CAGR to project the future course of reduction in deprivation is entirely incorrect. The deprivations remaining now (lack of nutrition, for example) are more difficult to crack. Many data points indicate reduction in the rate of poverty decline, if not reversal, in the post-pandemic period. The 2019–21 Survey was substantially a pre-pandemic survey. The actual state of deprivation in 2022–23 can only be assessed by another NFHS.

A closer perusal of the NITI Aayog paper, if you take arithmetical averages and not compound averages, reveals a different picture that arithmetical MPI poverty reduction was not extraordinary during the Modi government, compared to the period between 2005–06 and 2013–14. The NITI Aayog paper states in Graph 1 that the headcount ratio of MPI poor was 55.34 per cent in 2005–06, 29.17 per cent in 2013–14 and 11.28 per cent in 2022–23. Therefore, the MPI poverty reduced by 26.17 per cent (55.34 per cent minus 29.17 per cent) in eight years of the UPA government whereas it reduced by 17.89 per cent in nine years of the Modi government. The annual average reduction was far higher in the UPA period than the Modi period, as per NITI Aayog's own data. In absolute terms also, as 17.89 per cent reduction in headcount ratio reduced multidimensional poverty by 25 crore in nine years of Modi government, 26.17 per cent reduction in headcount ratio in eight years of the Manmohan Singh government would have reduced poverty by about 36 crore.

Consumption Measured Poverty

Poverty, in simple terms, is the inability of a person or a household to consume adequate goods (principally food) and essential services to maintain a minimum standard of living. The consumption benchmark converted into monetary value equals poverty measured in income. Lack of consumption resulting in deprivations translates into poverty measured from deprivations. Let us take stock of India's poverty situation from the consumption perspective.

The consumption method measures consumption of requisite goods and services directly. The standards of consumption are determined, e.g. so many kilocalories in food. India developed a massive consumption-based poverty measurement system in the 1970s which, in fact, worked as the model for the world. India last measured consumption and poverty based on consumption in 2011–12 (68th round of the NSS).

HCES 2022–23 does not provide consumption poverty estimates

The NSSO conducted a Household Consumption Expenditure Survey (HCES) between August 2022 and July 2023 to generate estimates of household monthly per capita consumption expenditure (MPCE) and its distribution separately for the rural and urban sectors of the country, for states and union territories, and for different socio-economic groups.

The summary results of this HCES: 2022–23 were released on 24 February 2024 in the form of a factsheet. I have discussed the HCES comprehensively in Chapter 4—Consumption.

No poverty estimates were included in this survey. The NITI Aayog CEO, however, claimed the next day, 25 February, that poverty in India had reduced to less than 5 per cent.

There was no basis for his claim. The consumption basket for defining the poverty cut-off was not prepared. Nor was the consumption data collected applied to such a consumption basket. Accordingly, there was no estimate, forget credible estimate, of poverty reduction in the HCES 2022–23.

India remained without any consumption-based poverty estimates during and till the end of the Modi government's tenure.

Income-Based Poverty

The income method determines the monetary value of the requisite minimum consumption of goods and services to arrive at the poverty cut-off. India's income poverty estimates were also last worked out in 2012, based on the household survey as part of the 68th round undertaken in 2011–12.

For 2011–12, using the Suresh Tendulkar Committee (2005) methodology, the then Planning Commission had estimated per capita income of Rs 816 per month in rural areas and Rs 1,000 per month in urban areas as the poverty cut-off. It translated, for an average family of five members, into a poverty cut-off of Rs 4,080 in rural areas and Rs 5,000 in urban areas. For this income poverty, it was estimated that 25.7 per cent of people in rural areas (216.5 million), 13.7 per cent in urban areas (52.8 million), in all 21.9 per cent (269.3 million) persons were below the poverty line in 2011–12.

While India does not have income-based poverty estimates since 2011–12, the World Bank does bring out income-based poverty estimates from time to time, including that of India. The latest World Bank extreme poverty cut-off is $2.15 per capita per day income in 2017 purchasing power parity (PPP) dollars.

The extreme poverty cut-off of $2.15 per capita per day in 2017 PPP dollars equalled Rs 44.40 in 2017. According to the World Bank's estimates, 10 per cent of India's population was poor in 2019, the year when the second term of the Modi government began.

The World Bank website has the last extreme poverty estimates for 2021 (latest available). Extreme poverty in India had increased to 12.92 per cent in that year, partly due to the impact of Covid-19. For the estimated population of 141 crore in 2021, the number of extremely poor in India worked out to be 18.22 crore.

The World Bank also has other measures of income poverty at $3.65 per capita per day and $6.85 per capita per day in PPP 2017 dollar cut-off. According to these cut-offs, 44.05 per cent and 81.76 per cent of India's population was poor in 2021.

India still has an unflattering income poverty challenge to overcome. It is no point in claiming and celebrating elimination of poverty in India at the present juncture.

Global Hunger Index

There is one more measurement of poverty in the form of nutritional deficiency in children, mothers and the population in general, as measured in the Global Hunger Index.

India registers slow progress on Global Hunger Index

The Global Hunger Index (GHI) is released every year. The last GHI during the tenure of Modi 2.0 was released in October 2023.

The GHI, using the UN's Food and Agriculture Organization (FAO) data and data published by respective countries, assigned scores to 125 countries on an overall basis and on each of the four building blocks—child mortality (proportion of children dying before age five), child stunting (low height for the age, which measures low birth weight and poor nutrition in the first 1,000 days), child wasting (low weight for the height, which indicates acute under-nutrition until children complete five years) and undernourishment (which measures general under-nutrition). Stunting and wasting of children together had one-third weight with child mortality and general under-nourishment accounting for the rest one-third each. The weighted score of these four benchmarks was the overall GHI score of a country.

To capture the absolute and relative states of under-nourishment, the scores were classified in five segments. Extremely alarming (GHI score ≥50) made the worst reading. Alarming (between 35 and 50) and Serious (between 20 and 35) also underlined a quite difficult situation. Moderate (between 10 and 20) indicated good progress and low (≤10) the most satisfactory position.

India with a score of 28.7 was in the 'Serious' category with a hopelessly poor 111th ranking (out of 125 countries) though its GHI score has been consistently improving—from 38.4 per cent in 2000 to 35.5 per cent in 2008 and 29.2 per cent in 2015. India's rank, however, has been continuously slipping—94 in 2020 and 101 in 2021. India's performance was the worst in South Asia with only Afghanistan behind India.

GHI measures long-term nutrition not food starvation

The GHI is not about counting people dying of starvation or a country enjoying food surpluses or facing food shortages. India successfully banished famines and stopped importing degrading PL480 wheat aid for feeding its teeming millions many years ago. Barring in only a few unfortunate countries in Sub-Saharan Africa, no one dies of starvation any more. India is a net exporter of wheat and rice. For the last three decades, India is truly atmanirbhar in food/calories.

The GHI is about chronic and acute under-nutrition, which leads to underdevelopment of the human body and brain. This under-nutrition is captured as chronic hunger in the GHI and is most evident in India's stunted and wasting children and, to a significant extent, in their mothers. That is where the GHI 2023 called out India's sub-optimal performance.

GHI 2023 did not make a grim reading for India in all the four constituent parameters. India did very well in the child mortality parameter. Its child mortality rate was in the best performance class of 'Low' with a score of 3.1. The GHI recorded India's consistently improving score with the child mortality rate coming down from 9.2 in 2000, to 6.8 in 2007, to 4.8 in 2014 and 3.3 in 2022. India has surely succeeded in making sure that its children don't die young.

India is, however, still not producing and rearing healthy children. India's child stunting rate was in the 'Alarming' category with a highly disappointing score of 35.5; although this had also come down from an 'Extremely Alarming' score of 54.2 in 2000. It was quite discomforting that there were only a few countries in Sub-Saharan Africa that had a child stunting score worse than India.

It was in the child wasting parameter, where we came out the worst with the score of 18.7 per cent, implying that almost every fifth child of less than five years was wasting. Child wasting, on top of child stunting, indicated the worst nutrition status of the children and their mothers. It is our shame that India continues to be the worst performer in the world for this benchmark. To put salt into India's festering nutritional wounds, India's performance on this front deteriorated during the Modi government period. Our 2023 GHI child wasting score of 18.7 per cent was worse than the average score of 18 per cent recorded for the period 2013–17), though it was lower than 19.3 recorded in 2022. Child stunting and wasting remains our Achilles heel.

India's own surveys confirm GHI findings

India's own surveys and data fully confirmed the GHI scores. The Fifth National Family Health Survey 2019–21 (NFHS-5 2019–21) reported that 35.5 per cent children under five were stunted and 19.3 per cent wasted in India. The GHI score of 35.5 for child stunting and 19.3 for child wasting for 2022 were exactly the same score as the NFHS-5's. The GHI 2023 records a minor improvement, though no later NFHS data set is available.

Misdirected and wasting food security programmes are our real problem. India spends massive budgetary resources, in lakhs of crores of rupees, in running programmes for tackling the issue of food security in general and under-nutrition in children. The Integrated Child Development Services

(ICDS), now reincarnated as Poshan-2, addresses under-nutrition in children by providing supplementary nutrition to children and expecting and lactating mothers.

The National Food Security Act (NFSA) addresses general under-nutrition by making it obligatory for the governments to provide 5 kg of wheat/rice/coarse cereals to every identified deprived person. There are over 81 crore Indians who get cereal nutrition under NFSA. The government doubled the NFSA food allowance in 2020 by launching an additional scheme—Pradhan Mantri Garib Kalyan Yojana (PMGKY), which ran until December 2022. PMGKY's additional foodgrains did nothing to improve GHI ranking as additional cereal provision could have impacted the nutritional status of children, mothers and the population in general. The government made the NFSA foodgrains free of cost (the nominal Rs 3/2/1 per kg charge was removed) from January 2023. This is not going to make any difference to India's nutritional status or GHI ranking either.

Poshan-2 and its earlier version ICDS, running for the last forty years, have been implemented in a dysfunctional manner and have not really succeeded in denting child stunting and wasting. We have to get our food security and women/children nutrition programmes right to make a real dent in the GHI.

Welfare/Redistribution Programmes

Inadequate labour incomes of the poor leads to lower consumption, which, in turn, results in various kinds of deprivations and poor nutritional status. While the programmes to impart necessary skills to help the poor improve their incomes are the real solution for addressing poverty, for the poor, who, for physical or other infirmities, cannot be expected to earn enough for their living and many others who, for social or other reasons, remain trapped in poverty, the government has to provide supplemental income or consumption support to save them from the consequences of inadequate incomes.

This supplemental support can be provided either in the form of income support which can be with or without conditions, used by the recipients to address consumption deficiency or in the form of direct consumption goods like food, fuel, housing support, etc.

I review, in this section, the working and performance of such welfare/redistribution programmes run by the Modi government, with particular emphasis on the second term.

Redistribution is inclusive development

The operation of modern production/value addition systems is such that capital—physical and digital—takes away a disproportionate share of value addition/income generated. The share of labour is relatively small.

More than 45 per cent of workers in India were employed in 2022–23 (as per the government PLFS) in agriculture and another 13 per cent in construction. Only 21 per cent of workers were employed in regular wage/salary jobs; 22 per cent were engaged in casual labour jobs and the remaining 57 per cent were self-employed, of which as many as 18.3 per cent were unpaid helpers in household enterprises.

The regular/wage/salaried employees earned between Rs 14,723 and Rs 21,026 on average during the year. Casual workers earned between Rs 265 and Rs 443 per day when engaged in work. The self-employed had smaller average earnings than the regular workers. They earned between Rs 5,302 and Rs 15,763 on an average per month.

Most of India's labour force does not earn enough to afford a decent life. The government therefore runs several programmes which are available to workers and employees in the workforce and in employment. The PM Kisan payment of Rs 6,000 per farmer is available to all farmers barring a very small section. The MGNREGA offers demand-based employment for 100 days to every worker who wants to avail this, irrespective of his normal wage earnings. Free rations are provided to 80 crore-plus people, including a large number of farmers and non-farm workers.

Only about 57 per cent of India's population in the working age is actually employed. A good proportion of the rest does not have any income. The surveys report about 17–18 crore Indians are at present multidimensionally poor. They desperately need government support to live.

The government taxes the rich and distributes the same to the needy and poor by way of running many poverty-reduction and life-support programmes. This is redistribution.

The Modi government operated a number of good programmes in the first term: Ujjwala for providing fuel for cooking and other necessities, electricity for utilizing time in an optimum manner, Swachh Bharat for sanitation and the like—which sought to take care of the dysfunctional economic ecosystem that prevents people from developing their skills and education and wastes considerable time in coping with them. In the second term, only the Jal Jeevan Mission had this trademark of meeting the utility needs of the people.

Let me take stock of large redistribution programmes run by the Modi government.

Free Food scheme

The Union Cabinet, on 26 March 2022, approved the extension of the Pradhan Mantri Garib Kalyan Anna Yojana (PM-GKAY) for six months (from 1 April to 20 September 2022), which meant that nearly 80 crore beneficiaries would continue to 'get additional 5 kg free ration per person per month in addition to his normal quota of foodgrains under NFSA'.

The PIB press release issued on the day further underlined that the government would spend Rs 80,000 crore on 24.4 million tons (MT) foodgrains, which would be distributed under the extended scheme. This meant that the government incurred a cost of Rs 32.8 per kg of foodgrains (Rs 80,000 crore divided by 2.44 crore tons) to provide the foodgrains free. The government measure was clearly populist as they asserted that ' . . . this PM-GKAY extension would ensure that no poor household goes to bed without food during this time of recovery' from Covid-19.

The primary motivation of PM-GKAY was to liquidate spiralling stocks with FCI. India's foodgrains production had steadily grown, including during the Covid-19 years, and was expected to exceed 316 MT in 2021–22 (285 MT in 2018–19). Foodgrains procurement had also gone up (100 MT in 2020–21 against 86 MT in 2019–20). The offtake under the NFSA (at subsidized rates of Rs 2/3 per kg wheat/rice) and other schemes (schemes other than PM-GKAY), however, had peaked in 2018–19 at 66 MT. There was some drop in the following three years (of about 5 MT). The government could not sell any foodgrains in domestic or export markets in four years until 2021–22. Consequently, the foodgrains stocks with the government were rising steadily—from 53 MT on 1 July 2017 to 82 MT on 1 July 2020.

While the NFSA foodgrains were adequate for meeting food energy requirements, the government, saddled with rising foodgrain stocks, decided to provide another 5 kg of wheat/rice free of cost to all 80 crore NFSA-registered persons when Covid-19 struck in March 2020. This did increase foodgrain offtake (32 MT and 41 MT distributed under PM-GKAY in 2020–21 and 2021–22). Still, there was increase in foodgrain stocks with the government (90 MT on 1 July 2021).

The official PBI press release on 23 December, after a Cabinet meeting, claimed that the government would provide free foodgrains to about 81.35 crore beneficiaries under the NFSA for one year from 1 January 2023. Minister Piyush Goyal further asserted, in the post-Cabinet meeting media briefing, that the Centre would spend more than Rs 2 trillion in this period of one year as food subsidy, and, in a bid to win over people's sympathy, Piyush Goyal claimed that this food subsidy would 'remove the financial burden of the poor and the poorest of the poor'. The Minister termed this, like every other decision of the government, 'a historic decision' and wanted the press folks to note that this reflected the 'sensitivity of the Prime Minister towards the beneficiaries of welfare schemes'.

What did the government actually decide on 23 December? On that day, the government made two decisions, one which was announced with big headlines and press statements. The foodgrains, which were being provided at Rs 3/2/1 per kg under NFSA, would be provided free of cost from 1 January 2023 for one year. The second was conspicuous only by the government's complete silence. What was left unsaid was that the PM-GKAY—the scheme which provided foodgrains free of cost—would not be extended beyond 31 December 2022. The net effect of the government's decision on 23 December was that the government would, with effect from 1 January 2023, provide 5 kg foodgrains only, instead of 10 kg foodgrains, per person per month. Further, the poor would be getting the 5 kg per person per month free of cost. In effect, the free of cost component of the PM-GKAY was converted into NFSA and the erstwhile PM-GKAY was abandoned.

Piyush Goyal's claim that the government took a historic decision of providing food security to 81.35 crore people of India free of cost was quite untrue. The government, from 1 January 2023, would be providing only half the foodgrains provided in the previous three years. Only the name of the scheme under which this quantity of foodgrains was provided free of cost was changed from PM-GKAY to NFSA. The name NFSA was changed back to PM-GKAY later.

The government had made NFSA foodgrains a classical and complete freebie. The average economic cost of foodgrains (rice and wheat together) distributed under NFSA is about Rs 30 per kg. At 5 kg per person per month to over 81 crore poor, the government needs approximately 50 million tons of foodgrains. This quantity of foodgrains freely distributed costs the government about Rs 1.5 trillion per year as subsidy. Some other commitments like cheaper foodgrains to a few other categories of people take the food subsidy expenditure to about Rs 2 trillion. The poor are only about 20 crore in India, whereas free NFSA/PM-GKAY foodgrains go to over 81 crore. More than three-fourths of foodgrains recipients are undeserving. The foodgrains subsidy expenditure on them is a kind of freebie.

Subsidized LPG cylinders

On 29 August 2023, the Modi government announced a subsidy of Rs 200 per LPG cylinder to reduce the price of a 14.2 kg LPG cylinder from Rs 1,103 per cylinder (in Delhi) to a 'more affordable' price of Rs 903 per cylinder. The 9.6 crore households covered under the Pradhan Mantri Ujjwala Yojana (PMUY), out of a total 31 crore domestic LPG consumers, were to get this subsidy in addition to the existing Rs 200, making the price Rs 703 per cylinder for them.

While the decision was aimed at pleasing the poor and middle-class households and was going to have a positive effect on retail inflation (estimated at about ~0.3 per cent), it raised several questions from the poverty elimination/ redistribution perspective.

Was Rs 1,103 the real cost/market price of an LPG cylinder for the oil marketing companies (OMCs)? Why did the government extend a subsidy of Rs 200 to non-PMUY consumers, who were not poor? Was the Rs 400 per cylinder subsidy to PMUY consumers an unnecessary freebie? If the real cost of an LPG cylinder was less than Rs 1,103, was there an attempted welfare window-dressing?

In a PIB note issued on 13 February 2020, the Ministry of Petroleum and Natural Gas (MoPNG) stated that the primary LPG price was determined based on the international market price of LPG and the government determines the subsidy to be provided to LPG consumers administratively under the then prevailing LPG subsidy scheme—PAHAL. In the same note, the MoPNG informed that on account of an increase in the international price of LPG during January 2020 from $448/MT to $567/MT, the price of domestic non-subsidized LPG cylinders was increased from Rs 714 per cylinder to Rs 858.50 per cylinder.

The Petroleum Planning and Analysis Cell (PPAC), under the administrative control of the MoPNG, tracks and reports international price movements in LPG like other petroleum products. The July 2023 Snapshot Report of PPAC informed that the international LPG price had come down to only $385/MT in July 2023, whereas the average international prices were $692.67/MT in 2021–22 and $711.50/MT in 2022–23. The LPG cylinder price revision data put out by Indian Oil Corporation on their website indicated that, for Delhi, the price per cylinder remained between Rs 719 and Rs 819 during 2020–21, between Rs 809 and Rs 949.50 in 2021–22, and Rs 949.50 and Rs 1,103 in 2022–23.

The LPG prices, thus, were not revised down from Rs 1,103 per cylinder fixed on 1 March 2023, although the international prices had come down from the average of $711.50/MT in 2022–23 to $385/MT in July 2023—a reduction of more than 45 per cent. If the LPG cylinder price was reduced in line with the 45 per cent reduction in the international prices, the domestic LPG cylinder price would be only Rs 607 per cylinder—Rs 100 less per cylinder than the price of Rs 703 per cylinder fixed for the PMUY customers after factoring in Rs 400 subsidy! The OMCs did suffer under-recoveries after the Ukraine-Russia war for some time in 2022–23. However, they had made up for these under-recoveries and reported healthy profits for the last two quarters of 2022–23. The subsidy of Rs 400/200 was perhaps a camouflage for the OMCs' real cost reduction of LPG cylinders.

On 4 October 2023, the government increased the LPG subsidy to PMUY customers by an additional Rs 100 per cylinder, making the effective cylinder price Rs 603 for them. On 8 March 2024, the government cut the general LPG cylinder price by Rs 100, bringing the normal price to Rs 803 per cylinder.

For PMUY beneficiaries, the LPG cylinder price got further reduced to Rs 503 per cylinder.

Housing for All

The Modi government took up the housing programme in a major way right after assumption of power in 2014. Their ambitious Housing for All agenda was eloquently captured in the address of the President of India to the Joint Session of Parliament on 9 June 2014: 'By the time the Nation completes seventy-five years of its Independence, every family will have a pucca house with water connection, toilet facilities, 24x7 electricity supply and access.' As part of this grand strategy, the government adopted Housing for All as its big priority under the rubric of the Pradhan Mantri Awas Yojana (PMAY), restructuring both the earlier housing schemes—Indira Gandhi Awas Yojana for rural areas and Rajiv Gandhi Awas Yojana for urban areas. For urban areas (PMAY-U), a target of 1.12 crore houses was set, based on demand survey. For rural areas, the targets set over the years amounted to 2.94 crore houses. Helping construction of about 4 crore houses with government support has indeed been a pioneering effort.

As per the background note released by the government on 13 June 2024, at the time of approval of a new scheme to construct 3 crore houses, the government had sanctioned a total of 118.64 lakh houses under the scheme until the conclusion of Modi 2.0, of which 114.29 lakh houses were grounded and 83.67 lakh houses completed.

Of the four components of PMAY-U—slum rehabilitation of slum dwellers, affordable housing in partnership with public and private sectors, subsidy for beneficiary-led individual house construction/enhancement and the credit-linked subsidy (CLS) scheme—the CLS claimed the largest expenditure. About 25.04 lakh houses were sanctioned under the CLS scheme. This is a central sector scheme, with the GoI bearing all the expenditure. As per the latest progress report, the GoI spent Rs 1.51 trillion on PMAY-U schemes (out of a total commitment of Rs 2 trillion). Of this, about Rs 60,000 crore was spent on the CLS scheme towards the present value of the interest subsidy due, paid fully upfront.

On 4 October 2023, the newspapers headlined an approval by the Expenditure Finance Committee (EFC) of a new affordable housing scheme to provide an interest subsidy of Rs 60,000 crore on home loans for the urban poor. This, however, was not taken up for government approval until the end of the second term.

In the rural areas, at the end of FY 2022–23, 2.41 crore houses are reportedly completed, as per a government press release dated 1 August 2023. About 53 lakh houses remained to be completed out of the targeted 2.94 lakh houses during 2023–24. For the purpose of completing these houses in 2023–24, the year before elections, the outlay of the scheme was jacked up from Rs 44,962 crore of actual expenditure in 2022–23 to Rs 54,487 crore in 2023–24 BE. However, the budget provision of the scheme was reduced to Rs 32,000 crore in 2023–24 RE, perhaps indicating the less than desired progress of the scheme during the year.

Jal Jeevan Mission

In the second term (2019–24) of the Modi government, there was only one new large beneficiary-oriented scheme—the Jal Jeevan Mission (JJM), which was formally announced by the Prime Minister on 15 August 2019. The JJM's goal was to provide every rural household with a functional household tap connection (FHTC) with a minimum service level of 55 litre per capita water per day (lpcd).

As on 15 August 2019, the day JJM was formally launched, there were 3.24 crore households in rural areas with tap water connections out of a total 19.24 crore rural households, indicating a paltry coverage of 16.8 per cent. As many as 16 crore rural households needed to be provided tap water connections in five years if the goal of providing every rural household with a tap water connection was to be realized. JJM succeeded the earlier National Rural Drinking Water Programme (NRDWP). The announcement of FHTC or Har Ghar Nal Yojana under JJM by the Prime Minister generated considerable momentum in the country, building on the excellent successes of Ujjwala, Swachh Bharat Abhiyan (SBA) and other beneficiary-oriented programmes.

The states provided aggressive timelines to attain the goal of tap water in every home. Goa aimed at doing it in 2020. Bihar, Puducherry, Telangana and Andaman and Nicobar Islands promised 100 per cent completion in 2021. Ten states, including major states like Gujarat, Haryana, J&K and Punjab, stipulated 2022 as their timeline for 100 per cent roll-out. As many as nine states committed for 2023 and the remaining eight by 2024. Major states like Andhra Pradesh, Maharashtra, Odisha, Rajasthan, UP and West Bengal promised to do so only by 2024.

The uncovered rural households were expected to be provided tap water connections in three modes: private connections, other schemes of the central/state governments and the JJM. The JJM website informs that, of the 16 crore households to be provided with FHTCs, 0.74 crore were to be covered by private FHTCs and 3.28 crore from schemes other than the JJM. The JJM was expected to cover the remaining 11.98 crore rural households.

The government approved schemes to provide connections to as many as 12.83 crore households—107 per cent of the required JJM target. Of the approved houses, the work could start for 10.46 crore houses—87 per cent of the target—as per the updates posted at the end of March 2024. Looked at another way, the work could not start for as many as 2.37 crore households.

The JJM saw the highest momentum in 2020–21 when as many as 3.23 crore houses were provided with FHTCs, possibly as these were low-hanging fruit to pick. The programme faced some challenges in 2021–22 when only 2.01 crore FHTCs could be provided. There was a small pick-up in 2022–23 when 2.33 crore FHTCs were provided. In the first four years of the JJM programme, 8.48 crore FHTCs could be provided, which was 53 per cent of the target. As many as 7.52 crore connections were still to be provided in 2023–24.

The programme was thus hopelessly out of reach to achieve the target at the beginning of FY 2023–24. In 2023–24, the JJM could provide 2.99 crore connections (as claimed on the JJM website), which left as many as 4.53 crore connections still to be provided as the programme period ended.

The government was quite liberal with the release of funds under the JJM. In three out of the four years until 2022–23 (except 2020–21), the government released more funds than were spent by the states. In 2019–20, the government released Rs 9,952 crore, whereas the expenditure was only Rs 5,999 crore. In 2021–22, the government released Rs 40,010 crore and the expenditure amounted to Rs 25,524 crore. In 2022–23, the amount released was Rs 54,742 crore, whereas the expenditure was Rs 51,006 crore. Only in 2020–21, the amount released was Rs 10,918 crore, whereas the expenditure incurred was Rs 12,542 crore.

When you relate the household tap connections provided during the year with the expenditure incurred in the respective year, it confirms that the FHTCs provided in 2020–21 (3,22,61,522 connections; a record under the programme) were relatively easier pickings as the expenditure incurred during the year was also quite low at Rs 12,542 crore. On an average, one FHTC cost the government only Rs 3,890. As the yearly expenditure piled up in subsequent years and the FHTCs released got lowered, the per FHTC cost shot up.

The government made serious efforts to roll-out the JJM during its term. However, at the end of its term, with more than 4.50 crore connections still to be provided—the tougher ones—the programme implementation was not as effective as the development programmes implemented during Modi 1.0.

No universal basic income scheme

Value addition in the global economy is increasingly becoming less and less labour-intensive.

This has accentuated the inability of households and individuals to earn enough income from their labour. The overall value addition is not adversely affected though. Machines and artificial intelligence are substituting human labour, in ways perhaps better than human labour.

This is leading to a situation where, while enough goods and services are available for meeting everybody's consumption, the income in the hands of households and individuals to buy these goods and services for consumption is shrinking. There is an increasing case for the governments to tax the income and wealth of the few who corner all the income, and redistribute it to all those who lack adequate income to support themselves.

This objective can be accomplished through what has come to be described as the universal basic income scheme. While 'universal' might be a misnomer as there is no need to provide basic income to the rich and middle classes, the idea of universal income is to provide adequate income support to the universe of people who need it.

India is still not in the situation of labour being excessively substituted by machines and artificial intelligence. However, in certain segments of the economy—like farming and mini and small businesses, in addition to those households which are headed by physically and socially handicapped persons—there is a justifiable need to bring a universal basic income scheme.

The Modi government instituted one scheme of this nature—the PM Kisan scheme, which provides Rs 6,000 per year to all farming families, about Rs 10 crore on average—as direct benefit/cash transfer in their accounts. There was no universal/targeted basic income scheme, though.

Reforms

I will discuss the redistribution programmes and the expenditure thereon in the chapter on Expenditures in Part VI. There are serious doubts about the right targeting and productivity of many redistribution programmes.

A good set of process reforms are needed to make expenditure programmes productive and well-targeted.

No enumeration of poor households and aggregate household benefits

The government runs numerous programmes to overcome poverty—primarily of three types.

The first type of programmes target specific deprivations, e.g. the free food programme targets nutritional deprivation. Many of these programmes have successfully eliminated the concerned deprivation, e.g. the Jan-Dhan programme has eliminated deprivation of a bank account. Some programmes have not made any desirable difference; free food for 81 crore Indians has failed to have an impact on nutritional deprivation.

The second set of programmes delivers cash or a cash equivalent directly to an individual/household, e.g. PM Kisan delivers Rs 6,000 to each farm household. The beneficiaries may or may not spend the cash to manage deprivations.

The third set of programmes are indirect in-kind delivery programmes. The government runs schools to provide education to poor students and maintains a chain of hospital services to provide safe deliveries.

The governments, though, function in a highly compartmentalized manner while delivering the multiple programme benefits. While the benefits under all three sets of the programmes finally land at the households, the government does not aggregate the benefits delivered at the household level.

It is absolutely necessary that all the benefits delivered under the central and state programmes are mapped to the households. This requires building a household poverty, benefits and outcome measurement system.

The most reliable method of measuring individual/household income, consumption, deprivation and government benefits delivery is to collect the requisite data for each and every household. The government spends lakhs of crores on the poverty programmes but does not spend a few thousand crores to institutionalize a universal household data collection system.

A comprehensive system of periodic universal household surveys will help the government and people in getting reliable information about each and every household and its income, consumption, deprivation and poverty status. The governments will be able to accurately identify the poor and their deprivations and design and implement general and customized poverty-alleviation programmes for all the genuine poor.

Only when we have such an institutionalized system, measure the actual status and intensity of poverty regularly, design and deliver the specific customized package of services to all the genuine poor and monitor the outcomes of the interventions made, will we be in a position to confidently talk about the real difference made to the extent and intensity of poverty in India.

The Modi government did not undertake the enumeration of poor households and aggregation of benefits delivered to each household.

Modi government ended up increasing freebies

Prime Minister Modi quite often cautioned people against what he termed 'revdi culture', under which political parties seek votes by promising freebies.

The governments, both central and state, spend substantial public funds on myriad 'welfare' and freebie schemes; many targeted at deserving sections of society and many that do not.

At the core of the general disgust against freebies is the feeling that many government schemes benefit undeserving people. Subsidies to industrialists, expenditures on bailing out loss-making PSUs, providing free/subsidized electricity to the well-off, fertilizers and loan waivers for rich farmers enrich the undeserving at the cost of the public exchequer and, therefore, are definitely freebies, and the public's disgust against such freebies is understandable.

It is not the states alone that run the populist schemes or provide freebies.

The Modi government, instead of pursuing the agenda of eliminating freebies, ended up providing larger freebies from the Central government. Three big schemes—free foodgrains under the PM Garib Kalyan Yojana, almost free fertilizers loaded with more than 90 per cent subsidies, and PM Kisan, between them, spend about Rs 4–5 trillion every year. A good proportion of these expenditures are freebies.

9

Climate and Pollution

Global concern for the environment—climate change hastened by the rising concentrations of carbon in the atmosphere and pollution in the industrializing developing world—has now assumed centre stage of global policy, production and trade engagements. At the same time, falling job opportunities, insufficient rise in wages, discriminatory practices for men and women and many other facets of the corporate and business world, resulting in decreased labour welfare, are also getting expressed in the form of an active social agenda. There is also developing anxiety at the governance of corporates as well as that of governments.

The whole of this agenda has been encapsulated in the E (Environment), S (Social) and G (Governance) or ESG movement all over the world. All the Sustainable Development Goals (SDG), piloted by the UN system, encompass the ESG agenda in its broadest sense. The GoI is obviously not oblivious of this global and local reality and priority.

I have reviewed the social agenda extensively in the last two chapters—Chapter 7 on Labour Income and Welfare and Chapter 8 on Poverty and Redistribution.

In this chapter, I take stock of the environment performance of Modi 2.0 as part of the two broad themes of climate change and pollution.

The governance performance will be assessed in Chapter 10—Governance.

Climate Change

Global concern and ambition captured in Glasgow Climate Action Plan

The Conference of Parties (COP) to the UN Framework Convention on Climate Change (UNFCCC) 26th Session (COP26) held in Glasgow, UK, in October–November 2021 summarized the global concern and ambition in climate change by expressing alarm and utmost concern that human activities have caused around 1.1°C of global warming to date and that impacts are already being felt in every region.

COP26 reaffirmed the long-term global goal to hold the increase in the global average temperature to well below 2°C above pre-industrial levels and to pursue efforts to limit the temperature increase to 1.5°C above pre-industrial levels, recognizing that this would significantly reduce the risks and impacts of climate change.

Recognizing further that the impacts of climate change would be much lower at the temperature increase of 1.5°C compared with 2°C, the Glasgow Climate Pact resolved to pursue efforts to limit the temperature increase to 1.5°C and noted that limiting global warming to 1.5°C required rapid, deep and sustained reductions in global greenhouse gas emissions, including reducing global carbon dioxide emissions by 45 per cent by 2030 relative to the 2010 level and to net zero around mid-century.

The stock-taking reports filed after the Glasgow COP kept reporting that the global action to reduce emissions was nowhere close to the desirable emissions reduction path. The first global stock-take concluded at the COP28 meeting with the commonly accepted dire conclusion that the world was not on track to limit global warming to 1.5°C and the window for meaningful change was fast closing.

India 'not a climate polluter'

In a reply to the Parliament in July 2022, the government dwelt on India's climate change policy and action. India's overall approach to climate change is informed by 'the foundational principles of equity and common but differentiated responsibilities and respective capabilities'.

India lays considerable emphasis on the fact that her historical cumulative emissions and per capita emissions have been very low despite being home to more than 17 per cent of the global population. India contributed only about 4 per cent of the global cumulative greenhouse gas emissions between 1850 and 2019.

Taking India's growing energy needs into consideration, the statement emphasized India's belief that 'all countries should have equitable access to the global carbon budget, a finite global resource, for keeping temperature increase within the limits set by the Paris Agreement and all countries must stay within their fair share of this global carbon budget while using it responsibly'.

India also wants the developed countries to take action 'for climate justice, and for undertaking rapid reductions in emissions during the current decade so as to reach net zero much earlier than their announced dates, as they have used more than their fair share of the depleting global carbon budget'.

India also wants 'transfer of climate finance and low-cost climate technologies', which have become more important for the implementation of climate actions by developing countries. It wants the UNFCCC to track the progress made in climate finance as it tracks the progress in climate mitigation.

Finally, even though India is not part of the problem, the policy statement emphasized that India is committed to being part of the solution and has done far more than its fair share. India's commitment to emission intensity reduction of the economy is an economy-wide target and not specific to any sector, including the transport and energy sectors.

Prime Minister announced India's net zero goal

Prime Minister Narendra Modi attended the COP26 Glasgow Climate Summit in November 2021 and, while addressing world leaders at the High-Level Segment for Heads of States and Government, made the big, though somewhat surprising (as there was no pre-announcement and public examination of this policy), announcement that India will achieve net zero carbon emissions by 2070.

As part of India's climate action plan to attain this goal, the Prime Minister made the following five specific commitments at the COP26:

1. Reach 500 GW non-fossil energy capacity by 2030,
2. 50 per cent of its energy requirements from renewable energy by 2030,
3. Reduction of total projected carbon emissions by 1 billion tons from then to 2030,
4. Reduction of the carbon intensity of the economy by 45 per cent by 2030, over 2005 levels, and
5. Achieving the target of net zero emissions by 2070.

The first four elements of the announcement relate to the commitments to be attained by 2030. It is not quite apparent how much these commitments, even if achieved, will contribute, to take India to net zero.

India updated NDCs

India furnished her updated nationally determined contributions (NDCs) under the Paris Agreement for the 2020–30 period in August 2022, taking on board the Prime Minister's announcements at COP26. The Paris Convention requires furnishing of NDCs only for the period up to 2030 for the present.

India's updated NDCs are a set of eight commitments. The first two commitments are philosophical, articulating India's basic societal approach for attaining the goal. This includes propagating a healthy and sustainable way of living based on the traditions and values of conservation and moderation, and to adopt a climate-friendly and cleaner path.

The third and fourth commitments are important from the energy transition perspective. India committed 'to reduce Emissions Intensity of its GDP by 45 per cent by 2030 from 2005 level' and 'to achieve about 50 per cent cumulative electric power installed capacity from non-fossil fuel-based energy resources by 2030' with an added rider to do it 'with the help of transfer of technology and low-cost international finance including from Green Climate Fund (GCF)'.

In terms of carbon sequestration, India made a fifth commitment to 'create an additional carbon sink of 2.5 to 3 billion tonnes of CO_2 equivalent through additional forest and tree cover by 2030'.

The remaining three commitments are broad statements of intent and lay down India's investment, administrative and implementational expectations and approach. India committed 'to better adapt to climate change by enhancing investments in development programmes in sectors vulnerable to climate change', 'to mobilize domestic and new and additional funds from developed countries to implement' mitigation and adaptation actions, and 'to build capacities, create domestic framework and international architecture' for quick diffusion of cutting-edge climate technologies and collaborative R&D.

The NDC update and the specific commitments admittedly do not add up to India's goal of net zero by 2070. The NDC update, however, did link this periodic update to the net zero goal by stating that 'India's existing NDC is a step forward towards our long-term goal of reaching net-zero by 2070': a step towards, not the action plan.

Transition to renewable electricity

Every ton of fossil fuel burnt produces roughly 3 tons of carbon dioxide (CO_2). CO_2 is primarily responsible for global warming. It is the energy requirement that makes humans burn fossil fuels; if it goes down, carbon emissions will reduce. To the extent energy use cannot be reduced, its replacement by renewable electricity can provide the solution. Transportation consumes the largest amount of energy.

The world energy requirement growth is plateauing and is expected to get on to the reduction path soon. However, the reduction trajectory is too slow for comfort. With climate change already upon us, witnessed in so many natural orderly phenomena getting disturbed, the world cannot bank upon only the reduction trajectory of fossil fuel-based energy use.

Renewables have to play a big role. As per Renewables 2024: The Global Status Report, the share of modern renewables (primarily wind and solar), in global energy grew from 8.7 per cent in 2009 to 13.3 per cent (5.5 per cent solar plus 7.8 per cent wind) in 2023.

Advancement in many non-fossil fuel energy generation technologies—most spectacularly in wind and solar electricity generation technologies—has raised hopes of replacing fossil fuels materially by 2050.

There is increasing electrification of energy; most machines and appliances are fast transforming into electric appliances—electric cars, electric kitchens, electric work-machines, electricity-run robots and what not. The technology to convert electricity into chemical, static or hydrogen energy to store and use at the time and place required is also making intermittent renewable electricity a steady state supplier of electricity.

India missed the 175 GW renewable energy (RE) goal

In October 2017, the government had set a target of 175 GW renewable power installed capacity by the end of 2022. This target included 60 GW from wind power, 100 GW from solar power, 10 GW from biomass power and 5 GW from small hydro power.

At the time of the announcement, as on 31 October 2017, India had a total installed power generation capacity of 331.95 GW from all resources. The installed renewable power capacity was 60.98 GW, making the installed renewable power share about 18.37 per cent. The photo-voltaic (PV) solar capacity was only about 15 GW. By the end of FY 2018–19, India's renewable power generation capacity increased to 78.32 GW, comprising 35.63 GW of wind power, 28.18 GW of solar power, 4.59 GW of small hydro power, 9.92 GW of bio-power (biomass, gasification and bagasse co-generation and 0.14 GW of waste-to-energy). In 2018–19, India added 8.53 GW of grid-connected renewable power.

India could reach 120.90 GW of renewable energy capacity by the end of December 2022 (against the target of 175 GW) assuming the 'by the end of 2022' target was the end of calendar 2022 only, comprising 41.93 GW of wind power, 63.30 GW of solar power, 4.94 GW of small hydro power, 10.21 GW of bio-power (biomass, gasification and bagasse co-generation and 0.52 GW of waste-to-energy).

India needed to add 114 GW (from 61 GW capacity at the time of the announcement of 175 GW target) in more than five years. India, however, added only 60 GW of capacity (12 GW per year on average) during this period, taking the renewables installed power to 121 GW. If India were to keep up the pace of 12 GW on an average per annum, the target of 175 GW would materialize only by 2027, five years behind the date, with 100 per cent time delay.

As appeared to be the case, even by the end of FY 2023–24, India did not achieve the target of 175 GW RE. As on 31 March 2024, India's cumulative RE capacity was 143.45 GW (still 31.55 GW short of target) comprising 45.89 GW of wind power, 81.81 GW of solar power, 5 GW of small hydro power and 10.90 GW of bio-power.

Modi 2.0 tripped on the renewable energy target of 175 GW by 2022 in a big way.

India casually announced 450 GW/500 GW RE goal

President Kovind, while addressing the Joint Session of the Parliament on 30 January 2020, announced the government's resolve to raise the renewable energy installed capacity target to 450 GW.

He said: 'Keeping environment conservation in mind, my Government has enhanced the target for producing renewable energy to 450 gigawatts.'

At COP26 in 2022, the Prime Minister mentioned India's ambition to reach 500 GW RE by 2030.

The Modi government never produced any break-up of the 450/500 GW RE target or any road map for its achievement. Earlier, NITI Aayog had produced a report titled 'Renewable Energy 2030 Roadmap', although largely a procedural road map without any target or strategy, in 2015 before the target of 175 GW was announced. No such document or report was provided before raising the RE target casually to 450/500 GW.

Domestic manufacturing of solar cells and modules did not take off

The government adopted a three-pronged strategy to push domestic manufacturing of the solar cells and modules which go into solar panels, which capture solar light to generate solar electricity. The PLI scheme for high-efficiency solar PV modules signified the largest intervention to encourage manufacturing in India. Limiting the bids in solar capacity auctions to the firms with high domestic content and an attempted move to limit the government procurement to only the Approved List of Module Manufacturers (ALMM) was the epitome of the second prong. Finally, using the customs duty protection was the third pillar of the strategy to get the cells and modules manufacturing going in the country.

The government quoted a report of the Centre for Energy Finance of the Council on Energy, Environment and Water (CEEW-CEF) of May 2022 titled 'Making India a Leader in Solar Manufacturing', to emphasize that setting up manufacturing capacities of 16 GW of polysilicon, 29 GW of ingot and wafer, 55 GW of cell and 58 GW of module, would require an estimated capital expenditure of around $7.2 billion.

To facilitate an investment of this magnitude, the government allowed 100 per cent FDI under the automatic route in the RE sector, although FDI from China was subject to the condition of approval under the government route. This is done under an omnibus clause in the FDI policy that FDI from an entity of a country that shares a land border with India or where the beneficial owner of an investment into India is situated in or is a citizen of any such country, is permissible only with approval under the government route.

In the first term, the government had operated the Modified Special Incentive Package Scheme (M-SIPS) Scheme, managed by the Ministry of Electronics and Information Technology (MeitY). The scheme provided subsidies for the capital expenditure—20 per cent for investments in Special Economic Zones (SEZs) and 25 per cent in non-SEZs. While the scheme was open to receive applications till 31 December 2018, the incentives approved continued to get disbursed during 2019–24.

The government (Ministry of New and Renewable Energy—MNRE) operated the PLI scheme for high-efficiency solar PV modules from 28 April 2021 (later termed as Tranche-I), with an outlay of Rs 4,500 crore. The scheme supported setting up of integrated manufacturing units of high-efficiency solar PV modules by providing incentives on sales of such modules.

Under this Tranche-I PLI scheme, the Letters of Award were issued to three successful bidders in November/December 2021 to set up 8,737 MW of fully integrated solar PV module manufacturing capacities with scheduled commissioning dates in November/December 2024. As per the information submitted by the beneficiary manufacturers, the government informed that an investment of around Rs 2,441 crore had been made till February 2023 by the three beneficiaries.

For the PLI scheme for high-efficiency solar PV modules (Tranche-II) with an outlay of Rs 19,500 crore, the scheme guidelines were issued on 30 September 2022 and the tender document for selection of solar PV manufacturers on 18 November 2022. The government allocated a total capacity of 39,600 MW (no capacities for polysilicon and wafers) to eleven domestic companies, with a total outlay of Rs 140.07 billion.

I have described the implementation of the scheme in Chapter 2—Industries. While no operational capacities were to come on board during the second term and accordingly, no disbursement of incentives was made, the parties that had got the allocations did take some steps towards implementing the scheme.

Unsuccessful attempt at limiting procurement to domestic firms

The preference to Make in India in public procurement in the renewable energy sector, issued vide an order dated 9 February 2021, prescribed that in public procurement of solar PV modules and solar inverters, only Class-I local suppliers with sufficient capacity and capability to supply goods, services or works with local content equal to or more than 50 per cent would be eligible to bid.

Under many of the operating developmental schemes of the MNRE, e.g. the CPSU Scheme Phase-II, PM-KUSUM and Grid-connected Rooftop Solar

Programme Phase-II, wherein government subsidy was given, it was mandated to source solar PV cells and modules from domestic sources.

The MNRE issued an 'Approved Models and Manufacturers of Solar Photovoltaic Modules (Requirement for Compulsory Registration) Order, 2019' on 2 January 2019 to enlist the eligible models and manufacturers of solar modules complying with the BIS Standards in a list called the 'Approved List of Models and Manufacturers' (ALMM).

The government made only the models and manufacturers included in the ALMM eligible for use in government projects, government-assisted projects, projects under government schemes and programmes, and open access/net-metering projects installed in the country, including projects set up for sale of electricity to the government under the guidelines issued by the Central government under section 63 of the Electricity Act, 2003. It was further specified that the 'government' included the Central government, state governments, central public sector enterprises, state public sector enterprises and central and state organizations and autonomous bodies. The government also intended to make the mandatory use of ALMM-listed solar modules for open access/net-metering projects.

The first ALMM for solar PV modules was issued on 10 March 2021. As on October 2023, the ALMM consisted of ninety-one module manufacturing facilities (all domestic) with aggregate solar PV module manufacturing capacity of 22,389 MW per year. In 2023, the government restricted the enlistment in ALMM to only those manufacturers making solar modules with minimum efficiency thresholds of 20 per cent for utility/grid scale power plants, 19.5 per cent for rooftop and solar pumping, and 19 per cent for solar lighting.

No ALMM for solar PV cells was issued.

The government placed, from 10 March 2023, the ALMM order in abeyance, which remained the case until Modi 2.0 was over. All projects commissioned by 31 March 2024 remained exempt from the requirement of procuring solar PV modules from the ALMM.

Customs duty protection

The government imposed basic customs duty (BCD) of 25 per cent on import of solar PV cells and 40 per cent on modules with effect from 1 April 2022.

The Ministry of Finance vide its notification dated 1 February 2021 also rescinded its earlier notification dated 6 January 2011, withdrawing the benefit of concessional customs duty on the items imported for initial setting up of the solar power projects.

The duty stayed on, though there are exemptions in some bilateral and regional trade agreements.

Climate change programmes lacked planning and coordination

The government's programmatic intervention for combating climate change primarily revolved around the National Action Plan on Climate Change (NAPCC), initiated by the UPA government in June 2008. Curiously, while most of the programmes of the UPA era were recast, substituted or rebranded by the Modi government, the NAPCC stayed unaltered throughout both the Modi government's tenures.

Its eight missions—Solar Energy, Enhanced Energy Efficiency, Sustainable Habitat, Water, Sustaining the Himalayan Ecosystem, Strategic Knowledge for Climate Change, Green India and Sustainable Agriculture—remained almost unchanged. The NAPCC requires all states to make their State Action Plan for Climate Change (SAPCCs).

The Executive Committee on Climate Change (ECCC) mandated, in 2021, that the Apex Committee for Implementation of Paris Agreement (AIPA) review the progress in the National Missions under the NAPCC. Strangely, there is no ministry effectively in charge of the NAPCC, though the Ministry of Environment, Forest and Climate Change (MoEFCC) is supposed to coordinate with the NAPCC. There are no specific budget heads in the MoEFCC to record expenditures on the NAPCC or in other ministries for its eight component national missions either.

It is almost impossible to assess the relevance and contribution of the NAPCC to India's policy and strategy for climate change or even its NDCs, which is indicative of great neglect.

Pollution

The emissions of global greenhouses gases (GHGs), which cause climate change, get globalized and their consequences are suffered by the world community collectively, irrespective of which countries or people contributed.

The emissions and generation of gaseous, liquid and solid substances that pollute the air, water and soil, in contrast, have a much greater localized impact, affecting the quality of life and health of the local, regional and national population more directly and immediately.

India has an acute pollution problem

Indian factories and cities unload pollutants and untreated organic material into our rivers, lakes and ponds. This makes their water unfit for drinking or bathing or both, depending on the extent of pollution. More than 320 out of 521 rivers monitored for water quality by the Central Pollution Control Board (CPCB) in 2016 were found to be polluted (whose water is not fit for drinking). A 2015

CPCB report found that the number of polluted rivers in India increased from 121 to 275, and to 351 in 2018.

In 2019, as per the World Air Quality Report, India had the highest population-weighted annual average particulate matter $(PM)_{2.5}$ exposure in the world at 83.2 micrograms per cubic metre $(\mu g/m^3)$ of air. The World Health Organization's (WHO) safe limit for weighted annual average $PM_{2.5}$ exposure is only 10 $\mu g/m^3$. India was in the least healthy category of exposure, between 75 and 85 $\mu g/m^3$. Over the period 2010–19, the country had seen the third-highest increase in exposure after Nigeria and Bangladesh at 6.5 $\mu g/m^3$ over this period. India's general quality of air suggests a state of emergency.

India's air, water and environment are all severely polluted. Modi 2.0 needed to address the pollution problem as an emergency.

Control of pollution scheme did not make much difference

The Control of Pollution scheme has been operational since 2018. The main objectives of the scheme is to monitor air quality across the country and take appropriate mitigation measures, besides monitoring water quality and noise levels.

There are four components of the scheme: a. financial Assistance for Abatement of Pollution (AAP) to the weaker state pollution control boards/ pollution control committees (SPCBs/PCCs) and to the central pollution control board (CPCB), b. managing the National Clean Air Programme (NCAP), c. measuring quality through the Environmental Monitoring Network Programme (EMNP), and d. conducting related research and outreach programmes.

Actual expenditure under the CoP scheme was Rs 599.91 crore in 2022–23 and pegged at Rs 848 crore in 2023–24 RE. The expenditure under the programme has gradually increased from Rs 409 crore in 2019–20. The funds under the scheme are essentially released to the CPCB, which, in turn, passes on most of it to the state pollution control boards.

The funds under the AAP component are spent on pollution abatement activities, including pollution assessment—source monitoring, monitoring of ambient air, water and noise, conducting technical studies and the like. This component functions more as maintenance of the system created to monitor quality.

The NCAP component, initiated in January 2019, supports a more focused intervention. The objective was to improve air quality in 131 select cities by reducing the PM_{10} concentration over the baseline 2017 by 20–30 per cent by 2024 (later revised to 40 per cent by 2025–26 relative to base year 2019–20). A total of 885 stations have been made operational to monitor air quality in these 131 cities. The MoEFCC Annual Report 2023–24 reports that city-level action plans had been prepared for all the cities. Further, ninety cities showed improvement in air quality in 2022–23 compared to base 2017 and fifteen cities conformed to national ambient air quality standards compared with six cities in 2017. Unfortunately, the extent of improvement in these ninety cities, even after the programme had run for more than four years, was not specified. Admittedly, in the forty-one remaining cities, the air quality deteriorated or stayed stagnant.

Environment Ministry kept diluting/postponing standards for thermal power plants

The MoEFCC notified eighty-one standards across industries, including for major polluting industries, such as thermal power plants, sugar industry, cement industry and fertilizer industry, among others. The implementation of standards, however, was not that satisfactory.

A case in point is the notification of stringent emissions limits issued for sulphur dioxide, nitrogen oxides, particulate matter, mercury and water usage in coal-based thermal power plants. The standards were first notified in 2015 and were to be complied with by 2017. In 2017, the power plants were granted a five-year extension (till December 2022) to meet the deadlines in a phased manner. Eleven plants in Delhi-NCR were to comply with the norms by 2019.

The MoEFCC kept diluting the standards after extending the deadline to 2019/2022. In June 2018, the water norms for units installed after January 2017 were diluted from 2.5 m3/MWh to 3 m3/MWh. In May 2019, the nitrogen oxide (NOx) norms for units installed in 2004–16 were diluted from 300 mg/Nm3 to 450 mg/Nm3. In March 2021, the MoEFCC issued a notification specifying new deadlines for compliance, with the norms based on the location of the coal thermal power plants. In September 2022, the MoEFCC further extended the sulphur oxide (SOx) standards deadline to 2024.

There was only limited progress in making the thermal coal plants comply with the environmental standards, diluted notably in the nine years ending March 2024.

Commission on Air Quality made little difference to Delhi air pollution

The government, in a bid to deal with the rising air pollution in Delhi-NCR, first brought an ordinance on 29 October 2020—the Commission for Air Quality Management in National Capital Region and Adjoining Areas Ordinance 2020—to put in place an oversight body which would have functions, including laying down parameters of air quality and environmental pollutants, to inspect premises violating the law and ordering closure of non-abiding industries/plants.

After a little flip-flop in which the Commission was denotified, a statutory commission was constituted on 23 April 2021 through the Commission for Air Quality Management in NCR and Adjoining Areas Act, 2021. The adjoining areas where the act is in force include Punjab, Haryana, Rajasthan and Uttar Pradesh, and adjoining areas of the NCR region and Delhi, where any source of pollution is located and is causing an adverse impact on air quality in the National Capital Region (NCR).

As per a press release issued by the government in 2023, the Commission for Air Quality Management in NCR and Adjoining Areas (CAQM) did undertake 'considerable action' for the prevention and control of air pollution in Delhi-NCR and adjoining areas, which resulted in 'general improvements in the AQI level' of the NCT Delhi.

The press release further informed that the commission adopted an airshed-like approach and issued a comprehensive policy to curb air pollution in the NCR in July 2022. The policy has sector-wise action plans for the prevention and control of air pollution in the region by various sectors contributing to air pollution. The commission also issued seventy-eight directions and eleven advisories, besides many executive orders to various agencies concerned in the NCR, including the state governments of Punjab, NCTD and various bodies of the central and the state governments in the region.

Separately, a Graded Response Action Plan (GRAP) was formulated and notified by the MoEFCC in January 2017 on the recommendation of CPCB for Delhi-NCR to tackle the issue of a sudden rise in air pollution levels. A comprehensive review of actions listed under GRAP was carried out by CPCB in 2020. Based on these inputs, the revised GRAP was published by the CAQM and further action was taken for its implementation.

While the government claimed improvement in air quality, the winter of 2023–24 witnessed the worst air pollution in Delhi and NCR. The 'End of Winter Report 2023–24: Spread and scale of air pollution crisis in India' issued by the Centre for Science and Environmental Analysis, noted that the 'toxic air pollution came back to trouble the public yet again this winter'. The air quality began to worsen much earlier than usual due to low rains in September–October and was made even worse due to low wind speed through the season. The report concluded that North and East India remained the most polluted regions of the country. The 'air quality in North India was significantly worse this winter compared to the previous winter'.

There was no improvement in the quality of air in Delhi, the seat of the Modi government, during 2019–24.

India adopting electric vehicles but at a slow pace

Electric vehicles (EVs) produce fewer greenhouse gas emissions than internal combustion engine vehicles—petrol and diesel-powered vehicles. Ramping up adoption of EVs is, therefore, one of the most important steps in reducing transportation emissions. The GoI has not adopted any specific target of the proportion of EVs in total passenger vehicles sold with reference to 2030 or any other year. The scheme—Faster Adoption and Manufacturing of Electric Vehicles (FAME)—did make a reference to manufacturing and selling 30 per cent of all passenger vehicles by 2030, more as intent than goal.

The Economic Survey 2018–19, citing NITI Aayog officials, estimated that 'if India reaches an EV sales penetration of 30 per cent for private cars, 70 per cent for commercial cars, 40 per cent for buses and 80 per cent for two and three wheelers by 2030, a saving of 846 million tons of net CO2 emissions and oil savings of 474 MTOE can be achieved'.

According to the Global EV Outlook 2023, the electric car markets saw 'exponential growth as sales exceeded 10 million in 2022'. Besides reporting the world hitting this important milestone, the Outlook also reported that 'a total of 14 per cent of all new cars sold were electric in 2022, up from around 9 per cent in 2021 and less than 5 per cent in 2020'.

According to the Outlook, three markets dominated global sales. China was the frontrunner, accounting for around 60 per cent of global electric car sales. More than half of the electric cars on roads worldwide in 2022 were in China. In Europe, the second-largest market, electric car sales increased by over 15 per cent in 2022, which also meant that more than one in every five cars sold was electric. Electric car sales in the US—the third-largest market—increased 55 per cent in 2022, reaching a sales share of 8 per cent.

The progress in India was more modest. The Outlook 2022 reported, 'Electric car sales are generally low outside the major markets, but 2022 was a growth year in India, Thailand and Indonesia. Collectively, sales of electric cars in these countries more than tripled compared to 2021, reaching 80,000. For Thailand, the share of electric cars in total sales came in at slightly over 3 per cent in 2022, while both India and Indonesia averaged around 1.5 per cent last year.'

India has a much wider EV market than cars—there are eight categories of EVs. In December 2022, 1,03,154 EVs were registered in India. Electric two-wheelers (E2W) were the largest at 64,348 vehicles. There were 30,348 e-rickshaws/e-autorickshaws as well. A total of 4,681 electric four-wheelers (E4W) and 142 e-buses were also registered.

EV sales reached 1,40,923 in March 2023 but fell to 1,11,356 in April 2023. The sales rose again to the highest monthly sales of 1,58,433 vehicles in May 2023 to fall back again to the lowest of the year, 1,02,547 in June. The sales kept rising every month thereafter reaching 1,53,466 in November before falling again to 1,40,892 in December 2023. On the year to year base, from December 2022 to December 2023, monthly sales rose from 1,05,009 EVs to 1,40,892 EVs, recording a growth of 35,883 EVs, which is about 34 per cent higher. A total of 7,141 electric cars were sold in December 2023.

The total EV market is recording good but not enough growth. Total EVs registered in the country in 2020 were 1,23,092. In 2021, it increased to 3,27,976 and in 2022 to 10,15,196. The annual growth rate was 166.4 per cent in 2021 and 209.5 per cent in 2022. Total EVs sold in India increased further to 15,31,891 in 2023. There was a slowdown in terms of both the absolute number and the percentage growth in 2023 compared to 2022. While the absolute increase recorded in 2023 was 5,16,695 EVs, which was lower than the increase of 6,87,220 recorded in 2022, the percentage growth of 50.9 in 2023 was much smaller than 209.5 per cent growth in 2022.

India's EV penetration seemed to be growing with a faltering/slowing rate, as Modi 2.0 completed its term.

FAME programmes made halting progress

The government approved the 'Faster Adoption and Manufacturing of Electric Vehicles in India Phase II (FAME India Phase II)' scheme to promote electric mobility on 28 February 2019, just before completing its first term. The scheme had an outlay of Rs 10,000 crore and was to be implemented over a period of three years (2019–20 to 2021–22) commencing from 1 April 2019.

The objective of the scheme was to encourage faster adoption of electric and hybrid vehicles in the country. Very specific targets were laid out—supporting 10 lakh E2W, 5 lakh E3W, 55,000 E4Ws and 7,000 e-buses. The scheme also provided for establishing a network of early charging infrastructure for electric vehicles. The scheme prioritized electrification of public transportation, including shared transport.

An incentive of Rs 10,000 per kWh of electric battery capacity for all electric vehicles was promised. For buses, the working rule was Rs 20,000 per kWh. The target for E3W was 5 lakh with a budget allocation of Rs 2,500 crore at the rate of Rs 50,000 incentive for 5 kWh and a maximum ex-factory price of Rs 5 lakh. A smaller number of four-wheelers (35,000) was also included for incentives at the rate of Rs 1.5 lakh per vehicle for 15 kWh capacity. The budget allocated was Rs 525 crore. The largest budget for demand incentives was for e-buses (Rs 3,545 crore) with each vehicle normatively assessed eligible for a Rs 50 lakh incentive with the ex-factory cost capped at Rs 2 crore delivered under the OPEX model.

The scheme was slow to take off. Only a total of 1.85 lakh electric vehicles had been incentivized under FAME II in two years, of which 1.40 lakh vehicles were in 2021. This poor performance led the government to liberalize incentives in June 2021. Demand incentive for electric two-wheelers was increased from Rs 10,000/kWh to Rs 15,000/kWh with maximum cap increased from 20 per cent to 40 per cent of the cost of vehicles.

There was some improvement but not much. The government claimed that till 6 December 2022, a total of 6.63 lakh E2W (along with 70,159 E3W, 5,375 E4W and 3,738 e-buses) had received incentives of about Rs 3,305 crore under the FAME India Scheme Phase-II. Thereafter, as per the press release of 5 December 2023, 11.53 lakh EVs had received incentives under FAME II. The FAME II dashboard indicated the number of EVs supported with incentives at 14.86 lakh as on 13 March 2024.

The actual expenditure data, however, tells a different story. In 2020–21, the government reported actual expenditure of only Rs 315 crore and for 2021–22 Rs 800 crore on the FAME II scheme. In 2022–23, the actual expenditure came down further to only Rs 500 crore. The provision for 2023–24 was also reduced from Rs 693 crore in the BE to Rs 318 crore in the RE, clearly indicating serious issues in the implementation of the FAME scheme.

The scheme, particularly E2W, ran into implementation problems. Two problems cropped up. The first issue related to non-adherence to minimum local content requirements. Quite a few E2W suppliers registered under the scheme allegedly violated the condition of minimum 50 per cent domestic value addition. Some major E2W suppliers were given notices in this regard and fines were slapped. The other issue related to bypassing the condition of a maximum ex-factory price of Rs 1.5 lakh per vehicle. To bring their E2Ws within this cap, it was alleged that many suppliers sold the battery as a separate unit, whereas the scheme conditions clearly prescribed the battery as part of the vehicle, or committed other irregularities. Many E2W suppliers were given notice to refund the excess price charged to customers.

The sale of EVs suffered. Their penetration (as a proportion of new vehicles sold) was still quite small at 4.97 per cent in 2022. While the proportion of new EVs shot up over 51 per cent of total sales (3.50 lakh out of 6.77 lakh), for three-wheelers, the proportion was quite small at 4.05 per cent (6.31 lakh out of 1.56 crore). For cars, it was only 0.99 per cent (33,205 out of 33.47 lakh).

On 25 June 2021, the government had extended Phase II of the FAME India scheme for two years, i.e. until 31 March 2024. On 9 February 2024, the government announced an increase of the scheme outlay from Rs 10,000 crore to Rs 11,500 crore. It was also clarified that the scheme was a fund- and term-limited scheme, which meant that the subsidies for incentives would be eligible till 31 March 2024 or till the time funds remained available, whichever was earlier.

On 13 March 2024, the government unveiled a new scheme—Electric Mobility Promotion Scheme 2024—to continue incentives for E2Ws and E3Ws to be sold after the expiry of FAME II. The scheme will have a total outlay of Rs 500 crore and is valid for four months from April 1 to July 31.

India's air quality remains toxic

The 6th Annual World Air Quality Report (WAQR) was released on 16 March 2024, disclosing air quality status of 134 countries based on measurement of their $PM_{2.5}$ average annual score. Seven countries met the WHO annual $PM_{2.5}$ guideline (annual average of 5 μg/m3 or less): Australia, Estonia, Finland, Grenada, Iceland, Mauritius and New Zealand.

India turned out to be third most polluted country with a score of 54.4 μg/m3, which is more than ten times higher than the WHO $PM_{2.5}$ benchmark, better than only two countries—our neighbours Bangladesh and Pakistan.

India scored another notorious distinction. Begusarai was found to be the most polluted metropolitan area of 2023 in the world. India is home to not only the four most polluted cities in the world but as many as forty-two cities out of the fifty most polluted cities were in India. Delhi was back as the most polluted capital of the world, the fifth time out of six editions of the WAQR.

Modi 2.0, without a doubt, did not think improving the quality of life by taking care of the air quality was any of its concern.

10

Governance

All things and persons are getting converted into data, which in turn is leading to the production of new digital products to use as inputs and consume, development of digital processes to transact goods, money and other services, and reshaping of human interactions through new mediums of communication—loosely referred to as social media. Digital or data governance is the single biggest policy and regulatory challenge today as data, digitalization and artificial intelligence impact the economy and society profoundly and in ways humans do not understand fully.

Companies are the principal mode of production in the global society. They have a non-human impersonal personality and financial liability limited to their issued capital. Companies, however, are ultimately owned by humans. These ultimately beneficial human owners claim and have all the profits, patents, technologies, assets and financial and social power of the companies they own. Their capital liability is, however, limited, which allows the beneficial owners of companies to take risks and actions which might harm other stakeholders of the companies—bankers, financiers, minority shareholders, suppliers, buyers, consumers and the like.

These critical elements and inherent character of companies make it necessary for corporate governance to be very carefully designed and regulated to bring a balance between the creativity and productivity of the companies on one side and the protection of financial and other stakeholders on the other. When the financial lenders see their loans turning non-performing, they call out the corporation concerned to bankruptcy.

The fiscal federal policies and actions impact the delivery of governance services both at the centre and state level materially, which, in turn, also impact the economy and businesses significantly.

I discuss these four key governance matters—data governance, corporate governance, bankruptcy and insolvency, and fiscal federalism policies and the record of Modi 2.0 in this chapter.

Data Governance

Criticality of data for the digital economy

All numbers, words, pictures, sounds, information, expressions and almost everything else that can be transformed into bits and bytes (essentially electrical on and off impulses and sets thereof) are data. Data is as critical to the digital economy as matter is for the industrial economy. All agricultural and industrial goods produced are made of some form of matter or the other. All digital goods and services produced, stored or transmitted are made of data and data alone.

The industrial economy was the most competitive and productive system of producing goods and services at scale. The emergence of the industrial economy in the eighteenth century led to mass production of almost every product all over the world. The industrial economy, however, killed customization, cutting cloth to the size of each one. The digital revolution provides the opportunity to bring back customization as a key differentiator of products and services.

Customization requires personal data: for example, the precise measure of all dimensions of the foot for making the best fitting shoes for each individual; individual preferences for delivering the products desired; even producing a car that meets the specific needs of an individual or family. The digital economy works, thrives and prospers by using all data, including personal data.

Government introduces and withdraws Personal Data Protection (PDP) Bill 2019

Personal data use and privacy protection thereof was governed by the IT Act 2000 and the Information Technology (Reasonable Security Practices and Procedures and Sensitive Personal Data or Information) Rules 2011 when the Modi government took office in 2014. The Rules 2011 defined sensitive personal data or information (SPD or I) to mean personal information relating to password, financial information such as bank account, credit card, debit card or other payment instrument details, physical, physiological and mental health condition, sexual orientation, medical record and history, biometric information, any detail relating to this data/information provided to body corporate for providing services and any of this information received by body corporate for processing, stored or processed under lawful contract or otherwise.

The 2011 Rules enjoined body corporates to adopt a privacy policy for the handling of and dealing in personal information, including SPD, obtaining consent in writing from the provider of the SPD for the purpose of usage before collection of information, disclosure of SDP to any third party with prior permission from the provider of information and transfer of information.

This data governance regime was completely outdated. In July 2017, the Modi government constituted a Committee of Experts under the chairmanship of Justice B.N. Srikrishna to deliberate upon a data protection framework for India. The committee presented its report and made comprehensive recommendations, along with a draft personal data protection bill on 28 July 2018.

The major recommendations included defining jurisdiction over the processing of personal data in India and abroad, defining personal data on the basis of identifiability, covering processing of personal data by both public and private entities, defining sensitive personal data, consent to be the lawful basis for processing personal data, reformulation of the relationship between the data subject and the data controller, cross-border data transfers of personal data and the role of the Central government. In addition, the committee recommended setting up an independent Data Protection Authority (DPA). The government could not complete its deliberations to take the next step of taking the PDP Bill to the Parliament before its first term concluded in May 2019.

The bill recommended by the Srikrishna Committee was examined by the Modi government after it returned to power in May 2019, taking into consideration feedback from people and institutions. The government introduced the Personal Data Protection Bill, 2019 (PDP Bill 2019) in the Lok Sabha on 11 December 2019. The bill was referred to a Joint Committee of the Parliament.

The PDP Bill 2019 made some significant departures from the PDP Bill 2018, including extending the obligations of significant data fiduciaries to the social media intermediaries (SMIs) and much wider access to the government than envisaged under the PDP Bill 2018, and empowered the government to exempt any government agency from the purview of all or specified provisions of the bill.

The PDP Bill 2019 was referred to a Joint Parliamentary Committee (Joint Committee) of both the Houses. The committee submitted its report on 16 December 2021. There were several dissent notes.

The committee viewed data as a public resource of immense national importance. Its view was reflected in the emphasis it laid on the 'need to design and setup processes to unify data sets across public sector, private sector, and academic and research institutions'. It viewed with 'equal concern' the 'sharing of personal information to third parties without notice or consent of individuals and the violation of sovereign laws'. The committee was worried about the health and other consequences of the breach of data and also proliferation of bots and fake accounts. It was strongly in favour of data localization and government control over data in the context of national security.

The committee expanded data protection, whatever it meant, to non-personal data as well and its regulation by a single DPA. It proposed extensive changes (counted eighty-one) in the PDP Bill 2019, styling it as Data Protection Bill (DPB) 2021. It made many recommendations that generated immense controversy as well.

The government found the DPB 2021 recommended by the committee going beyond the scope of a modern digital privacy law. On 3 August 2022, the government withdrew the PDP Bill 2019 from the Parliament. The government promised to bring a new personal digital data protection bill soon.

India gets digital personal data protection law in 2023

The government took some time to draft the all-new Digital Personal Data Protection Bill 2023. After the Cabinet approved it on 5 July 2023, it was introduced in the Lok Sabha on 3 August 2023. The bill was drafted in simple and business-like language and applied only to the processing of digital personal data within India where such data is collected online or collected offline and is digitized. It applied to the processing of such data abroad if it was for offering goods or services in India.

The bill provided for the processing of digital personal data in a manner that recognizes both the rights of the individuals to protect their personal data and the need to process such personal data for lawful purposes and for matters connected therewith or incidental thereto. The bill protects digital personal data (that is, the data by which a person may be identified) by providing for the obligations of data fiduciaries (that is, persons, companies and government entities who process data) for data processing (that is, collection, storage or any other operation on personal data) and the rights and duties of data principals (that is, the person to whom the data relates).

The bill was based on seven principles: a. the principle of consented, lawful and transparent use of personal data; b. the principle of purpose limitation (use of personal data only for the purpose specified at the time of obtaining consent of the data principal); c. the principle of data minimization (collection of only as much personal data as is necessary to serve the specified purpose); d. the principle of data accuracy (ensuring data is correct and updated); e. the principle of storage limitation (storing data only till it is needed for the specified purpose); f. the principle of reasonable security safeguards; and g. the principle of accountability (through adjudication of data breaches and breaches of the provisions of the bill and imposition of penalties for the breaches).

The bill was passed by the Lok Sabha on 7 August 2023 and by the Rajya Sabha on 9 August 2023. The President provided her assent on August 2023 and it was notified in the official Gazette on 12 August 2023.

Finally, after five years of the Draft Personal Data Protection Bill 2018 provided by the Justice Srikrishna Committee, India did have a personal data protection law—the Digital Personal Data Protection Act 2023 (DPDP Act 2023).

Twitter suit failed to rein-in excessive digital regulation

Twitter (now X) filed a suit in the Karnataka High Court questioning the government's authority under section 69A of the Information Technology (IT) Act 2020 to block accounts on its platform as disproportionate. The government had ordered Twitter to block about 1,500 accounts between February 2021 and February 2022 largely relating to the farmers' protests against the three farm laws. The government's orders were also challenged on the grounds of not being in compliance with the procedural requirement of Blocking Rules 2009 framed under the IT Act.

A long-standing tussle was on between the government and Internet platforms relating to the maintenance of the intermediary status of Internet platforms under section 79 of the IT Act. Intermediary Guidelines 2021 went beyond the scope of the IT Act and placed onerous obligations on Internet social media platforms. Some platforms did not comply with government orders fully. The ministers warned the social media companies to behave or shut shop in India time and again. The Karnataka High Court first granted a stay. However, in its final judgment delivered on 30 June 2023, the High Court not only dismissed Twitter's suit but also ordered exemplary costs of Rs 50 lakh to be paid by Twitter.

The judgment had important ramifications for the right of free speech and also in terms of expanding, rather than restricting, the scope of blocking orders under the IT Act. In sum, the judgment expanded the scope of section 69A to preventive action, which allows the government to block the information still not published. It also expanded the scope of information to include any information identifiable by a URL. The judgment also questioned the right of Twitter (the intermediary) to speak on behalf of the person whose URL was ordered to be taken down. Twitter, a foreign entity, was denied the benefit of fundamental rights on account of not being an Indian citizen.

Twitter, after paying part of the cost as required under the High Court rules, filed an appeal before the division bench of the Karnataka High Court, which was admitted on 6 October 2023. The case is still to be decided.

Government initiates process of framing digital markets law

The Ministry of Corporate Affairs (MCA) constituted a Committee on Digital Competition Law (CDCL), India's version of the Digital Markets Act, on the recommendations of the Report of the Parliamentary Standing Committee on

Finance on the subject titled 'Anti-Competitive Practices by Big Tech Companies', to examine the need for a separate law on competition in digital markets. The committee submitted its report along with the draft bill on Digital Competition Law. On 12 March 2024, the government placed the report and the draft bill in the public domain and invited public comments.

The bill seeks to make provisions for designating 'enterprises' as 'Systemically Significant Digital Enterprise' (SSDE) with respect to 'Core Digital Service' if it has a significant presence in the provision of any such core digital services in India. The 'core digital service' is widely defined to include (a) online search engines; (b) online social networking services; (c) video-sharing platform services; (d) interpersonal communications services; (e) operating systems; (f) web browsers; (g) cloud services; (h) advertising services; and (i) online intermediation services.

The bill proposes a criterion for designating an enterprise an SSDE if it meets any of the criteria in the two separate buckets prescribed. First is the financial threshold in each of the immediately preceding three financial years: turnover in India of not less than Rs 4,000 crore or global turnover of not less than $30 billion or gross merchandise value in India of not less than Rs 16,000 crore or global market capitalization of not less than $75 billion or its equivalent fair value of not less than $75 billion calculated in such manner as may be prescribed. Second is the user threshold in each of the immediately preceding three financial years in India: core digital service has at least 1 crore end users or the core digital service provided by the enterprise has at least 10,000 business users.

The draft bill, thereafter, imposes certain obligations for such SSDEs, which are elaborately described in the bill. The SSDEs, more commonly known as Big Tech, have opposed ex-ante designations and obligations imposed on them. As the Lok Sabha elections were declared three days after the draft bill was put in the public domain, further action is to be taken only by Modi 3.0.

Government tried to control deepfake and AI

In the wake of a couple of highly publicized deepfake instances in the latter half of 2023–24, the government, besides holding meetings with social media platforms about the need to curb such deepfakes, issued an advisory on 26 December 2023 for ensuring strict compliance with IT Rules. The directive specifically targeted growing concerns around misinformation powered by AI and deepfakes.

The advisory mandated that intermediaries communicate to the users clearly and precisely what content is prohibited, particularly those specified under Rule 3(1)(b) of the IT Rules. The advisory further emphasized that digital intermediaries must ensure that users are informed about penal provisions, including those in the IPC and the IT Act 2000, in case of violation of Rule 3(1)(b). The Rule 3(1)(b)(v) explicitly prohibits misinformation and patently false information.

In March 2024, another controversy broke, about one of the AI apps (Google Gemini) generating embarrassing content about the Prime Minister. The government issued an advisory immediately under the new IT Rules to the effect that platforms that are under trial or training will have to seek approval from the Centre before launching any AI products.

The government argued that if a product is under trial, it did not absolve the concerned social media firms from the consequences of the law, especially criminal law.

There were widespread protests against the 'high-handed' approach of the government with the potential to kill innovations. The government first clarified that the advisory did not apply to start-ups. Later, the government said the firms would not require to take prior approval.

The government sought, in the second term, to control large-tech firms and social media firms in the fast digitalizing world of communications by using its power to make rules and regulations or even stretching the same to issue advisories, which were issued as directives. It achieved only a limited success, though.

Insolvency and Bankruptcy

The equity contributed by the owners and the debt provided by the lenders make up the capital of any company. The equity owners are usually the owners and operators of the company, whereas the lenders have a somewhat distant relationship—they are certainly not sitting inside the company. The performance of loans for the lenders also by and large depend upon the performance of the owners and their managers. The debt, therefore, becomes the first and major casualty whenever any company makes losses, becomes sick or otherwise is not in a position to service the loans.

In India, banks have been traditionally the principal credit and debt providers to companies. Every ten years or so, after they were nationalized in the 1960s, banks have witnessed spikes of non-performing loans. In the 1980s, the non-performing loans ratio reached nearly one-fourth of total advances. Again in the 1990s and 2010s, the non-performing loans, especially in public sector banks, crossed 10 per cent of advances.

Indian policymakers tried various methods. Nothing really succeeded.

The Sick Industries Companies Act (SICA) was enacted in 1985 for the rehabilitation of sick companies that had lost more than 50 per cent of their net worth. The law kept owners in charge and expected the lenders to fund their schemes of rehabilitation. The law proved to be an utter failure.

The government, following the Narasimham Committee report, constituted numerous Debt Recovery Tribunals under the Recovery of Debts due to Banks and Financial Institutions Act 1993. The debt recovery tribunals proved to be as slow and inept in recovering non-performing loans as the civil courts that these tribunals replaced. Banks' claims kept accumulating in the debt recovery tribunals.

The government, thereafter, enacted the Securitization and Reconstruction of Financial Assets and Enforcement of Security Interest Act, 2002 (SARFAESI Law), which gave birth to two institutional developments. First, the banks could take over and enforce the securities it had from the borrowing companies and second, it led to the formation of Asset Reconstruction Companies (ARCs) to take over the debt from the lenders and resolve the same. Enforcement of securities made some difference in non-performing loans but the asset quality reviews undertaken in 2015 revealed the true extent of stressed/non-performing assets, which turned out to be in excess of 13–14 per cent.

Modi government enacts IBC

The Modi government succeeded in bringing the Insolvency and Bankruptcy Code (IBC) in 2016, which put owners at risk of losing their companies. A financial default entitled the lender to haul the defaulting company to the IBC tribunals (the NCLTs).

The moment the petition was admitted, owners were divested of the management control of their companies, which was put in charge of an insolvency professional. The creditors were put in charge of the resolution. With the incentives of owners and lenders materially altered in favour of lenders, it was expected that lenders would finally get the best value for their debts.

The performance of IBC in Modi 1.0, though not as good as expected, was nonetheless quite satisfactory, much better than any of the big policy/legislative measures taken to date.

As per the Report on Trend and Progress of Banking in India 2018–19, in 704 cases admitted by the NCLTs in 2017–18, Rs 4,926 crore (49.6 per cent) was recovered out of a total amount involved of Rs 9,929 crore. In 2018–19, the last year before Modi 1.0 completed its tenure, a substantial amount of Rs 70,819 crore was recovered out of the amount of Rs 1,66,600 crore involved in 1,135 cases (42.5 per cent). This data related to recovery by the banks.

The recoveries made through IBC were far higher than the recoveries through other means. The recoveries in 2018–19, through the Lok Adalats was 5.3 per cent (Rs 2,816 crore out of Rs 53,506 crore), DRTs 3.5 per cent (Rs 10,574 crore out of Rs 3,06,649 crore) and SARFAESI Act 14.5 per cent (Rs 41,876 crore out of Rs 2,89,073 crore).

While there were some issues and the government had also effected important amendments, there was enormous satisfaction at the success of IBC and enthusiasm for its ability to resolve issues when Modi 1.0 completed its tenure.

First signs of weakening IBC in 2019–20

The IBC corporate insolvency resolution process (CIRP) came into force on 1 December 2016. There were visible signs of the IBC process weakening in 2019–20, the first year of Modi 2.0.

The pace of institution remained quite strong. As many as 1,953 cases were admitted to CIRP under the IBC in 2019–20. This was more than the 1,894 cases admitted in the previous three years.

The IBC process results in disposal of the case filed in four different ways: a. appeal/review/settled, b. withdrawal under section 12A of the IBC, c. approval of the resolution plan (the real remedy under IBC), and d. commencement of the liquidation process. In 2017–18, 200 cases (28.37 per cent of those admitted) were disposed of and in 2018–19, 622 cases (53.99 per cent of those admitted). In 2019–20, the number of cases disposed of also increased appreciably to 1,060.

The pace of disposal, however, began stagnating in 2019–20 as, like 2018–19, 54.28 per cent of the cases instituted were disposed of during that year.

The bigger worrisome trend seemed to be getting established in terms of the value of admitted claims realized by lenders, the key rationale for the IBC. In 2017–18 (latest IBBI data, March 2024), in twenty cases of corporate debt resolution, financial creditors realized Rs 4,458 crore out of the total admitted claims of Rs 8,198 crore, with a recovery rate of 54.38 per cent. In 2018–19, with a recovery of Rs 1,11,441 crore out of the admitted claims of Rs 2,06,848 crore in seventy-five cases resolved, financial creditors had realized 53.88 per cent of their admitted claims.

2019–20 proved much weaker in the matter of recovery. Lenders realized Rs 41,826 crore out of the admitted claims of Rs 1,64,568 crore in 132 cases resolved, which gave them realization/recovery of 25.42 per cent only.

This weaker recovery rate was evident in case of another benchmark as well—the realization rate as a proportion of the liquidation value. The liquidation value is the value which is assessed to be realizable if the assets of the company are stripped and sold off. The realization value must always be much higher than the liquidation value, if the insolvency process, which sells the company as a going concern, is actually succeeding.

In 2017–18, the realizable value was 235.41 per cent of the liquidation value. It was as high at 232.01 per cent in 2018–19. However, in 2019–20, the realizable value as a proportion of the liquidation value dropped sharply to 166.02 per cent only.

These were unmistakable signs of the IBC process losing steam in 2019–20.

Government dilutes and suspends IBC

As part of the first set of announcements in the wake of the imposition of Covid-19 lockdowns, Finance and Corporate Affairs Minister Nirmala Sitharaman raised the minimum cut-off floor for approaching the NCLT under IBC and suspended the proceedings under the IBC for the Covid-19 period.

The official announcement on 24 March 2020 said:

> Due to the emerging financial distress faced by most companies on account of the large-scale economic distress caused by COVID 19, it has been decided to raise the threshold of default under section 4 of the IBC 2016 to Rs 1 crore (from the existing threshold of Rs 1 lakh). This will by and large prevent triggering of insolvency proceedings against MSMEs. If the current situation continues beyond 30th of April 2020, we may consider suspending section 7, 9 and 10 of the IBC 2016 for a period of 6 months so as to stop companies at large from being forced into insolvency proceedings in such force majeure causes of default.

The President of India promulgated an ordinance on 5 June 2020, to insert section 10A in the IBC which suspended filing of applications under Sections 7, 9 and 10 for defaults committed on or after 25 March 2020 for a period of six months. This was later extended to one year. With this amendment, no insolvency proceedings could be filed for any default arising on or after 25 March 2020 for a period of one year. This bar, however, did not cover the defaults arising before 25 March 2020.

The consequences in terms of fresh institutions of the IBC cases were quite immediate. The Annual Report 2020–21 of the Insolvency and Bankruptcy Board of India (IBBI) informs that only 499 new cases were admitted in 2020–21 under the CIRP as against 1978 in the year before. The disposal also came down to 614 (against 1,203 in the year before), which incidentally was higher than fresh institution, thus bringing down the pendency.

The trend of the IBC process resulting in lower claims realization continued in 2020–21. Of the 108 cases resolved against the admitted claims of Rs 1,27,200 crore, the realizable value approved was only Rs 25,551 crore (latest IBBI report). The realization value ratio regressed to only 21.66 per cent.

Several voices were raised, accusing the IBC process being gamed by vested interests.

IBC becomes resolution mechanism for financial service providers

The IBC process was meant for non-financial real sector companies. The government had introduced a Financial Resolution and Deposit Insurance Bill, 2017 (FRDI Bill) in the Lok Sabha on 10 August 2017, which was referred to the Joint Committee of Parliament for examination and report thereon. The joint committee had completed considerable work on the FRDI Bill. However, the bill was withdrawn by the government in August 2018 for further comprehensive examination and reconsideration of the subject. The government never brought the FRDI Bill, including in the second term of the Modi government.

Section 227 of the IBC authorizes the Central government to notify, in consultation with the financial sector regulators, financial service providers (FSPs) or categories of FSPs for the purpose of insolvency and liquidation proceedings. In fact, an annexure to the FRDI Bill prescribed the resolution process for financial firms. With the FRDI Bill withdrawn, the resolution process of financial firms like banks, NBFCs, mutual funds, insurance companies, etc., was left hanging.

In 2019, the government decided to provide a resolution framework for 'systemically important financial service providers' under the IBC. The Ministry of Corporate Affairs in November 2019 notified the Insolvency and Bankruptcy (Insolvency and Liquidation Proceedings of Financial Service Providers and Application to Adjudicating Authority) Rules, 2019, which provided a generic framework for insolvency and liquidation proceedings of systemically important FSPs, other than banks.

Under the new rules, only a regulator is allowed to refer a non-bank lender or housing financier to a bankruptcy tribunal, unlike in the case of companies that can approach a tribunal on their own, or can be brought to the NCLT by both the financial lenders and operational creditors.

The rules also prescribed a different process in place of the resolution professional-run and the creditor-led process of the normal IBC. The NCLT was empowered to appoint an administrator, who would prepare and bring out a turnaround plan. The administrator was to be nominated by the sector regulator, e.g. the RBI in the case of non-bank lenders and housing financiers. The registration or the licence of the FSP could not be suspended or cancelled during the bankruptcy resolution process. In case the resolution programme did not work out, the NCLT would take into account the views of the concerned regulator before passing its final orders.

The RBI brought an application before the NCLT to initiate CIRP against the NBFC Dewan Housing Finance Corporation Ltd (DHFL) in December 2019, which was duly admitted and an administrator appointed on the advice of the RBI. As per the resolution plan submitted to the NCLT, it approved the transfer of DHFL to Primal Capital and Housing Finance Ltd in 2021 after the RBI communicated their no-objection to it. The amount of claims admitted in this case were Rs 87,248 crore and the amount realized was Rs 37,167 crore.

No other financial intermediary or service provider's case was resolved under the IBC process during Modi 2.0.

Pre-packaged resolution process initiated but gained no traction

The government promulgated the Insolvency and Bankruptcy Code (Amendment) Ordinance, 2021 on 4 April 2021 to lay the ground for a pre-packaged insolvency resolution process (PPIRP) or pre-pack process in India. The PPIRP enables corporate debtors classified as MSMEs to have faster resolution with their voluntary participation. The IBBI notified the PPIRP Regulations simultaneously to enable operationalization of the PPIRP.

The government claimed that this would help the insolvent MSMEs to have a very quick resolution.

The pre-pack process adopts the 'debtor-in-possession with creditor-in-control' model and envisages a shorter timeline for completion. In the pre-filing stage, the corporate debtor and its unrelated financial creditors (excluding the related party creditors) complete certain requirements. Thereafter, the MSME corporate debtor files an application with the Adjudicating Authority. The unrelated financial creditor(s) have to approve the pre-package plan by a 66 per cent majority for the corporate debtor to initiate the process. The pre-pack process envisaged a shorter 120-day period for resolution as the resolution is principally assumed to have been agreed to before the formal case is filed before the NCLT.

The pre-pack resolution process did not catch the fancy of MSMEs. The first case was filed in September 2021. In a reply in the Lok Sabha in August 2023, the government stated that only six cases had been filed under the pre-pack process. Still worse was the fact that despite the pre-pack process being an almost pre-agreed resolution, only one case was actually resolved. Only a total of eight cases were filed in all under the pre-pack process and two were resolved in the second term of the government.

IBC resolution lost its mojo

The IBBI newsletter for January–March 2024 provided data relating to the resolutions and their financial outcome for all the years since 2016–17 ending with 2023–24, by the time Modi 2.0 completed its tenure.

In the first term, in which the IBC operated for two full years of 2017–18 and 2018–19, ninety-four cases were actually resolved. These cases had total admitted claims of Rs 2.15 trillion. The IBC process yielded realization of

Rs 1.16 trillion against these claims to the creditors, providing a decent recovery of 53.90 per cent.

The IBC resolution process began hobbling from the first year of Modi 2.0. The position relating to the first two years, 2019–20 and 2020–21, has been stated in the foregoing paragraphs.

2021–22 proved to be equally underwhelming. Creditors got Rs 47,523 crore against their admitted claims of Rs 2.11 trillion in 144 cases resolved during the year at 22.53 per cent realization to admitted claims. 2022–23 was somewhat better though not much. The resolution of 189 cases during the year with admitted claims of Rs 1.54 trillion led to realization of Rs 55,449 crore, which returned 35.94 per cent of the admitted claims to the creditors. In 2023–24, the realization of Rs 47,653 crore was 27.43 per cent of the total admitted claims of Rs 1.74 trillion.

For the five years of Modi 2.0, 853 cases with admitted claims of Rs 8.31 trillion were decided through the IBC resolution process. The creditors realized Rs 2.20 trillion only, which meant recovery of only 26.47 per cent of the claims to the creditors. This recovery performance was less than half of the recovery of 53.90 per cent seen during the first term of the Modi government.

In every manner, the IBC seemed to be losing its mojo. Total disposal of cases, through all the processes, including resolution and liquidation, stagnated. After a record 1,235 cases were disposed of in 2019–20, the annual disposal was in the range of 722–936 in the next three years.

The number of cases in which realization was less than 10 per cent of admitted claims began rising. In the quarter July–September 2023, in as many as twenty-five cases out of ninety-two cases resolved in that quarter, the realizable value was less than 10 per cent of the admitted claims. In almost an equal number of cases (twenty-six), the realizable value was less than even the liquidation value; in a few cases, the realizable value was less than 50 per cent of the liquidation value.

In 2022–23, the average time taken in the cases resolved was as high as 614 days.

It was unfortunate but appeared quite true that the IBC process was also heading towards becoming as routine and inexpeditious a process as the other recovery processes—DRT, Security Realization, etc.—had proved to be.

Corporate Governance

The Companies Act 2013 lays down and regulates the raising of capital and corporate governance rules for companies registered and operating in India. It is the listed companies that raise capital from the market and investors. The market access and corporate governance of the listed companies, therefore, becomes a primary concern. It is the Securities and Exchange Board of India (SEBI), which, through the listing rules, subjects the listed companies to the market access and corporate governance principles, practices and rules. SEBI brought about important policy and regulatory changes during the five years of Modi 2.0.

Action on Committee on Corporate Governance

SEBI had appointed a Committee on Corporate Governance headed by Uday Kotak to make recommendations on important aspects of corporate governance in 2017. The committee submitted its report in October 2017. SEBI accepted about forty of the eighty-one recommendations made by the committee without any modifications and another fifteen with modifications. The SEBI (Listing Obligations and Disclosure Requirements) Regulations 2015 (Listing Regulations 2015) were amended in May 2019 to give effect to these accepted recommendations.

SEBI's decision led to considerable resentment on some key matters like composition of the board of directors, separation of the post of chairperson and managing director, quorum, independent directors and the like. The government stepped in and SEBI reconsidered some changes. Some of these changes were carried through during Modi 2.0.

Until its amendment in 2018, the listing agreement provided for the appointment of separate persons to the position of chairperson and MD/CEO as a good governance practice on a completely voluntary basis. Following the recommendations of the Kotak Committee, SEBI, in May 2018, amended the listing regulations to mandate that the top 500 listed companies by market capitalization shall ensure that the chairperson of the board shall be a non-executive director and not be a 'relative' of the MD or the CEO. Considering the representations and also taking into account the views of the government-appointed committee, SEBI deferred the implementation of this provision in April 2020 until 1 April 2022. SEBI assessed the status as of 31 December 2021 and found that only 54 per cent of the top 498 companies (two did not report) were compliant with the deferred provision.

As the deferred deadline was approaching, the SEBI board reconsidered the matter in 2022 and decided to make the provision of separate chairperson and MD/CEO a voluntary provision, restoring the pre-2017 status.

The listing regulations provided for at least one woman director on the board of every listed company. This was in line with the requirement of the Companies Act. The Kotak Committee wanted to go a step further and recommended that there should be at least one independent woman director. The recommendation was accepted by SEBI and it was decided to implement it in a phased manner—first in the top 500 listed companies by 1 April 2019 and in the top 1,000 listed companies by 1 April 2020. The position remained unchanged thereafter.

SEBI changes provision relating to independent directors

The listing regulations as they stood in 2021 provided for the appointment and removal of an independent director in the first term through an ordinary resolution and in the second term by way of a special resolution.

SEBI amended the regulations in 2021, with effect from 1 January 2022, to provide that the appointment, reappointment or removal of an independent director of a listed company shall be subject to the approval of the shareholders by way of a special resolution only.

Taking into consideration the feedback from industry, SEBI modified the provision to the effect that the first appointment would be by way of a special resolution. However, in case of a special resolution failing, the appointment could be approved by an ordinary majority of all votes cast and the majority of the minority of the public shareholders. An independent director in the first term could be removed by following the process of his/her appointment.

Independent directors cannot be appointed for more than two consecutive terms with a term not exceeding a maximum of five years.

Business responsibility and sustainability reporting mandated

Recognizing that adapting to and mitigating climate change impact, inclusive growth and transitioning to a sustainable economy had emerged as major issues globally and that there is an increased focus of investors and other stakeholders seeking businesses to be responsible and sustainable towards the environment and society, SEBI, in May 2021, decided to introduce new reporting requirements on ESG parameters called the Business Responsibility and Sustainability Report (BRSR). This regulatory requirement upgraded the responsibility reporting first mandated in November 2015.

The BRSR seeks disclosures from the listed entities on their performance against the nine principles of the National Guidelines on Responsible Business Conduct (NGRBC) and reporting under each principle is divided into essential and leadership indicators. The essential indicators are required to be reported on a mandatory basis while the reporting of leadership indicators is on a voluntary basis. The BRSR is intended to have quantitative and standardized disclosures on ESG parameters to enable comparability across companies, sectors and time. The filing of the BRSR was made mandatory for the top 1,000 listed companies (by market capitalization) from FY 2022–23.

In February 2023, SEBI issued a consultation paper proposing a regulatory framework for enhancing the ESG disclosures, which consisted of applicability of BRSR Core, disclosures for value chain and specifications on assurance, including a glide path. Subsequently, on 29 March 2023, SEBI approved these proposals. Based on the recommendations of the ESG Advisory Committee and the consultation paper, SEBI, through a notification dated 14 June 2023 amended the Listing Regulations 2015 to introduce the BRSR Core for companies' value chain. Subsequently, on 12 July 2023, SEBI issued a framework prescribing the disclosure and assurance requirements for BRSR Core, ESG disclosures for value chain and assurance requirements.

The requirement stayed at this during the rest of Modi 2.0. The disclosures required under the BRSR are viewed as aggressive and world-class by companies. However, they have not changed much in terms of business management and servicing of the ESG goals. These are still seen more as compliance requirements than the path to follow towards a sustainable and competitive environment.

Government brings in differential voting rights

The Security Contract Regulation Rules 1957 (SCRR) framed under the Security Contract Regulation Act 1956 provides for various matters relating to listing of securities on the stock exchanges, including the provisions of minimum public shareholding of 25 per cent, subject to some exceptions, for all public listed companies.

For incorporating the shareholdings with differential voting rights (DVRs), SEBI amended its regulations/rules in line with the amendments in the Companies Act, 2013 in August 2019. Subsequently, on 19 March 2020, the SCRR were amended to harmonize the SCRR requirements with the implementation of the framework on DVR shares issued by SEBI.

The framework issued by SEBI for the issue of DVR shares contemplated the listing of ordinary equity shares as well as DVR shares. In light of this requirement, the SCRR Amendment Rules provided that both ordinary shares and DVR shares would have to be listed on the same stock exchange during the initial public offer (IPO) of the ordinary shares of the company. Minimum offer and allotment requirements as specified under Rule 19(2)(b) of the SCRR were not made applicable to the listing of DVR shares.

SCRR relaxes minimum shareholding requirements

The government amended the SCRR 1957 in January 2023 to assume powers, in the public interest, to exempt any listed entity in which the Central government or state government or public sector company, individually or in combination, directly or indirectly held a majority of the shares or voting rights or control from the provisions of continuous listing requirements of minimum public shareholding of 25 per cent.

With the assumption of this omnibus power, all that the Central government needed to do was to issue a notification exempting public sector listed companies from the minimum public shareholding requirement. It is quite ironic that the public sector companies are being shielded from having minimum 25 per cent public shareholdings whereas private sector listed companies are mandated to do it without exception.

SEBI's primary market advisory committee (PMAC) recommended that post-CIRP companies may be mandated to have at least 5 per cent public shareholding at the time of relisting and be provided a period of twelve months to achieve public shareholding of 10 per cent from the date of relisting and a total of thirty-six months from the date of relisting to achieve public shareholding of 25 per cent.

As part of this recommendation (5 per cent/10 per cent limits) was at a deviation from the public shareholding norms prescribed under the SCRR, SEBI decided to refer the matter to the government to amend the Rule 19A(5) of the SCRR. The government duly notified the changes.

Fiscal Federalism

The Indian Constitution confers independent taxation powers to the central and state governments. Still, there is a constitutional provision for sharing central taxes with the states as the taxation powers of the Central government allow it to raise a majority of tax receipts.

The centre and states have independent authority to raise loans and issue guarantees on the strength of their respective consolidated funds. Yet, the Constitution subjects the states, which owe a debt to the Central government, to obtain the permission of the Central government to raise loans.

Both the Central government and the state governments have full executive authority to spend on the subjects allocated to them from their resources and no authority to spend on the subjects allocated to the other. Yet, the Constitution permits both the central and state governments to provide grants for the subjects within the executive domain of the other.

Indian states are massive fiscal entities and have enormous independent fiscal powers. Yet, the various provisions relating to sharing of central taxes, subjecting states' borrowing to Central government's permission and authority to provide grants in the executive domain of the other have made the Central government assume considerable authority over state finances and fiscal decision-making.

I review the policies and performance of Modi 2.0 in the matter of fiscal federalism in this part.

Share in central taxes/constitutional transfers

Article 280 (3) (a) of the Constitution enjoins upon the Finance Commission, appointed every five years, to make recommendations as to the 'the distribution between the Union and the States of the net proceeds of taxes, which are to be, or may be, divided between them'. Article 270 of the Constitution, after the 80th Constitutional Amendment, defines the divisible pool.

Article 270 prescribes that 'all taxes and duties referred to in the Union List', 'except the duties and taxes referred in articles 268 and 269' and 'surcharges on taxes and duties referred to in article 271' and 'any cess levied for specific purposes shall be shared between the Union and the States'. As the articles 268 and 269 speak only of marginal taxes like tax on stamp duty and consignment sale, all the union taxes, which includes income tax, corporation tax, central GST and excise duties are currently shareable with the states.

The Finance Commission recommends three specific handles which the Central government can use to alter the effective share of states in central taxes.

First, the 'net proceeds', as defined in Article 279 of the Constitution means the proceeds of any tax or duty reduced 'by the cost of collection', which is required to be finally ascertained and certified by the CAG.

Second, the 'surcharges on taxes and duties' levied by the Parliament, effectively the Central government, as permitted under Article 271 allows increase, at any time, in any of the duties or taxes by a surcharge (except on CGST) for the 'purposes of the Union', and the whole proceeds thereof shall form part of the Central government revenues only.

Third, the Parliament/Central government can levy 'any cess' for 'specific purposes'. There is no specific provision in the Constitution regarding the cesses. It is generally understood that the Central government is empowered to use its executive authority to levy cess for any specific purpose. Numerous types of cesses have been levied in India—road cess, sugar cess, coal cess and so on.

The 14th Finance Commission recommended 42 per cent share of states in the central taxes. The 15th Finance Commission revised it to 41 per cent, only to make an adjustment for the change in the status of Jammu and Kashmir into two union territories of Jammu and Kashmir and Leh.

The Modi government, however, used its authority to levy surcharges and cesses substantially to partly undo the recommendations of the Finance Commissions.

Surcharges and cesses zoomed

The governments used to make extensive use of cesses in the pre-GST period. The GST subsumed, in its fold, all the cesses on the goods and services covered under the GST. After GST, only the GST Compensation Cess remained, which was also to expire in June 2022. It was, however, extended to June 2026 to clear the arrears and loans taken for providing compensation until June 2022. As no cesses and surcharges can be imposed on any goods and services covered under the GST without the express consideration in and approval of the GST Council, the Central government has not imposed any cess or surcharge on the GST products.

Petroleum products remained outside the GST and became the main arena of experimentation to convert the shareable basic excise duties on petrol and diesel into non-shareable cesses and surcharges.

When the Modi government took over for the second term, the applicable excise duty, inclusive of cesses and surcharges, was Rs 17.98 per litre on petrol and Rs 13.83 on diesel. The government raised the road and infrastructure cess on petrol and diesel by Rs 2 per litre in the July 2019 Budget, the first budget of the new government, raising the excise duties on petrol and diesel to Rs 19.98 and Rs 15.83 per litre respectively.

The excise duties stayed put at that level for the rest of the year. In May 2020, in the immediate aftermath of the Covid-19-induced collapse of crude petroleum prices in the world, the government unleashed and imposed massive cesses/surcharges on diesel and petrol. Effective excise duty, inclusive of cesses and surcharges, went up to Rs 32.98 per litre on petrol and 31.83 per litre on diesel. The duties remained perched at such high levels for the rest of the year even though the global crude prices reverted to their normal levels.

In November 2021, the government effected the first major reduction in excise duties—by Rs 5 per litre for petrol and Rs 11 per litre on diesel. The effective duties came down to Rs 27.90 per litre on petrol and Rs 21.80 per litre on diesel. The government effected another major cut in excise duties in May 2022. Excise duties, including cesses and surcharges on petrol, were reduced by Rs 8 per litre and on diesel by Rs 6 per litre, bringing the total effective excise duties to Rs 19.90 and Rs 15.80 per litre on petrol and diesel, respectively. After two years, the excise duties on petrol and diesel reverted to the levels that were prevalent in May 2020.

The excise duties remained at this level until the government delivered a parting shot in March 2024 by reducing the duties by Rs 2 each on both petrol and diesel. This brought the effective excise duties on petrol and diesel to Rs 17.90 and Rs 15.80 respectively, exactly at the level at which these duties were when Modi 1.0 went to the polls in March 2019.

In the first term, the government had virtually converted the excise duties into non-shareable surcharges and cesses. In 2018–19, the states' share in union excise duties was Rs 27,024 crore out of the gross excise duties of Rs 2,31,045 crore (11.7 per cent). The government increased overall excise duties in 2019 and 2020. At the same time, it further reduced the shareable component of the excise duties. As a result, in 2022–23, states' share turned out to be Rs 13,483 crore only out of total excise duty revenues of Rs 3,19,000 crore (4.23 per cent).

The treatment of excise duties is a prime example of how the GoI used (or misused) the cesses and surcharges to appropriate the union taxes, which are otherwise shareable with states, for itself.

Significant reduction of states' share

The recommendations of the 14th Finance Commission became applicable from FY 2015–16 and ran up to FY 2019–20. Thereafter, the period is covered by the recommendations of the 15th Finance Commission.

For the period covered by the 13th Finance Commission, the states got 27.6 per cent share (the recommended percentage was 32 per cent) in the GTR, which was about 87 per cent of the recommended percentage.

The Modi government, which implemented the 14th Finance Commission award, started chipping away the excise duties from the shareable pool right from 2014–15. The major yanking away of the shareable central taxes started in 2019–20. The share of states during the 14th Finance Commission period was 34.94 per cent during 2015–16 to 2019–20, which was about 83 per cent of the maximum recommended share in the GTR of this period.

The Modi government completely snatching away the excise duties after May 2020 and diversion of the customs duties from 2021–22 led to the states' share falling to only 31.62 per cent from 2020–21 to 2022–23, down to only 77 per cent of the maximum recommended share of 41 per cent.

In the first three years of Modi 2.0 (2019–20 to 2021–22), the actual GTRs were Rs 67,27,727 crore. The government transferred Rs 21,44,066 crore to the states, which amounted to 31.87 per cent. If the government had transferred to states 35.54 per cent of the GTRs, the states would have got Rs 24,58,311 crore. In the three years alone, the states lost Rs 3,14,245 crore. The loss of more than Rs 1 trillion a year was certainly a massive blow to the states.

During the five-year period of Modi 2.0, the central taxes transferred to the states amounted to Rs 42.22 trillion out of the GTRs of Rs 132.63 trillion (both Controller General of Accounts numbers). This amounted to only 31.83 per cent of the GTRs collected. Had the Central government transferred 41 per cent of the GTRs, the states would have got Rs 54.38 trillion. Had the Central government transferred 36.54 per cent share of the GTR (@87 per cent of 42 per cent, as was the case during 2013–14 and 2014–15), the states would have got Rs 48.46 trillion as their share of central taxes. The states lost between Rs 6.24 trillion and 12.16 trillion rupees in lower central tax shares on account of the self-serving cesses and surcharges policies pursued by Modi 2.0.

Finance Commission grants

The grants to the states as part of the award of the Finance Commissions, though not obligatory on the Central government, acquires the character of mandatory transfers once these are accepted by the government and included in the action taken report (ATR) placed in the Parliament.

The grants for local bodies are recommended in pursuance of the mandatory term of reference of the Finance Commission in Article 280 (3) (bb)—the measures needed to augment the Consolidated Fund of a State to supplement the resources of the Panchayats, and Article 280 (3) (c)—the measures needed to augment the Consolidated Fund of a State to supplement the resources of the Municipalities. The Finance Commissions have been recommending these measures in the form of grants and the Central government has always accepted the same without any change. Therefore, while these transfers are in the nature of 'grants', their real nature is closer to the 'share in taxes'.

Likewise, the recommendations relating to the assistance to the states for their respective State Disaster Relief Funds (SDRFs) have also been never tinkered with except in case of the recommendations of the 14th Finance Commission when enhanced transfer of 90 per cent, in place of the usual 75 per cent, was implemented.

The rest of the grants recommended by the Finance Commissions have not received such deference from the GoI. These grants have been routinely subjected to conditions not laid down by the respective Finance Commissions. In case of the 15th Finance Commission, the recommendations whereof came during Modi 2.0, the government decided not to accept certain recommendations at all as informed in the ATR placed in the Parliament on 1 February 2021.

The commission recommended providing grants to the state governments in eight different sectors, namely health, school education, higher education, agriculture, maintenance of PMGSY roads, aspirational districts and blocks, judiciary and statistics amounting to Rs 1,29,987 crore during the five-year award period. The ATR indicated the 'Government will give due consideration to sectors identified by the Commission while formulating and implementing existing and new Centrally Sponsored and Central Sector Schemes.'

Likewise, the commission recommended the state-specific grants amounting to Rs 49,599 crore for the award period. For these grants also, the ATR said: 'Keeping in view the untied resources with the State Governments and the fiscal commitments of the Central Government, due consideration will be given to the above recommendation.'

In 2019–20, 93 per cent of the grants (Rs 1.24 trillion out of Rs 1.34 trillion) recommended by the 14th Finance Commission had been transferred. In 2020–21, the percentage fell to 88 per cent of the grants (Rs 1.84 trillion out of Rs 2.10 trillion) recommended in the Interim Report of the 15th Finance Commission. The grants transferred were 89 per cent of the grants (Rs 2.07 trillion out of Rs 2.33 trillion) recommended in 2021–22, the first year of the recommendations of the 15th Finance Commission. The slide started thereafter. In 2022–23, grants of Rs 1.73 trillion were transferred out of the total grants of Rs 2.28 trillion recommended by the 15th Finance Commission (75.8 per cent). In 2023–24, as per the revised estimates, Rs 1.40 trillion were transferred out of recommended grants of Rs 1.98 trillion (70.92 per cent).

For the five years of Modi 2.0, the Central government transferred total Finance Commission grants of Rs 8,28,398 crore out of the total recommended grants of Rs 10,03,066 crore, i.e. 82.59 per cent. In the process, the Central government short-transferred Rs 1,74,668 crore to the state governments.

Interest-free fifty-year CapEx loans a kind of fiscal trap for states

The Central government was a big lender to the states during the 1990s, meeting about 50 per cent of their total annual borrowing. States' finances were in a big mess and the provision of autonomously flowing central loans was a major reason responsible for the same. Both the NDA government at the Centre and the states had to take significant policy steps to redress the situation from 2002–03 onwards by bringing the net loans to the states below zero for the first time that year.

The UPA government continued these reforms and discontinued central loans to the states in 2005–06. By 2011–12, the states were only returning loans to the Centre, dismantling the lender-borrower relationship between them in the process. The states' net-repaid central loans equalled 4.7 per cent of their borrowing that year. By 2019–20, outstanding central loans to states fell to less than Rs 75,000 crore. The day when states would break free from central debt-yoke was drawing near.

Modi 2.0 decided to change tack. Ostensibly to expand the capital expenditure, the Central government re-initiated the pernicious practice of lending to states in 2020–21 with an outlay of Rs 12,000 crore, which increased to Rs 15,000 crore in 2021–22. The scheme outlay exploded to Rs 1 trillion in 2022–23 (actuals Rs 81,195 crore). For 2023–24, CapEx loan outlay was budgeted to Rs 1.3 trillion (revised to Rs 1.06 trillion in RE).

The CapEx loans to states have been provided in two broad buckets—one is supposed to be an untied bucket (80 per cent of loans) and the other linked to conditions, reforms and specified expenditures (20 per cent).

The tied 20 per cent of CapEx loan outlay was provided in 2022–23 in five sub-buckets: PM Gati Shakti (Rs 5,000 crore), priority village roads (Rs 4,000 crore), incentives for digitization (Rs 2,000 crore), optical fibre cable network

(Rs 3,000 crore) and incentives for urban reforms (Rs 6,000 crore). All allocations were tied to many conditions. For example, the incentive for digitization was subject to six conditions, one of which was mandatory use of Aadhaar in all subsidy expenditures.

The government identified six new buckets with new categories of tied CapEx loans in 2023–24. Loans of Rs 3,000 crore were linked to scrapping old vehicles, Rs 15,000 crore to urban planning reforms, Rs 5,000 crore for making municipalities creditworthy to issue municipal bonds, Rs 2,000 crore to police housing, Rs 5,000 crore for constructing unity malls and Rs 5,000 crore for building children's libraries.

The Central government claimed to provide the bulk of CapEx loans—Rs 80,000 crore in 2022–23 and Rs 1 trillion in 2023–24—as loans without conditions. That was, however, not true. Serious fiscal and political conditions were attached to this supposedly untied conditions basket. The states had to agree to use only the central names for all CSSs (earmarking political credit to the Centre exclusively), even though states were funding more than 50 per cent of these CSSs' expenditure.

The states also had to accept a new procedure for release of CSSs' funds by creating a single bank account to make all transactions visible to the Central government. The states had to pay interest attributable to Central government funds to the Centre. An additional condition—integration of the state treasuries with the central fund management system—was prescribed for 2023–24.

Article 293(3) of the Constitution subjects a state to take the approval of the Central government for all its borrowing in case it has any outstanding loans to the Centre. By sweetening the CapEx loans with a longer repayment period of fifty years and charging no interest, the Central government lured the states to accept central loans for practically eternity as these fifty-year loans cannot be prepaid.

These CapEx loans were provided over and above the states' borrowing space of 3 per cent of Gross State Domestic Product (GSDP). However, that largesse was superfluous as the states, barring 2020–21, never, since 2005–06, borrowed in excess of 3 per cent of GSDP.

By providing the CapEx loans to the states, Modi 2.0 not only ensured that the states would continue to remain in its clutches (needing permission for borrowing every single rupee of loans every year) but also turned into subordinate entities by imposing several conditions.

Part IV

Engagement with the Rest of the World

11

Trade and Commerce

In today's highly integrated world, foreign trade and commerce serve to raise national productivity and incomes. Exports help in establishing new manufacturing facilities and servicing establishments that create employment.

Imports have been increasing as no country produces all the goods and services its residents need for consumption. They undertake programmes and expenditures to raise the quality of their residents' lives besides importing technology needed for production.

Imports, however, need to be paid for. This can be best done from the export income or one has to import capital or pay by running down foreign reserves/ gold/other precious metals. The current account balance, the difference between all trade and income inflows and outflows is, therefore, a very important factor in determining the external and internal stability of money—the foreign exchange and domestic currency.

In the national accounts, export-import performance enters into the expenditure side equation. The GDP equals consumption (private and government together) plus investment plus net exports, with net exports defined as exports minus imports. Therefore, if the net exports are positive, i.e. exports of goods and services exceed imports, the GDP of consumption plus investment gets a boost. On the contrary, if the imports exceed exports, net GDP gets dragged down to the extent of imports exceeding exports.

For example, for 2020–21, the exports of goods and services, at constant prices, were Rs 25.57 trillion, whereas the imports were Rs 28.67 trillion, with net exports being minus Rs 3.11 trillion. The GDP (excluding net exports) of Rs 139.98 trillion was dragged down by Rs 3.11 trillion of net negative exports leading to GDP coming at Rs 136.86 trillion.

Growth Performance

Modi government did badly on the foreign trade front in first term

In 2013–14, the year before Modi 1.0 assumed office in May 2014, India exported $314.46 billion worth of goods. Goods exports had gone down to an embarrassingly low level of $262.29 billion in 2015–16. Only in 2018–19, the last year of Modi 1.0, did India's exports, at $330.07 billion, exceed the nominal level of exports made in 2013–14.

India's goods imports, however, had continued to grow through 2014–2019, although at a lower rate. Goods imports, which were $450.21 billion in 2013–14, had declined for the next three years, bottoming out at $381.01 billion in 2015–16. Thereafter, imports increased at a good clip, reaching $514.08 in 2018–19, crossing the $500 billion mark for the first time.

India's goods trade balance was in the negative by $135.75 billion in 2013–14 and the deficit increased to $184 billion in 2018–19. India had recorded a trade deficit in every one of the previous forty years, but in 2018–19, the trade deficit was the largest ever.

Over the same period, India fared much better in services trade. The export of services rose from $151.8 billion in 2013–14 to $204.76 billion in 2018–19, increasing by $52.96 billion in five years. The import of services also rose—from $78.7 billion in 2013–14 to $126.36 billion in 2018–19, recording an increase of $47.66 billion in five years. In 2013–14, India had a surplus on services trade of $73.1 billion, which increased to $78.40 billion in 2018–19.

India, in 2018–19, recorded total exports (goods and services combined) of $534.84 billion and total imports of $640.44 billion, generating overall trade deficit of $105.60 billion. This was explained by a deficit of $184 billion in the goods account and a surplus of $78.40 billion in the services account. With India's GDP amounting to about $2.70 trillion in 2018–19, the deficit of $105.60 billion on the trade account (both goods and services) was of the order of 3.91 per cent of GDP, which certainly was quite concerning. These numbers are as per the data published by the directorate general of foreign trade (DGFT).

The RBI also publishes trade data as part of the balance of payment statistics. There is a small difference in the trade data between the RBI and DGFT on account of different conventions followed regarding the point of exports/ imports, receipts of payments and treatment of monetary gold.

RBI data for 2018–19 indicates that goods exports, imports and the balance were $333.24 billion, $517.52 billion and $180.28 billion respectively. For services, the export, import and balance were $208 billion, $126.06 billion and $81.94 billion respectively. The overall exports, imports and trade balance, as per RBI data, for 2018–19 were $545.25 billion, $643.58 billion and $98.34 billion, respectively. The overall trade balance was about $7.26 billion lower as per RBI data, which made it 3.64 per cent of GDP, nonetheless quite concerning.

DGFT does not publish data on current account, which aggregates trade data and transfers of incomes. For assessing where India stood in terms of the current account, one has to only use RBI data. Two kinds of incomes/outflows—primary and secondary—are taken into account to arrive at the current account balance from the trade account balance.

The primary income, which includes compensation received/paid for Indian employees working abroad and non-residents working in India, receipt/payment of interest, dividend, etc., on investments abroad or investment in India, amounted, in 2018–19, to $21.84 billion of inflows in India and $50.70 billion of outflows, resulting in net outflow of $28.86 billion.

The secondary income, which primarily includes personal transfers between residents and non-residents, had resulted in inflows of $76.64 billion (thanks to large remittances from the Indian diaspora) and outflow of $6.70 billion in 2018–19, generating a large inflow surplus of $69.95 billion.

Putting all the constituents together, trade account deficit of $98.34 billion, primary income deficit of $28.86 billion and secondary income surplus of $69.95 billion led India to record a net current account deficit of $57.28 billion in 2018–19, which was 2.12 per cent of GDP.

Merchandise trade continued to cause concern in second term

India's goods trade performance deteriorated further, on the precarious base of 2018–19, in the first two years of Modi 2.0.

As against exports of $330.08 billion in 2018–19, merchandise exports went down to $313.36 billion in 2019–20 and further to $291.81 billion in 2020–21. India's exports in 2020–21 were lower by $38.37 billion in two years.

Goods exports bounced back smartly in 2021–22 when they reached $422 billion on the back of global supply disruption caused by Covid-19 and the Russia–Ukraine war. The good performance continued in 2022–23 as well when merchandise exports registered their highest level in the second term at $452.17 billion. The last year of Modi 2.0 again witnessed a decline in goods exports with provisional exports coming down to $435.64 billion in 2023–24.

The volatile performance of goods exports made Indian exports' CAGR growth to be a small 5.71 per cent during Modi 2.0.

Goods imports mirrored the exports performance. From the level of $514.08 billion in 2018–19, goods imports declined to $414.71 billion in 2019–20 and to $394.44 billion in 2020–21. Imports in 2020–21 were $119.64 billion, less than in 2018–19. Like the goods exports, goods imports also jumped to $613.05 billion in 2021–22 and peaked at $716.50 billion in 2022–23.

Goods imports also declined in 2023–24 (provisional) coming at $661.04 billion. Goods imports also recorded a CAGR of 5.16 per cent.

The trade account deficit increased from $184 billion in 2018–19 to $225.40 billion in 2023–24, recording a CAGR of 4.14 per cent.

Services trade did quite well

Barring a temporary minor setback in the Covid-19 year of 2020–21, when the services exports at $209.36 billion experienced a slight decline from exports of $220.73 billion in 2019–20, services exports recorded excellent growth from $204.76 billion in 2018–19 to $254.53 billion in 2021–22, $325.45 billion in 2022–23 and $341.25 billion (provisional) in 2023–24.

Services exports recorded a decent CAGR of 10.76 per cent during Modi 2.0.

Services imports also grew during 2019–2024 but at a slower pace. They were at their lowest in 2020–21 during Modi 2.0 at $122.64 billion. Otherwise, services imports increased from $126.36 billion in 2018–19 to $140.65 billion in 2019–20, $147 billion in 2021–22, $180.14 billion in 2022–23 and $177.27 billion (provisional) in 2023–24. Services imports recorded annual growth of only 7.01 per cent during the five years of Modi 2.0.

The services export surplus grew handsomely as a result of excellent growth in exports and subdued growth in imports. The services trade surplus rose to $163.98 billion in 2023–24 against the surplus of $78.4 billion in 2018–19, growing at a significant rate of 15.90 per cent per annum.

Overall trade balance healthier

India's total exports (goods and services together) were $534.84 billion in 2018–19 and total imports $640.44 billion, with the total trade deficit amounting to $105.60 billion, (-)3.91 per cent of the US$ GDP of 2.70 trillion.

In 2023–24, total exports rose to $776.89 billion (provisional), whereas total imports amounted to $838.31 billion, leading to a total trade deficit of $61.42 billion, with a much smaller overall trade deficit of (-)1.72 per cent of US$ GDP of $3.57 trillion.

Reflecting the combined effect of goods and services exports and imports, the CAGR of total exports was 7.75 per cent and of total imports 5.53 per cent, leading to a significant lower CAGR of (-)10.75 per cent for the total trade deficit.

Excellent growth in 2021–22 and 2022–23

Looking at individual year performance during Modi 2.0, 2021–22 and 2022–23 turned out to be high performance years.

India recorded massive growth in exports in 2021–22 when goods exports grew to $422 billion from $291.81 billion the year before at a stupendous growth of 44.62 per cent. Services exports also had a decent growth of 21.58 per cent (from $209.36 billion in 2020–21 to $254.53 billion) that year. The combined tango of exports of goods and services led to India recording an unprecedented growth of 34.99 per cent in 2021–22, from $501.16 billion in 2020–21 to $676.53 billion. This impressive growth of exports cleaned up the backlog of exports decline from 2018–19 in the first two years of Modi 2.0. The goods, services and combined exports recorded a CAGR of 8.15 per cent, 5.87 per cent and (-)7.52 per cent respectively, for the first three-year period from 2018–19 to 2021–22.

Imports, however, grew faster than exports in 2021–22. The imports of goods in 2021–22 at $613.05 billion were 55.42 per cent higher than the imports of $394.43 billion in 2020–21 (against export growth of 44.62 per cent). Services imports at $147 billion recorded 19.86 per cent growth, slightly lower than the export growth of 21.58 per cent that year. Combined goods and services imports in 2021–22 at $760.06 billion recorded a massive growth of 46.99 per cent, whereas combined exports growth that year was 34.99 per cent

2022–23 turned out to be another excellent year for exports, although the growth momentum slowed down. Goods exports amounting to $452.17 billion recorded growth of only 7.15 per cent that year. Services exports, however, remained on the big upswing, recording still better growth of 27.86 per cent to $325.45 billion. The combined exports of goods and services at $777.62 billion also chalked out a decent growth of 14.94 per cent.

The import of goods and services both recorded a more concerning performance in 2022–23. Goods imports grew to another record-breaking level of $716.50 billion with the annual growth for the year still very high at 16.87 per cent. The services imports also recorded a growth rate higher than the previous year at 22.55 per cent. Consequently, the combined imports of goods and services during 2022–23 reached $896.64 billion, recording a very high annual growth rate of 17.97 per cent, higher than combined export growth of 14.94 per cent.

Consequently, the combined trade deficit reached the highest level of $119.02 billion during Modi 2.0.

Exports lost momentum in 2023–24

India's exports (goods and services combined) at $184.66 billion in the first quarter of 2023–24 were lower than the exports of $197.08 billion in the first quarter of 2022–23, registering a decline of $12.43 billion (6.30 per cent).

The absolute decline of $12.43 billion in the first quarter sounded ominous. India had recently decided to ban exports of white rice. Some other restrictions were imposed and these were expected to continue impacting exports in the coming quarters. India's merchandise exports seemed headed towards being lower than the exports in 2022–23.

Merchandise exports suffered the most in the first quarter, with merchandise exports at $103.89 billion declining by $17.09 billion over exports of $120.98 billion in the first quarter of 2022–23, contracting by as much as 14.13 per cent. Merchandise exports declined in all the three months—by $5.08 billion, $4.05 billion and $7.96 billion in April, May and June, respectively.

The worrying clouds of the first quarter seemed to be getting significantly cleared in the second quarter, although the merchandise and total exports growth was still in negative territory. Combined goods and services exports at $190.58 billion were almost flat (lower by 0.08 per cent) compared to the combined exports of $190.73 billion in 2022–23. Services saved the day with a positive export growth of 4.24 per cent ($83.38 billion in 2023–24 against $79.99 billion in 2022–23). Merchandise exports remained in the negative growth territory with exports of $107.20 billion falling 3.20 per cent short of the exports of $111 billion in 2022–23.

The third quarter of 2023–24 signalled positive recovery, albeit small, on goods trade as well. Merchandise exports of $105.66 billion were 1.06 per cent higher than the exports of $104.6 billion in 2022–23. Services exports continued to grow at 5.15 per cent with the third quarter exports amounting to $87.72 billion.

At the end of nine months in December 2023, merchandise exports ($316.76 billion) were still in the negative zone with a net shortfall of $19.53 billion, (-)5.81 per cent, compared to the previous year's exports of $316.76 billion in 2022–23. With services exports making positive contribution of $12.35 billion, the combined exports ($568.61 billion) were only $7.18 billion short of the combined exports ($575.79 billion) in the nine months of 2022–23.

The fourth quarter recorded positive growth in both merchandise and services trade, albeit at a low growth rate of 4.15 per cent and 4.02 per cent, respectively. Combined exports of goods and services reached $208.28 billion during the quarter.

Combined exports in 2023–24 ended up almost flat ($776.89 billion in 2023–24) against $775.82 billion in 2022–23. The merchandise trade ended up recording negative growth after two years of (-)3.28 per cent, whereas services exports growth came out to be a timid 4.85 per cent. The fact that services trade growth was only 4.02 per cent in the last quarter of 2023–24 added to the worrying clouds on the horizon.

Greater decline in imports improved overall trade deficit

There was a greater decline in imports in 2023–24 with the overall goods and services imports ($838.31 billion) declining sharply by (-)6.25 per cent over combined imports of $894.19 billion in 2022–23. Both merchandise and services imports declined. Merchandise imports declined by (-)7.42 per cent and services imports by (-)1.60 per cent.

This improved the trade deficit as well to $61.42 billion (against $118.30 billion in 2022–23).

Export Promotion

Foreign Trade Policy was quite unimaginative

India had issued the foreign trade policy (FTP) in 2015 and the next edition was due on 31 March 2020 for the next five years. The government kept postponing the new FTP and finally it was issued only on 31 March 2023, three years after it was due and barely a year before the term of Modi 2.0 was to get over. It is a misnomer to call this policy an FTP. The policy essentially documents ongoing government schemes/initiatives to promote exports and their procedural aspects.

The official release issued on the occasion mentioned that the key approach to the policy was based on four pillars: (i) Incentive to Remission, (ii) Export promotion through collaboration—Exporters, States, Districts, Indian Missions, (iii) Ease of doing business, reduction in transaction cost and e-initiatives, and (iv) Emerging Areas—e-Commerce Developing Districts as Export Hubs and streamlining Special Chemicals, Organisms, Materials, Equipment and Technologies (SCOMET) policy.

The FTP claimed, for export promotion and development, moving away from an incentive regime to a facilitating regime, based on a technology interface and principles of collaboration. The ongoing schemes of Advance Authorization, Export Promotion of Capital Goods (EPCG), etc., were continued (without any change) with process re-engineering and technology enablement for facilitating the exporters. FTP 2023, it was further claimed, codified implementation mechanisms in a paperless, online environment, building on earlier 'ease of doing business' initiatives. Some reduction in fee structures was provided for MSMEs to access export benefits.

Duty exemption schemes for export production will now be implemented through regional offices in a rule-based IT system environment, eliminating the need for a manual interface. It was promised that, during 2023–24, all processes under the Advance and EPCG schemes, including issue, re-validation and Export Obligation (EO) extension, will be covered in a phased manner for this transition. The cases identified under the risk management framework will, however, be scrutinized manually, it was caveated.

The government designated four towns—Faridabad, Mirzapur, Moradabad and Varanasi—as Towns of Export Excellence (TEE), in addition to the existing thirty-nine towns. The TEEs enjoy priority access to export promotion funds under the Market Access Initiative (MAI) scheme and can avail Common Service Provider (CSP) benefits for export fulfilment under the EPCG scheme. The status recognition norms were 're-calibrated' to enable more exporting firms to achieve 4- and 5-star ratings.

The FTP doubled down on the Districts as Export Hubs (DEH) initiative to promote exports at the district level. It was noted that the efforts to identify export-worthy products and services and resolve concerns at the district level would be made through an institutional mechanism—the State Export Promotion Committee and District Export Promotion Committee respectively, and district-specific export action plans would also be prepared.

Recognizing the necessity of an 'export control' regime, as part of the integration with export control regimes of partner countries, the policy announced a wider outreach and understanding of SCOMET among stakeholders to implement international treaties and agreements entered into by India. A robust export control system in India would provide access of dual-use high end goods and technologies to Indian exporters while facilitating exports of controlled items/technologies under SCOMET from India.

In terms of sectors of new emphasis, the e-commerce exports were recognized as a promising category requiring distinct policy interventions to realize export potential in the range of $200 to $300 billion by 2030. FTP 2023 outlined the intent and road map for establishing e-commerce hubs and related elements, such as payment reconciliation, book-keeping, returns policy and export entitlements. As a starting point, the consignment-wise cap on e-commerce exports through courier was raised from Rs 5 lakh to Rs 10 lakh. A comprehensive e-commerce policy addressing the export/import ecosystem, based on the recommendations of the working committee on e-commerce exports and inter-ministerial deliberations, was promised.

The EPCG scheme, which allows import of capital goods at zero customs duty for export production, was further rationalized by adding the Prime Minister Mega Integrated Textile Region and Apparel Parks (PM MITRA) scheme as an additional scheme eligible for benefits under the CSP scheme of the EPCG scheme, exempting the dairy sector from maintaining average export obligation and making battery electric vehicles (BEV) of all types, vertical farming equipment, wastewater treatment and recycling, rainwater harvesting system and rainwater filters, and green hydrogen eligible for reduced export obligation requirement under the EPCG scheme on being treated as green technology products.

For the Advance Authorization Scheme, which provides duty-free import of raw materials for manufacturing export items to domestic tariff area units, certain facilitation provisions were added in the present FTP, such as the apparel and clothing sector on a self-declaration basis to facilitate prompt execution of export orders. Benefits of the Self-Ratification Scheme for fixation of input-output norms were extended to 2-star and above status holders in addition to authorized economic operators.

Merchanting trade of restricted and prohibited items under the export policy, except for goods/items classified in the Convention on International Trade in Endangered Species (CITES) of Fauna and Flora and SCOMET lists, was permitted subject to compliance with RBI guidelines,

The government also introduced a special one-time amnesty scheme under the FTP 2023 to address defaults on export obligations to provide relief to exporters who have been unable to meet their obligations under EPCG and Advance Authorizations, and who are burdened by high duty and interest costs associated with pending cases. All pending cases of the default in meeting EOs of authorizations mentioned can be regularized on payment of all customs duties that were exempted in proportion to unfulfilled EOs. The interest payable was capped at 100 per cent of these exempted duties under this scheme. However, no interest was payable on the portion of Additional Customs Duty and Special Additional Customs Duty.

The FTP 2023 did not have anything in it to set exports on fire. It was a routine and no-real-change policy. Some of the announcements made, such as bringing a new e-commerce policy, did not see the light of the day. The exports declined for many months after the announcement of this policy.

Large electronics PLIs did make some difference

The PLI scheme for large electronics, which included manufacturing and exporting mobile phones in India, with a massive outlay of Rs 40,995 crore, was the first major initiative to promote exports from India.

The government talked a lot about the growth in electronics exports, which included both smartphones and electronics like laptops, etc. In the last few quarters of Modi 2.0, iPhones were manufactured and their exports did become a major highlight.

ITC HS Code 85171300 captures the exports of smartphones. In 2022–23, the DGFT carved out a separate class (HS Code) of smartphones as it entered the list of the top fifteen exports of India with a total export value of $10.96 billion. The largest smartphone export destination was the UAE ($2.57 billion), followed by the USA ($2.16 billion) and the Netherlands ($1.07 billion). As there was a heavy customs duty on it, the import of smartphones was only $1.41 billion in 2022–23. In 2023–24, smartphones exports rose further to $15.57 billion, recording outstanding growth of 42.15 per cent in the year. Smartphone imports, on the contrary, declined by 34.53 per cent to only $923.60 million.

Smartphones make up a major constituent of the broader group of electronic goods. Import of electronic goods had become India's big bugbear, rising to about $60 billion in 2018–19, second only to the import of petroleum products. India needed to bend the curve—upping the exports curve and flattening, if not lowering, the imports curve of electronic goods. The export-import performance of electronic goods during Modi 2.0 did offer evidence that India might be finally able to do so.

In 2018–19, the export of electronic goods amounted to $8.83 billion. After remaining nearly stagnant in the next two years (primarily on account of Covid-19 and lockdown disruptions) at $11.70 billion and $11.09 billion, the export of electronic goods spurted in 2021–22 to $15.66 billion and further jumped to $23.57 billion in 2022–23. Over four years, the CAGR of electronics goods exports was as high as 27.83 per cent. The imports, on the other hand, exhibited a much slower growth rate. Electronics imports were as high as $57.38 billion in 2018–19. They did grow to $77.27 billion in 2022–23, but that was a much lower CAGR of 7.23 per cent. There was a sobering message in terms of absolute growth. While the exports grew by $14.74 billion over the four-year period, the imports recorded an increase of $19.89 billion. The imports, in absolute terms, grew by $5.15 billion over exports. At $77.27 billion in 2022–23, the imports also remained at 328 per cent of the exports of $23.57 billion, with India running a large trade deficit of $53.69 billion in electronics trade.

Import of electronic goods increased to $89.67 billion in 2023–24, recording 13.24 per cent annual growth. Export of electronic goods during the year increased to $29.38 billion, growing by 12.46 per cent. Despite the record performance of smartphones, the overall growth in electronics goods exports was smaller than the growth in import of electronic goods. In absolute terms, the gap in imports and exports growth widened further.

There are unmistakable promising signs that the curve might be bending for smartphones imports and exports. However, the 2023–24 performance on the wider electronics goods trade continued to underline India's big dependence and vulnerability on electronics imports.

Duty and taxes remission schemes did not boost exports

There is a plethora of export promotion schemes, most of which have been running for a long time. Two schemes were initiated by the Modi government in the first term to compensate exporters for state taxes, which are difficult to identify and abate, and the remaining central duties (other than the most common taxes like GST, excise duty). The Merchandise Exports from India Scheme (MEIS), introduced in 2015–16, provided a specified percentage of incentive in the form of duty scrips on exports of most goods. There was a small service counterpart of MEIS—Services Exports from India Scheme (SEIS)—which provided incentives on exports of specified Mode 1 and Mode 2 services. The other scheme, termed Rebate of State Levies (RoSL) provided compensating incentives for state levies on textiles products.

The Modi government replaced MEIS with a scheme called Rebate of Duties and Taxes on Exported Products (RoDTEP)—with effect from 1 January 2021. MEIS had run into challenges with the World Trade Organization (WTO) as it provided export incentives unlinked to any uncompensated/rebated taxes or duties. RoDTEP cured that defect. It provides for reimbursement of taxes/duties/levies, levied at central, state and local level, which are not refunded under any other scheme or mechanism. The scheme takes care that such taxes/duties/levies are incurred in the process of manufacture and distribution of exported goods and their rates of refund are determined by a technical committee set up by the Department of Revenue. As there is a clear/plausible link between the taxes/levies/duties incurred in the manufacture of exported goods and the reimbursement thereof under RoDTEP, the scheme is WTO-compliant besides serving the purpose that MEIS was intended to serve. Similarly, the Rebate of State and Central Taxes and Levies (RoSCTL) scheme replaces the RoSL scheme and provides for reimbursement equal to state duties and central taxes levied on export of garments and made-ups. There is no real difference between the RoDTEP and RoSCTL and the two schemes can be easily merged. Both schemes remained in operation till the final year of the Modi government, i.e. until 2023–24.

The duty credits under MEIS duly tapered off after 2020–21. In 2018–19 and 2019–20, they were Rs 39,298 crore and Rs 39,046 crore, respectively. In 2020–21, the duty credits under the scheme came down to Rs 14,405 crore (there was a delayed effect as the MEIS was under review), which was partly made up in 2021–22, when duty credits provided amounted to Rs 20,984 crore. In 2022–23, the duty credits under MEIS were only Rs 1,028 crore, probably reflecting some delayed claims and sanctions. The MEIS/RoDTEP are pan-exports schemes. Their impact on exports is difficult to judge. As the exports flagged in 2019–20 and 2020–21, the MEIS/RoDTEP incentives had no effect on arresting the fall. Likewise, when overall exports jumped in 2021–22 and 2022–23, there was no apparent contribution of MEIS/RoDTEP either. MEIS/RoDTEP can be viewed more as serving the taxation principle that no duties and taxes should be exported.

In case of RoSCTL, however, we can see the impact more specifically. RoSCTL targets exports of textiles and made-ups. These two products are covered under the export group of readymade garments (RMG) of all textiles. Data is available for specific merchandise: a. RMG of cotton, including accessories, b. Cotton fabrics, made-ups, etc., and c. Manmade yarns, fabrics and made-ups. The exports of cotton fabrics and made-ups represent the RoSCTL incentives closest. The exports of readymade garments (RMG), as per data provided by the Apparel Export Promotion Council (AEPC), from 2019–20 to 2023–24 were $15.51 billion, $12.29 billion, $16.02 billion, $16.19 billion and $14.53 billion, respectively.

RMG exports have been quite static during Modi 2.0 with the exports in 2023–24 lower than in 2019–20. The larger influencing factors were the demand from the importing markets and the competition from other suppliers. RoSCTL probably made no real difference. However, as long as RoSTCL represents compensation for the taxes, duties and other levies embedded in the cost of the exported goods, there is no reason why these incentives should be tampered with.

Setting export targets does not help

The government cannot really promote exports of goods and services by setting export targets. It has also been trying to boost exports by providing tax, expenditure and other monetary incentives. There are numerous such schemes in operation. However, there is no evidence of any direct correlation between these scheme outlays and the targeted export performance.

In 2021–22 and 2022–23, exports boomed though there was no material change in the export incentive package. Before that, for seven to eight years, there was complete stagnation in exports despite the government continuing numerous export promotion schemes and also instituting quite a few new ones like MEIS. Merchandise exports declined again in 2023–24. The incoming slowdown in exports could not be arrested by the government schemes and targets.

Imports Control

Government could not reduce dependence on petroleum products imports

Import of petroleum products constitute a big chunk of India's imports. The crude oil prices were at one of the highest-ever levels in 2013, averaging $105.87 a barrel. India imported 144 million metric tons (MMT) of crude oil in 2013–14 costing $143 billion. Including the import of petroleum products, the import bill was $155 billion. As India also exported petroleum products of $61 billion, the net import bill was much less at about $94 billion.

India does produce crude oil (37.8 MMT in 2013–14) in her onshore and offshore blocks, and imports finished petroleum products as well (12 MMT in 2013–14). India has established a larger refining capacity than required for meeting its domestic demand. India could export 61 MMT of finished petroleum products in 2013–14. The entire import of crude oil (144 MMT in 2013–14), therefore, does not go towards meeting India's domestic petroleum products demand. There are some differences in opening and closing stocks of crude oil and petroleum products with the OMCs as well. Taking into account all these factors, the Petroleum Planning and Analysis Cell (PPAC) reckoned that India's import dependency (based on consumption) was 77.6 per cent in 2013–14, the year before the Modi government took over.

Worried by such an excessive dependence on the import of crude oil and petroleum products, Prime Minister Modi vowed in April 2015 to bring down this dependence from 77 per cent of its energy requirement (he meant petroleum products consumption) by 10 per cent by 2022 (i.e. to 67 per cent) and to 50 per cent by 2030. By the time the Modi government completed its first term in 2019, India's import dependence had gone up to 83.7 per cent in 2018–19, a full 6 per cent higher than 77.6 per cent in 2013–14. In 2018–19, the average crude oil import prices were much lower ($64.04 per barrel), yet the import of petroleum products went up to $140.92 billion.

The first milestone of 67 per cent import dependency by 2022 (December-end presumably) fell in FY 2022–23. The import dependency unfortunately kept rising during Modi 2.0. In 2019–20, the first year of the second term, it went up to 85 per cent. Import dependency came down a little in 2020–21 when a fall in the consumption of petroleum products on account of Covid-19 and lockdowns brought it down to 84.4 per cent. In 2021–22, import dependency increased to 85.5 per cent. In 2022–23, when economic activities picked up pace again, the import dependency rose to 87.3 per cent. The Modi government was 20 per cent off the target of 67 per cent. Instead of bringing down the import dependency to the targeted 67 per cent, the import dependency went up further to 87.3 per cent, deteriorating another 3.6 per cent from 83.7 per cent in 2018–19.

Oil prices did shoot up in 2022 in the wake of the Russia–Ukraine war, averaging $100.08 per barrel. Though India could get a good part of its imports from Russia at discounted prices, the crude oil import bill rose to $157.6 billion. Inclusive of petroleum products, the import bill cost India $184.4 billion in 2022–23. As India's petroleum products exports amounted to $57.3 billion, the net imports were $127.1 billion ($184.4 billion minus $57.3 billion). India's LPG imports had also gone up during the year and amounted to $17.1 billion, taking India's net oil and gas products external trade bill to $144.2 billion in 2022–23.

India regressed on oil import dependency during Modi 2.0.

Abortive licensing for digital devices imports

In a shocking move on 3 August 2023, the government placed imports of laptops, tablets, all-in-one personal computers and ultra-small form factor computers and servers under the 'restricted' category, making their imports permissible only under a valid licence. Some minor exemptions were provided but all imports of the computer devices on which India's digital services and exports are built were brought under government control with immediate effect.

There was an understandable outcry all around. The government officials and ministers first tried to sell the idea that this was done to advance the cause of Make-in-India, to make India Atmanirbhar in manufacturing computer devices. Then, they brought the security argument into play. None of these justifications went far. Late at night on 4 August, the day after, the government backtracked to make 'liberal transitional arrangements' and postponed the compulsory licensing to 1 November, announcing that import consignments will be cleared till 31 October 2023 without a licence for restricted imports.

The whole episode left no one in doubt that the government was trying to bring the dysfunctional licence-permit raj into the new-age economic value creator—digitalization.

India did not invent computers and its constituent IT hardware components and parts—chips, batteries, cameras, etc. Consequently, India does not build computer devices. We have a very small computer hardware manufacturing industry in the country, which is also hugely dependent on imports of semiconductor chips and other computer hardware parts. Our computer devices industry is more Assemble-In-India than Make-In-India. Even in this, we are not domestically competitive.

India, on the other hand, in the last twenty-five years, successfully built a massive information technology services export industry using the computer devices built by and imported from the rest of the world. We exported our information technology software services massively. As per RBI data, India received payments of $122 billion from the export of software services in 2021–22.

India's total imports of automatic data processing machines and units, which constitute the international system of classification HSN, under entry 8471, placed under the restricted list, was only $11.63 billion in 2021–22 (DGFT data). Software services exports brought ten times more foreign exchange than the cost of all the devices imported. Software services are the mainstay of India's services and total exports. In 2021–22, software services made up as much 48 per cent of total services exports and 18 per cent of all our total exports, all goods and services combined.

Liberal import of electronics devices have kept the prices of electronic products under control and input costs for the software industry low. The wholesale price index for manufacture of computer, electronic and optical products, which includes manufacturing of all computer devices covered by HSN 8471, has been only 1.45 per cent per annum for over a decade.

The government notification did not openly indicate that its objective was to restrict imports of computer devices from China though that was believed to be the real reason behind the move. About 80 per cent of the computer devices imported under entry 84713010 are sourced from China ($4.11 billion out of $5.33 billion in 2022–23—77.11 per cent).

MeitY operates numerous schemes to encourage domestic production of computer hardware. PLI schemes are the flavour of the season for encouraging manufacturing in India. The government announced a Rs 7,350-crore PLI scheme for IT hardware in March 2021. The scheme targeted hardware segments of laptops, tablets, all-in-one personal computers (PCs) and servers (all items covered by the entry 8471). The scheme extended incentives up to 4 per cent on net incremental sale over the base year 2019–20 for a period of four years (2021–22 to 2024–25).

The government approved fourteen companies under this PLI, promising to make IT hardware of Rs 1.6 trillion (approximately $20 billion). The scheme has not done wonders; the IT hardware PLI hardly saw any disbursement.

The government came up with the PLI 2.0 for IT hardware in May 2023 with an increased budget outlay of Rs 17,000 crore. This scheme increased the incentive to around 5 per cent and operational period to six years. The scheme application window was first opened until 31 July 2023 and later extended to 31 August 2023. Media reports suggested that forty-four companies applied. Twenty-seven applications were approved in November 2023 with a potential investment of Rs 3,000 crore. The provision of Rs 146 crore for the scheme in the 2023–24 Budget was reduced to Rs 70.42 crore in RE.

Instead of full-scale licensing, India put in place an import monitoring system, a faceless and contactless system, for electronics hardware, from 1 November 2023. The system, to remain valid until September 2024, requires the importers of computer hardware covered by the notification cited above to apply on the system to seek authorization for imports.

The system does not prescribe any conditions or restrictions in the matter of quantity, value or country. However, companies in the 'denied entity list' would not be granted authorization. Likewise, companies intending to import second-hand goods or refurbished items were not allowed to use the online system.

There was no specific restriction on applying for authorization through the online monitoring system for importing computer hardware from China or Chinese companies. It was widely suspected that the government would not grant authorization for import from Chinese companies. The provisional data for 2023–24 for the HS code 84713010, however, does not suggest any significant reduction in imports from China—$3.82 trillion out of total imports of $4.92 trillion (77.64 per cent).

12

Foreign Investment

Capital inflows from the rest of the world to the Indian government, businesses and households, normally described as capital account transactions, in the broadest sense, represent foreign investment in India. Indian residents and companies also make investments abroad; though such capital outflows are much smaller than the capital inflows which India receives.

Foreign direct investment (FDI) is the most durable and the largest source of capital account inflows in India's context. The outward direct investment (ODI) by resident Indians in the rest of the world is much smaller. FDI also brings with it foreign technology, management practices and, many times, access to export markets as well. FDI flows, therefore, are the most important inflows in the investment context. The government started keeping a detailed record of FDI inflows from 2000. The stock of FDI in India is, therefore, described with reference to 2000.

FDI has three constituents: a. inflow of new foreign investment, b. reinvestment of retained earnings, and c. disinvestment/repatriation of the FDI invested. The new FDI inflow is made up of new FDI flowing into the country in a particular year. This brings in additional foreign currency inflows.

FDI-invested companies generate profits—a part of which belongs to the FDI owners. While the companies distribute a part of the profits earned, the share attributable to the FDI shareholders in the retained earnings gets counted as FDI inflow. The sale of equity invested earlier and counted as FDI leading to its repatriation abroad is the outflow of FDI in that particular year.

While the terminology of FDI inflow is used loosely to describe all three situations: a. only fresh inflow of FDI, b. fresh FDI inflows plus retained earnings, and c. FDI inflows (fresh and retained earnings) minus disinvestments/repatriation, I will be using in this book, New FDI flows to describe 'a' (new inflows), Gross FDI to describe 'b' (new inflows plus retained earnings) and FDI to describe 'c' (Gross FDI minus disinvestment and repatriation).

Indian investors also take FDI out to other countries to invest in their companies and enterprises. This is described as outward direct investment (ODI). FDI minus ODI is also referred to as Net FDI.

The stock of Gross FDI in India, as per the DPIIT website, including reinvested earnings attributable to foreign investors, from April 2000 to March 2024, is $990.97 billion, tantalizingly close to $1 trillion FDI.

Foreigners invest in Indian businesses by net buying the shares of Indian companies as well in the market, mostly on the stock exchanges. These flows are collectively termed as foreign portfolio investors (FPIs). As per the National Securities Depository Ltd (NSDL) database, FPIs have brought a net cumulative inflow of $197.70 billion in equity stocks as on 31 March 2024. The FPI equity assets under custody (AUC) gain in valuation as well when their share prices go up. The total equity AUC of FPIs as on 31 March 2024 are estimated at $769.51 billion, as per NSDL data.

Foreign investment in debt takes place both by way of investment in Indian debt securities of the government and the corporates through FPIs as well as in commercial loans to Indian financial and non-financial entities, known as external commercial borrowings (ECBs).

Debt investment in India is also quite substantial. As on 31 March 2024, FPIs had a cumulative investment of $41.61 billion in debt, $17.75 billion in debt (voluntary retention route—VRR—a specialized route provided by the RBI) and $5.20 billion in hybrid securities; in all, $64.56 billion (NSDL data). The outstanding ECB borrowings were estimated at $222 billion at the end of FY 2022–23.

Foreigners/FPIs invest in Indian government debt securities by buying them in primary auctions conducted by the RBI and also in the secondary market through stock exchanges and the RBI's debt platform. FPI investment in government (sovereign) securities, listed on stock exchanges as on 31 March 2024, was $28.68 billion in debt, $0.17 billion in debt (VRR); in all $28.85 billion. The government's securities share in FPI-owned Indian debt was about 45 per cent.

Non-residents, mostly of Indian origin, keep significant amounts of deposits in Indian banks, besides making investments in stocks and debt. In 2022–23, gross capital account flows were $72.26 billion, including FDI of $41.01 billion and NRI deposits of $20.98 billion.

In this chapter, I review the policies and performance of Modi 2.0 with respect to FDI, foreign portfolio investments (FPI) and other capital account flows.

Foreign Investment in Capital Formation

All foreign capital inflows don't form capital

Gross capital account inflows comprise, besides FDI, portfolio investment, ECBs, external assistance from multilaterals, NRI deposits and others. Some accounts have negative receipts in some years. Capital flows take place in the opposite direction as well, such as direct investment by Indian companies abroad. The net capital account flows are, therefore, net of negative inflows and capital account outflows.

Certain capital account flows provide financial capital formation directly. FDI adds to the equity capital of the companies concerned. ECB and debt investment directly in the instruments of the companies concerned provide debt capital. FPI investments through the secondary markets, however, do not add to the financial capital formation directly.

The financial capital provided through FDI and direct debt flows, when used by the companies concerned in buying capital goods domestically or from abroad, adds to the capital formation in the economy. It is, however, not easily possible to establish a direct link between the foreign investment flows and the capital formation in the economy. However, it may be sufficient to assume that a good part of the FDI and direct debt capital flows do end up getting invested in capital formation.

In India, for the economy as a whole, the deficit on the current account, i.e. on account of imports of goods and services exceeding exports thereof, is met by the capital account flows. Still, usually, there is an excess of capital account flows, including the portfolio flows.

The excess of capital account inflows, which is the default case in most of the years, over the current account deficit, ends up adding to the foreign currency reserves. In a few years, when capital account flows are not enough to finance the current account deficit, there is a withdrawal from the RBI's exchange reserves.

Excellent capital account flows in first term

In the first term of the Modi government (2014–19), India received a total of $352.65 billion of gross capital account flows (from the RBI balance of payments data). The FDI flows at $205.14 billion ($35.28 billion in 2014–15, $44.907 billion in 2015–16, $42.215 billion in 2016–17, $39.43 billion in 2017–18 and $43.30 billion in 2018–19) constituted the largest FDI inflows in any five-year period. FDI inflows at 58 per cent of total foreign investment flows in 2014–2019 constituted the largest component of foreign flows as well.

FPI, volatile as ever, including being negative in some years [$42.19 billion in 2014–15, (-)$3.64 billion in 2015–16, $7.77 billion in 2016–17, $22.165 billion in 2017–18 and (-)$0.405 billion in 2018–19], also contributed handsomely with $68.08 billion during that period.

ECBs inflows were mostly negative but ended up with a positive contribution of $1.17 billion in five years. NRI deposits aggregated to $29.25 billion.

With outward ODI and portfolio investments amounting to $41.25 billion and $0.89 billion respectively during this five-year period, the net capital account inflows amounted to $310.61 billion. In the first term, there was an addition of $141.11 billion to the foreign exchange reserves as the deficit on current account amounted to $169.40 billion.

Weakening growth in second term

In the first four years of Modi 2.0, the aggregate capital account inflows pretty much equalled the inflows of five years of the first term.

India received $352.11 billion in gross capital flows. The FDI inflows at $209.17 billion ($56.006 billion in 2019–20, $54.927 billion in 2020–21, $56.231 billion in 2021–22 and $42.006 billion in 2022–23) crossed FDI inflows of $205.14 billion in the first term of the government. There were strong FDI inflows in the first three years, which began weakening in 2022–23.

There was significant compositional change in the rest of the components.

The portfolio flows proved to be particularly low in the first four years at $20.38 billion [$0.552 billion in 2019–20, $38.725 billion in 2020–21, (-)$14.071 billion in 2021–22 and (-)$4.828 billion in 2022–23]. In two out of four years, FPI lows were strongly negative.

NRI deposit inflows practically disappeared in four years, aggregating $1.27 billion only. ECBs, on the other hand, made a smart recovery, garnering $27.17 billion in flows. The other capital flows were the most abundant, bringing $47.04 billion.

2023–24 proved to be quite a roller-coaster ride.

FDI decelerated (particularly on account of disinvestments and repatriation) at $26.550 billion (RBI Bulletin May 2024—provisional) only. Portfolio inflows, on the other hand, hit the roof at $42.880 billion (more than double of the net portfolio flows of the first four years).

Foreign Direct Investment (FDI)

FDI is a capital account transaction, controlled and regulated under the Foreign Exchange and Management Act (FEMA). The capital account transaction has been defined as a transaction which alters the assets or liabilities, including contingent liabilities, outside India of persons resident in India, or assets or liabilities in India of persons resident outside India, and includes transactions as per section 6 of FEMA.

While the Department of Economic Affairs (DEA) in the Ministry of Finance is the administrative department in charge of FEMA and, therefore, of capital account transactions, the FDI policy has been placed under the charge of DPIIT. DPIIT takes the lead in development of FDI policy, which is, thereafter, implemented as capital account transactions through the Foreign Exchange Management (Non-Debt Instruments) Rules 2019 framed by DEA and administered by the RBI under the Foreign Exchange Management (Mode of Payment and Reporting of Non-Debt Instruments) Regulations, 2019 issued by the RBI.

Equity transactions are the principal capital account transactions which impact ownership and control over the operating financial and non-financial companies in India. The FDI policy framed by DPIIT defines, for the purpose of FDI policy, 'capital' as equity shares; fully, compulsorily and mandatorily convertible preference shares; and fully, compulsorily and mandatorily convertible debentures and warrants. In simple words, the equity shares and fully and compulsorily convertible preference shares, debentures and warrants constitute equity capital in which investment by non-residents is FDI.

FDI, in FDI Rules, has been formally defined as investment through capital instruments by a person resident outside India in an unlisted company, or 10 per cent or more the post-issue paid-up equity capital on a fully diluted basis of a listed Indian company. Fully diluted basis means the proportion of the equity capital if all the convertible debentures, warrants, etc. are taken as fully converted.

It makes no difference now whether 10 per cent or more investment in any Indian listed company is made by direct subscription to the shares issued by the company or acquired through stock exchanges or a combination of both. For unlisted companies, the condition of minimum 10 per cent equity holding does not apply. It has also been clarified that once a foreign investor acquires 10 per cent share in a listed company, even if its shareholding comes down to less than 10 per cent later, the investment will continue to be treated as FDI.

The RBI collects and publishes FDI data. Gross FDI is the total of fresh inflows of foreign investment in capital plus the unrepatriated share of profits belonging to the foreign direct investors.

Non-residents keep repatriating and/or disinvesting their FDI holdings. The gross FDI minus the repatriated/disinvested FDI constitute direct investment or foreign direct investment or FDI. To illustrate, India received gross FDI inflow of $36.05 billion in 2013–14. That year, foreign investors repatriated/disinvested $5.28 billion worth of their FDI investments. This brought an FDI inflow to India of $30.76 billion during 2013–14.

FDI rose and then fell

In 2018–19, FDI inflows were $43.30 billion.

FDI flows went up significantly in the first year of Modi 2.0, i.e. 2019–20 to $56.01 billion, rising by an impressive $12.70 billion (29.3 per cent) that year. Thereafter, FDI inflows stagnated for two years at $54.93 billion in 2020–21 and $56.23 billion in 2021–22.

FDI inflows in 2022–23 fell significantly to $42.01 billion, a reduction of over $14 billion in a year. FDI inflows in 2022–23 were less than the FDI in 2018–19. The falling trend accelerated in 2023–24. As per the provisional data released by the RBI, in 2023–24, FDI inflows fell to $26.550 billion, declining by a whopping $15.456 billion in a year. FDI inflows in 2023–24 were less than half of FDI inflows in 2019–20.

The drastic fall in FDI inflows was explained by a disproportionate increase in the repatriation from and disinvestment of FDI stock in India. While the gross inflows of FDI during the year were only fractionally smaller ($70.954 billion in 2023–24 against $71.355 billion in 2022–23), the repatriation and disinvestment were much higher at $44.404 billion in 2023–24 against $29.349 billion the year before.

Gross FDI inflows actually rose consistently in the first three years of Modi 2.0—from $62.01 billion in 2018–19 to $74.39 billion in 2019–20, to $81.97 billion in 2020–21 and further to $84.84 billion in 2021–22. The Gross FDI declined sharply to $71.355 billion in 2022–23 and remained at that level, declining marginally to $70.954 billion (provisional) in 2023–24.

The repatriation/disinvestment of FDI stock first shot up in 2020–21. From the very low level of $18.38 billion in 2019–20, the repatriation/disinvestment outflows increased massively to $27.05 billion in 2020–21. Thereafter, it remained steady at that level for the next two years—$28.61 billion in 2021–22 and $29.34 billion in 2022–23 before going off on a tangent in 2023–24 at $44.404 billion.

Both the trends were quite ominous for the future. Declining Gross FDI indicated that foreign investors were losing interest in the India investment story. Heightened disinvestment and repatriation suggested that foreign investors believed that the value of their investment had peaked and it was the best time for them to book profits and go home.

Net FDI also declined

The investment made by Indian residents in equity capital instruments of companies established and operating outside India (ODI) reduced from the FDI in India makes up the net foreign direct investment or Net FDI. The Net FDI can grow higher if there is greater FDI or the ODI outflows are smaller.

Indian investors had received FDI of $43.30 billion in 2018–19 and had made ODI investments of $12.59 billion. The Net FDI (FDI-ODI) was, therefore, $30.71 billion in that year.

We took note of the FDI inflows during 2019–2024 in the last section.

ODI flows were $12.993 billion in 2019–20 and $10.972 billion in 2020–21. In 2021–22, ODI outflows jumped to $17.644 billion. ODI outflows declined to $14.020 billion in 2022–23 before rising to $15.962 billion in 2023–24 (provisional).

High growth in ODI in the last three years of Modi 2.0 resulted in bringing down the Net FDI flows in 2021–22 to $38.587 billion only. 2022–23 proved to be very difficult from the Net FDI perspective, with the Net FDI amounting to only $27.986 billion in that year.

The Net FDI witnessed one of the worst ever years in 2023–24. With the FDI flows (minus repatriation/disinvestment) turning out to be $26.550 billion only and the ODI outflows remaining elevated at $15.962 billion, India received the Net FDI of only $10.588 billion in 2023–24.

FDI has a small share in India's capital formation

Provisional GDP numbers for 2023–24, at current prices, estimated the GFCF, the statisticians' term for capital formation, at Rs 91.07 trillion ($1,097 billion @ Rs 83 to a dollar); 30.83 per cent of Rs 295.36 trillion GDP.

Capital formation in India, at current prices, was 29.5 per cent in 2018–19, the last year of Modi 1.0. In 2020–21, it fell to 27.3 per cent of GDP. Thereafter, it began rising and in 2023–24 reached more than 1 per cent higher than the level of 2018–19. In 2021–22, the GFCF was Rs 67.86 trillion, or about $920 billion @ Rs 74 exchange rate, making up 28.9 per cent of Rs 234.71 trillion GDP.

Most of the capital investment in India is funded by domestic savers, primarily the households and corporates. FDI's share in fixed capital formation became still smaller in Modi 2.0.

In 2021–22, FDI inflows were $56.23 billion and, in 2022–23, $42.01 billion. FDI thus contributed, even if it is assumed that the entire FDI got used up in capital formation, only 6.11 per cent of capital formation in 2021–22 and 4.18 per cent in 2022–23.

It turned out to be much worse in 2023–24. For that year, provisional FDI inflows are estimated at $26.55 billion. With GFCF amounting to $1,097 billion, the FDI, at best, ended up contributing less than 2.5 per cent of the fixed capital formation.

More than the quantum of FDI investment in fixed capital formation, it is the quality of FDI investment in capital formation, which matters most in India's context as it brings new technology, management culture and productivity. India was also expected to be a beneficiary of the China Plus One pivot. Unfortunately, the FDI story in Modi 2.0, especially in the last two years, seemed to indicate worrisome portents for India's future economic growth.

Services dominated new FDI

The texture of new FDI flow has massively changed since the onset of the computer-technology revolution. New FDI in manufacturing is receding. Services are taking centre stage. This trend was accentuated during the Modi 2.0 period.

Computer software and hardware (essentially software services as there was very little new FDI in hardware during this period) was the largest new FDI receiving group during the five years of Modi 2.0. The FDI flow into these services was as much as $65.646 billion of the total FDI inflows of $258.843 billion received between 2019–20 and 2023–24. The computer software group, which also included the in-house global capability centres being established by the largest global corporations, received more than one-fourth of total new FDI inflows—25.36 per cent of the total new FDI received during this period. In 2020–21, the FDI inflow in this group was $26.15 billion (as much as 44 per cent of the new FDI of $59.64 billion received that year). The sheer dominance of the computer software (and hardware) group in FDI inflows is breathtaking. While there was a slowdown in FDI inflows after 2020–21, still, in each of the subsequent three years, it made up about 20 per cent of total new FDI inflows.

The DPIIT provides inflow data for the ten largest FDI receiving industry groups. Four of these are now made up of services. Besides, computer software and hardware services, the other three top groups are: a. services sector, which includes financial, banking, insurance, non-financial/business outsourcing, R&D, courier, tech, testing and analysis, etc. (primarily the financial services); b. trading; and c. telecommunications services. These four services received about 50 per cent of all fresh FDI inflows during Modi 2.0—$127.915 billion, which is 49.42 per cent of the total new FDI received.

Telecommunication services contributed significantly in 2019–20 ($4.445 billion). Thereafter, new FDI in telecommunication services ebbed, reflecting the sorry state of affairs in the industry. Trading services, mirroring the foreign investment dominance of e-commerce, continued to be quite strong with inflows between $2.6 to $4.7 billion received every year. Trading FDI inflows in five years was $20.377 billion, which constituted 7.87 per cent of the FDI received during this period.

Together, the top three FDI receiving groups—all services, received $121.415 billion of FDI, which was 46.91 per cent of total FDI inflows of $258.843 billion during Modi 2.0.

The services sector is the strength of India; it is the future of Indian growth. That is very clearly visible in the FDI inflows as well.

PLIs did not show up in the FDI inflows

The PLI on large electronics was expected to boost FDI in telecommunications as well. FDI in telecommunications spurted from 2016–17 when it went up from $1.32 billion in the year before to $5.56 billion.

There was a good show of FDI in telecommunications for the next three years with FDI flows amounting to $6.21 billion, $2.67 billion and $4.45 billion. The telecommunications sector took up the second to fourth position in the top ten FDIs during this period.

Beginning 2020–21, however, the FDI in telecommunications simply disappeared. The FDI fell to a paltry $392 million in 2020–21, was only $668 million in 2021–22 and $773 million in 2022–23. In 2023–24, it fell to $282 million only.

Automobiles, solar cells and modules and batteries were other groups which had seen significant announcements of PLI schemes. However, none of these PLIs actually received accelerating FDI during Modi 2.0.

FDI Policy Liberalization

Lays foundations of FDI regime for start-ups

The Press Note 1 (2022 series) mainstreamed capital instruments used by the start-up industry in the FDI policy.

The definition of capital in para 2.1.5 of the FDI policy was expanded by way of adding a note to the effect that equity shares shall include partly paid equity shares. This relaxation of partly paid was, however, not extended to preference shares and convertible debentures.

Para 2.1.9 was amended to bring in the capital instrument of 'Convertible Note', which has been defined to mean an instrument issued by a start-up company acknowledging receipt of money initially as debt, which is repayable at the option of the holder, or which is convertible into such number of equity shares of such start-up company, within a period not exceeding ten years from the date of issue of the convertible note, upon occurrence of specified events as per the other terms and conditions agreed to and indicated in the instrument. With this amendment, for start-ups, the condition of preference shares and debentures to be compulsorily and fully convertible has been given up.

As many start-ups are set up as limited liability partnerships (LLPs), this press note permitted foreign investment made by a person resident outside India on a repatriable basis in capital instruments of an Indian company or to the capital of an LLP. In case of investment being made by a resident Indian citizen but on declaration that the beneficial interest was held by a person resident outside India, such an investment can also be treated as foreign investment.

As many start-ups provide employee stock ownership plans (ESOP) to their employees/directors, which otherwise are capital instruments, the Press Note 1 (2022) brought in the definition of 'share-based employee benefits', which was defined to mean any issue of capital instruments to employees, pursuant to share-based employee benefit schemes formulated by a body corporate established or constituted by or under any central or state act.

The funding winter and removal of the exemption available to foreign venture capital funds from the angel tax in Budget 2023–24 neutralized relaxations granted to encourage FDI in start-ups.

Local sourcing requirement for single brand retail done away with in a round-about way

FDI of more than 51 per cent in single brand retail trading (SBRT) companies was made subject to the requirement of sourcing 30 per cent of the value of goods procured from India in 2012 when FDI in multi-brand retail trading (MBRT) was permitted. By their very nature, foreign-branded goods are usually imported from abroad and sold under the same international brand in India. The condition of sourcing 30 per cent material, intermediate or associated products from India, therefore, was unimplementable. The SBRT brand holders were also not very keen to bring their products to India with less than 50 per cent ownership for obvious reasons. The government wanted Apple to come and sell iPhone and other iconic products. Apple kept showing interest but did not take concrete steps to establish its brick-and-mortal retail stores.

In September 2019, the government decided to come to the rescue of Apple. The simplest way of doing this was to simply abolish the requirement of local sourcing for SBRT goods. For optical reasons, the government was not willing to do so. Therefore, they decided to adopt a round-about method of enabling the SBRT FDI investor to meet the local sourcing condition without actually using the material sourced in the manufacture of SBRT products.

The Press Note 4 (2019 Series) issued on 18 September 2019, permitted the following avenues to SBRT FDI investors to meet the 30 per cent local sourcing condition nominally. First, the quantum of domestic sourcing was allowed to be done in a self-certified manner. Second, the procurement requirement was allowed to be met over a period of five years at an average of five years' total value of goods procured. In simple words, no questions would be asked until at least five years of SBRTs setting up shop, i.e. opening the first store or start of online retail. Third, all procurement made from India by the SBRT entity would be counted towards local sourcing, irrespective of whether the goods produced were sold in India or exported. Finally, the SBRT entity was permitted to set off sourcing of goods from India for global operations towards the 30 per cent local sourcing condition.

The SBRT entity could literally buy anything from India for use in the name of global operations and simply export it. Once this press note was issued, the subject of 30 per cent local sourcing stopped being of any consequence. The government stopped monitoring whether anything was procured locally for making the SBRT products sold in India.

Apple expanded manufacturing of iPhones in India. From almost no manufacturing in India in 2018–19, Apple increased iPhone manufacturing in India steadily—from Rs 16,750 crore in 2020–21 to about Rs 1.92 trillion in 2023–24.

FDI in insurance sector further liberalized

The government modified the FDI policy in the insurance sector twice in its second term.

In 2020, through the Press Note 1, the government permitted 49 per cent FDI under the automatic route in insurance companies. 100 per cent FDI was permitted under the automatic route in intermediaries or insurance intermediaries, including insurance brokers, re-insurance brokers, insurance consultants, corporate agents, third party administrators, surveyors and loss assessors and such other entities, as may be notified by the IRDA.

There were some other conditions. Insurance companies were not to allow aggregate holdings by way of total foreign investment in its equity shares by foreign investors, including portfolio investors, to exceed 49 per cent of the paid-up equity capital of such insurance companies. The Indian insurance company was also required to ensure that its ownership and control remained at all times in the hands of resident Indian entities.

The FDI policy was further liberalized, through Press Note 2 (2021 series) on 14 June 2021. FDI limit through the automatic route was raised to 74 per cent from 49 per cent. There was no change in the case of insurance intermediaries. The condition relating to the insurance company remaining in Indian hands was made clearer and somewhat sharper. It was specified that, in an Indian insurance company having foreign investment, a majority of its directors, a majority of its key management personnel (KMP) and at least one among the chairperson of the board, its managing director and its chief executive officer should be resident Indian citizens.

Certain restrictions relating to repatriation of dividends and payments to foreign entities were also prescribed. It was enjoined that such insurance companies with FDI should take prior permission of the IRDA for repatriating dividend and making payment to the foreign group or subsidiary or interconnected or associate entities.

The insurance sector continued to be a good recipient of FDI during Modi 2.0.

Facilitating FDI in telecom

On 6 October 2021, through the Press Note 4 (2021 series), the government expanded the definition of telecom services (including telecom infrastructure providers Category I) for 100 per cent FDI through the automatic route.

The liberalized definition included all telecom services, including telecom infrastructure providers category-I, namely, basic, cellular, unified access services (UAS), unified license (access services), unified license, national/international long distance, commercial V-SAT, public mobile radio trunked services (PMRTS), global mobile personal communications services (GMPCS), all types of ISP services, voice mail/audiotext/UMS (unified messaging systems), resale of international private leased circuits (IPLC) mobile number portability services, infrastructure provider category-I (providing dark fibre, right of way, duct space, tower), other service providers and such other services as may be permitted by the Department of Telecommunications (DoT).

As I noted above, FDI in telecommunications kept reducing during Modi 2.0.

FDI in sectors witnessing domestic liberalization

Manufacturing

On 18 September 2019, through the Press Note 4, the government liberalized FDI in manufacturing, which had 100 per cent FDI under the automatic route, to include contract manufacturing (through a legally tenable contract, whether on principal to principal basis or principal to agent basis). Additionally, manufacturing companies receiving FDI were per permitted to sell their products manufactured in India through wholesale and/or retail, including through e-commerce.

No reliable data is available for FDI attracted in contract manufacturing.

Coal and Lignite

On 18 September 2019, through the Press Note 4, the government permitted 100 per cent FDI, through the automatic route, in coal and lignite mining for captive consumption by power projects, iron and steel, cement units and other eligible activities permitted under the Coal Mines (Special Provisions) Act 2015 and the Mines and Minerals (Development and Regulation) Act, 1957.

In the coal and lignite sector, 100 per cent FDI was permitted to set up coal processing plants, such as washeries. This was subject to the condition that the company would not do coal mining and would not sell washed coal or sized coal from its coal processing plants in the open market. It would supply the washed or sized coal to those parties who were supplying raw coal to coal processing plants for washing or sizing.

100 per cent FDI under the automatic route was also permitted in companies established for selling coal and for coal mining activities, including associated processing infrastructure, which covers coal washery, crushing, coal handling and separation (through a magnetic or non-magnetic process).

The government conducted about seven tranches of coal block auctions. No foreign company or investor got (probably no such investor bid for) any coal block.

Defence

Prior to 17 September 2020, FDI in the defence industry, which was subject to industrial licence under Industries Development and Regulation Act (IDRA) 1951 and manufacturing of small arms and ammunition under the Arms Act, 1959, was permitted up to 49 per cent under the automatic route. FDI higher than 49 per cent could be permitted through the government route for investments where it was likely to result in access to modern technology or for other reasons to be recorded.

Through the Press Note 4 (2020 series), the government raised FDI in the defence industry, as defined earlier, to 74 per cent from 49 per cent. FDI higher than 74 per cent could be considered through the government route in cases as permissible earlier.

The government reported inflow of Rs 494 crore in FDI in defence in August 2022. No further press notes were issued.

REITs

The government, through the Press Note 1 (2022 series), also amended the definition of real estate business, in which FDI is not permitted, to exclude real estate investment trusts (REITs), registered and regulated under the SEBI (REITs) Regulations 2014. It was also clarified that earning of rent/income on lease of property, not amounting to transfer, will not amount to real estate business.

FDI in space sector

The government further streamlined and liberalized FDI in the space sector in February-March 2024. The satellites sub-sector was divided into three different activities with defined limits for FDI in each activity. As per the FDI policy prevailing on that date, FDI was permitted in the establishment and operation of satellites through the government approval route only.

Up to 74 per cent FDI was permitted under the automatic route for satellites—manufacturing and operation, satellite data products, and ground segment and user segment. FDI beyond 74 per cent in these activities continued to remain under the government route.

Up to 49 per cent FDI was allowed under the automatic route for launch vehicles and associated systems or subsystems, and creation of spaceports for launching and receiving spacecraft. FDI beyond 49 per cent for these activities remained under the government route and would also require approval of the relevant sectoral regulator.

Up to 100 per cent FDI was permitted under the automatic route for manufacturing of components and systems/sub-systems for satellites, ground segment and user segment.

It was expected that the liberalized FDI regime in the space sector would facilitate integration of Indian companies into global value chains.

FDI liberalization in sectors taken up for privatization

PSU Petroleum Refiners

FDI has been permitted up to 100 per cent through the automatic route for many years in private petroleum and natural gas companies in the entire value chain—from exploration activities to marketing. In the existing oil and gas PSUs, without any divestment or dilution of domestic equity, however, FDI was permissible only up to 49 per cent through the automatic route.

The government put up BPCL for strategic divestment. To facilitate participation of foreign investors in the bidding process, the government brought out Press Note 3 (2021 series) on 29 July 2021 to allow foreign investment up to 100 per cent under the automatic route in case an 'in principle' approval for strategic divestment of a PSU had been granted by the government in the petroleum and gas sector.

This permissible incentive was not good enough to attract foreign investors to BPCL. None provided a serious bid. The government finally cancelled the BPCL privatization.

LIC

The government brought out the IPO of LIC in 2022. To increase demand for LIC shares, FDI was permitted to the extent of 20 per cent under the automatic route in the Life Insurance Corporation (LIC) vide Press Note 1 (2022 series) issued on 14 March 2022.

FDI in insurance companies permissible up to 74 per cent though the automatic route, partly mentioned above, was not strictly applicable to LIC as the maximum FDI permissible was only 20 per cent. The government, therefore, carved out a set of separate conditions for FDI in LIC. Three conditions were prescribed.

The foreign investment in LIC was made subject to compliance with the provisions of the Life Insurance Corporation Act, 1956, as amended and such provisions of the Insurance Act, 1938, as are applicable to the LIC. Like this, there were two other formal and nominal conditions. There was no possibility of any foreign investor acquiring any controlling interest in LIC as only 3½ per cent shares were being issued in the IPO. Even when 20 per cent shares would be divested, the necessity of securing management control in Indian hands, etc., will not really apply to LIC.

Government clamps down on FDI from China

On 17 April 2020, the government issued Press Note 3 (2020 series), modifying FDI policy for investment from China 'for curbing opportunistic takeovers/ acquisitions of Indian companies due to the current Covid-19 pandemic'.

Para 3.1.1 of the FDI Master Circular existing on the date provided that a citizen of Bangladesh or an entity incorporated in Bangladesh could invest only under the government route. Further, a citizen of Pakistan or an entity incorporated in Pakistan could invest only in sectors other than defence, space, atomic energy and prohibited sectors/activities, that too only under the government route.

By the above-mentioned press note, the government, to bring the FDI from China under the government approval route, expanded the stipulation earlier applicable only for Pakistan and Bangladesh. The revised prescription stated that an entity of a country which shares land borders with India or where the beneficial owner of an investment into India is situated in or is a citizen of any such country can invest only under the government route. For Pakistan investors, FDI in defence, space and atomic energy remained impermissible even under the government route.

The government also stipulated that in the event of transfer of beneficial ownership resulting in change inviting the situation mentioned above, such subsequent change in beneficial ownership would also require government approval.

Foreign news entry virtually denied

On 18 September 2019, through the Press Note 4, the government restricted FDI to only 26 per cent, that too under the government approval route, for uploading/streamlining of news and current affairs through digital media.

Portfolio Investment

FDI is sticky. When it comes, it stays. India received, from 2000 onwards, gross FDI of $917 billion (RBI data) up to 2022–23, including the reinvested earnings. While FDI of $220.6 billion got repatriated and disinvested, FDI of $696.7 billion (market value much higher) stayed with the invested companies.

Portfolio investment—the investments made by the non-resident investors in minority stakes—are more opportunistic. The FPIs make investments when they expect the equities to appreciate and sell the same when they believe the markets have matured or expect the market to go down for the foreseeable future for any reason to book their capital gains. The portfolio flows are therefore quite volatile.

They come in hordes when non-residents believe it is the right time to make an entry—the markets have crashed disproportionately, e.g. during the first wave of Covid-19—and they leave in hordes when they believe markets have risen to high levels. Of course, some of the portfolio investment stays on a net basis in any cycle, which has led to the stock of FPIs.

Net portfolio inflows, calculated by adding annual net portfolio flows, as per RBI data were $250.9 billion from 2000–01 to 2022–23. Net inflows are different from the market value thereof which, as noted above, exceeded $770 billion at end 2022–23.

Portfolio investment had a volatile outing

Portfolio inflows were quite robust during Modi 1.0. In these five years, a total net inflow of $67.18 billion came in as portfolio investment through FPIs. The last year of Modi 1.0, however, saw a net sell-off by FPIs, though of only $618 million.

In 2019–20, the pre-Covid-19 year witnessed a small net inflow of $0.552 billion.

The Covid-19 year 2020–21 was a yo-yo year with massive volatility. In the first few months, the FPIs sold off. However, by the middle of 2020–21, the FPIs started to move in and then made it into a big rush. For 2020–21 as a whole, there was a net inflow of a whopping $38.725 billion.

FPIs went into a reverse drive from 2021–22. While in the first few months, FPIs kept investing, by the middle of the year, a hefty sell-off began, resulting in the FPI portfolio witnessing a negative flow of as much as $14.071 billion. The outflow of portfolio investment continued in 2022–23, albeit at a smaller scale. FPIs took away $4.828 billion of portfolio investment in 2022–23.

In the first four years, two (2019–20 and 2020–21) witnessed net portfolio investment inflows of $39.277 billion, whereas the other two (2021–22 and 2022–23) saw net portfolio investment outflows of $18.899 billion. On a net basis, India received foreign portfolio investment of $20.378 billion.

The year 2023–24 witnessed FPIs pouring in, in a big way expecting perhaps the return of Narendra Modi at the head of a still stronger majority. FPIs brought in a whopping $42.880 billion in the year, taking total portfolio investment in Modi 2.0 to $63.258 billion.

Direct listing on GIFT city exchanges

The government had permitted Indian companies to raise equity funds abroad in the form of global depository receipts (GDRs) and American depository receipts (ADRs) from the 1990s. Foreign banks and other investment vehicles would create the depository receipts against the shares purchased and held in India of Indian companies which were subscribed to by overseas investors. Many public companies, including public sector companies, raised funds through these structures. While the popularity of these structures went down, particularly after SEBI started asking for the details of the beneficial owners behind the omnibus holdings of these ADRs/GDRs, there are still some surviving ADRs/GDRs.

In 2014, the government issued a policy direction to permit direct listing of Indian equities abroad. SEBI was to come out with detailed directions and operationalize the same. However, SEBI and the government could not resolve the problems of the omnibus structures and India's requirement of beneficial ownership KYC details.

Indian companies could not raise equity abroad by listing their securities abroad. The government decided in the latter part of 2023–24 to enable Indian companies to list their securities in the Gujarat International Finance Tec-City (GIFT) international exchanges at least to raise equity from non-residents. By the Companies (Amendment) Act, 2020, the government made enabling provisions in the Companies Act, 2013, to allow direct listing and brought these provisions into force with effect from 30 October 2023.

The government amended the Foreign Exchange Management (Non-debt Instruments) Rules, 2019, in January 2024 and notified rules for the Direct Listing of Equity Shares of Companies Incorporated in India on International Exchanges Scheme, i.e. the exchanges established in the international financial centre in the GIFT City, Gujarat. Simultaneously, the government also issued the Companies (Listing of Equity Shares in Permissible Jurisdictions) Rules, 2024, for making enabling provisions in the Companies Act.

This regulatory framework would enable public Indian companies to issue and list their shares in the international exchanges permitted and established in the International Financial Services Centre (IFSC), GIFT City. As of now, two international stock exchanges—India International Exchange and NSE International Exchange—are the permitted stock exchanges.

No securities were listed until the second term of the Modi government was over.

India moves to T+0 settlement

Settlement of trades in the stock exchanges don't take place simultaneously in what is otherwise the mode of payment—delivery versus payment or DvP. The securities have to be brought to the stock exchanges and the payments have to be arranged. In the physical settlement times, this used to take many days. Dematerialization of the securities, introduction of electronic trading and conversion of bank accounts into electronic bank accounts have made near simultaneous settlement of equity trades possible.

In the 1990s, the T+3 days settlement cycle was introduced. India/SEBI introduced T+2 settlement system in 2003, which was uniformly applied to all stock exchanges in India. In 2012, SEBI proposed the idea of T+1 settlement for the first time, which is where the situation stood when the Modi government took over in 2014.

SEBI, from 1 January 2022, provided flexibility to the stock exchanges to offer either the T+1 or T+2 settlement cycle. The stock exchanges were initially allowed to use different settlement options for different scrips. Beginning with the top 100 stocks, the T+1 settlement system was introduced on 25 February 2022 compulsorily. For the next 500 companies, it was introduced from March 2022. The transition to the T+1 settlement cycle for the entire equity market was completed for all the scrips from 27 January 2023.

The ambitions of SEBI to move as close to DvP did not end there. SEBI decided to introduce the T+0 settlement system, albeit on an optional basis, from 28 March 2024. The experiment was done successfully.

SEBI subjects FPIs to tighter disclosures of beneficial ownership

FPIs bring pooled funds of their investors for investment in Indian equities. Equity investment through the portfolio route or the FDI route is no different as far as rights of shareholders are concerned. While the FPI investment limit in a company is pegged at 10 per cent (after which it gets categorized as FDI), a number of conditions attached to the FDIs, such as the applicability of substantial acquisition of shares and takeover regulations or maintaining minimum public shareholdings in the listed companies, are not applicable to portfolio investors.

It is important to know who the natural persons are behind the FPIs. The ownership structures of most of the originating jurisdictions don't require the FPIs to go to the last natural person beneficial owner as well. To ward off the possibility of natural person beneficial owners in FPIs acting singly or in concert in violation of or in avoidance of the regulations made for guarding shareholding transparency or public goods, such as maintaining minimum public shareholding, SEBI tightened the regulations applicable to the FPIs in August 2023.

SEBI amended the regulations to specify that granular details of all entities holding any ownership, economic interest, or exercising control in the FPI, on a full look-through basis, up to the level of all natural persons, without any threshold, should be provided by FPIs holding more than 50 per cent of their Indian equity AUM in a single Indian corporate group and FPIs that individually, or along with their investor group, hold more than Rs 25,000 crore of equity AUM in the Indian markets. FPIs having a broad-based, pooled structure with a widespread investor base, ownership interest by the government or government-related investors, etc., which were seen as not posing any significant systemic risk, were exempted from these regulations.

There was a certain degree of opposition to these disclosure requirements. SEBI, on 21 March 2024, partially relaxed the requirement of making these additional disclosures for FPIs having more than 50 per cent of their Indian equity AUM in a corporate group if: i. the apex company (list to be made public by stock exchanges and depositories) of such corporate group had no identified promoter, ii. the FPI holds not more than 50 per cent of its Indian equity AUM in the corporate group, after disregarding its holding in the concerned apex company and the composite holdings of all such FPIs in the apex company is less than 3 per cent of the total equity share capital of the apex company.

External Commercial Borrowings

The commercial sector in India receives credit financing from domestic as well as foreign sources. The ECBs are an important source of foreign credit funding of the commercial sector. This source is also highly volatile.

ECB flows much higher

During Modi 1.0, there were mostly negative ECB flows in the first four years aggregating to a total of Rs 93,482 crore (RBI statistics). In the last year of the first term—2018–19, the government provided several incentives to encourage flow of ECBs, which resulted in a massive inflow of Rs 69,629 crore that year. For the first term as a whole, ECB inflows were in the negative for an amount of Rs 23,853 crore.

The incentives provided in the first term, such as no withholding tax on interest remittances and the big squeeze in availability of credit from the banks, led to ECB inflows in a massive amount of Rs 1.54 trillion in 2019–20 alone. The government then did away with the incentives, which brought the ECB flows in 2020–21 to a trickle of Rs 874 crore.

As many non-bank finance companies, including those owned by the government, such as PFC and REC, depend upon the flow of ECBs, the ECB funding again increased significantly to Rs 55,218 crore in 2021–22. However, repayment obligations and other considerations led to an outflow of Rs 32,458 crore on the ECB front in 2022–23.

For the first four years of Modi 2.0, India received net positive ECB flows of Rs 1.78 trillion.

Foreign Currency Sovereign Bonds

Foreign investment in GoI bonds declined during Modi 2.0

India did not permit foreign investment in GoI securities before 1991. From the mid-1990s, India began permitting foreign investment in GoI bonds in a cautious and limited way. There was incremental progress over the next fifteen to twenty years with specified categories of non-resident investors permitted to invest in government securities issued by the Centre and the states, though FPIs did not invest in state government securities at all. In 2013, the regime was significantly rationalized. Two broad classes of foreign investors—general and long-term investors—were created. They were permitted to invest in government securities and corporate bonds subject to limits prescribed—overall, for each class of investor and each type of security (GoI securities, state government securities and corporate bonds). The overall investment limit was fixed at $51 billion.

In 2018, the Voluntary Retention Route (VRR) was introduced to provide a less regulated regime for those FPIs that committed bond investment in excess of specified limits. The fully accessible route (FAR) was introduced in March 2020. With this, foreigners could buy and sell GoI bonds issued under FAR, without any restrictions. From 2021–22, all new GoI securities were designated as FAR securities. Until the end of 2023, GoI bonds of about $330 billion were designated FAR securities.

Foreign investment in GoI bonds kept on declining during Modi 2.0. FPIs held, on 31 March 2023, GoI bonds of Rs 1.31 trillion (about $16 billion @Rs 82/$). This amounted to only a little over 1.3 per cent out of the total outstanding GoI bonds of Rs 96.46 trillion (about $1.175 trillion). FPIs' investment in GoI bonds was much higher at Rs 1.43 trillion (about $20 billion @ Rs 73/$) on 31 March 2021, with FPIs commanding a share of 1.9 per cent out of total outstanding securities of Rs 76.34 trillion ($1.045 trillion). In fact, FPIs had the largest investment in GoI bonds in 2018. On 31 March 2018, FPIs owned GoI bonds of Rs 2.35 trillion ($36.30 billion @Rs 65/$) out of total outstanding securities of Rs 53.97 trillion ($830 billion), giving them a share of 4.4 per cent. It is worth noting that FPIs' holding of GoI bonds more than halved in five years (from $36 billion in 2018 to $16 billion in 2023).

FPI investment in GoI bonds depends on a few key parameters. The net dollar interest rate on the dollar-invested but in rupee-denominated GoI bonds (the coupon rate minus hedging cost) is the first key parameter. Depreciation of capital invested on maturity/sale of GoI bonds in dollars on account of rupee depreciation is the other. Appreciation of FPI investment until March 2018 and the steady decline thereafter (from $36 billion to $16 billion) is explained by the above two key factors.

Inclusion in JP Morgan Emerging Markets Bond Index (JPM-EMBI)

India has been exploring the possibility to get its GoI bonds included in the global bond indices for quite some time—at least since 2015. Two problems had proved to be intractable . One, restrictions like category-wise and security-wise limits on purchase/holding/sale on FPIs for investing in GoI bonds. The bond indices cannot work with such limits/constraints. Two, the insistence of the index providers to settle the bond transactions through Euroclear. In the last few years, the demand for tax exemption was also added. The FAR regime removed the first constraint. The bond index makers held out longer for Euroclear until JPM-EMBI blinked (other bond indices are still insisting). JPM-EMBI has also abandoned the tax exemption demand.

On 22 September 2023, the long-awaited announcement of including GoI securities/bonds (GoI bonds) in the JPM-EMBI finally materialized. With about $240 billion riding on the JPM-EMBI and the promised weight of 10 per cent in the index, the prospects of about $24 billion inflows coming to India in 2024–25 brightened (index inclusion has started in June 2024 with 1 per cent weight, which will rise to 10 per cent over the next nine months, i.e. until March 2025).

Indian policymakers heaved a sigh of relief more on account of the fact that the inclusion happened without the government providing any undue concession, such as exempting the withholding tax on interest/capital gains of the GoI bonds purchased through the index-aligned funds/vehicles. Hopes of this inflow providing a positive impact on the rupee have also been raised. The investment bankers and bond market wholeheartedly welcomed the development as well. The inclusion is undoubtedly significant.

Index-based investment is not influenced by the two factors highlighted above. Therefore, the inclusion in JPM-EMBI will surely bring in $24 billion of inflows. This was expected to take FPI investment in GoI bonds to about $40 billion by March 2024.

With inclusion in the JPM-EMBI, the present available routes for FPI investment (VRR, FAR, etc.) will turn into only alternative modes to the index route. With index-based bond investment becoming the global fashion, it is quite likely that FPI investment through the existing routes will get emasculated. FPI investment of $16 billion at the end of March 2023 was also expected to see a partial conversion in JPM-EMBI-based investment. Outflows of $5 billion–$10 billion from the existing FPI investments could not, therefore, be ruled out.

JPM-EMBI inclusion opened the path of GoI bonds' inclusion in global bond indices. In March 2024, the Bloomberg Index Services announced the inclusion of Indian sovereign bonds in the Bloomberg Emerging Market Local Currency Index and related indices in a phased manner from 31 January 2025.

At the end of December 2023, the RBI reported that the share of FPIs in the GoI securities rose to 1.92 per cent (from 1.36 per cent at end-March 2023). As the outstanding government securities at end-December 2023 were Rs 105.39 trillion ($1.27 trillion), FPIs were holding government bonds of $24.4 billion.

The impact of inclusion in bond indices was beginning to show up.

Real answer is Foreign Currency Sovereign Bonds

Despite inclusion in the JPM-EMBI index, the fundamental constraints associated with rupee-denominated GoI bonds still remain.

Foreigners make investments in dollars (other currencies). What matters to them are the total returns from investment in GoI bonds *in their currencies.* The losses and costs associated with conversion of dollars/foreign currencies at the time of purchase of rupee-denominated government securities, receipt of interest/returns and capital return at the time of sale would not go away upon inclusion in the JPM-EMBI. These will continue to impact the investors' total returns.

These constraints can only be overcome when India issues foreign currency-denominated sovereign bonds. Such sovereign bonds were announced in the 2019–20 Budget. The government, however, could not implement the announcement. India is the only G20 country which does not issue foreign currency-denominated bonds. India's real global bond inclusion and integration would happen only when India musters courage and begins issuing dollar/foreign currency-denominated GoI bonds.

13

Global Economic Integration

India's global economic and financial interactions with the rest of the world are best summarized in a statement, India's External Investment Position (EIP), which the RBI publishes quarterly. The statement provides details of the economic and financial assets that Indians hold in the rest of the world and the liabilities that India is subject to concerning the non-residents—both NRIs and the foreigners included.

India's external investment liabilities exceed India's external investment assets by a good margin, even after factoring in India's foreign currency reserves. As on 30 September 2023, India's external investment liabilities were $1,313.7 billion, whereas the private/non-reserve external investment assets and foreign currency reserves were $345.10 billion and $587.7 billion respectively, in all, $932.80 billion. India's external liabilities exceeded external assets by $380.90 billion as on 30 September 2023.

India's external liabilities are both in equity assets holdings and the debt India owes to the rest of the world. The EIP statement records both equity and debt flows in terms of net outstanding flows, not in terms of their market values. The FDI and FPI equity ownership of non-residents reflected in the EIP is thus far less than the market value of equity AUM. As per the EIP, India's equity liabilities (FDI plus FPI) were $652.30 billion ($497.7 billion in FDI and $154.6 billion in portfolio). Details of the market value of FDI equity assets owned by foreigners is not available anywhere at one place. The market value of foreign portfolio equity assets as on 30 September 2023 alone was $651.19 billion (NSDL data).

The outstanding liabilities position is reflected in more current values as the external debt rotates much faster. On 31 March 2023, as per the EIP, it was $637.20 billion. The government and the RBI publish a separate statement on the status of India's external debt. This statement provides detailed information about official and private debt, long-term and short-term debt and further break-up of official and private debt. As per RBI data, India's external debt stood at $624.65 billion as on 31 March 2023. There is quite a close correspondence between the two data sets.

Finally, the break-up of India's foreign exchange reserves in foreign currency assets, gold holdings of the RBI, India's special drawing rights (SDRs) holdings and India's reserve tranche position in IMF. India's foreign exchange reserves stood at $578.45 billion on 31 March 2023.

External Financial Integration

Good growth in foreign exchange reserves

India's foreign exchange reserves were $412.87 billion at the end of Modi 1.0 in 2018–19. The reserves increased to $578.45 billion after four years in 2022–23, recording an annual growth of 8.8 per cent. As on 29 March 2024 (the last working day of the financial year), India's foreign exchange reserves stood at $645.583 billion, which taken at the year-end 2023–24 level, meant that India's foreign exchange reserves grew by a handsome rate of 9.35 per cent per annum in the Modi 2.0 period.

The foreign exchange reserves had recorded massive increases in the first two years of Modi 2.0. At the end of 2020–21, the foreign currency reserves stood at $576.98, about 40 per cent higher than the reserves at the end of 2018–19. This was on the back of massive inflow of FDI as well as portfolio investment in 2020–21.

The foreign exchange reserves had continued to gather momentum well into 2021–22 as well. On 14 January 2022, the foreign exchange reserves reached the highest level of $634.97 during Modi 2.0 (until 1 February 2024). However, for various reasons, including the rise in oil prices and fall in equity prices on the stock exchange, the reserves fell to $607.31 billion by the end of FY 2021–22. The foreign exchange reserves fell further in 2022–23. The reserves remained virtually flat between 2020–21 and 2022–23, amounting to only $578.45 billion at the end of 2022–23 against reserves of $576.98 at the end of 2020–21.

There was a good accretion in foreign exchange reserves in March 2024. As on 1 March 2024, the reserves were $625.63 billion. On 29 March, the foreign exchange reserves rose to $645.58 billion. In a month, foreign exchange reserves rose by as much as $20 billion. It seemed the RBI wanted to build up the reserves to its highest level and depreciate the rupee-dollar exchange rate somewhat. The RBI bought quite aggressively in the last few working days and achieved its objectives.

SDRs and gold contributed a larger share

The IMF allocates its accounting currency special drawing rights (SDRs) to member countries, which, if held by the countries concerned, become part of their foreign exchange reserves. India held SDRs equivalent to $1.46 billion at the end of Modi1.0.

In 2021, the IMF successfully carried out a general increase of SDRs. India got 12,569.6 million SDRs in this quota increase, which at the exchange rate of $1.42 to an SDR, amounted to approximately $17.85 billion. This allocation increased India's SDR holdings to $18.89 billion at the end of FY 2021–22. India's SDR holdings were valued at $18.145 billion on 29 March 2024. The SDR holdings recorded a CAGR of 65.60 per cent in the five years of Modi 2.0.

The RBI has been consistently buying gold for its monetary/foreign exchange purposes since 2018. The RBI has now started disclosing its gold holdings in physical quantities as well. Between 2018 and 2023, primarily in the second term of the Modi government, the RBI bought gold of about 240 tonnes to raise its gold reserves to 817 tonnes as on 23 February 2024. The gold reserves valued at $52.16 billion on 29 March 2024 rose by $29.09 billion over the gold reserves of $23.07 billion at end-March 2019 and recorded a CAGR of 17.72 per cent during Modi 2.0.

The principal foreign currency reserves, which make up the bulk of foreign exchange reserves (about 90 per cent) had a relatively smaller growth of 8.17 per cent per annum during this five-year period, increasing from $385.36 billion at end-March 2019 to $570.62 billion on 29 March 2024. The last component of the foreign exchange reserves—India's reserve tranche position, primarily reflecting India's lending to the IMF for its operation—was much smaller at $4.66 billion at the end of FY 2023–24.

Foreign exchange reserves growth was not unprecedented

India had foreign exchange currency reserves of $304.22 billion at the end of 2013–14, just before the Modi government took over in May 2014. India's foreign currency reserves grew to $412.87 billion at end-March 2019 on the eve of the end of Modi 1.0. India's foreign exchange reserves grew by an annual growth rate of 6.30 per cent per annum during the first term.

This performance was far better than the reserves accumulation performance of the second tenure of the Manmohan Singh-led UPA government. In its five-year tenure, the foreign exchange reserves had grown from $251.99 billion at the end of FY 2008–09 to $304.22 billion at the end of 2013–14, recording a small growth of 3.84 per cent per annum. The second term of the UPA government had faced big turmoil in international currency markets, most famously known as the taper tantrum, which was partially responsible for arresting the growth of reserves.

The first term of the Manmohan Singh-led UPA government was, however, completely different from the foreign exchange accretion perspective. The Singh-led UPA-I had assumed leadership when the foreign exchange reserves were only

$112.96 billion (at the end of FY 2003–04). As the foreign exchange reserves grew to $251.99 billion at the end of FY 2008–09, the Singh-led UPA-I recorded a fabulous growth rate of 17.41 per cent per annum in those five years.

The Modi government accumulated foreign exchange reserves of $341.36 billion in ten years (2014–24) at an annual growth rate of 7.81 per cent per annum. The Manmohan Singh government added $191.26 billion of foreign exchange reserves in ten years (2004–14) at an annual growth rate of 10.41 per cent.

Over a full two-term tenure, the foreign exchange reserves accumulated at a higher growth rate per annum during the Manmohan Singh government than during the Modi government.

Excellent control of external debt

The Indian government borrows from multilateral lenders, such as the World Bank and the Asian Development Bank (ADB), and from bilateral lenders, such as the German KfW and others. The private sector borrows commercially from international lenders and also by issuing securities. A country's total external debt, both public and private, matter from the foreign exchange vulnerability perspective.

India's gross external debt outstanding on 31 March 2019 was $543.14 billion. The long-term debt (of more than one year residual maturity) was $434.72 billion. India's external debt grew to $624.65 billion at the end of FY 2022–23, recording a very low growth rate of 3.56 per cent per annum. The Modi government had recorded a similarly low growth rate of 4.01 per cent per annum in its first term as well when the external debt had grown from $446.18 billion in 2013–14 to $543.14 billion in 2018–19.

The uncontrolled increase in external debt during the entire UPA government period was primarily responsible for the taper tantrum in 2013. India's external debt was only $112.65 billion at the end of FY 2003–04. This external debt ballooned to $224.50 billion by the end of 2008–09, recording annual growth of 14.79 per cent per annum. Similarly, in the second term of the Singh-led UPA government, the outstanding external debt increased to $446.18 billion at the end of 2013–14, again recording an unsustainably high annual growth rate of 14.73 per cent per annum.

The UPA government added $333.53 billion to India's outstanding external debt in its ten years of government (2004–14), recording a big 14.76 per cent growth per year. The Modi government, on the other hand, has been extremely conservative and sensitive in not expanding the external debt. The external debt increased by only $178.48 billion during the nine years (2014–23) of the Modi government, recording a modest growth rate of 3.81 per cent per annum.

Commercial borrowings-financed investment expansion was primarily responsible for the big foreign exchange vulnerability created during the UPA period. External commercial borrowings grew from $22 billion in March 2004 to $62.46 billion in March 2009, rising by a whopping 23.20 per cent per annum. The growth of ECBs remained uncomfortably high in the second term of the UPA government as well, with outstanding commercial borrowings zooming to $149.35 billion by end-March 2014, again recording a hefty growth of 19.05 per cent per annum. For the ten-year period of the UPA, ECBs multiplied about seven times, recording a back-breaking growth of 21.11 per cent per annum.

In contrast, ECBs increased to only $216.56 billion at end-FY 2018–19 and $221.98 billion at end-FY 2022–23. ECBs recorded growth of only 1.91 per cent in the first four years of Modi 2.0 and 4.50 per cent in nine years. The firm control over ECBs by the Modi government ensured that India's external account remained largely unruffled.

External investment account liabilities witnessed subdued growth

India's external investment account liabilities are almost entirely private, though the government borrows from multilateral and bilateral institutions. The RBI breaks down these external liabilities in three major buckets of direct investment, portfolio investment and other liabilities. These broad buckets have further equity and debt-related divisions. These liabilities are recorded in terms of stock building up by accumulation of annual net flows. These are not based on the market values.

As at end-March 2019, India's total external investment account liabilities were $1,078.6 billion. These liabilities increased to $1,389.98 billion at the end of FY 2023–24 at a muted annual rate of growth of 5.20 per cent.

The direct investment liabilities were $399.2 billion at end-March 2019 (break-up in equity and debt securities is not available for the year). Direct investment liabilities grew to $542.52 billion, comprising equity and investment fund securities of $511.14 billion and debt securities of $31.37 billion at the end of March 2024. Outstanding direct equity-oriented liabilities recorded an annual growth rate of 6.33 per cent.

As selling and buying of securities at current market prices results in portfolio investment liabilities to the extent of the net of sales and purchases, the greater sell-off by the FPIs in the first four years of Modi 2.0 resulted in the book value of portfolio investment liabilities actually going down during this period before regaining the 2018–19 level in 2023–24. The outstanding portfolio investment liabilities were of the order of $260.3 billion, comprising $147.50 billion of equity portfolio and $112.8 billion of debt securities portfolio at the end of 2018–19. While the outstanding portfolio grew to $278.5 billion in March 2021, it came down to $243.5 billion at the end of March 2023, before recovering to $283.81 billion ($168.7 billion equity and $115.1 billion debt securities) at the end of March 2024. The portfolio liabilities recorded a tepid growth rate of 1.74 per cent per annum.

The other external investment liabilities include trade credits, commercial loans, currency and deposits and other liabilities. These liabilities increased from $419.10 billion at the end of 2018–19 to $563.66 billion in 2023–24, again recording a somewhat higher annual growth of 6.11 per cent.

External investment assets saw better growth

India is not a major foreign direct investor. Nor does India's policy and legal regime permit residents to acquire portfolio assets abroad. As a result, the extent of external assets owned by resident Indians is relatively small. At the end of FY 2018–19, the external investment assets owned by Indian residents amounted to $228.80 billion only, about 21 per cent of the external investment liabilities.

The external investment assets of resident Indians grew to $381.88 billion at an annual growth rate of 10.8 per cent. The direct investment assets at the end of March 2024—overseas direct investment or ODI and investment in overseas debt securities by Indians—at $242.27 billion constituted the largest component (almost 64 per cent) of the external assets portfolio.

Indian's presence in the portfolio investment segment is almost non-existent. The outstanding equity portfolio, on 31 March 2024, stood at only $8.5 billion and that of debt securities at $1.8 billion—in all $10.2 billion. The portfolio investment assets of non-residents (RBI book value) on that date were about twenty-eight times at $283.8 billion.

The other assets—trade credits, commercial loans, currency and deposits and other liabilities—external portfolio of Indians was also quite small at $129.33 billion at the end of 2023–24.

Wide gap between cost of liabilities and assets

The total external assets portfolio of India (other than foreign currency reserves) aggregated to $381.88 billion at the end of FY 2023–24. The external liabilities portfolio on that day was $1,390 billion. External liabilities exceeded external assets by a whopping $1,008.10 billion. The external liabilities and assets gap was almost three times the external assets.

India had built up $646.42 billion of foreign exchange reserves by the end of 2023–24. The reserves, owned by the government/RBI exceeded the total privately owned foreign assets by as much as $264.54 billion.

India's foreign exchange reserves have been built from the external capital flows, which is what constitutes India's external investment liabilities. The external account investment liabilities impose two costs: the cost of interest/return differential and the cost of foreign exchange depreciation. India's foreign exchange reserves earn for the RBI and the government much smaller interest/returns than the interest/returns which the Indians pay for the capital flows in equity and debt.

The broader external investment account position indicates the status of capital and technology wealth of the country. The countries, other than the natural resources exporters, with external liabilities exceeding external assets are largely capital and technology-dependent countries.

International Alliances

International Solar Alliance (ISA)

The vision of ISA, set up in 2015 on the sidelines of the Paris Climate Agreement, is grand: Let us make the sun brighter and the mission very appealing—Every home, no matter how far away, will have a light at home. The ISA claims to be promoting a green grid initiative on the notion of 'One Sun, One World, One Grid'.

India is the founder promoter of the ISA and has committed to fund 50 per cent of its cost. From the latest available Annual Report 2023, 119 countries have signed the ISA Framework Agreement and ninety-seven countries have become its members after signing and ratifying the ISA framework.

ISA, at the very initial stage, adopted a goal for mobilizing $1 trillion investment support for solar programmes in the member countries by 2030. It claims to have developed a strategic plan for the purpose. Its achievements have, however, been quite modest. By December 2022, as per its annual report, ISA had mobilized only $80 million (not billion) of investment support in member countries. It seems to have reconciled to a more modest goal of deploying $300 million of investment support by 2026 (Annual Report 2023). It would be quite an achievement if the ISA is able to mobilize investment support of $1 billion by 2030.

ISA seems to have lost its acceptance in member countries. In 2021, it received only $1,104 in contributions. In 2022, it received no contributions. It had small other income of 0.382 million in 2022. ISA's expenditures, though modest, were disproportionately large at $6.64 million. ISA's deficit was as high as $6.26 million in 2022.

ISA provides modest programmatic support. In its eight years of existence, it made less than $10 million in programme support. ISA hosted its fifth regional meeting in Kigali, Rwanda on 31 August 2023. Nine solar power demonstration projects, established through grants given by the ISA, were remotely inaugurated by India's Power Minister. These nine projects cost less than $1,50,000.

The ISA is grandiose in talk but quite small on the ground.

Coalition for Disaster Resilient Infrastructure (CDRI)

The CDRI, launched by PM Modi at the 2019 UN Climate Action Summit, has thirty members. It aims to promote resilience of infrastructure systems to climate and disaster risks, thereby ensuring sustainable development.

India is almost fully funding CDRI with a grant of about $64 million. CDRI operations have been quite small. It spends about $1 million a year, mostly in management salary and travel. CDRI has published its 2022–23 report as I close this book. It still exists. The short financial statement says it utilized $3.93 million during the year.

India–Middle-East–Europe Economic Corridor (IMEC)

On the sidelines of the G20 Leaders' Summit in New Delhi on 9 September, the IMEC was launched in the presence of leaders of the US, European Union (EU), France, Germany, Italy, Mauritius, the UAE and Saudi Arabia, as also the World Bank. An MOU on IMEC was signed by India, the US, Saudi Arabia, the UAE, EU, Italy, France and Germany without disclosing its details.

The IMEC was envisaged to connect India with Europe though the corridor's directions are set more in terms of Saudi Arabia and the UAE than India. The IMEC will comprise an Eastern Corridor connecting India to the Gulf region and a Northern Corridor connecting the Gulf region to Europe. The Gulf region is west of India but the connecting corridor was called the Eastern Corridor! The IMEC was not envisaged to be an all-land corridor as Pakistan sits between India and the Gulf region. The IMEC will be a mix of railway, ship-rail transit network and road transport routes.

These are the only sketchy details shared about the IMEC at its launch without any feasibility and economic viability study having been done! No comparative study was available to establish how this corridor will be more efficient and economically cheaper than the current transportation network through the Suez Canal. As there is an absence of any rail networks in the Gulf region and unstable territories between the Gulf and Europe, much of the investment for building the new rail network perhaps was to come from Saudi Arabia and other Gulf countries.

India had, in 2002, envisaged an International North South Transport Corridor (INSTC) linking India to Europe via Iran, Central Asia and Russia. The Modi government had been making a lot of effort to get this corridor going before the IMEC was launched, though there was no real progress.

The IMEC was also spoken of as an alternative to the Chinese Belt and Road Initiative (BRI). Not much has been heard about the IMEC since its launch ceremony. The Israel-Gaza conflict seems to have put further spokes in the way of the IMEC.

Global Biofuels Alliance (GBA)

PM Modi launched the GBA in the presence of leaders from Singapore, Bangladesh, Italy, the USA, Brazil, Argentina, Mauritius and the UAE, in an impressive show on the sidelines of the G20 Leaders' Summit 2023 hosted by India in New Delhi. Nineteen countries and twelve international organizations were reported to have agreed to join. The GBA will take on OPEC, asserted the Petroleum Minister after it was launched.

Biofuels—ethanol and bio-diesel, substitutes of petrol and diesel—have gained good traction in the world grappling to find answers for high prices and environmental unsuitability of hydrocarbons. India has primarily focused on ethanol.

The US is the leader in biofuels with over 50 per cent of global production, followed closely by Brazil with about 30 per cent of global production. India has only 3 per cent of the global biofuels share. Both the US and Brazil have large and durable surplus grains and other plantation materials to produce biofuels. Both are also self-sufficient in and exporters of hydrocarbons. India, on the contrary, does not have a steady surplus of grains/sugarcane to make ethanol. We are a big importer of crude oil and gas.

The US and Brazil did not take the lead for creating any global biofuel alliance; India did. Consequently, India will provide all the initial capital for setting up the GBA. Even with 20 per cent of petrol substitution by ethanol, India can at best reduce the demand for petroleum products by 4 per cent.

The objectives of the GBA are quite unspecific. It will expedite the global uptake of biofuels by facilitating technology advancements—it says. Will it fund technology development? Brazil has already developed cars that run on 100 per cent ethanol. The technology development is hugely capital-intensive. The GBA can never have resources to fund technology development.

That the GBA will shape robust standards setting and certification is stated as another objective. Setting fuel standards is quite complex and there are highly sophisticated and well-capitalized standard-setting bodies already in place. The GBA cannot do any standard-setting.

The GBA's true future was stated at the end of the press release: 'GBA will be offering capacity-building exercises across the value chain, technical support for national programs and promoting policy lessons-sharing.'

Again, nothing much has been heard about the GBA after its launch.

International Trade Agreements

India signs three trade agreements

India had ten regional trade agreements (RTAs)/free trade agreements (FTAs) with various countries/regions, which included Japan, South Korea, countries of the ASEAN region and countries of the South Asian Association for Regional Cooperation (SAARC) when the Modi government took office in 2014. In the first term, the Modi government was not much in favour of signing trade/economic cooperation agreements.

There was a policy shift in the second term. The government managed to sign three new trade agreements. The India–Mauritius Comprehensive Economic Cooperation and Partnership Agreement (CECPA) came into effect from 10 April 2021, the India–UAE Comprehensive Economic Partnership Agreement (CEPA) from 1 May 2022 and the India–Australia Economic Cooperation and Trade Agreement (Ind–Aus ECTA) with effect from 2 April 2022.

India and Mauritius signed the CECPA on 22 February 2021, which was the first trade agreement signed by India with a country in Africa. The agreement was described as 'a limited agreement'. The CECPA covered 310 export items for India, including foodstuff and beverages (eighty lines) and agricultural products (twenty-five lines). Mauritius was expected to benefit from preferential market access into India for its 615 products, including frozen fish and speciality sugar. With respect to trade in services, Indian service providers will have access to around 115 sub-sectors from the eleven broad service sectors, such as professional services, computer-related services and telecommunication. India offered around ninety-five sub-sectors from the eleven broad services sectors, including professional services and R&D.

The India–UAE CEPA was described as the first deep and full free trade agreement to be signed by India with any country in the past decade. The CEPA is a comprehensive agreement which covers almost all the tariff lines dealt in by India (11,908 tariff lines) and the UAE (7,581 tariff lines), respectively. India is expected to benefit from preferential market access provided by the UAE on over 97 per cent of its tariff lines, which account for 99 per cent of Indian exports to the UAE in value terms, including labour-intensive sectors. India offered preferential access to the UAE on over 90 per cent of its tariff lines, including lines of export interest to the UAE. As regards trade in services, India has offered market access to the UAE in around 100 sub-sectors, while Indian service providers will have access to around 111 sub-sectors from the eleven broad service sectors. Both sides also agreed to a separate annex on pharmaceuticals to facilitate access of Indian pharmaceuticals products, especially automatic registration and marketing authorization in ninety days for products meeting specified criteria.

The India–Australia ECTA was described as the first trade agreement of India with a developed country after more than a decade. The agreement encompassed cooperation across the entire gamut of bilateral economic and commercial relations between the two countries, and covered areas usually covered in trade agreements, such as trade in goods, rules of origin, trade in services, technical barriers to trade (TBT), sanitary and phytosanitary (SPS) measures, dispute settlement, movement of natural persons, etc. Eight subject-specific side letters covering various aspects of bilateral economic cooperation were also concluded as part of the agreement. The ECTA between India and Australia covered almost all the tariff lines dealt in by the two countries. India will benefit from preferential market access provided by Australia on 100 per cent of its tariff lines, which include all the labour-intensive sectors of export interest to India. India offered preferential access to Australia on over 70 per cent of its tariff lines, including lines of export interest to Australia, which are primarily raw materials and intermediaries such as coal, mineral ores, wines, etc. As regards trade in services, Australia has offered wide-ranging commitments in around 135 sub-sectors and most favoured nation (MFN) status in 120 sub-sectors which cover key areas of India's interest, such as IT and ITES. India has offered market access to Australia in around 103 sub-sectors and MFN status in thirty-one sub-sectors from the eleven broad service sectors, such as business services and communication services.

India had earlier walked out of the Regional Comprehensive Economic Partnership (RCEP) in 2019. Signing these three agreements indicated that India was getting interested in reducing its trade isolation. These trade agreements were too new to have any appreciable impacts during Modi 2.0.

Important trade negotiations remained inconclusive

India undertook negotiations with many other countries, including the UK, Canada, Bangladesh, Israel and the EU to conclude trade/comprehensive economic agreements with these countries during the Modi 2.0 period. While several rounds of discussions/negotiations were held, none of these agreements could be concluded by the time the Modi government completed its second term.

Many rounds of trade negotiations, including at the ministerial levels, had been held between India and Canada to conclude a free trade agreement. Around June 2023, the two countries announced that they were close to initialling the agreement during the year. However, on 1 September 2023, Canada announced a pause on talks on the proposed trade treaty with India. 'Trade negotiations are long, complex processes. And we've paused to take stock of where we are,' a Canadian government official said. The talks remained suspended thereafter.

The India–EU Free Trade Agreement (EU FTA) is under negotiation for ages. The third High Level Dialogue (HLD) for the EU FTA was held on 26 August 2023. During the discussion, the ministers took stock of the ongoing three negotiations between India and the EU, i.e. India–EU Free Trade Agreement, a standalone Investment Protection Agreement, and a Geographical Indications Agreement. It was apprised that both sides made good progress in all three negotiations. On 19 February 2024, India and the EU started the seventh round of negotiations in New Delhi. A lot of talks and negotiations but no firm step was taken towards conclusion of the India–EU FTA in ten years of the Modi government

There is greater urgency and mutual necessity to conclude the UK–India Free Trade Agreement (FTA) as the UK, after Brexit, has no bilateral trade agreement with India to regulate and promote trade between two traditionally enjoined countries. The Prime Ministers of the two countries have got involved at several stages and deadlines for concluding and signing the same were also fixed. The thirteenth round of negotiations for the UK–India FTA took place from 18 September to 15 December 2023. The round included sessions both in person, in London and Delhi, and virtual talks. As with round twelve, these negotiations focused on complex issues, including goods, services and investment. The fourteenth round of negotiations began in January 2024 but was officially closed in the middle of March by putting formal negotiations on hold as India headed into election campaign mode after the general election schedule was announced on 14 March. It was indicated that the talks would resume only after the elections.

The FTA with Sri Lanka remained in discussion. No mention was made of the FTA with Israel in the year-end 2023 information note issued by the government.

G20 Presidency

G20's original objectives have got diluted

The G20 Summit at the Presidents/Prime Ministers level was born in the global financial crisis in 2008 to coordinate immediate rescue of the international financial system and find durable solutions for its stability to generate sustained economic growth.

In the last fifteen years, the G20 did succeed in delivering at least three major real deals. First, quick and functional coordination smothered the global financial crisis and spawned new institutions and rules to bring about better financial stability. Second, the G20 built consensus on major taxation reforms and ushered in a Multilateral Convention on Base Erosion and Profit Shifting (BEPS-MLI) as well as agreements on minimum taxation of multinational corporations and taxation of the digital economy. Third, it did thrash out deals for infusion of capital in the World Bank and the IMF.

The G20 Leaders' Summit, however, got diverted into numerous other tracks—growth, taxation, trade, global warming, financial inclusion, infrastructure, digital economy, terrorism, money laundering and everything under the sun. Instead of finding solutions for the big and pressing economic and financial problems, it degenerated into a body that produced a lot of verbiage.

The character of G20 has also changed

The US was the most powerful economy in 2008 with $14.6 trillion GDP. China was a fast-growing but a relatively smaller economy with $4.5 trillion GDP. In 2023, with GDPs of about $26 trillion and $19 trillion respectively, the US and China are the two biggest and equally powerful economies.

The US–China trade war since 2018 and the Ukraine–Russia war in 2022 have upended the global supply chains and created two rival camps in G20. The US decision to impound Russian foreign exchange reserves and the joint US–EU decision to impose sanctions converted the G20 into two solid US–European and Chinese–Russian camps. The G20 now mirrors more trade, financial and currency competition and confrontation than coordination and cooperation.

The American regional banking system was in crisis in early 2023, impacting the global start-up ecosystem. The Indian Presidency was not bothered to coordinate and find solutions. In line with the G20 ethos, India also picked up its priorities for its Presidency. There was no real deal on any of these priorities.

The establishment of new powerful China-led multilateral development banks (MDBs)—Asian Infrastructure Investment Bank (AIIB) and New Development Bank (NDB)—and alternative global development assistance frameworks, e.g. the Chinese BRI, will further divide the G20. The G20 has already transformed from an action forum to a formal forum. In times to come, it might cease to exist.

India could not push on tough agenda

India's push for expanding the commitment on phasing-down coal to phasing-down hydrocarbons had to be dropped. Progress on the climate finance commitment of $100 billion remained stalled.

On re-capitalization of the MDBs, the Summers-N.K. Singh duo did produce a report recommending inclusion of global public goods as the third mandate for the MDBs and tripling of finance. The G20 communique merely left it to them to deal with the recommendations as they wanted.

India thought of playing a good Samaritan for finding a solution for the bilateral debt of low-income countries (LICs). The Chinese have a big chunk of it and refused to play ball, resulting in no traction. India wanted India's UPI accepted as the global best practice of digital public infrastructure (DPI). As the payment systems of many G20 members run more on credit cards and QR codes, they were nice but refused to bring DPI at the centre of payment systems.

On cryptocurrency, the status remained where it was when India's Presidency began. The failure to cut any new deal or make any significant breakthrough was not on account of any lack of effort by the Indian negotiators. The very nature of G20 and its increasingly dysfunctional character explain the surfeit of words and absence of action.

India made a good show of its G20 Presidency

India's Presidency delivered the consensus G20 New Delhi Leaders' Declaration on Day 1 of the meeting itself on 9 September 2023 and ushered in the African Union as a member of G20.

India also rustled up and announced two new international alliances— India–Middle-East–Europe Economic Corridor and the Global Biofuel Alliance.

India produced the longest-ever Leaders' Declaration with eighty-three paragraphs and thirty-nine annexed documents running into thousands of pages. However, there was no single ready-to-implement agreement/actionable point in it.

To make the best of the G20 Presidency, India decided to showcase it more for the domestic constituency. The notion of *Vasudhaiv Kutumbkam*, converted into a catchy logo 'One Earth, One Family, One Future' and many other events were used to drive home the point that the world was listening to India's civilizational ethos and leadership.

The 200-odd meetings of G20 ministers and working groups organized in many Indian cities, with roads and buildings decked up and visitors treated to the best of Indian cuisine and travel, showcased G20 to the Indian masses. India did create a big buzz around its Presidency.

It was no big deal, though.

Climate Engagement

Copenhagen promise remains unredeemed

The Copenhagen declaration committed the developed North 'to a goal of mobilizing jointly $100 billion a year by 2020 to address the needs of developing countries' (extended to 2025 by the Paris Agreement). As it happens in these negotiations, the commitment was couched in unspecific language.

At one place in the Copenhagen accord, the commitment was 'to provide new and additional resources'. It was also promised that 'a significant portion of such funding should come through the Copenhagen Green Climate Fund'. Developing countries hung on to this and expected industrialized countries to provide additional development assistance mostly in grant and concessional form. Later in the declaration, a somewhat dilutionary language was used to record that 'this funding will come from a wide variety of sources, public and private, bilateral and multilateral, including alternative sources of finance'. There has been massive wrangling over the definition of climate finance and the import of the $100 billion a year pledge. The developed North goes by the report which the Organization for Economic Co-operation and Development (OECD) produces annually, counting how many green dollars have flowed in.

The OECD report released on 29 May 2024 claimed that $115.9 billion was delivered against the $100 billion pledge in 2022, exceeding the commitment. The OECD counts funds flow through four sources: multilateral finance (multilateral funding tagged as climate finance as per their definition in the ratio of the shareholding of developed countries), bilateral finance (official development assistance—ODA, including concessional credit, aimed at serving climate finance objectives), export credits for green projects (though minuscule) and private finance (private debt and equity invested in green projects of developing countries).

There is very little new and additional grant finance in the climate finance claimed to have been delivered. Multilateral agencies, such as the World Bank and ADB, have directed a higher part of their normal financing for development projects for SDGs and tagged these as climate finance projects. There is considerable evidence that ODA did not increase. Private finance (FDI and debt) comes for green projects on purely commercial consideration, which would have been the case if there was no Copenhagen accord.

The Green Climate Fund (GCF) was established in 2010. Until 2016, it got equity contributions of only about $10 billion. India has received commitments of hardly $1 billion so far. Donald Trump, accusing India of being the big beneficiary of GCF at the cost of American taxpayers cut off American investment in GCF and walked out of the Paris Convention. The GCF has trudged along thereafter, providing financing of about $1–1.5 billion dollars to developing countries a year.

Government pitches for a loss and damage fund

India was in the forefront of the coalition that fought for common and differentiated responsibility of developed and developing countries in Rio in 1992. India was also in the lead when Barack Obama and others in the developed North agreed in Copenhagen in 2009 to provide climate finance of $100 billion per year by 2020. In the Conference of Parties (COP) 27 held in Egypt in November 2022, India again led from the front to negotiate the hard-to-get Loss and Damage Fund (LDF).

The relevant decision text noted that the COP 'establish a fund for responding to loss and damage, whose mandate includes a focus on addressing loss and damage'. To further restrict the recipient of the LDF, COP agreed to establish new funding arrangements 'for assisting developing countries that are particularly vulnerable to the adverse effects of climate change'. To make sure that no one entertains any expectations of new additional or grant resources, the COP decision further noted that 'these new arrangements complement and include sources, funds, processes and initiatives under and outside the Convention and the Paris Agreement'.

There could not have been a vaguer commitment for correcting climate injustice. The fund size was not specified. No new grant resources were committed. The LDF was envisaged to only complement and include resources earlier committed. It seemed that, like the $100 billion a year pledge and the Green Growth Fund, the LDF would also not deliver even $20 billion in the next ten years to developing countries.

The LDF was formally established at COP28 held in the UAE on 30 November 2023. It is structured on the lines of the Green Climate Fund. No specific fund size was prescribed. The COP28 decision invited the members to commit contributions. Some commitments were made. Germany committed $100 million with the whole of the EU committing $245 million. The UK committed at least $51 million, the US $17.5 million and Japan $10 million. The World Bank was assigned the responsibility to see through its settlement over a four-year period.

India might draw satisfaction that it achieved the LDF. However, expecting the LDF to provide any material resources to developing countries might be a chimera.

Part V

Money, Finance and Wealth

14

Currency and Money

Currency

The currency issued by the sovereign or a central bank or another authorized agency on behalf of the sovereign, with the people and the banks, termed the currency in circulation (CIC), is the primary mode of conducting monetary transactions, including payments, in any economy. In India, the RBI has been entrusted with the responsibility of issuing and managing the currency/CIC.

The currency is primarily in the form of currency notes, called banknotes. A smaller part of it circulates in the form of coins. The RBI is experimenting with digital currency, denominated e₹-W in wholesale and e₹-R for retail users from 2022–23 onwards. As at the end of 2022–23, the total CIC was Rs 33,78,521 crore. Of this, Rs 1,02,085 crore currency was with the banks and the remaining Rs 32,76,436 crore with the public.

The bank or currency notes in circulation at the end of 2022–23 were Rs 33,48,219 crore. Coins of denomination of Re 1 or more, including the Re 1 currency notes, legally called Rupee coin of Rs 29,542 crore were also in circulation. The small coins (less than Re 1) of Rs 743 crore and the digital rupee—e₹-W—worth Rs 16.39 crore were also part of the currency in circulation at the end of 2022–23.

Currency circulation exceeded pre-demonetization levels

The CIC at the end of 2013–14, just before the Modi government took office, was Rs 13.01 trillion. With the nominal GDP being Rs 112.34 trillion in that year, the cash/currency to GDP ratio amounted to 11.58 per cent.

The CIC at the end of FY 2015–16, the financial year before demonetization of Rs 500 and Rs 1,000 notes was carried out, was Rs 16.63 trillion and the GDP for the year Rs 137.72 trillion. The cash to GDP ratio at 12.08 per cent in 2015–16 had increased by 50 basis points over the previous two years. The

Modi government believed that the currency in circulation or the 'cash' was the primary source and the reason for black money in the economy.

The government decided to demonetize Rs 500 and Rs 1,000 notes in November 2016. Thanks to demonetization, the volume of the CIC plummeted first. Thereafter, with slower remonetization, the growth rate of currency decreased. It turned out to be just about 10.5 per cent per annum when the first term (2014–19) of the Modi government concluded, as against the growth of the CIC by 13.5 per cent per annum between 2000–01 and 2013–14. However, the ratio of cash to GDP had recovered to 11.31 per cent (CIC Rs 21.37 trillion and GDP Rs 189 trillion) in the final year (2018–19) of the first term.

There was a phenomenal growth of digital payments in the economy in the second term. However, the currency in circulation also kept growing unabated until the withdrawal of the Rs 2,000 note was announced in May 2023. The CIC reached Rs 33.79 trillion at the end of 2022–23. As the nominal GDP for the year was Rs 272.41 trillion, the cash to GDP ratio for 2022–23 had increased to 12.40 per cent, much higher than at the time of demonetization.

The currency in circulation to GDP ratio at the end of 2023–24 moderated to 11.90 per cent (CIC Rs 35.16 trillion and GDP Rs 295.35 trillion), which was higher than 11.58 per cent at the end of 2013–14, but lower than 12.08 per cent at the end of 2015–16 and, of course, much higher than 11.31 per cent at the end of 2018–19.

The demonetization objective of reducing cash in the economy had by and large come unstuck.

Coins usage is fast declining

Coins are minted in the four presses of the public sector company Security Printing and Minting Corporation of India Ltd (SPMCIL). As per the Annual Report 2020 of the RBI, a total of 120.32 billion pieces of coins (of Rs 1, 2, 5, 10 and small denominations) were in circulation at the end of FY 2018–19, with an aggregate monetary value of Rs 25,844 crore.

With the demand for coins gradually coming down, the RBI had begun reducing the indent to SPMCIL for new coins. The RBI placed indents for 30.60 billion pieces of coins in 2017–18 and 28.88 billion pieces in 2018–19.

In the first year of the Modi government's second term, the indent was marginally reduced to 25.10 billion pieces. The big push-down came thereafter. The RBI reduced the coin indent to only 3 billion coins in 2020–21, 0.8 billion in 2021–22 and 1 billion in 2022–23. Clearly, the RBI seemed to be closing the tap for minting new coins. As a result of this squeeze on new minting of coins, the coins in circulation increased to only 132.35 billion pieces at the end of 2023–24 with the monetary value of Rs 33,389 crore.

The government/SPMCIL has four mints—at Kolkata, Noida, Mumbai and Hyderabad—with the largest mint at Noida having the biggest minting capacity. With RBI indents getting reduced to a trickle, the SPMCIL had to close down some of the mints as they were left with no work.

Demonetization: limited gains but largely a misadventure

'To break the grip of corruption and black money', the Prime Minister had declared on 8 November 2016, 'we have decided that the five hundred rupee and thousand rupee currency notes presently in use will no longer be legal tender from midnight tonight.' Calling this demonetization a 'mahayagna' in the 'fight against corruption, black money, fake notes and terrorism', the Prime Minister called upon every citizen to participate in that 'Imandari ka Utsav' (festival of honesty) and 'Pramanikta ka Parv' (celebration of authenticity). This was the movement for 'purifying' the country, the Prime Minister asserted.

The currency in circulation (CIC) on 4 November 2016 was Rs 17.74 trillion. The demonetization of Rs 500 and Rs 1,000 banknotes on 8 November divested Rs 15.44 trillion of bank notes of their legal tender status, putting in motion a drastic move to take out as high as 86 per cent of currency out of circulation.

The Prime Minister perhaps expected some of the demonetized currency notes not to come back when he mentioned that 'the five hundred and thousand rupee notes hoarded by anti-national and anti-social elements will become worthless pieces of paper'. Further, linking 'cash' in circulation directly to the level of corruption and inflation, the Prime Minister did not fail to underline that there was 'no restriction of any kind on non-cash payments by cheques, demand drafts, debit or credit cards and electronic fund transfer'. Promotion of digital payments was not specifically mentioned as the objective of demonetization at that time.

In its annual report for 2016–17, the RBI reported that demonetized banknotes, formally called specified bank notes (or SBNs) under the Specified Bank Notes (Cessation of Liabilities) law, of an estimated value of Rs 15.28 trillion (98.96 per cent of demonetized notes) were received back as on 30 June 2017. A small amount of notes, not yet returned, were accounted for as well. The annual report mentioned that the SBNs held by district central cooperative banks, Nepal Central Bank and in the custody of law enforcement agencies under orders of courts were not part of the Rs 15.28 trillion banknotes returned.

Quite unexpectedly, 100 per cent of the demonetized notes were either received back or otherwise accounted for.

The CIC, or the cash, was also back to its pre-demonetization levels soon. On the first anniversary of demonetization in November 2017, the CIC had reached Rs 16.13 trillion (90 per cent of pre-demonetization level). By the close of FY 2017–18 (in the space of sixteen months), the CIC had reached Rs 18.17 trillion, crossing the pre-demonetization CIC in absolute numbers. The CIC, on the fifth anniversary of demonetization in 2022, exceeded Rs 29 trillion, having increased by about 65 per cent over pre-demonetization levels.

It was quite common for people to encounter fake notes while depositing cash in banks in the pre-demonetization period. Most bankers and people preferred to destroy such notes in place of formally reporting or lodging a police FIR. The RBI's reported Rs 274 million worth of counterfeit Rs 500 and Rs 1,000 notes in 2015–16 was certainly a gross under-assessment. The real culprit—the high-quality counterfeit notes—almost disappeared after demonetization, though there were numerous instances of poor fakes or copies being seized by the police. Instances of counterfeit notes financing terrorist activities in J & K and elsewhere were also not uncommon in the pre-demonetization period. There was a visible reduction in instances of stone-pelting and other terrorist activities after demonetization for quite some time.

The principal objective of demonetization was to make the black money hoarded in the large denomination notes of Rs 500 and Rs 1,000 worthless pieces of paper. Whether Rs 15-plus trillion of CIC returned was not hoarded as black money or the hoarders took advantage of legal and administrative loopholes in the demonetization implementation mechanism to change the colour of money from black to white, the fact was that the entire demonetized currency came back to the RBI. Nothing became 'worthless pieces of paper'.

The Income Tax Department surveyed the SBNs deposited in bank accounts and identified 17.92 lakh deposit accounts, which received deposits of Rs 2.5 lakh or more, aggregating to Rs 4.2 trillion (approximately 25 per cent of demonetized CIC) as suspicious. The department issued notices calling for explanations under the standard operating procedures (SOPs) established and scrutiny/inquiries were made. While the process is still not finally concluded, the inquiries did not seem to have yielded much in hard cash as tax. The government also announced an amnesty scheme—Pradhan Mantri Garib Kalyan Yojana—targeting holders of these SBNs to declare their black money. It proved a damp squib and netted less than Rs 5000 crore.

Expansion of digital payments is coincidental correlation. The immediate aftermath of demonetization with a massive liquidity squeeze saw people struggling to find ways to make payments for their day-to-day purchases. There was a rush to sign up for the digital payment wallet companies. As the economy remonetized, this forced resort lost steam. The government came up with many other promotional schemes for encouraging digital payments—no charges for use of cards on most government payments. Merchant user charges were also exempted/reduced. These measures did help but the expansion of digital payments at the end of one year after demonetization was hardly up by 10 per cent.

Building innovations like UPI for payments, use of QR codes and proliferation of good quality fintech companies gave a much needed fillip to the adoption of digital payments during Modi 2.0. This transformation also received considerable impetus during the Covid-19 pandemic. There is a real push to digital payments expansion in the country. India is fast adopting digital payments as the way of life.

Looking back to the demonetization shock administered eight years ago, one cannot fail to note the enormity of the measure in terms of its impact on the economy and people's lives. The forced formalization of India's large tax-evading informal economy was not worth the pain it caused in terms of loss of businesses and employment. Its impact on elimination of corruption and black money was hardly noticeable. It did have some impact, at least initially, on curbing terrorist activities and the injection of counterfeit money. On account of the sheer nature of the operation, its implementation was chaotic and caused considerable pain.

On the whole, it was a misadventure.

Rs 2,000 currency note withdrawn

By asserting that about 90 per cent of Rs 2,000 currency notes, which were issued prior to March 2017, were at the end of their productive life (normal lifespan of Indian paper currency notes, according to the RBI, is four to five years under its clean note policy), the RBI, on 19 May 2023, decided to withdraw the Rs 2,000 denomination banknotes from circulation. The measure did generate some excitement in the media and people as they saw this move in light of the demonetization of Rs 500 and Rs 1,000 currency notes undertaken in November 2016. 'Withdrawal' of Rs 2,000 currency notes by the RBI was in no way akin to demonetization.

The introduction of Rs 2,000 denomination currency notes at the time of demonetization in November 2016 was, in a sense, ironical. Demonetization was undertaken on the premise that high-denomination currency notes of Rs 1,000 and Rs 500 were most susceptible to be used for hoarding black money and the proceeds of corruption. Yet, the government used a much higher denomination note of Rs 2,000 to reflate the depleted currency in circulation (86 per cent of currency was illegitimized in one stroke).

The Rs 2,000 currency note was permitted to be introduced in 2015/16, when the RBI made a proposal to introduce Rs 10,000, Rs 5,000 and Rs 2,000 banknotes on the grounds that the notes of Rs 1,000 and Rs 500 were of too small a value! As Rs 2,000 notes were being printed at the time of demonetization in November 2016, it came in handy for remonetizing the economy temporarily.

In a way, the fate of the Rs 2,000 currency note was sealed even before it was introduced. The RBI, in its press release, noted that the objective of introducing Rs 2,000 banknotes had been met and its utility was over, once the currency notes in other denominations became available in adequate quantities. The process of reducing the circulation of Rs 2,000 currency notes for its eventual phase-out had started soon after demonetization. The total value of Rs 2,000 currency notes was about Rs 7 trillion when an in-principle decision was taken in July–August 2017 not to print any more Rs 2,000 currency notes. A small quantity of Rs 2,000 currency notes were printed in March–April 2018 to tide over the mini currency notes shortage crisis at that time.

From 2018 onwards, a gradual and unannounced process of withdrawing Rs 2,000 notes started. A good part of the notes received by the banks in their normal operation were returned to the RBI for destruction instead of being put back into circulation. A few months later, the banks started removing the Rs 2,000 tray from their ATMs. As a result, the quantum of Rs 2,000 currency notes in circulation had declined to Rs 3.62 trillion in May 2023, when the 'withdrawal' decision was announced.

Rs 2,000 currency notes retained their legal tender status during the withdrawal process. By 30 September 2023, when the time provided by the RBI for deposit and exchange of notes through the banking channels ended, all the Rs 2,000 currency notes except that of Rs 16,000 crore had been returned. The RBI gave another week for returning the Rs 2,000 notes through banking channels.

Rs 3.56 trillion of Rs 2,000 notes were in circulation at the close of business on 19 May 2023 when the withdrawal of the Rs 2,000 note was announced. The RBI kept issuing the status of return of Rs 2,000 notes from time to time. By the end of September, all but Rs 14,000 crore worth of notes came back. Thereafter, the process slowed down. RBI press releases stated that the Rs 2,000 currency notes in circulation had declined to Rs 8,470 crore at the end of February 2024 and Rs 8,202 crore at the end of March 2024.

Government did not bring out cryptocurrency bill

On 23 November 2021, the government signalled its intent to introduce the Cryptocurrency and Regulation of Official Digital Currency Bill, 2021 in the winter session of the Parliament. As intimated by the government to the Parliament, the bill sought 'to create a facilitative framework for creation of the official digital currency to be issued by the Reserve Bank of India'. The government seemed to have moved only marginally from its position to ban private cryptocurrencies as the Parliament Bulletin further said that 'the Bill also seeks to prohibit all private cryptocurrencies in India, however, it allows for certain exceptions to promote the underlying technology of cryptocurrency and its uses'. There was no more information on the contents of the proposed bill.

The government had earlier signalled its intent to introduce the Cryptocurrencies Bill in the Parliament in the Budget Session 2021. The government never followed it through. The government did not introduce the proposed bill in the winter session or in any other session of the Parliament until the end of its term in 2024.

The government's dilemma and lack of action was understandable.

Earlier, the RBI had sought to dissuade use of cryptocurrencies by issuing a number of press releases to warn people. When the warnings did not work, the RBI sought to secure the financial system of the country by directing entities regulated by the RBI, which pretty much covered the entire financial system as the RBI regulates both the banks and non-banks, to keep all cryptocurrency businesses—from mining to trading to investing—out of India's payment system. The net effect of this decision of the RBI was an almost total official ban on the cryptocurrency ecosystem in the country, intended to strike a killer blow to it. The crypto operators went to the Supreme Court. The Supreme Court, partly out of fascination for the new technology but more on account of the absence of any legal framework in the country making dealing in cryptocurrencies an unlawful business, struck down the RBI notification. This made all cryptocurrency-related businesses in India fully legit.

The government kept struggling to come up with a law to deal with the cryptocurrencies phenomenon. A committee, headed by the author, then Economic Affairs Secretary, in 2018–19, in which the RBI and SEBI were prominently represented, had recommended three major policy changes. First, a framework was proposed to enable India to proactively introduce a digital version of its currency—the digital Rupee. Second, a ban on the private cryptocurrencies as currencies was recommended. Third, the government was nudged to adopt a promotional policy framework to encourage the use of the blockchain-crypto digital technology in the financial system.

The report and draft bill of the committee made the crypto businesses and investors quite concerned. Further, the complexity of the cryptocurrency ecosystem in which capital, product, service, price and currency all get rolled into one single phenomenon—its platform cryptocurrency—proved too arcane for the policymakers, technologists and market players to understand, segregate and deal with.

Later, the government spoke of bringing out a discussion paper. It did not come. Then, while assuming the chair of the G20, the government, arguing that it required international cooperation to regulate cryptocurrencies, referred the matter to an IMF-led group. Nothing concrete emerged.

The government could never really get its act together after it put out the draft bill in the public domain in June 2019. Cryptocurrencies remained completely unregulated in India.

RBI digital currency had no visible impact

The Finance Minister announced, in her Budget Speech 2022–23, that the RBI would come out with a digital currency, more popularly described as a central bank digital currency (CBDC), during the financial year itself. The RBI issued a concept note on CBDC on 7 October 2022. In November and December 2022, the RBI launched pilots for both the wholesale CBDC and the retail CBDC.

The pilot in the wholesale segment, known as the digital rupee-wholesale (e₹-W), was launched on 1 November 2022, with a highly limited use case—settlement of secondary market transactions in government securities. The pilot in the retail segment, known as the digital rupee-retail (e₹-R), was launched on 1 December 2022, restricted within a closed user group (CUG), comprising participating customers and merchants. Eight banks were identified for phase-wise participation in the retail pilot project. The e₹-R is in the form of a digital token that represents legal tender rupee banknotes. It was distributed through the banks. The users could transact with e₹-R through a digital wallet offered by the participating banks with transactions taking place in person to person (P2P) and person to merchant (P2M) modes. It could also be converted to other forms of money, such as deposits with banks.

The digital Rupee did not catch up. At the end of the first year (2022–23), the total digital Rupee equivalent of Rs 16.39 crore was in circulation (less than two hundred-thousandth of CIC) with e₹-W amounting to Rs 10.69 crore and e₹-R Rs 5.70 crore. The e₹-R has been designed to circulate in the same denominations as that of physical rupees (there is also an e₹ of 50 paise). e₹-R of Rs 500 denomination is the most used form.

Not much happened during 2023–24. The RBI did not put out the digital currency in circulation during the year. One communication issued by the RBI Governor on 29 December 2023 claimed that usage of the e₹ exceeded the milestone of 1 million transactions on 27 December 2023. This was perhaps designed to tick the goal of reaching 1 million daily transactions in digital rupees during 2023. It seemed to have been helped by a few banks nudging their employees to do transactions using e₹.

At end-March 2024, e₹-R in circulation increased to Rs 234.04 crore but e₹-W almost vanished at Rs 0.08 crore. The entire experience of digital currency in two years of 2022–23 and 2023–24 seemed more of a formality, with the RBI going through the motions.

Money

The currency in circulation and the deposits with the RBI constitute the Reserve Money, which is the measure of the money originating from the central bank. At the end of 2022–23, the reserve money was Rs 43.87 trillion (CIC Rs 33.48 trillion). The bulk of the deposit money with the RBI was in the form of bankers deposits, which amounted to Rs 9.30 trillion.

The broad measure of money includes demand and time deposits with the banks, which can be used for making payments, which is the function of money. The broad money in India at the end of 2022–23 was Rs 223.44 trillion.

Money growth was not quite subdued

The broad money at Rs 95.17 trillion had grown at an uncomfortably high annual growth rate of 14.70 per cent between 2008–09 and 2013–14 (second term of the UPA). The broad money to GDP ratio was 84.72 per cent in the year before the Modi government took over for its first term in 2014.

Broad money growth dipped to 10.48 per cent per annum in the first two years of the first term of the Modi government, touching Rs 116.18 trillion at the end of 2015–16, in the year before demonetization. The broad money to GDP ratio was only a tad lower at 84.36 per cent.

Demonetization did have a perceptible impact on the growth of broad money as well with the broad money standing at Rs 154.32 trillion at the end of 2018–19. The five-year CAGR for Modi 1.0 declined perceptibly to 10.15 per cent, which brought down the broad money to GDP ratio significantly to 81.65 per cent.

In the second term of the Modi government, the broad money growth was not that subdued. As the CIC growth accelerated, as we saw earlier, the broad money growth slowed down but only marginally to 9.69 per cent in the first four years. At the end of the fourth year (2022–23), the broad money stood at Rs 223.44 trillion. The broad money to GDP ratio, in fact, was somewhat higher at 82.02 per cent at the end of 2022–23 as against 81.65 per cent at the time Modi 1.0 completed its tenure.

In 2023–24, the growth in CIC was quite subdued due to the withdrawal of Rs 2,000 notes. However, much higher growth in bank deposits led to the broad money expanding to Rs 248.31 trillion. This had the effect of increasing the broad money to GDP ratio to 84.07 per cent, almost at the level of 2013–14, when the Modi government first took office.

Reserve currency witnessed highest growth

The reserve currency comprises the currency in circulation and the deposits with the RBI. Both these components recorded significant growth during Modi 2.0.

The deposits with the RBI has two sub-segments: bankers' deposits and other deposits. Bankers' deposits grew at an annual rate of 11.24 per cent (from Rs 6.02 trillion in 2018–19 to Rs 10.25 trillion in 2023–24). The other deposits, though smaller in volume, grew at a much higher rate of 24.39 per cent (from Rs 31,742 crore in 2018–19 to Rs 94,536 crore in 2023–24). Together, the deposits component of the reserve money recorded an annual growth rate of 12.06 per cent during Modi 2.0. This growth was significantly higher than the combined deposit growth rate of 7.98 per cent per annum in the first term.

The CIC also grew at a high rate of 10.44 per cent per annum in five years (from Rs 21.37 trillion in 2018–19 to Rs 35.11 trillion in 2023–24). The reserve money (from Rs 27.70 trillion in 2018–19 to Rs 46.31 trillion in 2023–24) also recorded a significantly high growth rate of 10.82 per cent in the second term against the growth of 9.84 per cent per annum (from Rs 17.33 trillion in 2013–14 to Rs 27.70 trillion in 2018–19) in the first term.

Smaller deposits growth explained lower broad money growth than reserve money

The demand and time deposits with the banks constitute a big chunk of the broad money (about 85–86 per cent); time deposits alone making up more than 75 per cent of the broad money (Rs 187.40 trillion out of total broad money of Rs 248.31 trillion in 2023–24).

Both the deposits components had grown slower than the currency in circulation and deposits with the RBI. The demand deposits grew at 9.72 per cent per annum (from Rs 16.27 trillion in 2018–19 to Rs 25.87 trillion in 2023–24) in the five years of Modi 2.0, whereas the time deposits grew at 9.84 per cent (from Rs 117.22 trillion to Rs 187.40 trillion). Together, the demand and time deposits had grown at 9.82 per cent per annum (from Rs 133.48 trillion to Rs 213.27 trillion) against the growth rate of 10.05 per cent in the first term.

It might be a significant pointer of future trends that the growth in demand deposits during Modi 2.0 was significantly lower compared to the growth in the first term (9.72 per cent in the second term against 14.91 per cent in the first term). The growth in time deposits, on the other hand, was higher in the second term (9.84 per cent) against 9.47 per cent (from Rs 74.58 trillion in 2013–14) in the first term. This might as well be the impact of digitalization of bank deposits with virtual instant conversion of time deposits into demand deposits, making companies and non-corporate business keep lower amounts in the current and savings account.

Modi 2.0 was characterized by a slower growth rate of broad money (9.98 per cent) with the CIC growth (10.44 per cent) falling in the middle with the reserve money growth (10.82 per cent) turning out to be the highest.

Payments

UPI became synonymous with digital retail payments

The government, in a press release in December 2023, claimed that the initiatives taken by it and the RBI had resulted in the volume of Unified Payments Interface (UPI) transactions growing from 92 crore in 2017–18 to 8,375 crore in 2022–23, at a CAGR of 147 per cent.

The claim was perfectly justified.

UPI transactions continued to record scorching growth in 2023–24 as well. In October 2023, UPI recorded 11.41 billion transactions (against 7.31 billion in October 2022), generating over 50 per cent year-on-year growth. By the year-end, UPI had clocked 131.13 billion transactions, overtaking the previous year's total transactions of 83.71 billion by a wide margin of 47.42 billion, recording annual growth of 56.6 per cent. In 2023–24, UPI transactions averaged 10.93 billion every month (1,093 crore transactions) or 36.4 crore transactions every day.

UPI has transformed India's retail payments landscape significantly. In 2022–23, UPI transactions were 73.17 per cent of all non-cash retail payment transactions. In 2023–24, UPI transactions occupied more of non-cash retail transaction space, increasing further to 79.56 per cent.

UPI enables instant payment—big convenience to fast replace cash payments

Economy is all about buying and selling goods and services between two parties and transacting in assets. Money interposes and a transaction gets completed when a payment is made.

Payments are the linchpin of the economy. Payments made exactly at the point of transaction work the best. Cash serves this purpose very well but requires the parties to meet and exchange it. Cash has many other deficiencies, including non-availability of the exact amount, weight to carry and risk of loss.

UPI solves all these problems. The National Payments Council of India (NPCI) has digitally pooled all bank accounts into one single system. This enables UPI to make instant digital transfers through mobile phones and other devices. The instantaneous secure and convenient payments underline the stupendous success of UPI.

UPI has been widely adopted by crores of retailers and small enterprises; and also by more than 25 crore individual accountholders. It feels good to see the smallest of vendors and service providers in villages, small towns and metros nonchalantly accepting UPI/digital payments through mobile phones or QR codes.

The RBI does not collect and provide data of the quantum of retail transactions taking place in cash. Until 2018–19, it was anecdotally believed that about 90 per cent of all retail transactions were in cash. The RBI, however, provides data on paper-based transactions (mainly cheques). Such transactions had come down from 1.26 billion in 2013–14 to 0.71 billion in 2022–23 and further to 0.66 billion in 2023–24, falling by over 47 per cent since 2013–14 and nearly 41 per cent since 2018–19.

Both paper-based and cash transactions are getting rapidly substituted by UPI, though the currency in circulation also continues to grow.

It is high time the RBI conducts a comprehensive survey of all retail transactions to know the complete truth about retail payments—in cash, through UPI, total digital channels and paper based transactions.

UPI payments do not directly generate growth, though

The world is fast witnessing replacement of cash by non-cash payments. In OECD countries, it is through the use of credit cards, increasing used digitally. In China and East-Asian countries, it is mobile payments using QR codes and credit cards.

UPI is India's payment innovation. It is simple, less risky and most convenient. UPI may not be adopted by G20 and the global South, as India has tried (as other digital systems have permeated significantly and people have got used to them), its growth in India is unstoppable.

Very soon, paper-based transactions will dwindle to a trickle. Cash transactions may still be a significant method of making payments, but its role and proportion is expected to go down substantially.

Payments, though, do not generate GDP growth as their contribution to GDP is limited to the charges/value received by UPI service-providers (payments as such do not amount to any value addition). With fintechs and banks not allowed to charge anything for the UPI service, it has zero impact on growth.

Rupee Exchange Value

The rupee was in choppy waters in 2022

India's forex reserves exceeded $640 billion at end-October 2021, having risen by more than $72 billion in six months from $588 billion. The forex reserves continuously declined thereafter for some time. They were down to less than $600 billion in May 2022. The RBI's stated policy and strategy is to allow the rupee to float freely but maintain orderliness and stability in the forex market. The RBI had spent more than $45 billion in six months (October 2021–April 2022) to serve its policy objective. Yet, the rupee's nominal exchange value had depreciated from Rs 74.9 to a dollar on 31 October 2021 to Rs 77.7 on 19 May 2022. The rupee's dollar exchange value fell to Rs 82.18 to a dollar on 31 March 2023 and to Rs 83.38 at end-March 2024.

The global economy was definitely in a flux. The US and other major economies were raising policy rates and had begun to contract their balance sheets in view of unprecedented inflation. Covid-19 and the Russia–Ukraine war and consequential sanctions and trade realignment were also putting pressure on currencies all over the world. The currency waters were choppy and undercurrents for the rupee were quite weak.

Indian politicians like a 'strong rupee', which in practice implies that the rupee's nominal value in terms of US dollars should appreciate or at least remain stable and not depreciate. Collated with political preference, RBI's policy objective was thus to keep the nominal value of the rupee stable or if the rupee had to depreciate on account of fundamental factors, ensure that it happened in an orderly and gradual manner. India came very close to defaulting on its international obligations in 1991 but learnt a very valuable lesson—large forex reserves are the insurance against any speculative raid on the currency. The RBI wants to maintain as large the forex reserves as possible. Movement in forex reserves and the rupee-dollar exchange rate do impact domestic money supply, which in turn affects domestic prices and interest rates. For some time, the RBI was selling and buying dollars to raise profits for surplus distribution to Government. Inherent contradictions in these three policy objectives complicated the RBI's policy and actions operationally at times, which was the case in May 2022.

India's structural imbalances and vulnerabilities had come to the fore. India has a large international economy. We imported goods worth $612 billion and services worth $145 billion in 2021–22. Our imports were almost entirely denominated and paid for in US dollars. The US dollar is the de facto international settlement currency. India required $750 billion in US dollars to pay for these imports. India exported goods of $420 billion and services of $250 billion in 2021–22. The export earnings of $670 billion still left a foreign trade deficit of $87 billion. India runs a trade deficit almost every year. Whether you blame our excessive dependence on energy resources, electronics imports or our love for gold, our trade account remains structurally in deficit.

India received foreign investment flows of $80 billion in 2020–21 but foreign investment inflows plummeted to only $22 billion in 2021–22. Portfolio investments, the most volatile component, were $38 billion in 2020–21 but turned into an outflow of $15 billion in 2021–22. Perceptions about opportunity to make profits, movement in exchange rates, etc., influence the incentives of foreign investors. Loans and NRI deposits also have the same incentives. NRI deposits declined by about $3 billion in 2021–22. Commercial borrowing inflows are also declining—$5 billion in March 2022 as against $9 billion in March 2021. There was considerable structural volatility in the capital flows as well. The stock of all capital flows is reflected in the overall investment position. At end-December 2021, India had international assets of $926 billion (investments $293 billion and forex reserves $633 billion). Whereas India's external liabilities were $1,284 billion (FDI $514 billion, portfolio investment $277 billion, trade credit $113 billion, commercial loans $204 billion, NRI deposits $144 billion and other assets $32 billion). India had an international investment deficit of $358 billion at the end of December 2021.

Keeping the rupee strong has a cost. India's $600 billion forex reserves provide assurance that India will take care of a deficit in imports and exports, make sure that repayments of loans and interest is made on time and foreigners can repatriate their investments whenever they like. Forex reserves also keep the speculators away; however, they are maintained at a cost. India's outstanding external debt was $630 billion at the end of December 2021. India's foreign exchange reserves were also of the same order at $634 billion at that time. Indian borrowers paid on an average 5 per cent interest on its outstanding foreign debt. India deploys its forex reserves in foreign central banks and other institutions and roughly earned 1.5 per cent return in 2021. When India pays 5 per cent and earns 1.5 per cent, it costs India 3.5 per cent. This is the cost of maintaining the forex reserves. For $633 billion, it cost India $22 billion in 2021–22. This cost was higher than the entire expenditure on building national highways.

India was witnessing a very high order of inflation in 2021–22—more than 15 per cent in the wholesale price index (WPI) and about 8 per cent in the consumer price index (CPI). FPIs were net sellers of more than $25 billion in equity and debt in calendar year 2022. The RBI's forex policy can contribute to containing inflation and altering the behaviour of foreign investors to encourage them to bring more capital than take it out.

This will, however, require a change of mindset about a strong rupee. The RBI does not care that much about the domestic nominal value of the rupee. Likewise, we should stop worrying too much about the rupee's nominal dollar value. The RBI does not control global inflation, supply of dollars or its federal fund or other interest rates. It can, however, use its forex reserves to calibrate the demand and supply of US dollars for rupees to manage the current account deficit. Expectations about the movement of the rupee's exchange rate and relative interest rate differential determine the attitude of foreign investors, the Indian diaspora and traders. If the RBI ensures that domestic interest rates, including on government bonds, move to neutralize the increase in US interest rates and enough US dollars are supplied to take care of the trade deficit and other foreign exchange demand, there are good chances that the rush of capital outflow would also subside.

Certain decisions of the government complicated matters in forex markets. The decision to compulsorily blend imported coal with domestic coal might have led to a desperate rush to import coal at whatever cost. The decision to ban the export of wheat also hurt exports. Global energy prices stayed high for some time. The RBI was quite late in recognizing the inflation spiral in India. It did start raising interest rates but was well behind the curve. A compulsion to keep domestic interest rates low for financing large government borrowing programmes came in the way of the reversal of capital outflows. Choppy waters continued to rock the rupee boat for some time. The rupee fell below Rs 80 to a dollar by the end of March 2023.

RBI initiates measure for settlement of international trade in Indian rupees

The RBI issued a circular on 11 July 2022 to promote international trade settlement in Indian Rupees (INR). Vide this, the RBI put in place an additional arrangement for invoicing, payment and settlement of exports/imports in INR.

The broad framework for cross-border trade transactions in INR under the Foreign Exchange Management Act, 1999 (FEMA) required: a. all exports and imports to be denominated and invoiced in INR, b. exchange rate between the currencies of the two trading partner countries to be market-determined, and c. the settlement of trade transactions to mandatorily take place in INR.

For enabling the settlement of trade, the Authorized Dealer (AD) banks in India were permitted to open Special Rupee Vostro Accounts (SVRA) of the correspondent bank/s of the partner trading country. The arrangement made further envisaged that Indian importers undertaking imports through this mechanism should make payment in INR, which would be credited into the SVRA of the correspondent bank of the partner country, against the invoices for the supply of goods or services from the overseas seller/supplier. Likewise, Indian exporters, undertaking exports of goods and services through this mechanism, would be paid the export proceeds in INR from the balances in the designated SVRA of the correspondent bank of the partner country.

The RBI perhaps entertained hopes that surplus rupees would get generated in the SVRAs. The circular further provided the use of surplus INR for payments for projects and investments, export/import advance flow management and investment in government treasury bills, government securities, etc. Repatriation of the surplus balances was not envisaged.

The DGFT stated on 14 March 2023 that as many as thirty SVRAs had been opened by traders from eighteen nations. The Foreign Trade Policy (FTP) announced on 31 March 2023 promised to take steps to support international trade in INR in line with RBI regulations. The Government and RBI initiated negotiations with many countries, including Russia and Middle-East countries, to convince them to settle trade in INR.

The media reported on 4 May 2023 that India and Russia had suspended efforts to settle bilateral trade in INR, after months of negotiations failed to convince Moscow to keep surplus INR unrepatriated in international currencies.

Nothing came out of this initiative. The RBI's Annual Report 2023–24 merely notes that AD Category-1 Banks maintaining SVRAs as per the provisions of the RBI circular dated 11 July 2022 'are permitted to open an additional special current account for their exporter constituent exclusively for settlement of their export transactions, from November 2023'.

China and Russia have successfully settled international transactions in yuan and ruble and have also created an alternative to the SWIFT messaging system. India made considerable noise but did not move an inch forward.

Monetary Policy

Flood of liquidity to deal with Covid-19

The RBI brought in a flood of liquidity to deal with Covid-19. RBI Governor Shaktikanta Das started pushing the liquidity accelerator right from the word go, beginning with his unscheduled address to the media on 27 March 2020. Finance Minister Nirmala Sitharaman acknowledged its extent soon. While unveiling the government's $20 trillion stimulus package in May 2020 (10 per cent of India's GDP), she proudly asserted that 40 per cent of the stimulus package (Rs 8 trillion) was in the form of liquidity measures undertaken by the RBI. The RBI later provided fuller contours of its liquidity operations. In the Monetary Policy Report published in October 2021, the RBI informed that it took liquidity measures aggregating Rs 17.22 trillion (8.7 per cent of GDP) between 6 February 2020 and 30 September 2021. The budgetary/fiscal measures against Covid-19, to contrast with the liquidity measures and translated into actual fiscal expenditures from March 2020 to October 2021, did not exceed Rs 3 trillion.

Flooding the banking and financial system with liquidity immediately after completely locking down the country for twenty-one days was akin to a surgical strike. Governor Das maintained full flow of the liquidity measures for twenty months, keeping the financial system in a hugely surplus liquidity mode. There was an excessive systemic liquidity overhang in the system (more than $9 trillion at the end of October 2021).

Liquidity, besides serving the primary purpose of maintaining seamless payments in the system, takes care of one more important monetary policy purpose—the expansion of credit. This supports investments by businesses in newer projects and capacity addition and by households in durable assets, such as houses, vehicles, etc. Easier liquidity, accompanied by lower interest rates, does encourage businesses and households to borrow more and bankers and the financial system to lend more. Unfortunately, the banks could not expand credit during the post-Covid-19 period. The outstanding credit for the industry group (including all types of industries—micro, small, medium and large and also infrastructure) and the services group remained quite static overall and declined in many specific segments. Only agriculture (food credit and agriculture credit) and household credit (retail) maintained trend growth during this period.

Overall, credit grew by less than 6.8 per cent during that period. Outstanding industry group credit at the end of March 2020 was Rs 29.05 trillion and services credit Rs 25.95 trillion. Outstanding credit to the industry group was lower in absolute terms at Rs 28.95 trillion at the end of March 2021. At the end of August 2021, the outstanding industry credit was only Rs 28.20 trillion, about Rs 85,000 crore less than at the start of the pandemic. Services credit outstanding at the end of August 2021 was also only Rs 26.25 trillion, almost at the same level as at the end of March 2020. Surely, the liquidity measures of the RBI did not contribute to expansion of credit to industry or the services.

Policy about-turn on 4 May 2022

After ignoring consumer price inflation for some months (wholesale price inflation had also been extra-ordinarily high for long) under the illusion that inflation was transient and hoping it to subside on its own, the RBI finally changed course on 4 May 2022. The RBI took three measures: it raised the price of short-term funds it lent to banks (repo rate in central bank jargon) by 40 basis points to 4.4 per cent, sequestered an additional 1 per cent of banks' lendable funds by raising non-remunerative Cash Reserve Ratio (CRR—the RBI pays no interest on such deposits) to 5 per cent and announced that it would focus on withdrawal of accommodation while remaining accommodative.

Monetary theory stipulates that central banks can nudge banks to raise interest rates of credit by increasing the cost of central bank short-term funds, which then stifles the demand for loans. This, in turn, reduces consumption and investment demand, restoring demand-supply equilibrium and leading finally to the taming of inflation. Likewise, it is argued that when CRR is raised, banks' lendable funds are effectively reduced, curtailing the supply of loans. The RBI, by hiking repo rate and CRR, expected to contain credit growth and singe inflation.

The RBI's decision to continue with an accommodative stance, while beginning withdrawal of liquidity, however, kept the RBI ranged in the opposite direction. If the RBI kept supplying excessive liquidity/accommodation to banks by maintaining an accommodative stance, sequestering of lendable funds via a CRR hike would get effectively neutralized. The system remained in excess liquidity, though the cost of funds went up for banks. In a surplus liquidity situation, banks would not borrow from the RBI, making the repo rate hike quite ineffective. In a nutshell, the RBI could only send confused signals to banks and markets on 4 May.

The RBI's primary responsibility, after amendment of the RBI Act in 2016, is to maintain price stability (defined as maintaining CPI inflation in a corridor of 4 per cent plus/minus 2 per cent). Monetary stability is the obverse of inflation. The RBI, during the helmsmanship of Governor Shaktikanta Das, had, however, adopted two other objectives as its preferred objectives/missions. Supporting GDP growth was the first one and had been consistently articulated as the RBI's preferred goal since Shaktikanta Das took over in December 2018. The second one, reflected more in action, was to ensure smooth financing of large government borrowing programmes at low interest rates fulfilling the RBI's role, in India, as the government's debt manager. The RBI's 4 May policy action was an attempt to serve its three objectives.

The RBI tracks CPI, which deals with only part of the inflation problem (WPI witnessed double-digit inflation for many quarters during that period). CPI had also entered the upper inflationary corridor (between 4 and 6 per cent) for many months. However, the RBI kept ignoring this. The RBI had to act when CPI inflation crossed 6 per cent decisively in March. That explained raising the repo rate by 40 basis points and also the CRR. The RBI, however, did not want to hurt nascent growth or jeopardize financing of the government's borrowing programmes. This made the RBI announce that it would remain accommodative. This allowed the RBI to buy government bonds to address any ruffled feathers. Surplus liquidity in the system allowed a veneer of serving the growth objective as well. The RBI hoped to move along, serving these contradictory objectives.

More rate increases in 2022–23

The RBI decided to hike its short-term funds lending rate (repo rate) by 50 basis points on 5 August 2022. It continued to remain accommodative, though its official stance was 'withdrawal of accommodation' since the last policy meeting.

CPI inflation underplays the real inflation in India. WPI inflation was 15.18 per cent in June 2022 and had been running in excess of 13.5 per cent for the previous six months. India's economy-wide inflation (measured by GDP deflator, which is the difference between the nominal and real GDP growth rates) was also in excess of 10 per cent in 2021–22.

In August 2022, it was quite clear that the high inflation in India was largely the result of supply side dynamics in the real economy. India imports heavily. Prices of major import items—crude oil, edible oil, capital goods, electronics, etc.—had all gone up sharply. The foreign exchange rate had depreciated by more than 6 per cent in six months. This imported inflation was a major contributor to inflation. The RBI could not have done much about it. Domestic product prices were also rising. Food inflation was uncomfortably high at 7.56 per cent in June. Clothes and footwear inflation exceeded 9.5 per cent. Cereal inflation was inching upward with wheat and rice prices rising. The RBI again did not have much of a role to play in such domestic inflation as well.

Credit growth dynamics, however, changed from the second half of 2021–22. Credit demand picked up as the cost of building material and other commodities rose. Credit growth exceeded 8 per cent in January 2022 and steadily went up thereafter—11 per cent in April, 12 per cent in May, 13 per cent in June and 14 per cent in July.

The RBI raised repo rates for the first time in May 2022, from 4 per cent to 4.4 per cent. With two more rate actions thereafter, the repo rate had increased to 5.4 per cent by August 2022. Ironically, credit expansion accelerated in these months—from 11 per cent to 14 per cent. Clearly, the rate increases did not have any impact in controlling credit expansion. Inflation is the result of many factors—changes in the real economy, governmental policy actions and global inflation. The RBI policy could not have contributed or impacted these factors. The policy rate increase remained more of a proforma action.

RBI writes to explain failure to contain inflation

Containing consumer price inflation to a level as prescribed by the Central government, in consultation with the RBI, is the statutory responsibility of the RBI (Section 45ZA of the RBI Act) since 2016. The failure of the RBI to meet the inflation target requires the RBI to set out the reasons for this failure in a report (Section 45ZN) to the Central government. In addition, the RBI has to propose remedial actions and provide an estimate of the time period within which the inflation target shall be achieved. In the exercise of its powers, the Central government fixed in 2016 an inflation target of 4 per cent in terms of CPI, with upper and lower tolerance limits of 6 per cent and 2 per cent. Refixed at the same level in 2021, these remained the applicable inflation targets during the entire Modi 2.0 period. The Central government has further prescribed exceeding the inflation target in any three consecutive quarters as the standard of failure though the Central government has not prescribed what it would do with the report and what corrective action would be taken if the failure continued.

The RBI Act amendment created a Monitory Policy Committee (MPC) to meet six times a year and decide on monetary policy actions. However, the responsibility to maintain inflation in the target range is that of the RBI. CPI inflation had remained higher than the 6 per cent limit for more than three consecutive quarters. An RBI press release dated 3 November 2022 stated that a separate meeting of the MPC was held on that day 'to discuss and draft the report to be sent to the Government' by the RBI. The meeting was chaired by the RBI Governor and all the members attended. What report was drafted and when it was sent to the Central government has not been publicly disclosed until now. The government also refused to provide any information on the content of the report sent by the RBI, the course correction suggested and the steps taken.

CPI food inflation was 8.41 per cent in September 2022. Food and beverages have 46 per cent weight in CPI. Cereals and cereal products recorded inflation of 11.53 per cent while vegetables and spices inflation rose by 18.05 per cent and 16.88 per cent, respectively. Clothing inflation at 10.17 per cent and fuel inflation at 10.39 per cent were on the higher side as well. Proteins did not see much inflation—meat and products were 2.55 per cent, eggs (-)1.79 per cent and edible oils and fats 0.37 per cent. Services (health, transport, education, etc.) inflation was much lower at 6.06 per cent. It was only in the last quarter of 2022–23 that inflation came down to less than 6 per cent.

RBI targets the wrong index

The repo rate, along with the increase/decrease in money supply, is the principal instrument of the RBI's monetary policy toolbox for controlling inflation. The RBI uses the inflation measured by the CPI as its target for monetary policy purposes.

At the end of 2018–19, the year before the commencement of Modi 2.0, the CPI recorded an index value at 140.4. The applicable repo rate at that time was 6.25 per cent. The year 2019–20 witnessed CPI inflation of 5.84 per cent (CPI 148.6). As the repo rate was higher than the CPI inflation, the RBI reduced the repo rate regularly four times during the year before Covid-19 upended things (to 6 per cent on 4 April, 5.75 per cent on 6 June, 5.40 per cent on 7 August, and 5.15 per cent on 4 October 2019). On 27 March 2020, in the shadow of Covid-19 and the complete lockdown imposed by the government, the RBI brought down the repo rate to 4.40 per cent.

In spite of widespread supply disruptions, most particularly in the first half of 2019–20, the collapse of demand saw the CPI inflation dip to 5.52 per cent in 2020–21. Food inflation fell much more, to 4.87 per cent during the year. The RBI reduced the repo rate to 4 per cent on 22 May 2020 and then left it untouched during the rest of 2020–21.

CPI inflation raised its head in 2021–22. In the first two quarters, it was a moderate increase with CPI rising to 161.3 in June 2021 and to 163.3 in September 2021. However, the inflation rose alarmingly in the third and fourth quarters, consistently recording an increase of more than 6 per cent year-on-year with the CPI value rising to 166.2 in December and to 170.1 in March 2022. For 2021–22, the CPI inflation was quite high at 6.95 per cent. The food CPI inflation was still higher at 7.68 per cent. The RBI did not touch the repo rate during the year at all. By the end of the year, there was a widespread outcry on account of rising consumer inflation.

The RBI was forced to convene an off-cycle meeting on 4 May 2022 to raise the repo rate by 40 basis points to 4.4 per cent. It raised the repo rate in every single MPC meeting thereafter. The repo rate was increased to 4.9 per cent on 8 June, to 5.40 per cent on 5 August, to 5.90 per cent on 30 September, to 6.25 per cent on 7 December and finally to the high of 6.5 per cent in the 8 February 2023 meeting. In one year alone, the repo rate was raised from 4 per cent to 6.5 per cent, an increase of 2.5 per cent.

The CPI inflation was at the high of 7.79 per cent in April 2022 and low of 5.72 per cent in December. For the year as a whole, 2022–23 recorded consumer price inflation of 5.66 per cent. The CPI food inflation was only 4.79 per cent during the year.

The gyrations in the CPI inflation in India are caused by factors over which monetary policy has almost no control. The consumer inflation in April–May 2022 rose on account of increasing prices of certain food items like wheat on account of lower wheat production and some exports. This spurt in CPI inflation had nothing to do with the RBI repo rates. The CPI inflation went down in November–December 2022 because vegetables, fuel and some other commodity prices declined on account of favourable weather conditions and the decline in the international prices of crude oil. There was very little impact of the 2.5 per cent increase in the repo rate on these price movements and the CPI inflation in general. The RBI does accept that repo rates do not affect food and fuel prices.

The RBI implicitly argues that the repo rates are intended to target the 'core inflation'—the non-food and non-fuel inflation. Let us see whether this stands scrutiny in India's case. From the CPI, if food and beverages, which has a weight of 45.86 per cent, and fuel and light, which has a weight of 6.84 per cent, are excluded, more than half (52.72 per cent) of the CPI base disappears. Only what is left over is perhaps considered the 'core inflation'.

To get into the internals of this 'core inflation', let us see what is left out in the non-food non-fuel CPI. There are some commodities and some services. Two groups of commodities remain (weights in the bracket): One, paan, tobacco and intoxicants (2.38 per cent) and two, clothing and footwear (6.53 per cent). These commodities have a total weight of 9.91 per cent. Then we have housing with 10.07 per cent, which essentially captures changes in the rentals in the urban areas. Finally, there are six groups of primarily services with total 28.32 per cent weight—household goods and services (3.8 per cent), health (5.89 per cent), transport and communications (8.59 per cent), recreation and amusement (1.68 per cent), education (4.46 per cent) and personal care and effects (3.89 per cent). This is the 'core inflation'—9.91 per cent weight of commodities, 10.07 per cent of housing rents and 28.32 per cent of services. Barring footwear and clothing, there are not many industrial goods in the 'core index'.

A cursory look at these items suggest that there is very little credit flow to these so-called core items. The concept of core inflation in CPI has been imported from abroad where this represents largely industrial products and commercial services. In India, industrial goods form the bulk of the WPI. The bulk of bank credit flows to these industrial sectors (including through retail loans like housing, vehicles, etc., which are also indirect loans for industrial goods). There are very few industrial goods in CPI. The services included are also hardly commercial services. Therefore, if there is very little credit flowing to these sectors, the tinkering with the repo rate does not impact CPI inflation.

WPI inflation had quite a different trajectory during the period 2019–2023. All commodities in the WPI rose by 6.35 per cent in 2019–20 and fell to 1.65 per cent in 2020–21. The RBI had brought the repo rate to only 4 per cent in May 2020. In 2021–22, the WPI increased by a whopping 9.33 per cent, crossing double digits over many months. The RBI kept the repo rate at a rock-bottom 4 per cent during the entire year. In 2022–23, the WPI inflation remained high overall at 9.11 per cent but fell to less than 5 per cent in the second half. The WPI inflation remained in the negative zone in the first half of 2023–24. The RBI kept targeting the wrong inflation index throughout Modi 2.0.

RBI policy, banks' profits and EMIs

The effective interest rates or yield on financial assets like bonds are more closely linked to RBI-determined repo rates. As yields go up when the RBI raises repo rates, the prices of bonds with lower interest rates go down. Banks and other holders of the bonds record mark-to-market losses. While there is no direct one-to-one relationship between bond yields and repo rates as many other factors also work, e.g. investment and government demand, it is far stronger than the relationship between the repo rate action and inflation. As financial markets have become very large—a multiple of India's GDP—investment bankers and bond market players watch RBI rate action with bated breath. Their commentary is often motivated more by their gains and losses than the policy's inflation impact.

The most direct impact of RBI monetary policy action in today's India is on two sets of players—banks and retail borrowers—people who take housing and other consumer loans or run their credit card bills. As the housing and other consumer loan interest rates have been mostly linked to repo rates as a benchmark, the banks immediately pass on the increase in repo rates to their loanees. To lull these loanees into inaction, the banks, instead of increasing their equated monthly instalments (EMIs), elongate the loan repayment period.

The current account balances do not earn any interest. The savings bank interest rates have not been increased until now when repo rates had gone up by 2.5 per cent. The difference between the loan interest rates and the current account and savings account (CASA) deposits, which all banks love, has widened by this margin. Old fixed deposits (FD) continue to earn only the old low interest rates and the new FDs see increases lower than the increase in loan rates. Banks' interest margin on fixed deposits also go up.

Consequently, banks' net interest margin rose quite sharply. This, accompanied by lower provisions on non-performing loans, explained banks' soaring profits in 2022–23 and also in 2023–24. Banks were quick to raise interest rates on loans to pass on the impact of increased CRR. While the increased CRR will transfer about Rs 5,000 crore of interest income from banks to the RBI, the banks will not lose any profits as they increase the loan rates.

CPI inflation is more impacted by non-monetary factors, such as weather (irregular monsoon, heat in winters, floods, drought, etc.) and government policy action (ban on exports, reduction in import duties, etc.). The people most impacted by RBI monetary policy action in India today are the retail borrowers who avail housing and other consumer loans. While they suffer, ironically, the banks make a lot of money at their cost.

Shenanigans of Economic Capital Framework

Broad contours of RBI dividend policy

RBI dividend/surplus transfers are a significant source of the government's non-tax receipts. In 2021–22, the RBI transferred Rs 99,122 crore to the government. RBI dividends followed a volatile pattern during Modi 2.0. In 2019–20, the RBI declared a dividend of Rs 1.76 trillion, followed by Rs 571.28 billion, Rs 991.22 billion, Rs 303.07 billion and Rs 874.16 billion in the next four years.

The Bimal Jalan Committee set the broad contours of the policy for provisions the RBI has to make while determining the dividends to be given to the government out of its annual surplus.

The RBI is required to keep the realized/cash reserves (created out of retained surpluses) between 5.5 per cent and 6.5 per cent of its total assets. It also has to maintain the valuation reserves (difference between the market value of financial assets and its cost of acquisition) between 13.5 per cent to 19 per cent to keep the total reserves (valuation plus realized) between 20 per cent and 24.5 per cent of total assets.

RBI earns low return on its assets

The RBI is an exceptional institution. Its resources/liabilities—primarily currency issued, bankers' CRR deposits and accumulated reserves and provisions—are almost completely costless. Whatever the RBI earns on its assets (interest and profit on sale), minus the small cost of printing notes, running the government banking system and other administrative responsibilities, turns into its surplus.

The RBI earns poor returns from its assets, though. Its assets are predominantly foreign currency assets—Rs 48.02 trillion out of total assets of Rs 70.48 trillion at end-March 2024. It also held rupee securities of 13.63 trillion, gold assets of Rs 4.39 trillion and loans, advances and other investments of Rs 4.43 trillion. The RBI earned a total income of Rs 2.76 trillion in the year, which was only 3.60 per cent of its total assets.

This income, in fact, includes a significant amount of exceptional income which the RBI had to earn by converting unrealized valuation gains on its foreign currency assets by selling and buying securities at current prices. In 2023–24, such exceptional income was Rs 84,294 crore. Excluding this, the RBI's earning over its assets was Rs 1.91 trillion (2.71 per cent of its assets).

Rising US interest rates queered the pitch

Besides meeting the government's expectations to provide ever larger dividends, the RBI faced a major challenge to its surplus earning ability as global interest rates rose after Covid-19.

As the US interest rates started rising in the latter part of 2021–22, the valuation of the RBI's foreign currency assets (invested in low-interest-earning deposits and securities) started falling on a mark-to-market fair valuation basis. The RBI maintains an account—Investment Revaluation Account-Foreign Securities (IRA-FS)—to account for gains and losses on this fair valuation basis.

The RBI had to transfer Rs 94,250 crore to the IRA-FS account from its surplus in 2021–22 to cover mark-to-market loss, which was as much as 65 per cent of its total surplus of Rs 1.45 trillion and 124 per cent of its normal surplus of Rs 75,987 crore. Likewise, in 2022–23, the RBI transferred net Rs 71,239 crore to the IRA-FS account, which again was 33 per cent of its total surplus and 62 per cent of normal surplus.

In 2023–24, as the foreign currency interest rates peaked, the RBI could actually reduce the IRA-FS provision by Rs 22,268 crore, which increased its total surplus by that amount. As the RBI could take this change in fortune into consideration while deciding dividend for the government, the RBI could declare a record dividend of Rs 2.21 trillion to the government.

RBI delivered 100 per cent of normal surplus as dividend . . .

The RBI earned a total surplus of Rs 2.54 trillion in 2023–24 (Rs 2.76 trillion total income minus Rs 21,874 crore operational expenses). Of this, Rs 1.70 trillion was normal/ordinary surplus and Rs 83,995 crore exceptional/abnormal income. As the required transfer to keep the realized reserves at the maximum permissible limit of 6.5 per cent was only Rs 42,820 crore, the RBI transferred Rs 2,10,874 crore to the government as dividend, which was 124 per cent of its normal profit.

In the other years during Modi 2.0, the RBI had to struggle to raise exceptional profits from foreign currency sale/conversion to provide some dividend to the government as it was also required to set aside surplus to meet the IRA-FS provision requirement. In 2021–22, the RBI earned a normal surplus of Rs 75,987 crore and total surplus of Rs 1.45 trillion. Still, it could transfer only Rs 30,411 crore to the government as dividend: less than 40 per cent of its normal surplus and only 21 per cent of its total profit, as it had to transfer an enormous amount to the IRA-FS.

Still, over a five-year period during Modi 2.0, the RBI transferred as much as Rs 4.50 trillion as dividends to the government (received by the government during FY 2019–20 to 2023–24). During this period, the RBI earned Rs 4.57 trillion as normal surplus. The RBI gave the government dividends equal to 98.51 per cent of its normal surplus.

Including the dividend for 2023–24, which the government has received in FY 2024–25, after Modi 2.0 is over, the RBI transferred Rs 6.60 trillion as surplus against Rs 6.26 trillion of its normal profits, giving the government 105.48 per cent of its normal profits.

. . . and had to transfer Rs 3.40 trillion to Contingency Fund

The Raghuram Rajan–Urjit Patel-led RBI had fixed the upper limit of 4 per cent of the RBI's total assets as cash/real reserves created in the Contingency Fund. Without any justification, the Bimal Jalan Committee raised the level of the contingency fund to 5.5 per cent and 6.5 per cent of total RBI assets.

To meet this excessive diktat, the RBI had to transfer Rs 3.40 trillion to the contingency fund in five years from the 2018–19 accounts to the 2022–23 accounts. This was 43 per cent of the total surplus the RBI earned during this period of Rs 7.91 trillion.

It was to meet this requirement and also to provide the government surplus equal to 100 per cent of normal profits that the RBI management had to generate abnormal income of Rs 3.35 trillion during this period by converting valuation gains on primarily foreign securities by selling and buying the same.

Why did the RBI create so much noise to establish cash/real reserves/ contingency fund of a high order of 5.5 per cent and 6.5 per cent? Why did the Bimal Jalan Committee have to do so much of intellectual gymnastics if the RBI was prepared to transfer 100 per cent of its normal profits to the government?

15

Savings and Wealth

GDP measures the domestically generated income by corporates, households and individuals in a year. It is the result of all the commercially remunerative work done and value added during a year. The income of a nation and her people grows in tandem with the growth of GDP.

All the income/GDP generated in a year is not spent on consumption of goods and services during the year. A good deal of the amount is saved as well, which gets invested into capital formation, building the capital/wealth of the people/nation. The GDP is a measure of flow, whereas the wealth/ capital is the stock of the current value of all the incomes saved and invested in capital/assets.

India, like many other countries, receives significant income transfers from the rest of the world in two forms. First, primary income from the Indian non-immigrant labour working abroad or income from travellers coming to India minus the primary income that Indian residents send to non-residents. Second, secondary income from the Indian diaspora sending remittances for maintenance of their extended family and assets in India or for new investment in assets.

GDP plus primary transfers are described as Gross National Income (GNI) and the GNI plus other transfers from the rest of the world is considered Gross National Disposable Income (GNDI). GNDI is the real final pool of income available for consumption and/or investment to Indians. The gross savings are, therefore, referred to in the context of GNDI. All savings-related aggregates make sense in their current values and not in the constant values; these are usually expressed/reported in nominal values/prices prevalent in the concerned year.

Higher incomes and consumption lead to a higher standard of living for the people/nation. The national/people's accumulated wealth shows up in the prosperity of the people/nation. The wealth/prosperity is most visible in the stock of real estate and other physical assets. With the greater financialization of the economy/assets, the investment/wealth in financial assets like shares and bonds has been rising far more rapidly.

The savings for GCF flows from four sources: a. non-financial corporations that produce the real goods and services, b. financial corporations that provide finances and financial services, c. general government comprising the central and state governments, and d. the household sector. The last is the biggest contributor to gross savings. In 2018–19, of the gross savings of Rs 60 trillion, the household sector contributed savings of Rs 38.44 trillion, which was in excess of 64 per cent of all savings.

The general government happens to be a usual dis-saver as both the central and the state governments combined run revenue deficits. In 2018–19, the general government was a net dis-saver by Rs 2.59 trillion. Financial corporations make a positive contribution towards the gross savings, although the real sector/non-financial corporations are the second biggest savers, after the households. The financial corporations contributed gross savings of Rs 3.54 trillion whereas the non-financial corporations contributed as much as Rs 20.61 trillion in 2018–19.

The corporations, both financial and non-financial, are directly or indirectly owned by the households. The non-financial private sector corporations are mostly owned by the households directly. Even the shares and bonds of the corporations owned by the mutual funds and other institutional investors or the government are indirectly owned by the households as they own the mutual funds/institutions which own the non-financial corporations and provide investible resources.

In the final analysis, almost all of the capital/wealth is owned by households (including single individual households) as the final beneficial owners of stocks and bonds in corporations are also the households and individuals. In a way, the capital/wealth of a nation is equivalent to the wealth of all its households.

Savings

Households primary contributors in gross savings

India generated GNDI, or the income which resident Indians can either consume or save/invest, of Rs 191.91 trillion in 2018–19, the last year of Modi 1.0. Of this GNDI, the gross savings amounted to Rs 60 trillion (31.27 per cent).

The bulk of the gross savings came from the GDP, but a portion also came from the net inflow of primary and secondary income from abroad. Of Rs 60 trillion of gross savings, GDP contributed Rs 57.09 trillion (95.14 per cent) and net inflows from the rest of the world (RoW) amounted to Rs 2.91 trillion. India was in deficit as far as net primary income transfers from the RoW is concerned (Rs [-]2.02 trillion in 2018–19). The net secondary and other income transfers of Rs 4.94 trillion in 2018–19 more than made up this shortfall.

The households contributed Rs 38.45 trillion to the gross savings of Rs 60 trillion (64.07 per cent). The corporations mustered up gross savings of Rs 24.15 trillion (40.25 per cent), of which the bulk of gross savings were contributed by the non-financial/real sector corporations—Rs 20.61 trillion (34.35 per cent of total gross savings). The general government made a negative contribution of Rs (-)2.59 trillion, i.e. (-)4.32 per cent.

Gross savings growth declined

In Modi 2.0, India's gross savings growth decelerated. In addition, there was significant compositional change as well.

The savings rate used to be much higher—about 35 per cent or so—during the UPA period. In 2013–14 also, the gross savings to the GNDI ratio was 31.40 per cent (gross savings Rs 36.08 trillion and GNDI Rs 114.90 trillion). This ratio declined marginally to 31.27 per cent in 2018–19 (gross savings Rs 60 trillion and GNDI Rs 191.91 trillion), signifying the stability of the gross savings rate, albeit at a somewhat lower level, during Modi 1.0.

The gross savings to GNDI ratio declined significantly in the first two years of Modi 2.0 (29.05 per cent in 2019–20 and 28.73 per cent in 2020–21)—a decline of more than 2.5 per cent of GNDI in two years. This perhaps mirrored the fall in national disposable income consequent upon contraction of GDP on account of lockdowns and a greater share of the GNDI going towards consumption.

The trend reversed from 2021–22 onwards, though not fully. In 2021–22 (second revised/final estimates), gross savings jumped to Rs 73.63 trillion, which was 30.78 per cent of the GNDI of Rs 239.25 trillion. The increasing trend faltered somewhat in 2022–23 with gross savings rising further to Rs 81.50 trillion (by about 10.7 per cent over the previous year), which was, however, a per cent less at 29.75 per cent of the GNDI of Rs 273.99 trillion (I RE). The gross savings ratio in 2023–24 was still 1.52 per cent lower than the last year of Modi 1.0.

Gross savings had grown at an annual rate of 10.71 per cent during Modi 1.0 (from Rs 36.08 trillion in 2013–14 to Rs 60 trillion in 2018–19). The annual gross savings growth rate was much lower at 7.96 per cent during the first four years of Modi 2.0, certainly a big cause of concern.

The GNDI data for the last year of Modi 2.0, i.e. 2023–24 are available as I close this book. It rose from Rs 191.91 trillion in 2018–19 to Rs 299.86 trillion in 2023–24 (PE) at a CAGR of 9.34 per cent. The gross savings numbers and their break-up for 2023–24 are, however, not available as the book goes to print.

Composition change reflected significant rise in corporate profitability

There was significant compositional change in gross savings during Modi 2.0.

In 2018–19, gross savings split between the households, corporations and general government was 64.07 per cent, 40.25 per cent and (-)4.32 per cent respectively. The corporations recorded a massive growth in their savings rate during Modi 2.0.

The non-financial/real sector companies' gross savings increased from Rs 20.61 trillion in 2018–19 to Rs 30.40 trillion in 2022–23. The gross savings of non-financial corporations recorded annual growth of 10.21 per cent per annum during this period. As a result, the share of non-financial corporations increased from 34.25 per cent in 2018–19 to 37.31 per cent in 2022–23.

With banks and other financial sector entities turning around in a big way, the gross savings of financial corporations also increased from Rs 3.54 trillion in 2018–19 to Rs 7.60 trillion in 2022–23, more than doubling in four years at a hefty annual growth rate of 21.08 per cent. The share of financial corporations in gross savings, as a result, increased from 5.89 per cent in 2018–19 to 9.33 per cent in 2022–23.

Together, the share of companies/corporations (both financial and non-financial) increased from Rs 24.15 trillion in 2018–19 to Rs 38.01 trillion in 2022–23, recording a robust growth of 12 per cent (against an overall savings growth rate of 7.96 per cent) raising the corporations' share in gross savings to as high as 46.63 per cent in 2022–23 (from 40.25 per cent in 2018–19).

With fiscal deficits of the government shooting through the roof, the general governments' dis-savings increased from Rs (-)2.59 trillion in 2018–19 to Rs (-)6.14 trillion in 2022–23, recording a highly discomforting annual growth rate of (-)24.06 per cent per annum, bringing their share in gross savings to (-)7.53 per cent.

Household savings suffered during this period and declined significantly. They increased from Rs 38.45 trillion in 2018–19 to Rs 49.63 trillion in 2022–23. Their annual growth rate was an unflattering 6.59 per cent, which brought the share of household savings in gross savings to 60.90 per cent (from 64.07 per cent in 2018–19).

The gross savings split between the households, corporations and general government of 60.90 per cent, 46.63 per cent and (-)7.53 per cent respectively, could not have more poignantly captured the shift of income and savings from households and general government to the corporations in Modi 2.0. Good evidence of a K-shaped post-pandemic recovery!

Public financial corporations the star performer

The national accounts provide granular details of the corporation savings split into public corporations (owned by the government and other public sector companies, including departmental entities like Railways) and private corporations, and further split into financial corporations and non-financial/real sector corporations.

The public financial corporations (primarily public sector banks and LIC) had generated savings of Rs 1.78 trillion and public non-financial corporations (public sector enterprises primarily) of Rs 2.51 trillion in 2018–19, totalling Rs 4.29 trillion. As the total corporation savings (including private sector) amounted to Rs 24.15 trillion in 2018–19, the public corporations had a share of 17.75 per cent in total corporation savings.

Savings from the public financial corporations shot up to Rs 4.62 trillion in 2022–23, at an annual growth rate of 26.93 per cent, though the savings from non-financial public corporations grew at a tepid 6.23 per cent per annum to Rs 3.19 trillion. As a result of the spectacular growth in public financial corporations' savings, its share in total public corporations' savings increased from 41.51 per cent in 2018–19 to as high as 59.12 per cent in 2022–23. The share of public corporations (financial and non-financial) of Rs 7.81 trillion commanded a higher share of 20.56 per cent out of total corporations' savings of Rs 38.01 trillion in 2022–23.

The turnaround in the profitability of the public sector banks and also insurance and other companies was responsible for the high growth in savings in public sector corporations and the overall share of public corporations going up in the total corporation sector gross savings.

Total household savings fell precipitously

Household savings are the primary source/creator of household wealth. The NSO provides granular data of households divided into two broad groups of financial savings (currency, deposits, shares, bonds, etc.) and physical assets (houses, consumer durables, computers, laptops and the like).

Households also borrow and incur financial liabilities (loans for house building, cars and other durables). Gross financial savings minus financial liabilities makes up the net financial savings of the households. The savings in physical assets and net financial savings add up to the gross savings of the household sector.

India's total household savings (data is always in current rupees) were Rs 22.85 trillion in 2013–14, the year before the Modi government took over. Total household savings grew to Rs 38.45 trillion in 2018–19, recording a CAGR of 10.96 per cent, not a roaring rate of savings but still a decent one. The household savings carved out 20.34 per cent of GDP in 2018–19.

In 2021–22, the total household savings were assessed at Rs 47.42 trillion (second revised/final estimates)—20.10 per cent of the GDP (Rs 235.97 trillion). In the first three years of Modi 2.0, the household savings grew by a CAGR of only 7.25 per cent. In 2022–23, the last year for which the savings data is available as on 31 August 2024, as I finish this book, households' savings grew to Rs 49.63 trillion (only 4.66 per cent over the previous year) at a CAGR of 6.59 per cent, which brought the households' gross savings to GDP ratio to a very low level of 18.42 per cent only.

The decline in gross household savings to GDP ratio of about 2 per cent in the first four years of Modi 2.0 (from 20.24 per cent to 18.42 per cent) is the most tell-tale sign of the households' stress and behavioural preferences to cope with the dire economic and pandemic situation they faced during the period.

In 2019–20, the first year of Modi 2.0, when the economy had slowed considerably to record GDP growth of only 3.3 per cent, households' savings remained flat (Rs 38.45 trillion like the year before). As they faced hard economic situations, households used their incomes on consumption rather than increasing savings for investment.

Year 2020–21 was the pandemic year. With severe restrictions on discretionary expenditure, households were forced to put a larger part of their reduced income (current GDP fell by 2 per cent) ironically in savings. The household savings shot up to Rs 45.06 trillion (final estimates) recording an exceedingly high growth rate of 17.18 per cent (the highest during Modi 2.0).

Year 2021–22 saw the opening up of the economy with all Covid-19-related restrictions gone. People had to spend more to maintain their consumption (thanks to high inflation) and discretionary spending also resumed. The household savings growth rate in 2021–22 fell to a lowly 5.25 per cent (the nominal GDP had grown by 18.85 per cent during the year).

Year 2022–23 also turned out to be quite hard for households. The nominal GDP grew by 9.50 per cent. However, due to the continued pressure of maintaining their consumption, households could save relatively less. Households' savings grew to Rs 49.63 trillion, recording a growth of a lowly 4.66 per cent during the year.

Households changed their savings pattern

Households altered their savings pattern materially during Modi 2.0. They reduced their financial savings and increased their savings in physical assets.

The gross financial savings of households were Rs 22.64 trillion in 2018–19 and rose to Rs 29.74 trillion in 2022–23 (I RE) recording a CAGR of 7.06 per cent, slightly higher than the overall household savings growth rate of 6.59 per cent.

There was, however, a sting in the tail as households increased their financial liabilities at a very high rate during this period. Their financial liabilities increased from Rs 7.71 trillion in 2018–19 to Rs 15.57 trillion in 2022–23, recording an annual growth of 19.20 per cent!

As a result, households' net financial savings actually fell in nominal rupees from Rs 14.92 trillion in 2018–19 to Rs 14.16 trillion in 2022–23 (I RE), recording a four-year negative growth of (-)1.30 per cent per annum.

The savings in physical assets displayed the opposite characteristics.

In 2020–21, unable to carry out housing construction and maintenance or even to buy durable assets, the savings in physical assets fell to Rs 21.35 trillion (final estimates) from Rs 23.09 trillion in 2018–19. In the next two years (2021–22 and 2022–23), however, households increased their savings in physical assets significantly—to Rs 29.68 trillion in 2021–22 (second revised/final estimates) and to Rs 34.83 trillion in 2022–23 (I RE), by 63 per cent in two years! This raised the four-year CAGR of household savings to a decent 10.82 per cent per annum.

Lowest net financial savings in forty-seven years in 2022–23

RBI data released in its September Bulletin shrieked: India's net household financial savings have come down to just 5.1 per cent of GDP, the lowest since 1976–77.

Net household financial savings is the difference between the addition to the stock of financial assets like currency, bank deposits, shares, etc. and financial liabilities like loans from banks. NSO provided updated/revised data for 2022–23 later in 2023–24.

In 2022–23, there was a blow from both ends. Inflow into financial assets amounted to Rs 29.74 trillion (I RE), which was 11.03 per cent of GDP (against 11.07 per cent of GDP in 2021–22) whereas increase in households' financial liabilities at Rs 15.57 trillion shot up sharply to 5.78 per cent of GDP (against 3.81 per cent of GDP in 2021–22). Clearly, Indian households were saving less and borrowing more.

Taken together, there was an alarmingly massive reduction in net financial savings in 2022–23 to 5.26 per cent from 7.26 per cent of GDP. For the GDP of Rs 269.50 trillion in 2022–23, this reduction amounted to a lower financial savings of a whopping Rs 5.39 trillion! In fact, the net financial savings had declined in 2021–22 as well—from Rs 23.20 trillion in 2020–21 to Rs 17.13 trillion. If net financial savings of Rs 14.16 trillion in 2022–23 are juxtaposed against net financial savings of Rs 23.20 trillion in 2020–21, the fall was an unprecedented amount of Rs 9.04 trillion in two years.

Households' financial liabilities primarily went up on account of household loans from banks rising sharply. The NSO data and RBI paper nailed it—bank loans went up to Rs 11.88 trillion in 2022–23 against Rs 7.70 trillion in 2021–22, a growth of 54.4 per cent in one year!

India's household sector had no option but to use its savings and borrow heavily to invest in physical assets—in better homes and home offices, in high-end consumer assets like cars, televisions, air purifiers, and in high-tech commercially productive assets like computers, laptops, smart phones, etc., to fend off and prosper in the post-Covid-19 reality.

Household preferences for financial assets underwent significant changes

The NSO collects and provides household gross financial savings data in six different asset classes (currency, deposits, shares and debentures, claims on government, insurance funds and provident and pension funds). If one looks at the preference for these different financial asset classes over the nine-year rule of the BJP (2013–14 to 2022–23), there are materially observable trends.

Households are clearly losing their preference for currency, deposits and claims on government.

Household savings in currency witnessed a CAGR of 22.8 per cent in the first term (from Rs 99,500 crore in 2013–14 to Rs 2.78 trillion in 2018–19. In the first four years of the second term, the growth rate turned negative at (-)3.84 per cent as the savings in currency plummeted to Rs 2.38 trillion in 2022–23. The total household savings in deposits (banks, non-banks and cooperative banks and societies, all included) were lower in the second term until 2021–22 (4.08 per cent in the first term and 0.78 per cent in the second term until 2021–22) with savings amounting to Rs 6.67 trillion, Rs 8.15 trillion and Rs 8.34 trillion in 2013–14, 2018–19 and 2021–22. The savings in deposits looked up well only in 2022–23 (Rs 11.09 trillion) raising the four-year CAGR to 8.01 per cent. The claims on government also witnessed a low growth of 4.63 per cent in the first four years of the second term with the savings in such instruments amounting to Rs 2.47 trillion in 2022–23 against Rs 2.06 trillion in 2018–19 (in the first term, the annual growth was an astounding 55.02 per cent).

Households' deployment of their savings in shares and debentures (in companies, cooperative banks and mutual funds) is not quite substantial in India. In 2013–14, households put only Rs 18,930 crore, out of their gross financial savings of Rs 11.91 trillion, in shares and debentures. There was, however, a distinct household preference for increasing savings in shares and debentures from 2014–15 onwards. By 2018–19, in the last year of Modi 1.0, the savings in shares and debentures went up to Rs 1.73 trillion (an increase of about nine times) in five years, delivering a stupendous annual growth of 55.65 per cent, which also raised the share of savings in shares and debentures in GDP to 0.92 per cent. There was a decline in households' savings in shares and debentures in the first two years of 2019–20 and 2020–21, but the steady growth trend resumed from 2021–22 when savings in shares and debentures rose to Rs 214 crore (0.91 per cent of GDP). In 2022–23, there was again a little slowdown with the savings in such instruments amounting to Rs 2.06 trillion, yielding a four-year growth rate of only 4.50 per cent.

Households' savings in insurance funds is substantial. These savings rose quite steadily (from Rs 2.04 trillion in 2013–14 to Rs 3.87 trillion in 2018–19) during Modi 1.0, rising from 1.82 per cent of GDP in 2013–14 to 2.05 per cent of GDP in 2018–19, recording a CAGR of 13.64 per cent. The savings flow in insurance funds continued to be reasonably healthy, with a growth rate of 9.02 per cent during the first four years of Modi 2.0 (rising to Rs 5.47 trillion) in 2022–23.

The government and the RBI have been trying to promote households' participation in government securities. This has, however, refused to catch up and has been quite volatile. Savings in government securities were only Rs 14,794 crore in 2013–14. They fell to only Rs 1,324 crore in 2018–19 and were quite low, even in nominal numbers, in 2022–23 at Rs 8,392 crore.

Household savings in provident and pension funds have been the steadiest performer over the last nine years (2013–14 to 2022–23). These savings rose handsomely at a nine-year CAGR of 12.43 per cent, increasingly growing from 1.58 per cent of GDP in 2013–14 to 2.14 per cent of GDP in 2019–20 and stabilizing at 2.12 per cent of GDP in 2022–23.

The currency savings to GDP ratio was 0.89 per cent in 2013–14. It rose to a higher level of 1.47 per cent in 2018–19. By 2022–23, the ratio of savings in currency to GDP came down to only 0.80 per cent.

Household savings in real estate kept declining

Household savings in physical assets (measured as GFCF) is estimated in four different classes of assets: real estate recorded as dwellings, other buildings and structures in national accounts, machinery and equipment—primarily household equipment including computers, air conditioners, refrigerators for households and plant and machinery in household enterprises, cultivated biological resources and finally, intellectual property rights. For understandable reasons, there is hardly any savings deployed by households in capital formation in cultivated biological resources and intellectual property products. Households primarily save and form capital by investing in real estate.

A constantly declining, though not very pronounced, trend is visible in households' GFCF/gross savings in physical assets. Total physical savings/GFCF, which (at current prices) was Rs 14.06 trillion in 2013–14 rose to Rs 22.89 trillion in 2018–19 and further to Rs 34.65 trillion in 2022–23. The physical savings/GFCF was 12.52 per cent of nominal GDP in 2013–14, which marginally fell to 12.11 per cent in 2018–19 and further to 11.73 per cent in 2022–23.

The fall in savings/capital formation in real estate assets was, however, very steep. In 2013–14, households had saved/invested Rs 12.48 trillion in dwellings, other buildings and structures, which was 11.11 per cent of the GDP of Rs 112.34

trillion of that year. In 2018–19, the savings/capital formation in the real estate sector turned out to be Rs 15.14 trillion, which was only 8.01 per cent of the GDP of Rs 189 trillion of that year. After falling further in the first three years until 2021–22, the savings/capital formation of Rs 24.83 trillion in real estate in 2022–23 rose marginally to 8.41 per cent of the GDP of Rs 295.36 trillion.

There was an unusual jump in the physical savings/capital formation by the household sector in plant and machinery between 2013–14 and 2018–19, when it rose from Rs 1.50 trillion to Rs 7.67 trillion. Thereafter, the investment of household savings in plant and machinery plateaued a bit, rising to Rs 9.69 trillion in 2022–23. Household savings/capital formation in plant and machinery rose from 1.34 per cent of GDP in 2013–14 to 4.06 per cent in 2018–19 and steadied thereafter at 3.28 per cent in 2022–23.

Wealth of India

Wealth increased but marginally

India abolished wealth tax in 2015. Indian statistical agencies do not collect data about the wealth in the country. For getting a sense of wealth in India, we have to resort to global publications. The Global Wealth Report (GWR), brought out by the UBS/Credit Suisse, has been providing wealth estimates consistently for about two decades. The GWR defines wealth as the value of financial assets plus real assets (principally housing) owned by all adults of that country minus their debts in current nominal US dollars and publishes it annually. It is a measure of private wealth, which actually is the real wealth of a nation.

Global wealth was estimated at $360.6 trillion at mid-point 2019. North America had the largest share with the total wealth estimated at $114.61 trillion. India's wealth was estimated at $12.61 trillion. In 2022, the global total private wealth increased to $454.4 trillion. India's total private wealth increased to $15.37 trillion. India's wealth grew by 5.07 per cent per annum during this period.

The GWR also provides estimates of per-adult wealth for the world, major regional groupings and some large countries, including India. India's per adult wealth was estimated at $14,569 in 2019 mid-point (GWR began providing wealth estimates at the year end from 2019 onwards) and at $17,299 at end 2019. In 2022, the per adult wealth in India was estimated by GWR at $16,500 in 2022. India's per-capita wealth grew at a rate of 3.16 per cent per annum since mid-point 2019, although it was lower at end-2022 compared to end-2019, largely on account of rupee depreciation in 2022. According to the GWR, there were 7.59 lakh adults with wealth above $1 million (dollar millionaires) at mid-point 2019, which rose to 9.12 lakh at the end of 2019.

North America has the largest concentration of wealth. In 2022, with $151.17 trillion of global wealth out of $454.4 trillion, North America had about a third of the global wealth. North America also led in terms of per adult wealth with an average adult wealth of $531,826 in 2022. Europe was the second richest area with total wealth of $104.41 trillion and per adult wealth of $177,731. China has become the third richest region of the world with total wealth of $84.49 trillion and per adult wealth of $75,731. Asia-Pacific (excluding China and India) follows closely behind China with total wealth of $77.97 trillion and per adult wealth of $61,154.

India, with total wealth of $15.37 trillion and per-adult wealth of $16,500, remains relatively wealth-poor with only the African region behind it with total wealth of $5.91 trillion and per-adult wealth of $8,345. The last region—Latin America—is better off than India but less than half as rich compared to China with total wealth of $15.07 trillion (almost equal to India) but higher per adult wealth of $32,760 as it has almost half of India's adult population.

There is enormous inequality (much more pronounced than the income inequality) in terms of wealth. The GWR 2023 finds that the wealth share of the global top 1 per cent adults was as high as 44.5 per cent in 2022. There were an estimated 59.4 million US dollar millionaires in 2022—a little more than 1 per cent of the global adult population. The report estimated 79,490 adults with wealth above $100 million and 7020 with wealth above $500 million. On the other side, as many as 52.5 per cent of adults owned less than $10,000 of wealth. India, with a population of 141.3 crore and an adult population of 931 million in 2022, had per-adult wealth of only $16,500 in 2022.

Wealth inequality is widening

The organization of value addition in the agriculture age was more equitable. As income and wealth flow from value addition, society was more egalitarian in the agriculture age. The organization and ownership of the value addition system underwent drastic changes in the industrial age. There was a larger concentration of value addition, income and wealth in the hands of fewer individuals and households. The trend has only accelerated further in the digital age with large platforms becoming the primary generator of value addition, income and wealth.

Income and wealth inequality data are not produced by the GoI or any of its official agencies. The Gini coefficient measures inequality by dispersion in the values, e.g. income, of a frequency distribution. A Gini coefficient of 0 indicates perfect equality with everyone in the distribution having equal value of the variable—income, consumption or wealth. A Gini coefficient of 1 on the other hand indicates perfect inequality with one person having 100 per cent of the variable value and everyone else nothing at all. The World Bank Gini coefficient value for India was 34.7 in 2015. It rose to a high of 35.9 in 2017. Thereafter, it fell consistently to 34.2 in 2021.

Inequality is more dramatically measured by capturing the share of income and wealth of the top 0.01 per cent, 0.1 per cent, 1 per cent and 10 per cent on the one hand and that of the bottom 10 per cent and 50 per cent on the other. A number of studies have been done from time to time to assess the state of inequality.

A study, 'Income and Wealth Inequality in India, 1922–2023: The Rise of the Billionaire Raj' published in March 2024, estimated that 'at the turn of the 21st century, in 2002, top 10 per cent wealth shares stood at 57.1 per cent while the top 10 per cent income share was 42.1 per cent, a gap of 15 percentage points. Over the next 20 years, top 10 per cent income shares rose faster and the gap reduced considerably, effectively halved to 7.3 per cent by 2022. On the other hand, we observe the exact opposite trend when comparing top 1 per cent income and wealth shares over the same period. In 2002, the top 1 per cent wealth share was 25.4 per cent compared to 16.7 per cent for incomes, a gap of 8.7 percentage points. Twenty years later, by 2022, the top 1 per cent wealth share had reached 40.1 per cent compared to 22.6 per cent for incomes, a gap of 13.4 percentage points'.

Other studies have also reflected similar results. There is an inescapable conclusion that wealth concentration is accelerating at a fast rate in India, faster than the concentration of incomes.

Mutual fund assets have grown quite well

SEBI publishes data of the assets under management (AUM) of the asset management companies (AMCs) managing through the mutual fund schemes.

As per this data, the AUM at the end of FY 2018–19, the last year of Modi 1.0, were Rs 23.77 trillion. More than 91 per cent of the assets were under open-ended schemes. Income and debt-oriented open-ended schemes constituted the largest segment with a total AUM of Rs 9.89 trillion, which made up 41 per cent of total AUM. Growth/equity-oriented schemes also made up a significant chunk of the AUM with a Rs 8.57 trillion assets portfolio making up 36 per cent of the AUM. Index funds have begun making their mark and with AUM of Rs 1.39 trillion, constituted about 6 per cent of total AUM.

The mutual fund industry grew up to a massive AUM of Rs 57.26 trillion as on 31 March 2024, marking the terminal year of Modi 2.0. Mutual fund AUM recorded a rise of 140 per cent over the AUM on 31 March 2019 (Rs 23.77 trillion) with a CAGR of 19.22 per cent. This certainly was quite impressive.

There has also been a significant churn in the different mutual fund asset classes.

Close-ended mutual funds became almost extinct with the AUMs under such schemes declining from 8.81 per cent as on 31 March 2019 to less than 1 per cent (0.46 per cent) on 31 March 2024. Open-ended funds constituted almost the entire universe of mutual fund AUM, with a share of 99.54 per cent of the total AUM.

Within the open-ended schemes, the growth/equity-oriented mutual funds and exchange traded funds (ETFs) have grown in size considerably. The growth/equity-oriented schemes, which had an AUM of Rs 8.57 trillion on 31 March 2019 (36.04 per cent), grew to Rs 24.74 trillion AUM (43.21 per cent). ETFs, which had quite a small presence in 2018–19 with AUM of Rs 1.39 trillion at March-end, grew manifold to Rs 9.62 trillion AUM, with a CAGR of 47.24 per cent, claimed 16.81 per cent of total AUM.

Income-oriented mutual fund AUM declined proportionally. Such schemes had AUM of Rs 9.89 trillion (41.62 per cent of total AUM) on 31 March 2019. Their AUM recorded a more tepid CAGR growth of 8.08 per cent to reach Rs 14.58 trillion (25.48 per cent of the total AUM) on 31 March 2024.

16

Credit and Finance

Finance is primarily a credit intermediation function—the financial intermediary takes savings from the savers and lends to the borrowers. Credit intermediation also takes place from the present to the future. In addition to receiving savings, the banking system, including the central bank, also create credit.

Banks are the principal actors in the credit business, taking deposits from savers to lend to the borrowers and also creating deposits in the process of lending. Non-banks, a wide variety of financial institutions, sometimes dubbed shadow banks, from housing finance companies to consumer durable financing institutions, are also important players in the credit market. There are other non-banks like asset managers and insurance companies, which also lend.

The advent of digital technologies have brought in many fintech firms as enablers and facilitators of credit delivery. Working with banks and non-banks, they have revolutionized credit-associated services, such as loan origination, credit profiling and collections.

The real economy runs on money, vastly enhanced by credit, customized for the needs of businesses, households and individuals. The finance function has become the biggest driving force in enabling investments and driving up the size and distribution of goods and services in any economy and also globally.

In this chapter, I review the policy and performance during Modi 2.0 for bank credit, non-bank credit, other credits, the government guaranteed credit schemes and the public sector character of the credit and finance business in India.

Bank Credit

Despite late boom, credit grew slower

Banks' aggregate credit witnessed two phases of expansion in Modi 2.0, one slower (until 2021–22) and the other faster (2022–23 and 2023–24).

In the first phase, banks' credit expanded from Rs 97.72 trillion in 2018–19 to Rs 118.91 trillion in 2021–22, recording a tepid growth of 6.76 per cent over three years. This credit growth was lower than the growth recorded during Modi 1.0, when bank credit expanded by 10.27 per cent from Rs 59.94 trillion in 2013–14 to Rs 97.72 trillion in 2018–19.

Credit growth picked up impressively from 2022–23. Outstanding aggregate credit expanded to Rs 136.75 trillion at end-March 2023, growing by a high 15 per cent during the year. The four-year credit growth, on the back of this performance, edged up to 8.77 per cent.

In the first six months of 2023–24 also, there was a scorching pace in credit growth. The outstanding bank credit jumped to Rs 151.51 trillion at end-September 2023, recording a growth of 10.8 per cent in six months (annualized more than 21 per cent).

On the last day of December 2023, the outstanding bank credit stood at Rs 159.6 trillion and at the end of the financial year in March 2024 at Rs 164.35 trillion. Bank credit grew by a massive 20.18 per cent during 2023–24.

For the five years of Modi 2.0, bank credit recorded a healthy CAGR of 10.96 per cent, higher than the five-year annual growth of 10.27 per cent during the first term.

Large industrial and infrastructure credit collapsed

Much of the real growth in manufacturing and infrastructure is built on the credit advanced by banks to large industry and infrastructure companies. The boom phase of large industrial and infrastructure credit witnessed in the UPA government period (2004–05 to 2013–14) had sputtered in Modi 1.0. In Modi 2.0, it was no better.

The outstanding banking large industrial and infrastructure credit was Rs 20.44 trillion at the end of FY 2013–14, the year before the Modi government took over in May 2014. At the end of Modi 1.0, the industrial and infrastructure credit stood at only Rs 23.65 trillion, recording almost no growth of 2.96 per cent per annum. Fresh credit simply stopped; this little growth perhaps represented more of ongoing disbursements in already sanctioned accounts.

At the end of the first three years of Modi 2.0 (at the end of 2021–22), the outstanding large industrial and infrastructure credit just did not move and stood at Rs 23.98 trillion (almost at the 2018–19 outstanding of Rs 23.65 trillion), recording a paltry CAGR growth of 0.46 per cent in three years. The situation had remained quite pathetic during this entire three-year period. At the end of 2020–21, after two years, the outstanding credit to large industry and infrastructure at Rs 23.56 trillion was less than the outstanding credit at the commencement of Modi 2.0, even in absolute/nominal numbers.

The situation improved somewhat in 2022–23 when the large industry and infrastructure group recorded growth of 3.63 per cent to take outstanding credit to Rs 24.85 trillion at the year end. There was only a further marginal improvement in the pace of credit growth in the first six months of 2023–24. The large industry credit outstanding at the end of September 2023 was only Rs 25.80 trillion, recording a growth of 3.8 per cent during the first six months (annualized about 7.5 per cent).

At the end of FY 2023–24 (on the fortnight ending 22 March 2024), the outstanding credit to large industry and infrastructure rose to Rs 26.51 trillion, recording annual growth of 6.72 per cent. This was the best annual growth that Modi 2.0 witnessed in the large industry and infrastructure segment.

This could, however, raise the CAGR of five years in Modi 2.0 to barely 2.32 per cent per annum. Despite all the capital expenditure and so many PLI schemes, credit to industry and infrastructure expanded at a rate (2.32 per cent) that was even lower than the 2.96 per cent growth generated during Modi 1.0.

Bank credit was no longer financing industrial and infrastructure growth in the country.

Small industry credit picked up in a big way

The micro, small and medium industry (MSMI) credit (MSM services credit is separately shown), which had collapsed in Modi 1.0, picked up a good pace in Modi 2.0. The MSMI credit (recorded in two segments: a. micro and small, and b. medium industry) in RBI publications, was Rs 4.72 trillion (micro and small Rs 3.48 trillion and medium Rs 1.24 trillion) in 2013–14.

The outstanding industrial credit in these two segments at the end of 2018–19, when the Modi government completed its first term, was also exactly the same at Rs 4.72 trillion (micro and small Rs 3.71 trillion and medium Rs 1.01 trillion). The outstanding credit for the medium industry segment had actually decreased at a CAGR of 4.07 per cent during Modi 1.0.

The Modi government and the RBI started providing regulatory accommodation and credit packages to the MSMEs (which included MSMIs) from 2019–20 itself, much before the onset of Covid-19. During Covid-19, the government provided 100 per cent loss guarantee of additional 20 per cent (which was raised upwards later) on the outstanding MSME credit.

As a result of these measures, the credit to MSMIs accelerated, unlike large industry, exhibiting good growth in Modi 2.0. The outstanding credit to micro and small industries grew to Rs 5.32 trillion at a good clip of 12.74 per cent annual growth in the first three years ending 2021–22. The same pace continued in 2022–23 as well, with micro and small industry credit growing to Rs 5.98 trillion, giving an overall four-year CAGR of 12.67 per cent. The medium industry displayed still better growth of 25.92 per cent over these four years, rising to Rs 2.53 trillion at the end of 2022–23. Together, micro and small industries and medium industries' bank credit outstanding at end-2022–23 stood at Rs 8.52 trillion on the back of a decent 15.91 per cent annual compounded growth in the first four years.

The credit expansion to micro, small and medium industries continued at a scorching pace in 2023–24 as well. At the last fortnightly reporting Friday of 22 March 2024, outstanding credit to micro and small industries rose to Rs 7.28 trillion and to medium industries to Rs 3.04 trillion. Together, outstanding bank credit to MSMEs reached Rs 10.32 trillion, recording annual growth of 21.15 per cent during 2023–24.

With bank credit more than doubling (increased by 118 per cent) to MSMIs during Modi 2.0, the five-year CAGR also recorded a very healthy growth of 16.91 per cent.

The proportion of large industry and infrastructure credit has always been much higher in industrial bank credit. In 2013–14, it was over 81 per cent. In 2018–19 also, it exceeded 83 per cent. Thanks to expansion of MSMI credit in the second term, the proportion of large credit came down to 74.47 per cent in 2022–23. At the end of 2023–24, it fell further to 71.98 per cent. However, as the proportion of large and infrastructure credit is still quite high, the overall growth of industrial credit during Modi 2.0 was nonetheless a tepid 5.35 per cent.

Big growth in credit to trade and NBFCs

Most services enterprises are MSMEs. The regulatory accommodation and guarantee protection provided to MSMEs covered the micro, small and medium service enterprises (MSMSEs) as well. In addition, the credit provided by the banks to NBFCs are also considered as part of the services credit. The credit to trade and credit to MSMEs constitute a big bulk of the bank credit outstanding towards the services sector.

In 2018–19, the outstanding credit to trade enterprises was Rs 4.80 trillion (both retail and wholesale trade included), which was 20.5 per cent of the total services sector credit of Rs 23.41 trillion. The outstanding credit to NBFCs at the end of 2018–19 was Rs 7.51 trillion, which constituted 32.09 per cent of the total services credit outstanding. Together, these two segments at Rs 12.31 trillion, had more than 50 per cent of the services sector credit outstanding at the end of 2018–19, the terminal year of Modi 1.0.

These two segments witnessed quite an impressive expansion of credit during Modi 2.0. Trade credit grew at a CAGR of 14.32 per cent in the first four years to reach Rs 8.20 trillion at the end of 2022–23. The NBFCs' credit witnessed a still better growth rate of 15.38 per cent per annum, reaching Rs 13.31

trillion at end-2022–23. Together, these two segments of the services sector had outstanding bank credit of Rs 21.51 crore, which increased close to 60 per cent (59.6 per cent) of the total outstanding services sector credit of Rs 36.09 trillion. The share of bank credit to trade and NBFCs increased from 50 per cent to 60 per cent in the first four years of Modi 2.0.

The RBI started putting some regulatory restrictions on unsecured and NBFC credit in 2023–24. Still, there was no significant let-up in the credit expansion to these two sectors during the last year of Modi 2.0 as well. On the last fortnightly reporting Friday of 22 March 2024, banks' outstanding credit to the trade sector was Rs 10.24 trillion and to NBFCs Rs 15.48 trillion, in total Rs 25.72 trillion, recording annual growth of 19.58 per cent. As the services sector overall recorded an annual growth rate of 27.20 per cent reaching Rs 45.90 trillion, the share of these two services fell a little to 56.03 per cent.

The two segments of trade credit and NBFC credit recorded significant annual growth of 15.88 per cent per annum during Modi 2.0.

Personal loans occupied top sectoral space

Textural transformation of the bank credit in India is best captured in personal loans replacing industrial loans as the top of the four formal sectoral divisions (agriculture, industry, services and personal loans) of outstanding bank credit. In 2013–14, the year before the Modi government took over, the outstanding credit to the industry (all segments of industry together) of Rs 25.16 trillion made up 42 per cent of the total bank outstanding credit of Rs 59.94 trillion.

In 2018–19, the year Modi 1.0 completed its first term, the industrial credit was still the largest sectoral credit (despite almost stagnant growth) at Rs 28.38 trillion out of the total credit outstanding of Rs 97.72 trillion, though its share had come down to only 29 per cent—a fall of 13 per cent in five years.

In the second term, the industry was dethroned from its perch and surrendered its prime position in 2020–21. The personal loans occupied the top spot that year with outstanding loans of Rs 30.09 trillion, whereas the outstanding industrial loans remained stuck at Rs 29.35 trillion.

Personal loans kept strengthening its relative position in the credit sweepstakes during the remaining three years of Modi 2.0. By 2022–23, outstanding personal loans rose to Rs 40.85 trillion and constituted almost 30 per cent (29.87 per cent) of the total outstanding bank credit. The industrial credit share slipped below 25 per cent that year.

In 2023–24, in the last reporting fortnight on 22 March, the personal loans stood at Rs 49.22 trillion (including the HDFC merger effect, Rs 53.36 trillion), recording stupendous growth of 20.49 per cent (excluding the HDFC effect) during the year.

The personal loans recorded a five-year CAGR of 16.40 per cent per year, the highest of all four segments with its share in outstanding loans (Rs 159.90 trillion, excluding the HDFC impact) growing further to 30.95 per cent.

The banks have always been viewed as intermediaries between households/individuals (taking their savings) and enterprises (lending for investment in capital formation). With the households/individuals themselves becoming the largest segment availing bank credit, the banks have now become major intermediators between households/individuals themselves.

Housing loans flourished despite rate hike

The total non-food bank credit rose from Rs 97.30 trillion in 2018–19 to Rs 136.55 trillion in 2022–23 recording annual compounded growth of 8.84 per cent.

Bank credit growth had spurted in 2022–23. In 2022–23, it grew by 15.37 per cent (from Rs 118.36 trillion in 2021–22). Housing loans, which were at Rs 11.77 trillion in 2018–19 rose to Rs 16.84 trillion in 2021–22 and further to Rs 19.36 trillion in 2022–23. Housing loans recorded annual compounded growth of 13.27 per cent over the four-year period from 2018–19 to 2022–23. In 2022–23, the growth rate was 14.96 per cent, close to the overall loan growth rate.

The RBI decided to make it mandatory for banks to link the new retail loan rates to external benchmarks from 1 October 2019. The Financial Benchmarks India Pvt. Ltd (FBIL), jointly owned by Fixed Income Money Market and Derivatives Association of India (FIMMDA), Foreign Exchange Dealers' Association of India (FEDAI) and Indian Bank Association (IBA), publish the benchmarks. Banks were allowed to choose from among the RBI repo rate, GOI 3-month or 6-month T-bills yield or any other benchmark rate published by FBIL to link their housing and retail loan rates. Banks can charge the credit spread they deemed fit over the benchmark.

Most housing loans shifted to external benchmarks, principally the RBI repo-rate. From February 2022 to July 2023, the RBI raised the repo rate by 2.5 per cent. The housing loan borrowers were hit very hard with their EMIs rising by as much as 30–50 per cent. Yet, the pressing need to buy new houses or modify their existing ones in the post-Covid-19 work from home/hybrid scenario made people take housing loans.

Housing loans kept flourishing and bringing good profits to banks. On the last reporting fortnightly Friday of 22 March 2024, outstanding housing loans rose to Rs 23.34 trillion (Rs 27.23 trillion including the HDFC merger impact), growing by a spectacular growth rate of 20.04 per cent. For the five years of Modi 2.0, housing loan growth, not considering the HDFC merger effect, of 14.58 per cent per annum was nothing short of extraordinary, also vindicating the effect of government housing programmes and households' preference to accommodate the demand of work from home growing very fast in the economy.

Banks turned profitable

Scheduled commercial banks (SCBs) together reported aggregated net loss of Rs 23,398 crore in 2018–19, the last year of Modi 1.0. This was perhaps for the first time that the Indian banking industry, as a whole, public and private sector banks included, reported an aggregate net loss. The public sector banks (PSBs) were making losses for some years. In 2018–19 also their net losses amounted to Rs 66,608 crore, almost three times of all the SCBs put together.

From 2019–20, the SCBs together came into profit with total net profits of all the SCBs amounting to Rs 10,911 crore although the PSBs still reported net losses of Rs 26,015 crore. The year 2020–21 marked PSBs' return to profitability as well, with the PSBs reporting aggregate net profit of Rs 31,818 crore. That year, net profits of all the SCBs increased significantly to Rs 1.22 trillion. The march of profitability continued in the other three years as well. The total SCB profitability jumped to Rs 1.82 trillion in 2021–22 and further to Rs 2.63 trillion in 2022–23.

This impressive turnaround in profitability of the banking industry (from a net loss of Rs 23,398 crore in 2018–19 to a high net profit of Rs 2.63 trillion in 2022–23) was scripted by two big factors—improvement in the net interest income of the banks and reduction in the provisions and contingency.

In 2018–19, the net interest income of all the SCBs was Rs 4.30 trillion with the interest income amounting to Rs 11.41 trillion and interest expenditure coming at Rs 7.11 trillion. In the four years of Modi 2.0, the interest income grew to Rs 15.47 trillion at an annual compounded rate of 7.91 per cent, whereas the interest expenditure grew to Rs 8.07 trillion only, at an annual growth rate of 3.23 per cent. Consequently, the net interest income of Rs 7.40 trillion grew at a fabulous rate of 14.53 per cent per annum during this period.

Higher interest income growth was largely on account of expansion in personal credit at a much higher rate of interest, including the housing loans for which the central bank linked the interest rates to the repo rates. As repo rates were increased by 2.5 per cent, the interest income automatically shot up. On the other hand, the banks could successfully delay the passing of higher repo rates to the interest on deposits. The higher net interest income saw some tapering off only in 2023–24, when there was pressure on deposits and the increase in repo rates stopped.

The other factor that improved the profitability of banks was the lowering of provisions and contingencies. In 2018–19, the SCBs had made a total provision of Rs 3.19 trillion. In 2022–23, they made a total provision of Rs 2.46 trillion.

The provisions and contingencies actually contracted at the annual rate of 6.98 per annum. A shorter provision of Rs 0.73 trillion in 2022–23 (compared to 2018–19) directly added to the net profits of banks.

There is one more element of banks' profitability—the other income—which tracks the movement in their investment portfolio interest rates and also the fee income. Both the components of the other income were favourably aligned during the first four years of Modi 2.0, with interest yields on government securities falling and the fee income expanding. The other income of SCBs grew by 9.51 per cent per annum.

The turnaround in banks' profitability was certainly one of the major highlights of Modi 2.0. Whether it is sustainable, however, is quite doubtful.

Payment banks literally ceased to exist as a class

On 11 March 2024, the RBI directed the Paytm Payments Bank Ltd to stop, with immediate effect, onboarding of new customers. By another press release, the RBI directed the Paytm Payments Bank not to accept further credits into its customer accounts and wallets after 15 March 2024. The Paytm Payments Bank ceased to exist as an operating bank at the close of FY 2023–24.

The payment banks as a class of banks had come into being only during the Narendra Modi regime. In August 2015, the RBI had given in-principle approval for eleven entities out of forty-one applicants to set up payments banks, which policy move at that time was hailed as a harbinger of a revolution in the Indian banking sector.

For various reasons—inbuilt financial unviability of the payment banks (e.g. they were not allowed to make any loans and their deposits per account were restricted to Rs 1 lakh) and digital payments made free of charge (merchant discount rate or MDR which the banks earn on payment transactions was abolished in 2018)—the payment bank lost the initial euphoria of telecom and other digital infrastructure companies setting up profitable digital payment banks. By 2019, six of the eleven payment banks either did not operationalize the licences or ceased to operate.

Only six payment banks were actually or notionally operating when the Modi government assumed office for its second term—Indian Postal Payments Bank (IPPB), owned by the GoI, Airtel Payments Bank, Fino Payments Bank, Jio Payments Bank, Paytm Payments Bank and NSDL Payments Bank. These six payment banks had total insured deposits of Rs 12,533 crore at the end of 2022–23. The payment banks earned Rs 4,952 crore income in 2021–22. As their expenditure was Rs 5,041 crore, predominantly operational expenses of Rs 4,882 crore, the payment banks were in operating and net losses in 2021–22 of Rs 87 crore and Rs 90 crore, respectively. In 2022–23, the payment banks did report a small net profit of Rs 121 crore.

The payment banks as a class is becoming extinct fast. Paytm Payments Bank is as good as gone. Fino Payments Bank initiated the process in July 2023 to get converted into a small finance bank. Other payment banks are not seriously operating and may survive, except perhaps for the IPPB, owned by the government.

The government owned IPPB had a paid-in share capital of Rs 1,655 crore as on 31 March 2023 with accumulated losses of Rs 962 crore. Its total income was only Rs 766 crore in that year. This payment bank continues to exist only because the government is committed to supplying unlimited capital to it. The other payment banks, quite small and not in the limelight, might trudge along for some time before they wind up.

Non-Bank Credit

After the government transferred regulatory control over the housing finance companies (HFCs) to the RBI and empowered the RBI to initiate a resolution process against the NBFCs, the RBI is the sole regulator of the entire spectrum of NBFCs in the country.

The NBFCs had loans and advances outstanding of Rs 28.74 trillion at end-March 2023 and their credit to GDP ratio was 12.6 per cent in 2023 against the credit to GDP ratio of 50.2 per cent for the SCBs.

NBFCs are a significant player in the credit space in India. There were 9,480 RBI-regulated NBFCs in the country at the end of September 2023.

RBI regrouped NBFCs in four layers

The RBI's principal concern as a regulator of NBFCs has been protecting the depositors' interests; NBFCs, except a small number of deposit-taking NBFCs, are not allowed to take deposits from the general public. For many years, the NBFCs universe was classified by the RBI, from the depositors' perspective, into four broad classes of credit-providing NBFCs: Deposit Taking or NBFCs-D, NBFCs-Non-Deposit Taking or NBFCs-ND, Asset Reconstruction Companies (ARCs) and Housing Finance Companies (HFCs).

The NBFCs-ND constituted the bulk with 9,330 NBFCs/financial companies categorized therein. There was also a further subdivision of NBFCs-ND into systemically important (NDFCs-ND-SI), defined as the NBFCs-NDs with asset sizes of Rs 500 crore or more, which numbered 507, and the remaining NBFCs-ND, classified as Other NBFCs-ND, which were much larger in number at 8,823. The RBI had stopped granting licences to NBFCs as deposit-taking NBFCs many years ago. There have been twenty-six of them for decades. The remaining comprised twenty-seven ARCs and ninety-seven HFCs.

In addition to these four credit-providing NBFCs, there were a few other types of NBFCs that focused on investments or on providing non-credit financial services. In all, the RBI had eleven classes of NBFCs.

The RBI implemented another grouping arrangement for NBFCs in October 2022 without altering the basic classification or character of the NBFCs. According to the new arrangement, there are four layers of NBFCs: base layer (NBFC-BL), middle layer (NBFC-ML), upper layer (NBFC-UL) and top layer (NBFC-TL).

The RBI wants to keep the top layer vacant unless it identifies some NBFC-UL as having developed a considerable rise in potential systemic risk. The RBI has designed standard regulatory arrangements for all three layers of BL, ML and UL. In case the RBI classifies an NBFC as NBFC-TL, the RBI will design a specific regulatory package for such an NBFC. RBI regulations are designed to keep at least the top 10 NBFC-ML in the category of NBFC-UL. Currently, there are fifteen NBFCs in the NBFC-UL.

The total asset size of the NBFCs was of the order of Rs 45.37 trillion as on 31 March 2023. The depositing-taking NBFCs, the NBFCs-D, had a total asset size of Rs 6.61 trillion and the NBFC-NDs of Rs 38.76 trillion on that date.

NBFCs' dependence on bank financing increased significantly

The NBFCs, unlike banks, have no access to current and savings account (CASA) deposits. In fact, there is no defined and dedicated source of finance for the NBFCs. NBFCs' usual (secured) borrowing resources are debentures, borrowings from banks and borrowings from financial institutions.

In 2018–19, of the total borrowing of Rs 20.03 trillion, the secured borrowings comprised Rs 11.07 trillion and unsecured the remaining Rs 8.96 trillion. The banks provided both secured and unsecured financing to the NBFCs, though the bulk of it was in secured mode. Of the total secured and unsecured borrowings in 2018–19, the NBFCs' borrowings from the banks amounted to Rs 6.10 trillion (Rs 4.90 trillion in secured borrowings)—30.44 per cent of all the borrowings of the NBFCs and 21.58 per cent of all their resources.

In 2022–23, the total borrowings of NBFCs rose to Rs 30.02 trillion, registering an annual growth rate of 10.65 per cent, although not a very high growth rate but indicating sufficiently that NBFCs' businesses were expanding quite well, having overcome the massive ILFS and liquidity induced slowdown in the first term. The borrowing of the NBFCs from the banks, however, grew at a much more rapid rate. The outstanding borrowings of NBFCs from banks at the end of 2022–23 amounted to Rs 11.33 trillion, which was as high as 37.78 per cent of total borrowings. More significantly, the borrowings of NBFCs from the banks grew at a much higher rate of 16.76 per cent CAGR.

Raising resources through debentures is the only way for the NBFCs, other than the twenty-six NBFCs-D, to raise resources from the public directly or indirectly. The government had granted certain concessions in its first term for popularizing debentures as the principal mode of raising resources for NBFCs (including doing away with the mandatory requirement of maintaining debenture redemption reserves).

The NBFCs do raise both secured and unsecured debentures. In 2018–19, NBFCs had raised secured debentures of Rs 5.21 trillion and unsecured debentures of Rs 3.41 trillion, totalling Rs 8.62 trillion. In 2022–23, the NBFCs raised total debentures of Rs 11.46 trillion (Rs 6.34 trillion in secured and Rs 5.12 trillion in unsecured debentures). Total resources raised through debentures grew by only 6.53 per cent during the four-year period of Modi 2.0, at a rate much smaller than the resources raised by NBFCs from banks. What was more disappointing was that secured debentures recorded an annual growth rate of only 4.64 per cent per annum.

The dependence of NBFCs on banks for raising lendable resources and the inability to develop debentures as their principal mode of raising resources was so evident and builds considerable risks for both NBFCs and banks.

Retail loans expanded the most

NBFCs tend to grab the lending space which the formal banking system cannot efficiently reach out to: loans that banks are reluctant to give, e.g. loans to builders and loans against shares, etc.; loans which they can provide faster and more efficiently, e.g. vehicle loans; or loans which are small and costly, e.g. microfinance loans, etc., in rural areas. Most of these are retail loans. They also provide loans to riskier large industrial clients.

In 2018–19, the NBFCs loans outstanding at the end of the year were Rs 22.95 trillion. These grew to Rs 34.27 trillion at the end of 2022–23, at an annual growth rate of 10.54 per cent. Of the six components making up NBFCs' outstanding loan portfolio, the loans to industry were the largest at Rs 9.31 trillion (large industry loans being Rs 4.65 trillion). The retail loans at Rs 5.99 trillion were the second largest with a share of 26.09 per cent. Services loans were Rs 4.11 trillion, with food credit being only Rs 200 crore and other non-food credit amounting to Rs 2.92 trillion.

Retail loans expanded at a much higher pace than the overall growth in NBFC credit. In 2022–23, after the first four years of Modi 2.0, retail loans grew to Rs 10.55 trillion at an annual growth rate of 15.20 per cent. The share of retail loans in overall NBFC credit increased from 26.09 per cent in 2018–19 to 30.77 per cent in 2022–23.

Of the retail loans, credit card receivables recorded huge growth at 22.03 per cent. Micro finance loans/SHG loans were not separately reported in

2018–19. In 2019–20, these loans were reported at Rs 43,802 crore, which rose massively to Rs 1.19 trillion in 2022–23, registering a massive CAGR of 39.44 per cent. In the retail loans space, advances to individuals against gold, not recorded separately until 2018–19, amounted to Rs 34,678 crore in 2019–20, which rose at an incredibly high rate of 55.81 per cent per annum in the next three years to reach to Rs 1.14 trillion in 2022–23.

The state of retail loans, particularly microfinance loans and loans against gold, indicated the difficult consumption environment the people of India were facing in the wake of the loss of income caused by lockdowns during Covid-19 and the disappearance of low-skill labour jobs from the economy.

The large industry loans also grew handsomely to Rs 10.20 trillion at a decent growth rate of 21.70 per cent per annum (contrast this from almost flat growth in loans from banks to large industry). The loans to services moved at a slow pace of 3.79 per annum as the banks expanded these loans, growing to Rs 4.77 trillion at the end of 2022–23.

Retail loans flying away, from both banks and non-banks, is the story of financing growth for Modi 2.0.

RBI saw fintechs with potential to transform the financial landscape

In its November 2020 Bulletin, the RBI said the following on the emerging fintech industry in India:

> The landscape of banking and financial sector has undergone a phenomenal transformation since 2008 global financial crisis (GFC), owing to financial technology firms, popularly known as 'FinTechs'. Both as creative disruptors and facilitators, FinTechs have contributed to the modern banking and financial sector through various channels including cost optimization, better customer service and financial inclusion. FinTechs have played an important role in unbundling banking into core functions of settling payments, performing maturity transformation, sharing risk and allocating capital.
>
> In India, FinTechs and digital players could function as the fourth segment of the Indian financial system, alongside large banks, mid-sized banks including niche banks, small finance banks, regional rural banks and cooperative banks. This segment has the potential to fundamentally transform the financial landscape where consumers will be able to choose from a broader set of alternatives at competitive prices, and financial institutions could improve efficiency through lower costs. India has emerged as the fastest growing FinTech market and the third largest FinTech ecosystem in the world. Today, we carry out complex financial actions

like sending or receiving money, paying bills, buying goods and services, purchasing insurance, trading on stock markets, opening bank accounts and applying for personal loans online using smartphones, without ever physically interfacing with a bank employee.

Covid-19 and lockdown disruptions engendered the ground for very fast expansion of the fintech industry. The industry came up with numerous products and latched on to the payment revolution brought in by UPI and other instant payment mechanisms in India.

Fintechs spread their wings far and wide

The fintech industry provides technology-based services across the entire financial landscape, which gets described as PayTech in the payment space, LendTech in the credit space, InsurTech in the insurance space, WealthTech in wealth management and so on.

This nascent fintech industry in India before the Modi government took over in 2014 (funding $0.2 billion in 2014) established stable and large levels of funding in the first term ($1.6 billion in 2015, $0.8 billion in 2016, $3.1 billion in 2017 and $2.8 billion in 2018) with total fintech funding exceeding $8.3 billion during 2014–2018.

The second term of the Modi government began very well in 2019 as far as fintech start-up funding was concerned, with fintechs receiving funding of $2.8 billion in 2019 and a slightly lower funding of $2.2 billion in the Covid-19 and lockdown-affected year 2020. $5.0 billion fintech funding in the first two years was quite encouraging and confirmed the fintech industry, establishing its roots quite firmly in India.

The year 2021 proved to be a blockbuster. In that year alone, Indian fintech start-ups received $8 billion of funding, almost equal to the total funding received in the entire first term of the Modi government. Everyone believed the fintech start-up industry was by then fully entrenched in India.

In 2022, the fintech start-up funding fell somewhat to $4.8 billion, which was not all that bad. However, in 2023, it floundered to its lowest level in Modi 2.0 at $2 billion.

Increasing funding of the fintech industry in India actually followed increased penetration of the fintech industry in providing financial services across the entire spectrum of payments, credit and investment.

The UPI is the biggest success story not only in India but all over the world. It is the two fintech companies—PhonePe and Google Pay, along with India's own fintech start-up Paytm—which actually scripted the UPI's grand adoption in India.

The fintech industry also enabled expansion of credit to micro and small enterprises, besides providing them services to digitize their accounts and financial management. The growth of start-ups like Groww have also turned the mutual fund industry into fintech-enabled services primarily.

The industry also came up with several new (and innovative) products, such as buy now pay later (BNPL), peer-to-peer (P2P) lending, payment aggregators and so on.

The fintech ecosystem established and thrived very well in India during the second term of the Modi government until the RBI got a little worried.

RBI started cracking the whip

The RBI began promoting tokenization of debit/credit/prepaid card transactions in January 2019 'to enhance the safety and security of the payment system in the country'. This was expected to be a parallel but alternative system to the prevailing practice of merchants recording the card details on file (CoF) and effecting payments using that. The voluntary promotion did not succeed.

In September 2021, the RBI resorted to compulsory tokenization. The circular it issued said: 'With effect from January 1, 2022, no entity in the card transaction or payment chain, other than the card issuers and card networks, should store the actual card data. Any such data stored previously will be purged.' Most e-commerce merchants like Amazon, Netflix, Flipkart, etc., made many representations. None of these were accepted and card tokenization became compulsory from 1 October 2022.

In June 2022, the RBI cracked the whip on fast-expanding and booming BNPL credits through fintechs, which also included e-wallets. The RBI's notification disallowed non-bank prepaid payment instrument (PPI) issuers from loading credit lines from banks. The move disentitled the fintech players from offering credit lines in partnership with NBFCs. The RBI circular said, 'The PPI-MD (master direction) does not permit loading of PPIs from credit lines. Such practice, if followed, should be stopped immediately. Any non-compliance in this regard may attract penal action under provisions contained in the Payment and Settlement Systems Act, 2007.' The RBI circular restricted this for only thirty-seven non-bank PPI issuers (bank PPI instruments were permitted), which included prominent non-bank PPI issuers including Bajaj Finance, Amazon Pay and PhonePe.

There were many more measures to control the expansion of the fintech industry in areas and providing services that the RBI considered not in the interest of the orderly development of the financial services industry and the financial stability of the country. The RBI also began taking measures for collecting information about the fintech industry and bringing in a regulatory structure.

In its development policy statement released along with the monetary policy statement on 8 December 2023, the RBI initiated steps to collect all 'relevant and timely information on FinTech entities, including the nature of their activities', which included within its scope non-conventional and 'emerging technologies like distributed ledger technology (DLT), artificial intelligence/machine learning (AI/ML) and so on', increasingly used by the fintech industry. For this purpose, the RBI proposed 'to set-up a Repository for capturing essential information about FinTechs, encompassing their activities, products, technology stack, financial information etc.', voluntarily, at least initially.

On 15 January, the RBI, to optimize the contribution of the fintech sector, placed on its website a 'Draft framework for recognizing Self-Regulatory Organizations (SRO) for FinTech Sector' for 'healthy balance between facilitating innovation by the industry on the one hand, and meeting regulatory priorities in a manner that protects consumers and contains risk, on the other'. The RBI argued that self-regulation within the fintech sector was a preferred approach for achieving the desired balance. Perhaps the RBI had second thoughts about establishing an SRO for the fintech sector later. No further action was taken until Modi 2.0 was over.

There was significant entity-specific regulatory actions on fintech players in January–March 2024, including on Paytm. By the end of the second term, the fintech industry was scurrying for cover.

Other Credit Institutions

There are quite a few other segments of the Indian financial market that provide credit to industry and households. I will briefly discuss the developments relating to All India Financial Institutions (AIFIs) in this section during Modi 2.0.

There were four AIFIs in existence when the Modi government began its second term—Export-Import Bank of India (EXIM Bank), National Bank for Agriculture and Rural Development (NABARD), National Housing Bank (NHB) and Small Industries Development Bank of India (SIDBI). The government set up a new AIFI—National Bank for Financing Infrastructure Development (NaBFID)—in 2021, which began some disbursements in 2022–23.

The four AIFIs disbursed a total of Rs 4.15 trillion in 2018–19, with NABARD accounting for the largest share of Rs 2.82 trillion. These AIFIs disbursed Rs 4.37 trillion in 2019–20, with SIDBI accounting for the bulk of the increase with its disbursements going up from Rs 75,463 crore in 2018–19 to Rs 1.08 trillion in 2019–20. While the NABARD disbursement stayed almost at 2018–19 levels, the disbursements from EXIM Bank and NHB actually declined during the year.

The year 2020–21 saw a big jump in disbursements from NABARD—from Rs 2.81 trillion in 2019–20 to Rs 3.49 trillion in 2020–21. NHB also recorded a significant increase, from Rs 17,180 crore in 2019–20 to Rs 42,823 crore in 2020–21.

The AIFIs' disbursements kept increasing in the next two years, primarily from SIDBI. NABARD disbursements plateaued at Rs 3.78 trillion in 2021–22 and Rs 3.64 trillion in 2022–23. SIDBI's disbursements rose to Rs 1.45 trillion in 2021–22 and then jumped to Rs 2.79 trillion in 2022–23. NaBFID joined the group with disbursements of Rs 10,045 crore in 2022–23.

NaBFID—almost a failed institution

The government has been establishing financial institutions in the infrastructure space for many years. The Infrastructure Development Finance Company Ltd (IDFC) was promoted in 1997. The Indian Infrastructure Finance Corporation Ltd (IIFCL) was established in 2006. The IDFC faded away with a remnant of it becoming an alternate investment fund (AIF), which was also sold off finally to another fund. With its bank part also becoming part of another private sector bank after merging with an NBFC, IDFC ceased to exist. IIFCL continues to exist but not as a major infrastructure-lending institution. In 2002–23, total disbursements by IIFCL amounted to only Rs 13,826 crore.

Yet, the government established another infrastructure financing institution in 2021, that too by getting a specific law passed in the Parliament. Not only creating NaBFID as a statutory corporation to promote and finance infrastructure development in the country, the government infused equity of Rs 20,000 crore in the first year (2021–22) itself. In addition, the government provided a grant of Rs 5,000 crore. NaBFID was expected to run up disbursements worth Rs 1 trillion in two years and Rs 5 trillion in five years.

The CMD of NaBFID kept promising that NaBFID would start making disbursements in 2021–22 and would be able to sanction Rs 1 trillion in 2022–23. NaBFID could not sanction a single rupee of infrastructure projects in 2021–22. In 2022–23 also, the sanctions amounted to Rs 18,561 crore only. The details of these sanctions were never made publicly available. Whether these sanctions represented refinancing of existing loans sanctioned by others or there was direct funding of infrastructure projects was not ascertainable.

At the end of 2023–24, NaBFID could claim to have a loan portfolio of only Rs 35,342 crore, which was not even 8 per cent of 'at least Rs 5 lakh crores' which the Finance Minister promised in her Budget 2021–22.

NaBFID was expected to be a vital cog in the roll-out of the National Infrastructure Pipeline (NIP). The NIP itself was slow to move during Modi 2.0. The contribution NaBFID played in its roll-out and infrastructure financing in three years of its existence was hardly inspiring. This institution is failing and it might as well be on its way to becoming another infrastructure set-up by the government that did not deliver much.

Emergency Credit Line Guarantee Scheme

Government announces guaranteed credit stimulus for MSMEs

On 20 May 2020, in the immediate backdrop of a stimulus package and the first wave of Covid-19 lockdowns, the government approved an Emergency Credit Line Guarantee Scheme (ECLGS) for pushing bank credit to MSMEs.

The government decided to underwrite/guarantee additional funding of up to Rs 3 trillion to eligible MSMEs and Micro Units Development and Refinance Agency Ltd (MUDRA) borrowers. The government agreed to provide 100 per cent guarantee coverage to such loans through the National Credit Guarantee Trustee Company Ltd (NCGTC).

The government approved a corpus of Rs 41,600 crore (which later increased to more than Rs 61,000 crore) for potential credit losses under the ECLGS. Initially, all MSME borrower accounts, with outstanding credit of up to Rs 25 crore as on 29 February 2020 (increased to Rs 50 crore on June 2020), which were less than or equal to sixty days past due as on that date with an annual turnover of up to Rs 100 crore, were made eligible under the scheme.

The banks and NCGTC-registered member-lending institutions (MLIs) were mandated to provide additional working capital term loans/additional term loans up to 20 per cent of the outstanding credit up to Rs 25 crore as on 29 February, 2020.

The government decided important features of the credit to be provided under the ECLGS. The tenor of the loan was mandated to be four years with a moratorium of one year on the principal amount. No guarantee fee was to be charged. The interest rates were capped at 9.25 per cent for banks and FIs, and at 14 per cent for NBFCs.

Made credit to small sector risk-free for banks

The RBI granted zero-risk weight for the credit approved under the ECLGS.

Vide a circular issued on 21 June 2020, the RBI stipulated that 'as credit facilities extended under the scheme guaranteed by NCGTC are backed by an unconditional and irrevocable guarantee provided by GoI, it has been decided that Member Lending Institutions shall assign zero per cent risk weight on the credit facilities extended under this scheme to the extent of guarantee coverage'. Zero-risk weight/zero capital on all the loans provided and guaranteed under the ECLGS!

The credit sanctioned under ECLGS attracted no guarantee fee. There was no capital charge. The interest rates were capped at fairly moderate levels. Only interest was required to be paid in the first twenty-four months.

Many versions of ECLGS

The government was quite confident that the scheme would be quickly implemented. The Cabinet decision, therefore, provided that the scheme would be applicable to all eligible loans sanctioned during the period up to 31 October 2020, or till the amount of Rs 3 trillion was exhausted, whichever took place earlier.

This optimism, however, turned out to be untrue. There were many pulls and pressures to make relaxations in the scheme conditions and extend it to many stressed sectors outside the eligibility determined in May 2020.

Consequently, as many as six subsequent versions of the scheme came out, which were designated as ECLGS 1.0, 2.0, 3.0 and 4.0 and three modifications 1.0 (additional), 2.0 (additional) and 3.0 (additional). These are summarized below:

ECLGS 1.0: provided 100 per cent guarantee for eligible credit facility to borrowers whose total credit outstanding (fund-based only) as on 29 February 2020 was up to Rs 50 crore and past due status did not exceed sixty days.

ECLGS 1.0 (Extension): provided additional 10 per cent funding support (in addition to 20 per cent) to existing and new borrowers of ECLGS 1.0 for the revised reference date of 31 March 2021.

ECLGS 2.0: provided 100 per cent guarantee for eligible credit facility to borrowers in the twenty-six sectors identified by the K.V. Kamath Committee on Resolution Framework vide its report dated 4 April 2020 and healthcare sector, whose total credit outstanding (fund-based only) as on 29 February 2020 exceeded Rs 50 crore but not Rs 500 crore with past due status of less than sixty days.

ECLGS 2.0 (Extension): provided additional support to existing borrowers of ECLGS 2.0 or new borrowers eligible under ECLGS 2.0 based on the revised reference date of 31 March 2021.

ECLGS 3.0: provided 100 per cent guarantee for eligible credit facility to borrowers in the hospitality and related sectors and civil aviation sector whose past dues were up to sixty days as on 29 February 2020.

ECLGS 3.0 (Extension): provided additional support to existing borrowers of ECLGS 3.0 or new borrowers eligible under ECLGS 3.0 based on the revised reference date of 31 March 2021 or 31 January 2022.

ECLGS 4.0: provided 100 per cent guarantee for eligible credit facility extended to eligible hospitals/nursing homes/clinics/medical colleges/units engaged in manufacturing of liquid oxygen, oxygen cylinders, etc., for setting up on-site oxygen producing plants.

Relaxations and concessions granted routinely

The government extended the scheme deadline and maximum outstanding loan ceiling from time to time until 31 March 2023, after which no further extension was granted. Many significant extensions/relaxations were made, though, for specific sectors.

For borrowers belonging to the twenty-six stressed sectors identified by the Kamath Committee and healthcare sector, the loan outstanding ceiling was fixed above Rs 50 crore to up to Rs 500 crore under ECLGS 2.0.

On 29 September 2021, the government notified raising of the credit limit by 10 per cent of the outstanding credit. Existing borrowers under ECLGS 1.0 and 2.0 were made eligible for additional credit support of up to 10 per cent of total credit outstanding as on 29 February 2020 or 31 March 2021, whichever was higher, raising the credit ceiling to 30 per cent of the total credit outstanding.

Businesses in sectors specified under ECLGS 3.0 (hospitality, travel and tourism, leisure and sporting and civil aviation) were allowed to avail credit support up to 40 per cent of their credit outstanding as on 31 March 2021 and to the maximum of Rs 200 crore per borrower.

On 30 March 2022, major relaxations were made for the travel, tourism and hospitality sector and the civil aviation sector. New borrowers in the sectors who had borrowed after 31 March 2021 and up to 31 January 2022 were made eligible to avail of emergency credit facilities under ECLGS 3.0. The extent of emergency credit facilities was massively increased for all such borrowers. All eligible borrowers (other than the civil aviation sector) were permitted to avail up to 50 per cent of their highest fund-based credit outstanding on any of three reference dates (29 February 2020, 31 March 2021 and 31 January 2022), as against the earlier limit of 40 per cent of the higher of their fund-based outstanding on either of two reference dates (29 February 2020 and 31 March 2021).

The eligible borrowers in the civil aviation sector were permitted to avail of non-fund based emergency credit facilities as well under ECLGS 3.0. They were allowed to avail up to 50 per cent of their highest total fund and non-fund-based credit outstanding on any of the three reference dates referred to above, subject to a maximum of Rs 400 crore per borrower. Further, to lower their cost of accessing non-fund-based credit, bank guarantees, letters of credit and other non-fund-based facilities sanctioned under ECLGS 3.0 were permitted to be issued without any cash margin and subject to a cap of 0.5 per cent per annum on the fee/commission.

On 6 October 2022, the government allowed credit support to airline companies, up to 100 per cent of their total credit outstanding (both fund-based and non-fund-based outstanding) as on the reference dates, subject to a cap of Rs 1,500 crore per borrower, whichever was lower. Of this, Rs 500 crore (over Rs 1,000 crore) was made available subject to the additional condition of promoters/owners infusing proportionate equity contribution.

The overall ceiling, initially announced for ECLGS at Rs 3 trillion was enhanced to Rs 4.5 trillion. An NCGTC letter dated 30 August 2022 extended the ECLGS from Rs 4.5 trillion to Rs 5 trillion.

On 31 October 2020, the government extended ECLGS 'by one month till November 30, 2020, or till such time that an amount of Rs 3 trillion is sanctioned under the Scheme, whichever is earlier'. The government on 30 March 2022 extended the timeline of ECLGS till 31 March 2022 or till guarantees for an amount of Rs 4.5 trillion were issued under the scheme, whichever was earlier. Further, the last date of disbursement under the scheme was also extended to 30 June 2022.

The Finance Minister announced in Budget 2022–23 that the ECLGS would be extended further. Following that, NCGTC, on 30 March 2022, extended the ECLGS till March 2023. The scheme formally closed on 31 March 2023. The last date of disbursement for fund-based facility and utilization of the first tranche for non-fund-based facility for airlines under ECLGS 3.0 (Extension) was revised from 30 June 2023 to 15 July 2023 on 29 June 2023.

Scheme took time to take off

Most loans covered under ECLGS had a repayment period of up to five years, in which interest was chargeable only for twenty-four months with the principal repayment only thereafter in twenty-six monthly instalments. There were in all 244 member-lending institutions—twelve PSBs, twenty-one private sector banks, eight foreign banks, ten small finance banks, two financial institutions—EXIM Bank and SIDBI, twelve cooperative banks, forty-two RRBs and 139 NBFCs.

The Department of Financial Services (DFS), operational controller of the ECLGS, informed that, as on 2 July 2021, Rs 2.73 trillion had been sanctioned under the scheme, of which Rs 2.14 trillion had been disbursed. The loans sanctioned could cross Rs 2.86 trillion on 24 September 2021.

It was stated on 25 March 2022 that the loans sanctioned under ECLGS had crossed Rs 3.19 trillion. The government informed the Parliament on 13 March 2023 that, as on 31 January 2023, the guarantees amounting to Rs 3.61 trillion had been issued under ECLGS, benefiting 1.19 crore borrowers. Of this, the number of loans guaranteed to MSMEs were 1.14 crore (95.18 per cent) and the amount of credit sanctioned was Rs 2,39,147.53 crore (66.16 per cent).

Non-performing loans started emerging

Soon, non-performing loans started emerging in the scheme. On 23 September 2021, NCGTC informed all MLIs who had not reported/missed to mark its

NPA data on the ECLGS portal within the stipulated time of ninety days from the date of the NPA.

As a one-time measure, such MLIs were allowed to enter/report such pending NPA data on the ECLGS portal on or before 31 October 2021. It was also brought to their notice that for all NPA accounts which were reported on the ECLGS portal with the delay, deduction from the claim amount to the extent of 1.5 per cent as penalty would be charged.

The RBI Financial Stability Report (December 2022) suggests that, of the Rs 2.82 trillion disbursed till September 2022, about Rs 2.20 trillion (78 per cent) was under ECLGS 1.0 and ECLGS 1.0 (Extension). The report also stated that one-sixth of the ECLGS amount availed has turned into NPA.

An evaluation report in March 2023 commissioned by NCGTC found the NPA ratio of PSBs under ECLGS was better than their overall gross NPA ratio. The NPA ratio of private banks (PvBs) is comparable to their overall benchmark. However, the NPA ratio of NBFCs is much higher under ECLGS. NPA ratios have fallen over time between ECLGS 1.0 and ECLGS 4.0. The NPA ratio was close to 11 per cent for ECLGS loans, which carry rates beyond 10 per cent.

NCGTC did not carry out any further impact assessment. At least, no such report was placed on its website after the first and last report of 20 March 2023.

Status of non-performing loans in March 2023

Credit sanctioned by different groups of MLIs and NPAs performed differently, as brought out in the NCGTC-commissioned evaluation study in March 2023.

Banks did the bulk of the sanctions: Rs 3.06 trillion out of total loans of Rs 3.62 trillion sanctioned (84.4 per cent), with the private banks claiming the largest share (Rs 1.61 trillion: 44.5 per cent). Foreign banks (Rs 8,510 crore), cooperative banks (Rs 3,601 crore), small finance banks (Rs 2,607 crore) and regional rural banks (Rs 811 crore) also contributed a little.

NBFCs with sanctions of Rs 31,258 crore, financial institutions with sanctions of Rs 5,786 crore and housing finance companies with sanctions of Rs 3,921 crore were the non-bank credit providers. A total of Rs 2.91 trillion loans were disbursed (80 per cent). Private banks had the best disbursing ratio (Rs 1.42 trillion; 88.75 per cent). PSBs were poor disbursers (Rs 1.03 trillion; 71 per cent).

A total of Rs 15,478 crore was marked as NPAs—5.32 per cent of loans disbursed. NBFCs had the largest proportion of NPAs (Rs 2,934 crore; 11.98 per cent). PSBs' NPAs (5.93 per cent) were higher than private banks' NPAs (3.73 per cent).

Only a much smaller proportion of the loans marked as NPAs were actually lodged as claims—Rs 2,374 crore (15.33 per cent of claims lodged). The government began settling the claims as well. Claims of Rs 1,102 crore were settled.

Public Sector Dominance of Finance Function

PSBs continued to shrink despite enormous capital infusion

The government had infused over Rs 3 trillion equity (including premium) in public sector banks (PSBs) between 2018 and 2022. A good part of this equity was used by the PSBs to write off the loans and advances classified as loss assets. At the end of FY 2016–17, the PSBs had a total equity of Rs 5.78 trillion. At the end of 2018–19, the total equity was Rs 5.97 trillion. Not much change.

Thereafter, in four years of Modi 2.0, the PSBs used a part of further capital infusion and profits earned to build reserves and surpluses. As a result, PSBs' total equity increased to Rs 8.95 trillion at the end of FY 2022–23, by Rs 2.98 trillion. PSBs' capital increased by 10.66 per cent per annum. Total equity capital of PvBs, not including foreign banks (FBs), small finance banks (SFBs) and payment banks (PBs) grew at 15.21 per cent CAGR per annum. The difference was that almost all PvBs could raise capital from the markets, whereas all the PSBs literally shunned the equity market and raised capital from the government.

With all the PSBs out of the prompt corrective action (PCA) framework and their equity capital restored beyond minimum regulatory requirements, the PSBs were expected to do much better during Modi 2.0 and gain market share in deposits, loans and assets. Still, the PvBs continued to gain market share on all three parameters at the cost of PSBs.

PSBs' total deposits grew from Rs 84.86 trillion in 2018–19 to Rs 117.10 trillion in 2022–23, growing at an annual rate of 11.01 per cent. PvBs' total deposits grew, in this period, from Rs 37.70 trillion to Rs 62.99 trillion at a CAGR of 13.69 per cent. PSBs' share in total deposits was 65.85 per cent in 2018–19, whereas that of PvBs was 29.26 per cent. As a result of relatively lesser growth in total deposits, PSBs' share came down to 61.41 per cent in 2022–23, whereas PvBs' share grew to 33.04 per cent. Despite massive capital infusion at taxpayers' cost, PSBs lost market share in deposits by roughly 1 per cent a year.

A similar trajectory was noticeable in case of loans and advances. PSBs' outstanding loans and advances of Rs 58.93 trillion, which made up 60.90 per cent of total outstanding loans, and advances of Rs 96.76 trillion in 2018–19, grew to Rs 82.84 trillion in 2022–23, resulting in a lower share of 57.85 per cent of the total outstanding loans and advances of Rs 143.19 trillion. PSBs lost a share of a little over 3 per cent of loans and advances in four years. PvBs, on the other hand, increased their loans and advances from Rs 33.27 trillion in

2018–19 to Rs 53.67 trillion in 2022–23, improving their market share from 34.39 per cent to 37.48 per cent.

The gap in the share of PSBs and PvBs is steadily shrinking.

Similar trends were visible in total assets and liabilities. PSBs, despite massive capital infusion and consolidation in fewer big banks, continue to shed their market dominance.

Government did not privatize two public sector banks

The Modi government displayed enormous political courage when Finance Minister Nirmala Sitharaman proposed privatization of two public sector banks (PSBs) in her 2021–22 Budget Speech. However, no follow-up action whatsoever was taken, although the Finance Minister had promised bringing amendments in the bank nationalization laws in the 2021–22 Budget Session itself.

RBI staff published a research paper in the August 2022 issue of the RBI Bulletin lauding the role of PSBs and arguing that what it called the 'big-bang privatization' of PSBs was no panacea. This created a deep apprehension that the RBI was against privatization. The RBI officially acknowledged that the article did create an impression in media that the RBI was against privatization of PSBs and, referring to the government announcement of privatizing two PSBs, clarified that the 'gradual approach as announced by the Government would result in better outcome'. No 'big bang action' or 'gradual approach' was taken by the government in the rest of the Modi 2.0 tenure.

Indira Gandhi nationalized twenty private sector banks in 1969 and 1980, at that time representing over 90 per cent of the deposits and loans in the banking system. This was admittedly done for purely political reason. The idea was to control nationalized banks to do politico-social banking—provide cheap loans to farmers, the poor and small businesses—to turn them into vote banks. Except for some gains in spreading banking to rural areas and channelizing of government benefits to beneficiaries, the nationalization of banks failed spectacularly. The poor ended up only providing cheap CASA deposits to banks. PSBs splurged in lending non-performing loans to industrial cronies.

Within twenty-five years of the first nationalization in 1969, the government started reversing the policy. New banking licenses were provided by the Narasimha Rao-Manmohan Singh government in the early 1990s to usher in new-age private sector banking. That policy worked. In the last three decades, the banking scenario has transformed enormously. The share of PvBs in growth of deposits and credit has consistently been higher than the nationalized banks by a wide margin for many years now. PvBs have generated more profits, fewer non-performing loans and fewer frauds than PSBs.

The Modi government adopted the policy of consolidating PSBs. SBI's subsidiaries were merged into SBI. Eight PSBs were merged into five larger

PSBs—Bank of Baroda, Punjab National Bank, Indian Bank, Canara Bank and Union Bank. Now there are twelve PSBs, including the behemoth SBI—six large and six small. Consolidation changed very little. Some branches were rationalized and common IT systems adopted. Risk assessment, banking culture, technically outdated staff, all continued unchanged.

The Finance Minister's Budget Speech 2021 laid down the government's CPSE privatization policy. Banks were included in strategic sectors in which the government could retain up to four PSEs. The policy allowed privatization of eight PSBs. The government made the opening gambit proposing to privatize two. These two PSBs were expected to be named soon after the Budget announcement. A NITI Aayog committee reportedly shortlisted two PSBs—Central Bank of India and Indian Overseas Bank—which was never announced officially. Despite a categorical announcement, the bill to amend the bank nationalization laws was not introduced in the Budget Session. Eight Parliament sessions, including the Budget 2022–23 and Interim Budget 2023–24 Session have gone by since then. There was no sign of the Banking Laws Amendment Bill.

Bank nationalization was simply abandoned.

Part VI

Budgets and Debt

17

Expenditures

Budgets are essentially about the expenditures the government intends to make in the ensuing year. Along with the expenditure budget for the coming year, the government also presents the revised estimates for the current year, taking into account information for actual expenditures for up to nine months of the year already gone by. As per tradition, the government also provides the actuals of the year gone by. All budgets thus have expenditure information for three years.

Expenditures are organized into four broad categories in the budgets: a. general services, b. social services, c. economic services, and d. grants and contributions. This classification is based on a long-standing government accounting convention.

The expenditures on running the government and what broadly would constitute sovereign institutions—the presidential secretariat, Cabinet, Parliament, election commission, CAG, among others—and also what is normally understood as public goods and services, such as defence, police, currency, foreign relations, are considered as expenditure on general services. Interest payment and pension expenditures are also classified as part of general expenditures.

Expenditures on welfare measures for the weaker and poorer sections of society, such as education, scholarships, health, subsidized food, etc., are classified as part of social services expenditures. Expenditures on agriculture, industry, infrastructure and other economic growth-promoting interventions and heads are considered as economic services expenditures. Grants and contributions expenditures, as the name implies, are made up of the grants and other transfers made to the state governments, foreign governments and other persons.

Expenditures are classified into revenue expenditure and capital expenditure depending upon the nature of expenditure.

Expenditures incurred on consumption or expenditures that don't constitute assets are revenue expenditures and expenditures that create assets—real estate, such as buildings and offices, machinery and infrastructure, and financial assets like loans and equity—are classified as capital expenditure.

Before 2016–17, India had the system of classifying expenditures into plan (new development) expenditures and non-plan (the rest) expenditures as well, which was abolished in 2017.

The current system of expenditure classification is quite dated and unrepresentative of their real nature.

Many expenditures that are in the nature of social welfare expenditures, such as the Rs 6,000 transfer to farmers under PM Kisan, are classified as economic services as these are budgeted under the agriculture head. Likewise, the fertilizer, food and LPG subsidies, also of the nature of social welfare expenditures, are classified as economic services. Many public goods and services expenditures like expenditure on improvement of environment under the budget of the Ministry of Forest and Environment or that on collection and maintenance of statistics by the Ministry of Statistics and Programme Implementation are wrongly classified as economic services.

I began doing a thorough reclassification of the expenditures incurred by the Modi government from 2021–22 into four clearly understandable categories.

I take out the expenditures that represent the cost of past liabilities and do not serve any public purpose during the current year, such as the interest payments and pension payments. In addition, I exclude the expenditures that are not that of the Central government, such as mandatory transfers to the state governments like Finance Commission grants and also capital expenditure loans to the states, which actually result in the expenditure of the states. Together, these non-current and non-Central government expenditures make the first category of expenditures.

The remaining expenditures (current and productive) are classified into three broad categories of: a. public goods and services expenditures (which broadly correspond to general expenditures minus interest and pensions plus such expenditures classified as part of economic services), b. welfare or distribution expenditures (which broadly correspond to social services but include such expenditures presently classified elsewhere) and economic growth expenditures (broadly corresponding to economic services minus expenditures wrongly classified therein). This three-way classification of current expenditures broadly corresponds to the principal functions of the government—public goods and services, redistribution and welfare and promoting economic growth.

An extensive discussion on the expenditures so classified year by year during Modi 2.0 can be accessed in my books on Budgets 2023–24 and 2024–25.

Expenditure Review

Decent expenditure growth but significant slowdown in last three years

The total expenditure incurred by the government in 2018–19 was Rs 23.15 trillion. There was an element of understatement as part of the food subsidy expenditure was paid off-budget from the NSSF and some other expenditures were excluded by being paid off-budget via FSBs.

Accumulated food subsidy arrears were cleared in one go in 2020–21, which made the total expenditures jump to Rs 35.10 trillion, and caused the total expenditures to record a year-on-year growth of an unprecedented 30.66 per cent over the expenditure of Rs 26.86 trillion in 2019–20. The two-year CAGR of total expenditures between 2018–19 and 2020–21 also jumped to 23.13 per cent.

Total expenditure growth slowed down thereafter. As per 2023–24 PE (published by the Controller General of Accounts or CGA), in the last year of Modi 2.0, the total expenditures were only Rs 44.43 trillion. The terminal year (2023–24) total expenditures exhibited a five-yearly CAGR growth of 13.93 per cent, a reasonably decent expenditure growth. However, the expenditure growth in the last three years (from 2020–21 to 2023–24) was only 8.17 per cent per annum.

Despite running very heavy fiscal deficits, the Modi 2.0 government remained quite expenditure-constrained in the last three years.

Disturbing growth in interest expenditures in last three years

Interest payments constitute the largest proportion of the total non-current expenditures. In 2018–19, interest payments amounted to Rs 5.83 trillion. They rose to Rs 10.64 trillion in 2023–24 (provisional).

Interest payments grew at a CAGR of 12.79 per cent during the five years of Modi 2.0, at a rate somewhat lower than the total expenditure growth of 13.93 per cent. However, the loose fiscal deficit policy followed by the government from 2020–21 onwards had its understandable adverse impact on the growth of interest payments.

While the interest payments in 2020–21 had grown to Rs 6.80 trillion, by a CAGR of only 8 per cent annually in the first two years, the interest payments growth shot up to a CAGR of 16.09 per cent in the last three years, at nearly double the total expenditure growth of 8.17 per cent during this period.

Current expenditure growth low

In 2021–22 (the year after abnormal expenditure growth on account of clearing off-budget liabilities), of the total expenditures of Rs 37.94 trillion, non-current and unproductive expenditures amounted to Rs 13.38 trillion; the remaining Rs 24.56 crore of expenditures being current and productive.

The total expenditures, non-current expenditures and current/productive expenditures increased to Rs 41.93 trillion, Rs 15.89 trillion and Rs 16.86 trillion respectively, in 2022–23, growing by 10.53 per cent, 18.74 per cent and 6.05 per cent, respectively. The current/productive expenditures recorded the lowest rate of growth.

As the actuals/provisional numbers for 2023–24 are not going to be available until the 2025–26 Budget is presented in February 2025, if we use 2023–24 RE numbers, current/productive expenditures recorded a similar tepid growth of 7.69 per cent in 2023–24, almost at par with total expenditure growth of 7.09 per cent and non-current expenditure growth of 6.11 per cent.

The total current/productive expenditures of Rs 28.05 trillion in 2023–24 RE recorded a two-year CAGR of 6.87 per cent only from the 2021–22 current expenditure of Rs 24.56 trillion.

No good growth in public goods and services expenditure

Expenditure on defence, police, organs of state, administrative services relating to public goods and services and environmental and scientific services make up the Central government's expenditure on public goods and services in India. The expenditure on public goods and services grew at a much lower rate of 9.49 per cent during Modi 2.0 (from Rs 5.26 trillion in 2018–19 to Rs 8.27 trillion in 2023–24 RE). From 2021–22 to 2023–24 RE, this expenditure recorded almost a similar growth of 9.08 per cent per annum.

There are three major demands for grants relating to defence expenditures (defence pension has been accounted for as non-current expenditure above)— defence (civil), which includes expenditure on most non-forces like coast guards, the Border Road Organization (BRO), and defence services (revenue), which takes care of the establishment expenditure of the armed forces, and defence (capital outlay), which accounts for capital expenditure on acquisition of defence assets. The overall defence expenditure grew by an annual growth rate of 9.82 per cent, from Rs 3.02 trillion in 2018–19 to Rs 4.82 trillion in 2023–24 RE. As is quite clear, the defence expenditure constituted almost three-fifths of total expenditure on public goods and services (57.37 per cent in 2018–19 and 58.22 per cent in 2023–24 RE).

The expenditure on Central Armed Police Forces (CAPFs) and grants for strengthening policing in the states was also significant (Rs 91,693 crore in 2018–19) but recorded a tepid growth rate of only 6.64 per cent per annum in five years, rising to Rs 1.26 trillion in 2023–24 RE. The expenditure on other administrative services actually recorded the highest annual growth at 13.34

per cent per annum, growing from Rs 96,697 crore in 2018–19 to Rs 1.81 trillion in 2023–24 RE.

The organs of state and sovereign institutions, which actually have a very small expenditure load, registered a very low expenditure growth rate of 5.26 per cent per annum, growing from Rs 3,544 crore in 2018–19 to Rs 4,579 crore in 2023–24 RE. The worst rate of growth was witnessed during Modi 2.0 in case of environmental and scientific services. The expenditure on seven scientific and environmental departments (science and technology, bio-technology, industrial research, earth sciences, environment and forest, space and statistics) was almost static (Rs 32,216 crore in 2018–19 and Rs 33,843 crore in 2023–24 RE) recording growth of less than 1 per cent per annum.

Welfare and freebies expenditure mushroomed

Welfare or redistribution expenditures can be better classified into five groups of expenditures: a. food and agricultural subsidies like those under PM Garib Kalyan Yojana (earlier NFSA) and fertilizer subsidies, b. expenditure on creating jobs and employment like that on MGNREGA and Livelihood Mission, c. direct transfers including PM Kisan and PM Awas Yojana (PMAY), d. indirect transfers such as PM Fasal Bima Yojana, and e. in-kind support such as expenditure on education, health or children's nutrition.

These welfare/redistribution expenditures, which also include many freebies, constitute about one-fourth of total expenditures. In 2023–24 RE, the redistribution/welfare expenditures amounted to Rs 10.35 trillion out of total expenditures of Rs 44.90 trillion, which was 23.05 per cent. In 2018–19, the redistribution expenditures were Rs 5.47 trillion (23.63 per cent of total expenditures of Rs 23.15 trillion).

Of the five groups of redistribution expenditures, the expenditures under what would fall most clearly in the freebies category—the food and agriculture subsidies and direct benefit transfers like PM Kisan transfers—grew at the highest rate. The food and agriculture subsidies were Rs 1.92 trillion in 2018–19 and grew to Rs 4.29 trillion in 2023–24 RE, recording a stupendous growth of 17.52 per cent per year. In 2020–21, the food and agricultural subsidies had skyrocketed to Rs 7.14 trillion thanks to the discontinuation of off-budget payment of food subsidies and clearance of past arrears. The direct benefit transfers saw a big jump, up on account of the government bringing out the pure freebie of PM Kisan in 2018–19 and scaling up PMAY significantly. As a result, the direct cash benefit transfers of Rs 67,057 crore in 2018–19 jumped to Rs 1.51 trillion in 2023–24 RE, again recording extraordinary growth of 17.62 per cent per annum.

Thanks to the massive scaling-up of the drinking water connections programme—Har Ghar Nal Yojana—(from Rs 18,412 crore in 2018–19 to

Rs 77,391 crore in 2023–24 RE at the rate of 33.14 per cent per annum), the indirect benefits (in-kind) transfers also recorded a very good growth rate of 11.30 per cent per annum (growing from Rs 1.86 trillion in 2018–19 to Rs 3.17 trillion in 2023–24 RE). School education (from Rs 48,441 crore in 2018–19 to Rs 72,774 crore in 2023–24 RE) and health, minus Central Government Health Scheme (CGHS) pensioners' expenditure (from Rs 51,730 crore in 2018–19 to Rs 73,329 crore in 2023–24 RE) actually witnessed very low growth of 8.39 per cent and 7.23 per cent, respectively.

The jobs and employment programmes also witnessed tepid expenditure growth of only 7.67 per cent per year (from Rs 80,097 crore in 2018–19 to Rs 1.16 trillion in 2023–24 RE). The employee pension scheme (EPS) recorded good growth of 14.78 per cent. So did the AJEEVIKA/Livelihood Mission programme (19.56 per cent). MGNREGA was perhaps underprovided in 2023–24 RE despite an increase in the allocation at the RE stage and recorded growth of only 6.83 per cent.

The worst performance was evident in the indirect benefits transfers group, with the total expenditures on such indirect benefits coming down from Rs 22,694 crore in 2018–19 to Rs 22,128 crore in 2023–24 RE, actually recording a negative annual growth of (-)0.50 per cent per year. The crop insurance programme is the largest in the group. As the programme witnessed a lack of interest by many states, the expenditure grew from Rs 11,937 crore in 2018–19 to Rs 15,000 crore in 2023–24 RE, recording a small growth of 4.67 per cent per annum. Other programmes—PM ASHA, social security schemes of DFS and social security schemes of social welfare departments, other than scholarships—actually witnessed a fall in the absolute amounts spent on them.

Infrastructure expenditures went through the roof

With PM Modi championing the virtues of capital expenditure and infrastructure-led economic growth, economic growth expenditures received the biggest boost in Modi 2.0.

The economic growth expenditures of the government can be classified into four broad sub-groups of agriculture, industry, services and infrastructure. The total growth expenditure in 2018–19 was Rs 3.50 trillion, which made up about a quarter of the total current expenditures of Rs 14.23 trillion. In 2023–24 RE, growth expenditures increased to Rs 9.42 trillion and became about a third of the total current expenditure of Rs 28.05 trillion. The economic growth expenditures recorded a massive CAGR of 21.89 per cent in Modi 2.0.

Within the economic growth expenditures, the infrastructure expenditures delivered a superlative performance. Infrastructure expenditures, at Rs 2.12 trillion, constituted 60.48 per cent of total growth expenditures in 2018–19.

In 2023–24 RE, the infrastructure expenditures, at Rs 7.20 trillion, captured a much larger space and constituted more than three-fourths of the total growth expenditures (Rs 9.42 trillion) at 76.44 per cent. The infrastructure expenditures CAGR skyrocketed to 27.74 per cent during Modi 2.0.

The government promotes industrial growth through several interventions. The PLI schemes, capital subsidy programmes, subsidies to neutralize exporting taxes, public expenditure in promoting industries like steel, heavy industry, coal, etc., make up the government's industrial growth promotion expenditures. Despite high-decibel support for programmes like PLI and a large-scale roll-out of Remission of Duties and Taxes on Exported Products (RoDTEP), the industrial growth promotion expenditures grew by only 13.92 per cent per year from Rs 57,977 crore in 2018–19 to Rs 1.11 trillion in 2023–34 RE.

Agriculture and allied sector growth expenditures were still more subdued at 10.25 per cent per year (from Rs 37,591 crore in 2018–19 to Rs 61,232 crore in 2023–24 RE). With the agriculture department's expenditures largely acquiring the colour of redistribution programmes, agriculture growth-promoting expenditures recorded only 4.21 per cent per annum growth (from Rs 16,681 crore in 2018–19 to Rs 20,505 crore in 2023–24 RE). The expenditure on the water resources programme did record a decent growth of 21.33 per annum (from Rs 7,422 crore in 2018–19 to Rs 19,517 crore in 2023–24 RE).

The government spends a much smaller budget on promoting services even if we include commerce, posts, culture, tourism and most of the non-industry expenditures of MeitY in services. The services growth expenditures were Rs 42,817 crore in 2018–19. These expenditures remained almost flat during Modi 2.0, recording an annual growth of only 2.92 per cent per year to Rs 49,443 crore in 2023–24 RE.

Capital Expenditure

In its first term (2014–19), bringing the fiscal deficit to 3 per cent of GDP was the big driving policy force for the Modi government. This naturally constrained capital expenditures as the pressure of unavoidable revenue expenditures consumed most of the space the fiscal deficits created.

The capital expenditure in the last year of the Manmohan Singh government (2013–14) was Rs 1.88 trillion. In the last year of Modi 1.0 (2018–19), the capital expenditure grew to Rs 3.08 crore. Consequently, the Modi 1.0 government could deliver capital expenditure CAGR of a not-so-impressive 10.4 per cent. This trend continued in the pre Covid-19 year (2019–20) as well. In six years (2014–15 to 2019–20), the capital expenditure expanded to Rs 3.36 trillion in 2019–20, generating trend annual growth of a little higher than 10 per cent.

It was the Covid-19 year (2020–21) that changed the government's expenditure policy priorities completely. The government abandoned its goal of bringing fiscal deficit down to 3 per cent of GDP and embarked on the bandwagon of boosting capital expenditures. The capital expenditure, in fact, became the unique selling proposition (USP) of Modi 2.0 from the time Nirmala Sitharaman presented Budget 2021–22. This continued to be her big Budget pitch in all the Budgets thereafter. In her Budget Speech 2022–23, she underlined: 'This substantial increase in recent years is central to the government's efforts to enhance growth potential and job creation, crowd-in private investments, and provide a cushion against global headwinds.'

It is considered axiomatic in the macro-economic world that new capital investments drive economic growth. However, it is not necessarily true of government capital expenditure. For the capital investment to drive GDP growth, it must meet two conditions. First, the increased budgetary capital expenditure should add to the overall capital investment of the public sector, not substitute it and, second, it should be productive, i.e. each unit of additional capital expenditure should generate additional output at an efficient capital output rate.

In the normal course, elevated budgetary capital expenditures from 2021–22, raised to Rs 10 trillion in the Budget 2023–24 (reduced to Rs 9.50 trillion in 2023–24 RE), should have contributed handsomely to the GDP growth in India. Headline budgetary capital expenditure, however, did not tell the complete truth. Let me relate to you the real capital expenditure story of Modi 2.0.

Budget speeches underlined shift to capital expenditure strategy

As noted above, capital expenditures became the most-talked-about fiscal policy instrument from the third year of Modi 2.0. The contrast in the two Budget Speeches of 2019–20 and 2020–21 and the four Budget Speeches from 2021–22 (including the 2024–25 Interim Budget) onwards could not have been starker.

The entire Budget Speech 2019–20 used the expression 'capital expenditure' only once, that too in the context of the required investment of Rs 50 trillion for Railways infrastructure between 2018–2030, which was, in fact, cited to provide a rationale for the then-emphasized need of public-private partnerships (PPPs) to unleash faster development and completion of tracks, rolling stock manufacturing and delivery of passenger freight services. Unfortunately, the government did not follow through on the PPPs in Railways thereafter.

The Budget Speech 2020–21 mentioned capital expenditure twice—once to underline that the government had unfailingly worked towards keeping up the capital expenditure during the year and, second, to emphasize in the last paragraph that a good part of the borrowings for FY 2020–21 would go towards capital expenditure, which was being scaled up by more than 21 per cent. The capital expenditure in 2020–21 was partly bogus actually, as it included a loan of Rs 79,398 crore from the general budget to Railways to cover operational losses caused by Covid-19 disruptions.

From Budget 2021–22, capital expenditure became the principal pivot of the government's policy. The Finance Minister began singing paeans of capital expenditure in every Budget. Under the title 'sharp increase in capital budget' in paragraph 48, the Finance Minister said eloquently:

> For 2021–22, I propose a sharp increase in capital expenditure and thus have provided Rs 5.54 trillions which is 34.5 per cent more than the BE of 2020–21. Of this, I have kept a sum of more than Rs 44,000 crores in the Budget head of the Department of Economic Affairs to be provided for projects/programmes/departments that show good progress on Capital Expenditure and are in need of further funds. Over and above this expenditure, we would also be providing more than Rs 2 trillions to States and Autonomous Bodies for their Capital Expenditure.

She linked the increased capital expenditure with implementation of the NIP, which had projects exceeding Rs 100 trillion. The NIP was largely forgotten later on. The capital expenditure was also the biggest talking point of her 2022–23 Budget Speech, where she spoke of the multiplier effect of capital expenditure. In paragraph 101, she doubled down on stepping up the capital expenditure sharply.

> Considering the above imperative (virtuous cycle of investment requires public investment to crowd-in private investment), the outlay for capital expenditure in the Union Budget is once again being stepped up sharply by 35.4 per cent from Rs 5.54 trillion in the current year to Rs 7.50 trillion in 2022–23. This has increased to more than 2.2 times the expenditure of 2019–20. This outlay in 2022–23 will be 2.9 per cent of GDP.

In her Budget Speech 2023–24, Nirmala Sitharaman termed capital investment the 'driver of growth and jobs' and jacked it to Rs 10 trillion:

> Capital investment outlay is being increased steeply for the third year in a row by 33 per cent to ₹10 trillion, which would be 3.3 per cent of GDP. This will be almost three times the outlay in 2019–20.

The Finance Minister wasn't as strident in her Budget Speech 2024–25 (Interim), presented on 1 February 2024. She turned somewhat superstitious in increasing capital expenditure outlay by 11.1 per cent to Rs 1.11 trillion. In para 61 of her Budget Speech, she said:

Building on the massive tripling of the capital expenditure outlay in the past 4 years resulting in huge multiplier impact on economic growth and employment creation, the outlay for the next year is being increased by 11.1 per cent to eleven lakh, eleven thousand, one hundred and eleven crore rupees (₹11,11,111 crore). This would be 3.4 per cent of the GDP.

From almost no mention in the Budget 2019–20 to making it the biggest talking point in the Budget 2023–24, the Modi government did come a long way in its attempt to establish capital expenditure as its biggest fiscal policy plank.

Headline budgetary capital expenditure growth highly impressive

In the five years of Modi 2.0 (2018–19 and 2023–24), the nominal/headline budgetary capital expenditure grew impressively from Rs 3.08 trillion in 2018–19 to Rs 10.01 trillion in 2023–24 BE (revised to Rs 9.50 trillion in 2023–24 RE), which amounted to a highly impressive CAGR of 26.6 per cent (25.30 per cent taking 2023–24 RE into consideration).

After recording a tepid budgetary capital expenditure growth of 9.1 per cent in the first year (2019–20), the budgetary capital expenditure growth took off impressively from 2020–21. Budgetary capital expenditure growth was 26.98 per cent in 2020–21, the first Covid-19 year, though it was triggered by the accounting loan of Rs 79,398 crore—from the general budget to the Railways budget.

There was a much higher annual budgetary capital expenditure growth from 2021–22 onwards. In 2021–22, the budgetary capital expenditure went up from Rs 4.27 trillion in 2020–21 to Rs 5.93 crore, recording an impressively high annual growth of 39.07 per cent. The year 2022–23 also witnessed a staggering high growth of 24.82 per cent when the capital expenditure went further to touch Rs 7.40 trillion. Budgetary capital expenditure growth continued to be quite bullish in 2023–24 with RE recording capital expenditures of Rs 9.50 trillion.

For the five years of Modi 2.0, the budgetary capital expenditure recorded a perhaps never-before CAGR of as high as 25.30 per cent per annum. The total nominal budgetary capital expenditure for the five years of Modi 2.0 was Rs 30.45 trillion, giving an annual average nominal/headline capital expenditure of Rs 6.09 trillion per year.

Loans and advances not Centre's capital expenditure

The budgetary capital expenditure actually comprises two parts—first, the 'actual' capital expenditure, which is incurred on constructing or acquiring physical assets like buildings, roads, railways, machinery and the like and also on making equity investment in public enterprises and, second, the 'loans and advances' given to the state governments, foreign governments and other enterprises and individuals. The loans and advances given to state governments, when incurred by them on actual capital expenditure, do lead to the capital expenditure, but that is the actual capital expenditure of the state governments, not that of the Central government.

Modi 2.0 witnessed significant growth in the loans and advances. They were only Rs 24,414 crore in 2019–20 and went up to Rs 1.63 trillion in 2023–24 BE (revised down to Rs 1.43 trillion in 2023–24 RE). The nominal budgetary capital expenditure of Rs 9.50 trillion in 2023–24 RE was, therefore, actual capital expenditure of Rs 8.07 trillion.

During the five years (including 2023–24 RE) of Modi 2.0, loans and advances aggregated Rs 4.52 trillion, which made up 14.83 per cent of total budgetary capital expenditure of Rs 30.45 trillion. In these five years, loans and advances recorded a much higher annual growth rate of 38.38 per cent as well, jumping from Rs 28,221 crore in 2018–19 to Rs 1.42 trillion in 2023–24 RE.

The budgetary headline capital expenditure, minus loans and advances, of Rs 25.93 trillion (Rs 30.45 trillion minus Rs 4.52 trillion) was still quite respectable at an average of Rs 5.19 trillion per year.

Growth capital expenditure was still smaller

The government incurs capital expenditure for creating infrastructure like railways, roads and metros and also for promoting the establishment of new plants and machinery to generate new economic output. The government also, however, incurs capital expenditure on many economically unproductive expenditures, such as buying arms and armaments for the defence forces and building public offices. These non-economic expenditures are quite important from the national security viewpoint and for delivering public goods and services, but such capital expenditures are not helpful in generating economic growth.

The government classifies the capital expenditure into three broad services: economic, social and general. The defence capital expenditure is included in general services. Therefore, the capital expenditure classified as economic services capital expenditure is the real capital expenditure for boosting economic growth and having some potential for crowding in private investment and bringing the multiplier effect to work.

Of Rs 6.25 trillion of actual capital expenditure in 2022–23 (Rs 7.40 trillion total budgetary expenditure minus loans and advances of Rs 1.15 trillion), the 'general services' capital expenditure was Rs 1.61 trillion. This included a capital outlay on defence services of Rs 1.43 trillion. We need to exclude the entire general services capital outlays from the total capital expenditure (excluding loans and advances) to ascertain the growth-promoting capital expenditure. Likewise, the small social services capital expenditure of Rs 121.66 crore also needs to be excluded. For the five years of Modi 2.0, the general services capital expenditure amounted to Rs 7.64 trillion and social services capital expenditure was Rs 47,649 crore. These two non-economic growth-promoting capital expenditures totalled Rs 8.11 trillion.

The exclusion of the Rs 8.11 trillion general and social services capital expenditure from the total capital expenditure brings the budgetary capital expenditure classified under the economic services capital expenditure closer to the real/actual/economic/growth-generating capital expenditure. Such actual growth generating capital expenditure was Rs 1.56 trillion in 2018–19 and Rs 6.16 trillion in 2023–24 RE.

For the five years of Modi 2.0, total real capital expenditure (excluding loans and advances), as we saw above, was Rs 25.93 trillion. Excluding the general services and social services capital expenditure of Rs 8.11 trillion, the economic growth-inducing capital expenditure turned out to be much smaller at Rs 17.82 trillion (annual average capital expenditure to Rs 3.56 trillion). The growth-promoting capital expenditure was reduced to 76.33 per cent of total actual capital expenditure during Modi 2.0.

Part of actual capital expenditure was phony

The government provided Rs 62,365 crore as 'equity' to Air India Assets Holding Ltd in 2021–22 to enable repayment/assumption of Air India Ltd. This was meant to take care of the past government guaranteed borrowings (Rs 36,254 crore), for repayment of past government-guaranteed Sale and Lease Back (SLB) lease rentals (Rs 12,357 crore) and for repayment of other past dues/liabilities (Rs 13,754 crore). This equity infusion of Rs 62,365 crore for payment of the lost loans/liabilities of Air India, not taken over by the new buyer Tatas upon Air India's privatization, was quite phony and can by no stretch of the imagination, be considered a capital expenditure.

There were a few other such equity infusions, most conspicuously in MTNL and BSNL to cover their losses and provide funds to pay the government licence fees or other dues. The government incurred capital expenditure of Rs 3,256 crore in 2021–22, Rs 54,542 crore in 2022–23 and Rs 69,224 crore in 2023–24 RE, aggregating to Rs 1,36,097 crore in the five years of Modi 2.0. Both BSNL and MTNL are fast losing their subscriber base. These have become marginal players in the telecom market. The capital expenditure incurred in infusing equity in these two public sector entities was certainly no real capital expenditure.

The total amount of such phony equity infusion in Air India Assets Holding Ltd and BSNL/MTNL, considered as capital expenditure by the government, amounted to Rs 1.99 trillion. This phony capital expenditure, excluded from the economic capital expenditure of Rs 17.82 trillion, brings down the net productive/growth-inducing capital expenditure to Rs 15.83 trillion for the five years of Modi 2.0.

The real budgetary capital expenditure at Rs 15.83 trillion during Modi 2.0 was way below the nominal budgetary capital expenditure of Rs 30.45 trillion. The actual growth-promoting capital expenditure amounted to only 52 per cent of the total nominal/headline budgetary capital expenditure, claimed by the Finance Minister as the capital expenditure.

Massive public sector capital expenditure substitution

The government makes capital expenditure through two channels—the budgetary channel and the public sector internal and extra-budgetary resources (IEBR) channel. The combined expenditure through these two channels constitutes the total capital expenditure of the government and public sector. The government presents the information relating to the total capital expenditure through the two channels in Statement No. 1 of the Expenditure Profile. A good part of governmental budgetary CapEx is actually incurred by the public sector enterprises themselves but not counted as their IEBR.

Capital expenditure through the budgetary channel was Rs 3.08 trillion in 2018–19, the last year of Modi 1.0, and through the IEBR channel it was Rs 6.08 trillion. Together, the government and public sector capital expenditure during 2018–19 was Rs 9.16 trillion. The IEBR channel of capital investment was much larger and accounted for almost two-thirds of the public sector (including government) capital investment.

During Modi 2.0, the total budgetary channel capital expenditure (including loans and advances) kept increasing, as I noted above (Rs 3.36 trillion in 2019–20, Rs 4.27 trillion in 2020–21, Rs 5.93 trillion in 2021–22 and to Rs 7.40 trillion in 2022–23). In 2023–24 RE, it amounted to Rs 9.50 trillion. On the other hand, the capital expenditure through the IEBR channel kept shrinking all the time until 2022–23 for which actuals data is available (Rs 6.42 trillion in 2019–20, Rs 4.78 trillion in 2020–21, Rs 4.38 trillion in 2021–22 and Rs 3.63 trillion in 2022–23). The 2023–24 RE numbers also vividly capture this declining trend as the capital expenditure through the IEBR channel was budgeted at only Rs 3.26 trillion in 2023–24 RE.

The shrinking IEBR channel is largely explained by the substitution of IEBR public sector capital expenditure by the budgetary capital expenditure, most prominently in the railways and roads sector. In nominal terms, i.e. without adjusting for inflation, the IEBR CapEx declined from Rs 6.08 trillion in 2019–20 to Rs 3.26 trillion in 2023–24 RE, shrinking by 46 per cent during Modi 2.0. The IEBR channel recoded a negative CAGR of (-)11.71 per cent.

Quite inevitably, the disappointing performance of the IEBR channel made the total government and public sector capital expenditure growth quite hollow and pulled down the CAGR of combined nominal budgetary capital expenditure significantly. The combined nominal capital expenditure (budgetary capital expenditure including loans and advances and public sector capital expenditure through IEBRs) turned out to be only Rs 12.76 trillion in 2023–24 RE.

This combined capital expenditure over the combined nominal expenditure of Rs 9.16 trillion in 2018–19 delivers a CAGR of only 6.87 per cent. Without doubt, this overall CapEx performance is quite pathetic as it does not account for even the inflation during this period. If we take into account budgetary capital expenditure (minus the loans and advances) plus the IEBR capital expenditure, the CAGR falls down further to only 5.01 per cent (Rs 8.87 trillion in 2018–19 and Rs 11.33 trillion in 2023–24 RE). If we treat economic services capital expenditure (including the phony equity CapEx) and the IEBR capital expenditure as the real CapEx, the outturn becomes still worse, with the capital expenditure growing from Rs 7.64 trillion in 2018–19 to only Rs 9.42 trillion in 2023–24 RE, giving us a CAGR growth of only 4.29 per cent per annum.

The CapEx growth story of Modi 2.0 is actually quite hollow.

Railways and roads capital expenditure massively substituted

The biggest growth in budgetary capital expenditure took place in two big physical infrastructure sectors—railways and roads. In 2018–19, the budgetary capital expenditure support for these two sectors was Rs 1.23 trillion (Rs 52,838 crore for Railways and Rs 69,759 crore for roads and bridges). In 2023–24 RE, the budgetary capital support for these two sectors shot up to a whopping Rs 4.91 trillion (Rs 2.40 trillion for Railways and Rs 2.51 trillion for roads and bridges). The CAGR growth in capital expenditure for these two sectors has been a stupendous 32 per cent per annum.

It is quite interesting and revealing, and no coincidence but the evidence of a deliberate policy, to note that as soon as the government started raising its capital expenditure from Budget 2021–22, it also began substituting an increasingly larger share of Railways and roads sector CapEx. Let me relate this hidden but gripping story.

Railways' capital expenditure in 2018–19 was Rs 52,838 crore from the budget and Rs 80,539 crore from the IEBRs, totalling Rs 1.33 trillion. The 2019–20 numbers were also quite similar to 2018–19. In 2020–21, the budgetary CapEx assistance to Railways actually declined to Rs 29,926 crore (in addition, the government gave a loan of Rs 79,398 crore) whereas the IEBR CapEx went up to Rs 1.25 trillion.

The churn and substitution began from 2021–22 and the roles of government capital support and IEBRs started reversing. The budgetary capital expenditure for Railways increased significantly to Rs 1.17 trillion in 2021–22, whereas the IEBR CapEx came down sharply to Rs 73,388 crore. The total CapEx of Railways increased to Rs 1.91 trillion. This trend—increasing budgetary CapEx and decreasing IEBR CapEx, with increasing overall capital expenditure— continued in the last two years of Modi 2.0 as well. The budgetary CapEx for Railways increased to Rs 1.59 trillion in 2022–23 and to Rs 2.40 trillion in 2023–24 RE. The IEBR capital expenditure declined sharply to Rs 44,727 crore in 2022–23 and to Rs 20,000 crore in 2023–24 RE. From the IEBRs funding over 60 per cent of Railways' CapEx in 2018–19, in 2023–24 RE, IEBRs' share had come down to a pathetically low level of 7.7 per cent.

We need to project what the IEBRs would have funded during Modi 2.0 to really understand the substitution effect. In the two years of 2018–19, the last year of Modi 1.0, and 2019–20, the first year of Modi 2.0, the IEBR channel had funded about 57.3 per cent of the total capital expenditure of Railways (Rs 1.61 trillion out of a capital expenditure of Rs 2.81 trillion). If the same rule (57.3 per cent of total CapEx) is applied to all the five years of Modi 2.0, the IEBR channel would have funded Rs 5.92 trillion of the total capital expenditure of Rs 10.37 trillion (actuals for the first four years and 2023–24 RE—Rs 1.48 trillion, Rs 2.35 trillion, Rs 1.91 trillion, Rs 2.04 trillion and Rs 2.60 trillion, respectively). As the IEBR channel provided only Rs 3.44 trillion of the Railways' CapEx (Rs 80,166 crore, Rs 1.25 trillion, Rs 73,388 crore, Rs 44,727 crore and Rs 20,000 crore, respectively), the government in effect substituted at least Rs 2.49 trillion of IEBR CapEx through the budgetary channel.

In the roads sector, the CapEx substitution takes place in the case of NHAI and proved to be worse than Railways. In the two years of 2018–19, the last year of Modi 1.0, and 2019–20, the first year of Modi 2.0, the IEBR channel funded Rs 1.36 trillion (Rs 61,216 crore in 2018–19 and Rs 74,988 crore in 2019–20), 66.86 per cent of total capital expenditure of NHAI of Rs 2.04 trillion (Rs 97,035 crore in 2018–19 and Rs 1.07 trillion in 2019– 20). During the five years of Modi 2.0, the total capital expenditure of NHAI, through the budgetary channel and IEBRs was Rs 6.49 trillion. NHAI contributed IEBRs of only Rs 2.05 trillion (stopped completely from 2022– 23). As a consequence, in the five years of Modi 2.0, the government provided capital expenditure support of Rs 6.49 trillion to NHAI whereas the total IEBR CapEx in this period was only Rs 2.05 trillion. If NHAI had funded 66.86 per cent of its total capital expenditure, its contribution would have been Rs 4.34 trillion. As NHAI provided Rs 2.05 trillion, the government substituted as much as Rs 2.29 trillion of NHAI capital expenditure through budgetary support.

The massive substitution had the effect of bringing down the overall capital expenditure growth to the low levels described in the paragraph above.

Capital increase narrative was quite hollow

There are two big takeaways with respect to the capital expenditure performance of the Modi 2.0 government.

First, there was a very high visible nominal budgetary capital expenditure growth. The Modi 2.0 government increased budgetary capital expenditure massively from the low of Rs 3.09 trillion in 2018–19 (the last year of its own government in the first term) to Rs 9.50 trillion in 2023–24 RE (in the last year of its second term). This highly visible increase generated a record CAGR of 25.30 per cent. The government claimed huge credit for saving the Indian economy and capital investment with this big investment.

Second, the real capital expenditure increase was very small. Loans and advances to the state governments and others don't constitute the Central government's capital expenditure. A good part of the so-called capital expenditure was incurred on non-economic assets, such as arms and armaments for the defence forces and phony equity investment to provide for the accumulated losses of Air India and BSNL. The biggest sleight of hand was in the form of substituting the capital expenditure incurred by the public sector entities by raising their own IEBRs by the budgetary support. The biggest capital expenders—Railways and NHAI—saw their total IEBR-funded capital expenditures being substituted by the budgetary capital resources. All this had the effect of neutralizing or cancelling out growth in the total capital expenditure (budgetary plus IEBRs), which grew by only 6.87 per cent per annum (at 5.01 per cent per annum if you only exclude the loans and advances given).

The high voltage capital expenditure narrative actually was quite hollow inside.

Subsidies

The government spends substantial budgetary resources on subsidies. Statement 7 in the Expenditure Profile lists what the government considers the subsidies and expenditure outlays thereon. There are more than thirty types of subsidies included in this statement. It categorizes the subsidies in five broad groups: a. food, b. fertilizers, c. petroleum, d. interest subsidies, and e. other subsidies.

Welfare or redistribution is a wider concept than the subsidies listed in Statement 7. Many welfare payments like PM Kisan handouts or contributions made to the Employee Pension Funds are not part of the statement on subsidies. I have grouped all the welfare and redistribution expenditures spread across the 102 demands in five groups and presented the principal trends in their expenditures during Modi 2.0 in the first part of this chapter.

In this section, I will deal with the subsidies listed in Statement 7, more particularly the four major subsidies—food subsidy, nutrient-based fertilizer subsidy, urea subsidy and petroleum subsidy—which the government considers major subsidies. The government provides monthly expenditure data on these subsidies as well on the CGA website.

Major subsidies constitute significant expenditures

The Modi government spent Rs 25.43 trillion in subsidies enumerated in Statement 7 in the five years of its second term (2019–20 to 2023–24 RE), averaging subsidies of more than Rs 5 trillion every year. The four major subsidies accounted for Rs 23.27 trillion (more than 91 per cent) of the total subsidies.

The total subsidies made up 13.62 per cent of the total expenditures of Rs 186.74 trillion and 21.6 per cent of the total current expenditures of Rs 117.71 trillion. The expenditure on four major subsidies of Rs 23.27 trillion was 12.46 per cent of the total expenditures and 19.76 per cent of the total current expenditures. One in every five rupees of effective current expenditures by the Modi 2.0 government was spent on major subsidies.

Other subsidies include two major credit-linked subsidies—interest subvention on crop loans and credit-linked subsidies for housing-for-all schemes. In 2022–23, the subsidy expenditure on these two schemes was Rs 17,998 crore and Rs 10,821 crore, respectively. Despite these two major subsidy payments, the total outgo on all subsidies, other than four major subsidies, were only a little over 8 per cent of the total subsidies expenditure during Modi 2.0.

Subsidies expenditures fluctuated quite violently during the second tenure of the Modi government. The amount spent on subsidies was as high as Rs 7.58 trillion in 2020–21, more than 3.82 per cent of the nominal GDP of Rs 198.01 trillion for that year. In the previous two years, the subsidy expenditures had added up to only Rs 4.85 trillion. The subsidy expenditures came down sharply in 2021–22 to Rs 5.04 trillion, though the same was still 2.13 per cent of the nominal GDP of Rs 236.65 trillion. On account of high fertilizer prices, the subsidy expenditure went up again to Rs 5.78 trillion in 2022–23. In the final year 2023–24 RE, the subsidy expenditures are estimated to have come down to Rs 4.41 trillion.

The fluctuating nature of subsidy expenditures comes out eloquently if you look at the yearly data in sequence. In the first year (2019–10), it was as low as Rs 2.62 trillion, rose to about three times in 2020–21, the year of the clean-up, to Rs 7.58 trillion and then tapered off to Rs 5.04 trillion and Rs 5.78 trillion in the next two years, before falling to Rs 4.41 trillion in 2023–24 RE.

Food subsidy mess cleaned up

The government did a major clean-up of the food subsidy mess in 2020–21.

In 2016–17, it had decided, in order to stay on course of the glide path to bring down the fiscal deficit to 3 per cent by 2018–19—announced in 2014–

15—not to release the complete food subsidy to the FCI. Instead, the unpaid part of the food subsidy was paid to FCI by providing a loan from the NSSF.

The food subsidy expenditure of Rs 1.01 trillion in 2018–19 (the last year of Modi 1.0) was only a partial payment of the food subsidy due to FCI for the year. In that year, the government provided FCI Rs 97,000 crore in loans through the NSSF. FCI repaid Rs 27,000 crore of food subsidy loans taken in previous years. Consequently, food subsidy to the extent of Rs 70,000 crore was the net paid through the NSSF loan in 2018–19. If these two are added up, the actual food subsidy bill for 2018–19 would have been Rs 1.71 trillion (Rs 1.01 trillion and Rs 70,000 crore).

At the end of 2018–19, NSSF loans of Rs 1.91 trillion were outstanding towards FCI, which would equal the food subsidy arrears of the three previous years, beginning 2016–17. In 2019–20, the NSSF lent Rs 1.10 trillion to FCI towards food subsidy and was repaid Rs 46,400 crore of the earlier years' loans. That year, therefore, food subsidy of Rs 63,600 crore was provided through the NSSF as a loan. As the food subsidy accounted for in the consolidated fund was Rs 1,08,688 crore, total food subsidy due for 2019–20 was Rs 1.72 trillion. The outstanding NSSF loans to FCI were Rs 2.546 trillion at the end of 2019–20.

In a welcome move, the government decided to clean the fiscal Augean stables by providing additional food subsidies equal to Rs 2.546 trillion to FCI to clear up all the outstanding loans of the previous years. The government provided Rs 5.4133 trillion of total food subsidy in the actual budget of 2020–21. This meant that the remaining expenditure of Rs 2.8673 trillion represented the food subsidy cost of that year, including the additional Rs 5 kg provided per unit under the PM Garib Kalyan Anna Yojana.

While this bold decision might have been partially motivated from the desire to show a large fiscal stimulus in that Covid-19 pandemic year, the net effect of the cleaned-up food subsidy arrears mess was quite appreciable and welcome.

The Modi government's total expenditure on food subsidy during the second term was Rs 14.24 trillion. If we take out outstanding NSSF loans of Rs 1.91 trillion at the end of 2018–19 as representing the food subsidy arrears of the previous term, the actual food subsidy expenditure during Modi 2.0 amounted to Rs 12.33 trillion or Rs 2.466 trillion per annum.

Fertilizer subsidies also shot up

The government has been budgeting fertilizer subsidy under two different heads—one, for nitrogenous (N) fertilizer as urea subsidy and two, for other fertilizer nutrients—principally phosphorus (P) and potash (K) as nutrient-based subsidy (NBS) since 2016–17. There are two different pricing formulas for urea and NBS fertilizers, with different implications for the subsidy outgo.

The urea subsidy regime works as a normative production cost (including a guaranteed return) minus the consumer price determined by the government. The government fixes the price/cost per urea bag. Normative cost minus the price per bag realized equals the urea subsidy. For the NBS regime—the government fixed the subsidy per kg for the three nutrients—N, P and K and also sulphur (S). The companies and cooperatives, including those government-owned and controlled, sell these fertilizers at prices determined notionally by them, taking into consideration the market cost and nutrient subsidy. In 2023–24, the government mandated that the consumer prices under the NBS regime would also be fixed in consultation with the government.

Fertilizer subsidy expenditure in 2018–19 was Rs 70,605 crore with the urea subsidy amounting to Rs 46,515 crore and NBS Rs 24,090 crore. The fertilizer subsidy expenditure increased to Rs 81,722 crore in 2019–20 primarily on account of a higher urea subsidy of Rs 54,755 crore. The urea subsidy bill had begun to shoot up as the government had decided to meet a greater proportion of the urea requirement from domestic production, which was costlier than the imported urea. There were also attempts to delay some fertilizer subsidy payments as well, in the interest of keeping the official fiscal deficit contained.

The government decided to clear up the fertilizer subsidy arrears in 2020–21 as well. The urea subsidy bill rose significantly to Rs 90,549 crore (the NBS subsidy bill also went up to Rs 37,373 crore) raising the total fertilizer subsidy to Rs 1.28 trillion. The international fertilizer and inputs prices started rising in 2021–22, making the fertilizer subsidy expenditure shoot up to Rs 1.54 trillion.

The year 2022–23 proved to be the worst.

The fertilizer subsidy bill depends on three key factors: the volume of fertilizer consumption, actual cost of fertilizers sold, and the government's policy decision regarding fixing the fertilizer cost/price per bag. In 2022–23, international prices shot through the roof (rose to $1,050 per tonne in April 2022 and $850 per tonne in September 2022 against normal monthly average prices of less than $400 per tonne in previous years) making the actual cost of fertilizer subsidies rise massively.

The government decided to keep the urea prices unchanged as well. In addition, it literally nationalized urea distribution, ordering all urea to be sold under a single Bharat brand at a single price. The volume of fertilizer consumption also increased. The government had kept the budget estimates at Rs 1.28 trillion, which had to be raised to Rs 2.37 trillion in 2022–23 RE. The actual fertilizer subsidy bill came still higher at Rs 2.51 trillion.

With the international prices returning to normality in 2023–24, the fertilizer subsidy expenditures have been estimated at Rs 1.89 trillion in 2023–24 RE (urea Rs 1.29 trillion and NBS Rs 60,300 crore).

In the five years of Modi 2.0, the fertilizer subsidies cost Rs 8.03 trillion and the average annual fertilizer subsidy bill was Rs 1.61 trillion.

Petroleum subsidies came back

The government has been providing subsidies on LPG cylinders and additionally on new LPG connections under PM Ujjwala Yojana (PMUY). There used to be a subsidy on the sale of kerosene to domestic consumers as well.

Petroleum subsidies had cost the government Rs 24,837 crore in 2018–19 with LPG and kerosene subsidies amounting to Rs 20,268 crore and Rs 4,569 crore respectively. Petroleum subsidies went up to Rs 38,529 crore in 2019–20, the first year of Modi 2.0. While the kerosene subsidy expenditure reduced marginally to Rs 4,443 crore, the LPG subsidies went up to Rs 34,086 crore.

Kerosene consumption has been going down thanks largely to the expansion of LPG connections in the country, which is reflected in the kerosene subsidies as well. In 2020–21, the kerosene subsidy outgo went down to Rs 3,260 crore. In 2021–22, it was as good as gone, with the subsidy outgo reducing to Rs 20 crore. From 2022–23, there have been no kerosene subsidy payments.

LPG subsidies illustrate more the government's wavering attitude towards it. In 2021–22, the government virtually decided to discontinue LPG subsidies except for the beneficiaries of Ujjwala scheme, that too restricted to the first few cylinders. Consequently, the LPG subsidy expenditure of Rs 35,195 crore in 2020–21 came down to only Rs 3,421 crore. LPG subsidy outgo remained low at Rs 6,817 crore in 2022–23 as well.

In 2023–24, the government had a change of heart (a more detailed description is in Chapter 8—Poverty and Redistribution). The subsidy per cylinder was increased to Rs 200 per cylinder (to Rs 300 per cylinder a little before the announcement of the Lok Sabha elections) to all the LPG-using families. As a consequence, the budget provision of Rs 2,257 crore in 2023–24 BE for LPG subsidy was increased to Rs 12,240 crore in 2023–24 RE.

Other Expenditures

Of the current expenditures of Rs 28.05 trillion in 2023–24 RE, after accounting for a capital expenditure of Rs 8.07 trillion (after excluding loans and advances, part of non-current expenditures) and subsidies of Rs 4.41 trillion, Rs 15.57 trillion of other current expenditures remain. A good part of this other expenditure is the establishment expenditure—Rs 7.67 trillion. The centrally sponsored schemes (CSSs)—Rs 4.60 trillion—constitute the other major constituent of this expenditure. The rest (about Rs 3.3 trillion) is accounted for by other miscellaneous central expenditures and transfers.

I have discussed the CSSs extensively in Chapter 8—Poverty and Redistribution, and FC transfers in the chapter on Governance. Establishment expenditure is mostly on public goods and services, which has been commented upon in the initial sections of this chapter. I propose to comment only on one aspect of establishment expenditure—the manpower cost.

Government decides to recruit 10 lakh people

The PIB issued a press release on 14 June 2022 reiterating a tweet by the Prime Minister on that day. The release said that the Prime Minister had reviewed the status of human resources in all departments and ministries and 'instructed that recruitment of 10 lakh people be done by the Government in mission mode in the next 1.5 years'.

The Parliament was informed in July 2022 about 9.79 lakh vacancies as on 1 March 2022 in the government.

Half of these vacancies did not exist

The information about the sanctioned and filled-in posts in the government as on 1 March is provided in the Annual Report of the Department of Expenditure. The data about the establishment strength of the persons in position in the ministries/departments, also with reference to 1 March of the year, is also published in Statement 22 of the Expenditure Profile.

There was a variation in the vacancy data in two documents published by the government. The Annual Report of the Department of Expenditure 2022–23 did state that total vacancies as on 1 March 2022 were 9.79 lakh while the filled-up posts were 30.56 lakh. Statement 22 (Budget 2022–23), however, stated that a total of 34.65 lakh posts were 'estimated' to be filled-up on 1 March 2022. The difference between the two data sets implied that there was an estimated 4.09 lakh less vacancies in the government as on 1 March 2022.

If you dig deeper into departmental data, two major differences explained this divergence. The Department of Posts had 4.22 lakh filled-in posts as per the Expenditure Statement 22, whereas, as per the Annual Report, only 1.77 lakh posts were reported as filled-in. Perhaps the Expenditure Statement counted in its estimates the extra-departmental employees of the Department of Posts as filled-in posts. The other major difference was in the case of Railways. Railways and Posts had been downsizing their strength for over three decades.

The Annual Report 2020 of the Railways Board informs that their employee strength had come down from 16.52 lakh in 1990–91 to 12.54 lakh in 2019–20, which is very close to the positions reported filled in at 12.20 lakh by the Department of Expenditure and 12.03 lakh in the Budget Statement. The vacancies of 2.94 lakh stated in the case of Railways in the Annual Report of the Department of Expenditure were, therefore, the posts that had long been abolished in the Railways. The government could not have treated these posts as vacant.

The strength of the Department of Posts, which employed 5.92 lakh employees (including 2.99 lakh extra-departmental employees, later converted into Gramin Dak Sevaks) in 1990–91, had come down to 4.22 lakh, as per the data in the Annual Report of the Department of Posts. This number is exactly the same as the posts reported as filled-in posts in the Budget Statement at 4.22 lakh. As all of the positions in the Department of Posts are occupied, the number of vacancies indicated in the Annual Report of Department of Expenditure was actually non-existent.

If you exclude 2.94 lakh vacancies in Railways and 2.25 lakh vacancies in the Department of Posts, a total 5.18 lakh vacancies were non-existent vacancies, although announced to be filled in by the Prime Minister.

Other vacancies were mostly redundant

The remaining 4 lakh-odd vacancies are also made up largely of clerks, accountants, stenos and Class-IV (now called MTS). In the digitalization age, most of these posts have become redundant. Accordingly, most of these vacancies have also not been filled in for many years for reasons of redundancy.

Effectively, there were very few vacancies to fill in to comply with the announcement made by the Prime Minister.

Government data shows no increase in filled-in posts

The Prime Minister did participate in five or six Rojgar Melas in two years since the announcement was made, in which reportedly about 2.5 lakh appointment letters were distributed.

A good part of these appointments were in the paramilitary forces and in Railways. Around 2.5 lakh appointments in two years were perhaps less than the new vacancies arising during this period.

The Department of Expenditure has published the actual data of posts filled as on 1 March 2022 in Budget 2023–24 and as on 1 March 2023 in Statement 22 published as part of the Budget 2024–25 (Interim).

As per these statements, the actual in-position strength of the government establishment on 1 March 2022 was 31.69 lakh and on 1 March 2023 was 31.67 lakh.

The strength of 31.67 lakh on 1 March 2023 is actually marginally less than the actual strength of 31.69 lakh on 1 March 2022.

The government data does not provide evidence of any net addition in filling in vacancies as announced by the Prime Minister.

18

Revenues

Revenues (mostly tax revenues and also relatively smaller non-tax revenues), non-debt capital receipts like disinvestment proceeds and net borrowings raised by the government fund the budgeted expenditures.

In this chapter, I will review the performance of the revenues, both tax and non-tax, and comment thereon. The disinvestment and other monetization receipts will be discussed in Chapter 19 and the borrowings and debt in Chapter 20.

After the performance review, I take up major policy developments and issues that came centre stage during Modi 2.0.

Tax Revenues

Corporation tax had a roller-coaster ride

Corporation tax receipts in 2018–19, the last year of Modi 1.0, were on a very high pedestal at Rs 6.64 trillion, as high as 3.51 of the nominal GDP of Rs 189 trillion of that year. The government announced the big bang steep cut in corporation tax rates in September 2019, which I will discuss later in the chapter.

More because of the tepid profitability performance of the corporate sector than the rate cut, the first year (2019–20) of Modi 2.0 turned out to be a horrible year from the corporation tax receipts perspective. Corporation tax receipts declined to Rs 5.57 trillion that year—an unprecedented negative growth of over 16 per cent from the previous year. As a proportion of GDP, corporation tax receipts declined to 2.77 per cent (GDP Rs 201.04 trillion).

The Covid-19 pandemic lockdowns buffeted the corporation taxes in 2020–21 and its collections declined once again, in absolute terms, dropping down to Rs 4.58 trillion (second consecutive double-digit decline by about 18 per cent). In two years, corporation tax revenues declined by almost one-third—an unprecedented and shocking experience in India's fiscal history. As a share of GDP, corporation taxes hit the bottom at 2.31 per cent of the low GDP of 198.30 trillion.

The year 2021–22, which witnessed the worst of the Covid-19 wave, turned out to be the turnaround year for corporation taxes. Business boomed; profitability boomed too. Many companies also switched over to the new tax regime of lower tax rates (22 per cent in place of 30/25 per cent plus surcharges) by this time. Corporation tax receipts rose to Rs 7.12 trillion, growing spectacularly by more than 55 per cent over the receipts of the previous year. The corporation tax receipts of 2021–22 could make up for the absolute decline of the previous two years and were 7.3 per cent more than the corporation tax receipts of 2018–19. As a proportion of GDP, it scaled back to 3.03 per cent.

Corporation tax performance steadied thereafter and assumed a more normal trajectory. The receipts of Rs 8.26 trillion in 2022–23 marked a 16 per cent nominal growth, which made the corporation taxes stay at 3.03 per cent of GDP (Rs 272.41 trillion).

The CGA reported provisional corporation tax receipts for 2023–24 at a slightly lower level of Rs 9.11 trillion, against the 2023–24 RE receipts of Rs 9.23 trillion. This registered annual growth of only 10.32 per cent. In terms of GDP ratio, it improved to 3.07 per cent.

The five-yearly CAGR of corporation tax was not impressive at all, coming at merely 6.54 per cent per annum, much lesser than even the nominal GDP growth of 9.43 per cent.

The two halves of Modi 2.0 could not have been more starkly different. While the corporation tax receipts in the three-year period (2018–19 to 2021–22) recorded a CAGR of only 2.38 per cent (it was big negative growth until 2020–21), the second period of three years (2020–21 to 2023–24 provisional) turned up a blockbuster CAGR of 25.79 per cent.

Similar trends are observed in the matter of corporate tax buoyancy. The five-yearly corporation tax buoyancy at 0.69 was disappointingly low. During the three-year period (2018–19 to 2021–22), the buoyancy dropped down to a pathetic low of 0.32. Buoyancy rose handsomely if you consider the three-year period (2020–21 to 2023–24) only to 1.81 per cent.

Taxes on income took off massively midway

The taxes on income (on all entities other than companies; predominantly individuals) did not get knocked out in the first two years of Modi 2.0, unlike the corporation taxes, despite the big slowdown of 2019–20 and the Covid-19 lockdowns of 2020–21.

During this crisis period of the first two years of Modi 2.0, income tax collections remained steady—at Rs 4.87 trillion in 2020–21 against the receipts of Rs 4.73 trillion in 2018–19, about 3 per cent higher than the base year.

The Covid-19 pandemic did impact the incomes of the poor adversely but for income taxpayers, it witnessed an unprecedented growth from 2021–22. The personal income tax collections jumped impressively to Rs 6.96 trillion in 2021–22, in the midst of the killing second wave, rising by as much as 43 per cent over the previous year.

The year 2022–23 proved still better for the individuals and other persons assessed as non-corporation taxpayers. Their incomes must have risen massively as the income tax collections of the government got jacked up to Rs 8.33 trillion in 2022–23, recording another blockbuster growth of 47 per cent year on year. In two years (from 2020–21 to 2022–23), the personal income tax collections rose by as much as 71 per cent.

CGA reported provisional personal income tax receipts of Rs 10.11 trillion for 2023–24. The personal income tax CAGR, which rose over all the five years of Modi 2.0, was a spectacular 16.41 per cent in 2023–24 RE. In 2023–24, personal income taxes grew at 21.32 per cent, a rate that was almost double the growth rate of corporation tax.

The excellent performance of personal income taxes was visible in both the halves. The CAGR during the three-year period (2018–19 to 2021–22) was a decent 13.75 per cent and quite impressive at 27.55 per cent in the second three-year period (2020–21 to 2023–24 RE). The five-year buoyancy was also impressive at 1.74.

Corporation tax receipts were 40 per cent higher than personal income tax receipts in 2018–19 (Rs 6.64 trillion against Rs 4.73 trillion). In 2020–21, corporation taxes slipped below the personal tax collections, but regained a small lead again in 2021–22. In 2022–23, however, personal income tax collections were higher than corporate taxes again. In 2023–24 RE, personal income taxes were about 10 per cent higher than corporation taxes.

Excise duties had an opposite out-turn

The government raised excise duties on petrol and diesel massively in May 2020, very soon after Covid-19 started spreading and international crude oil prices crashed. I will discuss the excise duty policy during Modi 2.0 later.

Excise duties boomed in 2020–21, when all other taxes tanked. The excise duties receipts turned out to be Rs 3.91 trillion that year against almost steady-state/stagnant receipts of Rs 2.32 trillion in 2018–19 and Rs 2.41 trillion in 2019–20. The show continued in 2021–22 as well, with the excise duties bringing in revenues of Rs 3.95 trillion.

The rise in international crude prices after the outbreak of the Ukraine–Russia war in February 2022 began to end the excise duty lottery. The government was forced to adjust the excise duties downward. Excise duty revenues witnessed a decline to Rs 3.19 trillion in 2022–23 and declined further to Rs 3.05 trillion in 2023–24 (provisional data).

The 2023–24 (provisional) excise duty revenues were higher than the revenues in 2018–19 (Rs 2.32 trillion), although the five-year CAGR was a tepid 5.65 per cent. The excise duty CAGR during the three-year period (2018–19 to 2021–22) was a robust 19.38 per cent and saw a large negative growth of (-)7.97 per cent in the second three-year period (2020–21 to 2023–24 RE). Understandably, the five-year buoyancy was also quite low at 0.60.

The excise duties were the only tax that witnessed a negative growth in 2023–24.

Government squeezed states of excise duty

The government used to collect excise duties primarily in the form of basic excise duties until 2013–14, which were shared with the states in accordance with the Finance Commission formula. In that year, the government collected Rs 1.03 trillion as shareable basic and special excise duties, out of the total excise duty collections of Rs 1.70 trillion. More than 60 per cent of excise duty collections were shareable with the states in 2013–14, before the Modi government took the reins.

By 2017–18, the situation changed significantly. That year, of the excise duty receipts of Rs 2.59 trillion, the shareable basic excise duties were only Rs 1.17 trillion, about 45 per cent of total duties. In 2018–19, the last year of Modi 1.0, the proportion of shareable basic excise duties came down further to 30 per cent.

The Modi government continued gnawing at the excise duties in Modi 2.0 by increasing the share of non-shareable road and infrastructure cess (non-shareable excise duties) in the first three years. In the 2021–22 Budget, the government brought in another non-shareable agriculture and infrastructure cess, which added to the non-shareable excise duties in the last three years.

The road and infrastructure cess revenue increased from Rs 51,266 crore in 2018–19 to Rs 67,371 crore in 2019–20. The basic excise duties receipts correspondingly decreased from Rs 69,352 crore in 2018–19 to Rs 61,769 crore in 2019–20. Even in 2020–21, when overall excise revenues zoomed to Rs 3.90 trillion from Rs 2.39 trillion in 2019–20, a rise of almost 63 per cent, basic excise duties further declined to Rs 54,060 crore.

The whittling away of shareable excise duties reached its lowest point in 2022–23 when only Rs 25,459 crore was collected as basic excise duties, out of Rs 3.91 trillion (a mere 6.51 per cent of total excise duty collections).

Non-shareable excise duties have been collected under numerous heads—additional duty on motor spirits, additional duty on diesel, special duty on motor spirits and so on. From 2022–23, the government merged these three non-shareable duties into a single special additional excise duty. In addition, there are two cesses. In the same year, a duty re-engineering was done by increasing the component of agriculture and infrastructure cess and decreasing the road and infrastructure cess.

Accordingly, the road and infrastructure cess came down from Rs 1.08 trillion in 2021–22 to Rs 59,232 crore in 2022–23 and further to Rs 44,300 crore in 2023–24 RE. On the other hand, agriculture and infrastructure cess receipts have gone up from Rs 48,065 crore in 2021–22 to Rs 53,300 crore in 2023–24 RE.

While the composition change from one type of cess to another or merging of three non-shareable duties into one non-shareable duty did constrain the government, the hollowing-out of basic excise duties kept the states deprived of their due share in excise duties.

Customs duties growth a result of change in accounting

Customs duties receipts were Rs 1.18 trillion in 2018–19. In 2019–20 and 2020–21, customs duties revenues were Rs 1.09 trillion and Rs 1.35 trillion, respectively. Customs revenues dipped in the normal year 2019–20 and recorded a CAGR of only 6.95 per cent in the first two years of Modi 2.0.

In 2021–22, however, customs duty receipts spiked up to Rs 2 trillion, recording an eye-popping growth of over 48 per cent in that year. While a good part of this abnormal growth could be explained by the massive increase in imports during that year, a change in the accounting system also contributed.

The government used to pay duty exemption scrips under the export promotion scheme—Merchandise Export Incentive Scheme (MEIS)—and recognize the customs duty receipts by excluding the duty scrips amount claimed/encashed during the year. From 2021–22, the government started recording claims/encashment of export promotion scrips as expenditure under the new scheme—RoDTEP, which replaced MEIS—and treats the amount so spent as customs revenue with a separate heading: Through Debit in Ledger Due to Various Scrip Based Schemes.

In 2021–22, customs duty revenue recognized through this mode amounted to Rs 21,377 crore. This accounting revenue grew to Rs 43,283 crore in 2022–23 but fell to Rs 24,684 crore in 2023–24 RE.

The overall customs duty revenues (Rs 2.33 trillion; PE) recorded a reasonably decent CAGR of 14.62 per cent during Modi 2.0.

GST revenues made up for underperformance of initial years

In 2018–19, the overall GST receipts (CGST, SGST, IGST and compensation cess) were Rs 11.75 trillion. In 2023–24, the overall GST receipts grew to Rs 20.18 trillion, recording a five-year CAGR of 11.42 per cent. As the nominal GDP grew by 9.43 per cent during this period, the overall GST revenues had a positive buoyancy of 1.21.

The Central GST or CGST receipts were Rs 4.58 trillion in 2018–19, which increased to Rs 8.21 trillion in 2023–24 (provisional), recording a CAGR of

12.38 per cent. The CGST grew at a CAGR about 1 per cent higher than the CAGR of overall GST collections.

Gross tax revenues (GTR) of the government includes the leftover IGST in the Consolidated Fund of India (CFI) and the GST compensation cess receipts. The GST for GTR purposes, therefore, means CGST, IGST (leftover) and compensation cess.

The GoI GST receipts grew from Rs 5.82 trillion in 2018–19 to Rs 9.57 trillion in 2023–24 (provisional) receipts, recording a CAGR of 10.48 per cent. This was on account of two reasons. First, the government had changed its policy of retaining some undistributed IGST (Rs 28,944 crore in 2018–19) to proactively distributing IGST (-)Rs 5,026 crore in 2023–24 provisional). Second, the CAGR growth in GST compensation cess was much smaller at about 8.9 per cent.

Consumption did suffer in India during the pandemic period as evidenced in CGST receipts. The CGST receipts, at Rs 4.58 trillion in 2018–19, were flat at Rs 4.56 trillion in 2020–21 and could grow to only Rs 5.91 trillion in 2021–22, generating a three-year CAGR of only 6.28 per cent, which we can take as the end of the Covid-19 period.

CGST revenues shot up from 2021–22 onwards, rising to Rs 7.19 trillion in 2022–23 and to Rs 8.21 trillion in 2023–24 (provisional). In the three-year period (from 2020–21 to 2023–24 provisional), the CGST CAGR was as high as 21.65 per cent despite reverting to a more normal CAGR of 14 per cent in 2023–24 (provisional).

Centre's net tax revenues grew at a higher rate than the GTR

The gross tax revenues or the GTR is the sum total of all the tax receipts of the GoI (before sharing with states). The GTR (from Rs 20.80 trillion in 2018–19 to Rs 34.65 trillion (CGA PE) recorded a five-year growth of 10.74 per cent, a decent one but nothing to celebrate about. The GTR had a buoyancy of 1.14 during Modi 2.0.

The GTR is shared between the Centre and the states. GTR minus national calamity contingency duties (NCCD) and the GTR attributable to the UTs are supposed to be shared with the states in accordance with the Finance Commission formula. The government can alter the distribution by increasing the share of cesses and surcharges in the GTR. This is precisely what happened in Modi 2.0. The distributable GTR (excluding NCCD) was Rs 20.79 trillion in 2018–19. It increased to Rs 34.56 trillion in 2023–24 (provisional) recording a CAGR of 10.70 per cent.

The share of states in the distributable GTR grew from Rs 7.61 trillion in 2018–19 to Rs 11.29 trillion in 2023–24 (provisional). This yields a CAGR of only 8.21 per cent. The compounded growth of the states' share in the GTR of the Central government (8.21 per cent) in Modi 2.0 was sharply less than the growth of distributable GTR (10.70 per cent).

The states' loss was reflected in the higher share of the Central government in its tax revenues. The net tax revenues of the Central government (distributable GTR minus share of states), however, grew from Rs 13.17 trillion in 2018–19 to Rs 23.27 trillion in 2023–24 (provisional) at a CAGR of 12.05 per cent.

The states' share grew at an annual growth rate of 8.21 per cent (7.72 per cent if 2023–24 RE is taken into consideration) at a much lower rate of growth than even the nominal GDP growth of 9.43 per cent, whereas the Centre's tax revenues increased at an annual growth rate of 12.05 per cent (12.02 per cent for RE), much higher than the growth rate of GDP. In terms of buoyancy, the states' share in central taxes recorded a tepid buoyancy of 0.87 only, whereas the Centre's share grew at more than a respectable buoyancy of 1.28.

Modi 2.0 ripped off the states.

Direct Taxes Policy

Big bang corporation income tax cut in 2019

Indian companies were subject to income tax with a basic rate of 30 per cent in 2014–15 when the Modi government took charge for the first time. This tax rate was considered quite high and cited as one of the principal reasons for India not attracting investment in manufacturing, including from non-residents. There were other distortions like investment and other exemptions and incentives to companies clawed back by the levy of minimum alternative tax (MAT).

As acknowledged by Finance Minister Arun Jaitley in the 2015–16 Budget, despite the high corporate tax rate, the effective tax rate on companies was only about 23 per cent. The government, therefore, proposed in that Budget to reduce the rate of corporate tax from 30 per cent to 25 per cent in a staggered manner over the next four years. Some reduction did take place, largely for the smaller companies, but the corporation tax rate stayed at 30 per cent at the end of the first term of the Modi government.

The first Budget of Modi 2.0 presented in July 2019 also did not propose any drastic reform in corporation tax.

All of a sudden, just before the visit of Prime Minister Modi to the US, in September 2019, where he was to share the big platform with the then US President Donald Trump, the government made the significant move to ring in a low corporate tax regime.

The Parliament was not in session. The government could not have amended the Income Tax Act by way of a finance bill or a regular amendment bill. Instead, it brought out the Taxation Laws (Amendment) Ordinance 2019 to achieve its objectives.

The new corporation tax system allowed any domestic company an option to pay income tax at the basic rate of 22 per cent subject to the condition that the company would not avail any exemption/incentive. These companies were not required to pay any MAT either. To attract new investment in manufacturing, the government allowed any new domestic company, incorporated on or after 1 October 2019 and making fresh investment in manufacturing (later extended to electricity generation companies as well), an option to pay income tax at the rate of only 15 per cent subject to the condition that these companies would not avail any exemption/incentive and commence production in a new manufacturing facility on or before 31 March 2022 (subsequently extended one year at a time to 31 March 2025).

What impact did this bazooka have on corporate tax receipts?

The government produces a statement—Revenue Impact of Tax Incentive under the Central Tax System—as part of the Receipt Budget.

This statement provided useful information about the impact of the corporation tax cuts effected in 2019–20. The latest statement is available in the Budget 2023–24 (no such statement was included in the Interim Budget 2024–25) and has the information for 2020–21.

The effective corporation tax rate is the ratio of total tax receipts, including surcharge and education cess, paid by the companies to the total profits before taxes (PBT).

The statements—Revenue Impact of Tax Incentive under the Central Tax System, relating to the respective years—inform that in 2017–18, the effective tax rate was 29.49 per cent and for FY 2018–19, the last year of Modi 1.0 and the year before the tax cuts were effected, the effective corporate tax rate was 27.81 per cent.

The corporate rate cut, the evidence suggests, resulted in an immediate reduction in the effective corporate tax rate. For 2019–20, the year in which corporate tax rates were slashed to 22 per cent, with the removal of most exemptions, the effective tax rate fell to 22.54 per cent. For 2020–21, the second year after the corporation rate tax cut, the effective tax rate reduced further to 22.20 per cent.

The effective tax rate in 2020–21 was very close to the base rate of 22 per cent and lower than the base rate, inclusive of surcharges and cesses. The corporate tax rate cuts had got fully transmitted really fast.

The impact relating to the manufacturing company dimension of the corporate tax cuts was not so visible. In 2019–20, 1.37 lakh profit-making manufacturing companies had filed their returns and their effective tax rate was 21.95 per cent. As this was the year in which the low tax rate of 15 per cent was enacted, no new manufacturing company could have been registered and come into production. The effective tax rate of 21.95 per cent in 2019–20 can, therefore, be taken as the base effective tax rate of existing manufacturing companies.

For FY 2020–21, 1.44 lakh profit-making manufacturing companies filed income tax returns. Their effective tax rates surprisingly shot up to 25.68 per cent. Even if it is assumed that only a few new manufacturing companies might have come into production to claim the low tax rate of 15 per cent, why did the effective tax rate of manufacturing companies go up by over 3.73 per cent in 2020–21? Maybe the subsequent year's data would clarify this.

Personal income tax rates tinkered with every now and then

Ruing the fact that India was 'largely a tax non-compliant society', Arun Jaitley brought down the income tax rate in the minimum slab (up to Rs 5 lakh) from 10 per cent to 5 per cent in Budget 2017–18, levying at the same time, a surcharge of 10 per cent on individuals with annual taxable income between Rs 50 lakh and Rs 1 crore while keeping 15 per cent on assessees with annual taxable income in excess of Rs 1 crore unchanged.

Other than this, nothing notable happened on the personal income tax front in the first term of the Modi government. In the Interim Budget 2019–20, however, the government brought in a 'master-stroke' . Clearly with an eye on the ensuing Lok Sabha polls and the middle class taxpayers—the salary earners, pensioners and senior citizens—deviating from the established practice of not announcing any major policy decisions in the Interim Budget, officiating Finance Minister Piyush Goyal granted a full rebate to all individual taxpayers with taxable annual income up to Rs 5 lakh. As the deduction of Rs 1.5 lakh available under section 80C was continued, Piyush Goyal could claim that the persons with gross total income up to Rs 6.50 lakh were not required to pay any income tax.

The Modi 2.0 government, however, substantially modified the personal income tax rates regime in the Budget 2020–21.

Terming the Income Tax Act 'riddled with various exemptions and deductions', which made compliance by taxpayers and administration of the Income Tax Act by the tax authorities 'a burdensome process', and also claiming 'to provide significant relief to the individual taxpayers and to simplify personal income tax regime', Finance Minister Nirmala Sitharaman announced 'significant reduction' in income tax rates for the 'individual taxpayers who forgo certain deductions and exemptions'.

The bargain offered by Nirmala Sitharaman was raising Piyush Goyal's limit of tax rebate to Rs 7 lakh and an additional layered reduction in the income tax rates applicable up to the taxable income of Rs 15 lakh. The rejig in the tax rates in all amounted to the lesser incidence tax of Rs 75,000. To get this relief, the taxpayers had to forgo many deductions like 80CC for savings, interest on housing loans, etc. The new alternative taxation system offered no real additional advantages and, therefore, did not attract, barring a fraction, of about 6.5 crore individual taxpayers filing returns to the new scheme.

To make the alternative system more attractive, Nirmala Sitharaman made a few more changes in the 2023–24 Budget and made the income up to Rs 7.50 lakh non-taxable. In addition, certain benefits like standard deduction, etc., were also permitted in the alternative taxation regime. The new tax regime became clearly beneficial for all individuals with taxable income up to Rs 15 lakh. The government also made the new regime a default regime.

The income tax slabs and tax rates reforms or complications brought from the Interim Budget 2019–20 to the 2023–24 Budget, whichever way you look at it, brought about three significant changes in the personal taxation regime.

First, the overall number of personal income tax returns went up significantly (to 8.18 crore for assessment year 2023–24 against 5.3 crore in assessment year 2016–17) as the small income taxpayers filed returns to claim the tax deducted at source (TDS). Secondly, the number of effective taxpayers (excluding those who filed zero tax returns) contracted sharply from the pre 2019–20 years (estimated to be about 60 per cent less), and third, the overall personal income tax collections recorded a decent growth rate, as I noted in the previous section.

Government laid the ghost of retro tax to rest

The capital gains made on transfer of equity or any other asset, which derives its value from the underlying business in India were and are capital gains made in India. The government has every justification to tax such capital gains. However, to tax something, the authority of an explicit law authorizing it is needed. Unfortunately, when Hutchison made massive capital gains by selling its equity in a non-resident company which controlled the Hutchison-Essar telecom business in India to Vodafone, such capital gains were not specifically taxable in the country. The government raised a tax demand on the buyer Vodafone for collecting tax on the capital gains that the seller Hutchison made, which blew up to over Rs 30,000 crore. The Supreme Court struck down this demand in 2012.

The government lost the case. To make the taxability of such capital gains abundantly clear in law, the government amended the Income Tax Act and framed detailed rules to collect this tax. Tax laws usually have only a prospective effect. In this matter, however, the government used its sovereign power to make such capital gains transactions taxable retrospectively. This raised howls of protests; some called it tax terrorism. The government raised retrospective tax demands in seventeen cases exceeding over Rs 1 trillion but could recover only about Rs 8,000 crore, including by seizing and selling shares of an Indian affiliate of Cairns.

Two of the largest such affected parties—Vodafone and Cairns—took the government to international arbitration tribunals and won. Cairns obtained orders for seizing overseas assets of the Indian State and its instrumentalities like Air India to recover its money. The government filed appeals but the chances of it succeeding were very slim. This constantly hanging sword must be causing enormous embarrassment to the government.

There were three ways to put an end to it: first, the government could have implemented arbitration tribunal orders; second, the government could have settled it bilaterally with Cairns and others; and third, the government could have undone the retrospective taxation law itself. Though belatedly, the government chose the third option. It allowed the government to neutralize the arbitration awards and frustrate ongoing cases. The cash cost to the government was not very large—only about Rs 8,000 crore, which was to be refunded or assets released.

The government did frame the necessary rules. The amendment law made retrospective tax assessment orders deemed as never passed subject to fulfilment of three 'specified conditions'. There were: withdraw pending court cases, withdraw pending arbitration and enforcement cases and give an undertaking not to pursue any remedy in the matter.

The parties accepted the conditions, withdrew the case and the government refunded the retrospective tax collected and released the assets/shares seized. A bad chapter in the history of India's taxation laws finally came to an end.

Black money law did not make much difference

The International Consortium of Investigative Journalists (ICIJ), a Washington-D.C. based non-profit, comprising 280 'best investigative reporters from more than 100 countries and territories' literally opened a huge Pandora's box when it released its first report on the Pandora Papers on 3 October 2021 titled 'Offshore Havens and Hidden Riches of World Leaders and Billionaires Exposed in Unprecedented Leak' on its website icij.org. ICIJ had earlier released investigative reports as well—the Panama Papers in 2016 and the Paradise Papers in 2017.

In this first report, based on the Pandora Papers, ICIJ claimed that they could uncover the financial secrets of thirty-five current and former world leaders, more than 330 politicians and public officials in ninety-one countries, and also many 'fugitives, con artists and murderers'. There are thousands of individuals who figure in the Pandora Papers, which included over 380 Indians as well.

The Pandora Papers revelations were primarily about wealthy residents creating legal structures offshore to hold their assets in those jurisdictions for their own or their families' benefit. These structures are created primarily for two purposes: keeping the assets away in more secure and secretive places and to avoid tax on the wealth and income therefrom. Some of these structures have been created as companies. But, the most common mode of holding these assets abroad is in the form of trusts. Pandora Papers investigations unearthed thousands of such structures from papers leaked from twelve major international firms specializing in creating such trusts and other structures for holding wealth offshore, mostly in tax-avoidance jurisdictions. These structures holding the wealth are legal or illegal depending on the laws applicable to the creators of these trusts and the wealth transferred to such trusts, which would have to be examined on the merit and facts of each case.

Besides the applicable tax laws, India enacted the Black Money (Undisclosed Foreign Income and Assets) and Imposition of Tax Act 2015, to deal with the problem of black money, defined as undisclosed foreign income and assets of a beneficial owner who cannot explain the source of such investment.

The Indian Trust Act permits the creation of offshore trusts by resident Indians and also resident Indians to be beneficiaries of the offshore trusts created by non-residents. Therefore, creation of offshore trusts or being a beneficiary of such trusts disclosed does not automatically imply any wrongdoing unless such a trust violated any Indian law, including tax laws and the black money law.

The GoI issued a press note on 4 October 2021 taking note of the Pandora Papers and vowed to get these investigated by 'relevant investigative agencies' and to take appropriate action as per the law. A multi-agency group was established to monitor the investigation. For the disclosures made in the Panama and Paradise Papers, the government stated that undisclosed credits of Rs 20,352 crore had been detected thus far. The government did not disclose the final outcome—did these undisclosed credits lead to any final assessments and if so, what amount of tax was collected? Or, the undisclosed credits were explained by the concerned people leading to no action. The disclosures made as part of the Pandora Papers in 2021 also met the same fate.

In June 2024, the Courts held that the Black Money law could not be used for the 'offences' committed before its date of enactment, holding this provision violative of Article 20 of the Constitution.

Cryptocurrency trade virtually finished

Taxation of capital gains made on transfer of cryptocurrencies, such as Bitcoin, had been a grey area for many years. The government sought to address this matter by bringing necessary legislative changes through the Finance Act 2022.

A new section—115BBH—was added to provide that capital gains on transfer of any cryptocurrency, defined more generally as a virtual digital asset

(VDA), would be taxed at the rate of 30 per cent on the consideration received without allowing any deduction in respect of any expenditure (other than cost of acquisition) incurred or set-off of any loss on other cryptocurrency trade. The new provision came into effect from 1 April 2022. In addition, the Finance Act 2022 provided for a deduction of 1 per cent TDS to come into effect from 1 July 2022.

VDAs were defined quite widely by including a new clause—47A—in section 2 of the act. As per this clause, a VDA means any information or code or number or token (not being Indian currency or any foreign currency) generated through cryptographic means or otherwise, by whatever name called, providing a digital representation of value, which is exchanged with or without consideration, with the promise or representation of having inherent value or functions as a store of value or a unit of account and includes its use in any financial transaction or investment, but not limited to, investment schemes and can be transferred, stored or traded electronically. Non-fungible tokens (NFTs) and any other token of a similar nature were also included in the definition of VDAs.

The new law obligated the person responsible for making payment to ensure that tax had been paid in respect of consideration received in cases where the payment for such transfer was wholly in kind or in exchange of another VDA, where there was no part in cash or where payment was made partly in cash and partly in kind but the part in cash was not sufficient to meet the liability of TDS.

The regime instituted by the government for subjecting crypto-VDAs to 30 per cent tax on capital gains was quite harsh. No set-off of any loss including the loss suffered on other crypto-VDAs was permitted. No carry-forward of loss was allowed. No deduction of any cost related to crypto-VDA other than the cost of its acquisition was allowed.

The provision of TDS made the going quite tough and hard. The cryptocurrency exchanges were required to deduct 1 per cent TDS on gross value of transfers made by the seller. When the net consideration in cash was less than 1 per cent of the gross value of sales made, the exchanges had to ensure that payment of TDS was anyhow made by the sellers of crypto-assets before consideration was transferred to their account.

These provisions turned the world of blockchain-cryptography topsy-turvy. Quite apart from what was happening in India, cryptocurrencies were collapsing all over the world for various reasons. Bitcoin, the most popular cryptocurrency, fell to less than $20,000 (from the highs of $69,000 in 2021–22). Market capitalization of cryptocurrencies fell to less than $1 trillion at end-September 2022 from $3 trillion a year before.

The government's capital gains regime for VDAs proved quite harsh for the cryptocurrency platforms/exchanges in India. Difficulties in implementing the

TDS provision made turnover on crypto-exchanges collapse by more than 70 per cent in a month. Complaints about some platforms being used to facilitate transfer of profits/funds from India and inquiries/freezing of accounts by law enforcement agencies also played a role. Some exchanges moved out; some effectively closed. The industry advocacy body terminated itself.

The world of cryptocurrencies was quite moribund in India by the time Modi 2.0 completed its tenure.

Indirect Taxes Policy

2017 GST reforms package by and large implemented

GST, institutionalized in India from 1 July 2017, made the entire country a single market, did away with border checkposts to make the flow of goods seamless, consolidated most indirect taxes into a single tax and made the tax process— registration to assessment—fully digital and business- and consumer-friendly.

The number of registered GST taxpayers increased significantly. As many as 64.38 lakh incumbent taxpayers shifted from the erstwhile fragmented indirect-tax regime. The number of registered GST taxpayers reached 14 million by the end of March 2023, more than doubling in less than six years. At the end of May 2024, there were 14.63 million registered and active GST taxpayers, comprising 12.79 million of normal taxpayers, 1.51 million composition taxpayers and the remaining number comprising input service distributors, casual taxpayers, tax collectors at source, tax deductors at source, etc.

The government made an ambitious decision in December 2019 of making e-invoicing mandatory for all GST taxpayers with an aggregate annual turnover of more than Rs 100 crore in any preceding financial year for all business-to-business supplies. The Covid-19 pandemic made the government grant some time and concessions. The date of implementation of the directive was extended in March 2020 to 1 October 2020; in July 2020, it was made applicable only to taxpayers with an aggregate turnover of Rs 500 crore or more.

The GST e-invoicing system began to roll out from 1 October 2020. 8.4 lakh e-invoices were generated on the first day, i.e. 1 October 2020, and picked up to reach 35 lakh e-invoices on 31 October 2020. The applicable turnover limit was brought down again to Rs 100 crore with effect from 1 January 2021. In the first six months of the roll-out, i.e. by the end of March 2021, a total of 39.81 crore e-invoices were generated by about 88,000 suppliers issued to more than 47 lakh recipients.

The e-invoicing regime was successfully extended gradually to most of the GST-registered businesses thereafter. The turnover limit was brought down to Rs 50 crore with effect from 1 April 2021, to Rs 20 crore with effect from

1 April 2022, to Rs 10 crore with effect from 1 October 2022 and to Rs 5 crore with effect from 1 August 2023.

The transition to e-invoicing seems to be a work in progress. In November 2023, 13.84 lakh (less than 10 per cent of all registered) were system-enabled to generate e-invoices. Of that, 7.75 lakh only had started generating e-invoices, including 41,800 assessees out of 69,395 total taxpayers in the Rs 500-crore-plus category.

The GST system has become almost fully implemented during Modi 2.0. It is 100 per cent electronic and all the processes, including filing of returns, payment of taxes, claiming of input tax credits and assessment, happen online. The robust digital infrastructure created under the GST system and network (GSTN) has enabled the government to undertake anti-evasion campaigns to spruce up GST performance. GST is here to stay in India.

GST compensation did cause considerable tension

Implementation of the 14 per cent guaranteed GST compensation to states for five years caused the biggest tension in the implementation journey of GST. These tensions were exasperated by the unilateralism of the GoI in the wake of falling GST revenues after the onset of Covid-19.

First, the GoI tried to renege on the guaranteed compensation taking a plea/excuse that the guaranteed 14 per cent growth was not applicable for the period of disruption caused by the pandemic. The states understandably protested. The meetings of the GST Council were conducted in quite a hostile atmosphere.

Thereafter, the government came up with a partial solution that the 14 per cent guaranteed compensation could be paid if the states agreed to receive a loan for the shortfall after using the GST compensation cess revenue, which the GoI would raise from the market to be repaid later from the GST compensation cess to be extended beyond June 2022. Many states wanted to get the 14 per cent GST growth compensation guarantee extended for another five years after 2022.

The GoI prevailed. It issued bonds and raised adequate amounts to provide for the GST compensation shortfall as back-to-back loans to the states. The GST compensation cess was extended for four years, i.e. until end-June 2026.

No extension of guaranteed GST compensation to the states beyond June 2022 was, however, made. By end-2022–23, the issue had gone into the background.

The CGST revenues increased quite well in the last three years of 2021–22, 2022–23 and 2023–24. The GoI could accumulate considerable unused GST compensation cess. By the end of Modi 2.0, however, looking at the possibility of a good GST compensation cess surplus left unused at the end of June 2026, the states started demanding that the surplus be shared with them.

The Supreme Court ruled in the Ocean Freight case (2022) that recommendations of the GST Council have persuasive value but are not binding on the Union and the states. This implied that the states continued to have the sovereign power to enact or amend the GST law in their respective states, even if the same was different from the GST Council's recommendation or the central enactment.

Online gaming got the GST stick

The online gaming industry has grown massively worldwide. There were an estimated 450 million online gamers in 2023. The gaming industry designs games and provides platforms for both competitive gamers and entertainment consumers. A lot of creativity, innovation, investment, technology and participation rides on the gaming industry. The government brought in the Central GST (Amendment) Act 2023, which changed the fortunes of the online gaming industry drastically.

Before this amendment, the law recognized the subtle distinction between gaming and betting/gambling. Section 65B(15) of the Finance Act 1994 defined gambling or betting as putting on stake something of value, particularly money, with consciousness of risk and hope of gain on the outcome of a game or a contest, whose result may be determined by chance or accident or on the likelihood of anything occurring or not occurring. 'Games' and 'contests' referred to in the definition were only those the results of which are determined by chance or accident. Games and contests with application of mind were not considered betting or gambling.

The GST law recognized the distinction between betting/gambling and online gaming. Besides horse racing, betting and lotteries, GST at 28 per cent was applicable only on gambling (GST Notification 11/2017—online gambling services; entry 999692). The same notification prescribed a lower rate of 18 per cent (under the heading 998439—other online content), which applied to the games intended to be played on the Internet, such as role-playing games (RPGs), strategy games, action games, card games, children's games, etc., the payment for which may be made by subscription, membership fee, pay-per-play or pay-per-view. Online games were, by and large, as per this notification, not betting or gambling. The gaming industry was paying 18 per cent GST.

There was considerable confusion in the minds of the GST administration whether to treat or not treat the payment/deposit for the prize pool of online gaming, as an actionable claim. The gamers make the real money deposits/stakes to win higher amounts than the amount staked. The platforms that provide online gaming services retain a part of the payment/deposit with the rest becoming part of the prize pool to be distributed to the gamers. The prize pool is indisputably considered an 'actionable claim'.

The CGST Act had provided that actionable claims, 'other than lottery, betting and gambling' were not supply of goods/services. As gaming was not gambling, the prize pool was considered not 'supply of goods/services' and hence, not subject to GST. However, some GST authorities assessed GST on the total prize pool, which was declared unlawful by the Karnataka High Court (GamesKraft case), which was later stayed by the Supreme Court.

The GST Council on 11 July 2023 decided to equate online gaming with gambling and betting and recommended a levy of 28 per cent GST on all real money online games, disregarding differences between games of chance and skill.

The GST is levied on the value added and not on the total value of output. The platform fees received by the gaming industry is the value added. The GST has to be levied only on the platform fee and other service charges received by the platforms. The total deposit (prize pool plus platform fee) is the actionable claim and is therefore not subject to GST. By equating gaming with gambling to deny the application of an actionable claim to the online gaming industry, the government clearly went for an overkill.

Usually, the platform fees are about 10 per cent of the total prize pool. Therefore, if 28 per cent GST is charged on 100 per cent of the prize pool, it actually amounted to 280 per cent of the actual value added.

The Parliament passed the Central Goods and Services (Amendment) Act 2023 to define 'online gaming' (inserted clause 80A in Section 2 of the CGST 2017) to mean 'offering of a game on the internet or an electronic network and includes online money gaming'. 'Online money gaming' (inserted clause 80B) was defined to mean 'online gaming in which players pay or deposit their money's worth, including VDAs, in the expectation of winning their money or money's worth, including VDAs, in any event including game, scheme, competition or any other activity or process, whether or not its outcome or performance is based on skill, chance or both and whether the same is permissible or otherwise under any other law for the time being in force'. Any Internet or online game that is played with a money stake is online money gaming. As the online money gaming and online gaming were defined specifically, the government can put GST both on online gaming and online money gaming, with or without making any further distinction.

A new class of 'specified actionable claim' (inserted clause 102A) was created to bring six types of actionable claims under it: betting, casinos, gambling, horse racing, lottery and online money gaming. These specified actionable claims would be treated as supply and hence, subject to GST on the full value of deposit/payment. A proviso to clause 105 made the organizers and arrangers of online gaming one of the six types of specified actionable claims as the suppliers under the GST Act and thereby responsible to collect GST and pay it into the government account.

The online gaming industry's fortunes went into a tailspin. The government's decision led to many court cases. The matter remained undecided until the end of Modi 2.0.

GST reforms did not touch MSMEs

The GST system works best when every business that supplies goods or services on commercial consideration becomes a GST-registered business and a part of the GST network. The strength of the GST system is a seamless flow of goods and services across all suppliers—big, small or tiny.

Misplaced considerations—socialist, small turnover, low profitability or lack of technology adoption—kept a big chunk of India's about 8 crore businesses outside the GST network in 2017. The suppliers of goods with less than Rs 40 lakh turnover (Rs 20 lakh for service businesses) were kept exempt from even registering under GST. Businesses with less than Rs 1.5 crore turnover were allowed to opt for a composition assessment that does not require invoice-based tax assessment.

These measures, supposedly taken for safeguarding the interest of small businesses, were actually not in their real interest. Small businesses became non-preferred partners for bigger businesses. Consumers also consider them less trustworthy and transact with them largely to avoid taxes. All these businesses—below the threshold or under composite schemes—also create enormous disturbance and discontinuity in the value-added chain and GST chain. The tax benefits MSMEs get are outweighed by the larger loss of market, credit and profitability.

Non-Tax Revenues

There are four non-tax revenue sources, which, besides impacting the fiscal health of the government, also indirectly provide evidence of the policy preferences of the government and its performance.

The surplus transfer from the RBI provides good clues about the prevalent interest rates in the economy, interest rate environment on foreign assets in which the foreign exchange reserves are deployed, the exchange rate movements and also their management by the RBI. However, from the government's viewpoint, the most important matter is how much of the surplus earned by the RBI is transferred to the government.

The dividend receipts, both from non-financial public sector enterprises, such as NTPC, Powergrid, Oil Marketing Companies, etc., and financial public sector enterprises, such as banks and insurance companies, indicate their relative share in the business and profitability performance.

The important economic services receipts such as those from the telecommunications (auction receipts, licence fee, etc.), roads and highways (toll receipts), petroleum (profit petroleum), etc., indicate successful implementation of key economic policies of the government.

Finally, the interest receipts do tell us about the loan policy of the government, interest rate environment and the performing/non-performing nature of these loans.

Let me first provide a comment on the performance of Modi 2.0 in respect to non-tax receipts, more specifically for these four major non-tax receipts.

Volatile and low growth in overall non-tax receipts

The non-tax receipts at Rs 2.36 trillion in 2018–19 were 1.25 per cent of the nominal GDP of Rs 189 trillion and 17.89 per cent of the net tax receipts of Rs 13.17 trillion. The non-tax receipts grew to Rs 3.76 trillion in 2023–24 RE, which turned out to be 1.27 per cent of the GDP and 16.17 per cent of the net tax receipts of Rs 23.24 trillion.

The non-tax receipts in the last year of Modi 2.0, as a percentage of GDP, remained almost at the same level as it was in the last year of Modi 1.0, but has fallen more than 1.72 per cent as a proportion of net tax revenues. Obviously, the non-tax revenue growth has been smaller than the net taxes growth.

The non-tax revenue growth has also been quite volatile and its pattern is different from the pattern visible in the case of taxes growth. It has wavered from year to year rather than going down during the Covid-19 period and recovered quickly in the post-Covid-19 period, as was the case with tax receipts.

In 2019–20, non-tax revenues jumped massively to Rs 3.27 trillion, rising by as much as 38.8 per cent. The very next year, it collapsed to Rs 2.08 trillion, in fact, less than the non-tax revenue of Rs 2.36 trillion in 2018–19. In 2021–22, non-tax revenues jumped again to Rs 3.65 trillion. 2022–23 saw non-tax revenues fall again to a low of 2.85 trillion. True to one year falling and another year rising, non-tax revenues were estimated at Rs 3.76 trillion in 2023–24 RE.

The non-tax revenues volatility is linked more to the volatility in the payment of dividend by the RBI out of the surplus it generated. The overall CAGR of non-tax revenues during Modi 2.0 at 9.78 per cent generated a lowly buoyancy of 1.04.

Telecom revenues performed well

The telecommunication services' non-tax revenues proved to be the star performer for Modi 2.0. Besides contributing a significant share of total non-tax revenues, the telecom services revenues rose to assume a large share of overall non-tax revenues during this period.

The government classifies the telecommunication non-tax revenues in three broad sub-groups: receipts from wireless planning and coordination organizations, which essentially represents the spectrum fees realized based on adjusted gross revenues (AGR), telecommunication licence fees and universal access levy.

Total communications services receipts were Rs 40,816 crore in 2018–19, which constituted 17.32 per cent of the total non-tax revenues of Rs 2.36 trillion. In 2023–24 RE, these revenues rose massively to Rs 93,541 crore, which was as high as 24.89 per cent of the total non-tax revenues of Rs 3.76 trillion.

The wireless revenues, the first of the three components of telecom revenues, received a major shot in the arm in 2021–22 when the government undertook certain reforms and cleaned out procedural and other cobwebs. The wireless telecommunication revenues, which were Rs 29,718 crore in 2019–20 and Rs 29,941 crore in 2020–21, rose dramatically to Rs 69,038 crore in 2021–22. The overall telecom services non-tax revenues in that year were Rs 85,828 crore.

The increase in telecommunication services revenues was despite the government revising the definition of AGR to applicable gross revenue (ApGR) in October 2021. The ApGR excluded certain non-telecom revenues, revenues earned from activities under a licence/permission granted by the Ministry of Information and Broadcasting, receipts from the Universal Service Obligation (USO) Fund and items of other revenue from the base of AGR. The telecom revenues though were aided by certain auction pre-payments.

A part role was played by a fiscal trick. The government provided equity support to BSNL from the budget which it used for payment of spectrum licence fee, fixed administratively for it. For example, Rs 19,808 crore was paid on account of administratively allotted spectrum in 2021–22. These payments also jacked up telecom revenues.

RBI surplus transfer

The RBI has been entrusted with currency management—a sovereign function of the government. In exercise of this function, the RBI issues banknotes/currency, which is its biggest liability. However, unlike other commercial enterprises, its currency liabilities have no cost to the RBI, barring a small cost of printing, storing and transporting it. The RBI also is a statutory regulator of banks. In exercising this function, the RBI, among other measures, mandates the banks to keep cash deposits with the RBI, on which normally it does not pay any interest. The RBI's liabilities are, therefore, uniquely no-cost liabilities.

The RBI deploys these resources/liabilities into rupee and foreign exchange assets primarily and earns interest and valuation benefits thereon. The higher the size of RBI liabilities or its balance sheet, the RBI usually earns more surplus. The RBI had assets/liabilities of Rs 70.48 trillion at the end of March 2024. Even if the RBI earns a net interest margin of 2 per cent thereon, it ends up making about Rs 1.41 trillion in surplus a year with such a balance sheet size.

The RBI's functions—maintaining liquidity, financial stability in domestic and foreign exchange markets, lender of the last resort (in times of crisis—rare), etc.—don't require the RBI to dip into any reserves. Its monetary authority takes care of all these monetary functions. The RBI, therefore, does not require to retain any part of the surpluses it earns. For this very reason, the RBI Act (Section 47) provides that 'After making provision for bad and doubtful debts, depreciation in assets, contributions to staff and superannuation and for all other matters for which provision is to be made by or under this act or which are usually provided by bankers, the balance of the profits shall be paid to the Central Government'. The first five heads of provisions don't require any significant amount to be provided for and the RBI has been doing it without anyone questioning it. However, the last 'which are usually provided by bankers' has been sought to be used by the RBI's top brass for retaining a good chunk of the surplus.

The RBI is no banker, it is the central banker. The central banks don't require any other provisions and many of them make no other provisions at all. Yet, in India, most particularly after 2015, the economic capital framework, designed and used to retain a big part of the surplus, has generated needless controversies. The effect of this controversy played out during the Modi 2.0 period principally. This entire period (2019–24) is covered by the recommendations of the Bimal Jalan Committee.

The RBI transfers surplus to the government usually in May–June after its financial year has ended on 31 March (earlier 30 June). Therefore, for the purposes of Modi 2.0, the surpluses that were generated from FY 2018–19 to FY 2022–23 are relevant for the purpose of non-tax income receipts of the government. The government accounts/budget does not disclose specific amounts of the surplus transferred by the RBI to the government every year. This can, however, be gleaned from the RBI accounts.

During this period of five years, the RBI earned a surplus (after its all operational expenses; in other words, before transfer to the government and to its contingency fund where it holds its free provisions) of Rs 7.91 trillion (Rs 1.77 trillion in 2018–19, Rs 1.31 trillion in 2019–20, Rs 1.20 trillion in 2020–21, Rs 1.45 trillion in 2021–22 and Rs 2.18 trillion in 2022–23).

The government receives the RBI surplus in the year it is declared and transferred to it. During 2017–18 and 2018–19, the RBI paid interim dividends of Rs 10,000 crore and Rs 28,000 crore respectively, during the operating year itself to the government. From FY 2019–20, no interim dividend was declared.

The RBI transferred Rs 1.48 trillion in 2019–20 against the dividend of 2018–19 (Rs 1.76 trillion minus Rs 28,000 crore), Rs 57,128 crore in 2020–21, Rs 99,122 crore in 2021–22, Rs 30,307 crore in 2022–23 and Rs 87,416 crore in 2023–24. In all, the RBI transferred a total surplus of Rs 4.22 trillion to the government during the five years of Modi 2.0.

The RBI transferred 57 per cent of its total profits/surplus to the government during Modi 2.0. The dividend transfer, in terms of normal RBI surplus, was close to 100 per cent. I have discussed this aspect of RBI surplus management in the chapter on Currency and Money.

Dividends and profit share from other public sector entities

The dividend receipts from the public sector entities (non-financial enterprises such as Steel Authority of India, Bharat Petroleum Corporation, NTPC, etc., and financial enterprises other than the RBI, which include the PSBs and LIC), are also a major source of non-tax revenues for the government. In the five years of Modi 2.0, the dividends and profit share receipts from the real sector public sector entities amounted to Rs 2.45 trillion, including Rs 50,000 crore in 2023–24 RE.

The dividends and profits share was highly subdued in the first two years of 2019–20 and 2020–21 (Rs 35,543 crore and Rs 39,750 crore, respectively). From 2021–22, the dividend performance turned the corner significantly, rising to Rs 59,294 crore in 2021–22 and Rs 59,953 crore in 2022–23.

The story about dividend transfers from the financial enterprises was quite pathetic during Modi 2.0. The head Dividend/Surplus from the RBI, Nationalized Banks and Financial Institutions recorded total receipts of Rs 4.53 trillion during 2019–20 to 2023–24 RE (Rs 1.51 trillion in 2019–20, Rs 57,128 crore in 2020–21, Rs 1.01 trillion in 2021–22, Rs 39,961 crore in 2022–23 and Rs 1.04 trillion in 2023–24 RE). Of this, Rs 4.22 trillion was transferred by the RBI alone. All the other financial institutions, including all PSBs, LIC and insurance companies, transferred only Rs 31,478 crore to the government as dividend in five years.

The first three years (2019–20 to 2021–22) were literally as good as lost as far as the profitability and dividend transfer from the financial institutions of the government was concerned. In 2019–20, these financial enterprises transferred merely Rs 2,602 crore. The next year (2020–21), they took a complete rest with not a single rupee being transferred as dividend. The year 2021–22 was as bad as 2019–20 with only Rs 2,231 crore transferred as dividend by the financial institutions. It was only from 2022–23, that the situation started looking up, with the government receiving Rs 9,654 crore in dividends. The 2023–24 RE assumes receipt of Rs 16,991 crore as dividend from financial enterprises of the government.

PSBs had taken a holiday in the first two years by not contributing even a single rupee as dividend to the government in 2019–20 and 2020–21. They made a modest contribution of Rs 2,231 crore in 2021–22. 2022–23 and 2023–24 saw the revitalized PSBs with a massive increase in their profitability being reflected in the dividend amount transferred to the government. In 2022–23, PSBs paid a total dividend of Rs 13,804 crore and in 2023–24, approximately Rs 18,000 crore.

LIC had been making a dividend transfer of about Rs 2,500 crore to the government for many years. In 2019–20, the first year of Modi 2.0, LIC paid to the government a dividend of Rs 2,611 crore. However, in the next two years, LIC did not pay any dividend to the government. It was not that LIC's profitability had received any big dent. It was primarily for building up reserves in the Shareholders Fund as LIC wanted to bring its IPO out in April 2022. For FY 2022–23, paid in FY 2023–24, LIC paid Rs 1,831.9 crore as dividend.

During Modi 2.0, the government received Rs 4.22 trillion from the RBI as surplus transfer, Rs 2.45 trillion from the real sector public sector enterprises and Rs 31,478 crore from the financial enterprises. In all, the government received Rs 2.76 trillion from the financial and non-financial enterprises and Rs 4.22 trillion from the RBI. Total dividend and surplus receipts amounted to Rs 6.98 trillion.

Income from petroleum and roads and bridges

Petroleum and roads and bridges are the two other important sources of non-tax income for the government.

The petroleum sector contributed a total of Rs 73,247 crore to the government in the five years of Modi 2.0 (Rs 11,841 crore in 2019–20, Rs 6,662 crore in 2020–21, Rs 20,037 crore in 2021–22, Rs 19,785 crore in 2022–23 and Rs 14,922 crore in 2023–24 RE).

The sector had contributed non-tax revenues of Rs 14,197 crore in 2018–19, the last year of Modi 1.0. The first two years saw a sharp decline. The revenue received a big boost in 2021–22 but again kept declining in the last two years, bringing it down to only Rs 14,922 crore in the last year. As a result, the CAGR of the petroleum sector during Modi 2.0 was a minuscule 1 per cent per annum.

The road and bridges sector (primarily toll revenues) contributed a total of Rs 85,521 crore in the five years of Modi 2.0 (Rs 10,394 crore in 2019–20, Rs 10,479 crore in 2020–21, Rs 14,330 crore in 2021–22, Rs 22,470 crore in 2022–23 and Rs 27,848 crore in 2023–24 (RE).

The road and bridges sector saw steady growth in revenues all through the five years of Modi 2.0, rising from Rs 103.94 crore in 2019–20 to Rs 278.48 crore in 2023–24. However, as the last year of Modi 1.0 (2018–19) had recorded a high non-tax revenue of Rs 19,866 crore, the CAGR during Modi 2.0 was only 6.99 per cent.

Three economic services—telecommunication, roads and petroleum—together TRP, if you'd like to call it, contributed a good chunk of the total non-tax revenues. The telecommunication sector contributed Rs 3.60 trillion (23 per cent of total non-tax revenues) during 2019–24. The contribution of the petroleum sector was Rs 73,247 crore (4.69 per cent). The roads and highways sector's contribution of Rs 85,521 crore amounted to 5.48 per cent of the total non-tax revenues. Together, these three sectors contributed Rs 5.18 trillion to the non-tax revenues kitty, which was 33.10 per cent of the total non-tax revenues of Rs 15.61 trillion during Modi 2.0.

19

Investment, Disinvestment and Monetization

Investing in public enterprises was the principal strategy of governments for decades after the Indian republic was established in 1950. The Jawaharlal Nehru government adopted, in the 1950s, the policy of entrusting the commanding heights of the economy to the public sector, which led to the setting up of numerous public sector enterprises. Later, Indira Gandhi expanded the public sector in the energy sector in the 1960s and 1970s by nationalizing oil companies, setting up new electricity generation companies and also by nationalizing the banks.

After 1991, the public sector enterprises juggernaut slowed down. The private sector was now permitted to enter all the industries reserved for the public sector. They could now establish banks, insurance companies and other financial intermediaries.

In the early twenty-first century, the Atal Bihari Vajpayee government started rolling back the public sector by privatizing some public sector enterprises. The policy of privatizing public sector enterprises was abandoned by the Manmohan Singh government. It was revived by the Modi government in 2015, but, barring the Air India privatization, no other genuine privatization was carried out.

In its second term, the Modi government jumped on the other side of the fence and made investment in public sector enterprises its preferred policy. Ironically, the policy of small-stake sales in public sector enterprises—disinvestment—which has been consistently adopted by all the governments since the mid-1990s, was also literally shelved by the Modi government in its second term.

The governments have made considerable investment in non-commercial enterprises, such as NHAI as well. These investments can only be partially recovered by monetizing the assets created. The roads built by NHAI can be monetized by granting concessions through various models like Toll-Operate-Transfer (TOT), Infrastructure Investment Trust (InVIT), etc. The Modi government announced a major policy of monetization but did not follow it through aggressively.

In this chapter, I discuss investment in public enterprises first as that has claimed a massive amount of budgetary resources in Modi 2.0. Thereafter, I discuss three aspects of recovering the investments made—privatization, disinvestment and monetization. Finally, I review the net investment and disinvestment.

Investment in Public Enterprises

The government provides the details of equity investment made in public enterprises in Statement 26 of the Expenditure Profile. This statement provides details for the equity investment made in each of the public enterprises and for each administrative ministry/department that has one or more such enterprises. The government makes no distinction between the class of public enterprises. It may be a purely commercial enterprise like the Gas Authority of India Ltd (GAIL), or a purely departmental enterprise like Railways, or a statutory authority set up for constructing a specific type of asset on a part-commercial-part-public-purpose basis, such as NHAI.

Some of these equity investments, in a budget-neutral manner, e.g. investment in the equity of PSBs and other financial institutions, such as insurance companies, EXIM Bank, etc., were made in this manner between 2017 and 2022. The government neutralizes the expenditure made in the equity investment by subtracting the investment made by such equity-recipient organizations in the debt securities of the government. While such equity investments do not increase the size of the budget, these expenditures are correctly captured in Statement 26 as equity investments.

Equity investments went up massively in Modi 2.0. In 2018–19, the last year of Modi 1.0, the government made a total equity investment of Rs 2.10 trillion in public enterprises, which included a heavy dose of budget-neutral investment of Rs 1.06 trillion in PSBs. In 2023–24 RE, total equity investment made zoomed to Rs 4.89 trillion, all from the budget.

Modi 2.0 would be remembered more for unleashing investments in public sector enterprises.

Total investment grew massively

With the PSB capitalization primarily undertaken in the last two years of Modi 1.0, total investment in public sector enterprises slackened to Rs 1.92 trillion in 2019–20, the first year of Modi 2.0. The second year (2020–21) witnessed the lowest level of equity investment in the second term, of only Rs 1.17 trillion.

The Modi government cottoned on to the magic of making capital investments from 2021–22, which manifested most in the form of equity investment. In that year, the government made equity investments of Rs 2.24 trillion. It was a big race thereafter, as the equity investment of the government substituted IEBRs of public enterprises.

In 2022–23, the total equity invested jumped to Rs 3.45 trillion and in 2023–24 RE to Rs 4.89 trillion. In three years (from 2020–21 to 2023–24 RE), equity investments made by the government in public enterprises more than quadrupled (418.6 per cent).

The CAGR of equity investment during Modi 2.0 has turned out to be 18.44 per cent, much higher than the total expenditure growth rate of 14.17 per cent. For the three-year period, from the lows of 2020–21 to the last year (2023–24), equity investment recorded a humungous annual compounded growth of 61.17 per cent.

It was Railways and roads all the way

In 2018–19, the last year of Modi 1.0, the government made a total equity investment of Rs 88,656 crore in the public sector enterprises of the Ministry of Railways (Rs 52,838 crore) and road sector public enterprise NHAI (Rs 35,819 crore) of the Ministry of Road Transport and Highways (MoRTH).

The equity invested in the enterprises of these two ministries did not see any major escalating activity in the first two years of Modi 2.0, with total equity invested amounting to Rs 99,533 crore in 2019–20 and Rs 75,988 crore in 2020–21.

The year 2021–22 provided the pivot. The penny dropped and the government unleashed a shower of equity investment in the enterprises of these two ministries. The investment in the public sector enterprises of the Ministry of Railways (MoR) grew to Rs 1.17 trillion (incidentally, higher than the total equity invested by the government in 2020–21 in all the public enterprises), recording annual growth of 291 per cent.

The Railways juggernaut kept plodding on with equity invested rising to Rs 1.59 trillion in 2022–23, recording annual growth of more than 35 per cent. This rose to an unprecedented level of Rs 2.40 trillion in 2023–24 RE, again growing at a stupendous annual growth rate of 50 per cent.

The government expanded equity invested in the enterprises of MoR at an unprecedented CAGR of over 100 per cent during the last three years of Modi 2.0. Even for the five years of Modi 2.0, the CAGR of equity investments in MoR enterprises was an incredibly high 35.36 per cent.

The pivot for NHAI, under the MoRTH, came a year later. From Rs 35,819 crore in 2018–19, after a small dip to Rs 31,691 crore in 2019–20, the equity invested in NHAI grew steadily to Rs 46,062 crore in 2020–21 (the pandemic year) and to Rs 57,061 crore in the second Covid-19 wave year of 2021–22.

The NHAI stopped raising any capital resources from the market on its balance sheet from 2022–23 onwards. Instead, the government supplied all the resources needed as equity. In 2022–23, the equity invested in NHAI zoomed to Rs 1.42 trillion, recording a jump of 148-plus percentage and further to Rs 1.67 trillion in 2023–24 RE. The five-year CAGR of the government's equity investment in NHAI at 36.12 per cent is as impressive as that of the Railways.

Together, the equity investment in the enterprises of the MoR and the MoRTH rose to Rs 1.74 trillion in 2021–22, to Rs 3.01 trillion in 2022–23 and to Rs 4.07 trillion in 2023–24 RE. The equity invested by the government in the public enterprises of these two ministries was 42.28 per cent of all the equity investment in 2018–19. This proportion kept steadily increasing to 51.97 per cent in 2019–20, to 65.09 per cent in 2020–21, to 77.87 per cent in 2021–22 and to 87.34 per cent in 2022–23, when it peaked during Modi 2.0. In 2023–24 RE, the final year of Modi 2.0, it came down marginally to 83.37 per cent.

With Railways and road sector enterprises claiming as high as 85 per cent of total equity investments made by the government, it would not be unfair to say that for Modi 2.0, public sector enterprises meant essentially the road and railway sector enterprises.

Investment in financial services stopped

The last two years of Modi 1.0 were all about keeping the government's financial enterprises afloat. PSBs were sinking. The insurance companies, with a dwindling solvency ratio, appeared to be heading into a crisis. Other financial enterprises, EXIM Bank, Indian Infrastructure Finance Corporation Ltd (IIFCL) and the like, were also in trouble.

Besides consolidating PSBs into a smaller number of banks, listing one general insurance company, the primary government intervention was the infusing of more equity to let the PSBs maintain the minimum prescribed regulatory capital ratios. For this purpose, the government did make large investments in these financial enterprises. In 2018–19, the last year of Modi 1.0, the government made an equity investment of Rs 1.10 trillion in public financial enterprises, which was as high as 52.36 per cent of the total equity investment of Rs 2.10 trillion. The bulk of these financial sector equity investments—Rs 1.06 trillion—went to the PSBs.

The financial sector equity invested remained quite high, though it declined in the overall numbers to Rs 83,298 crore in 2019–20, at 43.49 per cent. Of this, equity invested in the PSBs was Rs 65,443 crore. New candidates emerged for budget-neutral equity investments. Rs 5,798 crore was invested in the IIFCL and Rs 45.57 crore in IDBI Bank Ltd, which had been technically privatized the year before. Rs 2,500 crore was invested in insurance companies to recapitalize them and Rs 1,500 crore in EXIM Bank.

Equity investment in financial enterprises declined significantly in 2020–21 and amounted to Rs 35,817 crore that year, with the recapitalization of PSBs claiming an equity investment of Rs 2,000 crore only and that of the insurance companies another Rs 9,950 crore. The financial enterprises' share of equity investment that year declined to about 31 per cent from the otherwise depleted total equity investment of Rs 1.17 trillion.

In 2021–22, the government established another capital guzzling giant—National Bank for Infrastructure and Development (NaBFID)—and invested as much as Rs 20,000 crore in its equity. The equity investment in PSBs tapered off to only Rs 4,600 crore that year. Insurance companies still claimed another Rs 5,000 crore. With the stock of the road and railways sector rising, the share of financial sector enterprises in equity invested fell to 15 per cent that year.

From 2022–23, the government exited from making investment in public sector financial enterprises. No investment was made in PSBs, insurance companies or any of the public sector infrastructure enterprises. The only investment in this space was in the equity of the National Infrastructure Investment Fund (NIIF) under the Department of Economic Affairs, in which Rs 1,681 crore was invested that year. No investment was made through the Department of Financial Services. The share of financial sector public enterprises in the total equity invested by the government fell below 1 per cent in 2022–23. It was the same story in the 2023–24 RE. Equity investment of Rs 3,099 crore was made in the NIIF and the share of the financial sector in overall equity investment remained below 1 per cent.

The government made significant investment in recapitalizing the PSBs, insurance companies and regional rural banks (RRBs) during the first three years of Modi 2.0. Besides this recapitalization, the government also infused equity in EXIM Bank, IIFCL, IFCI, IDBI Bank, NaBFID and IRFC. A total equity investment of Rs 1.52 trillion was made in these financial enterprises during these five years.

PSBs received a total of Rs 90,043 crore (about 60 per cent) of total equity invested in financial enterprises. NaBFID received Rs 20,000 crore, insurance companies Rs 17,450 crore, RRBs Rs 6,085 crore, IIFCL Rs 5,798 crore, IDBI Bank Rs 4,557 crore, EXIM Bank Rs 3,550 crore, IRFC Rs 2,612 crore and IFCL Rs 1,500 crore.

Investment in financial enterprises almost stopped in the last two years, with only Rs 500 crore (IFCI Ltd) invested in 2022–23 in financial enterprises and Rs 1,600 crore in 2023–24 RE (Rs 500 crore to IFCI and Rs 1,100 crore in RRBs).

Very little investment in profitable commercial enterprises

The government made very little investment in 'commercial' public sector enterprises during Modi 2.0 or 2019–24. Worse, most of this equity investment was in enterprises that were loss-making or had no prospect whatsoever of ever making profit.

During Modi 2.0, the government invested equity in twenty-eight commercial enterprises. This included seven new public sector enterprises created out of the defence ordnance factories.

Rs 17,941 crore (9.32 per cent of a total equity investment of Rs 1.93 trillion) was invested in 2019–20 in commercial enterprises. Equity of Rs 17,198 crore (14.73 per cent of Rs 1.17 trillion) was invested in 2020–21 and Rs 29,928 crore (13.37 per cent of Rs 2.24 trillion) was invested in 2021–22. Equity investment in commercial enterprises shot up in 2022–23 as the government dumped more equity into loss-making enterprises to Rs 58,192 crore (16.89 per cent of Rs 3.45 trillion) and to Rs 1.01 trillion in 2023–24 RE (20.63 per cent of Rs 4.89 trillion).

The government dumped equity of Rs 26,386 crore in the perennially loss-making BSNL in 2022–23 and Rs 64,787 crore in 2023–24 RE. The equity investment in BSNL alone amounted to 45.34 per cent and 64.26 per cent of the total investment in commercial enterprises in these two years.

The government made equity investments during Modi 2.0 in five commercial enterprises of Indian Railways as well. This was in addition to the equity invested in Railways, which is not counted in the commercial enterprise. These five organizations are Bengaluru Suburban Transport Project by K-RIDE, Bhartiya Rail Bijlee Company Ltd, Dedicated Freight Corridor Corporation of India Ltd, Kolkata Metro Rail Corporation Ltd and National High Speed Rail Corporation Ltd. Almost the entire (95 per cent to 99 per cent) equity investment in these Railways enterprises went to the Dedicated Freight Corridor Corporation of India Ltd and National High Speed Rail Corporation Ltd. These two companies will never recover even operational expenses. The capital invested is as good as sunk.

Equity of Rs 14,316 crore, Rs 15,400 crore, Rs 25,094 crore, Rs 27,216 crore and Rs 31,883 crore was invested in these enterprises from 2019–20 to 2023–24 RE respectively. In the first three years (2019–22), the equity invested in these railways enterprises was as much as 79.8 per cent, 89.6 per cent and 83.9 per cent respectively, of the total equity invested in commercial enterprises. Only in the last two years (2022–24), did their share go down to 46.8 per cent and 31.6 per cent primarily because the equity invested in BSNL occupied the central space.

In the remaining twenty-two commercial enterprises (other than BSNL and five railway enterprises), the government invested merely Rs 19,001 crore in five years, which was 8.48 per cent of Rs 2.24 trillion invested in commercial enterprises and 1.39 per cent of the total equity investment of Rs 13.66 trillion. Barring GAIL, which received Rs 2,870 crore, no other organization seemed to be either listed or making profit.

The government has no entrepreneurial ability, which is amply proved by the kind of commercial enterprises the government sets up and then makes equity investment in. In almost all of these organizations, the government is the exclusive equity owner and there is no prospect of anyone else ever investing in these enterprises.

Dud equity investment portfolio expanded

In what can only be called a bizarre twist of the policy of minimum government, maximum governance, investment in public sector enterprises shot up sharply in Modi 2.0. The worst part was that the government made indiscriminate investments in the loss-making and will-never-make-profit commercial central public sector enterprises in addition to departmental and non-commercial enterprises like Railways and NHAI.

Jawaharlal Nehru and Indira Gandhi, the bêtes noires of the Modi government, were the architects of CPSEs and public sector investment in India. They created quite a few genuinely commercial and profit-making public sector enterprises.

The Modi government, which never fails to debunk the legacy of Jawaharlal Nehru, has proved to be, by its action, the biggest protector of the worst of the public sector enterprises.

Privatization

The Modi government made serious efforts to rejuvenate the privatization of the public sector enterprises in its first term. In 2015, the government announced a divestment policy intended to do genuine privatization. The government put Air India on the block soon after.

Unfortunately, it could not do much. The Air India privatization came very close to being consummated (the government did invite bids for 74 per cent share) in Modi 1.0. There were a couple of sham privatizations with the government's controlling or complete stake in a PSU being sold to another public sector enterprise—HPCL was sold to ONGC, REC was sold to PFC and IDBI Bank was sold to LIC.

The stage was set for real action on the privatization front when the Modi government assumed office for the second term in May 2019.

Government announced big policy tweak in Budget 2019–20

The government had been following the policy of divesting small stakes in listed CPSEs by way of selling them directly under the offer for sale (OFS) route or building small stakes of a number of CPSEs as part of an ETF. In some CPSEs, the government stake had already fallen to less than 55 per cent, severely diminishing the ability of the Department of Investment and Public Asset Management (DIPAM) to offer more stakes, even as small stakes. In Powergrid Corporation, which had the second-largest market capitalization among listed CPSEs in 2018–19, the government shareholding had fallen to only 51.34 per cent.

Minor stake sales were not yielding good disinvestment proceeds either. Generally speaking, the announcement of minority stake sales was followed by a fall in their share prices. The policy was not getting anywhere.

The government attempted a big policy tweak in Budget 2019–20.

The government announced that it would be 'open' to let its shareholding fall 'below 51 per cent to an appropriate level on a case-to-case basis' where deemed necessary, subject to the retention of management control. Further, to meet the situation of CPSEs where it was felt that public-sector shareholding should not fall below 51 per cent, the budget announcement further said that the government had 'decided to modify the present policy of retaining 51 per cent government stake to retaining 51 per cent stake inclusive of the stake of government-controlled institutions'.

This announcement marked a three-fold deviation from the earlier policy of selling only a minority stake.

First, the government was open to making a strategic sale or privatize by going below a 51 per cent stake on a case-to-case basis, which could mean selling the complete stake as well. Second, wherever it felt necessary to retain management control, it could go below 51 per cent provided it could retain management control. Third, it was also agreeable to applying the 51 per cent threshold, taking the composite stake of the government and government-controlled institutions together into consideration.

Unfortunately, the policy was not followed through. The policy announcement died a slow death.

Big privatization transactions announced

The Budget 2019–20 presented in July 2019 did not make any explicit announcement about the privatization of any particular public sector enterprise, though it signalled the government's intent to implement privatization seriously.

The government undertook preparatory work and finally in October 2019, it came out with a big bang announcement of making strategic sales in three new major public sector enterprises—BPCL, Container Corporation of India Ltd (CONCOR) and Shipping Corporation of India (SCI)—in addition to Air India.

The government offered its entire stake in BPCL and SCI and controlling interest in CONCOR. This privatization was expected to garner more than Rs 75,000 crore from their stake sale.

The Expression of Interest (EOI) for BPCL was issued on 7 March 2020. The EOI for CONCOR could not be issued during the year. For SCI, it was issued in August 2020 only.

There was serious optimism that the government would carry out these privatization transactions and India was on the verge of seeing big ticket privatization.

Air India privatized

The government made two major changes to the earlier abortive bid for selling Air India. It put on the block its entire 100 per cent stake in Air India to assure potential suitors that there would be no monkey on their back. Second, the government agreed to take over almost the entire debt on Air India, leaving only a very small part on Air India's books.

The Air India privatization transaction went through this time.

The government announced on 27 January 2022 that the Air India strategic disinvestment transaction was completed that day, with the government receiving a consideration of Rs 2,700 crore from the strategic partner (M/s Talace Pvt. Ltd), a wholly owned subsidiary of M/s Tata Sons Pvt. Ltd. The government transferred shares of Air India (100 per cent shares of Air India and its subsidiary Air India Express Ltd [AIXL] and 50 per cent shares of Air India SATS Airport Services Private Limited [AISATS] to the strategic partner on that day.

The acquirer retained a debt of only Rs 15,300 crore in Air India and AIXL. The Letter of Intent was issued to the winning bidder on 11 October 2021 and the share purchase agreement (SPA) was signed on 25 October 2021.

The government did bear a heavy capital loss, which actually was the accumulated loss for running Air India in the public sector. Besides losing Air India's equity of about Rs 30,000 crore, the government took over the debt of Air India in its 100 per cent-owned public sector enterprise—Air India Assets Holding Ltd (AIAHL).

First, Rs 29,464 crore of unsustainable debt was taken over by AIAHL from Air India on 1 October 2018, backed by the securities issued by the government. At the time of completing the Air India privatization in 2021–22, the government infused Rs 62,365 crore of additional equity in AIAHL to take over debt of an almost similar amount.

Air India privatization was a genuine privatization of a PSU. It made eminent financial sense for the government also, despite the heavy capital loss suffered. Air India was bleeding more than Rs 6,000–7,000 crore annually in operational losses. The privatization put an end to this financial sclerosis. Tatas, which owned Air India before it was nationalized in the 1950s, are expected to nurse it back to profitability and glory once again. There was no reason for the government to take over this highly service-oriented enterprise, which governments are most unfit to run.

After six decades of operating it inefficiently and losing the franchise of Air India all over (from one of the best airlines in the world to one of the worst airlines in the world), better sense prevailed and the government privatized Air India.

Formal privatization policy adopted

As part of its stimulus package, on 17 May 2020, the government announced that it would formulate a new CPSEs reforms policy. The official PIB press release stated:

'Public Sector Enterprises

- A new Public Sector Enterprise Policy will be announced.
- In strategic sectors, at least one enterprise will remain in the public sector but private sector will also be allowed.
- In other sectors, PSEs will be privatized.'

There was literally no follow-up action for the next eight months. In Budget 2021–22, the government came back with further articulation of the privatization policy as part of the CPSE policy.

In her Budget Speech on 1 February 2021, Finance Minister Nirmala Sitharaman announced a formal CPSE Policy. The new policy covered all the CPSEs, including financial sector enterprises—the PSBs and insurance companies.

The government defined the strategic sectors in the CPSE policy, though quite widely. The strategic sectors included: a. atomic energy, space and defence, b. transport and telecommunications, c. power, petroleum, coal and other minerals, and d. banking, insurance and financial services.

The strategic sectors included practically all the major and profitable CPSEs.

The policy further indicated that, in the strategic sectors, only a bare minimum presence of CPSEs would be retained with the other CPSEs either privatized, merged or subsidiarized with other CPSEs or closed. In the non-strategic sectors, the policy announced that all existing CPSEs would be privatized and those that could not be privatized would be closed.

Privatization of two banks and an insurance company proposed

In order to indicate the resolve of the government that it meant business and would start implementing the CPSE policy without any loss of time, Nirmala Sitharaman made another big and bold announcement in the same Budget Speech 2021–22.

The government decided to privatize two PSBs and one general insurance company, that too in FY 2021–22 itself. To make the government's intent and resolve completely clear, the Finance Minister asserted that a bill to bring about necessary legislative amendments in the bank nationalization laws for enabling privatization of PSBs would be introduced in that very Budget session.

To double down on the resolve to push an aggressive privatization agenda, Nirmala Sitharaman reiterated quite unambiguously in the same Budget that privatization of a number of CPSEs, announced in the previous years, which included BPCL, Air India, SCI, Container Corporation, IDBI Bank, the erstwhile Bharat Earth Movers Ltd (BEML), Pawan Hans and Neelanchal Ispat Nigam Ltd, would also be completed in 2021–22.

The track record of the government before the 2021–22 Budget was not very inspiring. Yet, the Budget Speech 2021–22 generated a widespread belief that the government intended to walk the talk this time.

Complete disappointment in performance

Quite uncharacteristic of the Modi government and, in complete contrast to the gung-ho spirit of Budget 2021–22, the government failed to take any action worth the name in implementing the privatization policy, announced so boldly.

It did not introduce the requisite amendments to the bank nationalization laws for initiating privatization of two PSBs in the Budget session, or during 2021–22 or even in its entire term. The second term ended with the announcement of Lok Sabha elections in March 2024. No action was taken in more than three years since the announcements were made.

The government did not even identify the two PSBs to be privatized. No sale of the government stake in the IDBI Bank was carried out.

On 4 March 2023, Finance Minister Nirmala Sitharaman said that the government was 'not in a crazy rush' to sell everything. She should have simply said that the government would not sell any PSE.

The big privatization reform agenda announced in May 2022, as part of the Stimulus Package and delineated in the CPSE policy laid down in the Budget 2021–22, completely petered out.

Promised transactions died a slow death

On 20 November 2019, the government accorded 'in-principle' approval for strategic disinvestment of BPCL. It was announced that the government would make a strategic disinvestment of the GoI shareholding of 53.29 per cent in BPCL (except its equity shareholding of 61.65 per cent in Numaligarh Refinery Ltd (NRL) and management control thereon) along with the transfer of management control to a strategic buyer.

The government called for bids for BPCL. Three bids came. None of them followed up as there were serious unresolved policy issues—effective pricing freedom and payment of subsidies on LPG cylinders to private owners upon privatization—to cite two.

The government officially called off the privatization of BPCL in May 2022. DIPAM issued a press release that stated: 'Multiple Covid-19 waves and geo-political conditions affected multiple industries globally, particularly oil and gas industry. Owing to prevailing conditions in the global energy market, the majority of QIPs have expressed their inability to continue in the current process of disinvestment of BPCL'. Primarily, it was the inability to resolve the two policy issues of pricing freedom and continuation of the LPG subsidy that dissipated all interest in buying BPCL.

Government equity in Pawan Hans Helicopters, along with the equity of ONGC Ltd, was put on the block. The government did find a successful bidder—Star9 Mobility Pvt. Ltd, which was a consortium of three companies. However, as per DIPAM, Almas Global Opportunity Fund (AGOF), one of the consortium members, had received adverse orders from the National Company Law Tribunal (NCLT) and the National Company Law Appellate Tribunal (NCLAT). The government disqualified the successful bidder—Star9 Mobility. Finally, the government announced the annulment of the expression of interest (EOI) process for the strategic disinvestment of Pawan Hans.

BEML is a listed company. In December 2019, the government gave an in-principle approval for strategic disinvestment of BEML Ltd to the extent of 26 per cent out of the then government shareholding of 54.03 per cent with transfer of management control to the strategic buyer. The government did invite preliminary bids for 26 per cent stake in BEML on 4 January 2021. Instead of carrying on with the process, the government decided to demerge non-core (essentially surplus land and building assets) into a separate company and to privatize only the core BEML. The demerger was approved by the Company Law Board in July 2022 and two demerged entities were listed on the stock exchange in September 2022. Government sources indicated that financial bids for privatization of the demerged BEML were likely to be called for in December 2022. However, the bids were never called for until the end of 2023–24.

Privatization of CONCOR was also approved in November 2019 with the government deciding to sell 54.8 per cent of its stake (retaining a minority stake of 24 per cent). However, this case did not move at all as it got stuck with the finalization of Railways' land usage policy. The DIPAM Secretary publicly said in October 2021 that privatization of CONCOR was not going to take place in 2021–22. In September 2022, the government approved a long-term leasing policy for Railways land. The decision confused the situation more than it cleared it. While the decision of levying 1.5 per cent of market value of land as land licensing fee was made applicable for the new leasing of land, the older land leases, which were subject to 6 per cent of industrial land value, would come under the new policy only when these land parcels were re-bid fresh. The decision clearly made CONCOR land parcels get stuck. CONCOR could not get these land parcels on new terms without fresh bidding or on completion of existing leases. There are more than sixty such land leases. The government kept announcing from time to time that fresh bids for privatization of CONCOR would be invited. No bids were called for before the government hung up its boots before the 2024 elections.

SCI also went through the same process as BEML. Demerger of non-core assets into a separate demerged entity was approved on 23 February 2023. Like BEML, there was very little likelihood of the SCI privatization transaction happening in 2023–24. It did not take place.

IDBI Bank was technically privatized in 2018–19 with the majority stake transferred to LIC. The transaction, which the Finance Minister referred to in her Budget Speech 2021–22, was for selling most of the remaining equity of the government, along with a good part of LIC stake to a private entity. A Preliminary Information Memorandum was issued in this case on 7 October 2022 for selling the government stake representing 30.48 per cent of IDBI Bank equity and the LIC stake representing 30.24 per cent of the IDBI equity (together 60.72 per cent stake). Several pre-EOI queries were received from some interested parties (not disclosed), as indicated on behalf of the government on 25 November 2022. The government reportedly received five responses/EOIs (not officially confirmed). The next stage was to invite financial bids. There was no word about that bid till the end of calendar 2023. Finally, the DIPAM Secretary indicated that the transaction would not take place during the term of the current government.

Failure to privatize a big policy failure of Modi government

The utter failure of the Modi government to carry out any privatization transaction in its second term, other than Air India, represents one of its biggest policy failures.

The government did create a crescendo of privatization in the first twenty months of its second term. It began to build momentum with the October 2019 announcement of a full/controlling stake sale in three major CPSEs—BPCL, CONCOR and SCI. The successful privatization of Air India strengthened the momentum.

Bringing the entire privatization programme within a comprehensive policy framework, announced in the Budget 2021–22 on 1 February 2021, indicated the seriousness of the government's resolve. The announcement of privatization of two PSBs and one insurance company raised the crescendo to its highest pitch.

There was a genuine sense of expectation that something big was about to happen. I thought 2021 would be the Modi government's 1991 moment to be remembered forever.

The disappointment, unfortunately, was as severe as the build-up of expectations. The government failed to act on any announcement. By the end of 2023–24, the privatization policy was buried deep.

The Modi government, it seemed, had amnesia as far as privatization was concerned. It did not even utter the word 'privatization' in any official policy announcement in the last twenty months of the government.

Disinvestment

The Modi government had demonstrated a creditable record in carrying out an ambitious disinvestment programme during its first term. The government continuously improved upon disinvestment receipts throughout its first term as well.

From Rs 32,620 crore in the first year (2014–15) to Rs 42,132 crore in 2015–16 to Rs 47,743 crore in 2016–17 to Rs 1,00,045 crore in 2017–18, the Modi government turned out improved performance every single year in the first four years. During 2018–19, the last year of its first term, the government could earn as much as Rs 94,727 crore in disinvestment proceeds.

For the five years of its first term, the government had set a disinvestment target of Rs 3.42 trillion. It achieved Rs 3.17 trillion. With a 92.79 per cent strike rate, it was indeed a highly creditable performance.

The second term disappointed as much as the first term buoyed.

Disinvestment floundered

As noted above, the Modi government established an impressive track record of disinvestment performance during its first term. In 2017–18 and 2018–19, the last two years of Modi 1.0, the government actually achieved 138 per cent and 118 per cent of the otherwise hefty Budget estimates of these years.

The disinvestment programme, however, turned into a miserable failure in the second term. The misery was worse, compounded by the fact that in the first three years, the Modi government had actually announced highly ambitious disinvestment targets.

For the three years of 2019–20 to 2021–22, the government announced disinvestment targets of Rs 1.05 trillion, Rs 2.10 trillion and Rs 1.75 trillion in the respective budgets. Disinvestment proceeds were also assumed accordingly.

The performance, however, was nothing short of an abject failure.

In the first year (2019–20), the government could muster Rs 50,304 crore, which was only 47.9 per cent of the target. 2020–21 proved still worse. The government could collect only Rs 32,815 crore in disinvestment proceeds against the highest-ever target of Rs 2.10 trillion. The worst was reserved for 2021–22 for which the government had lowered the disinvestment target to Rs 1.75 trillion. However, it could collect a miserable Rs 13,627 crore only as disinvestment proceeds during the year, which was only 7.79 per cent of the budget target.

It was a shame to see this pathetic performance in the backdrop of the stock market booming and the share prices of public sector enterprises rising smartly.

The government, thereafter, gave up the ambition of privatization and disinvestment in the last two years, i.e. 2022–23 and 2023–24. The 2022–23 target was fixed at Rs 65,000 crore only. The government achieved Rs 35,343 crore, 54.37 per cent of the target. For 2023–24, the disinvestment target was lowered again to Rs 51,000 crore. The actual achievement was again a disappointing low of Rs 33,122 crore (PE). The receipts/estimates of 2022–23 and 2023–24 RE included some monetization receipts as well.

For the five-year period of Modi 2.0, the government fixed the disinvestment target of a total of Rs 6.16 trillion in the Budget estimates. However, it could receive only Rs 1.65 trillion in disinvestment receipts, recording a dismal 26.82 per cent strike rate.

Very clearly, the performance was massively underwhelming.

LIC—the only major IPO

LIC had a paid-up equity of Rs 6,325 crore, divided into 632.50 crore shares of Rs 10 each, all owned by the government. The government/LIC filed a draft red herring prospectus (DHRP) on 13 February 2022 offering for sale (OFS) 'up to 3,16,249,885 Equity Shares' or 5 per cent of the total equity of LIC. The government wanted the IPO to be completed within FY 2022–23. However, the Ukraine–Russia war upended the markets. LIC resumed its front-page advertisements on 11 April 2022, urging its policyholders to open demat accounts for participating in its impending IPO.

The DHRP specified the number of shares offered for sale but did not indicate the price, but it could be indirectly inferred from the disinvestment receipts that the Government was looking for. The government had revised the disinvestment target to Rs 78,000 crore on 1 February 2022. By the end of February 2022, the government had collected only Rs 13,500 crore from disinvestments. As there was no other disinvestment proceeds likely to come in the last two months of 2021–22, it was fair to assume that the remaining Rs 65,000 crore were expected from the LIC IPO. If one takes 31.63 crore shares offered for sale and expected proceeds of Rs 65,000 crore, it indicated that the government was most likely looking to price LIC shares at about Rs 2,250 per share.

LIC is a humungous but a faltering behemoth. Its balance sheet size exceeded Rs 40 trillion, whereas the AUM of all the mutual funds together, at that time, was a little under Rs 38 trillion. LIC's market share of new business premium on 30 September 2021 was about 65 per cent, with the next largest life insurer commanding only a little less than 8 per cent market share. LIC assets attributable to non-participating policyholders exceeded Rs 15 trillion, after bifurcation in 2021–22, at the end of Q3 December 2021. LIC's embedded value (present value of future assets together with market value of net assets) assessed by actuaries reported in February 2022 was approximately Rs 5.4 trillion.

LIC's market share in the insurance business was, however, declining. In 2000, when life insurance was opened to the private sector, LIC had 100 per cent market share. In fiscal 2021, it had come down to about 65 per cent. In individual new business premium, private life insurers' share had already crossed 50 per cent in 2021. In the first eleven months of FY 2021–22, LIC's total premium growth was only 0.24 per cent, whereas industry growth was 8.43 per cent, bringing down LIC's share to 61.4 per cent. LIC also generated much lower returns on its AUM. In FY 2021, LIC's gross yield on life fund at 8.3 per cent was the lowest among the first six life insurers, with others earning between 8.6 per cent to 9.9 per cent. LIC's future profitability depended upon the growth of new premiums and better returns on its investments. On both fronts, LIC was faltering.

The DHRP disclosed that LIC's earnings per share (EPS) averaged Rs 4.47 per share in three fiscals (2019–21). EPS was only Rs 2.38 in six months of FY 2022. A desired price of Rs 2,250, LIC's price/earnings (P/E) ratio would have exceeded 500. Other life insurers had a high P/E ratio (81.46 for SBI Life and 94.26 for HDFC Life), yet a 500 P/E ratio for LIC was simply wild. To spice up profitability for shareholders vis-à-vis policyholders, LIC embarked upon increasing the share of non-participating funds (in these funds, the profit over assured returns go to shareholders only; not the policyholders). The share of non-participating funds, which was only 24.8 per cent at end-March 2021, was increased to 37 per cent by September 2021.

LIC earned a net profit of Rs 2,971 crore for its shareholders in FY 2021. In 2021–22, in the first nine months, it earned Rs 1,672 crore. It was likely to report profits in the range of Rs 3,000–4,000 crore for shareholders for 2021–22. At a mid-point of Rs 3,500 crore, the LIC EPS amounted to about Rs 5.5. A multiple of 100 to estimated EPS of 5.5 gave a price of Rs 550 for LIC shares.

The government finally decided to price LIC shares at Rs 949 per share and opted to sell only 3.5 per cent of its equity (approximately 22 crore shares) at a valuation of about Rs 6 trillion to raise about Rs 20,500 crore. This was still quite an overpriced offer and left nothing on the table for the potential investor.

The issue did get oversubscribed 2.95 times with government, public sector and some private sector entities also putting in substantial funds. The listing was quite tepid. In first trades on listing, LIC shares traded at Rs 872 against the issue price of Rs 949. At this price, all investors—including policyholders, employees and retail investors who got shares at a discount of Rs 40 to Rs 60 per share to the issue price of Rs 949—also lost money. It seemed someone started buying large quantities of LIC shares thereafter and the price inched up to Rs 900 per share. In the first twenty minutes, 2 crore LIC shares, about 10 per cent of the IPO, got traded. Despite a firm market the entire day, LIC shares remained subdued, trading at a near fixed price of Rs 875 for most of the day and closed at Rs 873.

The LIC share price continued downhill in the days and weeks following. It went down to less than Rs 650 at one stage. The LIC share price did cross its listing price in Modi 2.0 as it was nearing its term end from January 2024, by which time all the public sector shares had risen significantly.

All investors lost money, except those who had the patience to hold on to the share for about two years. Thereafter also, they could hardly gain a 10 per cent increase in its price.

Monetization

The government invests in the shares of its public sector enterprises. Such shares can be disinvested or the entire/controlling interest in such enterprises can also be divested and the public sector enterprise can be privatized.

The government also invests in many public sector enterprises, which don't have stocks in the conventional sense and accordingly, the shares of such enterprises cannot be disposed of. For example, the shares of departmental undertaking of Railways or NHAI cannot be sold off. The government can, however, monetize its investment by granting concessions in the assets created with public funds. NHAI roads can be given out in concessions such as TOT or under InVIT arrangements. Likewise, Railways assets or airport assets of the Airport Authority of India can also be monetized.

NHAI started doing TOT concessions in 2017–18. The then Finance Minister Arun Jaitley announced the first monetization policy in the Budget 2018–19. He announced that the 'Government would initiate monetizing select CPSE assets using InvITs from next year.'

To operationalize this announcement, the DEA had prepared a detailed list of monetizable assets of over Rs 3 trillion. A policy framework was proposed to nudge the line ministries and concerned CPSEs to undertake the monetization of their operational assets. DIPAM was entrusted with the task of driving the monetization agenda.

Not much happened in the first two years—2019–20 and 2020–21

The monetization agenda got into a slow grind thereafter. DIPAM viewed monetization as a kind of disinvestment or sale of land and buildings. It proposed a process to carry out monetization transactions that mirrored the process in vogue for disinvestment or privatization transactions. The process proposed by DIPAM was approved in the rush to clear the pending agenda before the general elections.

The process was notified on 8 March 2019. This order implemented the decision of the Cabinet taken on 28 February 2019 to delegate power in favour of an alternate mechanism (AM) for granting approval for disposal of assets and to lay down the detailed process for asset monetization. A key prescription in the Cabinet decision and the order issued was that the AM would set a threshold based on the value of asset(s) and/or any other criteria to determine the assets that would be monetized by the government through this mechanism. Assets below this threshold would be disposed of by the concerned administrative ministry/CPSE, etc. Later, in April 2019, a monetization threshold of Rs 100 crore was prescribed.

The government prescribed an overly bureaucratic process for asset monetization. Besides the AM, a Core Group of Secretaries on Asset Monetization (CGAM) was constituted under the chairpersonship of the Cabinet Secretary to recommend to the AM the process for asset monetization, threshold value of assets, selection of CPSEs and assets for monetization and the like. An Inter-Ministerial Group (IMG) was created to carry out exactly the same tasks to make recommendations to the CGAM.

Not much action resulted. Only a new InVIT was announced by the Powergrid, under the Ministry of Finance in August 2019.

Government adopts a comprehensive monetization policy in 2021

Finance Minister Nirmala Sitharaman announced a National Monetization Pipeline (NMP) on 23 August 2021.

Recognizing that monetization of 'operating public infrastructure assets is a very important financing option for new infrastructure construction', she announced that a 'national monetization pipeline' would be launched and an 'asset monetization dashboard' would be created for tracking visibility for investors.

NITI Aayog, not DIPAM, released the NMP book and policy. It was not clear who was in charge—NITI Aayog or DIPAM or someone else?

NMP was indeed ambitious

The NMP was quite ambitious in scope in terms of the type of assets proposed to be monetized. As the PIB note and the two volumes of NMP released by NITI Aayog indicated, the NMP included more than twelve line ministries and more than twenty asset classes. The sectoral width of assets identified for monetization included roads, ports, airports, railways, warehousing, gas and product pipelines, power generation and transmission, mining, telecom, stadiums, hospitality and housing.

The NMP eyed the assets of the government (such as stadiums), non-commercial organizations and authorities under the government (such as roads of NHAI, warehouses of FCI) and commercial CPSEs (such as gas and product pipelines of GAIL, power transmission lines of Powergrid).

Some of these assets had been taken up for monetization in the past (transmission lines, airports and roads). However, most of the assets offered for monetization in the NMP (railway lines, power generation plants) were new asset classes. The top five sectors—roads (27 per cent), railways (25 per cent), power (15 per cent), oil and gas pipelines (8 per cent) and telecom (6 per cent)—captured approximately 83 per cent of the aggregate estimated pipeline value.

The NMP envisaged a 15 per cent monetization target to be achieved in FY 2021–22, which implied that the government had to be able to monetize assets worth about Rs 88,000 crore in that year. The targets for the following three years were Rs 1.62 trillion in 2022–23, Rs 1.80 trillion in 2023–24 and Rs 1.67 trillion in 2024–25. More than 70 per cent of NMP was to be achieved during Modi 2.0.

The government had carried out monetization of three kinds of assets in the three years before the announcement of NMP: NHAI road assets, AAI airports and the transmission lines of Powergrid.

Monetization of NHAI road assets using the TOT model started in 2018. The contract for the first TOT transaction was signed in April 2018 when NHAI concessioned a road bundle of nine select stretches of national highways, of approximately 700 km, for Rs 9,681 crore to Australian company Macquarie Group. Another nine road stretches totalling 566 km were given to Singapore-based Cube Highways for a total capital payment of Rs 5,011 crore in November

2019. The NHAI's fifth TOT bundle was a smaller transaction involving a twenty-year lease of two road stretches of 160 km for an aggregate sum of about Rs 2,250 crore. The NHAI had carried out a total of three transactions before the NMP came into operation, for an aggregate amount of Rs 17,000 crore.

In all, the government had monetized a little over Rs 25,000 crore in four years before the NMP came into operation for about Rs 6,250 crore a year. A target of Rs 6 trillion or Rs 1.5 trillion per annum was certainly audacious.

Government's track record is nothing to write home about

Monetization of CPSE assets is more complex than privatization of CPSEs. It involves transfer of an operating asset or a company with operating assets to a private partner. Monetization transactions are for a long period of time. Six airports were given away for fifty years.

There are many questions about the appropriate choice of instruments. Privatization and divestments are simple transactions as these are standard transactions carried out only by selling equity. Monetization requires very comprehensive contracts to be structured and negotiated. It is difficult to standardize monetization transactions.

Monetization of warehouses, sports stadiums, power plants and ports would present another set of issues. Monetization of FCI warehouses would mean FCI handing them over to private operators to run. It would get a one-time payment but would pay for the services private contractors would render. The risk of mismatch in capital receipts and payment of services has the potential to create enormous problems.

No wonder the government could not push the monetization process. Sector by sector, it is more a story of misses than any hits.

No more airports (other than the six finalized in 2018–19) could be monetized. The process remained stuck in a policy logjam. Non-viable airports were bundled with the viable ones. The 2019 monetization template was abandoned. Despite constant noise that an additional six airports would soon be monetized, no bids were ever invited.

The new sectors for monetization announced in the NMP—Railways, power plants, gas pipelines—were simply not taken up. The incumbents pointed out all the problems they saw in monetization. The NITI Aayog and DIPAM leadership could not provide solutions or push. There was zero progress in these sectors. The Powergrid did not come out the second InVIT. Only the road sector continued to make small strides.

The government started resorting to questionable practices to show that its monetization targets were on track. Auctioning of coal blocks and other assets, which is, in fact, no monetization, began to be counted as monetization.

The government never officially put out a sectoral performance report of monetization. Some officials would informally tout out some numbers to some journalists about the incredible progress being made in monetization. Nothing really happened.

Poor numbers tell the story

All monetization proceeds don't land in the Consolidated Fund of India (CFI). The proceeds of InVIT issued by Powergrid were received by that company. The monetization of the assets of public sector enterprises accrue to the respective companies.

The monetization proceeds of the assets held by or owned by the government come to the CFI. The road assets of NHAI are owned by the government. The TOT or InVIT proceeds of these transactions, therefore, come to the GoI. Monetization of Railways assets also accrue to the government.

Of the top five sectors, the monetization proceeds for roads and Railways were to be received in the CFI, whereas the proceeds for the other three—power, oil and gas pipelines and telecom—were to go to the respective organizations. Of course, the government could always claw back at least a part of the monetization proceeds so received by these corporate bodies by way of special dividend.

No such contingency arose. Barring proceeds of one InVIT done by Powergrid, the proceeds of which were retained for meeting further capital requirements, no other public sector enterprise could achieve any notable monetization targets.

For the two sectors—roads and Railways—which the government expected to yield significant monetization receipts, Railways did not do anything. It was the roads sector that brought in monetization proceeds.

As per the Finance and Accounts published by the CGA, the government did not receive anything towards the proceeds of monetization of national highways in 2019–20. The proceeds started flowing in from the next year and yielded Rs 5,011 crore in 2020–21, Rs 1,011 crore in 2021–22 and Rs 10,662 crore in 2022–23. Data for 2023–24 is not still available. In all, less than Rs 17,000 crore were received towards the monetization of road assets in the first four years of Modi 2.0.

The road assets were to yield Rs 1.60 trillion in monetization. The receipt of Rs 17,000 crore, though woefully short of the target, was the best the government could deliver. Against the Rs 1.53 trillion planned from Railways' assets monetization, nothing could be achieved. Likewise, against the expected proceeds from warehousing (Rs 28,900 crore), aviation (Rs 20,780 crore), ports (Rs 12,828 crore) and stadiums (Rs 11,450 crore), which would have largely come to the government, almost nothing was achieved.

The government began putting a gloss on monetization numbers by counting the auction of coal blocks as monetization proceeds.

The monetization pipeline remained a pipeline only; literally no monetization proceeds flowed through it.

Net Investment

The government accounts for investments made largely as capital expenditures. The proceeds from disinvestment, privatization and monetization are accounted for as capital receipts. The government does not prepare any net investment account, which lists all investments made and all disinvestment/privatization/monetization transactions carried out.

As brought out above, the government made total equity investments of Rs 13.65 trillion in five years.

The disinvestment and privatization proceeds amounted to Rs 1.65 trillion only. The monetization proceeds contributed another Rs 17,000 crore. Taking note of the fact that some more monetization proceeds would come in 2023–24, we can assume total disinvestment and monetization proceeds to be Rs 2 trillion.

The investments outclassed disinvestments/privatization/monetization by 7:1. The Modi 2.0 government was a government of massive public sector investments and very little disinvestment, privatization and monetization.

It was a case of more government and less governance.

20

Deficit, Borrowings and Debt

The raison d'être of governments is to provide common or public goods and services to their people. The fundamental nature of public goods and services prevent these to be charged from their users/beneficiaries. Governments are, therefore, bestowed with the authority to collect taxes from the people to pay for the cost of the public goods and services.

In an ideal world, the government should be able to collect sufficient taxes to pay for the bouquet of the public goods and services being provided. In the real world, governments not only don't tax people enough, they also tend to spend on a number of goods and services that are not truly public goods and services—welfare and growth expenditures fall into this category. This leads to the mismatch between the expenditure requirement of the government and the taxes it collects.

This gap is the fiscal deficit.

Fiscal deficits are covered by the borrowings the government makes. There are numerous sources for borrowing the funds required. The government can issue bonds or securities in financial markets to raise funds or institute schemes of small savings to collect loans from people directly or subject its employees to contribute to pensions or provident funds, which become available to it as borrowings. There are ways to raise short-term, medium-term and long-term borrowings.

Borrowings lead to accumulation of public debt and liabilities, which need to be serviced for interest and repayment of principal. If a bigger proportion of the expenditure needs is funded by way of fiscal deficit, the borrowings might consume a good part of the tax receipts and lead to accumulation of unsustainable debt.

The fiscal deficit, borrowings and debt and liabilities policy and performance has a very big bearing on the effectiveness of the government, investments in the economy, inflation and public welfare and development in general.

In this chapter, I review the policies and performance of the Modi government relating to fiscal deficits, borrowings and debt/liabilities during its second term (2019–24).

Fiscal Deficit

Headline fiscal deficit went through the roof

The headline fiscal deficit, as per the Budget and accounts of the government, for FY 2018–19, the last year of Modi 1.0, was Rs 6.49 trillion. As the GDP for the year was Rs 189 trillion, the fiscal deficit turned out to be 3.44 per cent of GDP. It was quite close to the fiscal deficit glide path adopted by the government in line with the Fiscal Responsibility and Budget Management (FRBM) mandated fiscal deficit of 3 per cent in 2020–21.

The headline fiscal deficit jumped to Rs 9.34 trillion in 2019–20, the first year of Modi 2.0, rising by as much as 44 per cent over the previous year. The fiscal deficit was also much higher at 4.65 per cent relative to the GDP of Rs 200.75 trillion for the year. The government seemed to be getting quite uncomfortable with the fiscal deficits restraining its expenditure freedom. There was a clear signal that the government was in no position to abide by the fiscal deficit to GDP prescription of 3 per cent of GDP to be achieved by 2020–21, the following year, as mandated by the FRBM Act, as amended by Modi 1.0 in 2018.

The government abandoned all pretensions of sticking to the fiscal deficit rule in 2020–21, the first Covid-19 year. In fact, the government decided to use the occasion to clear off-budget food subsidy liabilities to FCI in that year (described in more detail in Chapter 17—Expenditures). The headline fiscal deficit for the year jumped to Rs 18.18 trillion, almost doubling from the year before. At 9.18 per cent of the GDP of Rs 198 trillion, it turned out to be more than three times the FRBM/statutory limit of 3 per cent of GDP for the year.

The government maintained very high fiscal deficits in the remaining three years of its second term. The fiscal deficit was Rs 15.85 trillion in 2021–22 (6.75 per cent of GDP of Rs 234.71 trillion) and Rs 17.38 trillion in 2022–23 (6.38 per cent of GDP of Rs 272.41 trillion). For the final year 2023–24 RE of Modi 2.0, the fiscal deficit was pegged at Rs 17.35 trillion, which was projected at 5.85 per cent of the advance estimates of GDP of Rs 296.58 trillion.

For the five-year tenure of Modi 2.0, the aggregate headline fiscal deficit was Rs 78.09 trillion, which turned out to be as high as 6.49 per cent of the five-year GDP of Rs 1,202 trillion.

The government had truly unleashed the fiscal deficit genie. An average fiscal deficit of 6.5 per cent of GDP for the five-year period of the government was truly unprecedented.

Highest-ever fiscal deficit

Restoring fiscal deficits (from 4.5 per cent in 2013–14 to 3 per cent of GDP) was the high policy priority of Modi 1.0 (2014–2019). It came pretty close to it achieving it by limiting fiscal deficit to 3.4 per cent of GDP in its terminal year 2018–19.

In complete contrast to the rigorous fiscal discipline approach of the first term, Modi 2.0 abandoned this approach completely in the second term (2019–24). Taking 2023–24 RE budget numbers (Rs 16.54 trillion) into account, Modi 2.0 ended up with the massive annual fiscal deficit average of 6.5 per cent of GDP as noted above. No government since 1991, the year when the economic and fiscal reforms began and fiscal deficits came to be recognized in budgets, ran fiscal deficits of such a high magnitude.

The Narasimha Rao government (1991–96) began controlling fiscal deficits. From the high of 7.6 per cent in 1990–91, the fiscal deficits averaged 5.5 per cent of GDP in its five-year term. Three more governments with five-year terms, before Modi 1.0 assumed power in 2014, also attempted to rein in the fiscal deficits. The Atal Bihari Vajpayee-led NDA (1999–2004) averaged a fiscal deficit of 5.3 per cent of GDP. The first Manmohan Singh-led UPA-I (2004–09), despite the global financial crisis, recorded a fiscal deficit average of 4 per cent of GDP. Despite running a lax stimulus policy, the Manmohan Singh-led UPA-II averaged a fiscal deficit of 5.2 per cent of GDP. The short-lived Deve Gowda (1996–98) and the first Atal Bihari governments (1998–99) also recorded smaller fiscal deficits of 5.2 per cent and 6.3 per cent in their respective tenures.

Modi 1.0 delivered the best performance since 1991, clocking a fiscal deficit average of 3.6 per cent of GDP. Modi 2.0 delivered the worst fiscal deficit performance, generating a fiscal deficit of 6.5 per cent of GDP.

Off-budget dimension of fiscal deficits

The Modi government used two off-budget expenditure practices in its first term.

The first method was to push certain expenditures out of the budget and accounts of the government through the use of two instruments—borrowing through what it described as Fully Serviced Bonds (FSBs) to pay for government expenditures such as the PM Awas Yojana subsidy and providing loans to FCI through the NSSF in lieu of food subsidy. The second method was to recapitalize the PSBs and other government-owned financial institutions in a fiscal deficit-neutral manner by adjusting the receipts of the proceeds of securities issued to the concerned institution against the expenditure of equity invested.

In 2018–19, the last year of Modi 1.0, the government raised off-budget borrowings of Rs 65,602 crore through FSBs and substituted the food subsidy of Rs 70,000 crore by providing NSSF loans of an equal amount to FCI. In all, the Modi government thus raised the off-budget borrowings of Rs 1.36 trillion in 2018–19.

The government also avoided a fiscal deficit of Rs 1.11 trillion by recapitalizing PSBs to the extent of Rs 1.06 trillion and EXIM Bank by Rs 4,500 crore in the fiscal deficit-neutral manner. If these two off-budget and fiscal deficit-avoided expenditures/liabilities are taken into account, the headline fiscal deficit of Rs 6.49 trillion for 2018–19 would get transformed into real fiscal deficit of Rs 8.96 trillion. As a result, the real fiscal deficit (including all off-budget liabilities) for the year was 4.74 per cent of GDP.

In 2019–20, the first year of Modi 2.0, the government raised FSBs of only Rs 22,000 crore. The NSSF loans, provided to FCI in place of food subsidy, however, went up to Rs 94,910 crore. Together, the off-budget expenditure/ liability thus was Rs 1.17 trillion. While the government provided recapitalization finance to IDBI Bank of Rs 4,557 crore, the equity recapitalization of PSBs went down to Rs 65,443 crore. In that year, the government also provided budget-neutral capital of Rs 550 crore to EXIM Bank and Rs 5,298 crore to the IIFCL. In all, the government made a budget-neutral capital investment of Rs 75,848 crore in 2019–20. The off-budget and budget-neutral liabilities of the government for the year aggregated to Rs 1.93 trillion and had the effect of increasing the headline fiscal deficit of Rs 9.34 trillion to real fiscal deficit of Rs 11.26 trillion. The real fiscal deficit to GDP ratio went up to 5.61 per cent in 2019–20.

The year 2020–21 was the year of cleaning up off-budget liabilities. The FSBs issued amounted to Rs 26,920 crore. The government cleared FCI liabilities of Rs 2.55 trillion during the year in addition to not meeting any food subsidy through NSSF loans. There was thus a reduction in off-budget liabilities of Rs 2.28 trillion in that year. The equity recapitalization expenditure was also reduced to Rs 20,000 crore. On a net basis, the off-budget and budget-neutral expenditure declined by Rs 2.08 trillion in 2020–21, bringing headline fiscal deficit of Rs 18.18 trillion to Rs 16.11 trillion. The real fiscal deficit, reduced to 8.13 per cent of GDP in 2020–22, was still the highest-ever fiscal deficit in India's history.

There were no off-budget borrowings in the remaining three years of Modi 2.0. Budget-neutral equity recapitalization expenditures also stopped, with only Rs 4,600 crore invested in the PSBs in 2021–22, which had a marginal impact of raising real fiscal deficit to Rs 15.89 trillion that year. For 2022–23 and 2023–24 RE, the headline fiscal deficit and the real fiscal deficit were exactly identical.

For the five years of Modi 2.0, the off-budget borrowings/liabilities actually amounted to a negative Rs 1.11 trillion, which meant that the government cleared off-budget liabilities of its first term as well during Modi 2.0. The fiscal deficit-neutral recapitalization expenditure/liabilities turned out to be an additional

Rs 1 trillion in Modi 2.0. On the whole, aggregate headline fiscal deficit of Rs 78.09 was trillion was reduced to real fiscal deficit of Rs 77.99 trillion.

It made only a marginal difference. The aggregate real fiscal deficit of Modi 2.0 remained unchanged at 6.49 per cent. The distinction or ignominy of running the highest fiscal deficit in India's history, headline or including off-budgets, will remain with Modi 2.0.

Violation of statutorily mandated fiscal deficit

The Modi government had vowed to adhere to the virtues of fiscal deficit discipline in its first term. As soon as the government took over in 2014, it committed to bring the fiscal deficit down to 3 per cent of GDP. In Budget 2014–15, Finance Minister Arun Jaitley announced a fiscal glide path as well.

In the 2018–19 Budget, the government got the FRBM Act amended to incorporate the hard target of attaining the fiscal deficit goal of 3 per cent of GDP by 2020–21 and, thereafter, to never exceed it.

As noted above, it was quite apparent in 2019–20 itself that the government had lost enthusiasm/commitment for fiscal discipline and bringing the fiscal deficit to the statutory limit. Using the opportunity of providing a stimulus in the wake of Covid-19, the government, in fact, decided to abandon fiscal discipline.

Finance Minister Nirmala Sitharaman paid only a kind of lip service to the fiscal deficit goal while consigning the fiscal deficit goal of the FRBM Act to the dustbin in her Budget Speech 2021–22 delivered on 1 February 2021. She casually said:

> We plan to continue with our path of fiscal consolidation, and intend to reach a fiscal deficit level below 4.5 per cent of GDP by 2025–2026 with a fairly steady decline over the period. We hope to achieve the consolidation by first, increasing the buoyancy of tax revenue through improved compliance, and secondly, by increased receipts from monetisation of assets, including Public Sector Enterprises and land.

The final fiscal deficit target/goal was revised upward—from 3 per cent, as prescribed in the FRBM Act to 4.5 per cent of GDP, discretionarily fixed in Budget 2021–22. The fiscal deficit target of 3 per cent by 2020–21 was postponed to 2025–26. These changes had no statutory backing as the FRBM Act was not amended. The logic of a 4.5 per cent target was not explained either, which made this an arbitrary exercise of authority. The government did not bring any amendment in the FRBM Act in any one of the subsequent three budgets of Modi 2.0.

It was a strange situation during the entire tenure of Modi 2.0. While the FRBM Act, a law that remained in force throughout its tenure, prescribed that the government could not run fiscal deficits in excess of 3 per cent of GDP after 2020–21, the government remained in flagrant violation thereof all through. By averaging fiscal deficit at 6.5 per cent of GDP for its entire second term, the government continued to cock a snook at fiscal discipline and the FRBM law.

Borrowing

The government raises its borrowing primarily through two major sources: market borrowings and small savings collections.

Market borrowing principal workhorse

The government issues market bonds/securities of various tenures—from one year to fifty years. Ten-year market securities are the most common instrument of borrowing and see the largest issuance. Short-term securities of less than one-year duration, generally referred to as treasury bills (T-bills), are issued for a varying number of days—14 days/31 days/91 days/182 days/364 days.

Issuance of government securities and T-bills together constitute the market borrowing of the government. The government also issues cash management bills (CMBs) for meeting temporary liquidity needs in addition to availing the ways and means advance (WMA) fixed by the RBI in consultation with the government.

Of the total fiscal deficit/borrowings of Rs 78.09 trillion in the five years of Modi 2.0, as much as Rs 50.73 trillion was raised by the government in the form of market borrowings (both long- and short-term), i.e. 65 per cent of its total borrowings/fiscal deficit. Rs 45 trillion of the market borrowing was raised in the form of dated securities/bonds and Rs 5.44 trillion in the form of T-bills and other short-term liabilities. The small remaining difference was accounted for by securities switching/buy-back.

The extent of market borrowing varied from year to year. Total market borrowings shot up from Rs 6.24 trillion in 2019–20 to Rs 12.40 trillion in the first Covid-19 year of 2020–21. In 2021–22, market borrowing declined to Rs 8.10 trillion to shoot up again to Rs 12.18 trillion in the next year (2022–23). In 2023–24 RE, the market borrowings stabilized to Rs 11.82 trillion.

In any year, the government raises market borrowing to fund its fiscal deficit and also to repay maturing market securities. The former is referred to as net market borrowing while the latter constitutes the gross market borrowing. In its second tenure, the Modi government raised gross market borrowing of Rs 59.02

trillion. Rs 14.03 trillion was used for repayment and the net market borrowing of Rs 45 trillion served to finance the fiscal deficit.

Small savings another significant source

Small savings accumulate in the NSSF. While some part of the net accruals in the NSSF go to a few states as loans and to other public financial institutions, the bulk of the net small saving accumulations are used in investing in Central government securities.

During Modi 2.0, a net investment of Rs 21.42 trillion flowed from the NSSF into Central government securities to fund 27.4 per cent of the overall fiscal deficit. Along with market borrowings of 65 per cent, small savings securities investment of 27.4 per cent made up about 92.5 per cent of the total borrowings/fiscal deficit of the government.

As the government kept small savings rates unchanged during 2020–21 while the market interest rates declined, there was a rush of savings flow in the NSSF in 2020–21. In addition, the government stopped using the NSSF for food subsidy substitution. Consequently, the flow of small savings in the government budget more than doubled to Rs 4.84 trillion in that year against Rs 2.40 trillion invested in 2019–20. In 2021–22, the flow of funds from the NSSF to the government increased further to Rs 5.51 trillion, building on the momentum of 2020–21.

The government kept the interest rates quite steady thereafter. The small savings flows stabilized. In 2022–23, Rs 3.96 trillion came into the government account from small savings and Rs 4.71 trillion in 2023–24 RE.

Other smaller sources

The external debt, which primarily represents the government borrowing from the official lenders—multilaterals like the World Bank and ADB and bilateral like Japan and France. The government keeps repaying the loans taken earlier. The net flows only (new borrowings minus debt repaid) are available for funding the budget. In the five years of Modi 2.0, the total flow of external loans as fresh additional resources was Rs 1.77 trillion only.

The flow in the State Provident Fund, which houses the general provident fund of Central government employees, has also been declining continuously as a result of all new government employees getting enrolled in the new pension scheme (NPS) in place of the provident fund. The total flow in five years, through the state provident fund, amounted to Rs 50,755 crore only.

The government accounts for net inflows in numerous public accounts (other than the state provident fund and the NSSF) as other borrowing receipts. These other receipts provided Rs 3.94 trillion (about 5 per cent) of borrowings contribution during the five years.

Finally, the government makes a cash withdrawal from its investment cash account in the RBI if total borrowings fall somewhat short of the requirement to meet fiscal deficit. If there happens to be some excess cash, it gets deposited in the same account with the RBI. A total of Rs 27,948 crore of excess borrowings went into the cash account during this period.

Aborted sovereign bonds

In the first regular Budget of Modi 2.0 in 2019–20, presented on 5 July 2019, Finance Minister Nirmala Sitharaman announced India's decision to issue sovereign bonds in foreign currencies:

> India's sovereign external debt to GDP is among the lowest globally at less than 5 per cent. The Government would start raising a part of its gross borrowing programme in external markets in external currencies. This will also have a beneficial impact on the demand situation for government securities in the domestic market.

All the G20 countries, except India, have issued foreign currency-denominated sovereign bonds. India was the only country not to have ever done so to finance fiscal deficit. The global stock of sovereign bonds exceeded $50 trillion in 2019 and made up over 60 per cent of the total global bond market. Raising sovereign bonds in foreign currencies is a routine matter for the rest of the world. The announcement made by Nirmala Sitharaman was intended to make India also join the party and benefit from global resources, which, as was noted, was expected to bring down the cost of government debt as well.

The market welcomed it and the yields on government bonds went down by about 12 basis points on the day of the Budget announcement, clearly demonstrating the lower cost advantage that the government would likely draw. The government, it was clarified in the post-Budget interactions, intended to raise about 10 per cent of its gross borrowing programme of Rs 7.1 trillion or about $10 billion, in foreign currency sovereign bonds during the year.

The announcement triggered considerable attention, reaction and debate in the media. Two groups of people—former RBI top brass, including Raghuram Rajan and Rakesh Mohan, and affiliates of the Rashtriya Swayamsevak Sangh (RSS), including the Swadeshi Jagran Manch—questioned the move. In the days to follow, the debate intensified as opposition from these quarters kept increasing.

The government had, in the late 1990s and also in 2018, toyed with the idea of issuing such foreign currency-denominated sovereign bonds. The 2019–20 Budget announcement was the first clearest and publicly made announcement. This also met with the same fate. The government did not issue any foreign currency-denominated sovereign bonds in 2019–20. There was no mention of sovereign bonds in the five budgets that followed. Neither were such bonds issued. Modi 2.0 simply kept it shelved.

Government came out with an alternate route

The foreign currency-denominated sovereign bonds were meant to allow FPIs and other non-resident foreign investors to invest in government bonds. India does want the FPIs and portfolio investors to keep investing in government securities.

Foreign investors were first permitted to invest in government securities in the 1990s. They could get their dollars in India and invest in rupee-denominated government securities. There were limits/quotas fixed for different classes of foreign investors.

As per the policy regime prevalent when Modi 2.0 took over in 2019, the investment limits were prescribed separately for two broad classes of foreign investors—long-term investors and the rest broadly described as the general category. The investment limit for long-term foreign investors was Rs 1.04 trillion and for the general quota, it was Rs 2.34 trillion, aggregating to Rs 3.38 trillion. There were other restrictions as well, e.g. foreign investors were not allowed to make investments in securities with a remainder maturity of less than one year, and a few more such conditions.

Foreign investors were not very happy about the complicated investment regime. To ease the cost of doing business for significant FPIs, the RBI came up with one policy carved out from the quota and restrictions regime.

VRR provided the FPIs greater operational flexibility in terms of instrument choices and some regulatory exemptions, provided they committed to invest a certain minimum specified amount in government securities (committed portfolio size or CPS) and invest at least 75 per cent of their CPS within three months from the date of admission in VRR. These commitments were relaxed to some extent in 2020–21. The VRR route led to some FPIs/non-resident investors shifting from the 'quota with restrictions' route to VRR; but there was no great take-off of VRR either. The global bond indices were not willing to include Indian government bonds in their bond indices.

To entice PIs and the companies running bond indices, the government came up with another innovation in Budget 2020–21. The Finance Minister announced that certain specified categories of Central government securities would be available fully for non-resident investors, i.e. without any restrictions specific only to foreign investors–no quotas, no VRR, no other restrictions.

The RBI introduced a channel called Fully Accessible Route (FAR) on 30 March 2020. All non-resident investors—FPIs, NRIs, OCIs and other entities— were permitted to invest in the specified/FAR-designated Central government securities—new or already issued—without being subject to any investment ceilings, applicable under the normal and VRR routes.

While the RBI maintained limits on FPI investments in Central government securities at 6 per cent of outstanding stocks of securities for 2021–22 with the division between general and long-term FPIs retained at 50:50, FAR securities were exempted from all limits and other restrictions.

Unfortunately, this innovation failed to attract FPIs. They continued to be net sellers. The non-resident's share of ownership of government securities continued to be low; in fact, it declined further—from 4.4 per cent in 2018 to 1.9 per cent (Rs 1.43 trillion) at the end of FY 2020–21. The FPI ownership of Central government securities declined in absolute amount to Rs 1.33 trillion at the end of 2021–22 (1.56 per cent of total Rs 85.29 trillion) and further to Rs 1.31 trillion (1.36 per cent of Rs 96.46 trillion) at the end of 2022–23.

With the announcement of inclusion of government securities in two global indices (described in detail in Chapter 12—Foreign Investment), the net inflows improved to Rs 2.51 trillion (2.34 per cent) in 2023–24.

RBI helped in lowering cost of borrowing

The government almost doubled the market borrowing in 2020–21 as we saw earlier. This heightened level of borrowings was not only fully financed but the cost of borrowing for the government also went down. The RBI did lend a helping hand in achieving this feat.

The RBI flooded the financial markets with abundant liquidity from March 2020 after Covid-19 struck. These helped bring down the general rate of interest in the economy, which assisted financial market participants to buy an increased supply of government bonds. The RBI also undertook unprecedented open market operations (OMOs) to buy a good chunk of government securities.

Almost the entire stock of dated government securities is fixed-interest-bearing. The RBI undertook several 'operation twist' programmes to lower the effective cost of outstanding dated securities. Under the operation twist, the RBI, on behalf of the government, bought existing higher yield/interest bonds to extinguish and sell lower interest shorter-term or same tenure security. While the entire operation was cash-neutral, the effective yield rate on the government securities exchanged/twisted came down, bringing the overall interest burden down also.

The Status Paper on Government Debt 2020–21 states that all these measures helped. Despite the government raising its borrowing requirement by several trillion, it could raise its borrowing at a really low rate of 5.79 per cent in 2020–21. To put this in perspective, the government's weighted average cost of borrowing was 7.77 per cent in 2019–20. The weighted average yield on outstanding dated government securities came down to 7.27 per cent in 2020–21.

There was one inevitable consequence. The RBI's ownership of government securities increased from Rs 9.79 trillion in 2019–20 to Rs 12.37 trillion in 2020–21 and further to Rs 14.18 trillion in 2021–22.

Government did not adhere to small saving schemes guidelines

There are three drivers of small savings flows—liberal tax incentives on schemes like public provident fund (tax-free interest and counting of investment made for section 80C incentive), higher than market rate of interest (on savings bank deposits, recurring deposits, fixed deposits and also saving certificates), and additional interest (over and above the liberal rate of interest on some specially targeted schemes (fixed deposits for senior citizens, etc.)

Many years ago, it had been decided that the government would be guided by a formula not to offer more than 0.5 per cent higher rate of interest than the corresponding maturity period bank/market instruments. Additionally, the interest rates were to be adjusted at the end of every quarter.

As we noted above, the interest rates plummeted during 2020–21. Yield on ten-year Central government securities, which were 6.3 per cent on 3 April 2020, fell to 5.88 per cent on 30 June 2020. The yields continued to decline in the second quarter (2020–21) as well, bottoming to 5.80 per cent on 21 July 2020, and ended at 6.02 per cent on 30 September 2020. At the end of the third quarter, yield on ten-year paper was 5.89 per cent and 6.06 per cent on the day of the 2021–22 Budget. As the government announced another bumper fiscal deficit and borrowing programme for 2021–22, the yields rose marginally to settle at 6.18 per cent on 31 March 2021.

The interest rates on small savings instruments were last adjusted/slightly reduced on 28 June 2019 for the second quarter (July–September 2019–20) and again on 31 March 2020. For the first quarter of 2020–21 (April–June 2020–21), savings bank deposits carried 4 per cent rate of interest, five-year time deposits carried 6.7 per cent, PPF interest rate was 7.1 per cent and five-year senior citizens savings scheme rate was 7.4 per cent.

Despite yields falling to sub-6 per cent in 2020–21, the government kept the interest rates on all the savings schemes unchanged throughout 2020–21. Quite obviously, the government did this in flagrant violation of the scheme guidelines. It was no wonder that there was a gush of inflows in small savings instruments/schemes in 2020–21.

A very unfortunate episode occurred on 31 March 2021. The Department of Economic Affairs (DEA) rightly issued a notification on 31 March, revising interest rates for the April–June 2021–22 quarter, aligning the small savings interest rates to market interest rates to a good extent in line with the formula. The interest rate, for example, on savings accounts was reduced from 4 per cent to 3.5 per cent, on PPF from 7.1 per cent to 6.4 per cent and on National Savings Certificates from 6.8 per cent to 5.9 per cent.

No sooner was the order issued, than all hell broke loose. The DEA had probably not factored in the likely impact of the order on the election campaign then going on in some states, including West Bengal.

In a bizarre twist, brazenly terming her own department's order an 'oversight', Finance Minister Nirmala Sitharaman tweeted to withdraw the order in the morning of 1 April. This fiasco ensured that the government did not revise the interest rates in the entire year of 2021–22.

Market interest rates started rising somewhat from the last quarter of 2021–22. When the interest rates rose further during the first three quarters of 2022–23, the government decided to raise the interest rates (raising interest rates is populist) on some small savings instruments on 31 December 2022 for the period applicable for the January–March 2023 quarter.

The interest rate on five-year National Savings Certificates was increased to 7 per cent from 6.8 per cent, on senior citizens saving scheme to 8 per cent from 7.6 per cent, on monthly income scheme to 7.1 per cent from 6.7 per cent, on Kisan Vikas Patra to 7.2 per cent from 7 per cent and on small savings deposits of one year to 6.6 per cent from 5.5 per cent.

The government did not revise the interest rates down, in line with the formula for almost three years (2020–21, 2021–22 and nine months of 2022–23). It revised the interest rates only upward for the quarter January–March 2022–23.

Besides abandoning market-aligned interest rates for small savings instruments, the government also introduced one more off-market saving product. Mahila Samman Savings Certificate Scheme 2023 was introduced in April 2023 to provide an opportunity to women to buy certificates carrying a much higher rate of interest of 7.5 per cent.

Debt

High fiscal deficits lead to high public debt—the debt raised on the strength of the CFI. This is the debt which ultimately is owed by the people of India to the people of India. In a way, the public debt represents the choice made by the representatives of the people of India to fund its public expenditures from debt to be repaid by future generations in place of taxes to be paid by the present generation.

The deposits raised in the public account also leave a surplus, which the government uses to fund its expenditure. These public account liabilities added to the public debt represent the true debt and liabilities of the GoI.

Debt binge

India's public debt was Rs 73.45 trillion at the end of FY 2018–19 when the term of Modi 1.0 ended. The public debt soared to Rs 152 trillion in 2023–24 RE when Modi 2.0 completed its term. India's public debt more than doubled in the space of just five years, rising by 106.94 per cent, registering a CAGR of 15.66 per cent.

Both the components of the public debt—the internal debt and the external debt—rose almost at the same growth rate. The internal debt went up from Rs 70.75 trillion in 2018–19 to Rs 146.62 trillion in 2023–24 RE, growing 107.24 per cent in five years at a CAGR of 15.69 per cent. The external debt also doubled from Rs 2.70 trillion to Rs 5.37 trillion at a CAGR of 14.77 per cent.

There was a reduction, though smaller, in total public account liabilities/ other liabilities during Modi 2.0. These liabilities declined from Rs 17.39 trillion in 2018–19 to Rs 16.73 trillion in 2024–24 RE, registering a CAGR of (-)0.77 per cent. This happened primarily thanks to the state governments stopping to take loans from the NSSF and the UPA-era special securities issued in lieu of subsidies to oil marketing companies and fertilizer companies declining upon part redemption. Incidentally, the off-budget liabilities incurred by the Modi government in the form of FSBs and food subsidy paid through NSSF loans did not figure in the outstanding liabilities of the government.

The reduction in other liabilities brought down the CAGR in overall debt and liabilities to 13.18 per cent for Modi 2.0—still a very high rate of growth in debt and liabilities.

Modi 1.0 was relatively restrained

The Modi government was reasonably restrained in incurring debt in its first term. The public debt went up from Rs 44.25 trillion at the end of 2013–14, marking the end of UPA rule, to Rs 73.45 trillion at the end of 2018–19. This resulted in a CAGR of 10.66 per cent, much less than the CAGR of 14.06 per cent in its second term.

Likewise, Modi 1.0 was more restrained in growing 'other liabilities' as well in the first term in contrast to the UPA period when they grew by 8.53 per cent. The other liabilities grew from Rs 12.44 trillion at the end of 2013–14 to Rs 17.39 at the end of 2018–19, recording a CAGR of 6.92 per cent.

The combined debt and liabilities grew from Rs 56.69 trillion at the end of 2013–14 to Rs 90.84 trillion at the end of 2018–19 at a CAGR of 9.89 per cent during Modi 1.0, much less than the growth rate of 12.56 per cent in ten years of UPA.

Lower inflation, higher debt pile-up

The CPI was 140.4 in March 2019. Despite an episode of high retail inflation beginning in early 2022, the CPI was at 177.2 in March 2023. The consumer price inflation recorded in the first four years of Modi 2.0 was 5.99 per cent per annum, touching the upper end of the inflation corridor at 2–6 per cent. In March 2024, the CPI rose to 185.8, which gave out five-year retail inflation of 5.76 per cent per annum.

The WPI was 119.8 at the end of 2018–19. As there was large wholesale price inflation during 2021–22 and 2022–23, the WPI rose to 152.5 at the end of 2022–23. The WPI recorded inflation of 6.22 per cent in the first four years of Modi 2.0. The WPI went into negative territory during 2023–24. With the WPI at 151.4 at the end of FY 2023–24, the wholesale price inflation during the five-year term of Modi 2.0, the annual growth of inflation came to 4.79 per cent.

With both consumer and wholesale price inflation during Modi 2.0 remaining under 6/5 per cent per annum respectively, annual growth in public debt at 15.66 per cent and in overall debt and liabilities at 13.88 per cent during the second term was in every which way quite unconscionable. Despite much higher inflation during the UPA term, the ten-year growth rate of public debt at 14.6 per cent and total debt and liabilities at 12.56 per cent was lower than the growth rate of public debt and total debt and liabilities during Modi 2.0.

Small savings and gold loans grew faster

Market loans (government securities of more than one-year term) is the largest component of the public debt of the government, constituting Rs 102.52 trillion at the end of 2023–24 RE out of the public debt of Rs 152 trillion (about two-thirds). Outstanding market loans recorded growth at 13.26 per cent during Modi 2.0, smaller than the overall public debt growth rate of 15.66 per cent.

The small savings securities issued to the NSSF by the government to borrow recorded a heftier growth during 2019–24. The small savings securities portfolio grew massively from Rs 6.09 trillion in 2018–19 to Rs 27.51 trillion in 2023–24 RE, more than quadrupling in the space of only five years. The small savings borrowings of the government grew by an astounding 35.2 per cent per annum during the five years of Modi 2.0.

The Modi government had introduced the sovereign gold bonds scheme and the gold monetization schemes in 2015. The initial pick-up was quite slow with total accumulations under the sovereign gold bonds scheme amounting to only Rs 7,336 crore at the end of 2018–19. In the second term, though, the scheme took off quite well. In two years, particularly (2020–21 and 2023–24 RE), there was a large inflow into the scheme.

In the five years of Modi 2.0, the outstanding accumulations under the sovereign gold bonds scheme reached Rs 70,000 crore, recording an astounding growth of 57 per cent per annum. There was smaller growth relatively in the gold monetization scheme, from Rs 2,854 crore in 2018–19 to Rs 9,430 crore in 2023–24 RE, displaying an annual CAGR of 27 per cent.

Special securities issued to the PSBs from 2017–18 had aggregated to Rs 1.86 trillion in 2018–19. The recapitalization programme entered a slower growth phase thereafter, peaking at Rs 2.68 trillion in 2020–21. It stayed at this level from there onwards. For the five years of Modi 2.0, the CAGR of special bank recapitalization securities turned out to be much smaller at 7.59 per cent. The recapitalization bonds to financial institutions, other than the PSBs, recorded a much higher growth rate during this period, increasing the outstanding portfolio from Rs 4,500 crore in 2018–19 to Rs 22,786 crore in 2023–24 RE; at a CAGR of 38.3 per cent.

Significant compositional change in ownership pattern

The outstanding debt raised through government securities is the biggest component of public debt. During 2023–24 RE, it crossed the Rs 100 trillion mark to reach Rs 102.52 trillion. Including the special securities converted into market securities, the total market loans outstanding were Rs 91.66 trillion at the end of 2022–23 and Rs 102.62 trillion at the end of 2023–24 RE. At Rs 83 to a dollar, the size of outstanding market loans is $1.24 trillion at the end of 2023–24 RE.

Banks had been subjected to high levels of pre-emption for many decades. High statutory liquidity ratios (SLRs) mandated the banks to invest in government securities. Over the last few years, the pre-emption is being watered down. This is reflected in the share of commercial banks declining in the total outstanding government securities.

At the end of March 2014, the banks owned 44.35 per cent of government securities (Rs 16.47 trillion out of Rs 37.15 trillion). In 2018–19, the banks' ownership stake came down to 40.28 per cent (Rs 23.85 trillion out of total outstanding securities of Rs 59.21 trillion). The commercial banks owned Rs 35.32 trillion of government securities at the end of 2022–23 out of total outstanding securities of Rs 96.46 trillion, bringing the banks' share in outstanding securities further to 36.61 per cent. At the end of FY 2023–24, the share of Central government securities held by the banks went up somewhat to 37.66 per cent out of outstanding securities of Rs 107.40 trillion.

The insurance companies, on the other hand, have increased their stake in government securities continuously. They owned Rs 7.26 trillion of securities, giving them a share of 19.54 per cent at end 2013–14. In 2018–19, their ownership increased to Rs 14.41 trillion, which amounted to 24.34 per cent of outstanding government securities. In 2022–23, their ownership and share increased to Rs 25.05 trillion (25.97 per cent). In 2023–24, the ownership share of insurance companies remained almost flat at 25.98 per cent.

The ownership of FPIs was majorly in the news as Modi 2.0 completed its second term, with two major bond indices including Indian government securities.

FPIs own a relatively smaller share of Indian government securities thanks to limits placed by the government/RBI on total ownership and changing margin advantage for FPIs on account of altering interest rates and hedging costs. In 2013–14, FPIs owned Rs 62,530 crore worth of Indian securities, giving them a 1.68 per cent share. In 2018–19, their ownership went up to Rs 1.91 trillion, increasing their ownership share to 3.22 per cent of total securities outstanding.

By the end of 2022–23, the ownership of FPIs had come down to Rs 1.31 trillion in absolute numbers and to 1.36 per cent in terms of their proportion. FPIs held the least amount of government securities at that moment, when there was widespread expectations of the foreign exchange flows to Indian securities on account of inclusion in bond indices.

The impact of bond indices inclusion was visible in 2023–24. FPIs increased their holdings of government securities at end-March 2024 to Rs 2.51 trillion (about $30.3 billion at Rs 83 to a dollar), raising FPIs' share to 2.34 per cent of outstanding securities of Rs 107.40 trillion.

Government avoided temptation to go back to old pension scheme

Five non-BJP states—Chhattisgarh, Rajasthan, Jharkhand, Himachal Pradesh and Punjab—reverted to the old pension scheme (OPS) by 2022–23. Andhra Pradesh provided an option for guaranteed pension equal to 33 per cent of the last pay.

BJP states also faced the heat though they managed not to roll back with considerable unease. The Centre was caught on the horns of a dilemma. While it refused the demand of states reverting to OPS to return the accumulated NPS corpus, it appointed, on 24 March 2023, a committee under the Finance Secretary T.V. Somanathan to look into the issue of improving the NPS.

For government employees, the OPS is a big bonanza—50 per cent of the last pay with DA thereon as pension for life, which also gets revised upward every ten years following Pay Commission awards. In addition, they get their contributions to the NPS back as general provident fund (GPF) contributions. In comparison, the NPS has relatively spartan benefits. The government pays only 10 per cent (raised to 14 per cent in 2018–19) along with salary. Employees contribute an equal amount to their NPS account in place of GPF contribution. Total accumulation, with returns, is the employee's total pension wealth, a part of which is annuitized as pension. NPS annuities vary but never yield a pension equal to OPS. There is no DA and no revision with Pay Commission awards. The OPS is about three times more beneficial to government employees than NPS.

India was in a fiscal mess in 2003–04. Most states used to survive on overdrafts from the RBI. Treasuries were routinely closed; the Assam treasury remained closed for about 240 days in one year. The NPS was introduced in 2004 by the BJP-led NDA, as part of a larger fiscal responsibility package, which included FRBM and swap of states' costlier debt. The Congress-led UPA continued with the reforms and nudged states to adopt fiscal responsibility laws and fiscal discipline. The NPS system was implemented in almost all the states. States' finances transformed. Despite shocks of the global financial crisis and Covid-19, states managed to live within fiscal deficit limits for almost fifteen years. The OPS has the potential of wrecking states' fiscal balance.

The Congress lost the assembly elections in Rajasthan and Chhattisgarh despite reverting to the OPS. The BJP won the Madhya Pradesh elections despite not adopting the OPS. Sensing the inability of reverting to the OPS to influence political results to any significant extent, the GoI, which was otherwise toying with the idea of diluting the NPS, did not make any announcement during the Budget session.

The Central government did well to stay on course of sustaining the NPS and not getting tempted to adapt the NPS or further weaken the rigour of the scheme.*

The pension liabilities of its civil servants under the old defined benefit pension scheme is a debt which the GoI owes. The NPS relieves the government of this liability.

---

* The Modi 3.0 government gave in substantially on 24 August 2024 by promising to pay a guaranteed 50 per cent pension to its NPS employees by announcing a modified scheme named the Unified Pension Scheme (UPS).

Epilogue

$10 Trillion GDP by 2035 Is Off-Track

$10 trillion goal had roots in Interim Budget 2019

While presenting India's ten-dimensional vision for the next decade in the Interim Budget 2019–20, Piyush Goyal, the officiating Finance Minister, articulated India's GDP ambition as follows (para 68):

> The NDA Government headed by Hon'ble Prime Minister Shri Narendra Modi has laid the foundation for India's growth and development for times to come. We have resolved many problems which were coming in the way of realising our full potential as a society and an economy. We are poised to become a Five Trillion Dollar Economy in the next five years and aspire to become a Ten Trillion Dollar Economy in the next 8 years thereafter.

This visionary statement implied that the $5 trillion GDP goal was to be attained in FY 2023–24 and the $10 trillion GDP goal by 2031–32. The BJP manifesto for the 2019 Lok Sabha elections also talked about the $10 trillion GDP goal. The Prime Minister mentioned the goal in a couple of his addresses in 2019–20.

I had, in my book *The $10 Trillion Dream*, decided to peg the $10 trillion goal to 2035, or FY 2034–35 and proposed a policy reform agenda to achieve the same.

Prime Minister Modi and the BJP government, after winning the Lok Sabha elections, however, decided to push the $5 trillion by 2024 goal more than the $10 trillion goal. While the $5 trillion GDP goal was spoken of every now and then (most stridently until 2022–23), the $10 trillion goal was only occasionally mentioned in the five years of Modi 2.0.

India missed the $5 trillion goal by a wide margin

The Prime Minister officially highlighted the $5 trillion goal for the first time in the meeting of the Governing Council of NITI Aayog held on 15 June 2019. He sought to make the states a partner in realizing this mission.

407

The minutes of the meeting recorded:

> While the goal to make India a 5 trillion dollar economy by 2024 is challenging, it is totally achievable too. There is a need for State governments to recognize their core competence and utilise their potential properly. If each State decides to increase its share in the country's GDP that will accelerate the process of achieving USD 5 trillion economy.

The call for 2024 was interpreted as 2024–25 in all official documents thereafter, including in the Budget 2019–20, presented by Nirmala Sitharaman on 5 July 2019.

India, however, missed the $5 trillion by 2024–25 mark by a wide margin, as explained in the prologue.

To recapitulate, India's GDP was $2.70 trillion in 2018–19, needing India to cover the gap of $2.30 trillion in six years. This required an average addition of about $380 billion to its GDP every year.

After four years, in 2022–23, India's GDP could grow to only $3.39 trillion. Modi 2.0 managed to cover the gap only to the extent of $690 billion in four years. Less than two years' work was done in four years! After five years, India's GDP could reach $3.56 trillion only, bridging the $2.30 trillion distance to the extent of $860 billion only. The average annual distance covered in five years of Modi 2.0 amounted to only $172 billion per annum, at about 45 per cent of the asking rate.

India has still to cover $1.44 trillion (about 1.7 times of $0.86 trillion covered in five years) in the final year of 2024–25. It is virtually impossible to achieve the $5 trillion GDP goal by 2024–25. Considering the progress of only $0.17 trillion in 2023–24 over the GDP of $3.39 trillion in 2022–23 and an average addition of $0.172 trillion GDP a year in the five years of Modi 2.0, it is unlikely that India will cross even the $4 trillion GDP mark in 2024–25.

Minister Piyush Goyal had assumed (read the Budget extract placed in the beginning of this epilogue) that India would attain $5 trillion GDP by 2023–24 itself. India missed this goal badly and is sure to miss it again by a wide margin in 2024–25.

The government did not formally recalibrate the target year of $5 trillion GDP goal to any other particular year. Government spokesmen like the Chief Economic Adviser (CEA) started talking about India reaching the $5 trillion mark by 2026–27. IMF projections expect India to go past the $5 trillion mark only in 2027–28.

Finance Minister Nirmala Sitharaman accepted the reality grudgingly but indirectly. On 10 January 2024, addressing industry honchos at the Vibrant Gujarat Summit, she said, 'Over the medium term, India could emerge as the world's third largest economy with GDP of over $5 trillion in FY 28.'

In 2023–24, the Prime Minister, other ministers and senior government functionaries stopped talking about the $5 trillion GDP goal. Two other goalposts became part of the government's rhetoric—the guarantee of India becoming the third-largest economy before the government completes its third term in 2029 and a Viksit Bharat by 2047.

India in serious danger of missing the $10 trillion goal

After missing the $5 trillion goal, India is in serious danger of missing the $10 trillion goal by 2035 goal as well.

India's GDP growth turned out to be around 5.69 per cent during Modi 2.0, i.e. 2019–24 with GDP, in current US dollars, amounting to $3.56 trillion in 2023–24 against GDP of $2.70 trillion in 2018–19. At this growth rate, India's GDP will grow to only about $6.50 trillion in 2034–35—a far cry from India's dream of $10 trillion GDP by 2034–35.

The possibility of attaining the goal of $10 trillion GDP in 2034–35 becomes harder if we take into account the depreciation of the US dollar. India's GDP goal was set in terms of US$ in 2019.

The rupee depreciates significantly both in terms of its real value and also in terms of the US dollar exchange rate. Setting the GDP goal in US dollar terms takes care of the rupee's depreciation vis-à-vis the global currency—the US dollar. Still, one downside is left uncovered even while setting the GDP goal in US dollar terms and measuring its progress. The US dollar also depreciates. The US dollar of 2024 is not equal to the dollar of 2019, when the $10 trillion goal was set.

The dollar, much less susceptible to depreciation since the 1980s, actually depreciated at a brisk pace after the Covid-19 outbreak. US urban CPI was 257.21 in October 2019, rising from 252.04 in October 2018. The outbreak of Covid-19 in 2020 did not lead to a spike in CPI initially. It began to rise later, growing to 260.23 in October 2020.

The US government's fiscal stimulus and the unleashing of liquidity by the US Fed led to a whopping increase in the CPI Index of 17.72 points or 6.8 per cent to 277.95 in October 2021 and further by about 20 points or 7.1 per cent to 297.71 in October 2022. Only in 2023 did it begin to moderate, though it was still quite high from a historical perspective at 307.79, rising by 10 points. In three years, the US urban CPI witnessed annual inflation of 5.67 per cent per annum. The US dollar depreciated by about 18 per cent against itself in three years.

The $10 trillion goal in 2019 was implicitly expressed in terms of the 2019 US dollar. The depreciation in US dollars, should, therefore, lead to adjusting the $10 trillion goal in current US dollar terms.

$10 trillion in 2019 equalled approximately $12 trillion in 2023, taking into account US dollar depreciation. If we assume further US dollar depreciation at the rate of 3 per cent per annum, $12 trillion in 2023 will be equal to a little over $15 trillion in 2034–35.

India's $3.56 trillion GDP in 2023–24 will require to grow at a dollar rate of higher than 14 per cent per annum to reach $15 trillion in 2035.

Under no scenario does it look feasible. The $10 trillion GDP goal by 2034 is as off-track as the goal of $5 trillion GDP by 2024–25 is.

Development Journey So Far

Making India a developed nation is every Indian's rightful ambition. Development requires high GDP growth and much more. Let me first take stock of India's growth and development track record.

GDP growth was in the dumps before 1991

India was a closed economy with a falling growth rate, high inflation, overvalued exchange rate, extraordinarily high import duties and bankrupt foreign exchange reserves in 1991. That year, on the verge of defaulting on its international payment obligations, India was truly in a big soup.

1991 was an apocalyptic moment. India was in a deep crisis, staring at an abyss—close to what later came to be symbolized as a Lehman moment. A look at the data for 1991–92 in the Economic Survey of 1992–93 can still send a shiver down one's spine.

The GDP in 1991–92 grew by only 1.4 per cent at constant prices; consumer price inflation was 13.9 per cent. Agriculture production had fallen by 2.8 per cent with food production contracting by 5.3 per cent; industrial production rose by a measly 0.1 per cent.

Money supply had spurted between 15 per cent and 19.5 per cent in the previous four years. The government was running large fiscal deficits financed by an unlimited overdraft from the RBI. Foreign exchange reserves were down to $2.2 billion in 1990–91, having plummeted by 33.6 per cent in the year. India was foreign-exchange bankrupt and on the verge of default.

India could have defaulted as many other developing countries had done in the 1970s and 1980s. Indian policymakers knew the ignominy, pain and dysfunctionality that defaulters faced. In the 1960s, Prime Minister Shastri, with India facing an acute food deficit, had begged Indians to eat only one meal a day so that everyone could at least eat something every day.

1991 reforms laid the foundations of faster growth

There were no easy choices but India decided to take the bull by the horns and embarked on the path of bold reforms. The reforms undertaken by India in 1991 were nothing short of extraordinary, risky and audacious. These reforms turned on their head the dystopian policies India was following for thirty-five years since Independence.

India's industrial economy was built on the twin pillars of reservations of basic and capital industry for the public sector and constraining the private sector under the asphyxiating yoke of the licence-permit raj. An inefficient industrial public sector had mushroomed in India in the quest for a utopian socialist pattern of society. Capital formation had shuttered with the efficiency of capital measured by capital-output ratio declining to its lowest rate in independent India.

In what was simply inconceivable in the India of the 1980s, the government abolished the reservation for the public sector and relieved the private sector from the slavery of the licence-permit raj. The reforms revived Indian industry, which has become globally competitive, at least in some areas.

India had become a closed, inward-looking economy under the mistaken notions that self-reliance and import substitution could build a strong Indian economy. Our exchange rate was highly overvalued to make imports a big attraction while exports had no takers. High tariffs had forced businessmen to become quota-seekers and smugglers. Foreign exchange inflows had grounded. Whatever the official aid and borrowings brought was used for unavoidable consumption imports and capital imports for the inefficient public sector. It was no surprise that foreign exchange reserves were totally depleted despite a massive import squeeze.

Instead of going in for quick-fix solutions like the rupee depreciation of 1965, the government decided to act tough and smart. Considerable foreign trade reforms were undertaken. Export subsidies were abolished. The rupee was substantially depreciated and a good part of export proceeds liberalized to be sold in markets at market-determined rates. Soon, the entire current account was liberalized and foreign exchange rates became more or less market-determined.

From being on the verge of default in 1991, India crossed the $100 billion reserves mark in 2003–04 and the $300 billion mark in 2007–08.

India was pathologically averse to foreign investments and technology before 1991. There was no concept of FDI or FPI or ECB. Technology imports were controlled with a tight fist and paltry royalty payments were only grudgingly allowed.

In a broad sweep of reforms in the 1990s, FDI was permitted in several sectors and technology imports and royalty payments liberalized. ECBs were also permitted from the middle of the 1990s. FDI stock crossed $100 billion in 2007–08 and $200 billion in 2011–12, from literally zero in 1990–91.

There were many other reforms. Ill-advised reservations for the small-scale sector, which had emasculated India's industrial growth, were done away with. The reforms unleashed in 1991 were truly massive.

Unfinished reform agenda in 2014

India reaped the gains of the 1991 reforms. Foreign exchange reserves had ceased to be an issue. India recorded phenomenal GDP growth after 2000. Extreme poverty was declining fast. Foreign investment had boomed. India had become a large market economy and had integrated globally in terms of trade, finances and immigration.

Yet, there was a significant unfinished agenda when the Modi government took over in 2014. There are two particularly important reforms that the governments did not take up between 1991 and 2014. One was privatization of the public sector and the second, reforms in agriculture.

The incumbent industrial and financial public sector continued unreformed after 1991. Some encouragement to bring a commercial orientation to the public sector was initiated. The government also stopped nationalizing the private sector and funding the capital requirement of the public sector. This was, however, not sufficient. The Vajpayee government took up privatization with some seriousness but could only touch the fringe.

The agriculture sector remained entirely untouched/unreformed. Probably the fact that India had become self-sufficient in agriculture by the 1990s made the governments quite complacent about it. The governments continued to do only more of the green revolution policies—higher MSP, subsidies extended to all agriculture inputs and also loan write-offs.

These two important unfinished reforms awaited the BJP government when it assumed power in 2014.

Modi government faltered in second term

The government began well by reposing faith in the maxim of minimum government, maximum governance. This implied that the government would follow policies and a reform agenda to unwind the public sector and liberalize agriculture.

In the first term, the Modi government initiated important indirect tax reforms by bringing out the GST system in 2017. Industrial insolvency was also sought to be addressed with the enactment of the IBC. Reforms were also introduced in the auctioning of public resources. Personal identification and building of the digital infrastructure stack was also taken up in a major way.

Unfortunately, however, nothing significant happened in the case of public sector reforms and agriculture reforms.

Barring Air India, no public sector enterprise—industrial or financial—was privatized in the ten years of the Modi government, though numerous announcements were made. Even disinvestment of minority shareholdings literally floundered in the second term. On the contrary, the government made enormous investments in the equity of sick and non-commercial public sector organizations (e.g. BSNL, NHAI and Railways).

In agriculture, not a single reform was carried out. An attempt was made to bring reform in agriculture marketing as part of the infamous three farm laws. The laws were abandoned midway to shut out farmers' protests.

Instead, there was an enormous expansion of subsidies and government in agriculture and farmers' lives. MSPs became larger with 50 per cent minimum profit (though not effectively implemented). Fertilizer subsidies rose to nearly 90 per cent of cost by 2022. There is a much larger public sector production of fertilizer. Urea distribution is effectively nationalized under a single brand—Bharat.

New fiscal resources-guzzling programmes like PM Kisan and doubled-up food allowance under PM Garib Kalyan Yojana for 80 crore Indians (for about three years between 2020–2022) assumed centre stage.

On 15 September 2022, Finance Minister Nirmala Sitharaman termed the 1991 reforms '*aadhe-adhure*' (half-baked). Instead, she argued that the direct benefit delivery schemes and infrastructure spending undertaken by the Modi government were the real reforms.

She could not have been more wrong. The Modi government not only did not take up the unfinished 1991 reform agenda, it made the situation worse by going back on some of the 1991 reforms.

The failures and underperformance in many sectors of the economy from 2019–20 to 2023–24 which resulted in a five-year GDP growth CAGR of an embarrassing 4.3 per cent per annum has been described in great detail in the twenty chapters of this book. Of course, there have been certain successes, which have been noted in the prologue and also in specific chapters. However, the successes were much smaller than the failures, which explains this gross underperformance.

Getting past Brazil, China, France and the UK was serendipitous

Most countries that India is now moving past have seen their growth peak at high per capita incomes.

India, with a GDP of $1.86 trillion, was the ninth-largest economy in 2013–14, with Brazil ($2.21 trillion), China ($9.57 trillion), France ($2.81 trillion), Germany ($3.7 trillion), UK ($2.79 trillion), Italy ($2.14 trillion), Japan ($5.21 trillion) and the US ($17.55 trillion) ahead of it.

It was quite a fortuitous coincidence that the GDPs of four countries—
Brazil, Italy, France and the UK—higher than India in the pecking order were
in the $2–3 trillion band, with India quite close behind in 2013–14. Indeed a
happy happenstance for Narendra Modi and the BJP.

Of these four countries, except Brazil, all three European countries—France,
the UK and Italy—had attained very high per capita incomes of $42,603,
$43,449 and $35,560 respectively, in 2013–14. Brazil's lower per capita income
of $12,259 was also nearly ten times India's per capita income of $1,438 in
that year.

All high per capita income countries invariably enter into the low GDP
growth orbit thanks to high economic prosperity and falling population. They
don't need fast economic growth at such high incomes, whereas developing
countries need to generate higher GDP growth to not only raise the country's
heft but also to improve the lot of their poor people.

Unsurprisingly, India, a poor developing country, despite a not-so-impressive
growth of about 7 per cent, in current dollars during 2013–22, could move past
these four countries to become the fifth largest economy.

Overtaking Germany and Japan will not make much difference

'When I first visited the US as a Prime Minister, India was the tenth largest
economy in the world. Today, India is the fifth largest and we will be the third
largest soon,' Prime Minister Narendra Modi said, with considerable visible
pride, in his address to the US Congress on 23 June 2023.

Germany and Japan are the two countries ahead of India in GDP terms at
number 4 and 3, respectively. Both countries are also very high per capita income
countries with declining populations. Germany's per capita income was $48,438
in 2022, whereas India's was only $2,389. Japan's case is bizarre. Japan's GDP was
$5.76 trillion in 2010 but only $4.26 trillion in 2022. The IMF projects, in the
World Economic Outlook (WEO) database April 2024, the GDP of Germany
and Japan to be $5.09 trillion and $4.65 trillion respectively, in 2027.

India becoming the third-largest economy is fairly given. However, reaching
this milestone in any specific year is not that certain.

The IMF projects India's dollar GDP growth, in my judgement, quite
optimistically, at 10.30 per cent per annum for four years (from 2023–24
to 2027–28) to reach $5.29 trillion in 2027–28. If these optimistic growth
projections are realized and depressing projections for Germany and Japan hold,
India will move past Germany in 2027–28 and Japan a year before in 2026–
27. In my judgement, however, India is unlikely to grow at 10.30 per cent per
annum in dollar terms for the next few years.

There are many other factors. Japan and Germany can attain better growth.
Japanese currency, which has depreciated massively to bring down its GDP in

dollar terms so badly, may reverse the course, raising Japan's dollar GDP. The Indian economy might grow at a lower nominal growth rate (in 2023–24, India's nominal GDP growth was only about 9 per cent). The Indian rupee might depreciate more against the US dollar, making GDP growth in terms of the US dollar much smaller.

Some analysts have already started talking of India overtaking Japan and Germany only in 2030. S&P Global projected in December 2023 that India would become the third-largest economy in the world by 2030. Most likely, the event of getting past Japan and Germany will take place in 2028–29 or 2029–30.

Again, if and when India moves past Germany and Japan to be the third-largest economy, it will not be on account of any special efforts of the government. It will be serendipitous.

India hardly budged in per capita income ranking

India's per capita income of $1,438 in 2013–14 increased to $2,389 in 2022–23, at a CAGR of 5.8 per cent.

India's rank, in terms of per capita income, was 147 (out of 189) in 2022–23 as per the World Bank per capita income tables.

In the last ten years, India overtook four out of eight countries ahead of us in terms of overall GDP to move to the fifth position. However, in terms of per capita income, India could overtake only seven to move to 147 in 2022–23. Hardly a great pace of development!

In these ten years, India moved ahead of Nicaragua, Uzbekistan, Mauritania, Nigeria, Ghana, Kenya and Lao PDR. On the other hand, Bangladesh, earlier seen as our poorer neighbour, overtook India during this period.

The per capita income of Brazil, Italy, France and the UK, whose GDP we have crossed, and Germany and Japan, which we will cross, remain far higher than us. We cannot even think of touching them.

India will prosper and Indians will experience real development only when the per capita income of the average Indian will grow to reach at least higher middle-income levels, if not the high income level; not when her GDP becomes the third-largest.

Viksit Bharat/Redefining Our Ambition and Goal

Tryst with destiny did not materialize

Nehru, delivering his 'tryst with destiny' speech at the hour of India's independence in 1947, felt relieved that India's 'period of misfortune' had ended. Believing that India was ready to 'discover herself again', Nehru dreamt of the 'future' bringing 'freedom and opportunity to the common man, to the peasants and workers of India; to fight and end poverty and ignorance and disease; to build up a prosperous, democratic and progressive nation'.

For the first fifty years after Independence, barring the brief Janata Party interlude during 1977–79, Nehru and the Congress party had an uninterrupted opportunity to translate his vision and dream into reality.

While Nehru laid the foundation of a vibrant and thriving democracy in India, established a large industrial base in basic and heavy industry, set up outstanding institutions of higher and technical education and built big dams, adoption of the wrong economic policy and model of a socialist pattern of society, and commanding the public sector meant that India witnessed quite a low GDP growth. This period coincided with high population growth, making the per capita income growth even more tepid.

India fell behind many countries in every economic development indicator—GDP growth, per capita income growth, investments, exports, productivity of capital and labour and whatever else you pick up.

Viksit Bharat@2047—is vague

Envisioning another tryst with India's destiny, on India's seventy-fifth independence anniversary, Prime Minister Modi called for making India a 'developed nation' by 2047.

In 2015, Narendra Modi had talked about doubling farmers' income and building a New India by 2022, the seventy-fifth anniversary of India's independence. In 2019, he talked about making India a $5 trillion economy by 2024 and a $10 trillion economy by the middle of the 2030s.

In 2022, when India completed seventy-five years of independence, he pushed the promise of New India into the background. Possibly realizing that even the goal of a $5 trillion economy by 2024–25 was also going to elude his government, he decided not to speak about it and shifted to reset the goal with reference to the 100th year of India's independence. He envisioned a developed India—a Viksit Bharat—by 2047.

The year 2023–24 was all about Viksit Bharat. From the Prime Minister to every Minister, from NITI Aayog to every think-tank or media platform, owned or sympathetic to the government, people only talked about Viksit Bharat in 2047.

The trouble is no one, including Prime Minister Narendra Modi, spelt out what Viksit Bharat meant. Sometimes, government ministers and functionaries talked about India becoming a $30 trillion or $35 trillion or $40 trillion economy by 2047. However, it was never officially mentioned that Viksit Bharat meant India becoming a $35 trillion or $40 trillion economy in 2047. Sometimes, Viksit Bharat was expressed in terms of big infrastructure development in the country and at other times in different contexts.

On 11 December 2023, the Prime Minister launched a 'Viksit Bharat@2047: Voice of Youth', which was also used as an occasion to address vice chancellors of universities, heads of institutes and faculty members in workshops organized at Raj Bhavans across the country. The initiative was envisaged as a platform for the youth of the country to contribute ideas to the vision of Viksit Bharat@2047. The press release mentioned that 'Viksit Bharat@2047 is the vision to make India a developed nation by 2047, the 100th year of its independence. The vision encompasses various aspects of development, including economic growth, social progress, environmental sustainability, and good governance, among others'. Again, nothing quite specific.

NITI Aayog was put in charge of Viksit Bharat and assigned to develop the road map for it. NITI Aayog organized its 8th Governing Council Meeting on the theme of 'Viksit Bharat@2047: Role of Team India' on 27 May 2023. The official press release noted that the 8th Governing Council Meeting provided 'an opportunity to create a roadmap for Viksit Bharat by 2047 in which Centre and States can work together as Team India'.

NITI Aayog promised to 'have the draft version of the plan ready' by December 2023. NITI Aayog CEO B.V.R. Subrahmanyam stated in November 2023 that 'a vision document is being prepared for India to become a developed economy of about USD 30 trillion by 2047, and it will be released by Prime Minister Narendra Modi in January next year'.

These deadlines came and went. The road map did not get ready by the time the elections for the next Lok Sabha were announced in March 2024. The government nonchalantly informed that the road map for Viksit Bharat would be presented along with its regular 2024–25 Budget.

The 2024–25 Budget presented on 23 July 2024 by the Modi-led National Democratic Alliance (NDA) did not provide the promised road map for Viksit Bharat. Another meeting of the Governing Council of NITI Aayog held on 27 July reportedly discussed an Approach Paper for Viksit Bharat (not publicly disclosed). The minutes of the meeting did not have any clarity regarding the definition of the goal. It only had the Prime Minister's exhortation to the states to work for it.

When the Modi government failed to achieve more specific GDP goals set in terms of a smaller five-year period, it makes very little practical sense to accept the rhetoric of GDP goals for twenty-five years ahead. Unfortunately, goals set in undefined and fuzzy terms like a 'developed nation', have still less likelihood of being attained or monitored for progress. There is no credibility of such goals.

India—a lower middle income country

There is no globally accepted definition of a 'developed country'. But, there is a standard classification of low income, lower and upper middle income, and high income countries done on the basis of per capita income.

The World Bank publishes the income-based classification of all its member countries every year. Accordingly, the per capita income cut-offs for inclusion in one or the other group also keep moving up every year, primarily depending upon dollar depreciation/appreciation against itself.

For 2023, the countries with per capita income of less than $1,135 are classified as low income countries (LICs), between $1,136 and $4,465 as lower middle income countries (LMICs), between $4,466 and $13,845 as upper middle income countries (UMICs) and those with per capita income higher than $13,845 as high income countries (HICs).

India started out as an independent nation in 1947 as one of the least developed countries (LDC), according to the UN system of development classification. With 80 per cent of her people extremely poor, India was categorized as a low income country (LIC) in the World Bank's classification of countries, based on average per capita income when this income-based classification started in 1978. It took India sixty years after its independence (in 2007) to move out of the class of LICs and enter into the lower middle income (LMIC group).

India today, with a $3.56 trillion GDP and a little over 140 crore people, has an average per capita GDP of less than $2,500 and is classified as a lower middle income country (LMIC). Global per capita GDP was about $11,750 in 2019 when India's $10 trillion GDP goal was set. It is approximately $12,500 now in 2024. Global per capita GDP is five times India's per capita GDP. The World Bank uses gross national income (GNI) per capita (in a methodology called the Atlas Method). India's GNI per capita in 2022 (the last available data) was $2,380 and India was placed at number 147 out of 196 World Bank member countries.

Let us define our goal in per capita terms

The World Bank classifies as many as eighty-three countries currently as HICs and another fifty-four countries are placed in the UMICs bracket. India is not among these 137 upper middle income and high income countries.

India, with a per capita income of about $2,500, is part of the LMICs group of fifty-four countries, along with all our neighbouring countries in South Asia.

Surely getting into the UMICs group in five to seven years and into the HICs group in the long-term should be a sufficiently motivating and challenging ambition for India.

Setting India's long-term growth and development ambition in terms of average per capita income is more apt as that conveys much greater sense in terms of average standard of life and consumption of the people of India relative to the rest of the world. Its quick relation to the World Bank classification of countries in low, middle and higher income categories also connects well with the relative standard of living.

We must therefore challenge ourselves to adopt and deliver the goal of making India a high income country. We may take India in the high income group as a developed country.

Let us adopt 2050 as our goal destination

There is one more change we must make in setting our long-term goal. India is a civilizational country with thousands of years of history. The British were here in India for about 200 years, in which the British Crown ruled India for only about ninety years. Linking our goals to independence from British rule is not a good clarion call for Indian people.

Indians—We the People of India that is Bharat (also called Hindustan)—adopted our Constitution in January 1950. We also made India a republic in 1950. In 2050, India will complete 100 years of being a republic. The vision of a truly Viksit Bharat should coincide with 100 years of the Indian Republic. This will also provide a reasonable window of twenty-five years, across five governments, to realize the vision.

The challenge of Viksit Bharat in per capita terms

It is fashionable now for political and industry leaders to tot up any number for India's GDP for the long shot—2040/2047/2050 or so on. Nirmala Sitharaman asserted on 10 January 2024 that 'India will be a developed country by 2047 with gross domestic product of $30 trillion even by conservative estimates'. On different occasions, Piyush Goyal talked about the Indian economy becoming 'a USD 40 trillion economy by 2047', 'a 30–35 trillion dollar economy by 2047', 'a USD 35 trillion economy by 2047' and some other numbers.

The government does not have a model to estimate the GDP for the next year while presenting the Budget. It builds a likely percentage growth over the advance estimates of the NSO for the outgoing year. The government failed to realize the $5 trillion goal by 2024–25 by a wide margin. It is also strange that the government spokespersons never specify which year's dollars they are talking about while giving wings to their imagination. There is no credibility of any of these high-sounding numbers.

However, you can change the fundamentals of the economy, growth and development only in the long term. For that, you need to pick up a long-term goal and then work policy reforms to get to that goal.

I think it makes much better sense to set India's long-term growth and development goal in terms of people's prosperity measured by average per capita income. The national GDP goal can be derived from that as well.

The World Bank cut-off for a high income country currently is $13,845 per capita gross national income (GNI) in 2022 dollars. For India's population of approximately 140 crore people in 2022–23, the high income $13,845 per capita GNI translates approximately into $19.38 trillion GNI in 2022–23.

India's nominal GDP in 2022–23 (I RE) was Rs 269.50 trillion. India's GNI, which is GDP plus net primary income of Indian residents from abroad, as per the NSO for 2022–23, was Rs 265.79 trillion. India's GNI was approximately 98.63 per cent of GDP in 2022–23, which is also the case for 2021–22 and 2023–24, as India has a deficit in the primary incomes. We can take the GNI as 98 per cent of India's annual nominal GDP. In such a case, India's required GDP for $13,845 per capita HIC cut-off would be $19.78 trillion or, say, $20 trillion.

India's dollar GDP in current US$ (IMF estimates) was $3.534 trillion in 2022–23. For India's population of 140 crore, it yields a per capita GDP of $2,395 or say $2,400. Per capita GNI at 98 per cent of per capita GDP works out to $2,347. The HIC per capita income cut-off of $13,845 in 2022 is 5.9 times higher than India's per capita GNI.

Closing an almost six times wide gap would be quite an ambitious goal even over a twenty-five year period. This, however, would be a real challenge, worth trying and vying for, for India.

The developed India/high income goal 2050

Let us assume a US$ depreciation of 2 per cent per annum for all periods up to 2050 for the purpose of revision of the World Bank HIC cut-off. In such a case, the World Bank's HIC cut-off of $13,845 in 2022 can be estimated to become $17,559 in 2035, $22,269 in 2047 and $23,632 in 2050.

We, as a nation, should set the goal of India achieving a per capita GNI of $23,632 in 2050 as the defining parameter of Viksit Bharat/Developed India.

As more people are familiar with GDP than GNI, taking India's GNI as typically 98 per cent of GDP, the estimated per capita GNI HIC cut-off, as stated above, will translate into per capita GDP of $17,917 in 2035, $22,723 in 2047 and $24,114 in 2050.

I am aware of many uncertainties surrounding these future calculations. The US economy might do better than it did in the last four to five years, resulting in lower depreciation than 2 per cent per annum or even an appreciation. In such a case, the nearly 75 per cent rise in the high income cut-off ($24,111 divided by $13,845) in 2050 may not happen.

However, one needs to work on a reasonably understandable number for India's dollar per capita GDP in 2050. We can take $24,111 as that per capita GDP for 2050. I would, considering the uncertainties around and the appeal of a number, suggest India adopt the goal of $25,000 per capita GDP in 2050 as its definition of Viksit Bharat/Developed India.

Estimating India's GDP for 2035, 2047 and 2050

For estimating India's GDP in any of the familiar target years—2035 (in the context of the $10 trillion dream), 2047 (government's ambition of Viksit Bharat) or 2050 (India completes 100 years of its Republic), we will need estimated populations of these respective years.

There are various estimates about India's estimated population in 2035, 2047 and 2050. We can go by the UN's estimates, which have the most acceptance. Accordingly, the estimated population of India in 2035, 2047 and 2050 can be taken as 156.8 crore, 166 crore and 166.8 crore.

The per capita high income GDP of $17,917 in 2035 for India's estimated population of 156.8 crore would mean a GDP of $28.1 trillion. Likewise, per capita GDP of $22,723 in 2047 for 166 crore people will equal a GDP of $37.7 trillion and per capita GDP of $24,114 in 2050 for a 166.8 crore population will mean a GDP of $40.2 trillion.

The $25,000 per capita GDP goal for 2050 for a 166.8 crore population will imply a GDP of $41.70 trillion.

If we succeed in raising the per capita income of Indians to $25,000 by 2050, India, under the assumptions regarding per capita HIC cut-off and India's population, India's GDP in 2050 should grow to $41.70 trillion.

It requires 10 per cent dollar GDP growth per annum

India's dollar GDP in 2023–24 is $3.56 trillion. To get to $41.70 trillion GDP in 2050, the asking dollar GDP growth rate would be 9.93 per cent per annum, or about 10 per cent per annum.

India has grown at about 5.53 per cent per annum in dollar terms in the last five years (2019–24) and at 6.76 per cent in the ten years of the Modi government. India has, however, grown at a rate higher than 10 per cent over a ten-year period in the past. India recorded a dollar GDP growth of 11.82 per cent per annum in dollar terms in the UPA period (2003–04 to 2013–14).

India can and has achieved a high dollar growth rate if the real GDP growth rate is quite high (about 8 per cent per annum), because the big real growth differential between India and the US results in the rupee appreciating against the dollar.

A tough task but worth trying for

Achieving 10 per cent per annum dollar growth over the next twenty-five years is a huge task but not an impossible one.

At the present juncture of India's development and growth, with the Indian population still growing at about 1 per cent per annum, India's enormous talent pool, especially in services, and the demand remaining strong for many decades as India rises from the lower-middle income country to upper-middle income country, an annual real GDP growth of 5 per cent for the next twenty-five years is literally a 'natural' rate of growth for India, even if it is business as usual.

If, however, India undertakes fundamental reforms, which I lay out in the next section, India can certainly generate another 3–4 per cent growth sustainably for the next twenty-five years.

When India generates 8 per cent annual growth sustainably for the next twenty-five years, it will be quite reasonable to expect a rupee appreciation of 1–2 per cent per annum, on an average, in the next twenty-five years.

That will yield India a 10 per cent dollar GDP growth for twenty-five years.

We must define the 2050 goal in intermediate periods also

India should, without any ambiguity or hesitation, express her per capita dollar income goal of $25,000 in 2050. Thereafter, the goals should also be expressed in intermediate milestones to keep monitoring the progress regularly.

The first major milestone should be set in terms of the completion of the Narendra Modi-led NDA government's term, which has assumed office on 9 June 2024. India's GDP of $3.353 trillion in 2022–23, if it grows at 10 per cent per annum until 2028–29, when the Modi–NDA government completes its third five-year term, will reach $5.94 trillion. India's GDP will cross the $5 trillion mark on the way, in current US dollars, in 2027–28 as well. Unfortunately, the setback of not attaining 10 per cent dollar growth in 2023–24 and the prospects of the current year (2024–25), make it seem difficult that the $5 trillion benchmark will be crossed in 2027–28.

The next milestone should be set with reference to 2035, our 2019–20 set date for the $10 trillion GDP dream. If India can manage to continue growing its GDP by 10 per cent per annum (from 2022–23 to 2034–35), our GDP will grow to $10.525 trillion, just a little higher than our $10 trillion GDP goal.

On the way, India will also enter the upper middle income country group as well.

Policy Reforms Agenda for $25,000 Per Capita Income Goal

I have evaluated the economic performance of the Modi 2.0 government in the prologue and twenty chapters of this book. These twenty chapters cover all aspects of the economy—value creation in agriculture, industry and services, consumption and capital formation, labour income and quality of life, governance, money and finance, foreign trade, investment and engagement with the rest of the world, and the government's finances, budgets and debt.

While making this evaluation, I have also brought up the successes as well as the failures of the Modi 2.0 government in undertaking the policy reforms needed for putting India on the path of a $10 trillion economy by 2034–35 and our redefined goal of $25,000 per capita income in 2050 to make India a high income country.

While evaluating the state of affairs, growth and reforms for each of the twenty segments of the Indian economy, I thought about the fundamental policy reforms that would help India get the best possible high growth in that segment. What are the fundamental reforms that can turn the performance of the Indian economy from an average 5–6 per cent dollar growth per year to 10 per cent dollar growth per year for twenty-five years?

I summarize below a set of fifty fundamental policy reforms, serious and tough, but absolutely necessary, organized under twenty headings corresponding to the twenty chapters of this book. I am quite convinced that making this major pivot in our policy framework would be critical for India to attain the ambition of $25,000 per capita income by 2050 and become a high income country.

Agriculture

1. Liberate and deregulate agriculture

Indian agriculture and farmers are most constrained by numerous restrictive laws and regulations. Farmers cannot buy land beyond the limits of a ceiling. They cannot legally lease land or enter into free contractual arrangements to grow their crops. Corporate agriculture is literally banned as the land ceiling laws apply to companies as well. There are artificial restrictions on Scheduled Castes (SC) and Scheduled Tribes (ST) and they cannot sell their land to non-SCs/STs in many states. There are also restrictions on sale of land for non-agricultural purposes and marketing of their products anywhere except the regulated markets where farmers are at the mercy of a cabal of a limited number of commission agents.

Agriculture needs to be liberated and deregulated. The land ceiling laws need to be repealed. Land leasing and contract farming has to be freely permitted. Restrictions on SC and ST farmers in the matter of selling their lands has to go. The agriculture marketing laws need to be converted from regulated markets to agriculture yards managed by farmers' and traders' associations on commercial principles. Farmers need to be freed to sell their produce in any manner through any of the marketing channels available to industrial product producers.

2. Degovernmentalize agriculture

Indian foodgrains agriculture, particularly cereals—wheat and rice—has become completely governmentalized, from land preparation/seeding to harvesting/selling crops. This has been done through a plethora of government subsidies for inputs—seeds, fertilizer, water, credit, electricity and others—which have distorted the inputs market. By continuing with the MSP system despite India having become a food surplus country, the government has not only governmentalized selling and distribution of these crops, but has created a vast vested interest therein.

Indian agriculture, including cereals, needs de-governmentalization and significant market orientation. Input subsidies need to be replaced with cash assistance to farmers on some objective basis—e.g. land area. Likewise, the MSP system needs to be disbanded by offering the MSP benefits to farmers in direct cash payments, again on a land area basis.

3. Freedom to farmers

On a rough estimate, all input and MSP subsidies, explicit and implicit, cost central and state governments put together approximately Rs 10 trillion a year. Indian farmers sow about 125 million hectares of agriculture land. The subsidies and support expenditure cost is about Rs 80,000 per hectare, more than the annual income a majority of Indian farmers earn from a hectare of land per year.

Discontinuation of all the subsidies and support delivered through hundreds of programmes, which have trapped farmers into overdependence on the government, and its replacement by payment of Rs 80,000 direct transfer to farmers will liberate farmers in India and give them complete choice of whatever crop they see giving them the most profit, buying whatever inputs they think is best for their crops and selling their produce anywhere in the market, whenever they want to sell and to whatever trader they are comfortable with. Of course, the government can design and calibrate the replacement programme over a period of three to five years.

This de-regulation, de-governmentalization, marketization of agriculture and replacement of subsidies with direct payments would bring down the dependence of rural people on agriculture for their livelihood. It is possible to envisage that not more than 10 per cent of India's labour, including farmers, would be deriving their livelihoods from agriculture by 2050 with others shifting to other remunerative avocations. Poverty among farmers would vanish and their incomes would multiply ten times in real prices.

Industry

India's industry needs to be developed as innovation-driven and globally competitive. This will require the government to leave out production of all private goods entirely in the private sector by unwinding the public sector producing private goods and services. The government must keep its support limited to the new future industries.

4. Get government out of production of private goods

The government is in the business of producing industrial goods directly through PSUs and it meddles in the functioning of private industry in ways that bring down competition significantly in many industries. The days of the licence permit raj are over but industrial production is still at the considerable mercy of the government. With industrialization and global value chains maturing in the world and the gap between global demand and supply vanishing, there is no case for infant industry or compensating for the lack of comparative advantage any longer, except possibly in a few futuristic industries.

The government must therefore stop all subsidies and other financial support to the industry, including most of the PLI schemes. The government must also privatize the PSUs engaged in the production of private goods and services. There is also a clear need for closing all the industry-specific ministries/departments like the Ministry of Steel, Department of Fertilizers, Department of Pharmaceuticals, etc.

5. Focus on futuristic industries only

There are clearly four futuristic industries where India lacks the basic technologies completely. The global production capacities in these industries are also in the establishment phase. The demand for these products are also expected to go up substantially in times to come. These are: electric transportation, including cars; solar cells and modules for renewable energy; batteries for storage and continuous power supply; and electronics, including semiconductors.

The government should first clear policy confusion about its objectives— make these in India or ensure their supply in India. I think it makes eminent sense to recognize that India is not a technology leader in any of these four industries at present. It also should be realized that the requisite production ecosystem is also completely absent. On the other hand, India needs renewable energy and its storage facilities to increasingly substitute thermal energy. India is also very good at building services on electronics invented and produced by others.

India should, therefore, focus on producing renewable energy and its storage by freely permitting imports of solar cells and modules as well as batteries. As the new renewable production comes up quickly, import of petroleum products and coal would also go down. In due course, to meet the growing demand, international manufacturers would establish their production facilities in India.

6. Institutional set-up for unincorporated enterprises

The organized sector (factories with twenty workers without use of power, factories with ten workers using power and certain non-factory specified establishments with 100 workers) is quite small in terms of numbers, about 3 lakh. Most enterprises in India—sole proprietorship, partnerships, association of persons, etc., usually indistinguishable from the households—are unincorporated.

The incorporated enterprises, including some small and medium enterprises, work under the system of registration, preparation of accounts, filing of returns and other regulatory arrangements, of the Indian Companies Act. The government, industry, public and other interested stakeholders have all the necessary information publicly available. These incorporated enterprises have easy access and acceptance for credit and equity capital. Government programmes can easily reach them. These enterprises have a recognizable identity.

The unincorporated enterprises lack all these. Some attempts have been made to bring some formality to larger unincorporated enterprises through the Udyam system, but it has not been able to reach more than 60–70 per cent of unincorporated enterprises. Even those who have registered under the Udyam system file no regular returns and have no organized periodic interaction. The Udyam system has not helped in improving their credit access either.

The government must reform the MSME Act into an Unincorporated Enterprises (Development and Regulation) Act, create a Registrar of Unincorporated Enterprises (highly decentralized to block level and completely digital) and institute a system of maintaining accounts and other information to provide a more solid footing to every unincorporated enterprise, including providing each one a unique business identity.

7. Do business with China

China is the global leader in electric cars and electronics. India imports most of its electronic components and equipment from China despite the government discouraging it in various ways. Chinese companies have highly competitive electric cars as well. Strangely, the current policy framework does not permit Chinese companies to establish a manufacturing base in India.

India must recognize that it is in its larger interest to do business with China in all the four futuristic sectors—electronics, solar cells and modules, electric cars and batteries. Therefore, the government must withdraw the press note regarding investment from the countries sharing land borders with India, which essentially targets and prevents Chinese investment in India in all these four critical areas.

Services

India has to seize the big service sector opportunity for becoming a high income country by 2050. India has tremendous talent and advantage in services—both digital and personal. India must aim to grow its GDP from services to more than two-thirds of its GDP from about 55 per cent today.

8. Open up services further

India needs to expand its services globally in many fields, such as accounting, legal, education, etc., where it has enormous competitive advantage. However, for the protection of small domestic service providers, such services are barred for foreigners in India, which also leads to Indian service providers being denied access in many countries.

The government must aggressively open up and seek concessions for Indian services from countries all over the world. India can offer concessions on manufacturing in trade negotiations to get concessions on services. Trading goods access for services access should be India's policy.

India's human resources are its biggest advantage. With the countries that produce about 70 per cent of global GDP currently having entered into the population ageing and declining phase, Indians have enormous opportunity to provide personal services as well. India must aggressively seek immigrant and non-immigrant concessions and visas for its massive service workforce.

9. Liberal data use policy

The future growth engine is data. It makes eminent sense to use Indian personal and non-personal data to build businesses and services. It also makes eminent sense for Indian companies to have access to global data to build services.

The digital personal data law should be notified immediately with some tweaking to do away with discrimination against large technology businesses and also limit the government's access to private data and digital services.

India must aggressively support building of digital services businesses to serve domestic and foreign clients. The government may encourage construction of vast data storage capacities by bringing a VGF programme if needed. The government should continue investing in building digital public infrastructure for public goods and services.

10. Sports, Travel, Entertainment and Personal Services (STEPS)

With manufacturing and industry becoming increasingly automated by mechanization and non-personal services, such as accounting, payments, finance, business process re-engineering (BPO) and even programming becoming increasingly automated in databases and machine processing, their employment intensity is likely to go down rapidly.

There are, however, vast opportunities emerging in sports (including gaming), travel, entertainment and personal services, which can be grouped together as STEPS. Personal services include health, nutrition management, education, coaching and many others.

India must seize this big opportunity in STEPS by investing in related infrastructure, fundamentally altering the education and training system and focusing on youth (until the age of twenty-five) in attaining nationally and globally competitive proficiency.

STEPS will be the next game changer in services.

Consumption

11. Reform the food subsidy programme

India's chronic malnutrition and under-nutrition (pathetic global hunger index ranking) despite the government providing free cereals to over 82 crore Indians (about 60 per cent of the population) has to be reformed.

The free cereals supply needs to be restricted to only those who are assessed to be poor after a comprehensive universal household survey. The poor so identified will also have to be given the option to either take free food from the government or take food coupons of an equivalent market amount to buy whichever cereal they consider best for them.

12. Bring out a nutrition-focused programme

All households that are identified as nutritionally deficient (which is different from being assessed as poor) must be put through an outcome-tested support programme. The reasons for someone being nutritionally deficient have to be assessed and informed to the concerned households. The government must provide them adequate financial support for buying the cocktail of consumables necessary to address the nutritional deficiency linked to outcomes laid down in terms of progress on the nutrition front.

Investment

13. Restructure capital formation in transportation

India's capital investment growth in the railways and road sectors is built basically on government capital expenditure and private CapEx supported by government subsidies.

The government CapEx in the railways and roads sector does not add much value to India's GDP in the second round, i.e. in production of goods and services, as the capital assets created in the first round do not contribute further value addition. These CapEx guzzling investments financed from high-cost debt will haunt India in times to come.

India needs to shift the rail and road construction programme to BOT bids with very liberal use of the VGF.

Infrastructure

India needs to build physical and digital infrastructure for 2050.

This will require profitable and private investment-oriented infrastructure like electricity and transport sectors to be left entirely to the private sector and withdrawal of the government therefrom. Infrastructure that has elements of public goods, such as roads and railway lines, will need to be shifted entirely to the public-private partnership (PPP) mode with government putting up the unviability cost.

Fully public infrastructure like community schools, hospitals, carbon sequestration, sewage treatment and the like will need to be constructed with private construction companies with the public works departments dismantled completely. PPP infrastructure will have to be competitively awarded and pricing determined transparently to provide a decent market return on capital invested.

14. Reform electricity distribution

There is enough evidence that privatization of electricity distribution and supply works wonders (the case of Delhi and Odisha) and continued monopolies of state government entities (almost everywhere else) in the distribution make electricity services sub-optimal, leads to large A&C losses, large financial losses for the government and higher electricity cost to commercial and industrial consumers. In addition, it discourages private sector investment in generation.

Over the next seven to ten years, the entire electricity distribution and supply system should be taken up for privatization by re-organizing the DISCOMs into two verticals—distribution and supply. The distribution entity would need to run only on charging for its wire services with complete open access and no cross subsidies. The supply business should, along with distribution, be freely opened for new licensees.

15. Reorganize Railways

The Railways today is like the state departmental electricity utilities of the 1960s, which used to have electricity generation, transmission and distribution all under one organization and the department of telecom, which used to establish and operate telecom services until the 1980s.

The Central government established NTPC in the 1970s with both generation and transmission organized in one company. Later, the transmission business was separated and Powergrid came into existence. Today, NTPC and Powergrid are two powerful companies in the generation and transmission space. Both are not monopolies. NTPC has about 20 per cent of generation capacity and new transmission is also incrementally passing to private transmission companies. The telecom monopoly of DoT, later corporatized in BSNL, was thrown open to private sector competition. 90 per cent of the telecom business is with private entities now, with consumers getting services of an international standard at a fraction of international prices.

The Railways needs to be reformed, taking on board the lessons of reorganization of power sector utilities and telecom utilities.

The track, passenger train, goods traffic and rail stations/goods yard businesses need to be separated into different companies. The track business, on the lines of Powergrid, should be converted into a Railgrid Corporation (keeping special purpose vehicles [SPV] like the Dedicated Freight Corridors Corporation separate). New rail track construction, like electricity transmission lines, should be thrown open to the private sector on a competitive basis with Railgrid participating as a competitor. The passenger trains business should be organized into a suitable number of consumer businesses, like Delhi/Odisha DISCOMs, and, over a period of time, privatized. So should the goods freight business. The rail stations and goods yard should also be organized into a suitable number of SPVs like airports and gradually monetized by giving them on fifty years lease on the pattern of airports privatized in 2019–20.

The reorganized Railways would, much before 2050, become highly profitable, service-oriented organizations.

16. Construct roads only on BOT

The government is constructing roads today through the EPC and Hybrid Annuity models, bearing 100 per cent of the cost of construction. On top of high land acquisition costs, both these models have escalated the government's road construction bill massively. The government also does not monetize the land parcels along the road stretches, letting go of an opportunity to meet part of the cost. Tolls recover only a fraction of the cost. The NHAI has gone bankrupt, forcing the government to pick up 100 per cent of the construction cost bill.

To get the private sector efficiency advantage of constructing and maintaining highways at a lower cost than the government and also reap the advantage of monetizing roadside amenities development, the government must construct the highways only on a BOT basis with regulated tolling. The government had imposed a limit of not awarding BOT projects through VGF if the viability gap exceeded 40 per cent. There is no rationale in limiting BOT projects to 40 per cent VGF and then meeting 100 per cent cost of the project through EPC/Hybrid Annuity.

The limit of 40 per cent VGF should be given up and all road projects awarded on a BOT basis, irrespective of VGF.

17. Monetize airports

The government had successfully monetized six airports in 2019/2020 by designing a business and consumer-friendly concession model. Consumers had to suffer no cost as the concessionaire was not subjected to any additional fees with all air-side charges kept within the regulator's domain. The concessionaire made money on cityside development and more efficient management of the airport terminal. The government got all its capital investment back and more than five times the share in revenue projected as the reserve price.

For very questionable reasons, the government did not use the same or any other model to monetize airports in the second term. The government must privatize/monetize at least fifty airports using the 2019 OMDA model.

Labour Income and Welfare

Industrial and infrastructure investment is highly capital-intensive. With increasing mechanization and automation, the labour density of manufacturing and infrastructure construction is reducing fast. Mechanization of agriculture will also render 70–80 per cent of farmers and agriculture labour jobless in times to come. It is only in services where the jobs are expanding and would continue to expand, but it is not enough to absorb the displacement from industry and agriculture.

The government is caught up in the time warp of providing employment to all. For this, it encourages surveys that artificially show higher employment. Instead of artificially jacking up labour workforce and employment statistics by including unpaid family helpers in the PLFS or producing higher new hires in the EPFO monthly surveys (often revised down later), the government should accept the reality of jobless industrial and agriculture growth.

18. Create a labour and payroll database

India does not register and recognize all of its labour force. There is complete fragmentation as well. EPFO registers and has data relating to the provident fund and employee pension scheme of employees working in defined classes of enterprises. The Employees State Insurance Scheme (ESIC) has some pay and benefits-related data. There is no integrated pay database for even these two organizations functioning under the same ministry. The government recently created a system of registering unorganized workers on a portal—eShram. About 30 crore informal sector workers have registered on this platform. eShram has very scanty data and no employment/payroll information.

India must create a national labour registration and payroll data platform to collect employment and pay status of all its labour (of twenty years or more in age), broadly divided in two parts: a. salaried, and b. self-employed.

19. Reskill surplus manpower for services

The education and skilling system needs to be overhauled for educating and reskilling the excess farmer and new labour entrants for the big opportunity in services—in India and abroad.

There is enormous scope for people's employment in healthcare, education, travel, entertainment, gaming, personal care, sports, finance, e-commerce and numerous other services, both on the traditional physical side as well as on the increasingly growing digital side.

The government must permit private schools, with a significant skills-oriented programme at secondary level, to undertake this massive reskilling campaign. The labour must pay for what they want to relearn and schools should charge the fees they consider apt for providing the education. Upon the labour-student acquiring the chosen skill, certified according to a quality examination by a standard setting body, the labour-student may be paid a lump-sum amount to cover a good part of her education and skilling expenses.

Invest in India's youth for reskilling them for STEPs.

20. Expand and restructure MGNREGA

MGNREGA is a backstop programme for labour that cannot find work elsewhere. Its basic construct of assuring 100 days of employment at a little less than minimum wages is perfectly fine.

What needs to change, however, is where the MGNREGA workers work today. MGNREGA labour either works on their own fields or gets employed on public employment works, such as deepening water ponds, digging pits, etc. The type of work taken up under MGNREGA is from the mindset of the 1960s and 1970s.

India needs to be cleaned up on pollution and carbon emissions to be an upper middle and later a high income country. The MGNREGA programme should be overhauled to be used for cleaning up our rivers, lakes, ponds, roads and other public buildings and structures of all the accumulated pollution and to undertake works to keep the villages and towns clean.

This restructured MGNREGA should be expanded to allow 200 days' work also and meet 100 per cent demand of jobless workers.

21. Institute a minimum basic income scheme

The reality of the future is that a much smaller proportion of the working age population will be able to produce all the agricultural and industrial goods and non-personal services for the requisite consumption needs of all.

A significant proportion of the labour force will adopt STEPS for employment and earning their incomes. Still, many able-bodied persons are likely to be left without jobs. Some might opt for the MGNREGA type of stopgap employment. However, a significant number of employable people might need hand-holding by the government.

For all those workers who are unable to get employment (despite acquiring the prescribed minimum qualifications/getting reskilled), the government should provide a minimum basic income linked to outcomes relating to their participation in voluntary social work and maintenance of specified health standards.

22. Reform the Wages Code

The consolidated Wages Code should be rewritten to provide for complete flexibility to design the wage package between the employer and the labour. The current construct of hundreds of minimum wages must be given up in favour of a state-level (or sub-state-level, if the state government so desires) minimum wage set in terms of minimum wages per day, per week and per month.

23. Reform the Workplaces Code

The Occupational Safety, Health and Working Conditions Code, 2020, should be replaced by a simple Hazardous Workplaces Code. This law, after defining workplaces comprehensively to include all factories, mines, plantations, office establishments, mobile vending carts, working homes, etc., should specify what constitutes a hazardous workplace.

The reformed code would require all non-hazardous workplaces to file an annual declaration about their status with no other compliances required from them. The code should classify and regulate hazardous workplaces appropriately, depending upon the nature of business.

24. Notify Social Security Code with consolidation of schemes

The Social Security Code provides important measures for addressing the welfare of informal and unorganized sector workers, including the new category of workers—contract workers, gig workers, platform workers and the like. Unfortunately, the rules under the code were not notified and the code remained unimplemented.

The government must immediately notify the code and create appropriate social welfare funds and schemes to provide social security to these workers. The government must also consolidate numerous schemes for unorganized workers, such as PM-SYM, Old Age Pension Scheme, Handicapped Pension Scheme, and so on, into the social welfare package under the code.

Poverty and Redistribution

25. Enumerate and classify all poor households

All households should be surveyed universally and first classified into non-poor and poor based on a well-defined and easily understandable criteria, e.g. the households adjudged nutritionally deficient and living in a non-permanent house. The poor should be classified into two broad categories—poor and poor only during emergencies.

A specific outcome-based food and cash support programme should be prepared for each poor household, in active consultation with the concerned household. The support delivery should be linked to specific outcomes in terms of improvement in nutritional standard, education, health and others.

The poor only during emergencies should remain duly identified and databased. Whenever any emergency affecting such household(s) occurs, the system should trigger an appropriate level of assistance.

26. Consolidate welfare programmes focused on households

The entire set of welfare/freebies programmes must be consolidated and refocused on households, instead of currently scattered departmental or thematic programmes. It is crazy to have hundreds of welfare/freebies programmes that are ultimately intended to reach India's households.

Climate and Pollution

27. Recognize pollution as an emergency

A wholesome environment is a prerequisite for good quality of life. The current state of air and water in the country is extremely bad. India was adjudged the most polluted country in the World Air Quality report, having seventeen of the world's twenty most polluted cities. The state of water quality in the Yamuna testifies to the general state of water quality in our country. India needs to recognize the pollution emergency in the country.

28. Make India air and water pollution-free

The Indian government spends next to nothing on controlling air and water pollution. Making India pollution-free is the best public good that the government can deliver to 140 crore Indians.

The government must adopt a goal of making Indian cities air pollution-free, i.e. the average air quality index (AQI) in a year should remain in the 'good' category, with an average reading of less than 50 during a year. A city-specific good air quality restoration plan should be made for all municipalities. The government must provide all the support needed for translating the plan into action.

29. Get to Net Zero by 2050

The government has declared its intention to make India a net zero carbon emission country by 2070. This is too far away. India should become a net zero carbon emission country by 2050 when we celebrate 100 years of our Republic. India also needs to get out of the victim mindset—it is the developed and industrially advanced countries who are responsible for carbon accumulation and therefore must pay for it—and adopt leadership of the climate movement.

Technologies have developed enough to generate clean power that is competitive to dirty thermal power. India should develop systems, policies and incentives to scale down and dismantle thermal power generation over a period of time. India must declare a total freeze on new coal thermal capacity creation.

India should actually seize the industrialization and service provision opportunity offered by energy transition and carbon sequestering. The carbon emissions control and sequestering can be India's chance to get rich as well.

Governance Reforms

Governance reforms are needed for affording true freedom of speech and assured protection of life and liberty. In addition, the governance systems need to be changed to ensure provision of equal opportunity to everyone. True federalism and decentralization are necessary for making people participate in governance.

30. Seize the digital opportunity

Seizing the digital opportunity requires two fundamental reforms. Make personal data the private property of the individual concerned. Allow all businesses to create non-personal data without any restrictions for their business use. Businesses should also have full freedom to enter into contracts with individuals for use of their personal data.

31. Build a functional insolvency regime for all businesses

India's insolvency regime needs to be put back on the rails to provide real and fast resolutions for businesses gone bad.

India does not have a functional insolvency and bankruptcy regime for financial sector businesses. The rules notified to deal with a couple of cases—e.g. DHFL—does not serve the need for a vast swathe of financial institutions in the country: NBFCs, insurance companies, banks and the like. The Financial Resolution and Deposit Insurance (FRDI) Bill 2017 was, by and large, the right resolution mechanism. With some necessary amendments to address due concerns of depositors, the FRDI Bill should be brought back and enacted to create a functional insolvency and bankruptcy regime for financial intermediaries.

The personal insolvency and bankruptcy provisions also need to be notified.

32. Restore fiscal federalism

The current fiscal federal regime requires massive rebalancing for India to become a truly fiscal federal country.

On the lines of GST, the governments should have no authority to levy cesses on non-GST goods and services, such as petroleum products and electricity. The existing cesses on petroleum products should be merged into excise duty. This will make all excise duties and cesses shareable.

The authority to levy surcharges on Central government taxes was always intended to be temporary to take care of the need for extra resources in times of war and emergencies. Surcharges have become large and a regular feature and have acquired the nature of tax. The existing surcharges on income tax, customs duty, etc. should be considered as taxes and shared with states. For the future, no surcharge should be allowed to be levied except in wars and natural disasters.

The states' borrowing authority should be fully respected. No state government should require the Central government's permission to borrow, within the limits permitted by its FRBM law, except when a state government has defaulted on its outstanding liability against the Centre.

Trade and e-Commerce

India's trade account needs to generate a surplus.

33. Make services exports the principal trade strategy

The promise of and big opportunity in services exports has to be realized to first make up the merchandise account deficit. India should go all out to increase services exports. In a few years, India's services exports should exceed goods exports.

Services export does not require any government support in the form of capital subsidy. The government may support the private sector's creation of service infrastructure and should also consider providing some income tax incentives against exports profit.

Foreign Investment

There are severe restrictions on Indians investing abroad in equity and enterprises. There are massive restrictions on Indians raising capital abroad.

34. Adopt foreign regulations for listing abroad

Indian corporates can raise equity capital abroad only following the regulations, requirements and practices followed in their respective stock exchanges. We cannot expect American investors to provide beneficial ownership details as per the requirements of the Prevention of Money Laundering Act of India or SEBI regulations. Permit Indian corporates to raise equity in all Financial Action Task Force (FATF) compliant jurisdictions following the regulations of the respective authority.

India should issue foreign currency-denominated sovereign bonds in select jurisdictions abroad. Other serious capital account reforms, such as liberalizing FDI regulations to remove conditions of Indian management, etc., are needed to make sure that India receives multiples of the FDI received today.

India should also liberalize outward flow of FDI from India. Equity investment abroad is actually a true barometer of any country's technology and investment leadership. India should become a net investor in place of a net FDI recipient on the way to our journey to 2050.

Economic Integration with the Rest of the World

35. Seek aggressive global integration

Global integration in communication, travel, education, immigration, payments, capital services and environmental impacts is real. The talk of deglobalization has a very insignificant and narrow relevance relating to production of goods.

In times to come, the world will move significantly towards one world. India needs to accept the reality and reform to take advantage of this opportunity.

We must aggressively pursue the establishment of Indian financial institutions abroad (in the private sector). India must see that Indian companies establish service establishments all over the world. We must develop protocols to share data with all trustable jurisdictions. We must improve our travel infrastructure to encourage the world tourist to visit India. We must open up our education industry for global leading universities to establish centres/full-fledged universities here and teach the world from India.

Currency and Money

36. Prepare for cryptocurrencies

Money is fast becoming digital. Money may also become a decentralized database account money (cryptocurrencies) in times to come. India has been successfully shifting to bank account-based digital money but needs to be open about the evolution of blockchain-oriented private cryptocurrencies, including stablecoins.

India must create the right framework for the establishment of a decentralized autonomous organization (DAO) in India. We must work on framing the rightful legal regime for DAO and blockchain-crypto organizations. We should also get into a partnership with the US and other European nations to get a sovereign-backed stablecoin.

Credit

Our credit system is severely constrained.

37. Sell off PSBs and general insurance companies

Keeping SBI as part of the sovereign asset management company, the government should let go of all other public sector banks, all the four general insurance companies and the non-banking finance companies it has. Their privatization, phased over a period of ten years, would do a lot to improve India's financial health.

The government's intrusion in credit decisions—through guaranteed credits or subsidized credit or write-offs—has to end.

38. Reform the financial sector

All artificial restrictions on foreign and Indian ownership of banks need to go. The restrictions on industrial companies on owning banks may stay but all restrictions on financial and other services companies owning banks should go.

Non-banks do not have a good source of raising lendable resources. Debentures need to be developed into non-banks' principal financing resources.

Wealth Is Becoming Increasingly Important

India is in the nascent stage of building wealth. Whatever wealth has been built is also hugely inequitable. The wealth and capital management industry is building up. Absence of a good and functional wealth tax system compromises incentives in wealth creation.

39. Reforms in real estate

The Integrated Land Information Management System under the Digital India Land Records Modernization Programme needs to be fast-tracked to build a national database of all land parcels with unique numbers. It should be available in the English language nationally. Likewise, a database of all buildings in India needs to be built up and updated regularly.

India should also consider moving towards the Torrens system of land and property registration and titling. India needs to have a national depository of all land and building titles.

There are large gaps in the regulatory architecture of real estate and financial assets. This calls for a deep-seated dose of reforms in real estate and financial assets.

Expenditures

40. Refocus CapEx on public infrastructure

The government has rightly enhanced budgetary capital expenditure. However, spending it all on transportation infrastructure to create trophy assets, which add very little value to GDP, makes it highly unproductive and wasteful. Whereas, the public infrastructure to transform India's water, air and waste management for eliminating pollution and carbon emissions go completely a-begging.

The government has to give primacy to public goods and services expenditure in place of capital expenditure, which serves the interest of private industry and misdirected freebies.

The government must spend about 3 per cent of GDP on making our soil, water and air clean and healthy, and also to make waste and dirt 100 per cent recyclable.

Revenues

41. Reform income taxes

Our current income tax laws tax labour incomes heavily and provide kid-gloves treatment for capital income. There is no difference in the two sets of income. In fact, the labour incomes deserve softer taxation treatment as these incomes fund consumption and improve the quality of life for almost 95 per cent of the people.

This objective can be achieved by taxing the capital incomes at the same rates. Additionally, the minimum tax slab should be fixed at four times the average per capita income in current prices on the assumption that one income taxpayer supports a family of four. As current per capita GDP is about Rs 2 lakh, the minimum taxable income threshold should be raised to Rs 8 lakh. The minimum taxable income threshold should be adjusted every two to three years. The maximum tax rate of 30 per cent should be applied for incomes higher than Rs 30 lakh. The income beyond Rs 8 lakh should be subject to 10 per cent tax rate. The 20 per cent slab may kick in at Rs 19 lakh.

The confused regime of options—between traditional with exemptions and alternative with very few exemptions—should be discontinued and the alternative assessment method with only a few defined exemptions and concessions should be made the only income tax assessment system.

Corporate income tax with 22 per cent as the applicable tax rate (no favourable treatment to manufacturing companies) should be cast in stone for at least fifteen years.

42. Complete GST reforms

The GST system of taxing goods and services production and the entire supply chain has settled in reasonably. Some systemic reforms still pending need to be completed.

Our nation must aim at ensuring that every producer of goods and services be registered under the GST system to create a complete tax value chain. This will require doing away with the minimum turnover threshold for registration under GST. Likewise, the differential compounded GST tax assessment system for smaller GST taxpayers must also be given up. The government can automate tax assessment based on every invoice issued by/payment made to the registered GST taxpayer.

Petroleum products, electricity, real estate construction and a few other goods and services currently outside the GST system must be brought into the GST system. The excessive taxation (higher than the applicable GST rate) element can be converted into non-VATable excises to be eliminated over a period of fifteen years. Finally, the GST slabs need to be reduced to three: 6 per cent, 12 per cent and 18 per cent.

43. Bring in wealth taxation

Currently, the capital gains on transfer of capital assets gets taxed as capital gains. The capital gains taxation regime, however, is highly convoluted with capital gains from different capital assets suffering tax at different rates, with different costs of acquisition allowed, and some capital assets not suffering any capital gains tax. Moreover, valuation gains are not subject to any tax at all, creating complex incentives between the distribution of income and retaining it. The addition to wealth valuation, the big value creation in today's world, remains completely tax-exempt, widening wealth inequality.

The government must bring in a wealth tax law. The capital gains provisions of the income tax law must be transferred to the wealth tax law and reformed to tax all capital gains at a uniform tax rate with a uniform acquisition cost system made applicable to all types of capital. The wealth tax law must also institute a valuation gains taxation system at a low rate of tax, say, 1–3 per cent of addition to the valuation of real estate and financial assets.

44. Institute negative value added taxation

Numerous methods have been tried to discourage carbon emissions—carbon credits, carbon taxes and so on. Pollution, which is a much bigger problem in countries like India, has not been subjected to such experiments, although emission of pollutants is quite similar to emission of carbons as far as these experiments are concerned.

The best way to deal with the problem of carbon and pollutant (specified) emissions is to institute a negative value added tax on net carbon and pollutant added (on a lifetime basis) at different stages of the production of goods, services and assets. A tax, maybe at a sin tax rate of 24 per cent, can be imposed on the value assigned to the net carbon and pollutant emitted. The government must bring this law immediately and extend it to all industries/producers over a ten-year period.

Investment and Monetization

45. Put a stop to investment in commercial public enterprises

India's fiscal policy in the last few years has junked disinvestment and privatization and instead taken up massive public investments, that too in commercially non-viable sectors and organizations. Sinking debt-financed resources by investing in irredeemable organizations like MTNL and BSNL is a criminal waste of scarce public resources.

This investment programme needs to be fully rolled back by putting asset creation in the transportation sector—railways, roads and metros, on a BOT basis, as noted above. Organizations like MTNL and BSNL need to be simply closed and their assets sold for whatever price they command. All loss-making organizations and organizations producing private goods and services should also be simply closed off.

46. Place market-significant PSEs under a sovereign asset management company

The profitable public sector enterprises should be classified into two groups—a. those which are industry leaders and play an important role in bringing competition and stability to the market, and b. those that have a minor market share.

The government must put the privatization agenda on the fast track to sell off all those public sector enterprises that have only a minor market presence. The major public sector enterprises with a dominant market role, such as NTPC, Powergrid, SBI, IOC and a few others, must be placed under a sovereign asset management company and run professionally on sound commercial principles under its watch. All the capital needed by the companies under the sovereign asset management company should be raised from the market.

47. Let go of financial enterprises

The nationalization of banks was a retrograde move which had massive adverse consequences for industrial and infrastructure investment in India. The government partly addressed the problem by licensing private banks. Similarly, allowing entry of the private sector in insurance, mutual funds, NBFCs and other asset management sectors also undid the excesses of nationalization of life and non-life insurance.

The government, however, is still dominantly present in the infrastructure finance sectors through power sector NBFCs. The decision in 2021 to set up NaBFID was the measure taken to make a government-owned institution fund the infrastructure in all other sectors, as the banks, who suffered heavily in funding roads, telecom and other infrastructure sectors realized in the last twenty years, stepped out of this financing.

The government must stop being a financier of infrastructure. NaBFID must be sold off and PFC, RFC, IIFCL, etc. privatized. The government must create all the right conditions (by reforming infrastructure profitability) for private sector financial institutions to finance infrastructure creation in the private sector.

Fiscal Deficit, Borrowings and Debt

48. Restore fiscal discipline

Fiscal deficit in excess of 6 per cent for five years running in Modi 2.0 has already started showing up in fast-increasing interest payments and will create many fiscal problems in the years to come.

The government must dedicate itself to the fiscal deficit rule of 3 per cent of GDP. As the current statutory mandate of achieving it in 2020–21 and maintaining it always thereafter is long gone, the government must amend the FRBM Act to substitute 2020–21 with 2028–29. As the fiscal deficit is estimated to be 5.1 per cent for 2024–25, getting to 3 per cent by 2028–29 will require a 0.4 per cent reduction every year. This fiscal consolidation and reduction path must be enshrined in the rules under the FRBM Act.

A severe penal provision must be built into the FRBM law if the government deviates from the fiscal consolidation path, including resignation of the Finance Minister.

49. Reform small savings

Small savings through government institutions like post offices were required to be promoted in the 1950s and 1960s when the presence of financial institutions in rural areas was very scanty. In today's world, every household/adult individual has a bank account, which also operates electronically. The government has singularly failed to keep the additional margin for small savings within the limit of 0.5 per cent of similar instruments/paper in the commercial sector. Most importantly, the state governments that promoted and needed small savings to fund their budgets have stopped taking small savings collections.

The government should discontinue all small savings instruments—recurring and term deposits, national savings certificates and so on. The interest rate on savings bank accounts in post offices should be made equal to the savings account rate of SBI. All the savings accountholders in the post offices may be given the option to shift to any of the public sector banks or the savings account in the India Post Bank, the payment bank operated by the Department of Posts.

The savings bonds issued through the RBI can be converted into a public savings bond instrument. If the government wants to incentivize some special social group, such as senior citizens, women's self-help groups, girl children, etc., an appropriate incentive (1–2 per cent) can be added to the RBI savings bond, issued as special RBI savings bonds to these interest groups.

50. Control public debt

Large fiscal deficits are building humungous debt. As most of this debt gets invested/spent on meeting revenue deficits and assets yielding dubious financial returns, the debt mountain is upending public finances. India's debt and liabilities are neither productive nor sustainable.

The government needs to repose its commitment to bring the debt and liabilities to 40 per cent of GDP, as enshrined in the FRBM Act. With Central government debt and liabilities over 55 per cent of GDP currently, doing it by 2024–25, as mandated in the FRBM Act, is impossible. The government must rejig the debt consolidation and reduction path to not later than 2030 and propose a yearly time frame to do so. The Finance Minister must resign if the government fails to stick to the debt consolidation path.

Acknowledgements

On 30 September 2023, the day my book *We Also Make Policy* was published and occupied a place in the top 100 bestsellers of the day, Manish Kumar, the thinking and entrepreneurial master editor at Penguin called. The idea of the book in your hand—*The $10 Trillion Dream Dented*—was seeded in that short conversation.

Manish, in fact, initiated me into writing books. A call from him in July 2020, in the midst of the Covid-19 pandemic and a few months after I had quit the IAS, explored the possibility of me writing a book on the Indian economy. My first book, *The $10 Trillion Dream: The State of the Indian Economy and the Policy Reforms Agenda*, was the result of what Manish saw in me as an author and his persuasion to make me take the plunge. That book, published in February 2022, dwelt on India's ambition of making a $10 trillion GDP economy, first expressed in the Interim Budget 2019–20 presented on 1 February 2019; incidentally, at the time when I was the economic affairs secretary in the Government of India and in charge of the budgets.

Our conversation on 30 September 2023 took the idea of $10 trillion economy further. We agreed that it is eminently necessary to make periodic assessments of the state of the economy and the progress India made towards realizing that goal. We also agreed that the best occasion to do so is to coincide this assessment every five years when one government completes its term.

As the Modi government was completing its second term in May 2024, we agreed that it was the most appropriate time to take stock of what the Modi government had done in realizing that dream, what reforms it undertook, what investments it made and what leadership it displayed. Our quick assessment was that the $10 trillion dream suffered a bit during Modi 2.0 for various acts of commission and omission. The dream, we concluded, had got dented. This book, *The $10 Trillion Dream Dented*, presents an evaluation of the five years of the Modi government's second term (2019–24) to you.

Manish's discovery of the author in me has flourished, as I have been able to write and publish five authoritative books on India's economy, budgets and policymaking in the last three years.

I can't thank Manish sufficiently in any words or in any other manner. I will simply say thank you very much, Manish.

I was a commerce and accountancy student and an administrative officer all my life until 2019. I wrote numerous notes on files but I had never written a book. The blogs I started writing after my innings in the government were rich in content but not the best example of writing skills.

I, therefore, got the manuscript of *The $10 Trillion Dream* edited by a professional editor, Aarti Menon. In the last three years, I have probably acquired and honed some writing skills. I did not, therefore, requisition the services of a professional editor this time. Still, I needed an assurance about the readability, accuracy and quality of the book.

Anjali Subhash, my wife and soulmate, has been the sounding board for all I write in books and opinion pieces. She has an immaculate sense of proportion and balance, which echoes the feelings of my readers. A chartered accountant by profession, she also has a knack for catching mistakes.

Anjali read the entire manuscript twice over. I thank her for all the time she invested in reading the manuscript and making the book readable and free of mistakes. I must also thank her for freeing me from most of the day-to-day responsibilities to allow me to focus on the book and my public engagements. Thank you very much, Anjali.

Manish did the structural editing of the manuscript and the lawyers had a serious look from the legal point of view. However, the back-breaking and eyes-tearing task of reading every single line and word of the manuscript fell upon Ralph Rebello, the master editor.

Ralph must have spent many days poring over the manuscript in an effort to transform it into a book of the class and quality which Penguin, as a publisher, is known for. Ralph suggested hundreds of changes to make the book conform to the Penguin style of writing and publication, identifying many sentences that did not make sense and ensuring that there were no gaps and errors. His contributions, I have no hesitation in admitting, improved the quality of the book massively. After his clearance, I feel fully assured that the book is worthy of readers' time and attention. Thank you very much, Ralph, for your diligence, hard work, imaginative editing and proofreading of the book.

Many professionals and executives in Penguin cooperate to make a book like this possible—in marketing, sales, contracting, reviewing and other areas. I thank all of them for their contributions.

Thank you Penguin, the publisher, for helping me transform the idea of this book, generated only eleven months ago, into a kind of authoritative commentary on the state of the Indian economy, the policy reforms and above all, our $10 trillion GDP dream.

A Note on Data Sources and References

This book is my sincere attempt to build an evidence-based, critical but fair commentary on the performance of the Narendra Modi government during its second term of 2019–24 (Modi 2.0).

The book has a very wide economic, financial and budgetary canvas of the Indian economy. I have drawn several conclusions about the performance of the Indian economy under Modi 2.0 and stated these in the book. I needed enormous amount of data to make these findings and draw these conclusions covering the macroeconomic dimensions, supply-side and demand-side economics, the factors of production and their incomes, poverty, savings, credit and wealth, India's economic and financial linkages with the rest of the world through trade, commerce, investments, technology and services, and much more. I also needed a whole lot of data about budgetary operations and the performance of the government.

For the sake of authenticity of the narrative in the book, I decided to almost exclusively rely on the official data sources, as far as possible. There is no dearth of official data, I must say.

Almost all the macroeconomic data has been sourced from the publications of the National Statistical Organization (NSO) and their periodic press releases. The National Accounts Statistics (NAS), published annually by the NSO, is the richest source of all macroeconomic data—gross domestic product (GDP), gross value added (GVA), consumption, capital formation, household savings and every other indicator.

It was fortuitous that National Accounts Statistics 2024 (NAS–2024) was published in August 2024, just a few days before I completed this book. NAS–2024 has the updated data up to the financial year 2023–24, the concluding year of Modi 2.0. Only a few deeper sectoral data is for the period up to the financial year 2022–23. I have used NAS data for most of the macroeconomic narratives in the book.

I created a number of statistical tables to draw inferences, ratios, compound annual growth rates, etc., to make a fact-based assessment of the economic performance of the Narendra Modi government. There is a set of seventy-five statistical tables, which I can publicly share if it is necessary.

The RBI publications—especially the annual statistical publication on the Indian economy, the annual reports and also the monthly bulletins—also came handy for macroeconomic, monetary and financial sector data.

Budget documents, Finance Ministry publications on debt and liabilities, and the monthly accounts brought out by the Controller General of Accounts (CGA) have been used extensively in the book, most specifically in the last four chapters focusing on expenditures, revenues, deficits, borrowings, debt and investments during Modi 2.0.

The book also relies heavily on the annual accounts of the ministries/departments and the press releases put out by the Press Information Bureau (PIB).

I have not used any private copyrighted book, document or other publication.

Scan QR code to access the
Penguin Random House India website